# Postmodern Perspectives on Indian Society

# Postmodern Perspectives on Indian Society

S.L. DOSHI

RAWAT PUBLICATIONS

Jaipur • New Delhi • Bangalore • Hyderabad • Guwahati

ISBN 81-316-0188-9 (HB)
81-316-0189-7 (PB)



**Reprinted, 2010**



*Published by*
Prem Rawat for **Rawat Publications**
Satyam Apts, Sector 3, Jawahar Nagar, Jaipur 302 004 (India)
Phone: 0141 265 1748 / 7006 Fax: 0141 265 1748
E-mail: info@rawatbooks.com
Website: www.rawatbooks.com

*New Delhi Office*
4858/24, Ansari Road, Daryaganj, New Delhi 110 002
Phone: 011 2326 3290

*Also at Bangalore, Hyderabad and Guwahati*

Typeset by Rawat Computers, Jaipur
Printed at Nice Printing Press, New Delhi

*To*

NARESH BHARGAVA
*and*
USHA BHARGAVA

*the towers of my strength*

# Contents

# Preface

It is difficult to define postmodernism. The word is highly used today, it is equally much misused. Its critics define it as a word of rejection. There is a saying: if you want to kill a dog, call it mad. In the similar strain, if you disagree with anything, want to reject anything, call it postmodern. Postmodernism thus is a cliche which is often used for rejecting anything.

It would be tragic to look at postmodernism in such a lighter way. It is a theoretical framework which helps us to understand the reality of social phenomena. The Enlightenment Project in Europe combined with modernity, in its initial stages of development, gave a sigh of relief to the liberal humanist ideology. But soon it went wrong. The benefits of modernity were mostly cornered by the elites and the high-ups of the society. Modernity in its turn came to oppress the human kind and turned it into certain set ways of thought and actions not always in its best interest.

In India, modernity has been hijacked by higher classes, upper caste Hindus and the corrupt politicians. The lower castes, tribals and the subalterns are out of the benefits of modernity. The emancipation of the disadvantaged groups is nowhere in sight. To combat the challenges of the masses of people, modernity has in a sophisticated way, created meta-narratives as coined by Jean-Francois Lyotard. These meta or grand narratives have been established as universalizing theories. Marxism, democracy and capitalism are glaring examples of grand narratives created by modernity to defeat the cause of subalterns who are characterized by 'culture of silence'.

The grand narratives have also given fundamentalism reasserting itself. There is eco-fundamentalism, academic fundamentalism and in the economic realm, there is market fundamentalism. Political and nationalistic fundamentalism (cultural nationalism) has put their trust in grand narratives. For example, in the US, thinkers like Francis Fakuyama have put all faith in political system; M.N. Srinivas in India has established that the high-caste Hindus are the only imitation models for the plural groups of the country. Wherever we see in this country, modernity has created rather new traditions or the old traditions are reinterpreted as grand narratives.

Postmodernity has a colossal task to perform. Institutional authority – religious, educational, economic and developmental – has been rejected and condemned by the postmodernity. Postmodernity's enemy is, therefore, modernity. It looks with skepticism all the vague notions of progress. It argues for the rejection of universalistic beliefs.

The methodology which is applied to study social phenomena assumes prime importance in social science. Sociology's methodology is functional. And, the functionalism heavily charged with empiricism has played much havoc with Indian society. Dialectical studies are exceptions in Indian sociology. The perspectives of functionalism, which have been applied in the study of Indian religion, caste, class, family, village and tribals, have given us a distorted image of Indian society. We are put to a land which is embedded with status quo, and conservatism. The functional sociologists 'educate' us that there is subtle change in Indian society, a 'radical change,' but it is 'adaptive'. The axiom is: there is change. The reality is: there is no change. It is all a gimmick of verbose.

In the present study, we have applied the perspectives of postmodernism to analyze the major social institutions of Indian society. Our findings show that Indian society is increasingly becoming postmodern. Our position in the study may be contested. I wish, I may prove to be wrong. But I am satisfied that I have said what I wanted to say.

Like any other study, the present one is a collective endeavour. My friends have always stood by my side to encourage me to complete the work. Prof. K.L. Sharma has remained all along my life as my friend and guide; B.K. Nagla and his wife Madhu Nagla are quite charitable to me; N.K. Bhargava and Usha Bhargava have extended all help to me. The book is dedicated to both of them. S.L. Sharma worked hard to prepare the bibliography. I owe him much.

At my family level, Tushar and Pankaj have made all efforts to keep me comfortable and happy. Pankaj's wife, my daughter-in-law, Sulochna has taken all pains to take care of me despite her busy life. I sincerely owe them much. The younger ones, Purbi, Bonnu, Nanhi and Krishna have all done minor errands with a smile on their face.

**S.L. Doshi**

# 1

# Postmodernity: What?

Postmodernity is not a theory or discourse on psycho-social risk, danger and despair; rather it tries to understand the nature of contemporary autonomous individual, diverse and differentiated, and secular challenges facing the modernity, identity and tradition. Besides, all its silver lining, it also suffers from inconsistencies and contradictions. In USA and Europe, it is a cliché to say that they are living in a postmodern world. The concept of modernity in these countries is one of the most used and abused terms. Despite such a status of postmodernity, no sociology in this world is complete without a debate on postmodernity along with modernity.

## Indian Sociology

Contemporary literature in sociology is different from its predecessor's. We are even today busy writing on our traditional themes of family, caste, kinship, marriage, religion and village communities as well as creating insignificant and trivial literature, all but in name, has appeared. Most of the sociologists and they are no ordinary celebrities, by any standard, have argued that we have been mistaken about 'modernity'; in fact, we are far away from modernity or in Jurgen Habermas' words, "modernity is an incomplete project in India".

Functionalism is the central ideology of our present conventional sociology. It is the overarching guiding paradigm of Indian sociologists. They constantly argue that Indian society is in a process of rapid transformation. And, to them, the massive change is 'adaptive change'. The argument is something like this: There are traditions in India, which have not been changed, they still maintain their status quo; at the most they have been adaptively modernized. This is how functionalism has put Indian sociologists into a closed iron case. They have put on blinkers.

**Culture Change**

Sociologists of contemporary India have been very vocal in stressing the importance of cultural change. It means change in values, customs and manners. Social anthropologists are no exception to this trend. All this has put on the backseat the need to understand the hard realities of life which the ordinary people have to face. The concepts which have become the prime treasure of sociology and social anthropology include sanskritization and westernization, little and great traditions, parochialization and universalization, organization of traditions, dominant caste and caste functionalism. This is all that the sociologists and anthropologists mean by cultural and social change.

Change for whom or for what? Dominant castes, twice-born castes and the higher ranks of society are the imitation models for the lower castes, scheduled tribes and the other backward classes. If the disadvantaged groups have to undergo the processes of cultural change, they have to follow the values, customs, beliefs and lifestyles of the higher castes. In this process of the so-called cultural change, the sociologists have never argued for the loss of identity of lower groups.

It seems there is a well-planned, long-drawn strategy to convert the poor and marginal sections of society to what is today called 'cultural nationalism'. The concept of sanskritization was used first by M.N. Srinivas to describe the process of cultural mobility in the caste hierarchy of Indian society. The term used at first was *Brahminization.* Such a contribution by an eminent sociologist was given to the succeeding generation of students; decade after decade, with the hope that the lower castes would transform themselves on the lines or model of the higher and dominant caste. What would be the effect of this gigantic process on the lower or subaltern castes? The knowledge of these processes of cultural changes, included at academic level at the university, is always and invariably in the form of the courses on sanskritization and its allied processes. The topics and themes of caste ranking, caste politics, joint family, and village unity have long remained the sociological pedagogy of all Indian civil services as also regional services. The image of sociology that our sociologists have built up can hardly be called to be satisfactory. One often cannot see the wood for the trees. Being bare bones it urgently needs flesh and sinews.

**An Overdose of Civilization**

The structure of society that India once had during the times of Mohanjodaro or the epics or the golden period of ancient India does not exist today. Our civilization was great indeed. But, the traditions which developed through this period have ceased to have any substantial existence. How can and do we justify our contemporary existence by clinging to the concepts of glorified joint family, caste and *Panch Parmeshwar*? Our perspectives of understanding and analyzing society are sadly, in a real sense, merely mythological, that is, lop-sided and distorted.

**Rejection of Modernity**

Sociology in our country has shown an extravagant fondness for ethnicity and modernity. First, it was the turn of ethnicity. Our anthropological literature is very rich in ethnicity. We have made fantastic claims on the achievements of our village communities. For instance, Henry Maine and C.T. Metcalfe have reported that village communities were little republics, having had nearly everything that they want within themselves, and almost cut away from all foreign relations. What these British anthropologists proclaim needs authentic evidence.

This period of the celebration of ethnic glorification was followed by a period of a more realistic assessment. Modernity bears the stamp of rationality. This period was marked by colonialism in India and feudalism in its princely states and in its villages. It was accepted that sociology would do something substantial to guide our struggle for independence. Sociological studies and objectives were for a freer, more egalitarian society. The victimization and enslavement of the subject people was beyond any description. That was the time when the British administrators-turned anthropologists, such as Hu Hon, Risley, O'Malley and others, were busy writing about caste, tribe and village and giving impetus to a new view of the then Indian society. In the European context, sociological studies fired visions of rapid and even revolutionary social vision. In India too, sociology has been expected to play the same role.

During the period of colonization and feudalism, the Indian anthropologists and sociologists followed the same track. G.S. Ghurye was greatly engaged in writing about caste, class, race, familial and sexual behaviour of American females. Our celebrated anthropologist Iravati Karve was busy writing on complexity and rigidity of caste and kinship. Anthropologists and sociologists created a 'valuable' ethnology without paying any serious attention to the gathering crises of the country. It was felt that they were themselves alienated from their own society.

What we have sought to maintain is that either our sociologists have over enthusiastically followed the western ideology of social sciences or have clinched only those local or domestic issues which did not have any relevance for the Indian society. The question is, if challenged, how would our sociologists respond to their lack of social responsibility? It appears that the non-social scientists and writers have written much about the damaging role that colonialism and feudalism played in Indian polity. And, these writers have been punished for their patriotism. Sociologists claim that they study the society in a very objective way. Have they kept any record of the fact of their suffering imprisonment for studying the impact of colonialism and feudalism?

Modernism, it is said, emerged in India during the British period. Quite earlier to modernism, Europe experienced enlightenment. It refers to the 18th century which stretches from England's Glorious Revolution (1688) to the outbreak of the French Revolution (1789). Enlightenment has been defined as dispelling darkness of ignorance, fear, and pseudo-religions, superstitions; of removing all the shackles from enquiry and debate. It opposed the traditional powers and beliefs of the church and raised questions of political legitimacy. Rationality, as opposed to blind, traditional faith, became the central point of discourse. It is to this project of enlightenment that science and technology became the major achievement of this upheaval. This was the epoch which assured to bring about a world radically transformed. The desire to master nature developed into the dream of mastering society and history.

Modernity went a step further. It made attempts to give a death blow to conservative tradition. It has been described variously. But there is a broad consensus among all writers on modernity that it involves a belief in the possibility of human progress; rational planning to achieve its objectives; a belief in the superiority of rational thought compared to religious faith and emotion; trust in the ability of technology and science to solve human problems; a belief in the ability and rights of human beings to shape their own lives; and the reliance upon manufacturing industry to improve living standards.

Society developed hand in hand with modernity. Durkheim, Max Weber and Karl Marx tended to believe that societies could and would progress. It was also thought that scientific principles would be used to understand society, and that rational thought could be employed to ensure that society was so organized as to fulfil and meet human needs. About two hundred years have passed since the working of the processes of modernization in India set in. But nothing substantial has happened. It has been difficult to get out of the rut. But winds of change have begun to blow, at least, through the urban society. Rural sector cannot be left far behind.

Our sociologists took up the theme of modernity sometime in the beginning of seventies. But, the perspectives adopted by them were erroneous. For instance, Yogendra Singh and Milton Singer discussed the issue of modernity in the idiom of tradition and civilization. Yogendra Singh is bilinear in approach. It appears he cannot analyze Indian modernity only in the context of India's tradition. For him traditions mean hierarchy, holism, continuity and transcendence. Actually, Yogendra Singh seems to be very much influenced by Louis Dumont. Dumont is notoriously known in India for his doctrinaire functionalism. He makes straightjacket classification of western and Indian societies, the former being egalitarian and the latter hierarchical. In other words, Indian society is a traditional society and the western society a modern one. Yogendra Singh is so much obsessed by the civilizational depth of India that he concludes by saying that a strange kind of adaptive transformation is taking place in India which makes traditions to take to modernity. Obviously, Yogendra Singh is very much influenced by India's civilization and British inspired functionalism.

Milton Singer, yet another advocate of civilizational approach and functionalism, argues:

> The movement of modern nationalism in India, as in most other countries, has always shown a strong interest in the recovery or reinterpretation of India's traditional culture.

Singer argues that civilization in India is the greatest bond of providing continuity to the society and tradition is the source which creates opportunities of job, employment as well as academic – for example, research and creativity – for the people. Singer concludes his observation by referring to Jawahar Lal Nehru who was a modernist.

Modernism failed the society in the west. The euphoria of enlightenment and modernity has left people disenchanted. The sociologists of these countries moved along with the times, more or less, abandoning modernity. As is the situation today "... the centrally of the west as the promised land of modernity stands not only eroded and decentred but also dispersed". Lewis Mumford's *Myth of Machine* (1967), Pitrim A. Sorokin's *The Crisis of Our Age* (1945) and K. Polanyi's *The Great Transformation* (1944) had already provided glimpses of the postmodern imagery of societies many decades ago. The west has ceased to be the centre of social inspiration. Daneal Bell's famous volume, *The Cultural Contradictions of Capitalism* (1976), has presented a poignant diagnosis of generally ailing segments of American society and demonstrated successfully the dissociation of norms from values and of means from ends, relating to processes of production, consumption and politics. "Modernity, in its post-war phase, suffered a credibility crisis, and this crisis made suspect the ruling assumption of modernity, namely, the assumption that science, reason, and rationality would lead to the making and shaping of a sane and sensible society."

The new sociology, which is increasingly becoming popular in the west, criticizes modernity and suggests that sociologists should say goodbye to tradition and ethnology. They should rather take up the problems which plague the contemporary society. The western people now do not care to read sociologists who write on the discourse of tradition and modernity. Haralambos and Holborn observe:

> People no longer believe in the inevitability of progress, the power of science to solve all problems, the perfectibility of humanity or the possibility of running societies in a rational way. People are more pessimistic about the future and much less willing to believe that the truth can be found in grand theories or ideologies such as Marxism. There is now a much wider variety of beliefs and most people are unwilling to accept that one set of ideas gives the absolute truth and all others are false. This seems no simple recipe for solving the problem of the world.

The contemporary sociology that we have created in India is not a substantive sociology. It does focus on modernity but specifically on the transformation resulting from it which has been analyzed only as adaptive culture change. The social structure in this process does not experience any radical change; it retains its identity, content and structure. The changes are only superficial displaying a modern facility. Tradition, civilization, culture and norms are the only arching characteristics of the Indian model of modernity.

There are, however, only a few exceptions to this kind of analysis of modernity. Rajendra Singh (2001), however, is one such sociologist who has examined new social movements in his book with the perspective of postmodernism. He considers modernity and postmodernity as the co-processes of most contemporary societies. He argues: "Postmodernity symbolizes both, a critique of modernity as well as a new apperception of the current nature of social processes and the consequent emergence of a new conception of society and social movement."

## Challenge to Tradition, Modernity and Identity

The mainstream sociology that we have today or which we have inherited does not have any grain of societal reality. It is all contained in verbose statements. There is nothing substantial – all unnecessary words, creating confusion. Those of the sociologists who have analyzed the impact of modernity invariably talk about tradition. And the term 'tradition' is used with reference to civilization. The whole treatment of civilization is in the terms of Samuel Huntington's influential book, *The Clash of Civilizations and the Remaking of the World Order* (1996). The difficulty with Huntington is that he classifies civilizations largely on the basis of religion. He contrasts civilizations as 'Islamic civilization', 'Hindu civilization', 'Buddhist civilization' and so on. Milton Singer, Yogendra Singh and others explain modernity in terms of tradition and the tradition is a part of Hindu civilization. Hierarchy, holism, continuity and transcendence are all sectors of Hindu mythology.

Milton Singer is a doctrinaire functionalist. His view on modernity is, therefore, essentially civilizational, that is, functionalist. His depiction of tradition runs as under:

> The word 'tradition' connotes the act of handing down and what is handed down from one generation to another. It means both process and product. A civilization may be thought of then as a structure of tradition, that is, as a persisting form of arrangements for the handing down of cultural substance within a great community, the community that civilization .... The local community within a civilization is ideationally, intellectually, and often morally, 'heteronomous' – dependent on norms coming to it from without.

If we carefully analyze the essays contained in Milton Singer's edited volume, *Traditional India* (1975), we will soon find that it is Hindu India to the exclusion of Muslims, Christians and Jews.

With Yogendra Singh's thesis that India's traditions, such as, hierarchy, caste, holism, continuity and transcendence, are in a state of adaptive transformation, and are getting modern. He also wants to convey that Hindu civilization is getting modernized. He has, however, a soft corner for Islam and modernization in India.

But he does not take into account other ethnic groups of the country such as Sikh, Jain and Buddhist.

The civilizational approach taken by sociologists and anthropologists in the study and analysis of the impact of modernization in India is obviously sectarian and biased. Civilization has continuity; it carries with it an organization of traditions. But it is not always that civilization and for that matter, traditions are not without diversity. Amartya Sen, in his *Identity and Violence* (2006), while rejecting Samuel Huntington's thesis of civilization clash, expresses his views:

> Civilizational clash suffers from foggy perception of world history which overlooks, first, the extent of internal diversities within these civilizational categories, and second, the reach and influence of interactions – intellectual as well as material – that go right across the regional borders of so-called civilizations.

The functionalist sociologists forget that the impact of modernization is not similar on all the traditions. And, therefore, to consider modernity with tradition is theoretically wrong. If we look at the Indian experience of modernity, the fallout is not satisfactory. Our expectation with the modernity was that it will provide us all-round development; millions of our villages will get self-sufficiency; agriculture would enable the people to fulfil their livelihood needs. It was believed that green revolution of sixties would strengthen the poor peasant. But modernization did not bring any worthwhile change in the poor status of the farmers. At the urban level, the general masses are alienated. Similar is the output of our democracy. Adaptive transformation experienced in the wake of modernization has made Indian society a victim of despair. At this stage of our discussion on the challenges given by modernity and modernized traditions, we cannot do better than to quote V.S. Naipaul who observes in his *India: A Million Mutinies Now* (1990):

> With industrialization and economic growth people have forgotten all reverences. Men honoured only money now. The great investment in development in over three or four decades had led only to this: to 'corruption,' to 'criminality' of politics. In seeking to rise India had undone itself. No one could be sure

> of anything now; all was fluid. Policeman, thief, and politician: the roles have become interchangeable. And with money – the money of which the crowded, ugly skyscraper towers of Bombay spoke – many long – buried particularities had been released.

Modernity has played havoc in this country. People of older generation do not even hesitate to say that the earlier times were far better than the present epoch of modernity. Their life was easy; there were no business hurry and flurry. Modernity, that is, belief in the possibility of human progress, has proved false. The high-ups in the society have cornered most of the benefits of urbanization, democracy and centralized planning. And to our surprise, sociology developed along with its all the abuses of modernity. It continues to sing the song of cultural change, using the terminology of epistemology. What we guess is that non-professional sociologists have done better services to society than the professional ones. They have very tightly locked the iron cage of functionalism. It is their methodology, theory and ideology all over. When the colonial rule oppressed the mass of people, when people lived an inhuman life, our sociologists were engaged in creating caste, kin, food raising and village profiles. If India's best village studies, such as *Village India*, *India's Villages*, and *Indian Village*, are translated into many of the regional languages, the buyers would be only a 'tiny' fraction of society. Contrariwise, the works of Hindi writers such as Prem Chand, Fanishwar Nath Renu and Jāi Shankar Prasad, who have written about the pathetic life of Indian peasants, have run into several editions. Even after the death of these writers, the frequency in the editions of these books has not diminished. There is no dearth of sycophancy in the community of sociologists. When S.C. Dube's *Indian Village* appeared in 1955, it was acclaimed to be a classical study. It had drawn the attention of sociologists and social anthropologists, nationally and internationally. Dube ventilated through this study "the basic underlying factors which shape the making of Indian society and culture".

Interestingly enough, when the flood of village studies came out in the earlier part of the sixties, the Government of India had launched Community Development Programmes (CDPs) in the country. The government had nothing to learn from village studies. The studies were taken to be every Indian's fund of commonsense knowledge. *Indian Village*, by any standard, was not more than a telephone directory. It could have proved to be informative for the foreign audience. But Dube had set the ball rolling and during a single decade, several village studies came up.

**Challenge to Tradition and Modernity**

Postmodernity is a challenge to contemporary modernity in India. It was due to modernity that the disadvantaged people suffered. Social stratification became sharp. Caste and religious identity took the shape of fundamentalism. The ethnic elaboration which sociologists and anthropologists made in their works proved to be harmful to the Indian social order. Modernity, democracy and capitalism worsened the already deteriorating status of the poor and the subalterns. Sociology and sociologists were not concerned with this section of society but following the idiom of functionalism, they were very much writing about hierarchy. Their model of imitation was Louis Dumont.

There were, however, a couple of intellectuals both – Indian and foreign – who tried to understand India's societal reality more objectively. For instance, A.R. Desai made ground coverage of the struggle for India's freedom and the situation of poor people. His Marxian perspective aside, Desai worked as an authentic analyst of Indian society. Democracy, capitalism and urbanization have been highly vulgarized and democracy in India is a mere sham. For an ordinary man in the street it has become difficult to bear it any more. He is increasingly becoming uneasy and rebellious. V.S. Naipaul (1990) gives the following warning:

> In the 130 years or so since the mutiny – the last 90 years of the British Raj and the first 40 years of independence begin increasingly to appear as part of the same historical period – the idea of freedom has gone everywhere in India. Independence was worked for by people more or less at the top, the freedom it brought has worked its way down. People everywhere have

> ideas now of whom they are and what they owe themselves. The process quickened with the economic development that came after independence; what was hidden in 1962, is not easy to see, what perhaps was only in a state of becoming has become clearer. The liberation of spirit that has come to India would not come as release alone. *In India, with its layer below layer of distress and cruelty, it had to come as disturbance. It has to come as rage and revolt. India was now a country of a million little mutinies* (emphasis added).

V.S. Naipaul argues what modernity, democracy, industrial revolution and capitalism have done for India is "group excess, sectarian excess, religious excess, regional excess and the beginning of self-identity". Sociology could not give any cautious signal to the intellectuals of the country. In all the earlier two hundred years of its history, this part of social sciences remained buried in the concepts of ethnicity, caste, kin, joint family and village communities. Added to it, there has not come out any exhaustive study, as a critique of modernity. Modernity, on the other hand, is even now acclaimed as some earth-moving cultural transformation.

In the country's national life there are political doctrinaires who more than often preach the ideology of cultural nationalism, that is, *Hindutva.* In the field of sociological intellectualism, there is no dearth of the practitioners of empiricism and sectarian historicism, who often write in the metaphor of culture, cultural change, its epistemology and history of traditions and hierarchy. As a matter of fact, sociologists have their own make-believe world. Non-sociologists are not allowed to enter their world. And, this permits a wide range of sycophancy among the sociologists. The mainstream sociologists have not created any theory of this discipline of studies and what they have to their credit are a few working hypotheses such as sanskritization, westernization and dominant caste system. These 'restricted' or limited-view concepts were created during the seventies and now after forty years they have continued to enjoy the same status. They form an inevitable part of the syllabuses of competitive examinations decade after decade which keep them kicking and alive.

**Why do Sociologists not talk about Postmodernity?**

Modernity has come to stay as long as it may have to in India. It has brought some changes in social structure. But, by and large, the changes are not basic to the Indian society. It appears that modernity has failed as a giant process of transformation or there are changes which have benefited only the higher castes and elites. Postmodernity has thrown a challenge to modernity. It was expected that with the coming of modernity, Indian society, mainly its subalterns, would come out of the rut and make progress. History would be forward looking. But it did not happen. Yogendra Singh raises this question in his *Culture Change in India* (2000) as under:

> Why is it that despite radical legislative measures to bring about change, the norms of social hierarchy, degree of empowerment of women and extent of religious and cultural tolerance remain confounded? Culture changes only slowly and adaptively, social anthropologists have variously explained it as being a result of the fact that a culture is always integratively continued. Each culture has a basic 'theme' or 'pattern' or 'symbolic code' which constitutes its core, and all changes in it are mediated by it.

The Indian society has been suffering terribly. Democracy has been abused. Economic growth has gone in favour of the rich. People have lost faith in science and technology. They have become aware, for example, of the damaging effects of pollution, the dangers of a future nuclear war and risks of genetic engineering. People have become more sceptical about the benefits of rational planning. As a matter of fact, people have lost faith in the loudly proclaimed political beliefs and grand theories that claim to be able to improve society. It has been a common observation in India that only modernity-inspired rationalism cannot solve the manifold complex problems of the masses.

In the western countries, people do not look for the solution of their problems in the classical thinkers, namely, Durkheim, Max Weber and Marx. Their idiom of theorizing is the totality of contemporary society. The advocates of the idea of postmodernism claim that the classic social thinkers took their inspiration from the idea that history has a shape – it goes somewhere and leads to progress – and that now this notion has collapsed. There are no longer any 'grand narratives' or 'meta narratives' – overall conceptions of history or society – that make any sense. Not only is there no general notion of progress that can be defended, there is no such thing as history itself.

What we are arguing is that sociology in the west is struggling hard for its survival. It has thrown a challenge to tradition and modernity. It has also discarded the methodology of abstract empiricism. It is not shy of condemning the modern theorizing and research methodology of our Indian experience which is altogether different. What the postmodern western sociology has abandoned in the west, we have borrowed it very gladly. Our quality of research is highly 'modern'. Even, the Indian Council of Social Science Research (ICSSR) and the University Grants Commission (UGC), which provide guidelines for project funding, lay much emphasis on empirical research. Such a research is nothing but a statistical report on some field data. It is believed widely that a research work in sociology should bring out as many statistical tables as possible. The richness of research is measured on the scale of abstract empirical data. And, to top to this faulty approach, there are no authentic, creative ideas which generously contribute to the fund of knowledge. Field work in these researches is carried out by the researchers in their drawing rooms. The word 'field' here is a misnomer. And, this 'technique' adopted by the sociologists from university departments to a tehsil headquarters college have become so popular that a mass of scholars have emerged as experts in sociology. The sociological 'field' is littered with such half-alive, half-dead figures of studies.

The meaning of sociology today has changed according to the new needs of society. Our problems are created by the misuse of tradition, modernity and identities. Quite a few sociologists have given legitimacy to tradition in the name of Hindu civilization. Surprisingly, when we scan western sociological literature on modernity and postmodernity, we do not find any reference to tradition in the index. And, in India, it is argued that modernity cannot be discussed without reference to tradition. It appears that *Hindutva* ideology has been introduced into sociology through modernity.

**Identity, the Root Cause**

Sociologists have created a huge literature on caste system. Castes are the oldest social formations of Indian society. These hierarchy-based divisions have not posed any challenge to the society. They were considered to be a part of our all-enveloping religion. And, there are ample evidences – all *shastric* – to prove that Indian society was essentially a caste-based society. But, with the coming of modernity to India, the society developed a caste identity. There has been a vigorous development of caste consciousness, which is called *casteism*. Politics plays a dangerous role to benefit from caste identity. This identity has many faces. It also has a role to play in voting behaviour, economic development and social change. In his recent work, Amartya Sen puts forward the thesis that most of current fire of India is due to the conflicting identities of the people – religiously and linguistically divided.

Amartya Sen diagnoses the structure of identity and says that a person has multiple identities. When sociologists argue that caste identity is culture identity, they are mostly mistaken. When S.C. Dube tried to measure the impact of community development, he did so by taking Rajput village and other caste villages in his book *India's Changing Villages*. To him, culture, that is, caste is a major determinant of development. The tendency of sociologists has been to assess secular themes in the perspective of culture and culture for them has always been religion, caste and fundamentalism. Amartya Sen is very specific when he clarifies the concept of identity:

> Our cultural identities can be extremely important, but they do not stand starkly above and aloof from other influences on our understanding and priorities. There are a number of qualifications that have to make while acknowledging the influence of culture on human lives and actions. First, important as culture is, it is not uniquely significant in determining our lives and identities. Other things, such as class, race, gender, profession, politics, also matter, and can matter powerfully .... Second, culture is not homogeneous attribution – there can be great variations even within the same general cultural milieu. Culture interacts with other determinants of social perception and action. For example, economic globalization brings in not only

more trade, but also more global music and cinema. Culture cannot be seen as an isolated force independent of other influences. The presumption of insularity – often implicitly invoked – can be deeply delusive.

## Need for New Theories of Society

In the foregoing pages, what we have tried to explain is that sociology as an intellectual discourse has certain obligations towards the society. In the past, the mainstream sociology has not done anything worthwhile for the improvement of Indian society. Its methodology – functionalism – has always remained conservative and pro-capitalist. In the name of culture and culture transformation, it has always talked about adaptive pattern of change. The western sociology has been straightforward. When it found that the founding fathers of sociology – Durkheim, Max Weber and Karl Marx – ceased to have their relevance, they without any hesitation, abandoned them; even the modern theorists – Talcott Parsons, Robert Merton, Peter Blau – have also been rejected. Hardly anyone cares to read them. They have lost their relevance in the attempts to solve the problems of their society. Now, they are trying postmodern thinkers. Stuart Hall et al. (1988) express their disenchantment with the outcome of the processes of modernization. They argue that the contemporary western countries are constantly a state of flux:

> Our world is being remade. Mass production, the mass consumer, the big city, big brother state, the sprawling housing estate, and the nation-state are in decline; flexibility, diversity, differentiation, mobility, communication, decentralization, and internationalization are in the ascendant. In the process, our own identities, our sense of self, our own subjectivities are being transformed. We are in transition to a new era.

## Postmodern Society and Postsociology

The modernity which India witnessed during the last about two hundred years has been a study of society as a whole or in totality. During this period sociology developed as a mainstream (conventional) sociology. The modern perspective has not succeeded in understanding the reality of our society. As a consequence of it, postmodernity has taken over. Society is now seen as a reality too devoid of centrally binding and cohering entity to be conceived of as a totality.

We do not argue that postmodernity in India will solve many of our problems. But, for one thing, we are certain. We as sociologists should throw a challenge to modernity, tradition and ethnicity, and above all to science. We have tried all these perspectives to analyze the problems of our society. The conventional paradigm of sociologists, characterized by historicism, cultural nationalism, functionalism and totality, must be given a vibrant goodbye. For sociology, taking to postmodernism and using its perspective to analyze present Indian society, it is a trying time. Let us join ourselves this venture.

# 11

# Theorizing Modernity and Postmodernity

> All intellectual disciplines and institutions take for granted that not everything has been said, written, or recorded; that words already heard or pronounced are not the best words (Lyotard, 1989: 37). We live in an imperfect world, one that will always be imperfect and therefore always harbour injustice. But we are far from helpless before this reality. We can make this world less unjust; we can make it more beautiful; we can increase our cognition of it (Wallerstein, 1999:250).
>
> Postmodernism seeks not only to deconstruct the accepted social categories but to depict a world produced by and producing multiple discourses. The critical position points to the Eurocentric character of the 'grand narratives' both in their meaning and in the way they support global power relations (Seidman, 1919: 139).

If postmodernity has questioned and challenged modernity, the former will not also be without challenge in the future. Lemert (1992: 245) has rightly observed, "sociological theory itself must challenge the authority of all theories of the world". Seidman (1991: 190) further adds that "sociology's legitimacy in the future rests on its encouragement of an open, reflexive, elaborated culture of public debate on the meaning and moral character of our social arrangements".

The emergence of the popularity of postmodernity in Europe and its beginning in India promises a bright future for sociological theorizing. Postmodernity is a disputed thought in our country. A section of sociologists maintain that there is hardly any existence of modernity in India. Indian society is still a feudal society or semi-feudal/semi-capitalist. It is an incomplete project. Others, however, are optimistic and suggest that postmodernity is very much alive in India. We have taken a position in the present work that postmodernity in this country is increasingly becoming pervasive. This position has motivated us, first, to identify the major parameters of postmodernity, and secondly to apply these parameters for an analysis of India's social institutions, social themes and problems. Admittedly, we have sociology which evaluates family, kin, caste and village communities from the framework of tradition and modernity. Such an analysis has proved that we have not witnessed any meaningful and substantial societal transformation. Whatever social change we observe is adaptive social change. People, the subalterns, it is certain, have rejected this kind of modernity. Modernity has, in fact, cheated the masses of people.

The present work on postmodernity is a fresh approach to understand the traditional Indian society. The new look at the institutions would perhaps help us to better understand our contemporary society. To begin with, we would first identify the perspectives on postmodernity at a general or global level. Secondly, we would try to understand the meaning of postmodernity in terms of India's experience. And, finally, we would put forward some of the social themes which are disputed and termed as problematic in contemporary India.

## Postmodernity: A Historical Backdrop

The European society lives today in a postmodern world. Though the concept is, by now, very familiar, it has not yet been precisely defined. The difficulty in defining postmodernity is that it has not yet enough empirical evidence to enable us to come to some broad generalizations. Despite this, Stuart Sim (2005:VII) says:

> Yet it is striking that few people can say with any sense of assurance what that term 'postmodern' actually means or involves. Some theorists have suggested that it is as much a

> mood of mind as anything else. But they do not seem to be agreed that it is widely in evidence... In a general sense, postmodernism is to be regarded as a rejection of many, if not most, of the cultural certainties on which life in the west has been structured over the past couple of centuries. It has called into question our commitment to cultural progress (that national economics must continue to grow, that the quality of life must keep improving indefinitely, etc.) as well as the political systems that have underpinned this belief.

The emergence of postmodernity is accounted for several reasons in the west. It is alleged that in its history, that is, during the era of modernity, human kind was oppressed. It is because of it that postmodernism is critical of universalizing theories, that is, grand narratives or meta narratives as they have been dubbed by Jean-Francois Lyotard. These theories are authoritarian in their outlook. It has been surmised that fundamentalism which we find in the west and India, has created terrible religious conflicts. Stuart Sim attributes the event of 9/11 – when the World Trade Centre in New York was bombed and demolished by religious or holy fanatical warriors of rabid, irrational fundamentalists. They were brought to public eye in the form of grand narratives. The grand narratives are now acknowledged as threat to people all over the world. India, too, has its share of grand narratives in the context of its great tradition and small historical ups and downs, its victories and defeats, its absorption of invaders as well as its failure to come to terms with fanatical, bigoted violent hordes. These traditions draw their strength from epics, Brahmanas and scriptures. Those who advocate cultural nationalism promote religious fundamentalism on these mythological texts. Postmodernity reconstructs all these meta narratives.

The history of the word 'postmodernity' goes back to 1870s, and although it proceeds to crop up periodically over the next few decades, sometimes with positive, sometimes with negative connotations, it is only in the latter half of the 20th century that it comes to take on the precise meaning of a reaction against modernism and modernity. We can run through some of those usages briefly to see how the concept has achieved its current form.

Earlier, the meaning of postmodernity was related to art and painting. The English painter John Watkins Chapman suggested that any art that went beyond impressionism, the revolutionary new art style of the period, would be definable as 'postmodern painting'. By 1917, the concept was used in terms of militaristic and anti-humanistic culture which was prevalent in Europe during the war. During 1920s and 1930s, the concept in America was used for religious matters. Arnold Toynbee, the British historian, in his celebrated work, *A Study of History*, mentioned that the period from 1835 onwards was the "postmodern age of western history". During this period, there was cultural decline – it was the period of two world wars. It is clear that postmodernity had its affiliations to fine arts and fashion.

Stuart Sim (2005), while tracing the history of the development of postmodernity, concludes:

> Postmodernity has proved to be in the field of architecture as a conceptual term. The architectural theorist, Charles Jencks, has done more than anyone to popularize postmodernism as a theoretical concept, particularly in the series of editions of his best known book – *The Language of Postmodern Architecture* (first edition, 1977). Jencks was highly critical of modern architecture, which he thought had lost touch with the general public.

Jencks illustrated the revolt against modern architecture by bulldozing of the award winning Pruitt-Igor housing complex in St. Louis, Missouri in 1972. It showed the public mood for rejecting modernity. Modernity or modern architecture was found to have alienated people from the community. Jencks favoured architecture which freely mixed the old and new styles.

Thus, postmodernity had its first revolt against modern architecture sometime in the middle of the 20th century. In the later part of this century, it appeared in ecology movement, which found technology and factory harmful, environmentally. 'Green' political parties were formed in many western European countries to criticize the evil environmental effects of technology and industry.

Many creative artists reverted to older styles that audiences felt more comfortable with, rather as Charles Jencks was calling on architects to do in their field. Philosophers and cultural theorists reacted against theories such as structuralism, which reduced the world to a series of interlinked systems with their own internal dynamic or 'deep structure'. The workings of the entire world could be mapped out in terms of these deep structures, which dictated how all systems operated. To explain the importance of postmodernity during this period of intellectual despair, we will quote again Stuart Sim, who says:

> Structuralism in dominance in mid-century intellectual enquiry (particularly in France) which led to a reaction, collectively called poststructuralism, which increasingly came to challenge the assumptions on which structuralist analysis rested. Whereas structuralists emphasized similarity and interconnectedness, poststructuralists emphasized difference and open-endedness. Structuralism was a universalizing theory, post structuralists spent their time demonstrating how such theories must always fall: the battle lines were drawn.

Historically, therefore, postmodernity subsumes poststructuralism. In its initial stages of development, it came as a part of art and painting. When the art in its impressionist form was not acceptable to people, a new art form was invented. During the world war period, postmodernity took to militaristic form of expression. Culture declined during this period. And, then, it again appeared in the form of modern architecture. The idea of deep structure and its analysis appeared in France as a theory of structuralism. This was rejected by postmodernity. Historically, postmodernity is rebellious. It rejects all the overarching theories of the totality of society for example, Durkheim's theory of social fact, religion (sacred and profane), and solidarity of society. It also denies Karl Marx and argues that Marx's attempt to find general pattern of history was inevitably doomed to failure. Postmodernist theorists outrightly give up all such theories, which sought to develop overall interpretations of social change. Postmodernity, in short, has a history of reaction, rejection and rebellion.

## General Temperament of Postmodernity

Postmodernity has developed its temperament through the condition and forces of culture that Europe and US witnessed during the 20th century. It has emerged out of the abuses of modernity including democracy, capitalism, industrialization and political failings. Grand marriages, especially in the form of fundamentalism, market autonomy and grand theories of universalization, have put the present society on the verge of destruction and darkness.

Not only in the field of religion, there are meta narratives also in the realm of market fundamentalism. Market fundamentalism was coined by international financier George Sorus to describe "the restricted, unregulated laissez-faire capitalism favoured by the International Monetary Fund (IMF) and the World Bank. These institutions tend to impose this model on failing economies around the globe, sometimes as in the case of Argentina, with quite disastrous results. Market fundamentalism demands the dismantling of the state sector (encouraging privatization programmes for all state-owned industries), low interest rates, and an open market for capital". For the IMF and the World Bank the needs of the market came first. The fact is that in modern capitalistic system, faith is put on the grand narratives at the expense of its impact on individuals, and that market is the authority which cannot be called into question.

It is temperamently not accepted by postmodernity. In any case, to support grand narratives, Lyotard argues that traditional societies have evolved methods of value judgment without having to resort to any overarching grand narrative as a method of validation. In these societies, even ordinary traditions take the form of narratives. In fact, Lyotard distinguishes between grand narrative and little narrative (little tradition). He says that our culture should be based on the grand narrative rather than on little narrative, as the latter cannot have any control over the former.

What is particular about and peculiar to postmodernity is that it does have any regard for authority, whether that of state or any institution or holy books and holy men. The notion of postmodernism is inherently characterized by dissent, rebellion, pluralism, cultural difference and skeptical of authority.

Postmodernism blows away anything which is interpreted as grand narrative. When development becomes a project for a state, postmodernity rejects it as an environmental problem; or when pro-life advocates bomb abortion clinics, the postmodernists do so in the name of grand narratives, or if there is any commitment to authority, the postmodernism would fight it out saying that it is doing so because authority of any kind is a grand narrative which they rejected. To cut it short, we would say that in today's world, postmodernism confronts an array of such narratives, modern and pre-modern, that refuse to accept any challenge to their authority.

## Postmodernism: A Philosophy

Postmodernism, as it began from France, is considered to be a system of philosophy. Probably, the leading figure in this respect to be mentioned is Jean-Francois Lyotard whose book, *The Postmodern Condition: A Report on Knowledge* (1970), is widely considered to be "the most powerful theoretical expression of postmodernism". Lyotard's plea that we should reject the grand narratives (that is, universal theories) of western culture because they have now lost all their credibility, sums up the ethos of postmodernism, with its disdain for authority in all its many guises. There is no longer any point in engaging with, for example, Marxism, so the argument goes; rather we should ignore it as of no irrelevance to our lives. Postmodern philosophy provides us with the arguments and techniques to make that gesture of dissent, as well as with means to make value judgements in the absence of overall authorities.

When postmodernism is described as a philosophy, it takes skepticism as its central point of argument. It is said that whatever we have received as our inherited wisdom, tradition, culture, and political norms must be put to a sceptical enquiry. Stuart Sim puts postmodernism to the test of philosophy when he says:

> Scepticism is essentially a negative form of philosophy, which sets out to undermine other philosophical theories claiming to be in possession of ultimate truth, or of criteria for determining what counts as ultimate truth. The technical term to describe such style of philosophy is *anti-foundational*. Anti-foundationalists dispute the validity of the foundations of

discourse, asking such questions as what guarantees the truth of your foundation (that is, starting point)? Postmodernism has drawn heavily on the example set by anti-foundationalist philosophers.

To some thinkers, postmodernism is only a branch of philosophy and should be discussed as such only. But, there are sociologists who argue that postmodernism, by all consideration, is a social science and should constitute the syllabus of sociology. Without entering into this conflict, we would include Lyotard, Jean Baudrilard, David Harvey, Anthony Giddens, Michel Foucault, Jacques Derrida, Fredric Jameson, etc., as postmodern sociologists rather than philosophers.

## Modernity and Postmodernity

Postmodernity is linked to modernity. Durkheim, Max Weber and Karl Marx have been defined as modern thinkers. Modern theories are claimed to provide a comprehensive and definitive theory of society. Such claim by modernists is not acceptable to postmodernists. Before considering the issue of the linkage of modernity with postmodernity, it must be said that both these have differential approaches to study sociology. For example, modern sociological theory, such as that of Weber, Marx and Durkheim, believes that it is possible to find out the objective truth about society, whereas postmodernism does not.

Commenting on the distinction of modernity and postmodernity, Haralambos and Holborn write:

> Modernity and postmodernity are terms used to describe different eras in the development of human societies. While some people believe that western societies have moved from modernity to postmodernity, others do not agree. Thus, the debate about modernity and postmodernity includes arguments the extent to which society has changed and about the sort of theoretical approach that should be used in sociological studies.

## Modernity

During the pre-modern era, the simple societies, free of heavy argumentation, such as tribal and primitive, believed that religion, superstition and tradition formed the basis of social life. There was no conception of social change as 'progressive'. They believed that quite like the changes in seasons, social change was also circular.

Modernity involves the following concepts:

> A belief in the progress of human conditions, rational planning to achieve objectives, a belief in the superiority of rational thought as compared to emotion; faith in the ability of technology and science to solve human problems; a belief in the ability and rights of human beings to shape their own lives; and a reliance upon manufacturing industry to improve living standards.

Our classical sociologists believed that it was possible for universalistic theories to solve the problems of society and lead it to progress. It was further thought that rational planning helps us to meet human needs through proper organization. For most of its history, sociological thinking has been dominated by such approaches. However, some thinkers, including some sociologists, believe that modernity is being or has been replaced by an era of postmodernity.

Modernity is a distinct and unique form of social life which characterizes modern societies. Modern societies began to emerge in Europe from about the 15th century, but modernity in the sense used here could hardly be said to have existed in any developed form until the idea of the 'modern' was given a decisive formulation in the discourses of the enlightenment in the 18th century. In the 19th century, modernity became identified with industrialization and the sweeping social, economic and cultural changes associated with it.

Stuart Hall et al., discussing the historical evolution of modernity, write as below:

> Modernity has had a pristine past and complex historical evolution. It was constituted by the articulation of a number of different historical processes, working together in unique historical circumstances. The processes included the political (a rise of the secular state and polity), the economic (the global capitalist economy), the social (formation of classes and an

advanced sexual and social division of labour), and the cultural (the transition from a religious to secular culture). Modernity, one might say, is the sum of these different forces and processes; no single 'master process' was sufficient to produce it.

## Meaning of Modernity

Generally, the meaning of modernity is associated with the sweeping changes that took place in the society and particularly in the field of art and literature, between the beginning of Second World War and the late 1950s. There is, however, no clear demarcation by reference to date, and although the term 'postmodern' has been increasingly used to describe changes since the Second World War, there are some who argue that modernity persists, and others who see its demise as having occurred much earlier. When modernity is explained in terms of history, it is said that the world first experienced renaissance, and then, enlightenment and thereafter modernity and postmodernity. As a matter of fact, there is much disagreement on the precise dates of the beginning and end of modernity. There appears to be a general consensus on its meaning and social formations. In a broader way, modernity is associated with the following:

1. Industrialization and urbanization
2. Development
3. Democracy
4. Capitalism
5. Superiority of power
6. Free market
7. Optimism
8. The search for absolute knowledge in science, technology, society and politics
9. The idea that gaining knowledge of the true self was the only foundation for all other knowledge
10. Rationality

A discussion on modernity in social sciences is considered to be fashionable today. India witnessed modernity during the British rule. Before this, we had feudalism of ancient and medieval periods. Our country has suffered immensely at the hands of feudal and colonial rulers. Though modernity has been introduced in this country soon after the downfall of Mughal empire, we got democracy despite having industrialization and urbanization after the attainment of independence and the promulgation of constitution. It is reasonable to ask the question: how are we so much interested in the theory and processes of modernity? It is certain that the European countries experienced modernity in the aftermath of enlightenment, and India after the operation of constitution. But, why are people so much involved in modernization after the lapse of such a long span of time? It is not difficult to explore the answer to this question. There are a large number of factors, which explain our concern for modernity. Before we attempt to define modernity, let us look at the intensification of its processes.

## Intensification of the Processes of Modernity

Modernity is that distinct and unique form of social life, which characterizes modern societies. Modern societies began to emerge in Europe in about 15th century, but modernity in the sense used today could hardly be said to have existed in any developed country until the idea of the 'modern' was given a decisive formulation in the discourses of the enlightenment in the 18th century. In the 19th century, modernity got identified with industrialism and the sweeping social, economic and cultural changes associated with it. In the 20th century, several non-European societies – for example, Australia and Japan – joined the company of advanced industrial societies. Today, modernity has become a progressively global phenomenon.

Now, we shall discuss some of the important processes, which led to the development of modernity.

## Enlightenment: The Age of Reason

Enlightenment is described by the historians as the age of reason. It was premised upon a belief in the universality of reason and the universal character of scientific explanation. Modernity emerged out of this scientific nature of human society. It became clear to social scientists that if nature can be explained in terms of reason, why not society be explained scientifically. It discouraged traditional understanding of society.

The emergence of modernity thus traces back to enlightenment. Enlightenment was renaissance, humanism and the recovery of classical thought in the city states of Italy from 15th and 16th centuries. Modern science, therefore, came through enlightenment and it was during this period that the tradition of theology was questioned by scientific reasoning. The hegemony of traditions was very strong in Europe during this period and it received its first blow from modernity. It was in 1732 that Voltaire in his *Philosophical Letters* took a pleasure in mocking the conventional system of his French compatriots:

> In Christian Europe, people gently aver that the English are fools and madmen: fools because they give their children smallpox to keep them from having it, madmen because they light-heartedly communicate to these children a disease that is certain and frightful, with a view to preventing an evil that may never befall them.

The scientific shift to modernity was given by Voltaire whose role model was Isaac Newton. It was the beginning of empiricism in modernity. It had its main citadel in England. In Europe, a reverse process had taken place in the methodology of modernity. Here, rational systems of thought had taken precedence over empirical science.

All these developments in the structure of enlightenment influenced the emergence of modernity. In fact, not only economic factors were responsible for the appearance of modernity, the phenomena of empiricism and rationality too contributed to it.

### Hegemony of the Ideology of Profiteering

There were some other historical events too that intensified the process of modernity. In Western Europe, industrialization had come along with the ideology of capitalism. The desire for mass production urged the mercantile community to find out new markets for the sale of their product. Profiteering intensified the desire for building capital empires in other countries also. Weber, for the first time, linked religious ethics with the spread of capitalism. The Christian Europe got the idea that heaven could be brought down to earth by more and more profiteering. The will to enhance capitalism obliged Europe to go for colonialism. More and more markets had to be captured and kept under their jackboots. The East India Company started its business in India just in quest for new market. Along with capitalism and the urge for profiteering, modernity became a reality not only in Europe but also in parts of Asia and Africa. Industrialism has an inherent tendency to go for the development of technology, rationality, capitalism and progress.

### Political Revolutions

The 18th and 19th centuries in Europe witnessed a spell of revolutions. There was the French Revolution, the Bloodless Revolution in Britain and the War of Independence in America. These revolutions gave a death blow to monarchy. It was a period of total collapse of feudalism. In Eastern Europe also, there was a decline of monarchy. These political upheavals gave a new ideology of liberty, freedom and fraternity. Individualism occupied a prime place in society. Modernity received its ideological content from these eventful changes.

### Intersection of National and International Conditions and Processes

It is obvious that modernity is created not by one cause only. There are other causes too. There were processes within the society and also exterior to society, which contributed to the emergence of modernity. The west established its identity owing to its own endogamous development in Europe and America, and the developing countries through their external relations with western countries through colonialism.

In the process of development, modernity created a cluster of institutions, each with its own pattern of change and development. These institutions developed in different parts of the world in differential conditions. Modernity thus created the institution of nation-state and an international system of states, a dynamic and expansionist capitalist economic order based on private property, industrialism, the growth of large-scale administrative and bureaucratic systems of social organization and regulation, the dominance of secular, materialist, rationalist and individualist cultural values, and the formal separation of the 'private' from the 'public'.

### Modern Capitalism

There was capitalism in some form or the other before the advent of modernity. But, in the aftermath of urbanization, industrialization, colonialism and democracy, capitalism took a modern form. Modernity made capitalism an international affair. There emerged capitalist market relations at a global scale. These relations in turn provide modernity with its economic dynamics for growth and expansion. However, modern capitalism is not without its pattern of social inequality, particularly distinctive class relations, based on those who own and control the means of production and those who only have their labour power to sell. These social divisions have persisted over time, while becoming more complicated as a result of the emergence of new social strata and occupational groupings. It is also modern capitalism which has created distinctive social patterns of gender, racial and caste divisions.

### Birth of Counter-culture of Socialism to Capitalism

Z. Bauman looks from a different perspective as to what gave emergence to modernity. In Western Europe and America, the industrial revolution and democracy gave rise to capitalism. This, however, did not happen in Eastern Europe. Here, there was the birth of a counter-culture, called socialism. According to it, the emancipation of man is not with capitalism, it is with the ideology of socialism. Socialism, on the other hand, gave birth to a new kind of modernity, which was based on one-party rule.

If we look at the processes that shaped the destiny of modernity, there emerged two basic forms which were scientific and secular in their content – industrialization and urbanization – thus creating two distinct strands of modernity.

### The Triumph of Liberalism

The objective of enlightenment was to attain social justice for the mankind as a whole. This justice could be materialized only by economic development. Thus, liberalism triumphed over feudalism and created a model of social justice and progress. As a matter of fact, liberation is the dominant ideology of the western democracies, which has its roots in enlightenment thought. It is opposed to political absolutism in all its forms – be it monarchist, feudal, military or communitarian. What is important in this respect is that it is the triumph of liberalism which has given the values of private property and free exercise of religion, speech and association to modernity. The emergence of individualism is largely due to the impact of liberalism.

Thus, modernity has passed through a long period of its evolution and development. It has seen many ups and downs. Whatever we have in the conceptual framework of modernity is the result of multiple processes. Admittedly, modernity has always made an upward move but it has not always been a smooth walk. At the end of the Second World War, Europe lay devastated and divided. The emergence of Nazism and Fascism had shattered any complacent views of Europe as the cradle of progress in the world. The holocaust appeared to negate Europe's claim – a claim made with particular force since the enlightenment – to represent the pinnacle of civilization. Some philosophers even began to think of the enlightenment as the origin of domination and totalitarianism in the west. This kind of thinking is advanced by Horkheimar and Adorno. The war itself, moreover, had destroyed millions of lives, wrecked Europe's infrastructure, and left the world increasingly polarized between the democratic-capitalist west and the communist east.

The real blow came to modernity in 1989. If modernity means freedom, progress and emancipation of the poor and the downtrodden, the year of 1989-90 was the year of the disintegration of Soviet Russia. The changes of political regime, which swept through Central and Eastern Europe during this period, brought about a total transformation in Poland, Hungary, East Germany, Bulgaria, Czechoslovakia and Romania. The disintegration of Soviet Russia meant the death of socialism and all that it meant. It was claimed that capitalism remained the only alternative for the development of society. As a result of this shake up, the division between the democratic-capitalist and state socialist worlds, created in the aftermath of the Second World War, began to disappear. The pattern of intensive rivalry between the superpowers, perhaps the single most significant feature of world politics in the second half of the 20th century, was almost at a stroke, transformed.

Modernity has had a long span of life. It started with the enlightenment and passed through a number of intensive processes. The last stroke, which came in the event of 1989-90, gave a decisive character to modernity. Modernity, therefore, today is characterized by capitalism, democracy and secularism. At this stage of our discussion, we should also mention that modernity is multidimensional. Its form, which is found in America or Europe, is not the same as in Asia or Australia. Quite like its form, modernity has its consequences also which vary from society to society.

## Multiple Faces of Modernity

We have argued that a contemporary comprehension of postmodernity is not possible without going into some of the major features of modernity. The discussion is still more important when we move from western modernity to Indian modernity. Modernity is not a monolith in its content and structure. It varies in space and time. The modernity, which Europe witnessed, has not been experienced by India. Social milieu and historical epochs determine the course of modernity. For instance, in India, postmodernity is not opposed to modernity, it is, in the end, opposed to those classes which have largely cornered the benefits of modernity – the affluent, the rich, the high-castes and the urbanites. We, therefore, argue that there is no single form of modernity; there are several modernities. Similar arguments run for postmodernity: there is no single postmodernity, there are several post modernities.

# III

# Postmodernity: Themes and Perspectives

Postmodernity may be treated as the result of a controversial development or the growth of sociological studies. There are sociologists who believe that postmodernist theories can help solve many of our problems. There is a historical evidence to demonstrate that enlightenment and modernity have failed to critically and realistically analyze the malaise of our contemporary society. Besides, there is no single or monolithic form of postmodernity. However, there are its several variants. Despite differentiations in postmodern conditions of life, most of the postmodernists share the view that the condition of living of the general masses has to be improved and made better. In developing countries such as India, it is expected that the benefits of development which have long been enjoyed by the higher classes, must be equally made available to the disadvantaged or subaltern people. The higher classes must also share the benefits of education and technology. Postmodernity is expected to make a shift of benefits from rich to the poor, from higher and middle classes to the lower classes. The heterogeneous ethnicity should have societal legitimacy. Expectations are several. What is required is to test the credibility of postmodernity in raising the status of the lower classes. It cannot be assumed that postmodernity would have a long life the world over. There is no guarantee of it. Today, it celebrates diversity, pluralism and secularism; tomorrow, who knows it may have the fate of enlightenment and modernity. There is only one assurance of change.

Postmodernity has made a vigorous entry into the corridors of social sciences. There are sociologists, such as Habermas, who claim that modernity is still incomplete in the west and before yielding, it has yet to conquer a few ports. Anthony Giddens argues for the trial of a social reflexibility; and Castell pleads for the application of the concept of 'network society'. There are sociologists who have devoted much of their intellect in writing on postmodernity, but deny that they are postmodernists. Among them is Michel Foucault.

There is yet another sociologist, Ulrich Beck, who also rejects postmodernism. Rather than living in a world 'beyond the modern', he argues, we are moving into a phase which can be termed as 'second modernity'. The second modernity refers to the fact that modern institutions are becoming global, while everyday life is breaking free from the hold of entrenched tradition and custom. The old industrial society is disappearing and is being replaced by a 'risk society'. Beck sees it as risk or uncertainty. The management of risk is the prime feature of the global order. Beck argues that in the contemporary world what is important is that the nature of risk is changing.

The shift from modernity to postmodernity has not been cakewalk. There were problems with enlightenment and modernity and there are problems with postmodernity too. We know it all well enough. The postmodern thinkers like Baudrillard, Foucault, Habermas and Beck are also familiar with some of the features and failures of postmodernity. But we are pessimistic about the methodology, ideology and epistemology of postmodernity. Here, we take an opportunity to try it out. And, we try it in our Indian society.

### Is Postmodern Sociology Suitable for Indian Society?

The present book-length study is about postmodernity and its impact on Indian society. Since 1857, ethnography, that is, anthropology replaced history and the colonial rule made efforts to understand the reality of Indian society. There was partition of the country into India and Pakistan. And, as a result of it, a huge exodus took place in both the countries. The sub-continent was fractured and the society had appalling experiences with millions of refugees. During this period, the Indian Constitution was framed and was enforced. The fundamental rights formed inalienable part of the basic framework of the Constitution and the reservation of weaker sections reshaped the whole structure of society. It was for the first time that caste and its hierarchy got disapproval from the state. Discrimination, based on caste, creed and sex, was replaced by preferential discrimination by the state in favour of the disadvantaged.

The Indian society witnessed a historical upheaval. Caste, religion, and a large number of ethnicities along with widespread development programmes in villages run through democratic institutions, secular and capitalist nation-state. It has been a gigantic effort to transform the fragmented India into a nation. The sociologists contributed very little to the study of intertwined and complex affairs of this country. There were problems of astronomical vastness, that is, of population exodus, challenging development programmes, fundamentalism, decentralization of family, kin, and village communities, deterioration of the lower castes and poor and gender inequalities and other issues. There has been advancement in technology. Technology has not only acquired more teeth, but has also become subtle. It is now conquering more fields, and is now more variously applied. The society has rapidly turned into a media society. But our sociologists remain clung to the old doctrine of functionalism. For India, the postmodernity's enemies are not only political failings, modernization, corruption and unemployment, but also globalization and weakening nation-state.

Our objective in the present work is, firstly, to note and analyze the prime characteristics of what is called universal postmodernity. Second, we will look at the postmodern characteristics at the local level, that is, at the levels of village, region and the state. These characteristics are termed as perspective for our analytical purpose. Our intention here is to get a perspective of the various Indian institutions to see how many things they stand for. We bid goodbye to functional theorizing. We would take a similar postmodern perspective on religion, secularism, ethnicity, democracy, polity, culture, film, and several other social aspects which constitute our society.

Our methodology to bring out the perspectives would be to take up the theoretical contributions of sociologists and non-sociologists in terms of their substantial contribution to postmodernity. In this case, our emphasis would not be so much on the postmodern thinker but on his contribution. This approach appears suitable to scan out unnecessary or superfluous, as these characteristics, as thinkers have not constructed any integrated theoretical framework of the kind of mainstream thinkers. Here is a distinct and exclusive theory. For instance, Michel Foucault advanced important ideas about the relationship between ideology and discourse in relation to modern organizational system. According to Foucault, power works through discourse to shape popular attitudes towards phenomena such as crime, madness or sexuality. Take another postmodern thinker, Jean Baudrillard – a French scholar, who believes that the electronic media has destroyed our relationship with our past and created a chaotic, empty world. He argues that the present social life is influenced above all by signs and images.

For illustration, we have quoted some postmodern thinkers to show that there are some perspectives in each thinker and these perspectives constitute the yardstick for analyzing various aspects of Indian society. It is hoped that such an analysis of postmodern perspectives would help us to better understand the emerging new Indian society.

To sum it up, some of the major characteristics of postmodernity, drawn from different authors, in a systemic way, are presented as follows:

## Meta or Mega Narratives

Meta or mega narratives are also called grand narratives. The concept comes from Jean-Francois Lyotard. Lyotard is known for his renowned book, *The Postmodern Condition* (1979). He tried to make a synthesis of Freud and Marx. He believes in postmodernism. He says that postmodern is not a new epoch or the beginning of a new era. It is really a recurrent historical phase within modernism. As he puts it, the postmodern is "undoubtedly part of the modern". We have had postmodern phases earlier too within modernism and we will have them again. A work can become modern only when it is first a postmodern one. Whatever denials Lyotard might make, his analysis of postmodernism well bestows on him the status of a postmodernist. For him, the best definition of postmodernism is the presence of meta narratives. He says:

> Simplifying to the extreme, I define postmodern as incredulity towards meta narratives.

In other words, all statements against universalizing theories are false. Since the major meta narratives that Lyotard attacks are associated with the enlightenment and modernity, he rejects these. Lyotard's *The Postmodern Condition* (1979) has an interesting background. It was first published in 1929. During this year, Lyotard was commissioned by the Canadian government to submit a report on the status of knowledge in the most highly developed societies in the west. It is here in this book that the word 'postmodern' was used to describe the state of knowledge.

Meta narratives, the central notion of postmodernity, were used for the first time in *The Postmodern Condition*. Basically, postmodernity is a kind of social movement. When there is any kind of disenchantment with modernity, postmodernity emerges.

Society has fragmented into so many conflicting spheres of knowledge. Knowledge is never coherent. It is the task of postmodernity to study multiple knowledges about society and people. The present society is beset with several problems. It is becoming increasingly multicultural and our lifestyles are becoming more and more cosmopolitan. The reality is that there is no agreement among scholars and even students about what is worth believing or even knowing anymore.

The postmodern condition mainly focuses on science. Officially, Lyotard was expected by the Canadian government to report on the state of affairs of knowledge. It is here that Lyotard informs that the present society is in such a frightening state of despair that the only solution lies in the coming of postmodernity. For such a society, Lyotard argues, there cannot be a universal or timeless body of knowledge.

### Lyotard Rejects Meta Narratives and their Characteristics

Why does Lyotard reject meta narratives? The cause of rejection of meta narratives by Lyotard is simple and definite. He says that the underlying assumption of both scientific and cultural narratives is that all the societies are uniform and their ethnicity, identity and problems are the same. This assumption of meta narratives is not acceptable to Lyotard. The societies and their kit of knowledge are in a damaging state of affairs. They have become irreparable and degenerated. On the other hand, the meta narratives and the theories propounded by their authors have failed to do justice to the mankind. These theories, their impact and their application are, in fact, responsible for the degeneration of society. They cannot be allowed to continue as such any more. We shall have to generate new knowledge for the 'health' of this society.

### What are Meta Narratives?

Lyotard's definition of postmodernity lies in his thoughts on narratives. By narratives, he means, grand narratives. The grand narratives are also called meta narratives or mega narratives by Lyotard. The thing, which is told or narrated or described in detail, is a narrative. For instance, a story is narrated. There is a technical meaning of narratives in Lyotard's conceptualization. Anthony Giddens (1990) has explained Lyotard's meaning of meta narratives as under:

> Meta narratives are broad overarching theories or beliefs about the operation of society and the nature of social change. Marxism and functionalism are examples of meta narratives that have been employed by sociologists to explain how the world works. Postmodernists reject such 'grand theories', arguing that it is impossible to identify any fundamental truth underpinning human society.

### Types of Meta Narratives

There are two major types of meta narratives which have been attacked by Lyotard: (1) emancipatory, and (2) scientific. Emancipatory meta narratives are associated with the notion of reason, experience, skepticism of religion and traditional authority. These appeared in sociology from the time of enlightenment which pleaded for secularism, liberalism and democratization of human society. Lyotard argues that these emancipatory meta narratives (functionalism and Marxism) are responsible for creating possibility of war, totalitarianism, and the yawning gap between the rich and the poor. The degeneration in education, environment and employment are all due to meta narratives. These need to be condemned and rejected.

Lyotard was attracted more towards scientific narratives. Actually, these constitute the term of his enquiry. One very bold observation of Lyotard in this connection is that there is no truth in scientific knowledge. Science has no direct access to truth. The white coat wearing laboratory technicians who appear on TV channels – more than often do so to convey to us that their brand of tooth paste makes the strongest of the tooth – are only giving knowledge about their pseudo-scientific prejudicial experiment. They are mere propagandists or lop-sided purveyors of their brand. This view is not based on any scientific truth, based on a truly scientific experiment. This, in fact is a mere shadow of truth if not a travesty of it. Thus, truth is limited by the institutions in which it is created. Truth can never be universal, nor can it be timeless.

### *Meta Narratives are Totalistic Only*

Lyotard considers the meta theories of conflict and functionalism as totalistic theories. Totalization means comprising or constituting a whole or entirety. The functional theory claims to study all the societies of the world. In other words, functionalism is universal. It stands for an 'ordered' society. Contrariwise, the conflict theory argues that society is never consensual. It is always charged with conflict: the history of all the societies is the history of class war. The totalistic theories exercised their dominance during the period of modernization. Functionalism preached the ideology of capitalism, elitism, totalitarianism, and in short, status quoism. Marxism, on the other hand, promised a classless and stateless society. Lyotard declared a war on totalizing meta narratives:

> It is time to make 'war' on such totalistic perspectives. And, modernity is pre-eminent of grand narratives.

### *Meta Narratives have Legitimization*

The tragedy of the modern society is that it has given full legitimacy to the hegemony of meta narratives. The kind of democratic order, which is never for the people or, by the genuine people that we have today all over the world, is legitimized by the meta narratives. Functionalism in India has become a truism for almost all the so-called eminent sociologists. Lyotard refers to the destruction of Jews by the Nazis as commented upon by Zygmunt Bauman. Their destruction or mass killing/genocide is supported by the meta narrative theory of the superiority of Aryan race as claimed by Hitler. Meta narratives are never neutral; they are invariably partial and prejudicial. And, these narratives have enjoyed the legitimacy of the society, the state, and above all, the intellectuals.

### *Narratives are Language Games*

Lyotard finds a subtle relationship between emancipatory and scientific narratives. Wittgenstein for the first time argued that both these narratives are characterized by 'language games'. Lyotard says that social relationships are like games that require language in order to participate. Such languages are the minimum relationship required for society to exist. Language games are, from Lyotard's point of view, the social bonds.

### *Narratives are Forms of Knowledge*

Lyotard generally talks about emancipatory or cultural narratives and scientific narratives. Both these narratives are forms of knowledge. But these forms are different. The cultural narratives include denotative and definitive statements such as: one should have vegetarian diet as it keeps a man non-violent, the means to an end should be in accordance with the values of the society, always do good to others, and so on. Denotative statements depict how to live, how to listen, how to eat. Normally, the cultural narratives give some pragmatic or down-to-earth rules to the people. The society is thus bound together by these cultural narratives. These narratives carry knowledge as they have legitimacy of the society. This legitimation does not come from some external source but from the simple fact they do what they do, that is, from within.

Scientific narratives as forms of knowledge are also denotative statements. For scientific narratives, the reference is only to truth. In cultural narratives, the denotative statements include cultural and social know-how whereas, in scientific narratives the denotative is truth. Viewed from this perspective, the scientific narratives do not have the element of sharing and, therefore, they do not establish any social bonds. Commenting on the difference between scientific narratives and emancipatory or cultural narratives, Ritzer (1997) writes:

> Science, in contrast, accepts only denotative statement. In other words, it is only 'birth value' that determines the acceptability to scientific statements. Unlike narratives, science is not a direct and shared component of the social bond. Although there are these and other differences between (cultural) narratives and science, the fact is that they are both language games and one is no more or less necessary than the other.

### *Cultural Grand Narratives are Fables, Myths and Legends*

Lyotard is very critical of grand meta narratives. Much of the legitimacy of these narratives has gone away. The fact is that the present society has increasingly become plural in its culture and ethnicity. And, the grand narratives have failed to cope with the plurality of society. Lyotard writes:

> With the decline of the grand narratives, legitimacy becomes plural, local, immanent. There will necessarily be many discourses of legitimation. Legitimation descends to the level of practice.

Devoid of any grassroots legitimacy, the grand narratives have no legs to stand on. They make only fancy stories. Functionalism and conflict as forms of meta narratives and their advocates Simmel, Marx, Dahrendorf, Durkheim, Weber and Parsons have come down and collapsed as packs of cards. The narratives constructed by them as general theories of society have lost all their relevance today. Describing the irrelevance of meta narratives, Lyotard writes:

> Narratives are fables, myths, legends, fit only for women and children. In other words, science questions the legitimacy of narratives and in process, helps to legitimize 'legitimation' as a problem. Science wants everyone to believe that it offers legitimate, 'true' knowledge and it criticizes narratives for being illegitimate and untrue.

Lyotard argues that science has always been in conflict with narratives. Judged by the yardstick of science, the majority of them have proved to be false. In his work, Lyotard has defined the forms of knowledge. He defines knowledge and comes to the conclusion that scientific knowledge never gives us the whole, immutable, final truth. Science makes successive approximation to truth. And, when the meta narratives do not carry any such truth, why accept them, he asks. Some of the key ideas of Lyotard regarding scientific truths are given below:

#### *Status of Knowledge is Always Altered*

Knowledge is never universal. It is always altered when the traditional society becomes modern and the modern society takes a turn to postmodern society. This transition has been under way since at least the end of the 1950s. The pace of knowledge is faster or slower depending on the country and within countries it varies according to the sector of activity. If the knowledge had given the truth, it would have never changed. Science, therefore, does not give the absolute truth. It simply cannot, by its very nature.

#### *Scientific Knowledge is Never Neutral*

Lyotard argues that scientific knowledge is a kind of discourse. It is a framework of thinking. Foucault has proved it at length that our knowledge about madness, sexuality and punishment has changed from time to time all through the periods of history. It clearly shows that knowledge in all its respects is a discourse. There is nothing like neutrality of knowledge. It is fair to say that for the last forty years, the leading sciences and technologies have had to do with language: phonology and theories of linguistics, problems of communication and cybernetics, modern theories of algebra and informatics, computers and their language, problems of translation and the search for areas of compatibility among computer languages, problems of information storage, telematics and the perfection of intelligent terminals, paradoxology. These facts speak for themselves.

### *Technological Transformation of Knowledge*

Scientific knowledge in our present information age is subject to technological transformation. Cybernetics is the best way for the transmission of our acquired knowledge. Knowledge is also commercialized through machines. It is reasonable to suppose that the proliferation of information-processing machines is having and will continue to have much of an effect on the circulation of learning as did advancements in human circulation (transportation systems), and later, in the circulation of sounds and visual images (media). Knowledge, thus, would become common to a layman through technological devices.

### *Nature of Knowledge cannot Remain Unchanged in the Technological transformation*

When knowledge is technologically transformed, it tends to become quantitative. The fact of the matter is that in this age of technological development, the nature of knowledge cannot remain unchanged. We can predict that anything in the structure of knowledge, which cannot be transformed through machines, is abandoned and consequently the direction of research will change. We tend to accept only those researches, which are translatable into computer language. The producers and users of knowledge must now possess the means of translating into these languages whatever they want to invent or learn. Along with hegemony of computers come certain logic systems, and therefore, a certain set of prescriptions determining which statements are accepted as 'knowledge statements'.

In the case of our country, whatever knowledge is generated from the field – anthropological or sociological – is put into computers. The moment that knowledge comes out of a computer, it is taken as legitimate knowledge. The national social science research body – Indian Council of Social Science Research (ICSSR) – makes all efforts to sanction technological aid to research. And, anything that comes in large quantity is held in high esteem. As a result of the proliferation of such researches, there is a flood of research findings, which hardly enrich our treasure of knowledge. There is, thus, a constant change in the nature of our knowledge.

### *Knowledge in the Present Era has Become a Commodity*

When the celebrated Hindi poet, Tulsidas composed verses for *Ram Charit Manas,* he did it for his own self-satisfaction (*Swant-Sukhai*). The voluminous classical composition was not a piece of commodity. It never earned him any amount of money. But, in the present era, knowledge is produced in order to be sold. Such knowledge is for new production. Obviously, the production of knowledge is for exchange. Lyotard comments on the present nature of knowledge:

> The relationship of the suppliers and users of knowledge to the knowledge they supply and use is now tending, and will increasingly tend, to assume the form already taken by the relationship of commodity producers and consumers to the commodities they produce and consume that is the form of value. Knowledge is now and will be produced in order to be sold, it is and will be consumed in order to be valorized in a new production: in both cases, the goal is exchange. Knowledge ceases to be an end in itself; it loses its 'use-value'.

### *Knowledge is the Principal Form of Production*

Technological assistance is quite useful in the production of knowledge. In such a situation, knowledge works as the form of production. Those who own a larger body of knowledge are considered to be more powerful and rich. In the post-industrial and postmodern age, science has increased the productive capacity of a nation-state. The difference between the developed and developing countries is that of the production of knowledge. What is important in the content of knowledge is the information richness. The nation-states, which are endowed with more information, are considered more powerful. It is conceivable that the nation-states will one day fight for control of information, just as they battled in the past for control over territory, and afterwards for control of access to and exploitation of raw materials and cheap labour.

Ward (1997) has condensed some of the assumptions of science, which prevailed in the earlier stages of modernity. These are enumerated as under:

(1) Science is progressive; it leads us to complete knowledge.
(2) Science is unified thought. It has various fields of specialization, such as chemistry, biology, zoology, geology, technology, engineering, medicine, etc., but deep down they all share the same goal and theoretical formulations.
(3) Science has universal nature. It works for the good of all of us. Its aim is to find out the total truth. This truth will work for the benefit of the total human life.

The scientific assumptions, which worked during the early periods of modernity, still function with the same vigour. Look at the Indian TV. Switch over to any channel, and there is a flood of advertisements. Most of these advertisements prescribe solutions to your varied ailments. All these advertisements push their commodity with some kind of scientific assumption underlying them. Not only that, simple articles of daily use are also recommended with a strong dose of scientific assumption. In Europe, things have taken a different turn. Lyotard claims that around the end of the Second World War, most of the scientific myths had collapsed. What has survived today is not the big scientific narratives but the little sciences.

### *Scientific Assumptions Collapsed and hence Rejection of Narratives*

In a long period between enlightenment and mid-20th century science justified itself by claiming that it needs no justification. This is to say, it took advantage of the idea that its activities were pursued in the name of the timeless meta narratives of progress, emancipation and knowledge. By appealing in this way to ideas, whose meanings are taken to be self-evident and universally agreed, science was able to masquerade as a single project objectively carried out for the good of human race. But, after the Second World War, it was realized by the world community that the scientific assumptions, which ruled over the human mind, had collapsed. We shall discuss this next.

**Some Basic Characteristics of Meta or Grand Narratives**

Reading Lyotard's account of grand or meta narratives, we describe below some of the prime characteristics of narratives:

(1) The theories which provide universal explanations are basically false. The Marxian theory of economic determinism is an example of grand narrative. It is a totalling theory which claims to explain the global society. In Indian context, the theory of the origin of caste or the conceptual framework of sanskritization is not valid.

(2) Grand narrative is authoritarian. It restricts the individual creativity.

(3) Narratives enable traditional societies such as our own to evolve methods of value judgement without having to resort to any overarching grand narratives as a method of validation.

(4) Lyotard also pleaded for little narratives because culture depends on it. As a matter of fact, little narratives promote pluralism. In our country, we have multiple little narratives such as varying marriage patterns, family size, modes of worship, fasts and festivals and dietary folkways.

(5) In grand narratives individuals are oppressed and find themselves being sacrificed to the objectives of those controlling the grand narratives.

(6) Roland Berths observes that it was through narratives that we made sense of our world. In our society, we understand the meaning of the words like mother, woman, religion and war through our grand narratives of epics, history, local wars and rivalries.

(7) Grand narratives discourage initiatives and crush any one raising his head to bring about reforms. Traditions rule the backward societies in the name of grand narratives.

(8) The present trend of cultural change shows that in most of the countries, fundamentalism, that is, grand narrative, is on the decline. However, religious fundamentalism is on the increase. Most of the major world religions have given rise to fundamentalist religious movements. Christianity, Islam,

Hinduism, Judaism all had their holy warriors. Even now, we have a few in our north-west.

(9) Postmodernity claims to have a prestigious status in social sciences. The status is due to its attack on modernity. Modernity is nothing but grand narratives. And, these grand narratives shield or defend stagnant social life, psyche and ethos. In India too, what are stated to be traditional, are grand narratives.

(10) Narratives have given rise to a variety of fundamentalisms. There is market fundamentalism, economic fundamentalism, political fundamentalism, national fundamentalism, etc.

(11) Grand narratives are negative aspects of postmodernity. Postmodernity is also a theory of rejection. And, it calls each tradition, each custom and each classical and foundational theory as forms of grand narrative. If postmodernity wants to kill any theory, it first labels it grand narrative.

(12) There is a grand strategy in postmodernity to fight the grand narratives. It is simple: we should cease to believe in narratives. And, the narratives would whither away, unread, unattended.

(13) Grand narratives have done much injustice to the subaltern people of the colonial India. A large number of people of these sections of society were denied benefits of hospitals, or better health insurance or basic literacy. The meta narratives of modernity, thus, historically drown the voices of the people who practised the 'culture of science'.

(14) Meta narratives promote dissent in principle or "dissent from everything possible". Thus, both Marxism and modernism have become easy targets of dissenting impulse within postmodernism.

(15) Lyotard has associated narratives with language games. He says that life revolves around language games. Narratives by themselves are nothing. These are just telling of stories, myths, legends and tales. It is the principle of language game, that is, of essence. In this game, the narrator has the unalloyed legitimacy. These language games are replaced by scientific denotative games. In games, it is not important who is speaking.

(16) Meta narratives tried to find out the truth or the final truth. Postmodernity has abandoned any search for truth – absolute or ultimate. Science does not have the objective to find out the ultimate and final truth. Instead, researchers in postmodernity struggle to find the usefulness or saleability of the theme under study.

Concluding the study of the prime characteristics of postmodernity we would only say that grand narratives or meta narratives are the central themes which provide a rebellious edge to postmodernity. Narratives spare nobody – enlightenment, modernity or history. Such a destructive weapon has its usefulness not only in the western countries but elsewhere in the developing countries too. Its fight in the west is against modernity; in the developing countries, it is against tradition as well. Modernity and tradition are its enemies.

**Little Narratives**

Grand narrative is authoritarian. In the fast changing society, Lyotard argues that these narratives have lost their relevance. He, therefore, pleads for 'little narrative'. Little narratives are put together on a tactical basis by small groups of individuals to achieve some particular objectives. The groups, which celebrate little narratives, are groups of coalitions of interests. These groups do not exist for a long period. They survive till the time the objectives of the little narratives are fulfilled. One might regard individual as the ultimate little narrative seeking to resist the power of authoritarian grand narratives, such as the state.

In Indian context, little narratives are exemplified by little traditions. We have several caste groups. And, there are castes which have made their coalitions to attain certain developmental and political objectives. There are certain cultural or customary celebrations, which are observed by certain little narratives restricted to particular areas. For instance, the celebrations of *Dushehra* or birthday of Gandhiji is characterized by little local or regional little narratives. Little narratives are the basic elements which make the fabric of ethnicity.

Postmodernity is closer to the masses of people. It belongs to the local grassroots. It also gives strength to diversity. Pluralism, multi-ethnicity and multi-lingualism which constitute the little narratives, are some of the basic characteristics of postmodern sociology. Diversity goes to such an extent that in some of the north-east Bodo villages, each village has its own dialect. In backward countries, the little narratives exclusively take the form of traditions. It is not essential that little narratives should draw heavily from grand narratives. Sometimes they do, sometimes not.

## Simulation Society

Postmodernity is characterized by simulations. Simulations are images about society. There is nothing real about society. It consists of signs and images. And, these images of society flow from media. Thus, simulation is an image of something that does not exist and has never existed. It is Baudrillard who has given the concept of simulation, that is, signs and images, of the reality of society. Quite like other conventional and postmodern sociologists, Baudrillard made an attempt to understand the reality of society. He is well known for his book *Simulations* (1983). He is widely seen as a postmodern thinker. Quite like Lyotard, he sees societies as having entered a new and distinctive phase, and relates this change to language and knowledge. Unlike Lyotard, he is rather pessimistic about the consequences of this change, seeing it as a kind of a trap from which escape is impossible. Explaining the importance of signs and images in the market, Baudrillard has been commented upon by Haralambos and Hobborn (*Sociology: Themes and Perspectives,* 2000):

> Baudrillard argues, in contradiction to Marxists, that society has moved away from being based upon production and being shaped by the economic forces involved in exchanging material goods. The central importance is of the buying and selling of signs and images, which have little, if any, relationship to material reality.

Our visit to market would show that we purchase a thing because of the image its manufacturer creates. For example, we go for a tooth paste, say Colgate. Its image about cleaning the teeth is created by its manufacturer. The image that the paste cleans our teeth like a shining pearl is false. In fact, the teeth cannot be as white and shining as a pearl. Signs and images never have one to one correspondence with reality. And, therefore, we, in the market, do not purchase the product, but only its signs and images.

**Concept of Simulation**

Features of contemporary life, such as fashion, environmental design, opinion polls, theme parks, telecommunications and cybernetics have all been rolled together in Baudrillard's hands as manifestation of the single, shiny new regime of simulation. The meaning of simulation, as given by Baudrillard, is interpreted by Ward (1997) as under:

> Baudrillard uses simulation in a bewildering variety of ways, but often seems to mean by it little more than a generalized realm of reproductions, images, representations and models.

Baudrillard has elaborated the concept in his book *Simulations* (1983). He cites the examples of simulations as Disneyland, psychosomatic illness, America's Watergate scandal, and hijacks. Ward (1997) makes the meaning of simulation very clear:

> Dictionaries link simulation to the fake, the counterfeit, and the inauthentic. Baudrillard retains these meanings to a certain extent, but pushes them considerably further, so that simulation can no longer be seen clearly as the opposite of truth. We might naturally assume that simulation either duplicates or is emitted by a pre-given real. In this sense we might think that simulation and reality have a necessary attachment to each other. But, for Baudrillard, this connection has long since snapped, so that simulation can no longer be taken as either an imitation or distortion of reality, or as a copy of an original. In Baudrillard's dizzying cosmos there is no firm pure reality left against which we can measure the truth or falsity of a representation and electronic reproduction has gone so far that the notion of originality is (or ought to be) irrelevant.

Kenneth Thompson argues that Baudrillard, quite like many of the literary theorists, has taken a linguistic stance in his explanation of simulation. He has analyzed linguistic or symbolic codes purely in terms of their internal relationship without reference to some external objects that they might be supposed to represent. He has argued that words have relationship with words and not the real object. Viewed from this perspective, Baudrillard's theory of commodity culture removes any distinction between object and presentation. In their place, he pictures a social world constructed out of models or simulations which have no foundation in any reality except in their own. In fiction, the characters and the events are purely imaginary but the story represents the reality. The Hindi novelist, Prem Chand once wrote in one of his prefaces that all the dates, years and places given in his novel are creations of his imagination and even the story itself is his own creation. But it represents the reality of society.

Mark Poster (1988) has explained the meaning of simulation and argues that it is a real piece of imagery. It has no relationship with any reality. He writes:

> A simulation is different from fiction or a lie in that it only presents an absence as a presence, the imaginary as the real. It also undermines any contrast to the real, absorbing the real within itself. Instead of 'real' economy of commodities that is somehow bypassed by an 'unreal' myriad of advertising images, Baudrillard, now, discerns only a hyper reality, a world of self-referential signs. He has moved from the TV which, however, never completely erases the commodity it solicits, to the TV newscast which creates the news if only to be able to narrate it, on the soap-box opera whose daily events are both referent and reality for many viewers.

Baudrillard's favourite example which he repeats time and again of simulation is Disneyland. It is presented as imaginary in order to make us believe that the rest is real, when in fact nothing is no longer real. It is no longer a question of a false representation of reality, but of concealing the fact that the real is no longer real. As a matter of fact, Baudrillard's postmodern message is that the media images do not merely represent reality; they are reality, because their meaning derives from their position within a system of signs, not from some referent in a real world outside that system.

Baudrillard says that even our day-to-day needs are structured by signs and images. To some extent this structuring has come to India also where a few parts of the country are near postmodernity. When we go for food shopping, we choose between designer foods, health foods, exotic foods, saline-junk foods, luxury foods, natural foods, traditional foods, convenience foods and ethnic foods. Others are 'fast foods' and 'junk foods'. Out of these foods, we choose the ones which suit our image. Perhaps, our image is that of the film actress, Kajol or the cricketer, Sachin Tendulkar. Recently, a cosmetic manufacturing company has come out with a variety of cosmetic items which it claims are favourites of film actress, Madhuri Dixit. These items have made Madhuri Dixit as she looks and as she is presented by the media. And, yet another image is of Sachin Tendulkar, the famous cricketer, which is sold for anything through media, ranging from biscuit to motor tyre, car, motor bikes, cold drinks, tooth paste and even *gutkha.* All these examples show that we respond to images thrown by the media. We are nothing more than a type.

Baudrillard has discussed the simulation society in all its details. "At this stage of the development of simulations, we are at a point where we suffer from cancer and viruses. These viruses are of social nature. Our efforts to eliminate all negativity has left us with a declining ability to defend ourselves. We are vulnerable as the 'boy in the rubble' was to germs. Like the AIDS patient, we are all becoming immune deficient. Because our defences have disappeared, we are coming to be destroyed by our own antibodies, by the leukemia of the organism." Thus, to Baudrillard, "our total prophylaxis is lethal".

### Power and Knowledge

Postmodernity is interpreted differently by different sociologists. And, therefore, its characteristics do not make for an interlinked mainstream. Each postmodern sociologist has his own understanding of social reality. For instance, Michel Foucault provides an influential and moving view of power. He suggests that power is found in all social relationships and is not exercised by the state. His concept of power is intimately linked with knowledge: power/knowledge produce each another. The extension of the power of the state, therefore, involves the development of new types of knowledge which enable it to collect more information about and exercise more control over the population.

Postmodern sociology has been powerfully influenced by Foucault's thinking. He has conducted specific empirical studies of the origin of the human sciences and the asylum, medicine and the births of clinical practices and crime and the Carceral system.

Village gossips in India are feared enough. The villagers can face a tiger in the forest but are immediately scared of the village gossips. The gossips go with the presumption that there is a definite knowledge behind them. This is precisely the power of knowledge. In the present-day proliferation of electronic system, there is an enormous amount of data. These data are stored in places that are accessible to governments, to those individuals, corporations and institutions whose requests for such knowledge are deemed legitimate, but the same data are often not accessible to or easily accessible to the subjects who have contributed the information. In the present postmodern world, only those nations are powerful who have large treasure of knowledge or data.

Max Weber was the thinker who for the first time defined power. It was the ability of a man or a group to influence one man's or group's behaviour. Thus, Weber's classical definition of power was influenced by Foucault. Foucault, through his case studies, hypothesized that power is related to knowledge and those who have big power are big knowledgeable entities.

### Discourse

Yet another popular aspect of postmodernity is discourse. Postmodernists often talk with reference to discourse. The use of this term is fashion for them. Anthony Giddens defined discourse as the "framework of thinking in a particular area of social life". For instance, the discourse of criminality means how people in a given society think and talk about crime. In India, often, the social scientists discuss fundamentalism as a discourse. Discourse, thus has been become the terminology of postmodernity. The origin of discourse is from the writings of Foucault. According to him, "it refers to self-contained systems of thought, belief, or social or political practices governed by internally accepted regulations and procedures". Foucault pointed out, how medicine, for example, became a discourse, in modern times, but we can also speak of politics or art or even sexuality as discourse. Even, we can say that modernity and postmodernity too are discourses.

It must be mentioned here that a discourse may come and go, it does not have any universal truth that can hold over time. They are based on power relations. Foucault says that each era or epoch has its own discourses. According to him, "Most discourses are repressive and deserve to be challenged".

In India, there are discourses in religion, tradition, modernity and education which need to be contested. Take the case of patriarchy. The women's movement opposes patriarchy but with no secures. And, there are religious traditions which are blindly followed by the people. Both new and old discourses are repressive. Postmodernity defines discourses as the vehicle of rebellion.

## Deconstruction

It was during the 1960s that Jacques Derrida coined the concept 'deconstruction'. It is considered to be a prime characteristic of postmodernity. When Derrida talked about deconstruction, he had in his views the text. A text is not only written material but includes also painting, architecture, information system and all attempts of representation. Deconstruction, therefore, is a mode of reading which exposes a text's internal differences and attends to its repressed contradictions or inherent vulnerabilities. A deconstructive reading can turn a text's logic against itself by showing how the logic of its language can differ from and play against the logic of its author's stated claims, but also because deconstructors tend to seize on the inconsistencies, inequalities or hierarchies, which are expounded or glossed over either by a text, by whole discourse, or even by an entire system of beliefs. For instance, the hierarchies found in the caste system are by any standard illogical. Ram Deo is a great saint of Rajasthan, he was born of an untouchable. Hierarchically, he is ranked at the lowest level of caste system. But, his sainthood raised him to the status of a big, great man. If the text of Ram Deo is deconstructed, the whole discourse of Ram Deo would crumble down.

Deconstruction of what? Obviously, it is deconstruction of text. In the paraphrase of postmodernity, as Derrida says, "there is nothing outside the text". It would be more accurate to state that the world is constituted by text. We have several texts in our Indian society. These texts are written or are things of material products. We accept these texts without any criticism. Actually, we are so much obsessed by the texts that we never put them to examination in terms of logical inconsistencies and inequalities, which characterize these texts. Postmodernity, according to Derrida, uses deconstruction as a careful analysis of a discourse.

A discussion on deconstruction is incomplete if mention is not made of binary oppositions. Western society has a tradition of binary oppositions. Derrida argues that modernity accepts these oppositions or opposites without any deconstruction. Night-day, friend-enemy, dark-white, order-chaos, high culture-popular culture and male-female are some of the traditionally accepted binary oppositions. These oppositions need to be examined. Deconstruction is the means by which we can reverse and dismantle the oppositions. Actually, the binary oppositions suffer from hierarchies of values cherished by the masses. For instance, in India, there is a binary opposition – Sawarn-Dalit, i.e., high-caste Hindu and the subaltern. The high-caste Hindu values consider the lower caste people as backward. Thus, Derrida's deconstruction helps to understand the reality of society in a postmodern society.

### Death of the Author

Ronald Barthes is a Marxist literary critic. He has given a very 'notorious' statement when he says that there is *death of the author* in postmodernity. He says that the author is not to be regarded as the final arbiter of a text's meaning. In Barthes' view, authors have come to be considered as authority figures thus placing the reader in an inferior position. He called for the death of a certain conception (more precisely, the death of a certain conception of the author, the author as authority figure) in order to free the reader to be creative. Reading was no longer to be considered a passive process. But, instead, it is an active one in which the reader was fully engaged in the production of textual meaning. The birth of the reader, as Barthes put it, was to be achieved at the expense of the author.

During the prime time of the modernity, the tendency was to treat author as cultural icon rather than authorship as such, and the 'death of the author' is an implicitly anti-traditional notion much in keeping with the liberationist tenor of the 1960s when it was devised.

Looking to the Indian situation, the notion of the 'death of the author' as developed by Barthes applies very well. M.N. Srinivas, S.C. Dube and other eminent 'priests' of sociology are alive today though they died while they were actually alive. Most of their concepts such as sanskritization, westernization, modernization and dominant caste, occupy a prestigious place in our day-to-day discussions.

Postmodernity hardly accepts anything which is modern. What is required today is to apply these basic characteristics to our present-day or contemporary Indian society. This society has always rejected the culture of the people, that is, the subaltern culture.

### Pluralism

For postmodernity, pluralism is the article of faith. It says that in the cause-effect scheme that there is no single cause for an effect. There is no reason, there are reasons; there is no cause, there are causes. Lyotard argues that there is no absolute notion of truth or authority. Barthes, quite like Lyotard, observes that the texts are no longer to be seen as having central meanings that critics should be striving to reveal, instead, sources of plural interpretations. Postmodernists insist that whether in political and intellectual domain, there is no single authority, there is no hegemony. For them, even truth is seen as plural, that is, not reducible to one central meaning that excludes all others.

Postmodernity believes in diversity and diversity means pluralism. As there are no universalizing theories, each group of people have their ethnic identity. In countries like India, where there are several cultural identities, the only alternative left for the masses of people is pluralism. K.S. Singh, in his *People of India* project, says that there are ninety-one culture areas in the countries. These culture areas attribute pluralism to Indian society. When postmodernists apply this perspective to understand Indian society, they take into consideration the pluralist form of society.

**New Identities**

In the traditional societies, identity of an individual was known by his race, nationality, caste, religion and language. Postmodernity has weakened the identity of an individual on such criterion. Globalization has a new focus to change the structure of postmodernity. In this era, globalization has a pluralizing impact on identities, producing a variety of possibilities and new positions of identification, and making identities more political, positional, more plural and diverse, less fixed, unified or trans-historical. The identities in postmodern era have thus become multiple.

Earlier, in India, identity was marked by caste, religion, region or state. This has now almost weakened. Globalization, economic growth, development, industrialization, education and industrial capitalism together have provided new identities to an individual and to individualism. A new dimension in identity has also emerged. In some parts of India, people have tried to reaffirm their religious, caste and regional identities. For instance, Jats and Rajputs of Rajasthan, and Jains, Vaishyas and Brahmins of the country as a whole are struggling to get benefits of reservation on one excuse or another. Amartya Sen elaborately discusses the relationship of identity with violence. In this context, he refers to religious fundamentalism. Earlier, identity was a mark of understanding an individual in the name of village, caste and religion. Now, with the increase in postmodernity, identity has raised its ugly head to create disturbances in the society.

**Popular Culture**

Enlightenment and modernity had developed an elite culture in the society. Differentiation was the mark of elite or high class, high-caste culture. Their cultural practices remained restricted to the high-ups in the society. The elites of this class had their own music which was classical. In fact, the artists got an extravagant patronage from the rich. Modernity attempted to break down the division between high culture and folk culture. But, with the coming of postmodernity, this distinction between elite culture and folk culture has been rejected. The modern culture, which was elite culture, has now come up to stand on equal footing.

### Consumerism

Sometimes the postmodern society is defined as a consumer society. Mass media encourages consumerism. Consumerism is associated with lifestyle. It was during the late 1980s and early 1990s that postmodernism entered the everyday life of people. During the period, when modernity was in its full form in Europe, there was industrialism that went hand in hand. And, industrialism encouraged mass production. It was followed by Fordism which reached the peak of post-Fordism. Development brought out new forces which gave rise to postmodernity. Postmodernity gave a new direction to production. Then came a shift in the production pattern. Market became a gigantic force to a new culture of consumerism. Individuality got strengthened and it produced specialized items, which enriched varying lifestyles. Obviously, postmodernity got rooted into consumption rather than in production. In this change, overemphasis was put on the needs of the individual. And, mass media, signs and images took control of the people's choices. Perhaps, one of the most noticeable areas of growth in consumer markets has been women's fashion and men's too. Older as well as young men articulate their identity through a conscious selection process of consumption involving clothes, hairstyles and body decoration. Food ways, clothing, body decoration and houses, new and varied kinds of buildings have given a new identity to postmodernism. In India, consumerism has also invaded the market. Not only higher and middle classes but the lower classes too in the urban areas have experienced the taste of postmodern lifestyle. In this era of information technology, lifestyle has also undergone changes in the remote villages. Local leaders ride on motorbikes and there are beauty saloons and English medium schools proliferating everywhere in the rural sectors.

### Dissent

Postmodernity has developed a special attitude of dissent for modernity. Its history has been to disagree with anything and not merely modernity. There is no concept in postmodernity for approval or appreciation. It is mostly dissent. The history of postmodernism shows that it all the time uses a vocabulary which is negative. Terms like subjectivist, fragmentary, arbitrary, defeatist, wilful are indicative of dissent.

### Multiculturalism

One of the differentiating characteristics of postmodern society is its multiculturalism. Our national leaders, when they make a public speech, often start with the phrase: "We the people of this community..." By the term 'we' they convey the notion that we are common people, have a common lifestyle and common values. But such a phrasing would not be acceptable to postmodernists. They argue that the community is never 'one'. It has varying ethnicities, feelings, religious followings and linguistic learnings. It is never possible to think of a community as a large family. There is enough fragmentation in a society.

Lyotard's *The Postmodern Condition* (1984), commissioned by Qubec's Council des Universities, is a wonderful document on the state of scientific knowledge and information. Lyotard finds out the state of scientific knowledge and informs us how it controls the society. He says that science is never a superior form of knowledge. It cannot find permanent answers to everything; it only comes up with temporarily valid opinions, and seeks to solve merely immediate, local problems. There are eternal questions it cannot answer, eternal verities, beyond even against its advancing frontiers.

There is splintering of knowledge because human beings in a society are never uniform. They are multicultural, multi-ethnic. Thus, the science which is developed and created in postmodern society is not coherent. It can no longer be valued for the contribution it makes towards human progress. Postmodern science has given up the idea that one day the sum of all knowledge will add up to a state of perfect information. Lyotard strongly believes that postmodern science has become a mass of incompatible little things with no goal other than to generate further research.

**Anti-historical**

The Marxists argue that human history is always progressive development of the means of production – a steady increase in human control over nature. Along with the progress of history, alienation has also increased. There are Marxist postmodernists who accept Marxism and go to the extent to observe that grand narratives of Marx are even today relevant. Fredric Jameson is one of them, who besides being a postmodernist, defends the historical materialism of Marx.

Postmodernity, by its tradition, strongly rejects history. It was Fukuyama who used the term 'end of history'. The conception of 'end of history' is based on the worldwide triumph of capitalism and liberal democracy. In the wake of the 1869 revolutions in Eastern Europe, the dissolution of Soviet Union and a movement towards multi-party democracy in other regions, Fukuyama argues, "the ideological battles of earlier eras are over. The end of history is the end of alternatives. No one any longer defines monarchism, and fascism is a phenomenon of the past."

The whole Marxian thesis of the revolution for socialism has been transformed by the Marxist postmodernists. They have challenged the idea that any one class, structure or factor can single-handedly explain history or bring about change. The ideas of Foucault, Baudrillard and others reject Marx. The post-Marxist tendency of these authors seeks a less reductive view of history and society and tries to formulate a more radical version of democracy than Marxism has often provided. It aims to address political theory to a more chaotic social landscape full of fluid identities and diverse social groups. It asks whether revolution is still possible in an age apparently without agreed values, and whether radical gestures can have any effect in a world which seems able to absorb all attempts at subversion.

### Farewell to Class War

Social formations have undergone massive change due to modes of production. The society has gone through Fordism to post-Fordism and mass production to flexible production. It has become a consumer society. It is more capital-intensive than labour-intensive. Peter Berger argues that in the postmodern society, the place of industrial labour has been taken over by the knowledge class. This class is highly paid and occupies a place of status in this society. It is said that such a development in industry has ended the primacy of class-based politics. Add to it is the increase in social pluralism and multi-polity of social groups. Jameson, a Marxist, also admits that one of the most profound social phenomena is the emergence of a whole range of small-group, non-class political practices, micro politics. These groups give rise to new social movements such as that of women, ecologists, regional autonomists which take the form of class war. And, here is the farewell to class conflicts. The days of labour unrest have now become a thing of the past.

### Goodbye to Systemic Approach

Foundational theories of Durkheim, Marx and Weber have their boundaries limited to systems. Parsons' theory of system is a typical example of boundary maintenance. A system is a complex unit of some kind, with boundaries within which the parts are connected, and within which something takes place. Parsons distinguishes three systems: the cultural, the personality, and the social. The cultural system includes the values and norms which influence an individual's choices. The personality system involves an individual's motivations and need-dispositions that govern, alongwith the norms, the choice he makes. The social system is based on the interrelations between actors. With the social system, Parsons looked at roles, equilibrium and the pattern variables.

System has least possibility of change outside it. It has a strong tendency to pattern maintenance. This approach, that is, the whole system theory is rejected by postmodernists. Its inherent tendency is flexibility. And, flexibility is against system. What is this postmodern flexibility? Postmodernity made a shift from mass consumption of Fordian type to flexible production. In this shift, there is a new pluralism of products, and a new importance for innovation. In postmodern society, flexible manufacture is linked with innovative organization. In this shift, the focus is on the needs of the customers. And, the customers needs are ever changing. The production changes with the needs of the customers. For example, General Motors took nine hours to change the dyes on its presses in the early 1980s. The Toyota has lowered the time to two minutes. The history of demand flexibility and innovation in production clearly states that postmodernity is against any theory of 'system'.

Add to it, the rejection of meta narratives. Meta narratives are based on system theory. Functionalism and conflicts theory are, in fact, system narratives. Postmodernity, at least negatively, has vehemently rejected system approach to society. Its efforts to theorize the present broken world, on the other hand, have yet not yielded any hopeful result. But, the battle is ongoing. Whether postmodernity succeeds to build a new social theory or not is not known but what is certain is that it has bidden a goodbye to the system approach.

### Science is 'Little Science'

During the postmodern period, once for all, big science has become little science. Around 18th century onwards, i.e., modern times, faith was placed in science as the source of enlightenment. For instance, instead of answering to religion as the guarantee of truth, political and economic fields claimed to have the standing of science. In sociology, all the founding fathers, tried to develop and establish it as a discipline. It was assumed that scientific knowledge could (1) get behind mystification and mystery of existence, and superstition; (2) reveal the facts about the world; and (3) lead human beings to a brighter day. It was further believed that science is progressive and universal.

Lyotard and a few other postmodernists demystified some of these assumptions of science. Lyotard was, in fact, officially appointed to find out the state of knowledge of science. He claims that around the end of the Second World War, these myths had collapsed. It is a science, which is responsible for the destruction of our environment; it is a science, which has created chemical weapons and this leads us to believe that science may be anything but surely not progressive. Approaches like 'chaos theory', quantum mechanics have highlighted uncertainty in some measure. Because of these it has become harder to see science "as the activity of a rational mind confronting a concrete reality".

A new development has taken place in the post-industrial production. Research has made a place in commercial enterprise as a result of which there has been rapid growth of computerized means of information processing. The outcome of this has been that theories and discoveries are now judged on the basis of performance and efficiency rather than truth or purpose. Scientists are now primarily interested in putting out work which will both generate further research findings and add to their own power and prestige within the academic 'market place'.

The big science of modern period has now become little science of postmodern period. The reasons for this are as follows:

1. Science is not coherent.
2. It is not progressive.
3. Postmodernity has abandoned the idea that one day the sum of all knowledge will add up to a state of perfect information.
4. Science has become a mass of incompatible little sciences with no goal other than to generate further research.

Concluding his research on the state of knowledge, Lyotard writes that the postmodern science now ceases to be a superior form of knowledge. Knowledge is splintered. Lyotard writes in his report:

> The splintering of knowledge is paralleled by a wider sense of social and culture disintegration. There are many echoes in fields as diverse as political theory, cultural theory and art criticism.

## Conclusion

One of the greatest virtues of postmodernity is that it is imprecise. Although it has now been around for a long time, it still has refused to settle down or solidify into a single meaning. We have seen that each postmodernist has his own perspective of the term. Baudrillard interprets the postmodern society as a simulating society only; for Derrida, it is a fragmented society; for Foucault, it is the knowledge power relationship, which defines this society. And what is worse, each scholar characterizes the contemporary society as postmodern and at the same time denies himself to be a postmodernist. We might say that postmodernism practices what it preaches, in that it continues to mean different things to different people and to have sometimes bewildering range of applications in different areas. It remains stubbornly elusive. In this way, it allows ideas to stay mobile, constantly re-inventing themselves and adjusting to changing circumstances.

It is difficult indeed to provide some agreed-upon characteristics of modernity. Despite fluidity, it is certain that postmodernism is against (1) ideas about depth and essence, and (2) the total and universal. Further, it is agreed upon by all postmodernists that (1) it is superficial and provisional, and (2) later in terms of fragmentation and difference. To write this in conclusion about postmodernism, we can do no better than to quote Glenn Ward (1997):

> The term 'postmodernism', however, slippery and contradictory it might be, it offers a way into debates about contemporary societies, cultures and lifestyles.

# IV

# Postmodernity in Post-colonial, Post-feudal Indian Society

Postmodernity is rooted in the social milieu of a nation-state. Postmodernity, as understood and propounded by Lyotard, Baudrillard, Derrida and Jameson, has emerged from the societal background of European and American society. Its structure is not uniform all over the world. There is no single postmodernity, in fact, there are several postmodernities. There were several social, economic and political upheavals in Europe from 18th to 20th century. Industrial revolution, French Revolution and a series of other radical changes brought about the epoch of postmodernity. In these countries, modernity had done much harm. There were two world wars; there was Soviet Russia's socialism, unprecedented rise of industrial capitalism, emergence of market as a strong economic force and, above all, intensification of information technology. The whole of Europe had become a mass society.

When postmodernity began to take its shape and structure in western society, modernity had already done immeasurable harm to the people. Pollution and environmental decay had struck roots. There was massive unemployment. The intellectuals in these western countries soon realized that enlightenment and modernity were their enemies. To define postmodernity in

European context, one element of it would be to say that modernity on the whole has done much harm to the people. The form of postmodernity, which is presented to us by postmodern European thinkers and writers is, therefore, specific to European history of modernity with its concepts and phenomena of political and economic upheavals, class war and industrial capitalism. Information technology and its intensification promoted Baudrillard to think of simulation society. It was contextual to European society that made Foucault to redefine power and show its relationship with knowledge.

## India's Variant of Modernity/Postmodernity

We have been arguing that the modernity/postmodernity, which we have had in our country, is altogether different from the US and European modernity/postmodernity The societies are different; their histories are different. European society had experienced democracy long back. In India, democracy came only during the postcolonial period when it attained independence. Sociological writings about modernity and postmodernity also present erroneous views about the real situation of society. Distinctively, in India, postmodernity had not to fight against modernity. Unlike Europe, here, modernity was not its enemy. Let us examine in some details the situation of modernity and postmodernity in pre-colonial, pre-feudal India.

India has had a mix-up of modernity and postmodernity. It was for the first time that Henry Maine and Charles Metcalfe mentioned that India's villages were autonomous. They did not experience the authority of any superpower. They in themselves were 'little republics'; self-reliance was the medium. It was postmodernity: differentiated, autonomous, diversified and self-sufficient.

The phenomenon of postmodernity of rural India has been supported by L.I. Rudolph and Susanne Rudolph in their recently published work, *Postmodern Gandhi and Other Essays* (2006). In this work, the authors consider *Hind Swaraj* as one of the evidences of Gandhi's being a postmodernist. In fact, Gandhi considered village as an autonomous unit of society. When the draft Constitution of India was submitted to Gandhi (he was not a member of the Constituent Assembly), he tore it up and said that for him there was no India without villages. It is said that on the insistence of Gandhi, village panchayats were given a constitutional status. Thus, there was postmodernity in India even before there was modernity.

Milton Singer, M.N. Srinivas, Yogendra Singh, Dipankar Gupta and others have observed that modernity in India came during the colonial rule. Yogendra Singh (*Modernization of Indian Tradition*, 1973), tracing the beginning of modernity in India, writes:

> Modernity in India started mainly with the western contact especially through establishment of the British rule. This contact had a special historicity, which brought about many far-reaching changes in culture and social structure of the Indian society.

Dipankar Gupta (*Mistaken Modernity*, 2000) takes a different view of modernity. He seems to argue that there are multiple modernities. But, for him, it would be wrong to "equate modernity with technology and with other contemporary artifacts". He considers modernity as attitudes "especially those that came into play in social relations". It should be characterized by "dignity of the individual, adherence to universalistic norms, elevation of individual achievement or privileges or disprivileges and accountability in public life".

As a matter of fact, both Yogendra Singh and Dipankar Gupta look at Indian modernity without taking into consideration the social condition of India. What is characterized as modernity by Yogendra Singh consists of technology, printing machine, steam power, steam engine, national legal code, bureaucracy, and English language brought or introduced by the British Raj. Dipankar Gupta does credit the British to have brought modernity. He prescribes certain social indicators to attain modernity. To him, "India is still unmodern". If we support the viewpoint presented by Yogendra Singh that modernity in India began from the establishment of British rule, then, it would tend to raise certain questions, which need to be considered carefully. We have been arguing that both modernity and postmodernity do not have any single variety, prevailing universally. Obviously, modernity and for that matter, postmodernity in India is particularly specific to Indian society. In the following pages, we shall argue that Indian modernity and postmodernity are not what they are defined by Yogendra Singh and Dipankar Gupta. In the west, postmodernity makes a sharp attack on modernity. There, postmodernity has justly argued and established that most of the abuses and failures in that society were due to modernity. Modernity was responsible for environmental decay, pollution, slums, unemployment and bureaucratic rationalism.

In India, the situation has been different. The technology, rationalization, codified law, freedom and justice, which the Britishers brought with them, have benefited the higher groups, higher castes and the higher and middle classes. Modernity became subservient to these sections of society. If it is argued and there are several sociologists who agree to it that the British are credited with having brought modernity to India, then several questions would come up: Who benefited by it? Who used the technology? And, which classes of people took the advantages of the British 'imported modernity'? These questions need quick answers.

## Indian Postmodernity

When in 1950s India took to planned development, there were a large number of projects launched throughout the country. Community development projects took care of village agricultural extension and along with it there were gigantic projects for industrial development. Jawaharlal Nehru, who was the Prime Minister of the country, was described as the architect of modern India. In his speeches he used to reiterate that these development projects were the pilgrim centres of modern India. For him, Bhakra Nangal, Jamshedpur, Tatanagar and Nilokhadi agricultural centres were achievements of what he called modern India. Nehru considered technology as the infrastructural ingredient of modernity. Dipankar Gupta denies all these developments as mistaken modernity. Gandhi, on the other hand, showed his dissent against technology and technological products. For him, postmodernity was a better solution for human development and dignity. The discourse of postmodernity with all its future possibilities is rooted in our social structure. We argue that postmodernity is particularly relevant and essential to Indian society. It is unlike as in the western society, where it had to fight against modernity.

Here, in this country, postmodernity had to fight not so much against modernity as against the dominant caste groups and the rich and powerful *Jagirdars* and *Jamindars*. These are the groups that have largely cornered the benefits of modernity during the colonial and feudal period. It was unfair to the tribal people, the backward castes and the disadvantaged masses who did not have any share in the modernity, which characterized the colonial and feudal period. The non-participation of these people clearly shows that modernity during this period was restricted to the privileged groups only. In this context, postmodernity targets not only the modernity which was limited in influence, but also the dominant groups in India.

## Postmodernity and the Struggle for Independence

While discussing the concepts of modernity and postmodernity, we find that there was a contradiction between the two groups – the elite group or the group of the cronies of colonialism and feudalism and the group of real and authentic freedom lovers and fighters. The historians belonging to the imperialist school of ideology have argued that the struggle for independence was not a people's movement. It was, on the other hand, a product of the needs and interests of the elite groups – both caste and class, who used it to serve either their own narrow interests or the interests of their respective groups. These groups were sometimes formed around religious or caste identities and sometimes through political connections were built around patronage. Clearly, it was the modernity of the elite group which gave rise to postmodernity.

The enemy of postmodernity during the colonial period was, therefore, not modernity but the groups of high-caste Hindus who had hijacked modernity. There emerged a new historiography led by Ranjeet Guha who argued that postmodernity was a consequence of the subaltern people. The struggle for independence was successful due to the participation of the mass of people.

Commenting on the perspective of subaltern history, Bipan Chandra and others (*India's Struggle for Independence*, 1988) say:

> For proponents of the subaltern history, the basic contradiction in Indian society in the colonial epoch was between the elite, both Indian and foreign, on the one hand, and the subaltern groups, on the other, and not between colonialism and the Indian people. They believe that the Indian people were never united in a common and anti-imperialist struggle, that there was no such thing as the united Indian national movement.

The characteristics of postmodernity, as given by the mainstream postmodern proponents, do not fully apply to India's situation. What is found here is that in urban and industrial centres there was a particular type of modernity. The dominant groups took to English as their medium of education, sent their children for higher education to England, rolled themselves in conspicuous consumption and led a lifestyle of what Dipankar Gupta calls 'intoxicated Indians'. This section of society was called 'modern Indian society'. There was another counterpart of this society which could be called 'postmodern society'. The postmodern society bore the influence of Gandhi, Vinoba Bhave and a few others. Postmodernity in India's context is autonomous, multi-ethnic, differentiated and decentralized. In the present era of postmodernity, untouchability has almost gone, old hierarchies based on caste are no longer available, and inter-caste marriages are invariably increasing.

### Post-colonial and Post-feudal India

Indian sociologists tend to look at India in a stereotyped way. They are at their core traditional. If one cares to scan the literature on postmodernity of the west, it would be easy to find that there is no mention of the word 'tradition' with reference to modernity or postmodernity. In India, the situation is different. Here, we cannot even think of modernity or postmodernity without mentioning the term 'tradition'. Writing on modernity, the Indian sociologists, in their historical fashion, brought the word 'tradition' as the starting point of thought and writings. It is a mistaken belief that Hindu or for that matter, Islamic or Sikh traditions are homogenous. There is much heterogeneity in our traditions. And, when we do not take note of the diversity, we simply propagate for cultural nationalism.

It must be emphasized that in its ethnicity the Indian society is, to a great extent, religious. It is only in our polity that we struggle to attain secularism. Secularism was one prime idiom when we were struggling to keep up our national unity. Secularism has been indispensable to fight against strong divisive tendencies in the form of communalism. In such a situation, there seemed no justification for analyzing modernity in the perspective of tradition. Besides the theme of tradition, modernity has not come to us in the context of totality of societal reality. India's social reality has two major dimensions. A large part of India had been British India or the colonial India; and the remaining one was, for all intents and purposes, feudal India in the form of states. The feudal India is also known as consisting of princely states. When M.N. Srinivas observes that the colonial rule introduced modernity in India, he does not include the princely states in it. And, it has further not been identified what groups or classes this modernity, affected in the colonial India. Indian sociology in this respect has been blinkered. To talk about modernity without reference to feudalism would make several of the statements of sociologists, false or lop-sided.

Homi K. Bhabha (*The Location of Culture*, 1994), who has examined the state of postmodernity in post-colonial world, particularly India, says that the experience of postmodernity in western or westernized, industrialized and capitalist countries or regions is different from those in other developing countries. It is this experience of post-colonial countries which makes postmodernity different in India. Commenting on post-colonial postmodernity, Eleanor Byrna (*Postmodernism*, 2005) writes:

> What are commonly viewed as characteristically postmodern concerns might easily be found in the context of colonial and anti-colonialism narratives and histories and identities that colonialism produces both for colonizer and colonized.

The colonial state of affairs in South Asia was very unlike and indeed fundamentally different from that of western countries. It is because of the colonial-feudal difference that we consider India's postmodernity a distinct phenomenon. Postmodernity and modernity ran parallel in this country. As mentioned earlier, India's villages were almost diversified – autonomous and structurally republican. India on the whole rejected modernity, as is known by the theory of Hind Swaraj, proposed by Gandhi. We were against colonial power and colonial products. We were against foreign goods and we boycotted anything and everything, which was not of Indian origin. Such an experience of India shows that there was postmodernity in India and at the same time modernity too, and that the latter was hijacked by the dominant groups of the country.

Aijaz Ahmed (*In Theory*, 1992), a Marxist critic, argues that modernity in the Third World, particularly, India, was not for the benefit of the general masses. And, therefore, there was postmodernity which took differentiation, diversity and fragmentation as the ethos of the people. His concern for the post-colonial Indian runs as under:

> Those who live with the consequences of that long past, good and bad, and in places where a majority of the population has been denied access to such benefits and modernity, as hospitals or better health insurance or even basic literacy, can hardly afford the terms of such thought.

Surely, there was printing press, English as a medium of instruction, political awakening, railways, a network of communication (though very scanty) and uniform legal code in post-colonial India, but the life of the people was very miserable. There were numerous cases of injustice, unbearable in the extreme. Bipan Chandra and others (*India's Struggle for Independence*, 1988) observe:

> The new courts and legal system gave a further fillip to the dispossessors of land and encouraged the rich to oppress the poor. Flogging, torture and jailing of the cultivators for arrears of rent on land revenue or interest on debt were quite common. The ordinary people were also hard hit by the prevalence of corruption at the lower levels of the police, judiciary and general administration. The petty officials enriched themselves freely at

the cost of the poor. The police looted, oppressed and tortured the common people at will.

Post-colonial India had its counterpart in feudal India. The feudal India included about 600 princely states, which were ruled by Rajputs, Jats and dominant high-caste Hindus. They were privileged to rule over the masses on the basis of the theory of divine right of kings. These rulers did not have any universalistic norms of governing. The only law was the rule of the thumb. Quite like the colonized people, these princely rulers tortured and oppressed the common people. Traditionally, they imposed certain taxes to enrich the royal treasury. Forced labour – *begar* – was imposed on them and they were obliged to submit to it. Strangely enough, the feudal rule exempted the higher castes, and the Rajputs of all hierarchies from the custom of taxes. The Brahmins were exempted from the oppression and tortures of the princely rules. We have elsewhere mentioned (more in *Feudalism and Subaltern Tribes*, 2003) that feudalism in India was the rule of the dominant castes.

The benefits of modernity in these states were taken over by the high and dominant castes. The people, that is, the masses were overwhelmed by the burden of tradition. Royal traditions, the royal fasts and festivals, royal deities were made to force down the throats of the people. When the sociological writings about the post-colonial and post-feudal states were made available to us, we felt greatly grieved. When M.N. Srinivas (he belonged to the feudal state of Mysore) reports about modernity in British India, he does not comment on the status of ordinary people in post-colonial society. It was Milton Singer (*Traditional India*, reprinted in 1935), the pet student of Robert Redfield, who tried to establish "the modern nationalism in India, as in most other countries, has always shown a strong interest in the recovery or reinterpretation of India's traditional culture". He further observes that "with the achievement of national independence, this interest has received an official defiance".

Milton Singer's anthropological writing has been erroneous. All through our struggle for independence, we tried hard to reform and recast our conservative traditions; we abolished discrimination based on caste, creed and sex; we raised the age at marriage; we encouraged women's education; we empowered village panchayats; we improved the status of tribals and legislated protective and development safeguards for the weaker sections. The age-old conservative tradition was not allowed to tighten its stronghold on the poor people. The western sociologists and anthropologists had developed monomania for the Indian tradition.

There are two more studies which need to be mentioned. They are influential writings of postmodern India: those of Yogendra Singh (*The Modernization of Indian Tradition*, 1973) and Dipankar Gupta (*Mistaken Modernity*, 2000).

Yogendra Singh has written a full-length book on tradition and modernity. He very powerfully puts forward Singer's idea of tradition and concludes that tradition is central to India's civilization. Traditions, both for Hindus and Muslims, consist of hierarchy, holism, continuity and transcendence. Yogendra Singh writes:

> Hierarchy was ingrained in the system; of caste and sub-caste stratification but also in the Hindu concepts of human nature, as seen in its belief system, occupational life cycles (*ashramas*) and moral duties (*dharma*). Holism implied a relationship between individual and group in which the former was encompassed by the latter in respect of duties and rights, which had precedence over community or *sangha* and not the individual. This substitution of individual by collectivity persisted all along the line of traditional social structure, i.e., family, village, community, caste and political territory or nation. Communalism in traditional social system was reinforced through the value of system of continuity which in Hinduism was symbolized by the principles of *karma*, transmigration of soul and a cyclical view of change. The principle of transcendence also posited the view that legitimation of traditional values could never be challenged on grounds of rationality, derived from the non-sacred or profane scales of evaluation. It formed a super-concept contributing to integration as well as rationalization of the other value themes of the tradition.

Yogendra Singh has very brilliantly analyzed the relationship between tradition and modernity. He argues that the organization of tradition is such that it provides depth and continuity to the integration of Indian society. The strength of tradition is such that it enjoys legitimacy with the masses. Even a poor peasant would not hesitate to sell or mortgage his trivial property to the village 'baniya' only to observe a tradition. The central reason for village poverty, which is reported by agricultural economists, is his commitment to the observation of various items of tradition, which are related to the life cycle.

Admittedly, there was technological and scientific modernity during the post-colonial period. But it could not influence the ancient mores and modes of Indian society to any large extent. The values of modernity are rejected or subordinated to the values of tradition. At best, the traditions are modernized to some extent, i.e., they have got a facelift but the core of traditions continue to remain the same.

As for modernization in India, we find a growing trend that traditional role-structures are giving way to modern ones. But persons following these roles often retain categorical values of tradition instead of imbibing those of modernity. We have already mentioned how caste itself is adopting many functions which properly belong to rational corporate groups. Generally, ritual order and religion, which are essentially based on categorical values of a traditional nature, do not suffer any decline, nor is there an easy possibility of their disappearance in near future.

Thus, Yogendra Singh says, modernization of tradition, that is, traditions has undergone an adaption change or transformation, but substantially they have not changed. Our argument is that what people call modernization is not really so. It is technological modernization. Yogendra Singh also accepts, and hopefully, we, too, are right in our analysis that the modernization of tradition is substantially, technological modernization. What people have done in the process of modernization is that they have retained the value structure of traditions, the values of our civilization and have benefited from the facilities given by modernity. They will travel by air, railways, road transport, use the banking facilities but, at the same time, exhibit their trust and belief in the birth of a son and dislike or even kill a daughter who would not continue their genealogy; they will go on the pilgrim of four *dhamas*, take holy bath in the Ganga and all this through the technological aids of modernity. Thus, for villagers of the grassroots level, modernity means technology, education, media and other such things. These are not to be mistaken for progressive, humanistic ideas. For them, even capitalism, industrialism, democracy and other such things of modernity are acceptable. They are very clear on this score. Their robust commonsense is alive and kicking, for they have faith in their tradition.

Looking to the ground reality of the country, it appears that what has been called as modernity of post-colonial India was a fake modernity. The tradition had a dominant, even overwhelming, role during this period.

The real fight during post-colonial period was not between tradition and modernity; it was between reform and post-modernity. The emphasis in this period was on 'small' things – small is beautiful. Jaya Prakash Narain, a reformist and also a revolutionary – the architect of 'Total Revolution' – gave the notion of autonomy to each district of India. In this way, there would be more than 300 federal states. His socialist ideology was characterized by minutest decentralization. So far as diversity and differentiation are concerned, he was a postmodernist.

There was yet another trend of transformation in the post-colonial India. The liberal ideology of our national leaders – Vivekananda, Tilak, Gandhi and others – was reforms of the traditions. Even the colonial rule pleaded for some soft dose of reforms. Legislation made in the realm of marriage and the ban on 'sati' was only brought about on humanitarian grounds. The British did not want to impose modernity on Indian society. There was merely an attempt to affect some low-level reform. It was also a part of their imperial policy to understand the ethnic character of India. They saw to it that 'reform' did not become a revolution endangering their rule.

The idea of understanding India's ethnicity came to the British after the upheavals of 1857. Surely, for a colonial power, land and revenue were the prime pillars of its continuity and sustenance. But, the rebellion of 1857 which quickly led to general agrarian revolt, obliged the colonial power to understand the ethnic structure of India. Writing about the importance of the study of traditions and ethnicity, Nicholas B. Dirks (in Saurabh Dube (ed.), *Postcolonial Passages*, 2006) observes:

> To put the matter in bold relief, after 1857, anthropology supplanted history as the principal colonial modality of knowledge and rule. In even bolder terms, I would label the late nineteenth and earlier twentieth century colonial state in India as the ethnographic state.

What Nicholas Dirks wants to argue is that India has been a 'great' diverse and plural state. It has scores of ethnicities and each ethnicity has its own identity – Bengali, Punjabi, Gujarati, Marathi, Marwari and so on. These distinct identities are differentiated and maintained through periods of India's cultural history. The *distinctness* and *differentiation* make traditional India a postmodern India and never a post-colonial modern one.

Yogendra Singh, in his yet another work (*Culture Change in India*, 2000), expresses his fear of the possible loss of India's indigenous culture in the wake of globalization and increasing contacts with the west. Modernization has made its inroads and has eroded the earlier cultural unity of Indian society. Though Yogendra Singh is not bold enough to accept that the rise of ethnicity heralds the coming of postmodernity, he confidently admits that the new rise of ethnicity carries most of the characteristics of postmodernity.

## Rise of Ethnicity and Increasing Identity

The study of ethnicity during post-colonial period was enlarged because of the need of the Britishers to understand India's grassroots culture so that the possibility of mutiny kind of upheavals does not arise in future. In other words, the Britishers wanted to frame their culture to keep the agitated castes calm and people undisturbed and complacent. In such a situation, the identity of people was caste identity. Being traditional, caste identities kept them within their cultural boundaries. And, it was celebrated by the British rulers.

But soon after the removal of imperial power and the constitutional safeguards, the post-colonial ethnicity increased substantially. The weaker sections having protective and developmental safeguards took benefit of their constitutional status and identity. Ethnic identity was celebrated with new power of reservations and privileges. Identity became a tool of development. There were several competing demands – formation of new states, identification as minority groups and distribution of development on ethnic basis and legitimacy. Yogendra Singh argues that in India there is a coincidence of development and ethnicity. He writes (*Culture Change in India*, 2000):

> These developments coincide with growth in the feeling of ethnicity. Ethnicity at its root, lies in the consciousness of identity and cultural self-awareness of a community or communities which share a common political and economic destiny.

What we have been arguing here is that in post-colonial society, the processes of modernization, including industrialization, capitalism and democracy, encouraged ethnicity and thus these have resulted in the initiation of postmodern social processes of culture change. As, at present, Indian society is the kaleidoscopic interplay of tradition, modernity and postmodernity. It could be wrong to take the view that in the processes of change, tradition comes first followed by modernity and finally postmodernity. Empirical history demonstrates that all the three processes can operate simultaneously. People's disenchantment is observed for all the three processes from time to time. Traditions have outlived their time; modernity is many a time fake and it works for the benefits of the dominant class/caste and political groups of the society; and postmodernity, which is based on pluralism, differentiation, autonomy and self-identity, may bring out disintegrative tendencies in the society.

Perhaps modernity has done much harm to the society. The dominant castes, elites and religious leaders have fanned the fire of fundamentalism. Fundamentalism has several dimensions – religious, casteist, linguistic and regional. Amartya Sen (*Identity and Violence*, 2006) relates identity based on religion with violence. Describing the extent of religious fundamentalism, Sen writes:

> Despite our diversities, the world is suddenly seen as a federation of religions and civilizations. In Britain, a confounded view of what a multiethnic society must do has led to encouraging the development of state-financed Muslim schools, Hindu schools, Sikh schools and young children are powerfully placed in the domain of singular affiliations well before they have the ability to reason about different systems of identification that may compete for their attention.

In Indian situation, postmodernity has waged a bitter battle against tradition. Despite modernity and postmodernity, the traditions keep the society divided into ethnic boundaries. The political coalitions which we find functioning right from the Centre to municipality and Gram Panchayat levels, are nothing but the manifestations of tradition. And, what is worse, the traditions carry with them religious, caste, linguistic and regional identities.

## Modernity and Technology

Dipankar Gupta, another influential writer on modernity (*Mistaken Modernity*, 2000), argues that modernity does not mean technology only. It would be a mistake to define modernity exclusively in terms of the availability of technology such as television, media, transport, communication and lifestyles introduced by these artifacts. If we deny technology as a valid criterion of modernity, then, to Dipankar, India has yet to attain modernity. For him, modernity is that which "gives dignity to the individual, observes universalistic norms, accepts individual achievement versus privileges by birth and considers the accountability of the individual in the public life". All in all, for Dipankar, "developed modernity is characterized by an attitude of equality with, and respect for others".

Dipankar's notion of modernity is abstract and very much limited. Those scholars who have worked and analyzed modernity in western societies have unanimously agreed to include democracy, capitalism, industrialism and state surveillance as prime conditions of modernity. And, Dipankar has left out all these characteristics ruthlessly. Instead of talking about tradition and its relationship with modernity, he defines the latter in terms of common sense characteristics. Dipankar is not wrong; he has written the article for lay readers of daily or weekly newspapers. The article seemed to be so fascinating to him that it became the title of his book which carries non-serious material for the ordinary people of the street. As a writer of the article, he does display himself as a sociologist. Whatever the book contains is for the public consumption, it is not for sociologists, only for boosting sale in the market.

Stuart Hall and others (1993), while defining postmodernity, argue that modernity in the west re-made the traditional society. The new modern society, characterized by mass production, mass consumption, big city, big brother state, gave way to postmodernity which is flexible, diverse, differentiated, mobile and decentralized. Dipankar Gupta fails to take into account all the characteristics of modernity, or even those of postmodernity.

## Postmodern Gandhi

A breakthrough in the analysis of postmodernity has been made by Lloyd Rudolph and Susanne Rudolph (*Postmodern Gandhi*, 2006). They consider Gandhi as postmodern. Their analysis of Gandhi, who is considered to be a 'sanatani' or Hindu, highly religious, and tradition – true and conservative, as a postmodern, is bound to surprise and shock his millions of followers out of their wits. What makes Gandhi a postmodern is his fondness for decentralization, panchayats, village industries, Swadeshi orientation and rejection of big and gigantic factories. Gandhi argues that values occupy a central place in the day-to-day life of the people. Truth, non-violence and manual labour constitute the value structure of society. Rudolph and Rudolph are justified in applying the parameters of postmodernity on the actions and personality of Gandhi.

Partial absence of technology in the developing countries subscribes to postmodernity. Basically, an individual is autonomous. He is required only to stick to the universalistic values of a wider social order.

## Ethnicity and Postmodernity

With the broadening and intensification of modernity, information technology has made media a powerful weapon of transformation. Television, mobiles (cellular), newspapers and a variety of other sources have created an overarching impact on our culture. India's traditions and its ethnicity have undergone vast changes. It was believed that with the rise in modernity, our ethnicity, customs and traditions would soon meet their death. But this has not happened. Despite the frightening rise of modernity, there has been an unprecedented growth of ethnicity. Our hypothesis is that the more there is intensification of modernity, i.e., rise in technology and computer science, the more there is a corresponding growth of ethnicity. People are happy – they share the benefits of electricity, electric gadgets, transport vehicles and means of communication. What they have done is to utilize the modern innovations for the strengthening and enriching of traditions and customs. Earlier, traditional fairs were attended by a few people only, now, the number swells to thousands. There are enough transport facilities to carry the people to the fair.

One wonderful consequence of technology is that it has given enough time to a person for leisure. Pilgrimage has become more a fashion among the masses than a sacred obligation to fulfil. Towns are common centres for life and living even for villagers. Technology, media and modernity have helped the people to revitalize their waning traditions. Each region has become conscious of its ethnic, traditional and historical identity. During the last two decades, new temples have been rediscovered, innovated. New gods have been invented and the forgotten saints have received new memorials. Their birth anniversaries are celebrated with extravagant expenditures and astonishing fanfare. There is enough evidence to support our hypothesis that rise in technology obviously leads to the growth, enriching and strengthening of traditions and ethnicity. And, the rise of ethnicity ultimately gives rise to automation, differentiation and diversity to a particular culture area. It is the birth and development of postmodernity. Differentiated ethnicity, autonomous ethnicity and self-conscious ethnicity constitute the structure of postmodernity.

Our hypothesis needs to be exemplified with some empirical evidence. K.S. Singh, in his studies of Indian communities, reports that the 91 culture areas of the country maintain their autonomous status and celebrate each festival with pride and glory. The Punjabis have their *Bhangra* dance which cuts across the boundaries of Punjab. The state of Gujarat is known for its folk dance of *Garba*, observed during nine days of the worship of Goddess Amba, preceding the celebration of Dushehra. Though, Gujarat being a highly industrialized state, people remain very busy all through the year, but celebrate *Navratras* and perform *Garba* with full enthusiasm. The markets remain closed and the late nights are made vibrant by the all-costly orchestra. The impact of *Garba* can also be seen in the adjoining states of Maharashtra, Rajasthan and Madhya Pradesh.

Cultural festivals are symbolic of the influence which ethnicity exercises on the public culture. In the cultural region of Bundelkhand, there is a public ceremony of *Alhaudal* – a heroic piece of bravery by Alha and Udal. Maharashtra celebrates *Tamasha*, which is a mass festival. In the state of Rajasthan, which has more than nine culture regions, there are cultural festivals like Teej and Gangaur.

The cultural festivals observed by different culture regions show that despite heavy industrialization, urbanization, democratization and secularism, no depreciation is observed in the celebration of these festivals. Modernity, in other words, makes no inroads in the tradition; contrariwise, the forces of modernity and technology have strengthened and enriched the structure of ethnicity. And, we have all through our discussion been arguing that more ethnicity means more postmodernity. With the increase of ethnicity, there is a corresponding increase in the identity of an individual.

### Little Traditions

Lyotard gave the concepts of grand narrative and little narrative. Grand narrative, to him, is authoritarian and therefore he coined the phrase 'little narratives'. Little narratives are put together on a "tactical basis by small groups of individuals to achieve some particular objectives". In Indian society, we have some little narratives which fulfil the local needs of ethnic groups. They are something like little traditions. Little traditions are specific to localities such as a culture area, or a region as a part of a state. Food habits, dress patterns, festivals, linguistic groups and things of the kind of public culture are parts of little narratives. These little traditions indicate the existence of postmodernity. *Bhangra, Tamasha, Garba* are all little narratives which fulfil the objectives of religion or ritual and entertainment.

**Food Habits and Food Ways**

Each culture area or sub-culture area has its staple food and food ways. In fact, there is culture in food or food in culture. People relate vegetarianism and non-vegetarianism with religion. Sometimes, these are also aligned with ecology. For instance, the people of Bihar, Bengal and coastal regions, notwithstanding their caste and religious affinity, consume fish. It is a kind of vegetable and is also available in the vegetable markets. For the people of these regions, fish and rice are the staple food.

There are also states in the country for whom wheat and maize are the staple food. Quite like food habits and food ways, there are food preferences also. It is said that Brahmins are very fond of sweet preparations; the Gujaratis like to have spicy snacks (*Namkins*), with a smattering of sugar, and South Indians have their specified food dishes. All the food varieties and beverages constitute postmodernity's little narratives. According to the mainstream of sociology, these are the ingredients of little traditions.

We have discussed little narratives in detail because we want to stress the point that there is phenomenon of authority in grand narratives. Marx, Weber and classical thinkers have been rejected by postmodernists as they suffer from authority authoritarianism. Their theories are said to be universalistic, and that is not acceptable to postmodernity. In all situations, postmodernity is anti-authoritarian. For Lyotard, little narratives are only 'tactful' to attain some objectives. In the case of India, the little narratives are not tactical. These are realities of grassroots level. For ordinary people, the grand narratives are cumbersome, difficult to apply. And, therefore, people celebrate the alternative of little narratives.

Little narratives in Indian situation do not carry even a grain of authority. These are happy-go-lucky celebrations. But, the little narratives indicate that there is postmodernity in the varieties of ethnicities of the country.

**Language and Dialects**

Much has been written on the diversity of Indian society. K.S. Singh's *People* of *India* enumerates 4,635 communities, which also include scheduled tribes, scheduled castes and other backward classes. There are 18 national languages. And, the number of dialects go beyond 1,652. There are three language families in the country – Indo-European, Dravidian and Austro-Asiatic. Indo-European language family has eleven languages including Punjabi, Sindhi, Hindi, Gujarati, Udia, Kashmiri, etc. Dravid language family consists of Tamil, Telugu, Kannada and Malayalam. In the third language family are included Mundari, Dhumia, Santhali, Khasi and other such tribal languages. The states have been organized on the basis of these officially recognized languages. There is no separate state for Hindi and Sindhi speaking languages. Here we do not want to enter into any debate on the issue of languages; we only want to mention that the federal units of the Indian Union are divided into linguistic zones. South India has its well marked line of demarcation from the North, so far as communication is concerned.

**Religion and Rituals**

K.S. Singh's *People of India* informs that there are five major religions in India – Hinduism, Buddhism, Sikhism, Jainism and Islam. Besides, there are also some important religions of tribals, Parsis and Jews. The Hindus constitute 76.47 per cent, the Muslims 12.6 and the tribals 8 per cent. In this connection, it should also be mentioned that Hinduism is not homogeneous; there are three major sects in it – *Vaishnava, Shaiva* and *Shakta.* Homogeneity is not also found in Buddhism, Sikhism and Jainism.

Each religion has its traditions and rituals, which are legitimized by its followers. Though there is enough authority in any structure of religion, the performance of rituals permits a great degree of autonomy. Each Muslim should practise *Namaz* – prayer to Allah – five times during the day and if possible take pilgrimage to Mecca once in his lifetime. But, this ritual enjoys some degree of autonomy. A follower can opt out of the ritualistic prescription. But, in this respect, at least Islam is an exception. Even, a little violation can be treated as intolerable, in Semitic sects or religions.

The same applies to Hindus and Sikhs. The argument which we want to make is that religious traditions and rituals differ from religion to religion. Differentiation and limited autonomy give existence and strength to postmodernity. In fact, modernity in its processes of change brings some resilience in the traditional rigidity and ultimately the authoritarian hold of these forces gets weakened.

We have discussed the diversity of Indian society. It has been a long and cherished theme of historians and sociologists. There is nothing new to deal with it here. But we only want to demonstrate that this diversity has enabled the individual to get rid of the authoritarian hold of traditional institutions and permits him to enjoy his autonomy.

### Lifestyle

One of the prime characteristics of postmodernity is a particular lifestyle which an individual or a group adopts. Technology is a money-minting device and in this age of modernity and postmodernity everyone wants to earn as much as possible. Accumulation of money makes a man a consumerist. A person who has enough consummation to his credit, gets a new identity. The older industries have gone out of existence. Earlier, traditional identities – son of a *Jagirdar, Zamindar*, or of high-caste Hindu – got the higher status readymade. It is the achievement which merits high now.

The new lifestyle gives a person a postmodern identity. He is a computer engineer, a film actor, a scientist and an advocate of human rights. The clothes or the brands which a person uses give him a special status in the society. Everything in the society – a house, a car, even a pen with which he writes, are items of lifestyle. In fact, the consumer market has become rich in fashion, cosmetics and lifestyle accessories. Increasing ethnicities do not demand either mass production or the post-Fordism production. Postmodernity stands for specialized and differentiated production and it is because of it that there has come about a shift in the production system. Lifestyle changes are due to several reasons. The impact of Green Revolution in agriculture during the 1970s, the industrial revolution and the growth of advanced technology, emergence of new vocations, increasing horizons of technical and academic education have all brought about radical changes in the lifestyle of the people. Yogendra Singh (*Culture Change*, 2000) provides a profile of the lifestyle changes that are found in the city and country:

> Most of these changes have long been in the process of emergence and crystallization. The forces of industrialization and developments in agriculture had a major impact upon the consumption style of people. The Green Revolution in agriculture during the 1970s gave spurt to changes in the consumption style of villages which till then was largely a preserve of the residents in cities and metropolises .... The NSS data show noticeable decline in the consumption of cereals both by the rich and the poor in India. The shift is towards consumption of milk, poultry and meat products. It is a phenomenon universal to the process of economic development.

Yogendra Singh also discusses changes that have come at other levels of lifestyle. For instance, there is electrification in the villages. People also use kerosene on a larger scale. There has been expansion of road networks right from village to the state and national highways. Providing details of the lifestyles of the people, Singh further writes:

> Following the Green Revolution, the country is now going through a White Revolution, it being the largest gross production of milk in the world. The per capita consumption of milk, however, remains still inadequate. The use of synthetic material for utensils, jars and cans is now common.... A remarkable change in the style and pattern of woman's wear has taken place. It is marked by a shift from saris to *salwar-kameez*. The middle classes are increasingly taking dresses marked by the multinationals. The uses of cosmetics, soaps and detergents have

reached all sections of the people of India. The vocation of beauticians, and the number of beauty parlours and health clubs, etc., have grown very rapidly.

Lifestyle changes are very many. And, these changes are more observable in the youths and adolescents. However, the elder people do not remain untouched by the new lifestyle coming to the fore by postmodernity.

The modernity-postmodernity combines have released some powerful forces which have shaken the traditional lifestyle of the people. The new lifestyle has adopted a tactful method to compromise with the new forces. For instance, the traditions which have ritualistic values are adopted without any contest. The marriage ceremony is performed in a patterned dress – red sari for the bride and a turban for the groom. In a similar way, festivals are celebrated according to the prescribed norms. The traditions are resilient and change takes place according to the compulsions of the times. This is what Yogendra Singh calls adaptive change.

## Marginals and the Crisis of Identity

The question of identity is being vigorously debated in social theory. In essence, the argument is that the old identities, which stabilized the social world for so very long, are now in decline, giving rise to new identities fragmenting the new modern individual as a unified subject. The so-called crisis of identity is seen as part of a wider process of change, which dislocates the central structures and processes of modern societies and undermines the frameworks which gave individuals a stable status.

The history of the development of the concept of identity in India is very interesting. During pre-colonial and post-colonial periods, the individual did not have his personal identity. His identity belonged to his caste, village and religion. As an individual he was not considered seriously. The caste identity was fixed or paramount. He was in a hierarchical order which, even if he liked, he could not change. His caste or religious identity was by birth.

The situation of the untouchables was quite miserable. They were so and so by birth, which was their only identity; they were ill-treated; they were not allowed to enter temples, attend school and change their occupation. Besides, the identity of the backward groups – the subalterns and the marginals – was determined according to their caste belongingness. For the purpose of competing with high-castes, these groups did not have any status to do so. They were treated inhumanely.

It is not that these groups were not conscious of their humiliating identity. There were some social movements, such as that led by Ambedkar and Gandhi, which tried to change the identity of these groups to a respectable status. The alternatives to identity changes were closed. Most of these groups reconciled themselves with the servile, docile acceptance of low identity on traditional divine grounds. Their identity, divine dispensation was the explanation, if any.

When there came modernity, there was a shift in the identity of the individual, though emphasis continued to lay with the caste and religion. Some enlightened sections of society, which believed in achievement, tried to propagate the India of equality and freedom. These modern values were strengthened by the struggle for independence. It was for the first time that Gandhi mobilized the ordinary people to participate in the freedom movement. Even women who lived in *purdah* came out openly to rebel against the colonial and feudal rule. It was unhistorical to find that notwithstanding caste, class, sex and regional differences, all sections of people rubbed their shoulders with one another. There was a marked shift in the identity of a person from parochial level to the level of country.

The attainment of independence and the promulgation of constitution bestowed a new identity upon the people. India now became a democratic, secular, socialist/capitalistic and industrial society. A flood of new identities made in-roads in the life of the people. Though the sociologists argued that Indian modernity came during the British period, the reality is that massive modernity was observable only after the promulgation of constitution. Now, the individual became the smallest unit of federal democracy. Adult franchise became the power of the individual, and the power of collectivity – caste panchayat, religious sects and other such organizations lost their legal legitimacy. Individual in the context of modernity acquired a powerful identity.

The scheduled castes, scheduled tribes and other backward classes along with women and weaker sections of society got a new identity through the provision of reservation at various levels. Those of the people, who had, all through the history, a downtrodden identity, got a new identity – a package of protective and development safeguards. This elevated the identity level of the disadvantaged groups. These groups occupy, now, prestigious positions in all walks of the nation's life. They have entered into government jobs and exercise power at different levels of public institutions.

Postmodernity has become a part of their life. In traditional Indian society, their identity was monolithic, that of untouchables or backward people. But these untouchables fragmented till now, and each of their fragments now enjoys a distinct identity. Identity goes with the ethnic fragment. For instance, there is a strong social heterogeneity among the scheduled castes. There are also about 400 scheduled tribe groups and each group has its own differentiated identity.

## The Coming Crisis of Identity

Postmodernity is a historical phase and going with it are the privileges – safeguards – of the scheduled groups. Initially, the safeguards were given for a period of ten years. But, the groups could not reach the level of development which the common people in the country had almost attained, so the privileges have been extended for a further period of ten years and are continued even now after more than six decades of independence. But, for one thing we are certain – the privileges cannot be given for an indefinite period. On long-term basis, what would be the identity of these scheduled groups? Would they like to be identified as *Chamar, Bhangi* or *Bhil* (tribal group)? How would the society resolve such a crisis of identity?

As, at present, the scheduled tribes have adopted several of the customs, rituals, festivals and ceremonies of the caste Hindus. In this respect, they are closer to the intermediate or lower castes. The big parties propagate the ideology of cultural nationalism and according to it they make it known that the tribals are Hindus. But, the tribals do not get entry into the caste system. Caste by its structure and cultural connotation is hierarchal. And, the tribes are only structural. For them, there is no hierarchy. Santhal, Gond, and Bhil are autonomous groups. Structurally, thus, the caste is different from tribe.

In the present era of postmodernity, it is expected that the tribal groups would not accept the authoritarian rule of the Hindu grand narratives. If the tribals are not assigned a respectable status in the caste hierarchy, they would not identify themselves as Hindus. What is interesting is that the advocates of cultural nationalism call the tribals as Hindus only but not a Hindu caste, say a Rajput, or a Kayastha. In such a situation postmodernity seems to be the only saviour of the scheduled groups. Our guess is that after the descheduling of these groups, including that of scheduled castes, they would nevertheless continue to identify themselves with their original name, that is, tribe.

With the economic growth the identity of the marginal groups has changed considerably. It was unheard of the untouchables to be elites and affluents. Now, there are elite untouchables, they may be the creamy layer. A few of them have become regional, state and national level leaders. It shows that the creamy layers of the marginals have really attained higher status in the hierarchy. What is found in the Indian society is that with the weakening of the authority of the higher castes and the consequent rise of the lower castes with their increasing and fragmented ethnicities, the postmodernity has benefited the latter. Under the garb of modernity, the higher castes exploited the marginals. Modernity and its benefits were traditionally utilized by the rich people, including the high-castes and public leaders. They had greater resources, more money and higher education. This provided them opportunities to fully avail themselves of the facilities of modernity.

With the coming up of constitutional provisions, the marginals have become conscious of their privileges and have also come forward to avail themselves of benefits of the postmodern denial of high-caste authority. Individualism, which was central to the wider framework of modernity, now changed to its newer form or *avatar*. The individual of the modern period was described as the 'sovereign individual' who was embedded in each of the key processes and practices which made the modern world. Analyzing the status of modern individual, Foucault (*The Subject and Power*, 1986) writes:

> Individual was the subject of modernity in two senses: the origin or 'subject' of reason, knowledge and practice; and the one who bore the consequences of these practices – who was subjected to them.

The postmodern individual is the result of advanced capitalism. He is a figure of the isolated, exiled or estranged individual, framed against the background of the anonymous and impersonal crowd. The individual that we had in modern India has acquired a new form. He is autonomous, free from the authoritarian dominance of high-castes, elites and public leaders. But, this autonomous individual is a broken individual. He is highly disenchanted – a disillusioned person. The marginals are examples of postmodernity's disenchantment.

There are today two distinct situations in this country: the disenchantment created by the modernity of the dominant castes, and secondly, the increase in different ethnicities. Modernity works not on prophecy but reason, not on hierarchy but equality, not on vocation or calling but work, not on sacred meanings but pragmatic instrumentalities and rational legal rules govern day-to-day life of the people. Such a modernity is forcibly taken over by those who have money power and the marginals are left high and dry. The affluent groups even in villages have reasons to be satisfied with the benefits of modernity; they have capitalistic agriculture, official status in the Panchayat Raj and all the comforts of modernity; the marginals and the poor have only to suffer disillusionment and disenchantment from such a kind of modernity.

The second distinct situation of modernity is that it has created development in different areas of life. Development coincides with growth in the feeling of ethnicity. Ethnicity at its root lies in the consciousness of identity and cultural awareness of a community. With the rise in ethnicity, there increases revolt against the authority of the high-castes, the cultural elites – their functions and customs. In the long run or along with it postmodernity gets a boost among the marginal and disadvantaged groups. Yogendra Singh (*Culture Change in India*, 2000) correlates the relationship between economic growth and rise in ethnicity as under:

> The process through which communities transform themselves into ethnic group may be many, such as, minority status due to migration to other countries, acute consciousness of alienation due to exploitation within their own country of residence as for example, due to uneven levels of developmental opportunities. This feeling, which is rooted essentially in existential deprivation of ethnic groups in relation to the dominant communities, is sharpened by projection of deprivations into symbolic idiom of politics.

**Concluding Observations**

Postmodernity, in a broader way, has a negative approach towards many perspectives and themes in sociology and social sciences. Many of the traditions and cultural certainties on which Indian social institutions – caste, kin, religion, family, village and linguistic groups – have remained structured over the past couple of centuries, are interwoven with tradition and change. Even our liberal sociological theorists argue that India has a deep-rooted civilizational depth and this cannot be eroded with the present strength of our social change including that of globalization and market domination.

Postmodernity all in all, thus, rejects traditions. In India, however, the situation is different. Here, our theorists argue that the power of modernity has brought about changes in the traditions themselves, changes despite traditions. But, instead of giving a death blow to traditions, modernity itself is getting a facelift – experiencing an adaptive transformation. Our national leaders, however, had a different strategy to deal with the traditions. They wanted to reform the traditions themselves or at least, put new interpretations on them, in the light of earth-shattering scientific changes worldwide.

We have argued in the present chapter that quite like modernity, postmodernity in India is unlike the postmodernity in the west. Postmodernity is rooted in the social structure and ethnicities. We have a history of colonial and feudal rule for a couple of centuries. These were the dark ages of our country. The country remained diversified through all these periods of history. Each petty feudal state fought against the other. The colonial rule had adopted the policy of divide and rule. Such a disruptive rule ended with the creation and increase of multiple diversities. Before independence, the country was socially and culturally fractured and fragmented. The definition of postmodernity has to be sought against such a social and historical background.

There are sociologists who have argued that despite alarming diversity, the country all through these years had unity. The idiom is: unity in diversity. Take, for instance, M.N. Srinivas, who argues that the unity of the country was maintained by cultural forces. The four *dhamas* of Hindu pilgrimage – Badrinath, Dwarka, Puri and Rameshwaram – keep the whole country tied together. But, such a unification of the country is only a grand narrative – it is nothing more than a myth. A Hindu is expected to visit these *dhamas* once in his life. Such a unity does not provide any opportunity for day-to-day functional relations, neither trade, social nor economic.

Besides M.N. Srinivas, K.S. Singh in his, *People of India* argues that there are plural ethnicities and identities in cultural India. But, what is striking in multi-ethnicities is that they tend to create linkages between diverse regions. How the linkages operate and how do they work, is not analyzed by K.S. Singh. His *People of India*, was a government sponsored enterprise. It is in reality a study of caste, which is termed as community. An official document cannot study caste and therefore it is labelled a community study. And, second, a government document is obliged to conclude that different ethnicities add to the integration of the country. Varying ethnicities hardly release integrative forces.

What is termed as cultural unity is, in fact, our political unity. The makers of our constitution were aware of this diversity and they could not find a way to abolish it. They, therefore, legitimized the multi-ethnicities and made provision to permit the ethnicities to operate as they like with the condition that those would not interfere in the functioning of other ethnicities and the state. The coalition governments that we find in India these days are the direct outcome of multi-ethnicities. And, strangely enough, not a single day goes without a change in the structure of ethnicity. Day in and day out, new local and regional temples are getting erected; new gods are emerging and fresh anniversaries of great men, saints and sadhus are being planned and even executed. All these changes vividly show the importance of a rise in ethnicity. The promoters of ethnicity know it well that they are working within the framework of the constitution.

In India, postmodernity has yet another favourable ground for its acceptance. Traditions are central to Indian ethnicity. As elsewhere, they die very hard. And, in their death, they tend to give rise to new traditions. In all possibility, the ethnicities grow unabated. Postmodernity, therefore, is acceptable to lower sections of society. The bearers of postmodernity would thus be these very sections. It should also be mentioned here that the postmodernity, which is closer to the poor, is not against capitalism or industrialism, which are the sources of employment and opportunities of education now. What is crucial to it is that it vehemently rejects the institutional authoritarianism, including that of caste, state and religion.

Before we close this chapter, we would observe that there is very little sociological research material in the country. It suffers terribly from grand narratives. The theoretical concepts of dominant caste, sanskritization, westernization and universalization are based on totality and universalization. They are against the core characteristics of postmodernity. It should be accepted that postmodernity, multiple traditions and ethnicities by their nature are divisive. What makes unification of India's diversities are not the ethnicities and postmodernity, it is the representative democracy and political order. Those who argue that religion and culture are the unifying forces of Indian society, suffer from the notion of grand narratives. Most of such sociologists are doing Hindu sociology; they are victims of cultural nationalism and advocates of the theory and ideology of functionalism.

India, at present, is going through the processes of modernization and postmodernization. Culturally, it is plural, multi-ethnic and multi-linguistic. Politically, it is democratic, industrial, capitalistic and secular. In the paraphrase of postmodernity, there has been in India, a variant of poststructuralism. It rejects the principles of structuralism. The strongholds of the structuralist paradigm were deconstruction and feminism. The theme of poststructuralism has not been touched in the present work. We have restricted ourselves only to postmodernity.

# V

# Fundamentalist World of Dogma and Danger

The dictionary meaning of fundamentalism is "a belief in the literal truth of the Bible, a movement in the 10th century Protestantism emphasizing such belief". Second, "it is a movement stressing strict adherence to a set of basic principles or beliefs especially in religion". As a matter of fact, fundamentalism is a general attempt to get to the basics, or fundamentals, of belief, setting aside any sophisticated theological argument of doctrines. In Christianity, it has generally come to be used for an approach based on a literal interpretation of the Bible. In Islam, it applies to those who claim to take an uncompromising approach to applying the *Shariah*, or the religious law.

In India, one of the epics, the *Ramayana*, gives description of Rama in his exile to forests – *Vanvasa*. He is accompanied by his wife, Sita and brother, Laxman. They move on foot, bear all the pains of forest, suffer the rough road and sleep under the open sky. The same Rama, by his divine power, constructs a bridge to Sri Lanka. All this description has to be accepted, as it is fundamental. Otherwise, a modernist or a postmodernist would question: Rama who constructed a bridge with the help of animals like monkeys, how could he not dare to tame a lion or two, to ride on and move along the forest? But such questions are untenable, for it is fundamentalism to show respect to all that which is written in the *Ramayana*. *Ramayana* is a grand narrative and it has to be accepted as it is.

Anthony Giddens (*Sociology*, 2001) has defined fundamentalism in sociological perspective:

> It is belief in returning to the literal meanings of scriptural texts. Fundamentalism may arise as a response to modernization and insisting on faith-based answers, and defending tradition by using traditional grounds.

Fundamentalism, thus, has its roots in traditional, historical prejudices and modernity. It looks at postmodernity with enmity. Postmodernity is against authority of traditions and modernity. Before the advent of modernity, there was also fundamentalism. But, it was, in the Indian context, interpreted by the colonial and feudal rule. The fundamentalists today mobilize themselves on the rules of rationality and bureaucracy. This has given rise to new strength in them. There is relationship between fundamentalism and postmodernity. The postmodernity has cried aloud against grand narratives. The universalizing theories tried to establish the authoritarian generalizations on the society. This was rejected. The postmodernity also rejected modernity in the west. In India, however, it did not happen. Here, in our situation, modernity was dominated by high-castes, elites and affluent groups. The authority of these groups continued to survive. And, they exercised their influence and authority. Fundamentalism attacks postmodernity as it is against authoritarian domination.

Despite the claims of postmodernists that there is weakening of grand narratives, the facts are otherwise. Fundamentalism is a grand narrative. It has its various dimensions. There is religious fundamentalism, market fundamentalism, political fundamentalism, and development fundamentalism. Fundamentalism also takes the shape of terrorism. In most of the cases, fundamentalists are also terrorists.

Postmodernists deny authoritarian dominance; contrariwise, the fundamentalists and terrorists show all faith in and commitment to authority. The postmodernists are skeptical about everything. The fundamentalists do not argue, they are committed to faith. Stuart Sim (*Postmodernism*, 2005) differentiates fundamentalism and postmodernity as below:

> Institutional authority is once again accepted unquestionably, obliged blindly, and allowed to direct the individual's life in the name of a larger cause. *Faith, rather than reason or skepticism, becomes the basis of the cultural process* (emphasis added). In its more extreme form – as with the Taliban regime in Afghanistan – Islamic fundamentalism is effectively a return to a pre-modern society, where almost all the modern world is rejected (with the significant exception of its weaponry).

Fundamentalism is a movement of the authoritarian-minded people. It gives them safety and security in an individual believer. The postmodernity does not have any such assurance. Admittedly, both fundamentalism and postmodernity are cultural movements. But it is clear, there is a larger market for traditional system of beliefs. In India, traditions and cultural practices have a great role for the origin and growth of fundamentalism. The ethnic formations make coalition with fundamentalism and as a consequence of it the social order gets polluted. The social pollution gets severe when it links itself with politics. In fact, fundamentalism in India is politicized and has weakened our democracy too.

## Fundamentalism and Postmodernity

We have earlier argued that in India's social structure, both modernity and postmodernity work simultaneously. Surely, modernity has many more hills to scale. But, it is industrially developed, democratically mature, economically progressive and powerful enough to maintain its sovereignty. Postmodernity, likewise, is rooted in our diversity, decentralization, village autonomy and denial of authority of caste and custom.

A new breakthrough has been made by modernity. It has given fundamentalism to religious, political, caste and market groups. Earlier, both Hindus and Muslims, Hindus and Sikhs, and high-castes and lower castes lived together. Even, in Indian villages today, one can find a temple and a mosque huddled together. There was peace. Festivals and ceremonies were not of a particular group only, but of the whole village. Iravati Karve reports that the son-in-law of a village person was treated as the son-in-law of the entire village. There was no fundamentalism.

With the coming of modernity, the dominant groups all of a sudden got embedded and influenced by the values of rationality, bureaucracy and ethnic consciousness. With some group interests and political developmental benefits they turned to fundamentalism. Fundamentalism is a very complex phenomenon. It also gives rise to revivalism. It reinterprets the tradition, reconstructs the local history and gives new meaning to the existing situations.

There are several fundamentalisms in Indian society. No ethnicity is without any fundamentalism. And, it is the modernity which is responsible for the rise of ethnicity and fundamentalism. Commenting on the rise of fundamentalism, Stuart Sim (2005) writes:

> Postmodernist philosophers may argue that grand narratives are in decline, but the growing popularity of religious fundamentalism around the world suggests this may be an over-optimistic assessment. Most of the major world religions have fundamentalist movements; Christianity and Islam are the most prominent, but Hinduism and Judaism have their committed activity as well. Fundamentalism was coined as a term to describe radical Protestant evangelism in early twentieth century America. Christianity was reduced to a set of fundamental beliefs (such as the virgin birth of Christ) that could not be questioned by adherents. Central to this outlook was the Bible, which in the more militant forms of fundamentalist thought is taken to be literally true. There are similar attitudes in Islam with regard to the Quran.

In Indian context, fundamentalism is to some extent a reaction to postmodern skepticism towards authority and has been described as an authority-minded movement. In the beginning religious fundamentalism was not very rigid. The colonial powers encouraged it to some extent. It was at a later stage that modernity with the coalition of competing ethnicities created ground for fundamentalism. Such a development brought it in complicity with postmodernity. Postmodernity rejects authority; and fundamentalism accepts it with all faith and belief. Faith cannot be debated, nor can it be argued. It is only to be practised and followed.

## Variants of Fundamentalism

Besides religious fundamentalism, there have emerged some new fundamentalisms which originate from the contemporary society, which is characterized by growing economic growth, rivalry among political parties, and increasing assertion by ethnic consciousness. Globalization has created market fundamentalism, rivalry from international trade and cultural impact. Fundamentalism in India is also traceable to the realm of academics.

All Sanskrit scholars – writers of *shlokas* or poetry – are considered to have created universal truths. They are axiomatic – above time and space. Even law courts quote the *slokas* of these scriptures in support of justice given by them. The idiom which goes is simple – quote a line of *Vedas, Ramayana* or *Mahabharata* and whatever you have said becomes truth – the reality of society. Tulsidas, Kabir, and even Shakespeare, have been divine creatures. Whatever they composed is said to be self-evident; no further evidence is necessary. This is what postmodernity calls the authority of the grand narratives – an example of fundamentalism. *Ramayana* or for that matter no scripture can be wrong. It is the belief in these scriptures and their writers that carry universal truth.

The situation in the academics of sociology is in no way different. Karl Marx, Max Weber and Talcott Parsons are equally 'worshipped'. They have been our 'priests'. Some of these worshipped priests have lost their relevance but they are very much in our syllabus. There are some sociologists in our contemporary India who have become totally outdated. But, whatever they have said about caste, family and village has stood the test of time. These are all trends of fundamentalism. The message is clear: if Sanskrit *shlokas* and *shastrakars* and Hindi literature poets are not wrong, how can sociologists be wrong. We do not argue and should not argue that whatever the writers of fundamentalism have said is wrong; what we emphasize is that their statements need to be deconstructed. Our concern here is only to say that there are several variants of fundamentalism and these are creations of modernity – rationality and bureaucracy. These are also products of competing ethnicities and identities. Amartya Sen holds the opinion that besides other forces of fundamentalism, competing identities are the major reason.

Market fundamentalism is yet another variant of fundamentalism. Adherents to this variant have blind faith in it. The term 'market fundamentalism' was coined by the international financier George Soros to describe "the unrestricted laissez-faire capitalism favoured by the International Monetary Fund (IMF) and the World Bank". These institutions tend to impose this model on failing economics around the globe, sometimes, as in the case of Argentina, with quite disastrous results. Market fundamentalism demands the dismantling of the state sector (encouraging privatization programmes for all state-owned industries), low interest rates, and open market for capital. With the liberalization of Indian economy during 1990s privatization was allowed to have strong influence in the control of market. Disinvestments in public sector get much encouragement from the state. What has happened today is that market is regarded as an authority which could not be called into question.

Fundamentalism is also observable in politics and political parties. Long back, during the Prime Ministership of Jawaharlal Lal Nehru, the Congress Party decided to design an Indian society on socialistic pattern. It was resolved that too much concentration of money would not be in the hands of a few business houses. Efforts were made to bring socialism on the ground. Public sectors were created as mechanisms to decentralize the national money. The market fundamentalism did not accept such a state policy.

In this context, it is interesting to mention thinkers like Francis Fukuyama, who brought about a new epistemology in the western thought. Fukuyama's controversial book, *The End of History and the Last Man*, came into prominence in 1992. This presented one of the first philosophically ambitious interpretations of the collapse of Soviet type communism in 1989. Fukuyama argued that there is no future for communism and socialism in the world. And, in the times to come, capitalism would survive. Such interpretations of capitalism have become fundamental truisms of political ethos. No power in the world can defeat the growth of capitalism. Quite like capitalism, democracy would also continue to stay in the world.

Fundamentalism is so structured that it does not tolerate dissenting views. No one can go against Tulsidas, against Marx, and Weber and for that matter, against S.C. Dube and M.N. Srinivas. The final truth has been laid down by these great priests of their respective realms. On the other hand, the postmodernity has to combat against the increasing fundamentalism. Postmodernity has a different approach to modern society, the fundamental society. It entails commitment to dissent, pluralism, cultural difference and skepticism towards authority. It finds itself in direct conflict which such systems, which substitute the authoritarian collective will for the individual. Postmodernity, for all purposes, is against grand narratives whether in sociology, academics, arts or literature.

We now turn to discuss some of the major variants of fundamentalism which have influenced the Indian society. India is a democratic, sovereign, secular, capitalistic and plural society. It is now increasingly realized that modernity in India was not the modernity of the masses; it was rather a preserve of the dominant groups. Postmodernity, which denied the authority of the higher groups, elite institutions, encouraged pluralism (multi-ethnicities) and dissent, also promoted fundamentalism. In our country, as we have reiterated, postmodernity's fight is against fundamentalism. Our traditions, as sociologists argued, have very marginally taken to adaptive changes. They have been revived with the new money received from technology, new traditions are created; new ethnicities and identities constructed. All these trends lead the people to fundamentalism. Postmodernity has to arm itself against this new threat.

Fundamentalism is rooted in identity. And, a person has not one identity but several. He is a businessman, a craftsman, a party boss, a Hindu or a Muslim. Out of several identities, one or two become predominant. The predominant identity results in fundamentalism. Amartya Sen argues that of all the identities, religious identity is most dangerous. In a lighter vein, he reports the crude beliefs that the Muslims and Christians have:

> It can take form of beliefs exemplified by U.S. Lieutenant, General William Boykin's blaring and by now well-known remarks describing his battle against Muslims with disarming

> coarseness: "I knew that my God was bigger than his" and that "the Christian God was a real God and (the Muslim's) was an idol." The idiocy of such dense bigotry is, of course, easy to diagnose and for this reason there is, I believe, comparatively danger in the uncouth hurting of such unguided missiles.

Muslim and Hindu fundamentalisms have been explained by political scientists and historians. Recently, Amartya Sen has also attempted it from civilizational perspectives. The political scientists argue that the communal theory initiated by the colonial rule is responsible for encouraging fundamentalism. The two-nation theory explains the division of country into India and Pakistan. There have been fierce Hindu-Muslim riots during the colonial and post-colonial eras.

Fundamentalism is associated with terrorism. As is observed today, most of the terrorist acts are engineered by Muslims. How is it that wherever in USA or Britain, there are terrorists activities, the Muslims are held responsible. When there was horrifying event of September 11, in the USA, of the attack on WTC tower, the blame was put on Muslims. The event has been diagnosed by civilizational theory. It is described as the *clash of civilizations*. The author of this theory is Samuel Huntington (*The Clash of Civilizations and the Remaking of the World Order*, 1996). He says that the world is categorized into a number of civilizations such as 'the western world', 'the Islamic world', 'the Hindu world' or the 'Buddhist world'. These worlds are categorized on the basis of religion. And, therefore, the event of September 11 was a clash between the western civilization and the Islamic civilization. There are several scholars who have disputed Huntington's theory. For instance, it is erroneous to categorize India as Hindu civilization, for there are a large number of people who are non-Hindu. The Sikhs have a major presence, as do the Jains. India is not only the country of origin of Buddhism; the dominant religion of India was Buddhism for over a millennium, and the Chinese often referred to India as the 'Buddhist Kingdom'.

When Huntington's theory was discussed in India's media, it was acclaimed by the politically active 'Hindutva', movement. Let us not forget that religion is not the all-encompassing and exclusive identity of a Hindu or a Muslim. A Muslim could take a confrontational view of another Muslim. Besides the Muslim identity, a Muslim is also a Rajasthani or a Bihari, he is an intellectual and also a poor person. This is not fundamentalism. This is merely an identity. But, when a Muslim takes Quran as his final authority, he shows all commitment to it and considers his faith as unabiding, it is a situation of fundamentalism. For a Muslim, in his hierarchy of identities, when religion tops, he is likely to become a fundamentalist.

## Muslim Fundamentalism

Muslim fundamentalism can be properly analyzed when we look from historical, social and cultural perspectives. Though Islam believes in community brotherhood or it is a rational group founding small groups of the country. When they are found in villages, they mix up with the local people and start speaking their dialect. It is the politics, which makes them to take to fundamentalism, which might give some relief. In India, the Muslims have experienced a history which also encourages them to pursue the path of fundamentalism, which might give some relief. In India, the Muslims have experienced a history which also encourages them take to the path of fundamentalism. Fundamentalism can also be seen in a game like cricket, when there is a match between India and Pakistan, the emotions are at their peak.

### *Advent of Islam*

The advent of Islam is traced back to 6th century, when the Muslims lived a nomadic life in Arabia. Barbaric practices like female infanticide, human sacrifice and others were the norm. Prophet Mohammad was born in this setting. He was disturbed by the happenings around him and took up the task of reforming the then existing society by preaching Islam. He, along with his ever-growing followers, had to cross insurmountable barriers to achieve a relatively humane and civilized society in that epoch.

Yousuff Kasim (*Seminar*, 416) delineates the reforms introduced among the Muslims of earlier periods:

> The following path-breaking commandments were advocated which other Semitic religions of that period had not advocated:

drinking was banned as it was considered instrumental in the emergence of all animal instincts in human beings; usury which was causing large-scale impoverishment was prohibited; slavery was discouraged (not banned); females were given the right of inheritance upto half that of the males; some semblance of democracy was introduced by creating an electoral college which elected the leader; a system of redistribution of wealth through zaket was made compulsory; idol worship and human sacrifice were banned; widow marriage was encouraged; and equality between haves and have nots and those belonging to different tribes during congregations for prayers inculcated a feeling of brotherhood in society.

These and many other changes created a dedicated mass of followers who zealously tried to spread the message of Islam far and wide. During the lifetime of Prophet Mohammed and four Caliphs, the spread of Islam was due to its lofty ideals and the sincerity and good examples of those who led.

### *Core of Islamic Religion*

We will address two questions here: What are core Islamic beliefs that pertain to both women and men? And, how do the Muslims take to fundamentalism? Admittedly, the Muslims are exposed to modernity and postmodernity. Despite all this, they are today poor and disadvantaged. They are illiterate; they live in *ghettos*. But, the Muslim history shows that when they came to India as invaders, they were a daring kind of people who, on one hand, converted the lower castes to Islam and, on the other, looted a large chunk of property in the form of gold and silver. Ghori and Ghajnavi made several attacks on the states of their smaller native rulers. It was on the strength of their sword that they continued their regime in India till the downfall of the Mughal empire. It is proved, they have the potentiality to stay on and settle in a foreign land.

The status of Muslims in India has swung from sublime to ridiculous. Let us see if their religion gives them strength and the present weakness. Is it the religion which makes them fundamentalist or a group withdrawing from modernity and postmodernity. Before we analyze the core of Islamic religion, we must mention that all Muslims are not fundamentalists, nor were all Hindus. The Muslims are excellent, generous; they are artists par excellence, they are all-influential writers, administrators, politicians, army men, sportspersons and what not. Only a handful of men turn to fundamentalism and terrorism. Any deep survey would show that fundamentalism is for political power and supremacy.

Islam came after Judaism and Christianity. It borrowed from the Old Testament but sought to liberate its followers from the hegemony of an organized church, to eliminate the structured religious hierarchy and to leave its followers in control of their observances. The performance of rituals, community progress and even marriage ceremonies were left to the individual. There was to be no intermediary between an individual and God, since each one was required to pray and make other observances privately. Shahid Lateef (*Seminar*, 416), interpreting the Islamic religion, writes:

> The Quran was a guide to collective belief and behaviour. It was also mindful of customs and traditions of the Arab culture of the time and those of the Christians and the Jews. The *Hadith* and the *Sunnah* comprising the sayings and the life of the prophet were to provide additional guidance. These gained importance and even proliferated, after the death of the prophet as Islam spread to non-Arab cultures and made many cultural compromises and adjustments.

If we look at Islam from comparative plane, we would find that followers of other religions are different. There is monotheism, daily prayers, fasting during Ramjan, charity and pilgrimage. It is this core that links most Muslim individuals and societies to each other rather than law and cultural accretions normally associated with Muslim societies. Shahid Lateef pens down the particularistic character of Islam in India:

> Islam in India is of the core beliefs shared by all Muslims, notwithstanding many variations in regional customs and the political exigencies of the community.

The core Islamic values thus are : (i) belief in the Quran, and (ii) on the prophet Mohammad's sayings. In other words, for a Muslim, Quran is the word of God, directly revealed by Prophet

Mohammad. *Hadith* is based on the authorized collection of the reports of Mohammad. Islam is theoretically not a closed religion. Some attempts were made to bring changes in the Islamic core and *Hadith* – it is called *ijtihad*. The objective of this effort was to make some innovative interpretation in the 10th century in *Hadith*.

Rashid Talib ('The Problem', *Seminar*, 46) gives all efforts made by reformers like Sir Syed Ahmed Khan, the poet Iqbal and Jamal al-Din Afghani and Mohammed Abduh in West Asia to bring some changes in the interpretations of *Hadith*. Rashid Talib comments on such attempts of reinterpretation of Islam:

> Many attempts all over the Muslim world during the 18th and 19th centuries and the impact of western colonialism were made to update Islam by these *mujtahits* among others through the route of *ijtihad*. However, all such efforts proved to be in vain.

### Modernization and Islam

Principally, Islam has not been so conservative as to reject modernization. Quite like Hindu traditions, the Islamic traditions have also made certain adaptive changes but the Muslim conservatives, following of the values of Islam, have made them to accept the authority of Ullema. It is difficult for a Muslim to change his religion. In the wake of industrialism, capitalism and democracy, a few Muslims have seriously taken to modernization. At a later stage, when we would discuss Hindu fundamentalism, we would argue that the Muslim genocide in Ahmedabad (2002) was not much on religious grounds, but was primarily on mercantile competition. In a few areas of trading, the Muslims were far ahead of Hindus. The competition between the two trading groups was cut-throat indeed. The objective of engineering genocide was to wipe out the Muslim traders.

The disturbances of Ahmedabad very clearly show that Muslim dominant groups have had most of the benefits of modernization. It is only the Muslim marginals and they are in sizeable number, who have not gained much from modernity. Their religion is basically immune to change as is evident from its history.

Islam has no space for modernity and postmodernity. It is basically committed to core values of religion. The nature of Islam is based on the individual. The Quran has placed the obligation of being morally responsible on individuals, since neither church nor clergy were required to enforce compliance with its tenets. Fundamentalism, or denial of modernity and postmodernity, is therefore, due to the individual consent to religion. The Friday prayers are not for collective worship, they are only opportunities to bring the adherents of Islam together and create feelings of solidarity.

It was believed at the time of the division of country that there will be no conflict emerging from two religions – Hindu and Islam. Each country would have its separate way of worship. But that did not happen. Today, the relations between the two countries are not smooth and cordial. All these events show that fundamentalism is not a major reason of terrorism. On the other hand, the attacks made by Muslims in medieval period on India were motivated by the spreading of their religion. However, they also converted lower castes to Islam. They also took huge money with them. The Mughals also demolished hundreds of temples and constructed quite a few mosques. It further strengthens the thesis that fundamentalism does not have its roots in religion. It is a perverted individual, an anti-social individual; it is a miscreant individual who adopts fundamentalism. And, whatever the reason, a Muslim is not prepared to bring any change in his religion. And, the history of religion shows it evidently that followers of Islam are not ready to accept any modernization. Their religious traditions are also not prone to change.

### Islamic Socialization

The values, norms and lifestyle of the individual are determined by the wider process of society. As it happens in other societies, the Muslims also experience the impact of religion on their personality. Fundamentalism has several allurements for an individual: it helps him to fulfil his nationalistic feelings; gives him easy money and bestows on him a terror figure. It is the choice of the individual to accept fundamentalism or go for other identities of a politician, a leader, a scholar or an ordinary man. What is particular about religious fundamentalism is that the individual has an abiding faith in and commitment to Islam. This faith is uncompromising and the individual becomes a trusted 'holy warrior'.

### *Madarsa*

A sectarian primary school, which is meant to orient its pupils to the basic tenets of Islam. Madarsa is considered to be the elementary agency of a Muslim socialization. It is not necessary for every Muslim individual to enter into Madarsa. It depends on the family to opt for or opt against Madarsa education. The Hindu fundamentalists decry Madarsa and say that it is this school, which prepares Muslim youths for fundamentalism and terrorism.

Edna Fernandes has very recently come out with a book, (*Holy Warriors*, 2006) which candidly explores bigotry among various religious groups of the country and tries to find out the extent of fundamentalism found in India. She gives details about a Madarsa, which has international status in the Muslim world. It has the support of *Darul-Uloom* or the House of Knowledge. It was established nine years after the 1857 Indian Mutiny.

*Darul-Uloom* is not only a school or Madarsa. It is a school of thought, a global movement based on Sunni Islam, which believed in the return of austerity of Sharia law, rejected the modes of modernity or western influence and "preached a true Islamic society that could be found in the Quran and the original teachings of the Prophet Mohammed, the credo that began in the small Indian town as a rejection of western imperialist hegemony in the mid-1800s was now resonating across the Muslim world 150 years later".

The Deoband School or Madarsa, as it is known, is an international centre for socializing the Muslims. Deoband is a small town situated in the western Uttar Pradesh. Whole of its population is Muslim. The Deoband life is on the Sharia pattern and women are kept in *purdah*. Introducing the Deoband Madarsa, Fernandes (2006) writes:

> The aim of Deoband was simple: to take a Muslim child and steep him in the ways of orthodox Islam, educate him in

> Quranic studies, Sharia, Fiquh, Hadith, Arabic, Persian, Urdu, Islamic history and scriptures until in his mid-twenties, he was ready to go forth into the world as a messenger of God. On graduation, these messengers of God established Madarasas across the Islamic region, thus exporting the Deoband message of orthodoxy. Since its birth 150 years ago, thousands of Deoband affiliated Madarasas had been set up worldwide with particular strongholds in the tribal regions of Pakistan and Afghanistan.

Fernandes elaborately discusses the impact of Madarsas in infusing the spirit of fundamentalism and terrorism. Perhaps, Afghanistan is the only country which has created a model of true Islamic society. Taliban is the creation of Afghanistan's Islamic ideology.

Deoband should not be taken as an ordinary Madarsa. There are about 3,500 students drawn from India, United Kingdom, Saudi Arabia, Bangladesh and Burma (now Myanmar). Its alumni's reach ranged from Africa and America to the West Indies and Yemen. Thus, Deoland has been a hotbed of fundamentalism. The Talibanis of Afghanistan are from Deoband.

Islam does not have any faith in modernization. It has always remained against the western culture. The Muslims believe that return to the past secures the life hereafter. The old way was the path to salvation and thereby justify acts that alienated much of the non-Islamic world. Fernandes interviewed the old Mufti of Deoband whose rulings were dispensed across the Islamic world and followed assiduously. Mufti Habur Rehman explained the objectives of Islam in the following words:

> Consumerism is totally against Islam, it does not follow the principles of humanity and morality. Islam does not believe in consumerism, consumerism is purely worldly thinking. Islam believes in two ways: one life here and one life hereafter.

Habur Rehman further explains another Islamic concept:

> *Jihad* is a religious term. It demands that we have to make an effort for the propagation of Islam. If there is opposition anywhere we are not allowed to do and perform our religious duties so that we can raise arms against the enemy. This type of effort is called *Jihad.*

In the Deoband Madarsa, teaching is not about expansion of the mind but conditioning it. Muslim fundamentalism is known for several reasons. *Darul-Uloom* imparts training in the teaching of Islam. And, Islam being based on individualism gives an open choice to opt for it or reject it. But, there are equally other forces for the promotion of fundamentalism and terrorism among the Muslims. We have mentioned it earlier that in India, Muslims are among the poorest, least educated and most marginalized sections of society. They have gone from being the ruling classes during the Mughal era to the underclass of post-independence India. For many Muslims, the meaning of equality under the Constitution and in the fine speeches by secular leaders, had little substance in a country where they were still at the bottom of the pile. The rise of Hindu nationalism in 1990s and the new millennium had exposed the Indian Muslims to a new form of politics – one that openly derived the secular ideal and called for a Hindu Raj under which Muslims must know their place.

In any discussion on fundamentalism and terrorism it must be said candidly that an ordinary Muslim, living in India's village, is a first rate-Indian. His identity, every inch, is Indian. The history of our villages, the literature – regional and parochial – show it vividly that the Hindu temple and the Muslim mosque are located close to one another. Our struggle for independence shows that both Muslims and Hindus fought jointly against the imperial power. The village habitation is not based on religious differences. There has never been any trouble between the two communities. If Id was a festival of Muslims, it was also a festival of the Hindus. Death of a Muslim was mourned by the whole village, notwithstanding any religious affinity. The dialect of both the communities was common, even the occupations were the same.

Islam was there during the historical period, but there was amity and cordiality between the two segments of society. There was no trace of fundamentalism before the coming of elections and party politics. The secular ideology created an atmosphere of living together and tolerating each other. There was identity for belonging to a caste or a religion. The Muslims have either their occupation as religious identity and the Hindus have their caste identity. It is the party politics, which divides the country into caste and religion. What we argue is that fundamentalism is not the creation of religion, nor is Hindu fundamentalism religious. Most of the fundamentalism is social and political. Historically, it must be admitted that the Muslims as outsiders invaded this country several times. It is proverbial for Surat in Gujarat that it was an idol of gold (*Surat Yane Sona ni Murat*). The Muslims looted it. Somnath was also a victim of several Muslim invaders. These invaders had an objective of preaching Islam. And, Islam preaches that it should cover the whole world under its umbrella. The religion of the invaders also prompted them to demolish several temples and *matths*.

Centuries have gone and the Hindus now cry for the demolition of Muslim mosques as their temples were reduced to ashes by the grand forefathers of the present Muslims. How the son could be punished by the crime committed by his father. The Muslims increasingly realize that they are being victimized for no fault of theirs.

To conclude our discussions on Muslim fundamentalism, we would make a few conclusions. Our objective in this chapter is not to centralize on fundamentalism. It is not our issue. We want to drive home that modernity has been like a cake in India to be consumed by the dominant groups who are Hindus, Muslims, Sikhs and several tribal groups. Sharing of the benefits of modernity created a severe battleground for these dominant groups. The poorest of the Muslims have by now lost the battle. They are buried in illiteracy, poverty and unemployment. It is in the name of religion that they are dragged into fundamentalism and terrorism. In the name of religion, women are not generally allowed to attend schools; they are obliged to observe *purdah*; and they are given a low status on the pretext of religion. Religion is such a strong force that the marginals tend to move towards fundamentalism and terrorism. It is difficult to identify the rich and affluent people who recruit themselves as fundamentalists. The masses of poor are mobilized to 'sacrifice' themselves for the so-called cause of religion. The higher class, at best, is required to finance the fundamentalist and terrorist groups. On the other hand, the benefits of modernity are absorbed by the upper sections of society.

The Muslim groups, which are educated and rich, have implemented a conspiracy to keep the marginals in perpetual backwardness. The denial of modernity to the Muslims is not by the people but they are put in such a position of poverty, illiteracy and backwardness that they cannot afford to avail themselves of the benefits of modernity. Nor can they accept postmodernity. Postmodernity is totally against grand narratives, such as the dictates of Ullema, his authority and the Arabian culture and traditions.

The status of Muslim women is also pitiable. They have to observe *purdah*, accept polygyny and agree to divorce as their fate. The Committee on the Status of Women (1972-74) found that "Muslim women belonging to the impoverished strata of society were overwhelmingly in favour of changes in Muslim Personal Law, especially in regard to unilateral divorce and bigamy. But Muslim women from the educated middle class were as vehemently opposed to any change and certainly not the change by government legislation."

By striking a conclusive note on Muslim fundamentalism, we would say that all major religions in India – Hindu, Sikh and Christian – have some type of religious fanatism. A thousand-year history of invasions and colonial rule, partition by the British and alienation of minorities within post-independence India sowed the seeds for sectarian divide. Religious insecurity in a modern, increasingly godless world helped that divide to lead to the growth of Muslim fundamentalism. Hindu fundamentalism also contributed to the growth of Muslim fundamentalism. This radicalized the fundamentalism on both the sides – Muslim and Hindu.

Perhaps modernization and postmodernization might have weakened the strength of Muslim fundamentalism, had the community not rejected social change. Poverty, unemployment illiteracy and a host of other factors have pushed the Muslim community to fanaticism. As a matter of fact, postmodernity suits well to the Muslims. Individual autonomy, authoritarian denial and love for technology might have discouraged the Muslims to accept fundamentalism. The ordinary Muslim masses are prone to accept social change but their illiteracy and poverty makes them conservative and fanatic. They believe that only their religion can save them. It is this option which pushes a handful of men to fundamentalism. But, the analysis of Muslim fundamentalism is incomplete without a thorough and comparative understanding of Hindu fundamentalism.

## Hindu Fundamentalism

Fundamentalism is a movement or belief calling for a return to the basic text of religion. It lives in the past. We have discussed above Islamic fundamentalism. Compared to Islamic fundamentalism, Hindu fundamentalism is new. It appeared during the period of our struggle for independence. Two-nation theory is based on Muslim fundamentalism. It was argued that Hindus and Muslims were religiously two distinct communities and if these communities were separated into two nations, the problem would be solved. But, this did not happen. The Hindus created a new identity. They argued that India belongs to Hindus and the Muslims are outsiders. Muslims should be driven out or should be given the status of secondary citizens.

### *Variety of Hindu Fundamentalism*

Hindus constitute an ethnic group. It is a cultural formation. And, what is a caste group? Both anthropologically and sociologically, caste is social and cultural. It is very difficult to differentiate caste from religion. There are several theories which show that caste has its origin from religion. If caste is religion, there is caste fundamentalism also. Most of the castes in India have their temples and what is worse, the marginalized castes have now created their own temples. Thus, there are as many castes so there are as many temples. The whole question of fundamentalism is related to identity. Caste identity is common today. When we discuss Hindus fundamentalism, we are concerned with caste fundamentalism also.

K.S. Singh, in his *People of India* project, reports that there are more than four thousand communities, that is, virtually castes in India. Each caste has its own identity, its nomenclature and differentiated culture. In other words, there are several fundamentalisms in the country. Such a hypothesis is not acceptable to the advocates of cultural nationalism. For the sake of Hindu votes they put various brands of caste identities into a single Hindu fundamentalism. This is a grand narrative charged by falsehood and sham.

However, those who have theoretically diagnosed fundamentalism agree to its two-fold division. Its one variant is political. Its one objective is to transform fundamentalism into nationalism. It is argued that Hindus, notwithstanding their schisms, are in a majority and therefore they are entitled to have *Hindu Raj*. The second variant of fundamentalism is cultural or non-political. *The Frontline* (Vol. 21, March 13-20, 2004) argues:

> Hindus who have percolated to the nooks and corners of South India and the routes of fundamentalism have often been socio-cultural and educational rather than political. In the north fundamentalism took to the acquisition of power. In their effort *Hindutva* forces were helped by the fact that they had the Bharatiya Janta Party in power at the Centre. The BJP became a political force to spread its net in the north. It gave a new identity to majority of Hindus. As the fundamentalists often do the Hindutva forces dealt with the past of the country. It took to the Indus Valley Civilization and argued that it was a Hindu culture. The Vedas, the epics, the Bhagwat are all carriers of Hindu culture. On the basis of culture and ancient scriptures, the Hindutva forces planned to bring together the followers of differentiated religious faiths. Religion, that is, Hinduism became a vehicle for cultural unity of the country. Nationalism was defined as cultural nationalism. Vedas are the cultural heritage of the nation.

But, a culture is not the only ingredient of nationalism. There is economy, there is polity, there is language, and there is geography and several other elements, which constitute a nation. If we give prominence to only one element, the holistic character of nationalism gets lost. The comments made in *The Frontline* (Vol. 21, No. 6, 2004) argue:

> The concept of cultural nationalism, conceived and propagated by Hindutva, is based on a misrepresentation of the nature of national identity. Nationalism like democracy is indivisible with its constitutive elements – political, economic and cultural – intermeshed with each other. Privileging any one of these attributes tends to undermine the holistic character of

nationalism. There is no denying the importance of culture in the make up of national identity; yet culture alone does not mould the nationalism of any country.

The Hindutva brand of fundamentalism not only talked about cultural nationalism, it also evolved a strategy to bring heterogeneous Hindu elements together. For instance, it started constructive programmes of education, medicine and public works to draw the tribal groups into the Hindu mainstream. They gave Hindu identity to the tribals. They were labelled as Hindus. Their traditional naming pattern was changed to Hindu naming pattern. The Hindutva forces entered into the arena of politics through culture.

Culture in the contemporary Indian society has lost its meaning and relevance. It is anything which fulfils our interest. Even sociologists show their fondness for the use of culture for anything which they please. We have earlier mentioned that sociologists are propagating 'Hindu sociology' in the name of culture. The concept is very notorious. It must be used with care.

We further elaborate the Hindutva way of working. It has created a large number of organizations which are called cultural organizations. Explicitly, these organizations have no relation with politics or any movement. *Rashtriya Swayam Sevak Sangh* (RSS), *Vishwa Hindu Parishad* (VHP), *Bajrang Dal* and a large number of organizations covering all the sectors of society – youth, women, marginals, tribals, students, trade unions, urban and rural. The Hindutva umbrella is very large – extended and wide. All these are clubbed together and are known *Sangh Parivar*. These satellites of Hindutva are concerned with culture only. Politics is denied to them. It is interesting to know how does culture work. Hindu fundamentalism, therefore, is not religious; it is cultural. And, nobody can object the cultural practices.

### Hindutva Movement in the South

We have said earlier that the variant of Hindutva movement is different in South India. The trend of Hindu fundamentalism has taken to cultural approach. It is similar to the approach taken by Gandhi in our struggle for independence. Gandhi argued that to fight against the colonial rule, it was necessary to mobilize the masses of people right from the grassroots. He, therefore, started creative work, that is, *Rachnatmak Karya* (constructive work). The NGOs were created to establish schools, night schools, hostels, health centres, women development and reform movements. An elaborate scheme was drawn which mainly worked in the villages. Such a constructive work would prepare the ordinary people to work for freedom struggle.

The Hindutva forces in the south are functioning on Gandhian line. In the states of Kerala, Tamil Nadu and Karnataka, schools, hostels and medical centres are either launched by the state or the non-governmental organizations. Hundreds of temples were constructed and many more renovated in these states. The Hindutva strategy has been to arouse religious fundamentalism which in the long run would lead to the attainment of political power. For both the variants of fundamentalism, the ultimate objective is to gain political power.

### *Savarkar and Fundamentalism*

Vinayak Damodar Savarkar was the main progenitor of *Hindutva* ideology. His thesis was simple:

> A Muslim or a Christian, even if born in India, could not claim to possess the qualities of *Hindutva*. The essentials of Hindutva are a common race (*Jati*) and common civilization (*Sanskrati*).

The Hindu fundamentalism is a very wide and precise concept. Only birth in India does not make a person Hindu. He must belong to the same race and share the same culture. Hindu fundamentalism considers both race and culture, that is, religion, as the central theme of its formation. The theory of this fundamentalism also gets support from M.S. Golwalkar:

> Hindutva excludes all non-Hindus from the ambit of the nation. Hindutva, therefore, serves as an ideological justification for the construction of India as a Hindu nation.

The idea of Hindu nationalism was also supported by Atal Behari Vajapaye, a BJP stalwart and the former Prime Minister of India. He made a statement that the demolition of the Babri Masjid is an expression of national sentiments. The Hindutva ideology is considered to be the national ideology. Those who reside in the national territory are all Hindus. The ideological and theoretical framework of Hindutva, thus, totally excludes the Muslims and their existence in India. This makes both the fundamentalisms opposed to one another. The Muslim fundamentalist spares no effort to bring togetherness among the Muslims of the world. It is because of the spirit of communityness-*biradari* – that Muslim fundamentalists draw their strength from world over.

Hindu fundamentalism has to work within the national boundaries. It has also to exclude some Hindu-like castes such as Jains, Sikhs and others. Despite these restrictions, Hindutva forces have adopted an aggressive policy of homogenizing the diverse groups among the Hindus. *The Frontline* (Vol. 21, No. 6, March 13-26, 2004) comments on the Hindutva ideology of homogenization:

> Many were taken by surprise when Dalits participated in the Gujarat pogrom and when adivasis supported the Bharatiya Janta Party in the recently held elections to the State Assemblies. But it is not altogether surprising as the ideology of Hindutva has been at work among these groups for a long time in order to inculcate a Hindu identity in them. An indication of this change is the transformation in their worship pattern. Their traditional places of worship are being refashioned as Hindu temples and their modes of worship are being replaced by those of the Brahmanical order. The Hinduization thus taking place amounts to cultural denial and oppression.

Hindu fundamentalism has created a crisis of identity. The Dalits have no identity. If they call themselves as a scheduled caste, their Dalit identity or their original name is lost. What is worse, they are not given a place in the caste hierarchy. The only identity which the Dalits possess is that of a downtrodden caste. And, if they call themselves a Hindu, they are lost in a vast sea of diversity.

### Origin of Hindu Fundamentalism

During the colonial period, the seeds of fundamentalism were sown. The colonial rulers encouraged it. And, as a consequence, the Muslims became more fanatic and hardened. If we look at the forces of modernization during this period, there were three cultural forces:

(1) Muslim and Hindu are two distinct entities – two civilizational cultures and, therefore, they should develop seperately.
(2) Gandhi as the prime leader of freedom struggle who advocated pluralism, low statelessness, minority rights and advanced participation of civil society. He argued for a localized society. This was a notion of postmodernity.
(3) The third cultural force was that which Jawahar Lal Nehru propounded. He was in favour of secularism, capitalism and parliamentary democracy.

We cannot discard these forces which explain the origin and development of fundamentalism.

Jawahar Lal Nehru was the architect of modernization. He favoured liberalism. The Muslims, on a broader plane, were generally against modernity. They were inspired by religious culture and opted for the creation of Pakistan on cultural grounds. They tried to build Pakistan as a nation on the consideration of religion, language and culture. Creation of Pakistan has been a major force for the growth of fundamentalism and terrorism. Now a nation, Pakistan has entered in the arena of promoting fundamentalism. All these historical factors have mobilized the Hindus to take their historical revenge.

Babri Masjid was demolished in Ayodhya by the *Kar Sewakas* arguing that it was originally the temple of Lord Rama. Hindu fundamentalists have a plan to build a Ram temple at the site of the demolished mosque. The matter is under the consideration of court. The Muslims countered the event of mosque demolition by burning the rail compartment carrying Hindu *Kar Sewakas* at Godhra station. The Hindus did not allow it to go as a ghastly event only. Revenge was taken and in 2002 the Gujarat society became a victim of Hindu-Muslim tension.

### Fundamentalism and the Politics of Yatras

The Hindutva ideology made all efforts to bring diverse groups of the country together as a political power. It used different cultural formations for this purpose. Describing the role of *yatras* in the consolidation of varying Hindu groups in Ahmedabad and other parts of the country, Achyut Yagnik and Suchitra Sheth (*The Shaping of Modern Gujarat: Plurality, Hindutva and Beyond*, 2005) observe:

> Sangh Parivar also tried to consolidate its social base through a series symbolic *yatras*. In 1983, the VHP organized its *Gangajal Yatra* or *Ektamata Yatra* from Haridwar in the foothills of the Himalayas to Rameshwaram in Tamil Nadu and another from Gangasagar in West Bengal to Somnath. Their aim was to rise above caste, sect and denominational differences and invoke the spirit of unity among all Hindus, the RSS, the Arya Samaj, the Rotary Club, the Lions' Club and also more notably Jain Sampradai, Vaishnava Parivar, Sikh Sampradai, Buddha Sampradai, and Bharatiya Dalit Varg and Sangh. The central mobilizing symbol to unite all Hindus was *Gangajal*, water from the Ganga, the holiest of all rivers for Hindus.

The Hindus included Buddhist, Sikh, Jain and the charitable organizations such as Lions' Club and the Rotary Club. The spread of Hindu umbrella has indeed been very wide. The objective of these *yatras* was to mobilize the Hindu masses – hundreds of castes to take a pledge for the construction of Ramjanmabhoomi at Ayodhya. Then, there was *yatra* from Somnath to Ayodhya in 1996. Somnath is a Shiva temple whereas, Ayodhya is the birthplace of Lord Rama. The *yatra* made an effort to establish a linkage between two Hindu traditions – Shaivite and Vaishnavite. Explaining the significance of the *yatras* for the provoking Muslim fundamentalism, Achuyat Yagnik and Suchitra Sheth (2005) write:

> Each yatra mobilization left behind a trail of communal classes. The first in the series, Ram Janki Dharma Yatra, led to violent Hindu-Muslim clashes in a number of towns of Sabarkantha and Kheda districts including Virpur town, located on the borders of these districts, where tribals from surrounding villages attacked Muslims. It was probably for the first time in the recent history of Gujarat that Muslims were attacked by tribals. The second yatra of Ramshila Pujan precipitated Hindu-Muslim riots on a much wider scale and 180 towns and

villages were affected. The last two yatras brought in their wake clashes in the towns of north, central and east Gujarat as well as in thirty-three villages of south Gujarat where tribals attacked isolated Muslim households.

### *New Fronts for Hindu Unification*

The experience of *yatras* gave new wings to the Hindu forces. It was increasingly realized that there were two sectors of Hindu India, which could organize to help Sangh Parivar to attain power. The VHP sponsored Bajrang Dal in 1984. It was its youth wing and provided muscle power to it. Bharatiya Kisan Sabha (BKS) was the creation of RSS. Although, the BKS did not incorporate any Hindu God into its name, it projected as its symbol Balram, the elder brother of Lord Krishna who carried a plough as his weapon. This farmer organization was created mainly to help the RSS.

It must be mentioned that recruitment to Bajrang Dal and BKS was made from amongst the youths belonging to the poor and other backward classes of cities and towns. The *Kar Sewakas*, who actively worked for the demolition of Babri Masjid, belonged to these youth organizations. Whenever there is call for *bandh*, its hundred per cent success is assured because of the strong and heavy muscle power ruthlessly exercised by these youth organizations.

### *The Aftermath of Babri Masjid Demolition and Yatras*

The Hindutva forces had shown their strength by several actions which charged Muslim fundamentalism with eagerness to do something in retaliation. In the riots following the Babri Masjid demolition, Surat, with 190 deaths, accounted for more than half of the total deaths in Gujarat. In many areas, a number of houses belonging to Muslims were burnt and scores of people were roasted alive. Even children were not spared, women were gang raped, many in front of their family members. As many academics have reported, the city witnessed unprecedented brutality in the course of the riots. *India Today* reports:

> In spite of such horrible violence, there is no feeling, shame or sadness in anyone. The communal elements among the Hindus consisting of many traders and professionals believe that this was going to happen. One businessman said: "Muslims will never dare to raise their heads in Surat now. They will have to learn to live in an inferior position as benefits a minority".

### *Carnage of Communal Tension, 2002*

Fundamentalism of Hindus and Muslims has been witnessed by Gujarat, Madhya Pradesh, Uttar Pradesh and Rajasthan several times. The riots which took place in Ahmedabad during February-March 2002 are unhistorical. During earlier riots, the weapons used were petrol and kerosene. A new development in 2002 was the use of cooking gas cylinders as explosives. Cylinders were taken from the victim's house, bundled in cloth which was set on fire and then put back into the house, where it would explode like a bomb, destroying the house and setting everything ablaze.

The rioting mob included larger groups of middle class and upper class men and women who missed no opportunity to loot the Muslims shops and take the goods to their houses. In the 2002 riots the participation of Dalits and tribals was huge. From all accounts, it was an anti-Muslim violence. Yet another dimension of 2002 violence was the participation of business community. The Hindu business community was not coming forward to help the victimized Muslims. There were economic reasons for this withdrawal of the Hindu community. We shall have opportunity to discuss it at a later stage. Suffice it to say here that market fundamentalism played a vital role in the communal disturbances of 2002. The violence of 2002 was against the Muslims who suffered the most. Second, the violence had the state patronage and it helped the fundamentalists to fulfil their targets. Achyut Yagnik and Suchitra Sheth (*The Shaping of Modern Gujarat*, 2005), who are also 'insiders' to Gujarat society, have made a dare-devil statement about the brutalities caused on Muslims by the high and middle class Hindus:

> In 2002 there was not only arson, mass rape and mass burning but eyewitness accounts from the majority community conform

> that young children thrown into the fire and wombs of pregnant women were ripped apart and mother and unborn child were burnt. Instances were also reported where the bodies of burnt women were sexually mutilated with sticks and rods and desecrated by the mob.

The extent of fundamentalism which the Hindu castes showed in Ahmedabad in 2002 is unprecedented. All sorts of slogans were raised conveying the meaning that the Muslims would be wiped out from India. How do we analyze such a situation from the perspective of modernity and postmodernity. Modernity is democratic, it is rational and bureaucratic, and creates strong state surveillance. The high-caste Hindus, dominant castes and the middle class in Gujarat are embedded in these core characteristics of modernity. These groups have heavily benefited from modernity. The Jains, *Baniyas* and Patidars of Gujarat are all economically well placed. Their percentage in the state and central services is also quite high. These groups also constitute the professional and intellectual class of the society. The state is headed by Sangh Parivar.

Considering all these factors of Hindu fundamentalism, it could be safely said that religion, rituals and what is more, the cultural formations of Hindutva elements are responsible for the growth of Hindu authoritarianism. In other words, in India, modernity, that is, bureaucracy, capitalism, democracy and rationality have contributed to the creation of fanaticism. Democracy in the form of majoritization has gone in favour of Hindus. The extended version of Hinduism, which is manifest in several movements engineered by the Sangh Parivar, clearly shows that the consolidation of diverse castes and ethnic groups has strengthened the Hindu identity and feeling of consciousness.

For India, violence seems to be the major outcome of modernity. It is the modernity of majority which is changed by fundamentalism. In Indian context, postmodernity has to fight with the modernity of high-castes.

### *Participation of Tribal and Dalit Groups in the Violence Raised by Hindu Fundamental Fanaticism*

For the violence of 2002 in Gujarat, the Hindutva forces have been claiming that for them Gujarat is a laboratory which is applicable at all-India level. Its findings are substantially useful for the annihilation of Muslims. If constructive work of development is done in the form of educational and medical facilities for the tribals and Dalits, they can be easily motivated to take part in violence engineered by the Sangh Parivar. In the scheduled areas of the country, viz., Bihar, Madhya Pradesh, Maharashtra, Gujarat, Rajasthan and Orissa where educational institutions, such as *Jan Jati Kalyan Parishad* and hostels are created, the tribals and Dalits can easily be motivated to join the fundamental upheaval.

But, there is another aspect of fundamental upheaval. In the scheduled areas, the tribals also reside along with the Muslims. The Muslims normally own larger part of land compared to the tribals. The poor tribals work as farm labourers with the Muslim big landowners. Along with it, the Muslims also advance loans to the poor tribals. The tribals in such a kind of economic relationship have developed antagonistic attitude towards the Muslims. On the other hand, the Jains and the *Baniyas,* who are traditionally associated with loan advancement to the tribals, find Muslims as their staunch competitors. They are always in search of an opportunity to harm the Muslim interests. The involvement of Dalits and tribals in violence created by Hindu high-castes is also because of the mercantile interest of the latter.

Yet another reason for the involvement of tribals and Dalits in the fundamental war is political. The advocates of cultural nationalism believe that the tribals and Dalits constitute a dependable vote bank in elections right from panchayats to the parliament.

Fundamentalism is only an excuse, a potential pretext. It is a mask through which the leaders get political power. When the tribals are drawn in fundamental upheaval, on one hand, they prove to be supporters of high-caste Hindus, and on the other, when they themselves contest elections in a reserved constituency, their victory constitutes a yes-men group in the power structure. It must be observed that in the democratic set-up like the one we have, the tribals and the Dalits are politically not mature enough to actively participate in the decision-making process. They are or they prove to be only supporters of the high-castes. They play the role of 'yes men'.

Hindu and Muslim fundamentalisms have a basic difference. The Muslims, when they become fundamentalists, are charged by the spirit of *Jihad* – the sacrifice for the cause of *Allah*. In *Jihad*, there is no place for skepticism. It is a matter of belief and faith. When Edna Fernandes (*Holy Warriors*, 2006) calls the *Jehadis* as holy warriors, she only wants to convey that fanatic Muslims follow the dictates of Quran quite blindly. Hindu fundamentalism does note have any such concept of *Jihad*. At best it is martyrdom. We have cases of martyrs who died for the cause of nation. It is the presence of *Jihad* that makes a religion strong or weak.

Hindu fanaticism may further be differentiated from that of the Muslim. Quran's legitimate interpretation is only through *Hadith*. Earlier attempts to revise and reinterpret *Hadith* have been foiled by Muslim reformers themselves. In such a situation, Quran's interpretation does not carry several variants. Among Hindus there are several interpretations of the scriptures and, therefore, there are several versions of Hinduism. The limitations of fundamentalism among Hindus are open. The specificity of Muslim fundamentalism has made it rigid, fanatical and conservative. It is because of it that the status of Muslim women has constantly remained low. Hindu fundamentalism is modernity-centric. And, therefore, its appeal to its followers is through culture. And, Hindutva culture is drawn from the Hindu sacred works. Its kit of concepts consists of Sanskrit and Hindi and in some cases local dialectic terms.

Normally, in any discourse on modernity and postmodernity, there is no scope for the inclusion of fundamentalism. But we have taken a stand that modernity and late modernity have aroused a new movement of fundamentalism not only in India but elsewhere in the world. During the last ten years, we have witnessed a variety of fundamentalisms – religious, academic, market, political, and so on. Such fundamentalisms draw their strength from the authority which these institutions possess. With fundamentalism, new identities have emerged. Fundamentalism is normally embedded in tradition. In loose words, one can say that fundamentalism gains much strength from traditionalism.

Hindu fundamentalism draws heavily from traditionalism. Llyod Rudolph and Sussane Hoeber Rudolph, in their earlier work, *The Modernity of Tradition* argued that in India traditions did not change but they were given a modern perspective and hence, the modernity of tradition. Yogendra Singh follows whatever has been concluded by Rudolph and Rudolph. He puts the same findings in his book, *The Modernization of Indian Tradition* (1994). He says that India's traditions have not made any substantial change but they have made certain adaptive changes. Both Rudolphs and Yogendra Singh have been obsessed with functionalism. Functionalists never believe in radical change. However, they sing the song of adaptive changes.

Thus, Rudolph and Rudolph and Yogendra Singh have constructed a grand narrative for making their work a piece of commodity. What Yogendra Singh says is that traditions are at the root of Hindu civilization. And, it is in the transcendence of traditions which keeps the civilization alive. It is nothing short of grand narrative. And, Rudolph and Rudolph have lifted four chapters from their earlier work *Gandhi: The Traditional Roots of Charisma*, and have written fresh four new chapters to be included in the new title, *Postmodern Gandhi (*2006*)*. To be precise, the sub-title of the book is 'and other essays'. These essays are from the earlier work published in 1983. The *Postmodern Gandhi* is an example of market fundamentalism. In the US, Europe and developing countries, postmodernity has a market for sale. And, the authors of the status of Rudolphs have made Gandhi a postmodern – hot saleable commodity. Again, an example of grand narrative which is termed as master narrative by Rudolphs.

In their effort to establish Gandhi as postmodern, the "Rudolphs describe him as an activist, a practitioner and a theorist". They further argue that Gandhi often talked about the importance of civil society quite like Habermas, who used the term 'public sphere' for civil society. What is surprising is that the Rudolphs are not an exception to the general community of sociologists who are fond of using verbose: imparting no meaning –

words without meaning. For instance, for Rudolphs, epistemology is a pet word used indiscriminately. Yogendra Singh is also in the habit of using such verbose.

Habermas used the term 'public sphere' to indicate that in a democratic country the civil society can be an effective weapon to pressurize the government. Gandhi did not use the term in this sense. It was an era of freedom struggle and he always referred to the general masses as the source of strength for him. If one is required to look at Gandhi from the perspective of sociology, he would be more close to Durkheim than Habermas. Durkheim considered society as par excellence – more than a God – *Janta Janardan*, that is, masses are God. But, the Rudolphs looked at Gandhi as a postmodernist; they were obliged to refer to Habermas. And, this is the glory of verbose.

Thus, it could be safely said that fundamentalism has been obsessed by religion. Much of fundamentalism is made by the observation of traditions and their practices. The deep cause behind fundamentalism is modernity. Rationality, bureaucracy and authoritarianism are the prime ingredients of modernity. And, through these elements, Hindus and Muslims are made into fundamentalists. But, such an analysis based on Muslim and Hindu fundamentalisms is a little hasty one. Let us study other fundamentalisms too – of Christianity, Sikhism and tribalism. Following the religious fundamentalism we would also dwell on market and political fundamentalism. And, this will be attempted from the perspective of modernity and postmodernity.

## Christian Fundamentalism

Postmodernity is against any idea of modernity or modernism. It argues that modernity has turned the contemporary society into a 'risk society'. It is a society of holocaust – an overarching danger. The postmodernists, all over the world, claim that they have won their battle against modernity. But it is not like this. There has emerged a new force of fundamentalism which seems to be stronger than modernity. Postmodernity is against the authority of institutions, such as caste, religion and region. The rejection of authority has taken a new avatar in the emergence of fundamentalism. As we have discussed earlier at length, fundamentalism has created an authority through religion, market, academics which cannot be faced single handedly. Stuart Sim in the 'Introduction' to his second edition (*Postmodernism*, 2005) writes:

> Postmodern theorists like to claim that we have crossed a watershed into a new world order where institution's authority no longer commands automatic respect, but it is clear that not just modernity but pre-modernity is fighting back and that grand narratives can still speak meanings, to large sections of the world's population.

Besides Islamic and Hindu fundamentalisms, Christian fundamentalism is no less active. There has been infiltration of the Republican Party in America by the Christian Right. "Activists have led campaigns at local, state and national levels to curb liberalizing legislation in areas such as sexual behaviour and abortion. Any move towards relativism is bitterly opposed; conformity, not difference, is the ideal sought."

In India, the Christian missionaries launched a lot of activities among the tribals and the lower castes. They approached the tribals with the mission of modernity and argued that Hinduism was full of superstitious traditions. These must be rejected. Christian religion, on the other hand, pleaded for modern education, technology and above all medicine. It was more powerful than their village local deities and Gods and Goddesses of Hindus as it belonged to the English people who had their empire spread over to the whole world. Christian God, the tribals were told, was much bigger than any God of the world.

Christianity got encouraged in the India's tribal world through the initiation of colonial and feudal power. As it was a 'foreign' religion and had the legitimacy of power holders, its acceptance was easy for the tribals. During the colonial rule, the tribals styled themselves as a modern people and worked as modern practitioners in the interior parts of the country. Their lifestyle got elevated to the level of high and intermediate castes; they took to cash crops, attained some education and in course of time took to the role of fundamentalists.

Today, there are 24 million Christians in India. They constitute 2.3 per cent of the total population. "The Portuguese are documented as the first to bring Christianity to India. But there is a tradition of belief in South India that the first missionary was St. Thomas, the Apostle who came to India in 52 A.D., landing on the palm-lined Malabar coastline in what is now Kerala." When St. Thomas arrived in Kerala, there were habitations of Brahmins, high priests and fishermen. St. Thomas himself was a fisherman from Galilea. Though, he was no match to the high-castes living in Kerala, he was no less than a miracle in this virgin land. Soon, he came to be known as 'Apostle of the East'.

It was in September 1542 that St. Francis Xavier wrote a report from Goa to Jesuits in Rome describing the response of local people towards Christian missionaries:

> More than four months have passed since we reached Goa here in India, a completely Christian city that is something to behold .... God our Lord must be greatly thanked for the fact that the name of Christ is flourishing in distant lands and among so many infidels.

Goa is the home of Catholic Christians. Francis Xavier has been an icon for India's Catholics. He was a missionary from the priesthood of the Jesuits or Society of Jesus, who was sent to Goa to bring God to the unbelievers. Writing about the first act of fundamentalism that was displayed by Christians for the first time in India, that is, Goa, Edna Fernandes (*Holy Warriors*, 2006) comments:

> Saint Francis Xavier, the ultimate crusader, the man who brought the Inquisition in India. The Inquisition was the blunt instrument of Christian fundamentalism and an institution of terror that left scars, imprinted on Goan society to this day. Its aim was to stop new converts to Christianity from slipping into the ways of this old religion. The converts of Hinduism found it hard to erase tradition, where culture and religion were intertwined. The Inquisition aimed to destroy that part of the Goan society, stripping out the Hindus ways and replacing it with a pure unadulterated Catholicism. It was a brutal process.

Goan society is plural. It has a tradition of religious tolerance. Christians, Hindus and Muslims co-exist despite centuries of religious warfare. But, the Inquisition made by Francis Xavier is even today not forgotten by the Goan converts to Catholicism. The Christians in Goa are faced with the problem of retaining their Goan identity. This has become uncomfortable for all the Hindu groups of the state. The Catholics, it is said, while implementing Inquisition, punished the wicked Portuguese, burnt them. Fernandes quotes the views of a Catholic convert who struggles for the survival of his Goan identity:

> We were Sardesais before we converted to Mirandas. Yet our family still retains parts of the old Hindu culture. We still give donations of rice and coconut to the local temple. This is the Goan identity, a fusion of the Indian Hindu, and the Portuguese Christian.

The situation of fundamentalism in Goa has a historical specificity. When the Christian missionaries entered the land of Goa, it was their dream to make it a place of Indian Christian identity. They succeeded in it. And, now, the people of Goa want it to have a homogenized Hindu identity. In present day Goa, Christian missionaries are against Hindu fundamentalism. They are antagonistic. Both Hindus and Christians are firmly committed to their respective traditions. And strange enough, both accept the normative expectations of modernity. That is, they are democratic, capitalistic and accept the identity of Goa. What distinguishes them is that they very richly follow the diktats of their religion. For them, the ultimate authority lies in their respective faiths. It is only the spirit of tolerance which permits the Goan plurality to survive. The BJP is trying to raise Hindu awareness in Goa. And, the Christians are working hard to give a strong notion to the country that Goa is a Catholic homeland for Christians. It is said that for the Goan people church is not just a religion. It is "a way of life".

### *Christian Fundamentalism in the North-East*

Northeastern states are geographically and politically sensitive states. These are the home of tribals such as Naga, Bodo and a larger number of smaller tribal groups. The whole tribal country is fertile with forests of pine, teak and bamboo. So far as horticulture and agriculture are concerned, 80 per cent of the world's herbal medicines are found here.

Some of the tribes, notably Naga, are described as head-hunters. "It is a legend in the Naga's culture that a warrior is judged by the number of heads he takes. They say, the more heads a man takes, the longer is his life. When women married, they looked not at wealth, but the number of heads in a man's house. This man must be from a tradition of great warrior." The Nagas are also described besides head-hunters, as dog-eaters. It is said that they are not 'like Indian'. The descriptions about Naga and Bodo have some resemblance. They are a different people in more than several ways. Racially, they belong to Mangolia stock, have a coppery red skin, slated eyes, and sculpted features. They are a handsome people, and gentle in nature, despite their fearsome reputation as warriors. Their language is part of the Tibeto-Burman group. Fernandes provides a differentiated portrait of the Naga community:

> Culturally, linguistically, genetically, and in terms of their religion, the Nagas differ from other Indians who, despite their regional differences, share other common characteristics.

The Christian missionaries have made their inroads in the northeastern states. Most of these tribal groups made insurgency against India in 1957. The tribal states were formed in the early 1960s. The Christian missionaries worked hard to bring the tribal 'savagery' to modernity. About 90 per cent of the tribals in this area are Christians. In their lifestyle, they display all the characteristics of an authoritarian society. In this respect, they have the norms of both modernity and postmodernity. Postmodernity has come to them in a restricted way. For instance, each village has its own dialect, its own autonomy. They are modern, for most of them have accepted western gadgets and artifacts. Their geographical isolation, the green cover and unlikely Indian appearance have made them fundamentalists not only in religion but in culture also.

What is particular about the fundamentalism found in the north-eastern states is that the tribals living in this part of country consider their religion as their prime identity. They say, they are westernized, belong to western religion (Christianity), have a language which is not Indo-Aryan or Dravidian, and above all their traditions do not match with the Hindu castes or Muslims. Racially, they belong to Mongolian stock and have no affiliations with the rest of tribes of the country. They are fundamentalists of the first rate whose identity is with their religion, church and tribal traditions.

The fundamentalism found among the tribals of the north-eastern states of the country is antagonistic to Hindus, Jains, Sikh and Muslims. There are some traders doing petty trading in these states. But they are identified as 'Indians' only. Such a situation makes these states semi-autonomous within the Indian Union. Nagaland is a good example. "In a bid to appease the desire for self-determination among the Naga people and end the insurgency which afflicted the state, the Indian government in December 1963 inaugurated the State of Nagaland. Under the Constitution (Thirteenth Amendment) Act, 1962 it is specified that Acts of Parliament in respect of Naga religion, customs, laws and procedures, ownership and transfer of land should not apply to the state unless the Legislative Assembly of Nagaland passes a resolution on it. By this, the Indian government hoped to protect the Naga identity within India, safeguard its resources and put a stop to secessionist sentiment."

The secessionist or fundamental attitude adopted by the Nagas is observable when the British left India in 1947. "Despite having some Naga territories under British control, the Nagas had hoped that when the British departed they would allow Nagaland to become a sovereign state. The Nagas argued that their's had always been a separate nation for thousands of years, with no connection to India. India was Hindu-dominated, Nagaland was a Christian state and did not wish to have its identity submerged within the Indian Union."

Nagas' argument is clear: They lived as Christians and would like to identify themselves as a Christian people. Christianity has always been their way of life. The Jesus seemed to have been on their side. And, even today, they maintain their religious fundamentalism and regional identity within the framework of India's Constitution.

The tribals in most of the parts of India have accepted Christianity. And, the acceptance of Christianity goes to the constructive work done by the missionaries. Besides Goa, Kerala, and the north-eastern states, the missionaries have also worked in the heartland of the country. Bihar, Orissa, Madhya Pradesh, Gujarat, Maharashtra and Rajasthan are other pockets where the Christian missionaries have some substantial work to their credit. The Christians in these points have demonstrated their fundamentalism and the problem of identity to the Union/state. It was the strength of their fundamentalism that gave them Chhattisgarh and Jharkhand. Though the Christian tribals in these states were not much vocal, they used political force with the non-Christian tribals to put their demand for a separate state.

### *Insurgency-centric Fundamentalism*

The fundamentalism of Hindus and Muslims was agitational and sometimes terrorist. But, the Christian tribals, mostly in the north-eastern states have taken to insurgency as a weapon for the attainment of their identity. It appears that for any reason, the fundamentalism inspired by it is a potential force. Hindus have sometimes taken to violent fundamentalism, as for instance, the demolition of Babri Masjid and the Ahmedabad genocide of 2002. The Bombay blasts of 1993 is also an example of violent fundamentalism. It could be further said that religious fundamentalism is an excuse, the overarching objective being the fulfilment of political power. Sometimes, the political parties also use it for their benefit. Insurgency is a big word, but it also includes violence for an antagonist group.

It would be misleading to think that modernity has washed away the authority of the traditions. A new authority has emerged in the present era. In India, for instance, the state does not discriminate among individuals on the basis of caste, creed and sex. The reality is that caste, religion and reason have flourished at the instance of state discrimination. The secular leaders miss no opportunity to fulfil the demands of religious and caste leaders. Political interests have promoted religious and caste fundamentalism. These are some of the new appearances of modernity which have to be combated. The battle between modernity and insurgency is a new phenomenon. There is terrorism and Nazism. These have also to be fought out.

Postmodernity in India has several challenges. Most of the religious traditions belonging to several castes and ethnic groups are found prevalent in villages and have to be removed. What is urgently required in India is to annihilate the grand narratives. Some of the grand narratives have appeared as a result of the processes of modernization. These have to be identified and combated.

## Sikh Fundamentalism

The Sikh community is found all over the world. The community is famous for its enterprise and creativity. It turns everything to profit. Ludhiana in Punjab is known for garment manufacturing. It makes woollens, shirts and fabrics for export. Leather and sports goods are also made in Punjab. Besides the industrial entrepreneurs, Sikhs are also skilled agriculturists. The credit of the success of Green Revolution in the late sixties and seventies goes to Punjab. The state still remains the bread-basket of India. Wheat, rice, pulses, sugarcane are just some of the crops grown here. In many ways, Punjab is known all over India as a potential economic superpower.

Sikhism was founded by Guru Nanak. Guru Granth Sahib is the sacred work, a holy book like Bible for Christians and Quran for Muslims. Historically, Sikhism emerged out of the injustices done to them by the Mughal emperor, Aurangzeb. Anandpur Sahib is the pilgrim centre of Sikhs which took its present form in 1699. It is here that the tenth Guru, Govind Singh urged Sikhs to become warrior-saints against their Muslim conquerors. He said that the Sikhs are Khalsa – the pure ones. Describing the incident of Khalsa faith at Anandpur Sahib, Fernandes observes:

> Guru Govind Singh's view of the religion had been irrevocably shaped at the age of nine, when his father, the ninth Guru Tej Bahadur, was executed in Delhi by the Mughal Emperor,

Aurangzeb. Tej Bahadur had gone to plead the case of the Kashmiri Pandits who had asked for his intervention after facing threats to convert from Hinduism to Islam. In the Emperor's court, Tej Bahadur was also advised to renounce his faith or face death. He chose death. He was beheaded on November 11, 1675. The site of his death is marked by a Gurudwara on Old Delhi's Chandni Chowk. Before his body could be quartered, a devotee stole away the Guru's head and bore it on horseback to the Punjab where it was cremated at Anandpur Sahib.

The death of Tej Bahadur Singh inspired Guru Govind Singh to pledge the Sikhs to prepare themselves to defend their faith unto death if necessary. The Khalsa faith thus is born of the desire for a distinct Sikh identity.

The Sikh identity or the identity of Khalsa consists of five 'k's': *kes*: they would keep their hair and beard uncut; *kangha:* they would wear a comb in their hair; *kachha*: they would wear an undergarment shorts; *kara:* they would wear a steel bracelet on their right wrist; and *kirpan*: they would be armed all times with a small sword. Alcohol, tobacco and meat from animals who bled on death were prohibited. The molestation of Muslim women was prohibited.

Guru Govind Singh's formation of Khalsa panth was not merely symbolic. He waged battles, built fortifications to protect his domain, developed arsenals of weapons for the holy cause and made clear in writings that he meant to defend the faith of Sikhism with deed as well as word.

### The Decade of Sikh Fundamentalism

Since the fall of Mughal empire, the Sikhs had become antagonistic to Muslims. Their *dharam yudh* or the battle of faith had historically made them fundamentalists. First, there was the Bhindranwale's mission who reasserted the traditional Sikh identity through the five 'k's' set out by the Tenth Guru at Anandpur Sahib. Bhindranwale, during his travels to Punjab's villages, baptized hundreds of people and urged all Sikhs to bear weapons and shun alcohol and tobacco. He stressed that the ways of Khalsa should not be forgotten. The second event which exhibited Sikh fundamentalism was the assassination of Indira Gandhi, followed by anti-Sikh riots. Third, the demand for Khalistan was also an event which showed that fundamentalism could help the people to have their own holy states.

In the case of Sikhism, it could be said that political ends could be attained by the practice of fundamentalism. Admittedly, Sikhs had become fundamentalists during the time of the fall of Mughal empire but this fundamentalism has continued till the present day. They seem to have a soft attitude towards Muslims but at present, particularly after the anti-Sikh riots that followed the assassination of Indira Gandhi, they seem to show some kind of malice towards Hindus.

### Bhindranwale's Mission

Bhindranwale was born in 1947 in the village of Rode, near Moga in Punjab. He asserted the Sikh identity and argued that they should never forget the ways of the Khalsa. He was against Hindu domination and advised that the Sikhs should be up in arms against Hinduism. In 1982, the Akalis launched a *dharm yudh* and its main objective was to drive out the Hindu community from Punjab. Bhindranwale was an icon of orthodox Sikhism. He moved to one of the guest houses of the Golden Temple with his band of men. It is here that he planned for Sikh separatism.

The state could not tolerate the provocations that Bhindranwale and his fundamentalist band of men showed. And, as a result, in June 1984, the first phase of Operation Blue Star took place. Commandos stormed in the main entrance of the temple, coming under fire from all sides. The causalities were heavy. The Akal Takht was heavily fortified, protected by high machine guns that were deployed at regular intervals. Brar described it as a bastion of automatic weapons. After two days of combat, the Akal Takht was reduced to rubble. Bhindranwale was killed, together with his lieutenants. Many pilgrims died in the firefight, unable to escape. The news swept across the world, inflaming Sikh sentiments in India and abroad. In London, one Khalistan hardliner appeared on BBC news and called for the assassination of Mrs. Gandhi. For the Sikhs, the storming of the Golden Temple was no less than a sacrilege.

The Sikh religious identity today is in danger. The younger generation is under the influence of modernity. The traditional Sikh identity is giving way to western education and lifestyle. One very serious loss to this generation is the loss of Punjabi language. Those residing overseas or other states of India, do not have Punjabi as a medium of instruction. They have increasingly taken to the regional language of the state where they reside. In the field of non-religious identity, postmodernity has made its way out. Gurudwara does not exercise that much authority as is required by Sikhism. The ordinary Sikh has cordial relations with both Muslims and Hindus. Sikh fundamentalism in the context of postmodernity has been weakened.

### Caste Fundamentalism

Caste fundamentalism has increased because of the influence of modernity. The dominant and influential castes in different culture regions have raised their competing demands. For instance, the Yadava caste has its strong power bloc. It has its domination in state power structure. In the state of Rajasthan, the Jats and the Rajputs have a considerable influence in making political decisions. In Gujarat, castes of Vaishnav, Baniya, Patidar and Jain exercise their fundamentalism not only in politics but also in business. In the state of Maharashtra, the Marathas are a dominant caste in matters of political decisions. So have the Reddys in Andhra Pradesh.

Before the spread of modernity in these states, the dominant castes had only cultural or power influence. Rajasthan and Madhya Pradesh had the feudal rule. The feudal mindset is enriched today due to education, and capitalism and power acquisition. Some of the 'modern' castes today in their respective areas have become powerful and exercise considerable influence. There are also fundamentalists who have a determining role in the rural areas where people still have respect for the feudal system.

### Mercantile Fundamentalism

Both the Muslim and Hindu fundamentalisms can be seen in the carnage of 2002. Many explanations are given to account for the Hindu-Muslim tension. One very strong reason for this conflict is forwarded on the basis of the mercantile nature or ethos of the Gujarat society. Admittedly, the Godhra rail incident is said to be the immediate cause of 2002 Ahmedabad riots. But, the mercantile ethos of Gujarat is equally responsible for communal tension. Gujarat is basically a trading community. There is cut-throat competition between the Hindu-Muslim communities in the market. Though these communities are based in urban centres, the spread of communalism is also found in rural areas. Achyut Yagnik and Suchitra Sheth call Gujarat a mercantile society. They have traced mercantilism from the earliest times. They explain the mercantile ethos of Gujarat as below:

> For almost a thousand years merchant communities – Hindus, Jains, Muslims and, later Parsis – not only dominated the economic sphere but also wielded influence in Gujarat society and power in political affairs. They set the norms for 'higher culture' and became representatives of Gujarat for the outside world.

Gujarat's ethos of mercantilism is largely due to its strategic location within Asia and its parts along the northern centre of the Indian Ocean. The Muslim communities which are involved in trading include Bohras, Khogas and Memons. Among Hindus are found Baniya, Jain and Patidars. These communities dominate the business and trade. The Hindus found Muslims as their major rivals in the market. After the Godhra incident, the Hindu traders made a plan to annihilate the Muslim trading communities. It is reported that they identified the leading Muslim traders of not only Ahmedabad, but Surat and Vadodara also. It was believed that the communal tension would wipe out the Muslims from the market. The government also had its latent approval to such a kind of mercantile fundamentalism. Thus, the perspective of economic fundamentalism is said to be the major cause of Hindu-Muslim tension of 2002 in Gujarat.

## Concluding Observations

Indian society is traditional. It traces its civilization from the Vedas. It is a diverse society. Its geography is also diverse. What holds such a plural society together? There are several explanations, one of the powerful explanations is that its varied ethnicities establish linkages with the ethnicities of what is called country or nation. Before independence, the various princely states and the presidencies of the British empire were divided into political units. Each feudal state was a separate unit. These units in some cases had friendly alliances and in some were rivals and antagonistic. Despite such diversity, the unifying linkages of ethnicities maintained some cultural unity in the country. Such a unity was possible because a large number of ethnicities were, in fact, caste and religious ethnicities. The lower castes and their ethnicities always remained at the bottom.

When there was emergence of modernity, it worked as a band for integrating the country. Modernity has always been a high-caste or dominated caste modernity. The lower groups had no substantial contribution to such a kind of integration. Modernity in its wake brought democracy, secularism industrial capitalism and plurality. These factors in turn contributed to the unity of the nation. As the things stand today, ethnicities divide the countries, so do the caste and religious traditions. The coalition governments that we find at the Centre and in states are nothing but a coalition of the political interests of varying ethnicities. Ethnicities and traditions in India are political phenomena.

Modernity is not without its failures. In the western society, modernity has created such risks and dangers that postmodernity has waged a war against it. In India, modernity has taken a different turn. It has created fundamentalism among religious groups, regional ethnicity, caste rivalries and linguistic factions. India's market in the field of economy has given rise to unregulated laissez-faire capitalism. This kind of market capitalism is supported by International Monetary Fund (IMF) and the World Bank. The control of market is increasingly going out of the hands of states. There is disinvestment in private sector. Economic growth has gone in the hands of capitalists and the marginals have become downtrodden.

Postmodernity in India is recent. It has a commitment to dissent, pluralism, culture difference, and scepticism towards authority. This scepticism has also given rise to political fundamentalism and the new life, which is fused by modernity, tradition and ethnicities, has posed fierce challenges to postmodernity. Before we strike a concluding remark on postmodernity, we would say that it would not solve many of our problems. But let postmodernism be a tryst phase of our national development.

# VI

# India's Grand Narratives and Emerging Little Traditions

Indian society has evolved through a long process of social changes. Since the attainment of independence, it has witnessed massive changes. Earlier, there were changes also in colonial rule. All these changes have been analyzed and diagnosed by social scientists. By the beginning of 1950s, systemic and planned development programmes were launched and implemented by the government and non-governmental organizations. The main objective of these development programmes was not only economic growth but also social and cultural development.

We, in this country, have witnessed colonialism, feudalism and modernism. Our Constitution is the valid document for its present and future development. The policies adopted by various governments from time to time are within the broader framework of the constitution. Besides variation in the acceptance of policies, there has been consensus to attain modernity as our national goal. India, in this broader context, is democratic, plural, secular, capitalist, and has strong belief in scientific and rational ethos.

There have been efforts towards building India as a nation. Such efforts are made according to the provisions of the constitution. Thus, the democratic-secular-capitalist-rational model is constitutional and valid. But, there are other models also left to the choice or option of the general masses. If there is a larger consensus on any of the alternatives of the form of nation, the votaries can transform the direction of change and by majority even replace the constitution. It is all a democratic process.

**Functional Ethos**

Indian society has been studied thoroughly by sociologists. Some of the aspects of society have received an exaggerated attention. For instance, we have enough studies on ethnicities. There has been a spate of village studies. During the early period of sixties, a larger number of village studies came out for publication. Some of these are designated as classical. It followed the period of the studies on family. There has been much debate on the definition of family and its jointness. Studies on caste have never been lesser. These studies are exhausting. The foreign sociologists also joined their Indian counterparts in the study of caste. The focus of this enquiry was to construct theories on the origin, functioning and change of caste system. The changing aspects of caste in villages also became a hot topic of analysis.

In all these themes studied by sociologists, the perspective has always been social and cultural change. A detailed study of the syllabus of any university or all the universities of India will immediately show that caste, family and village have been the consistent themes of study for the students. Nothing belonging to Indian society or everything constituting Indian society has been studied by sociologists. Along with social change, social stratification has also been an inevitable part of these studies.

Recently, social change is studied with the perspective of modernization. It has been argued that modernization in India is responsible for effecting massive change both in the rural and urban centres. It has also been analyzed that social change is observable in most of the communities of Indian society, viz., Hindus, Muslims, Jains, tribals and minor groups.

It is the perspective which gives new meaning and interpretation to the text. What postmodernists call 'deconstruction' (Derrida) is nothing but a mode of reading "which exposes a text's internal differences and attends to its repressed contradictions or inherent vulnerabilities, its strategy is also interventionist, and it is political also". Our objective in the present study is to analyze the

Indian society from a different perspective – the perspective of postmodernity. The change in perspective could present a new reality of Indian society. Admittedly, Indian society as mentioned above, has been elaborately studied by sociologists. But it has been studied, and we emphasize it with all our power, with the perspective and ideology of functionalism. Those whom we consider to be icons or great 'priests' of sociology, have all employed functionalism to be their prime methodology, theory and ideology. They all belong to the consensus theory.

There are, however, some sociologists who have studied Indian society from the perspective of conflict theory. But their conflict ideology is only doctrinaire. They do not look into the trends of neo-functionalism and the historical forces which have disintegrated Soviet Russia. The reality of Indian society which we find today is much oriented to the Hindu ideology – Hindu traditions caste hierarchy, holism, continuity and transcendence. Indian functionalism is strengthened and enriched by the inputs made or borrowings from A.R. Radcliffe-Brown and Louis Dumont.

Functionalism is a theory or a methodology based on the notion that "social events can best be explained in terms of the functions they perform, that is, contributions they make to the continuity of a society – and on a view of society as a complex system whose various parts work in a relationship to each other in a way that needs to be understood". Functionalism assumes that the parts of society are integrated in such a way that they provide stability and order to the society. Talcott Parsons calls the integrated society a system, which sociologists in India have studied (most of the parts of society) from the perspective of functionalism. Such an approach is exemplified by the statement of Yogendra Singh, who is the doyen of sociology. He writes at the beginning of his most influential book, *Modernization of Indian Tradition* (1973):

> These essays are an attempt to analyse the processes of modernization in India from a *systemic* (emphasis mine) sociological perspective. From two concepts which have been used here to analyse the forces of modernization are 'social structure' and 'tradition' .... Modernization in these *systems* begins either from

the emergent and endogenous sources, or through contact with forces – outside the systems.

Systems of Indian society – family, caste, and their politics – are studied as functional units. Social structure of the system is held together by the functioning of party. Our understanding of Indian society is thus characterized by capitalism, conservatism and status quoism. We argue that the Indian institutions should be studied with the perspective of postmodernism. It will provide new insights into the whole of our analysis. Our comprehension of society would change radically and we would have a fresh vision for changing it.

In the west, functionalism has faced sustained attacks since late 1960s. On the other hand, it was a period when it saw its beginning in India. Our village studies, studies on family and caste are all embedded in functionalism. Postmodern perspective to understand Gandhi is perhaps the first one made by Rudolph and Rudolph (2006). What we want to stress here is the point that in any deconstructive analysis of a discourse the perspectives accepted give refreshingly new ideas. Such an attempt to analyze Indian social structure is novel.

## How Does Postmodernism Look at Society?

Earlier, we have critically examined the major attributes of postmodernity. We only reiterate here some of its specificities which are helpful to apply to India's structural formations. Basically, postmodernity is a cultural movement. Its concern in India is to demolish the cultural edifice created by modernity and traditions. Postmodernity, by its nature and temperament is skiptical towards traditions constructed through Vedic times to different phases of India's history. It is negative. It is built on two pillars: grand or mega narratives and little narratives.

Mega or grand narratives are also termed as master narratives. In India's sociology we have grand traditions and little traditions which help us to analyze and interpret social and cultural change. Grand narratives are universalizing explanations of culture change. They are immemorial and go beyond time and space. The best example of grand narrative is that of Marxism which looks at all human history and social behaviour through its theory of dialectical materialism. The core content of a grand narrative is the authoritarianism which holds good for its believers. And, postmodernity is the deadliest enemy of any kind of authoritarianism whether it flows from caste, ethnicity or religion.

Little narratives are creations of individuals or groups of individuals who resist the authoritarianism of grand narratives. Grand narratives oppress the creativeness of the individuals. Marxism cannot be denied. In India, likewise, Ghurye or Srinivas can never be rejected. They constitute the structure of India's sociological grand narratives.

Grand narratives and for that matter, the grand traditions in India, have discouraged individual creativity.

Yet another specificity of postmodernity is fragmentation. It is said that "in postmodernization a thousand flowers bloom". There is a fantastic variety of cultural forms in a region or state. And, in this variety, no culture form is dominant. For example, popular music has fragmented into a wide variety of styles, each with its own audiences, choosing with its own preferred style to go with its chosen lifestyle. As variety becomes the order of the day, it becomes difficult for any particular style to claim to be superior to all others. Fragmentation relieves the people from the authority of classical culture.

Let us take the example of fragmented popular culture. In the state of Gujarat there is a popular form of culture known as *Kathiawadi* culture. The people of this region have Gujarati as their language of communication but their accent differentiates them from the Gujarati-people of central or south Gujarat. Similarly, the popular forms of dance also vary from one culture region to another. Likewise, there is differentiation or fragmentation in western Uttar Pradesh and eastern Uttar Pradesh in the practice of popular culture.

When modernity was dominant among the high-castes and affluent classes, their culture forms and types were considered superior in the society. With the declining influence of modernism among the high-castes and elites, there has been identification of their culture with the popular culture of masses. One more specificity of postmodernity is that it is pragmatic in its approach and does not isolate itself from the people who are at the grassroots level in the society. It must be stressed here that postmodernity takes a departure from the privileged classes.

## Social Change in India

As stated at the outset, India has witnessed massive social change. The change is visible in all the institutions such as family, caste, kinship, village, polity and economy. All these social institutions constitute Indian society. There are sociologists who have with great labour and intelligence studied these institutions. They have identified the processes which bring change. Modernization seems to be a huge force affecting social change. Yogendra Singh (*Modernization of Indian Tradition*, 1973) has identified the changes brought about in some of our social institutions. There are forces outside the society and forces from within the society. Explaining the functions of these forces on the social structure, Singh observes:

> Modernization in these systems begins either from the emergent and endogenous sources, or through contact with forces outside. These two bases of the initiation of social change should be analysed both at the levels of social structures and traditions.

D.N. Majumdar, S.C. Dube, G.S. Ghurye, Andre Beteille, M.N. Srinivas, Yogendra Singh and a few others have studied social change in Indian society. As a result of these studies, some theoretical constructs have come up. These concepts can hardly be labelled as theories. They are a little less than a theory and a little more than a concept. However, these concepts help us to analyze social and cultural change. The concepts have emerged out of the ideology of functionalism. They relate to caste, village, region, local and great tradition.

Modernization has influenced the content and direction of social change. Much analysis of the process of modernization has not been done by sociologists. All of them have identified modernity with social and cultural change. But what does modernity mean has hardly been made manifest. Our strategy here is to look into the changes brought about with the perspective of modernity and postmodernity.

A strong tendency of functionalism is that it believes in progress. It looks at history in an evolutionary way and says that it leads invariably to progress. Future is bright, it is shining. This is not shared by postmodernity. For postmodernity, the future is skeptic. It looks at our present traditions and processes of modernization with great suspicion. It argues that the present civilization is no better than the preceding ones. Modernization brought in its wake democracy, capitalism, technology and economic growth. But this has not given any relief to the marginal people. They continue to suffer from the institutional authoritarianism. State, caste, education and development continue to exercise their authority over the individual. And in such a struggle, the autonomy of the individual is shackled.

The central notion of postmodernity is the little narrative. Jean-Francois Lyotard, in his *Characterization of Postmodernity*, gave the idea of grand narratives, that is, all-embracing explanatory theories. These grand narratives suffer from authoritarianism and therefore Lyotard suggested the construct of little tradition. It is a form of ethnicity which gives expression to the feelings of local people. An individual could be called the ultimate little narrative seeking to resist the power of authoritarian grand narratives. What we feel in India, the little tradition is a specialized type of the process of cultural change. As a matter of fact, little tradition is a movement which keeps the masses integrated at the lowest level.

We have discussed above some of the particularities of postmodernity, which have close relevance to the analysis of some of the major aspects of Indian society. Our approach takes a departure from the earlier and some of the contemporary approaches such as ethnographic, historical and functional. Hopefully, such an exercise would help us to do better.

## Change in Caste

In functional methodology, caste is a system which works by integrating several castes. Each caste is also an ethnic group. These groups have witnessed social and cultural change owing to the functioning of inside and outside processes. Whether inside or outside of the structure of caste, these forces are characterized by modernity. Modernity itself is a grand narrative, which creates a large number of myths and falsehoods. The term 'modernity' is comprehensive and includes several variables such as democracy, state power, industrial capitalism, economic growth and progress. Some very important attributes of modernity are education, technology and village development.

Sociologists have created voluminous literature in India about caste, village and family. This has given us certain concepts, which help us to analyze social change in India. Here in this chapter, we discuss the change with the help of a few concepts. First, we provide the functional approach, which analyzes the societal aspects of India. After having done it, we shall interpret the social change with the perspective of postmodernity. This enables us to put forward the alternative analysis of the institution. Our objective is to understand the reality of India's social structure.

## Functional Analysis of Sanskritization

In his study of the Coorgs in Mysore (*Religion and Society among the Coorgs of South India*), M.N. Srinivas coined the concept of 'sanskritization' to analyze social change in Indian society. He found that the lower castes, in order to raise their position in the caste hierarchy, adopted some customs of the Brahmins and gave up some of their own, considered to be impure by the higher castes. For instance, they gave up meat-eating, consumption of liquor and animal sacrifice to their deities; they imitated Brahmins in matters of dress, food and rituals. By doing this within a generation or so, they could claim higher positions in the hierarchy of castes. To denote this process of mobility, Srinivas first used the term 'Brahminization'. Later on he replaced it by 'sanskritization'.

Srinivas explains caste mobility through the process of sanskritization. Sanskritization, according to him, means the culture of higher castes such as Brahmins, Rajputs, Jats and Baniyas. And, the term 'culture' in this respect consists of beliefs, values, customs, manners, food habits, dress patterns and the broader way of life. Srinivas saw the possibility of lower castes making position higher in the traditional caste hierarchy. He ("A Note on Sanskritization and Westernization" in *Caste in Modern India and Other Essays*, 1962) writes:

> A low caste was able in a generation or two to rise to a higher position in the hierarchy by adopting vegetarianism, teetotalism, by sanskritizing its ritual and pantheon. In short, it took over as far as possible, the customs, rites and beliefs of the Brahmins, and the adoption of the Brahminic way of life by a low caste seems to have been called 'sanskritization' ... in preference to Brahminization, as certain Vedic rites are confined to the Brahmins and the two other 'twice born' castes.

In his later modification of the concept, Srinivas includes castes other than Brahmins also. The imitating castes also include tribals and other groups. Srinivas has made a cultural model for the analysis of caste system. He argues that (1) there is a change among the lower castes; (2) the change is of culture, particularly beliefs, rituals, customs and ideology; and (3) the culture is obviously of Brahmins and twice-born castes. The lower castes marched towards this kind of change with the belief that their move towards higher caste purity would give them some higher status in the caste hierarchy.

What is the central message of culture and social mobility advocated by Srinivas? The sociologists, who claim to have made elaborate studies on sanskritization, give following findings:

(1) Sanskritization emerged out of the study of the Coorgs. It related to the locality of Mysore state.
(2) The sociologists gave it the status of a universalistic concept, which could be applied to the caste mobility all over the country. And, tons of ink has been consumed for such an analysis.
(3) The imitation was based on the make-belief that ritual or cultural superiority would in course of time make the lower castes as powerful as the higher castes. They worked on the thesis that Sanskrit scriptures bestowed a group or a caste with the political domination in a region.
(4) The sociologists analyzed sanskritization as a process of change in social structure. Yogendra Singh labels it as a

"general process of acculturation of vertical mobility of groups".

(5) Sanskritization has been presented as a theory of social change. It, however, did not bring any substantial change in the status of lower castes and untouchables. It was because of the refusal expressed by the higher castes. Yogendra Singh observes: "Not only some form of deviance by the lower untouchable castes from the sacred Hindu norms was tolerated but at one level their effort to follow the norms monopolized by the upper castes was stubbornly resisted. Status in caste being ascribed by faith, the changes of smooth mobility to high-caste positions were more or less closed".

Sanskritization has been assigned a status of prestige in any theoretical writing having a bearing on sociology. It appears that there is political footage to sociological concepts. When Srinivas was localized to M.S. University, Baroda, the concept did not get any air of popularity. His shift to Delhi made the concept a hot topic of discussion not only in India but elsewhere in the world too, and Delhi University became a common and popular place of visit for American and European scholars.

## Westernization: The Processes of Social and Cultural Changes Brought from Outside

Though Srinivas defines westernization as a process of change applicable to the whole Indian society, he in reality talks about cultural change in the caste system. Defining westernization, he writes:

> Westernization includes changes brought about in Indian society and culture as a result of over 150 years of British rule, the term subsuming changes occurring at different levels... technology, institutions, ideology and values.

The concept is very comprehensive and includes humanitarianism and rationalism. It is because of the wider scope of westernization, all efforts of reform, education, democracy, capitalism and modernization are parts of it. In his later modification of the concept of westernization, Srinivas uses the term 'modernization'. When, in the beginning, he explained culture change, he only meant changes brought about by the western countries, particularly England. And, hence, westernization. The term 'modernization', which he has preferred to use later on, has had wider scope. It included all the processes which were borrowed from outside – US and Europe.

As far as the fondness of Indian sociologists goes, they have an obsession for the study of culture and tradition. Sanskritization is the study of caste and culture; in the similar way, westernization is the study of caste and culture. In all their efforts to study, for sociologists, culture is central. Srinivas writes:

> To describe the social changes occurring in India in terms of sanskritization and westernization is to describe it primarily in culture and not in structural terms.

Westernization or modernization includes scientific attainments, technological development, educational development, and rise of nationalism, new political culture and leadership. Modernization has its impact on caste and the higher castes grab all opportunities to take to its benefits. Both sanskritization and westernization work simultaneously to influence the caste/culture. Srinivas explains culture change through these concepts.

Postmodernity, however, has another explanation. It does not accept the authoritarianism of any institution, including caste. Though Srinivas explains culture change on the basis of empirical data collected from South India, his approach to the problem is functional. He assumes that the higher castes have political power and because of it the lowest castes imitate them. In the long run, they will also be able to attain the status of power group. They will get their due place in the larger caste hierarchy.

According to postmodern perspective, Srinivas' whole analysis of sanskritization and westernization suffers from functional conservatism. Basically, all over India, the lower castes have been imitating the culture of the higher castes. The period of freedom struggle, led by Tilak and Gandhi and other leaders, is characterized by reform movement. Gandhi spoke against untouchability, Ambedkar stood for the eradication of castes. In such a situation, it was probable for the lower castes and tribal groups to abstain from bad and impure practices. Eating the flesh of dead animals and drinking excessively brought disrespect and condemnation to the lower castes. The imitation of higher castes, as Srinivas says, by the lower castes is never for power or higher status in caste hierarchy. Postmodern perspective looks at the imitation quite differently. The lower castes were conscious of the fact that the higher castes oppressed them all through the colonial and feudal periods. They were degraded because of their unrespectful practices. The freedom struggle initiated the reform movement among the lower castes not only with the objective of raising their status in caste hierarchy, but imitating the culture and customs of higher castes also to give up backwardness and illiteracy. The lower castes were broken down by the atrocities committed by higher castes. The best way to compete with the higher castes was to follow clean habits of teetotalism, daily bath and observance of *vratas*. Thus, the notion of sanskritization, as propounded by Srinivas from the postmodern perspective, is quite untrue. To put the concept in a universalistic mode of explanation is in no way valid. At best, the explanation seems to be tenable for the region of Mysore only.

There is yet another assumption taken by Srinivas. He says that sanskritization in the long run takes the lower castes to a higher caste in the caste hierarchy. It might take two or three generations. But this did not happen. Such an optimistic view is characterized by functionalism. Functionalism, as an evolutionary process, looks at history as progressive. Postmodernity does not believe in the theory that social change invariably leads to progress. And, in the case of sanskritization, it has been proved that the contention of postmodernity is right.

The functional perspective has put the concepts of sanskritization and westernization to the highest level. There are, it is believed, no parallels to these twin concepts to explain culture change among the lower castes. The postmodern perspective rejects the two concepts merely as grand narratives. They have no universalistic application; they only apply to the castes; they enhance the caste authoritarianism and never lead to progress.

What is worse is that sanskritization and westernization are reduced to the status of Hindutva ideology. The religious scriptures such as the Vedas, the Geeta and the epics constitute the sanskritic-cultural values of the higher castes and the lower castes are explained as the receivers of this culture. Sociology, as an objective and scientific social science, has thus been lowered to a sectarian level.

Yet another perspective of modernization is the standard of living. Those willing to imitate the higher castes, Srinivas says, have taken to modern dress pattern, lifestyle and consumerism. But imitation of these material artifacts does not show any sanskritization. Wherever technological, market and economic growth go, there is marked change in the customs, rituals and beliefs of the people. It is no borrowing of or imitation of sanskritic values. It is natural for modernization to create such an impact on caste.

Sanskritization is now gaining a new travel. What Srinivas calls the imitation of the values, beliefs and customs of higher castes, is nothing but acceptance of the modernized way of life. If the higher castes began availing themselves of the benefits of modernization such as democracy, capitalism, progress and technology, the lower castes are doing the same. It is erroneous to interpret that they are imitating the higher castes for status elevation; the fact is that the lower castes are coming closer to postmodernism.

Postmodernity is pragmatic. It is negative in its approach. What lower castes have been doing is to outrun the status of higher castes. What is important in this respect is that the lower castes have now got certain privileges granted by the constitutional provisions of protective and developmental safeguards. Development and economic growth are the assured sources of livelihood for these people. And, the higher castes feel their traditional status terribly threatened. So far as the findings of Srinivas are concerned, he also says:

> The Brahmans who constitute the top of the varna hierarchy have since time immemorial enjoyed the most respectable position in the caste system. They form the priestly class, have the monopoly over the study and interpretation of the Hindu

> scriptures and sacred texts through institutionalized means. As custodians of the Hindu tradition, a stricter conformity with the ideal norms of Hinduism was expected from them; this expectation progressively became less and less strict for the castes lower down in the hierarchy until for the lower and untouchable caste the widest deviation from the ideal norms was tolerated.

When Srinivas reports that the higher castes, particularly the Brahmins, have gone for westernization in the process of social change, it was not possible for lower castes to resort only to the imitation of higher castes. They also looked upward and immediately adopted modernization. Social change does not happen step by step. The community can jump over one phase of change to another. Postmodernity has a tendency to provide as many choices as possible. And, the lower castes, as any others, are always ready to avail themselves of the choices at their disposal.

When we look at the concepts of sanskritization and westernization from the perspective of postmodernization, they appear to be little narratives. The change was limited to the Coorgs and the wider society of South India. But, when the sociological analysts explained these in terms of universalistic social change, the concepts assumed the form of grand narratives – they became myths only. It was thought that to give the concepts an all-India explanatory status would obviously elevate the status of the architect of the concepts – M.N. Srinivas – to national and international planes. And that happened. But, the concepts in the perspective of postmodernity have proved to be a sham formulation. As we have politics in political parties, so there is politics of sociology also.

## Great and Little Traditions: A Systemic Approach to Indian Society

Sociologists have analyzed social change in Indian society with the help of concepts constructed by foreign anthropologists. This foreign-oriented sociology is invariably functional. It looks back at the Indian civilization for social change analysis. We have earlier referred to Milton Singer's edited work *Traditional India: Structure and Change* (1975), in which he has brought out about 19 articles. These articles cover various aspects of Indian life such as 'Ram Lila', 'The Indian Merchant', 'Class and Cultural Traditions in India', 'Religion and Anavils of Surat', 'A Sikh Village' etc. The articles are nothing but short descriptive stories about the rudimentary aspects of India's social life.

The articles do not show any trace of India's traditions and society. The status of Milton Singer has been very high and his edited work enjoys much status. But, earlier to this study of traditional India, Milton got a few research articles published in learned journals of sociology during the end of the fifties. In his work on India, Milton has tried to analyze social change in traditional India. His basic ideas on social change relate to 'civilization' and 'social organization of tradition'.

At a later stage, McKim Marriott also joined Singer and tried to study civilization and tradition as a unifying factor of India's unity. The traditions, which consist of cultural performances, manifest various practices of the social institution. There is a constant interaction between little and great traditions. Explaining the social structure of these traditions Milton Singer (*Traditional India: Structure and Tradition*, 1975) writes:

> These cultural performances are institutionalized around the social structure of both little and great traditions. Those persisting and important arrangements of roles and status appearing in such corporate groups as castes, sects, or in teachers, reciters, ritual leaders of one kind or another, which are concerned with the cultivation and inculcation of the great tradition, form the social structure of this tradition. The social structure of the little tradition consists of its own role-incumbents such as the folk artists, medicine men, tellers of riddles, proverbs and stories, poets and dancers, etc.

These two traditions have regular interactions. The great tradition influences the little tradition and so does the little tradition influences the great tradition. The interaction between the two affects one another and has led to social change in India. Milton Singer puts his conclusions as below:

> The weight of the present evidence seems to me to show that, while modernizing influences are undoubtedly changing many aspects of Indian society and culture, they have not destroyed its basic structure and pattern. They have given Indians new alternatives and some new choices of lifestyle but the structure is so flexible and rich that many Indians have accepted many modern innovations without loss of their Indianness. They have, in other words, been able to combine choices which affirm some aspects of this cultural tradition with innovative choices.

The great tradition has the potentiality of universalizing the materials in its possession to little tradition. As a matter of fact, the 'matters' originate from the little tradition itself and the latter without any hesitation accepts these in its cultural performances. Universalization of great tradition means downward movement of civilization to the grassroots level. But, in this transformation, there is every possibility of civilizational elements to get changed or modified at the level of little tradition.

## Multiple Traditions

Functionalist sociologists have advanced yet another explanation to analyze great and little traditions of social change. Yogendra Singh labels these explanations as 'multiple traditions'. His argument is that Indian society is not only a caste or Hindu society. It is plural and secular also. The great and little traditions or sanskritization and westernization have only limited application to caste society. This gives the idea of multiple traditions. Yogendra Singh comments:

> The dominant feeling of some social scientists is that Indian society or culture could not be described fully either through the dichotomy of the sanskritic and western traditions or that of the little and great traditions. Indian tradition is far too complex, and consists of a hierarchy of traditions each of which needs to be analysed in order to unravel all the ramifications of change.

S.C. Dube (*The Study of Complex Culture*), showers all praises on M.N. Srinivas for constructing the two concepts, which help us to explain social change in India. But he immediately argues that

Hindu philosophy does not have only one scheme of thought. It has several schools. And, the little and great traditions fail to take into consideration the variants of great tradition and little tradition. Dube writes:

> As far as little and great traditions are concerned, there is apparently no precise definition ... where there are more than one great or near great tradition, each with its canonical texts and ethical codes, the situation becomes all the more confusing .... It may also be added that the great tradition-little tradition frame of reference does not allow proper scope for the consideration of role and significance of regional, western and emergent national traditions each of which is powerful in its own way.

The concepts of great and little traditions, sanskritization and westernization, parochialization and universalization have been utilized to analyze cultural change in India. Structural change remains largely unattended. We have in earlier chapters mentioned that sociologists have an obsession with culture and tradition. And what does culture mean? It means norms, values, and rituals and in substantial terms everything else and nothing else. For sociologists, what they call sociology is actually anthropology. In the kit of the so-called major concepts, caste is everything. And, anthropologists are everything. Interactional aspects of social structure are lost in oblivion.

## Postmodern Perspective and Social Change Concepts

The processes of social change in India, which has passed through the historical phases of pre-colonial, colonial and post-colonial, have not been taken into account while analyzing social change. Modernization has an overarching influence on these processes. The struggle for freedom was an all-India event, which included Srinivas' Mysore also. Freedom struggle and the national leadership gave new values to caste. There was emergence of the values of freedom, liberty and equality. A new literature in regional languages was created. The attainment of independence led to the division of country and there were violent riots both in India and Pakistan. A new category of people emerged in both the countries, who were designated as refugees. The problems of these uprooted people could not be explained through the so-called major concepts of great and little traditions. The nature of these concepts, being cultural, that is, caste-oriented and borrowed from US anthropologists, was not helpful enough to include the complexity of Indian society.

We had modernity in India during the colonial period and its aftermath but this modernity became the pristine possession of higher classes and castes. The little tradition originating from locality created a kind of unity which spread upto the region and sometimes state. The rise of little tradition indicates the emergence of ethnicities which ends up in the gaining of political power. The postmodernity along with modernity does not give the lower castes any sanskritic benefit but a gain of power.

Srinivas has altogether neglected the impact of modernity and postmodernity on lower castes. He being a Brahmin himself, was much influenced by Hindu way of thinking. In the present situation of social change, his concepts of great tradition and little tradition have lost all relevance. Those embedded in the spirit of modernity, are now not prepared to accept the hegemony of high-castes. Inter-caste marriages are on the rise and those violating the rules of endogamy are not heard of given any penalty. There is enough material which shows that all over the country the traditional panchayats or caste associations are on the decline. Dominance of caste means dominance in exercising political power. And, the new change, which is observable at the village level is that the scheduled castes and scheduled tribes have cornered much of the benefits of modernity. Now, a tribal is a modern tribal.

Concluding the discussion on culture change in India through the concepts of great and little traditions, we find that these concepts have limited value. These might be the 'mightiest' contributions produced by the discipline of sociology ever since its birth. These might have contributed substantially to the strength of functionalism in India, but from the perspective of modernity and postmodernity, the concepts need to be scraped. A sociological theory or for that matter a valley of concepts survives in a discipline on its own merit and not on the merit of its creator. After all, it is the relevance or usefulness of the theory which counts.

Modernization is community or society specific. It is the challenges, which the society throws to the processes of modernization. The processes are rejected or accepted. The analysis of cultural change made by sociologists does not look at the colonial and postcolonial history. In the princely states, the society was divided into two clear divisions. There were on one side the Jagirdars, Zamindars and higher castes who enjoyed special privileges in the colonial and post-independent India. They were sycophants and luckiest of the groups who exercised power. Culture change in this respect did not benefit the higher castes. The concepts of little and great traditions only helped the lower castes to satisfy themselves that they are moving towards a 'pure society'. They were vegetarians, teetotallers and sacred people.

Culture change did not give any substantial material benefit to the lower castes. The benefit from modernity presupposes adequate sources of livelihood. So, to ride in a car, to have higher education, to live in a furnished house, to use all technological means, one should have adequate money. Analysis of culture change, in religion, ritual and other aspects of society, does not bring any change. If the tribals of Madhya Pradesh, Gujarat and Bihar take to Bhagatism, that is, become puritanic, it does not bring them closer to modernity. They have enough of hens, eggs and goats to eat, but they cannot consume these by themselves, as they are Bhagat tribals. All these 'local products' have to be brought to the market.

The efforts of sociologists, including that of M.N. Srinivas, S.C. Dube, Yogendra Singh and others, to explain the importance of concepts which help to analyze culture change, do not carry any importance. It is merely an eye wash to carry forward the tradition of change. Modernity in India has never been the concept of poor people. In the name of culture change, sociologists have lulled the poor segments of society. Admittedly, a society has its own culture – its religion, rituals, dance, riddles and literature, but it does not provide any loaf of bread. This is what Srinivas has contributed to Indian society.

We make yet another attempt to look at the concept of culture change in Indian society from the perspective of postmodernity. Postmodernity is anti-authoritarian and the efforts made by lower castes to imitate the beliefs and customs of higher castes, show the latter's willingness to submit to the dominance of the former. But, at the same time, lower castes' efforts to take to westernization, indicates the rejection of the dominance of the higher castes. Acceptance and rejection are simultaneous. In this case, the privileges obtained by the lower castes from the constitution tends to strengthen the claims of lower castes. Reservations in educational institutions, government services and public institutions further make their status high.

## Little Traditions and Little Narratives

There is difference in little traditions of cultural change and little narratives of postmodernity. Little traditions according to Milton Singer and McKim Marriott, are grassroots traditions. These are found at the village level in the cultural performances of the ordinary men. Local festivals, ceremonies, fairs, fasts and dances constitute little tradition. What is important in this respect is that these grassroots traditions, which are primordial ethnicities, cooperative and integrate themselves and form great tradition. Thus, the great tradition is embedded in caste, communities and traditions. In the process of social change, the great tradition assumes a universalistic form. The little tradition, looking at its local situation, deviate from the norms of great tradition.

The postmodernity's little narrative is slightly different from little tradition. When Lyotard constructed grand narratives, he defined it as an all-embracing explanatory theory. These grand narratives oppressed the individuals and compelled them to accept whatever is there in the narratives. Postmodernity rejected the grand narratives and suggested the forming of little narrative. The little narrative resists the power of grand narratives. Viewed from this perspective of little narratives, the little traditions do not oppose the great tradition. On the other hand, they have all choices to amend, transform and reject the great tradition. Second, there is no feeling of authoritarianism with the great tradition. Third, it is the little tradition, which forms the great tradition. What is important in little tradition is that it gives diversity to the culture of local community. Food ways, dialects, dress patterns and cultural performances differentiate one little tradition from the other. They give little tradition an individuality. India's diversity is thus closer to postmodern diversity. Little traditions and graying ethnicities are, therefore, postmodern features of India's cultural change.

### Social Change in Indian Society

In the preceding pages we have looked at cultural changes. These changes are subjected to postmodern analysis. It is interesting to find that sociologically, modernization, has not much influenced India's traditions. There is a rich conceptual body of literature in sociology which obliges us to conclude that despite peripheral changes, the core of our traditions remains the same. Yogendra Singh (*Modernization of Indian Tradition*, 1973) puts his final analysis of the impact of modernization on Indian tradition:

> Our analysis reveals on the contrary that these microstructures have responded with great *adaptive capacity* (emphasis added) to the demands of modernization. Caste has today become a major structural network of modernization in the Indian social system. It has permeated some of the major structure forms, such as local political bodies, voting behaviour and power structure forming itself into a corporate group without, however giving its social functions.

Having discussed the impact of modernization on Indian tradition and culture from functional and modern-postmodern perspectives, we now look as its impact on social structure. Cultural and social structures are differentiated in terms of values, norms, ideology and interaction patterns in corporate bodies. Modernization, as a process of social change, has influenced and brought transformation in the society.

Caste, kinship, family, class, occupational groups, educational institutions, health care centres are all social structures. These structures are the networks which provide opportunities for interaction. The members of these groups meet together in varying statuses. In interaction, they observe certain cultural values, norms and ideology. With the change in culture, there is corresponding change in social interactions. In any configuration of social structure, there is a substratum of values, customs and cultures.

The stability of social structure is contingent on culture. Yet, as abstraction, structure forms a higher level than culture. A structural analysis of change consists of demonstrating the qualities and nature of new adaptations in the patterned relationship, and when a joint family breaks and becomes nuclear, caste group is replaced by leader, popular choice, etc. From a functional standpoint, such explanation consists essentially of pointing out how the different activities fit on top of one another, and are consistent with one another, and how conflicts are contained and prevented from changing the structure.

India is very rich so far as ethnographic studies are concerned. The British officials-turned-anthropologists in India conducted a large number of studies on caste, family and village. Emphasis in these studies has been on the traditional forms of these institutions. The great traditions of Vedas, epics and scriptures were taken as the cutting point for contemporary analysis. Henry Maine, for instance, found villages as "little republics", whereas O'Malley described Indian joint family as a large structure consisting of as many as 500 members at a given time. Indian anthropologists were not behind their British counterparts.

Much ethnographic literature has also been generated on the society of tribals. At this stage of description, we must say that most of our ethnography was created on the information given by the servants of British administration. The servants were not accountable to anybody and they parted with information according to their fancy. Though British anthropology had a long tradition of fieldwork as is evident from the works of Rivers, the Britishers in India did not do any such fieldwork. Their ethnography, at best, was only an official output.

Social structure was studied by Indian anthropologists. They also did not do much fieldwork. G.S. Ghurye made an extensive study of caste and occupation in India. It has all been borrowed from the scriptures and Sanskrit texts. Iravati Karve's study of kinship behaviour in India does involve vigorous fieldwork but her studies on caste, family and linguistic groups are based on secondary sources.

What is important in this connection is that the ethnographic material which we have generated does not have any broad abstractions or generalizations. The studies conducted after the 1950s, refer to development programmes which were implemented both in the rural and urban areas. Giving details about structural studies conducted by sociologists Yogendra Singh writes:

> In most structural studies in India, the ideal-typical formulations and statements are not clearly indicated, although an implicit recognition of these is present. The differentiation roles and shifting nuclei of authority in family, the change of caste and tribe in the power structure, emergence of new factions and dominant castes in villages, the spread of bureaucratic administration, the emergence of youth organizations, new labour movements, urban growth and industrial-demographic changes in leadership, etc. are some structural studies which offer valuable clues to social change in India. In these studies, however, methodological orientation does not remain uniform which merits brief discussion.

Our objective in this chapter is to apply perspectives of modernity and postmodernity to the culture and social change witnessed in India's society. Having discussed the cultural change, we now shift to social change. There are studies on family, marriage, kinship, and rural and urban communities, which would be analyzed with the help of the perspectives of modernity and postmodernity. Such an effort would provide new insights into the interpretation of our society. It is difficult to find the reality about Indian society. There is no truth about it. But, we can, at least, strive to move towards truth and reality.

### Neglected Aspects of Social Change

In the aftermath of independence, and the promulgation of Indian Constitution, there were several social and cultural upheavals. First, due to the division of the country, a massive migration of people from Pakistan to India took place. And, in the same way, people from India left for Pakistan. There was a severe breakdown of kinship ties in both the countries. Not only the kinship ties severed, the pilgrim centres of Sikhs, Muslims and Hindus also remained divided. Queer enough, both the countries – historically and politically – do not have cordial relations. Consequently, at the international level, the kinship relations and religious affinity continue to suffer till today. The future does not predict to be rosy. Massive migration has also affected trade, commerce and economy.

The refugees who came to India had to develop a new pattern of relationship. In Pakistan, where they resided, they were mostly an agriculturist class. Some of them were landlords, Jagirdars and Zamindars. They found their stay in India quite uncomfortable. There was no spare land for them. They had limited options to take to a settled life. Most of them took to business as their vocation. Since they were not educated, they could not enter into public and private services.

All this happened between the end of the forties and the beginning of the sixties. The sociologists during this period were terribly busy in conducting studies on caste and family. We could only find two such studies: one by R.N. Saxena of the Institute of Social Sciences, Agra and the other by U.T. Thakur, who happened to be a postgraduate in sociology from Bombay University. Saxena was closer to Dehradun and therefore he had opportunities to interact with refugees who had concentrated there in large numbers. Thakur's book entitled, *The Sindhis*, has been published by Bombay University itself.

Besides these two works, we have no other full-length study on the refugees. Bombay had long remained a centre of sociological study, and Sindhis have their 'home' in Vilaspur but no study till now has come from this university on refugees. The social and cultural change, which the refugees (mostly Sindhis) have experienced after they came to India, could have been the richest literature on rehabilitation, produced by Indian sociologists. The Sindhi migrants today are found spread all across the country; they have learnt the local languages and dialects and very successfully perform cultural practices. All this happened in the country when our sociologists were mostly engaged in administering their research schedules on caste and family in towns and cities.

Functionalism has remained such an obsession with the sociologists that they have always been conservative in taking to new areas of study. Social change has occurred in a large number of social sectors but the sociologists have always been keen to study caste and family. The disadvantaged groups, marginals, weaker sections and tribals have recently got a new stratification wherein there are leaders, elites, and affluent classes. Stratification of these groups is almost absent. Social change among these groups is also pronounced. But such studies of tribals and marginals have been left for anthropologists. And, the anthropologists are busy in conducting ethnographic studies.

### Conflict Approach

Social studies on caste, kinship, village and linguistic groups pertaining to social change have been mentioned above. We shall refer to these groups at a later stage. Here, we only want to point out cultural and social changes from the perspectives of modernity and postmodernity. Social change, which is observed in the institutions, is largely studied with the functional methodology. But such an explanation is inadequate. There are a few sociologists who have studied social change with the perspective of conflict theory.

Marx gave the theory of conflict. According to him, all human history and social behaviour go through the process of dialectical materialism. According to dialectical materialism, all human history has been the history of class struggle. Marx argues that this is only the truth of society. Some studies have been conducted in India on the conflict theory. The difficulty with these theorists is that they have failed to develop a scientific tradition of thinking and research. None of them has given any theory of social change as is developed by neo-Marxist, Althusser. Indian conflict theorists are doctrinaire Marxists.

D.P. Mukerji, a Marxist sociologist, has analyzed social change in India in terms of modernity. He makes a mix of modernity and Vedanta. He mainly focuses upon the encounter of the Indian tradition with that of the west which, on the one hand, unleashed many forces of cultural contradiction and, on the other, gave rise to a new middle class. These forces, according to him, generated a dialectical process of conflict and synthesis which must be given a push by bringing into play the consumed energies of the class structure of Indian society.

A.R. Desai (*Social Background of Indian Nationalism*), the Marxist sociologist, has discussed social change from the perspective of dialectical approach. He argues that the nationalism which emerged in India is from the material conditions created by the colonial rule. It is during this period that with the coming of industrialism and economic growth there appeared class consciousness. The class developed antagonism towards the British rule and a feeling of nationalism was becoming apparent. Explaining his thesis about the coming nationalism, Desai observes:

> Indian nationalism was in fact the outcome of the new social, material conditions created in India and the new social forces which emerged within Indian society, as a result of the British conquest. It was the outcome of the objective complying of interest .... While recognizing the progressive role played by the introduction of modern education in India, it would be incorrect to conclude that Indian nationalism was the child of their education.

Thus, A.R. Desai's thesis of the background of nationalism in India is based on the historical and materialist interpretation of social and cultural factors.

## Application of the Perspectives of Modernity and Postmodernity

We have discussed social change in India with the help of functional and conflict perspectives in the preceding pages. These changes are evolutionary. The approach taken in these themes is based on modernity. Modernity is a very comprehensive phenomenon and involves the notions of progress, rationality, democracy, capitalism and industry. The changes which are observed in different institutions of society, are considered to be parts of modernization. They carry the elements of social change for social progress. The social change that we have in our country is towards modernization. In this context, modernization leads to reformation. The age-old traditions relating to marriage, status of women, removal of caste inequalities are all parts of the wider programme of reformation.

When postmodernity looks at the dialectical analysis of change, it is found to be only a great narrative. Great narrative is a universalistic explanation and when D.P. Mukerji and A.R. Desai analyze social change, they have no input, that is, empirical evidence, to support 'their' Marxism. They pick up the theoretical threads from Marx and apply it to India. There were some material conditions in India during the Mughal period – Akbar was a great emperor, there was property in his kingdom and the religion which he synthetically developed – Din-e-Ilahi – had the potential to develop some nationalism, but Marxism, then, was not applicable for A.R. Desai.

D.P. Mukerji, in fact, had very weakly applied Marxism in his analysis of modernity. For potmodernity, the conflict explanations advanced by sociologists-Marxists are, therefore, mere historical inadequacies. In all these dialectical explanations, only mechanical applications are made. There is lack of adequate specificity. Yogendra Singh's assessment of dialectical social change in India runs as below:

> An important limitation of the dialectical approach for studies of social change in India is the lack of substantial empirical data in support of its major assertions which are often historiographic and can easily be challenged. In theoretical terms, however, this approach can be most viable for analysis of the various processes of change and conflict in India provided it is founded upon or sound tradition of scientific research.

Cultural and social processes of change have been examined in this chapter with the help of the modern and postmodern perspectives. The analytical perspectives alter our insight and understanding of social change that we are experiencing in India's society. The culture change explained by functionalists is conservative and only shows the evils of modernity. Modernity in India has never gone in favour of the disadvantaged and subaltern people. The higher groups and the affluent have reaped the harvest of higher and professional education, green revolution, technology and industrial capitalism and the marginals have to satisfy themselves with the cultural borrowings of the modernized groups. In terms of cultural achievements, there is no material gain to these people.

Whenever the sociologists discuss cultural and social change, they are not tired of referring to tradition. And, it must be stressed that their traditions are invariably Hindu traditions. In the name of cultural change, a large number of our sociologists have built up an empire of 'Hindu sociology'. Where would it lead the Indian society and ultimately the Indian nation nobody knows.

Postmodernity, though sounds very high, is closer to the masses. It has removed the differences between popular and elite culture; it has stripped of the higher classes and castes from authoritarianism; it is critical of everything and anything; it is down-to-earth. Viewed from such a wider perspective of postmodernity, it could be said that whatever cultural and social change has come in Indian society, is for the benefit of the 'modernized' groups and corporations.

# VII

## The Family: Traditional, Modern and Postmodern

We are quite rich in family studies. Some of our sociological stalwarts conducted pioneering studies in this area. I.P. Desai, K.M. Kapadia and Andre Beteille made a beginning. Gujarat and Maharashtra are the prime fields which have attracted the attention of our sociologists. In the beginning, Iravati Karve made an analysis of family as is found in the scriptures. G.S. Ghurye provided a mythological portrait of the family structure.

The sociological studies are characterized by functionalism. There has always been a stress on discussing family in terms of its traditional structure. There cannot be any discourse on Indian family without reference to joint family. Iravati Karve, in her analysis, has brought out certain characteristics of joint family which have become standardized. She cannot be contested; nor rejected. I.P. Desai, in his popular work on the family in Mahaua (Bhavanagar), goes to the extent of saying that family in India invariably means joint family.

Admittedly, the family sociologists have brought out the forces which have changed the family structure and have created disintegration. Our sociology is so much overwhelmed by status-quoism that it cannot apply other perspectives to find out the exact form of family. What is strange is that changes in family are discussed but the theoretical concepts of modernity or postmodernity are not applied to the analysis. The studies thus remain merely examples of 'abstract empiricism'.

When families were studied in Gujarat, they were not passing through any crisis. Even today, family in Gujarat is safe and the members show all allegiance to it. We should know that both Gujarat and Maharashtra have a mercantile culture wherein business in joint family is always beneficial. Breakdown of joint family is not often. The studies on family, therefore, are only passion of the sociologists. In the west, and particularly in the US, where a large number of Gujaratis go to work, try to live in a joint family. Joint family is a craze for them. The Gujaratis, notwithstanding caste belongingness, consider themselves affiliated by kinship ties – every man is addressed as *Bhai* (brother) and every female a *Ben* (sister). In such a well-suited family structure, what prompted the sociologists to take up family studies is non-understandable.

## Postmodern Family in the US and Britain

The United States of America has reached to a form of family which could be postmodern family. The American sociologist, Judith Stacey (*In the Name of the Family: Returning Family Values in the Postmodern Age*, 1993) believes:

> Contemporary societies such as the U.S.A. have developed the postmodern family .... I use the term 'postmodern family' to signal the contested, ambivalent, and undecided character of our contemporary family cultures. Like postmodern culture, contemporary western family arrangements are diverse, fluid and unsolved. Like postmodern cultural forms, our family today admits unlikely elements in an improvisional pastiche of old and new.

Stacey's characterization of American family as postmodern makes it clear that it is the structure of family which determines the form of family. The American society is plural, secular, fluid, differentiated and diverse and accordingly the family has become so, that is, postmodern.

Anthony Giddens (*The Consequences of Modernity*, 1990), the British sociologist, argues that major changes have taken place between people who are sexual partners in a family. These changes are traced by him in what we call 'high modernity families'. Giddens explores that family in Britain initially was based on economic circumstances. The married couples hardly kissed and caressed. At a later stage, there developed families emerging from romantic love. Romantic love is egalitarian in nature. It is based on physical attraction. In such families, the man was dominant as he was the breadwinner. The divorce in these families was uncommon. Pre-marital relations were rare and unheard of. The British family, as described by Giddens was, by and large, a modern family.

### Indian Family: From Tradition to New Contexts

When Iravati Karve discussed the pattern of family in India (*Kinship Organization in India*, 1990), she laid down certain conditions for its form. Accordingly, the members of joint family (1) lived under one roof, (2) took food prepared from one hearth, (3) owned common property, (4) had common worship, and (5) possessed generation depth, that is, two or more generations lived in a family.

The traditional Hindu joint family has witnessed certain changes due to education, modernization, industrialization and mercantilism. Besides Iravati Karve, I.P. Desai, K.M. Kapadia, A.M. Shah and others have also studied family and its types in India. What is missing in these studies is that much stress has been put on the structure, functioning and changes in the traditional family. No attention has been paid to the practices that the members of the family observed. It must be mentioned that all the members of the joint family had similar practices. Some are engaged in business, a few have jobs in public/private sectors and others are ready to avail of any employment opportunity. There are variations among the members on ideological basis. All these practices need to be explained in the family form.

The status of family that we find in sociological research belongs to 70s and 80s. The family that we find today is in its new look. With the national ideal of two children for a family, the higher castes are in dilemma. Quite a good number of families send their children for higher and specialized education to centres of science and technology. Such highly trained students either go abroad or take up employment in multinational companies in metropolitan cities. Such youths say goodbye to their family. This leaves the parents at their original home – sure loneliness embitters their old age.

Again, industrialization has also complicated the situation. It is difficult for the new generation to get employment at the place where they reside. They are obliged to go out in search of employment elsewhere. The traditional joint family in such situations cannot keep its jointness. Today, jobs in private sector are so much scattered in terms of space that the possibility of traditional family can hardly be kept intact. Besides, earlier, the marriages were contracted with a specified caste marital area. But, now, a wider space in the country is open for negotiation of marriage. Added to it are the increasing incidences of inter-caste and inter-religious marriages. The daughter-in-law, who hails from an alien cultural and linguistic area, finds her in-laws' house quite strange.

The crisis of traditional family in India is not simple. It is much complicated. Not only the joint family is in trouble today, the nuclear family is also not without its share of agony. If the parents join their son at latter's workplace, their accommodation in the big or metropolitan city becomes much expensive and if they decide to stay behind at their native place, the old age problems loom large.

The family is in crisis at the village level too. The problem is not of its breakdown. It is the new form which it is gaining. Land in the villages is scarce. Whatever land is ploughed, is not sufficient to provide a viable subsistence to the family members. At the national level agriculture has now ceased to be a gainful occupation. Its contribution to national income does not hold top priority any longer. The small farmers and the landless cultivators are left high and dry in such an agricultural economy.

Thus, the main problem of family is neither of nuclearity nor of jointness. It is of survival. Indians or any other community cannot survive without family. The problem is to maintain a form which provides livelihood to the people and a promising welfare and future to its members. What appears strange and ridiculous about the Indian sociologists is that they take up a subject for research which does not have any inherent problem. And, at the end, the sociologists themselves generate some problem which has no relevance to the study. If, for instance, the joint family is breaking, and the nuclear family is emerging, how does it affect the society. But, the sociologists are not able to prove that the joint family is not breaking and are only accepting some adaptable changes. Joint family must exist and it is the only objective of sociologists. To prove this, they would go to any methodological extent.

The changes that we find in Indian family are not particular to India or the family only. These are general. But, the fact remains that western sociologists have shown seriousness about changes in their family. For instance, Ulrich Beck and Elizabeth Beckgernsheim, the German sociologists, argue that changes in family life and relationships are being shaped by the development of modernity. Modernity is characterized by individual choice, in contrast to an emphasis on following tradition in pre-modern societies. However, they characterize this process as involving individualization rather than collectivism.

## Individualization

Prior to the promulgation of Constitution, the Indian society was predominated by holism. And, holism implied "a relationship between individual and group in which the former was encompassed by the latter in respect of duties and rights; what had precedence here was community or *sangh* and not the individual. This subsumption of individual by collectivity persisted all along the line of traditional social structure, e.g., family, village, community, caste or political territory or nation."

Caste and village were considered to be the decision-making collectivities in traditional India. The Constitution of India, for the first time, considered individual as the last and smallest unit of society. Individual was responsible for his own decision-making. He decided whom to vote; he decided whether to educate his children; he decided the destiny of his family. In the pre-modern society, it was the tradition which determined the decision. In the gender relations, though the head of the family takes all decisions but there are large number of women in the family who are educated, who are working women and who receive a fat salary packet. All these new roles drew their strength from individualism. For Constitution, individual is the centre of all government activities. This has much affected the form of family and its practices. Though the women find it difficult to rebel in a joint family, they would assert their right in matters of family disputes.

What distinguishes the colonial-feudal family from the contemporary family is that the latter is empowered with the value of individualism. Along with this, the modern family is also influenced by the notions of democracy, capitalism, technology and above all freedom and liberty. The higher and middle classes are embedded in these values. The newly developing subalterns have now assumed the power of reservation and this has made them vocal about their rights. They may not be much educated, they may be poor – even below the poverty line, and they assert their rights and privileges in an organized way.

A large number of social forces are working today in Indian society. Perhaps, the most forceful power is that of modernity. The family forms, whether nuclear or joint, are influenced by these new forces. And, in the new social context of constitutional individualism, development and capitalism, it is difficult to analyze the forms and practices of family. In this connection, we have to make some broad observations: one, it is not important to indulge in the debate of joint and nuclear family. It is hardly relevant for Indian family. Second, the family forms in India must be analyzed in our present milieu of modernity and postmodernity. But we propose to take up this issue after we have diagnosed the analysis made by sociologists.

### Indian Joint Family

Family assumes all importance in Indian society. The identity of an individual is known by his family name only. In the South Indian society, the name of an individual goes with his father's and village's names. In the regions of Gujarat and Maharashtra, the official records carry the individual's name along with his place of residence. All over India, at the police stations, an individual is identified by his family and place of residence. During the colonial and feudal times, the family name carried with it the status of the family in terms of his caste. Caste was a dependable criterion of an individual. Now, with the constitutional abolition of castes (also creed and sex), family is not identified by caste.

K.M. Kapadia (*Marriage and Family in India*, 1956) studied family structure in 1955-56. The universe consisted of 1,345 families from Navasari of Surat district in Gujarat. It was an empirical study but adequate evidence was gathered from mythological and historical resources. The study thus combined mythological, historical and empirical methods. On the basis of his findings, Kapadia defines joint family as that which consists of two major characteristics: (1) common property, and (2) generational depth, i.e., two or more generations.

Iravati Karve's, as mentioned earlier, definition of Indian family is considered to be classical in sociology. In her, *Kinship Organization in India* (1990), she has given common roof, common hearth, common property, common worship and generational depth as basic determinants of joint family. Karve is criticized by her later generation of sociologists who say that in the present circumstances of industrial capitalism, it is difficult to share a common roof or a hearth. Migration and urbanization have made many of the things difficult for joint family.

Yet another study of family from Gujarat is by I.P. Desai (*Some Aspects of Family in Mahua*, 1964). Mahua, a town of Bhavanagar, has now become a district headquarters. It is inhabited not only by Hindus but by Jains and Muslims too. Desai goes with the assumption that the word 'joint' is added to family by the British anthropologists. In India, for Desai, the family is invariably joint. Whenever we talk about family in India, we mean by it joint family. He interprets jointness unlike K.M. Kapadia and Iravati Karve. Desai defines joint family as below:

> It is interesting to note that words used for joint family in most of the Indian languages are the equivalents of translations of the English word 'joint family'. The family is the group wider than the nuclear group, is not unknown to the European society. Yet

> strangely enough, the joint family came to be understood as the conglomeration of nuclear families for all purposes instead of a qualitatively different family that befogged our understanding and the study of the family in India. Any two or more nuclear families who are legal partners in business could not make a joint family. To the Indian the family is that which is the 'joint family' in English. The concept of family as nuclear family is still not the Indian concept. Consequently, the nuclear family to the Indian is not the same as it is to the Englishman or the American today.

Desai differentiates Indian family from the western family. The issue that Desai raised in his study requires a thorough investigation. Desai talked about jointness in the family. Members of joint family are united by some linkages. These linkages keep the members come together. And then, what are the linkages: residence, food, worship, property, and mutual kin obligations. But, the jointness need not be full, it could be partial. For instance, the members of a family may have separate residences but common property; may have common food but different worship. These elements of jointness may determine the degree to which a family may be called 'joint'. Desai offers four categories of concept of family type:

> I-a, household and wife only; I-b, uni-member household; II-a, husband, wife, and married sons, without children and other unmarried children; II-b, the above group, with other relatives who do not add the generation depth; III, three generation groups of linear descendants; and IV, four or more than four generations of linear descendents.

Under the category of nuclear family type I-a to II-b, his study shows that such families in Mahua (Gujarat) constitute 61 percent of the total; types III and IV which he defines as joint families make the rest of the 39 per cent.

Desai makes a distinction between the nuclearity or the jointness of family types as a structural phenomenon and degrees of sentiment of jointness in each family type derived from the relationships as obtaining among living in one household and between the relatives who are living in another household either in Mahaua or outside. Evaluating the structurally nuclear and joint families on the sentimental criteria of jointness, Desai finds:

> That 70 families in Mahua which are classified as nuclear on structural criteria comprise the 'high' category on the scale of the sentiment of 'jointness'; 51 such nuclear families are in the 'higher' category and 6 families in the 'highest' category on the scale of sentiment of jointness. (The scale of sentiment of jointness runs from zero, low, high, higher to highest categories). The nuclear on the zero scale of sentiment of jointness are only 21 and those on the low scale are 112 in number. Excluding the 5 per cent families where sentiment of jointness is zero, 95 percent of the total sample families have sentiment of jointness ranging from low to 'highest' degree.

### Change in Family

Sociologists have argued that the different forms of family which we find in India are due to social change. There has been much change since the ancient times. As the plurality of cultural and social structure goes, the family forms also experience variation. It means if we want to set a composition form of family structure, we should look at a comparative study. Pauline Kolenda (*Differences in Family Structure in India*, 1987), an American sociologist, made such a study in India between 1967 and 1982. She has tried to find out regional differences in family structure. She has also tried to identify the cultural specificity of a region and has studied the family structure in this context. She argues that the regional structure determines the form of family to a great extent. Kolenda has studied 26 families and concludes that it is not possible to give any common definition of family. However, she agrees that joint families are largely found in higher castes and big landowners. The lower castes and the landless labourers do not like joint family. It must be observed that Kolenda does not agree with the traditional definition of family given by Indian sociologists. K.M. Kapadia, Iravati Karve and I.P. Desai refer to the culture region of Gujarat where Hindu religion has its predominance. Desai has been a strong advocate of Gujarati culture and therefore goes with the assumption that family in India in all situations is joint. Family form varies with the status of social structure. In other words, when the sociologists discuss family, they are predisposed to joint family. And, according to them, it is the higher caste only which has kept the heritage of Hinduism intact.

We do not have any authentic sociological research about the family structure of scheduled castes, scheduled tribes, Muslims and Sikhs. Sociologists are so much overwhelmed by the Hindu tradition or national culture that they look only at the Hindu family and at the high-caste Hindus. There is enough ethnic and anthropological material which vividly shows that the tribals all over India do not have any form of joint family. Similar is the situation with lower castes.

## Forms of Family in South India

What we have been trying to argue is that the change in the perspective of analysis, presents a different reality of social phenomena. The sociologists have studied family from the perspective of functionalism and the ideology of national culture and this gives us some idea about family. Quite like joint family, particularly in North India, there is also prevalence of joint family system in South India like a family form called Tarvad. South India is a very wide area covering different linguistic groups and states. Karnataka, Andhra Pradesh, Tamil Nadu and Malabar have patrilineal and patrilocal forms of family. These states have joint family system. But there are in this region some groups or castes such as Nayar, Tiyan, Mopola (Muslims) and Bunt who have matriarchal system. The matriarchal system among these groups is called Tarvad. Tarvad is a matriarchal family which consists of eldest woman as the head of the family along with her brothers and sisters. Tarvad does not have any marital kin, all the members are related by blood. The Tarvad form of family, these days, is passing through crisis. With the increasing rate of migration, the family is breaking.

There is very scant literature on the study of Tarvad. Whatever we get from these studies only show the reiteration of the approach of joint family. These studies warn us that with the rise of modernization, the future of matriarchy and the Tarvad is bleak.

## Changing Family

Studies on family show ample concern for the changing family and its disorganization. The Gujarati sociologists, including Iravati Karve, have spent much ink to show that the 'joint family' is changing rapidly. Yogendra Singh has examined the impact of modernization on family structure. He refers to a large number of studies conducted both in the city, town and village. He is excellent in generalizing the findings:

> Changes in the structure and functions of joint families in India are thus following a reconciliatory pattern, a pattern common in the cultural changes in the Indian society. In mate selection, the principle of personal choice, especially in urban family, is today increasingly reconciled with parents' approval; the wife's freedom in middle-class homes to work outside in offices and schools operates within the traditional framework of the husband's approval; and sometimes the approval of the husband's or even wife's parents. Such reconciliations are, however, not without tensions which is an inalienable aspect of change, and in spite of these changes, the traditional world-view of the joint family still prevails.

Yogendra Singh's analysis of the family studies, conducted in India, is a classical example of the use of functionalism and functional ideology. He admits that there are inter-caste marriages, there are working women and there are tensions also. But these tensions are resolved by the Parsonian framework of tension management through reconciliation and compromise. Social change might be forceful, but the joint family still prevails.

The studies on family do not have any academic and useful relevance in our present era of social change. First, the sociologists who pioneered these had eminent status in sociology during fifties to seventies. Whatever they initiated was taken as a gospel. And strange enough, even today, it goes through one syllabus to another, one academic session to succeeding sessions. These have become recurrent aspects of our universities.

## Why Study Joint Family?

What led the sociologists to study family as an important aspect of Indian society? Were their social tensions regarding family in

Gujarat, Mumbai or elsewhere in the country? The sociologists who started the study of family have not pronounced any problems with the family. Perhaps their problem was that the joint family which forms the vital part of Indian society was breaking down. If the joint family breaks down (and surely not the family itself), it is feared that the whole society would crumble. Once, Iravati Karve (*Kinship Organization in India*, 1960) observed that it is essential to study family, caste and linguistic groups to understand Indian society. She was correct. But, Indian society can equally be studied with nuclear family or family of any form.

But the family has had several problems. The basic problem with the family is that ideologically it suffers from holism or collectivism on one hand, and individualism on the other. Karve describes joint family as a 'small world'. In the past, traditions kept the people together. But, with the promulgation of Constitution, individual becomes the smallest unit. It replaced the family. For governmental purpose, family is now only a part of wider society. It is like any social structure.

The ideology of individualism weakened the domination of the head of the family in a joint family. Even the new generation of family has started rebellion against the elders. Individualism thus has become a challenging force in a joint family. Our sociologists seemed to have overlooked such an important force of social change.

Karve, Kapadia and Desai have all defined joint family within the perspective of functionalism and a non-Marxist approach. Their one-point programme was to defend the breakdown of joint family. They were very keen to identify the forces, which helped the people to live together in the joint family. This led them to study common property, generation depth and common worship. But the relations between mother-in-law and daughter-in-law were altogether forgotten by these studies. In Indian regional languages, mother-in-law is often portrayed as a villain in the family. How harmony is maintained in such conditions among the female members of the family is a crucial problem which needs to be investigated. Dowry, and dowry deaths are other problems of family. The sociologists who studied family in Gujarat or Maharashtra did not think about all these events of inhuman acts.

Thus, their only concern was nuclearity or jointness. The functionalist ideology does not stir the sensivity of the society. All the time, and in all situations, they cling to the status quo. And, if there occurs some change, it should be within the system.

In a joint family, the central issue is about the authoritarianism of the head of the family. The family now in the new circumstances is more or less democratic. For an average man, ideology matters much. The family members are influenced by several ideologies – political, economic and cultural. Ideologically, no family – nuclear or joint – is free from ideology. But this aspect of the structure of joint family has always remained untouched by the sociologists of family.

### Family: Modernity and Postmodernity

Modernity does not mean only development of science, technology, education and industrial capitalism. It means several things together and this has affected the family structure. Industrialization, for instance, has changed the place of work. It has led to urbanization. A new rationality has emerged in business administration. All these forces of modernity have given a death blow to joint family. To talk about modernity and jointness in present situation is completely irrelevant.

In some senses, modernity is against tradition. Enlightenment gave the ideology of secularism and liberalism. When the modernity made its inroads in Indian society, it brought with it secularism, democracy and scientific ethos. When we interpret Indian family and its researches as are available to us, it could be safely said that the primary institution is moving towards a modern family. Before we describe the forms of family prevailing today in India, we would say that it cannot be discussed in the context of India's religion, rituals and ethnicity. The nature of Indian society has undergone radical change. It has ceased to be a colonial-federal society. Though the Indian Constitution has nowhere defined society, but the government policies have been straight forward to say that it is a democratic, socialist, secular and rational or science-oriented society. Its ethos consists of economic development and egalitarianism.

There is enough evidence to say that the present form of family, notwithstanding different regional cultural varieties, is nuclear. The government policy in this respect is unambiguous – it says that a person should not have more than two children. It comes down to an average family of four persons. Thus, the government stands in favour of a nuclear family. It is possible that in such a family size, there is possibility of other blood kin members such as grandparents and unmarried brothers and sisters. In such situations, the size of nuclear family might increase but the family continues to remain as a non-joint family. This is one aspect of the contemporary modernity of family.

Another aspect of family is that of welfare and property. The family of middle class makes all efforts for the development of its members. Children are educated in higher and advanced schools, colleges and institutions. Competitive examinations are a craze today, employment opportunities are keenly contested. This was not possible in a joint family where the collateral siblings belonged to different parents.

From the perspective of postmodernity, it could be said that in the present form of nuclear family, the domination of the head is considerably diluted. In the present family, the women are more or less equally educated; show a wide range of expertise and there is a democratic ethos pervading all the members. There are instances of pre-marital sex relations, divorce and inter-caste marriages. Though we do not have factual data about the frequency of inter-caste marriages, the media reports that these are many. The family thus becomes modern, keeping people of various regions, linguistic groups, castes and ethnicities together.

The pattern of family which has emerged today could be called heterogeneous in terms of ideology and religious belongingness. Postmodernity is characterized by diversity and differentiation. For example, in a family, there is enough political orientation. The father could be member of a Hindutva political party; the son, a Marxist and the daughter, an activist working for the mobilization of women. Such an ideological heterogeneity is a common feature in contemporary family form. This is how a postmodern perspective would look at family. Traditional joint family, more ore less, remains homogeneous. Deviance of any kind is not looked with approval.

The new family can be looked upon as a secular institution. Though a family has its own ancestral deity, its own tradition of worshipping a particular god or deity, it displays itself as a secular family imbibed by the spirit of democracy and scientific ethics. This is not possible in a joint family. From the perspectives of modernity and postmodernity, the present form of family is, by and large, a secular family.

Normally, a joint family follows a common occupation, which is the traditional occupation. The researches done in sociology tell us enough about the jointness or nuclearity of family, but we know little about the occupations which the family members follow. Does the joint family follow the traditional occupation, i.e., agriculture, carpentry, tailoring or pottery, we do not know much about it. However, K.S. Singh (*People of India*) informs us that the new generation of the joint family is increasingly leaving its hereditary occupations. For instance, the occupation of priesthood is not followed by the young generation. It pays little.

The new form of family gives all freedom to the selection of occupations. A Brahmin may open a shoe store or sell liquor. The traditional occupations are no more the monopoly of castes. The nuclear-hetero sexual family, which we have now in India, is occupationally free from following traditional occupations. It is modern.

## Subalterns and Their Family Forms

The sociological researches have mainly covered the high-caste Hindus. Their discussion on nuclearity and jointness revalues sound Hindu families. And, though they mention about Muslims, Jains and Sikhs (as I.P. Desai, and K.M. Kapadia) they only restrict themselves to high-castes. Thus, the family studies are, in fact, studies on Hindu high-castes. In their spirit of Hinduism, they do not forget to mention that the non-Hindus also have borrowed the Hindu joint family. Such is the influence or dominance of high-caste Hindus that even non-Hindus have imitated the joint family system. It must be mentioned here that the Muslim and tribal family forms are basically different from Hindu. In the name of family the sociologists have developed in India a Hindu sociology. When we apply the perspectives of modernity and postmodernity on the family descriptions, we find that the nuclear families have been moving towards secularism and modernity. The authoritarianism of the head of nuclear family, in all respects, is democratic. Even, in villages, as the studies report, the women take their decisions in Panchayat Raj Institutions (PRIs). The political parties in the elections design their strategy at the level of individual rather than family. Family approach during elections is a matter of the past. It is clearly an evidence of the decline of the authority of the nuclear family's head. Postmodernity is obviously, again, institutional authority.

The reservations, given to subalterns - scheduled castes, scheduled tribes and other backward classes, have created a new sub-society in the wider Indian society. The reservations have empowered the segments of society. Earlier, in India, a person was identified by the caste he belonged to. His status was tagged with his caste. Such a hereditary belongingness based on birth is now not in occurrence. A casual visit to a scheduled area would show that the non-tribal groups remain in constant tension with the dominance of tribals who occupy positions of prestige and power. It must be observed that though masses of tribals have not amassed any material gain but they are much assertive of special privileges they have obtained from their scheduled status. In public places - hospitals, police stations, bus stands and government offices - they would not miss any opportunity to create a scene of rebellion, or anger. This has given new form to their family. Their families now have become new power stations. Right from the family of the Sarpanch to the family of the Member of Parliament, the scheduled tribe or caste family enjoys a privileged position. The tribal family is, therefore, a privileged family. The new form of family found among the subalterns is accountable to the impact of modernization and decentralization of power. In this new form of family, the patterns of relationships have also changed. There is no trace of the bride wealth - *dapa* and the gender relations in these families are based on equality. Before the emergence of modernity, the tribals did not have much of a sophisticated life. The verbal relations were marked by the use of filthy language. Women were often addressed by abusive language. But it no more prevails. Women occupy high places in panchayats and municipalities.

Earlier, hierarchy in the caste system was determined by birth in a caste. Now, this is not found. Contrariwise, the status of a subaltern is determined by his belongingness to a scheduled group. The new context created by modernity has provided varying forms to family. Power, occupation, education and residence in a city have altered the shape of the subaltern family. It would be funny in this context to discuss anything about nuclearity and jointness of family. Modernity, which was in earlier times a preserve of high-castes and elites, has now shifted to subaltern groups, their leaders, elites and well-off sections.

Postmodernity operates in a cultural context. The form of Indian family, therefore, needs to be analyzed within the framework of immediate culture surrounding the family under study. For all purposes the studies done by sociologists are of Hindu families. What lacks in these studies are the cultural and social practices performed by the members of family. There are rituals pertaining to birth, marriage and death. It is said that in a joint family those who reside out of the household, are also invited on occasions of the observance of rituals. Even, those who live away from the family come together to celebrate the rituals. This also contributes to the sentimental jointness of the family. The argument of this kind only shows that the sociologists were determined to establish the jointness of family.

Postmodernity interprets such an event in a different way. It argues that the kinship ties of the family also go beyond kinship network to social network. Marriages in a family are also attended by friends, well-wishers, neighbours and in the case of villages, the whole villages. Such a large and heterogeneous participation in the affairs of family does not make it joint. It is simply a case of cultural postmodernity.

Before we close our discussion on Indian family with the perspective of postmodernity, we would strike a note on Derrida's concept of deconstruction and family. If we look at the texts, say *Mahabharata, Ramayana, Puranas* or for that purpose the works of

G.S. Ghurye, K.M. Kapadia and I.P. Desai (they all belonged to Bombay School of Sociology), we would find that their source of family discussion is largely drawn from the Sanskrit works and scriptures. Kapadia and Desai added fieldwork to support their mythological findings. Reading a text of the kind of Puranas, epics and Sanskrit works requires considerable expertise. It is difficult, says Derrida, to find out the real meaning of a text. He says that "rather than attempting to find a true meaning, a consistent point of view or unified message in a given work, the deconstructive reading carefully teases out the internal differences and attends to its repressed contradictions or inherent vulnerabilities." Whatever, K.M. Kapadia and Iravati Karve found suitable to their analyses, they have drawn freely from these texts. There has not been any deconstruction. By going through a careful mode of reading perhaps new interpretations could come out.

To conclude our analysis of the application of modern and postmodern perspectives on Indian family, it could be said that whatever our sociologists have done is a futile exercise. In the new context of modernity and postmodernity, functional ideology can hardly help us. To argue that Indian family is by nature, sentimentality, mythology and history, a joint family neither solves the tensions and problems of family nor the nature of modern family.

Our view of Indian family is that it is modern-postmodern, small in size and democratic, secular. The present form of the family corroborates the new general social milieu of the country. It is rational and to a great extent secular. The prevalence of joint family even in a remote village is exceptional. The individual member of the family has now become autonomous and the authoritarianism of the family head has gone. The future of family form depends on the future of the structure of society. Society and family forms are complementary. There is no antagonism between the two.

# VIII

## Interpreting Caste, Village Community and Postmodernism

The caste system has been over-studied in sociology. There have been debates on the origin, development, functioning and structure of the caste system. Caste hierarchy has been one of the central themes for sociologists. In the new context of Constitution, the Indian society officially does not allow the existence and functioning of caste. The state does not distinguish among individuals on the basis of caste, creed and sex. There is no caste system.

As there was no use of studying nuclearity and jointness of the family, so there was no need to study caste stratification. The study of class was enough to show inequality in the society. But sociologists have linked caste with religion. They argue that caste has religious origin – it has come out from *Brahma* and thus has divine properties. Lord Krishna says that the four *varnas* have been created by Him. The argument given by the orientalists goes further and says that the institution of caste, which is divine, cannot be changed by any state or by any individuals anytime.

India had several social institutions. We had the practice of animal sacrifice, *sati* system and inhuman treatment meld out to widows. These institutions received scant attention from sociologists. They did not study these stratifications as caste fulfilled all the conditions of functionalism. And, therefore, it was obligatory for sociologists to study the caste system as it has existed, its nature and need. The American and European sociologists either joined Indian sociologists in this venture or themselves initiated such studies at micro level. Some foreign sociologists, notably Louis Dumont, have proved to be icons for Indian sociologists who have studied caste stratification. We are not against the study of caste system and its functioning but the sociologists should take care of other institutions as well.

### What Obliges Sociologists to Study Caste?

However, sociologists of all origins and shades have studied caste in an adequate way. It is, in all its meanings, "an ethnic group". Ethnicity defines individuals who consider themselves, or are considered by others, as sharing common characteristics which differentiate them from the other collectivities in society, within which they develop with distinct cultural behaviour. When the Jews are defined as an ethnic group, the caste is also defined as an ethnic group. Obviously, the Brahmin caste is different from the Agrawal, so are Palves from Jain. Each caste has its traditions, customs, rituals and ways of life and living. There are thousands of castes. K.S. Singh has enumerated more than 4,000 communities. Communities, for him, are castes.

What made sociologists to study caste at all levels of society – village to metropolitan? It is not merely an academic craze. There are some reasons which need to be explored. The flood of caste studies came soon after the independence. Before that we did not have any problem with caste. There were some abuses with lower castes; untouchability, drunkenness, eating the flesh of dead animals and illiteracy were the problems with the lower castes. Since our national leaders were conscious of all these evils of the caste system, they had an important task for reforming the castes – low and high.

The lower castes were backward but they participated in large numbers in our struggle for independence. During this period, we did not have any problem with the caste. Bipan Chandra and others (*India's Struggle for Independence*, 1988) argue that the movement for freedom was not a movement led by elites of the country. It was a mass movement. All the castes, without distinction of higher or lower, participated in the movement. The authors write:

> The movement in its various forms and phases took modern politics to the people. It did not, in the main, appeal to their pre-modern consciousness based on religion, caste and locality or loyalty to the traditional rulers or chieftains. It fought for no benefits on that basis. People did not join it as Brahmins, or Paridars, or Marathas, or Harijans. It made no appeal to religious or caste identities, though in some cases caste structure was used in villages to enforce discipline in a movement whose motivations and demands had nothing to do with caste.

The above statement clearly shows that during the freedom struggle, caste never appeared to be a problem. The movement is described both by subaltern and nationalist historians as a people's movement. Soon after the attainment of independence, what went wrong was that the caste, all of a sudden, became a fertile and tempting subject which attracted a number of academic studies. We shall have to find out historical reasons for the appearance of such studies.

Nicholas B. Dirks ('The Ethnographic State' in *Postcolonial Passages*, ed. by Saurabh Dube, 2004) says that the mutiny of 1857 engineered by the sepoys of British Army made colonial power cautious above the discontent prevailing in the general masses. Before that the English missionaries were already clear that caste was their single most obstacle to the realization of their objectives, "and spoke of the need to break potential converts or their castes in order to free their souls for possible conversion". Dirks further writes:

> Despite the fact that the fat-laden cartridges were speedily withdrawn and sepoys instructed to pack their own cartridges in grease of their choice, their use became the occasion for the first outbreak resistance in Meerut on 10 May, 1857. Eighty-five sepoys who refused the cartridges were placed in irons and sentenced to ten years' imprisonment.

Historians have debated the mutiny of 1857. Indicating about its course, Sir Sayyid Ahmad Khan blamed the revolt on ignorance and insensivity rather than on more fundamental causes. He wrote: "government has not succeeded in acquainting itself with the daily habits, the modes of thought and of life, and likes, and dislikes and prejudices of the people. As a result, government was ignorant not only of local modes of thought and of life, but of the grievances through which their hearts were becoming estranged."

The rebellions of 1857, accompanied by agrarian rebellions obliged the British Raj to systematically study Indian ethnicity. In the study of ethnography, much attention was paid to caste. The Indologist, Max Muller, wrote in April 1858: "among the causes assigned for the Sepoy mutiny, caste has been made the most prominent. By one party it is said that too much, by another too little, regard was paid to caste." Muller made it clear that caste as a social formation was little different from the racial, ethnic, religious and class differences and prejudices that were accepted in most arenas of European social life.

It was in the second half of the nineteenth century that the British colonial rule declared itself as an ethnographic state. H.H. Risely, who entered Indian Civil Service in 1873, became the Director of Ethnography for India. In 1901, the results of first census were made open to the public. Risely published the census data with some additions and revisions as *The People of India* in 1908. Risely observed that caste was the cement that held Indian society together. He was never in favour of the death of the caste system.

The Britishers used knowledge about caste and ethnicity for laying a strong foundation of their regime. It was also used for their political benefits. Whatever Risely wrote about caste in his last work, he effectively denied the capacity of Indians for the formation of an India of a single unified nationality. The caste was divisive. In 1903, the partition of Bengal was made on the basis of caste knowledge of Risely. It has thus become colonial knowledge that ethnicity including caste can be effectively used for divisiveness and politics.

Before we return to the question raised above that what has been the usefulness of caste studies, we would once again refer to

Risely. He was very much interested in the study of race. He argued that race could be successfully understood with reference to caste. He had a strong belief in Brahminical sociology of knowledge and concluded that the caste system as a whole can be interpreted through the Brahmin caste. Dirk (2004) writes about the role of Brahmins in his study of caste:

> He organized his entire understanding of caste structure and rank according to Brahminical indices such as the acceptance of food and water, the use of priests, origin stories concerning duties and obligations, and ritual proximity to and functions relating to Brahmins.

Risely's knowledge of caste was considered so much authentic that colonial rule accepted it for running the administration. The British Raj was convinced of the usefulness of ethnic data for establishing themselves in a foreign country. Dirks (2004) further writes:

> Caste might have been justified as a subject of study because it was seen as organizing many administrative matters from famine relief to criminality, but in the same breath it was constituted once again as a Brahminical ritual system in which the most esoteric forms of social distinction became the basis for administrative knowledge.

Edgar Thurston, who was appointed Secretary of State (Madras), appreciated the work done by Risely in connection with the Ethnographic Survey made in 1901. He argued that the data generated by Risely could be also useful in solving some of the problems of Europe. Using language that was a direct quotation from Risely, the Secretary of State wrote:

> The Census provides the necessary statistics: it remains to bring out and interpret the facts which lie behind the statistics. No clearer statement could be made of the colonial uses of anthropology of how by the late nineteenth century the British in India recognized that the task of *colonial rule was essentially ethnographic* (emphasis mine). Virtually no area of government policy or activity could be conducted without benefit of extensive anthropological knowledge. *The late colonial state was genuinely ethnographic state* (emphasis added).

Risely did not rigidly separate the ethnographic survey, which in the end was never formally completed, from the census, which stands to this day as a monument to Risely's general influence on colonial anthropology and administration. And, while Risely scripted much of the above justification for the conduct of ethnography, his interests were relentlessly 'scientific' rather than attuned to the needs of administration.

We have made a lengthy reference to Risely. He defined caste with reference to race; he considered caste as divisive; he used scientific procedures to study caste and considered Brahminic knowledge as a key to analyze caste. He did not really intend to create knowledge of ethnography for the practical use of running administration and create hierarchies in government work. The government used his ethnographic knowledge to great effect.

Why did the Indian anthropologists and ethnographers study caste, caste ranking, caste hierarchy, caste origin and caste changes and functioning? Surely, they did not know that their rich findings would be gainfully used by the government in independent India. None of the sociologists has made any such claims. But, these studies unintendedly turned in favour of the political parties and the general politics. Unfortunately, the Constitution denied vehemently the practice and behaviour based on caste. And, strangely enough, what was denied and forbidden by the Constitution was enthusiastically taken up for elaborate study by sociologists.

But, the caste studies proved to be of immense guidance for those contesting for power. If Risely supported the British for smoothly running their administration, the caste studies helped in providing enough material to the politicians for creating vote banks and developing election strategies. It would not be wrong to say that all the caste information is contained in the small briefcase of a petty politician. We have some evidence to demonstrate the usefulness of caste studies. The emergence of Jharkhand and Chhatisgarh is partly due to the empirical material laid down by the anthropologists. The concept of 'Diku' (non-tribal exploiting) mobilized the tribals of Bihar to stand up in arms against the caste Hindus. Bal Thakre, the Shiv Sena supremo, recently announced that Mumbai was exclusively meant for the sons of the soil, that is, only for the Marathas and not for the South Indians and Christians.

In Rajasthan, the Jats have openly come out against the Kshtriyas. The Meenas are against the Gurjars, the latter demanding the status of a scheduled caste. The whole country is rocked by competing caste rivalries and the demand for minority reservation is increasing. Even the Jains – an affluent group of traders – are agitating for minority status; the Brahmins who even today have cultural dominance are rallying for a reserved space. The burden for providing raw material to agitators and politicians lies on the sociologists. The situation today has reached such a stage that politicians and party bosses know better about caste than even the sociologists themselves.

We have earlier in this work mentioned that there has been a tremendous increase in the intensification of ethnicities. In a single caste, there could be more than one ethnicity. The ethnicities are tied up with a caste or group of castes. These sub-ethnicities work in collaboration for contesting power positions in public institutions. The data for multiple ethnicities are generated by caste studies. The concepts, such as sanskritization, westernization, parochialization, universalization, and dominant caste, have valuable political importance.

## Order and Change in Caste System

We have tried to interpret the sociological caste studies from a different point of view. Before applying any perspective – modern or postmodern – we have raised certain questions about the relevance of these studies in the context of prevailing social surroundings of the country. But, this has been a hasty step. First, let us see how these studies are looked at by sociologists and critics.

Caste has its origin in religion, that is, Hinduism. "The normative principles of Hinduism have been as meticulously systematic and closed as its empirical structure has been varied and amorphous. Often this latter attribute (eclecticism or amorphousness) of Hinduism is emphasized without any regard for the former, which gives an imperfect and incomplete picture of the Hindu culture. Behind the extreme degree of permissiveness and liberalism in beliefs and variety in ritual practices as admittedly canonical system, there exists a strictly logical view of phenomena in terms of which the principle of *order* and *change*, *being* and *becoming*, *creation* and *destruction*, *hedonistic-utilitarianism* and *spiritual transcendence* can be meaningfully explained. Implicit in this system of logic and metaphysics is a theory of society and culture which admits little confusion and has been formulated with extraordinary clarity."

The caste studies, which have been empirically conducted, contain strong factual data. The data are diverse relating to different cultural zones of the country. Notwithstanding the differentiation of caste, its structure and change, one could apply the principles of Hinduism and say that the changes in caste, whether political or economic, are merely outwardly. The caste system maintains its *order* and *change*. Order means the hierarchy of system. Modernization, technology, education and politics have not been able to change the position of a caste in the system. A member of an untouchable caste may become a cabinet minister (for instance, Jag Jeevan Ram) but he is not allowed to change his position in the caste hierarchy. Similarly, a Kshatriya despite his being a learned person cannot obtain the status of a Brahmin. Order or hierarchy of the caste system must be maintained. This kind of change is irrelevant for hierarchy.

Yogendra Singh (*Modernization of Indian Tradition*, 1973) explains great traditions in terms of cultural renaissance and changes in Indian society. He says that the Indian society revolves round the concept of caste. Caste is not static. It has also a cyclical order which brings some changes. Thus, caste is an *order* (of hierarchy) and also a social phenomena of *change*. But, the change does not interpret or transform the order. He writes:

> The twin basic concepts of this system are *order* and *change*. Order, both normative and social, is conceptualized through the principle of hierarchy and change, which is assumed to be the immanent nature of all phenomena, and of hierarchy combined with cyclical theory of growth and change introduces an element of dynamism in this theory of culture and society.

The great traditions thus consist of Hindu caste hierarchy and dynamism. It must be mentioned here that change in caste or great traditions does not disturb the caste hierarchy. Further, emphasizing the importance of hierarchy in caste system, Yogendra Singh argues that hierarchy is a decisive element of Hinduism. He writes:

> The principle of hierarchy could easily be called the ethos of the Hindu traditions cultural pattern. It permeates through most of the cultural categories. In an analytical sense, principle of hierarchy may be seen as governing the cultural structural at many points.

Not only Yogendra Singh, Louis Dumont (*Homo Hierarchicus: The Caste System and Its Implications,* 1970) also considers hierarchy as the dominant feature of Hindu tradition. According to him, tradition also carries with it the elements of 'holism' and 'transcendence'. The literature on caste is huge. It is difficult to take all these studies together and make common generalizations. However, it can be said that whatever changes that we find in caste are in the realm of values and norms. Generally, three major perspectives have been adopted to study caste. These are: (1) perspective of scriptures, (2) anthropological cultural perspective, and (3) caste as a structural and cultural phenomena.

The varying perspectives look at caste as an ethnic group, which is related to norms and values, race, occupations, mobility, religion and culture. Among these aspects of caste, perhaps, the most important is hierarchy. It has raised the question of dominance in a particular region. In the caste hierarchy, traditionally, Brahmins are at the top and the lower castes at the bottom. But this ideal type hierarchy is not found all over the country. For certain, the lower castes in any part of the country are not at the top or middle. They are invariably at the lowest level. The castes, which enjoy dominance in a village or region among other castes, have larger share of power in their possession. And, the dominant caste is that which has more land, power position in local organizations and which runs the whole village. In the total hierarchy of caste system, therefore, it cannot be said that Brahmins are at the top. However, the ritual position of the

Brahmins always remains at the top. We shall make an effort to find out the caste hierarchy from the empirical studies conducted by sociologists.

Yogendra Singh observes that the dominance of power of one caste over another is a key factor in the maintenance of the social structure of caste. He refers to a large number of caste studies to show the relative dominance of particular castes.

Likewise, Berreman (*Hindus of the Himalayas*, 1963) observes that in Senapur and Rampur the Brahmins were not the powerful or economically superior caste, but were subordinate to the Jats and Thakurs. The Kshatriyas or Rajputs were also found to be dominant in other North Indian villages, for example, in Mohana village in central U.P., Khalapur (John Hitchock, *The Rajputs of Kalapur*, 1963) village in western U.P., and in Kasandra (McKim Marriott, *Village India*, 1955) village in Gujarat and Ramkheri village in Malwa (Andrian C. Mayer, *Caste and Kinship in Central India*, 1960). Berreman observed that both the Rajputs and Brahmins as a pair constituted a dominant caste in the village of Sirkhanda in the Himalayas (Gerald Berreman, *Hindus of the Himalayas*, 1963). The warrior caste has been reported to be dominant in the Bisipara village studied by Bailey (F.G. Bailey, *Caste and the Economic Frontier*, 1957). "In the South Indian villages, Brahmins and Okkaliga as dominant caste have been noted by social anthropologists. The Havik Brahmins in village Tottagadde in Maland area of Mysore and Smarth Brahmins in the Kum, Bapettai in Tanjore (Tamil Nadu) have been observed to be dominant classes. Okkaligas are dominant in the village of Rampura" (Srinivas, in McKim Marriott (ed.), *Caste Ranking and Community Structure in Five Regions of India and Pakistan*, 1960).

We have referred above to some caste studies. As a matter of fact, in sociological research, there are a large number of caste studies and castes have also been studied within the context of a village. And, these studies come out with universalistic generalizations. To be honest, while making any valid statement on the basis of these studies, it could be said that these studies are grand narratives. But, before we apply postmodernity to these studies, let us refer to functionalists' views on these studies.

Now, a question raises: What castes are there that exercise dominance on the society? In other words, among all the castes, that is, in caste hierarchy, which caste has more powers as compared to others. Does hierarchy matter nothing in the exercise of power, at least, at village level only if not on a wide plane? Yogendra Singh makes a vigorous exercise to critically look at the question of caste dominance. His analysis runs as follows:

> The facts regarding dominance as analyzed with respect to the villages mentioned above lend support to this theoretical formulation since the reported dominant castes are Brahmin, Rajputs and Okkaliga, the first being in the upper the other two in the upper-middle and middle category of castes. This would indicate a continued structural stability in the caste system, especially with regard to villages where these studies have been conducted.

It must be observed that Yogendra Singh analyzes caste dominance within the area of the villages which have been studied. He is logical. But he takes up another issue, that of, challenge to caste dominance. And, he generalizes it to apply it to the total caste system. Here, he very conveniently forgets the villages under study and generalizes it to apply to a much wider area. Again, the issue of dominance in terms of dominant castes – Brahmin, Rajput and Okkaliga – has been identified by him on the basis of castes in villages. Methodologically, the functionalist sociologists have erred in making all kinds of generalizations on micro-studies.

It is further observed that the castes are changing. There is occupational change; there are inter-caste, inter-regional and inter-religious marriages. Dominance and power are specific to caste. Much stress has been put on the politicization of the castes. M.N. Srinivas is the chief architect of the studies on the status of caste in modern India. He combines both sanskritization and westernization (or modernization) in his analysis of caste. He is quite hopeful of the survival of caste. In one of his statements he says that caste has appeared in its new avatar – incarnation. The Indian Constitution says that for the purpose of state there is no caste while the sociologists say that on the strength of empirical data caste is eternal. It is gaining strength day by day. Srinivas writes ("Caste in Modern India," in Myron Weiner (ed.), *The Civilization of India*, Vol. II, 1961):

> The building of roads all over India, and the introduction of railways, postage, telegraph, cheap papers and printing ... especially in the regional languages ... enabled castes to organize, as they had never done before. A post-card news of a caste meeting themselves, and the railways enabled members scattered in far-flung villages to come together when necessary, while the availability of the cheap newsprint facilitated founding the caste journals, where aim was to promote the interests of their respective castes, it is usual to point out that railways and factories relaxed rules of pollution regarding eating and drinking and other forms of contact. But this is only one side of the story. The availability of cheap paper enabled caste disputes to be recorded, and this gave permanent form to rules and precedents which were till then dependent upon the fallible and, therefore, changeable memory of elders. I learn that several castes in Gujarat have their constitutions printed.

It is also argued by caste sociologists that the contemporary castes organize themselves into associations. A single caste may align itself with sub-castes with which it has communal and marriage relations. Such caste associations work as political interest groups. Pressure is exercised on state decisions and there are demonstrations and rallies. But such mega caste associations are limited to linguistic and cultural areas only.

Admittedly, the caste system has witnessed several changes. There is resilience in the system. The studies on caste elaborately show that despite changes, the order of the system remains intact. The functionalists have left no space to convey that castes have undergone changes but they do not touch the hard core of caste, that is, its order – Risely however stressed its racial aspect. The lifeline of the survival of caste is its order. Order is religious spirit. It is hierarchy. Railways have come, print paper has become cheap, and there are television, mobile phone and computer. Despite all these earth-shaking upheavals, no change has come in the hierarchical order of the caste. Pollution and purity, as qualifying values of caste differentiation, are no more in vogue; traditional occupations have become the thing of the past; inter-caste marriages are increasing and food taboos are no more applicable. Much has changed in the caste system, such as dress pattern, food ways and housing pattern. What is interesting is that the caste studies do not discuss issues relating to hierarchy. Louis Dumont has written much about caste. But the one single message which he gives to the Europeans is that the Europeans learn much about hierarchy from India's caste system. Hierarchy is religious, it can not be changed. And, therefore, despite huge changes, the caste remains the same. This is the position taken by functionalists. Yogendra Singh's final analysis on changes in caste runs as below:

> The castes as communal groups structurally persist. Changes are, however, taking place at other levels of their functional differentiation, such as their articulation as interest groups, as political microstructures and as communication networks for modernization. These functions caste largely performs either owing to the structural constraints or because caste alone in India provides an immediate and pre-existing structural framework for diffusions and mobilization of new role structuring, but these, in the absence of other fully differentiated voluntary associations, not only carry the imprint of caste but also articulate new activities through its social structure. In this form the social structure of caste undergoes changes which are meaningful to the process of modernization in India.

Caste is changing rapidly. But, the hierarchy of the caste system remains the same. Jan Breman (*Of Peasants and Migrant Paupers*, 1985), who has worked in Surat (Gujarat), reports that the tribals have developed caste characteristics but they are not included in the caste hierarchy. They may be called *tribal castes*. Nowhere in the country the Rajputs have assumed the status of Brahmins though they have become teetotallers. The caste studies, pertaining to a large number of village studies, have come to the conclusion that caste has used all 'adaptive mechanism' to assimilate and 'co-exist' with many structural changes. These studies bring out that there is a huge degree of resilience in this system which gives it adaptive and survival value.

### Caste and Postmodernity: Hyper-differentiation and Hyper-rationalization

Postmodernity has specific perspective to look at social institutions. Caste, which is basic to Indian society, was viewed by Risely as a divisive force which comes in the way of national unity. At its roots, caste, therefore, is a dangerous ethnic institution. It denies great narratives and perpetuates diversity. From the point of view of postmodernity, caste ends up in hyper-differentiation and hyper-rationality. Some of the writers, who adopt stronger claims for modernity and postmodernity, emphasize differences, rather than similarities, between members of social groups. They believe that it is the job of researcher to uncover and describe these differences rather than to make generalizations about the whole social group. Postmodernity believes in increased fragmentation of culture. And, the caste also tends to end up in diversity and fragmentation. We would apply perspectives of modernity and postmodernity on the caste situation that we find from various caste studies mentioned above.

## Modernity and Caste

M.N. Srinivas argues that India has become modern. It has many of the characteristics of modernity. Similar are the views of Andre Beteille and Yogendra Singh. The availability of a huge mass of ethnicities brings out the fact that people at the grassroots levels are increasingly becoming modern. There are caste associations, coalitions and federations which try to get as much share in the power politics as possible. In this game of power sharing, the true meaning of democracy has been lost.

Modernity believes in rationality and the castes which are equipped with education, technology and resources avail of all the benefits of modernity. The sociological studies have a queer position in the analysis of caste. They show their concern for social change. And, social change for them means modernization. All social change is not modernization. Modernization involves democracy, secularism, socialism, industrialism and capitalism. Modernization that we find among the higher castes is nothing but its abuse. Among the lower castes, including the other backward castes and the tribals, there are so-called creamy layers. These layers have joined hands with the high-castes and so the ordinary masses remain outside the benefits of modernity.

The lower castes have been betrayed on yet another count. They have been made to believe that caste is a divine formation. It cannot be disturbed. Its order is based on hierarchy and, therefore, no caste group can ever get an opportunity to change its status in the hierarchy. In such a situation, the benefits of modernity can only be availed of by those caste groups which have adequate resources. The dominant castes which have an access to power – Brahmin, Rajput and Okkaliga – favourably take to modernization. The creamy layers have now begun to reach higher status because of the benefits of protective and developmental safeguards.

Modernity has been identified with progress and all sections of society in India hog to take advantages of democracy, industrialism and capitalism. In this race for modernity, the master objectives of building India as a secular and socialist nation have been defeated. Equality is rejected. And, most of the cultural certainties constructed by caste have been accepted. Instead of rejecting the caste certainties, modernity, in the name of rationality and bureaucracy, has observed that the sociologists' notion about caste as a social and cultural formation is false. Caste changes, as the studies indicate, are no real changes. These are only cultural changes. There is no trace of change in the order of caste. Purity, pollution, and residence, or marriage rules are only at a superficial plane.

The caste studies further show that there are tensions in the inter-caste relations. These tensions sometimes become so severe that there is a fear of the breakdown of the system itself. But functionalists are not easily disheartened. They have an eternal faith in the resilience of caste system that no inter-caste rebellion can hurt the survival of the system. Caste can take over the role of politics, economics, and development and, what not. Its resilience is marvellous. Referring to Srinivas, Yogendra Singh comments:

> Among other forces which show caste resilience Srinivas mentions growing anti-Brahmanism in Madras which provides rationale for polarization of lower castes in the DMK movement; the rise of Mahars and Marathas as political groups in Maharashtra (which too had an undertone of anti-Brahmanism), the rivalries between the Kamas and Reddis in Andhra, both of whom first united to drive out Brahmins from power and following that, sub-divided among themselves

> to reap greater benefits of power. He also mentions the Lingayat-Okkliga rivalry in Mysore, where too anti-Brahmanism has been a catalyst for politicization of castes; and caste has been recognized as a factor for appointment to government posts and for offering seats in medical and engineering colleges; this however, could not have been achieved without a complicity of the Government of India, which amended the constitution in 1951 to give preference in services and educational institutions to the backward classes and members of the scheduled castes and tribes. The Rajput-Bhumihar rivalry for power in Bihar and scheduled castes movements of Shoshit Sangh in U.P. has also been noted by Srinivas, to be connected with increased mobilization of castes for gaining secular objectives. His conclusion is, the power and activity of caste has increased in proportion as political power passed increasingly to the people ('through constitutional reform and democratization') from the rulers.

Caste has taken to political activities. Both Srinivas and Yogendra Singh have come to the conclusion that the caste studies very clearly show that changes have come in the system. They agree with Lloyd I. Rudolph and Susanne Rudolph (*The Political Role of India's Caste Associations*) on the aspect of change in caste system and take the similar position:

> Modernity has entered into Indian character and society but it has done so through assimilation not replacement.

Yogendra Singh and Rudolphs argue that caste has changed. There has come modernity in its structure. But, at the same time they say that change is adaptive or assimilative. What does it mean? The order of the caste, that is, its religious character in terms of hierarchy has not changed. And, therefore, basically, caste has not changed. Such a kind of interpretation – adaptive and assimilative – is a goody-goody statement. It talks two things at the same time – caste has changed; caste has not changed. Such an approach to Indian society is the obsession for functionalism and tradition. This is how the Hindu sociology works.

Perspectives of modernity and postmodernity look at changing caste from a different point of view. It takes a firm position on the strength of data available through caste studies that castes have become modernized. With the working of the processes of modernization, what is life under the caste system. Most of the characteristics of caste predominantly stated by M.N. Srinivas, D.N. Majumdar, McKim Marriott and A.C. Mayer include: (1) restrictions on communality, (2) caste hierarchy, (3) religious disability on participation in functions, (4) ascribed status, (5) endogamy, (6) specific occupations, (7) social structure, and (8) values.

The characteristics of caste are traditional. These have largely become oblivious to change that is fundamental. Rules of communality have become irrelevant. Even marriage feasts are participated without any caste bar. Caste occupations have been replaced with secular occupations. Much of the polluted occupations have now been mechanical. Even non-lower castes have made their entry into municipal scavenging. Ascriptive status has gone in favour of achievement status. Reservations have upgraded lower castes to status occupations. Education is now no more the monopoly of the higher castes. Civil services are not exclusive to higher castes. Politics is highly democratized. It is also open to scheduled/lower caste people. The only pillar which could give identity to caste is endogamy. But this is also crumbling. There are also instances of inter-caste marriages. All these caste characteristics have been weakened. The biggest contribution of modernity is the remarkable achievement stated above.

There is one more aspect of caste which needs to be mentioned. Each caste has its own customs, traditions and rituals. These regulate the behaviour of caste members. Caste gets its survival through this behaviour. But, the decision-making power of the caste has now been weakened. The term ‘outcast’ is now not in vogue and caste members have always their choice open. They can go to the court of law. In such circumstances, caste remains only a mark of identity.

Now, the question of hierarchy – how does it matter if there is no change in hierarchy? Modernity gives identity to a person. It is the achievement or merit which counts. Secularism has replaced caste belongingness. The scheduled groups, such as tribals, lower castes and disadvantaged groups, will not face this problem of hierarchy. They have been denied a position in the caste hierarchy despite their taking to sanskritization. Since Srinivas coined this concept, three generations have passed and no lower caste has been able to enter into the iron-cage hierarchy. These groups have now taken to secularism and modernity. And they seem to be happy with this new untraditional status.

The lower castes and tribals were initially put into scheduled category for ten years. The government did not find improvement in their status. And, therefore, the period of scheduled list has been further extended many times. When will descheduling begin, is anybody's guess. The issue is now political and not developmental only. Whenever descheduling begins what would happen to these groups? Will they be able to break the iron-cage of caste hierarchy or the so-called order of caste? It is not possible. The Chamars, the Bhangis and other social groups might change their caste name but their position in the caste, as untouchables, would remain the same. The functionalists must be told: What is there in a name? There are Brahmins who serve as watermen in offices though they occupy top position in caste hierarchy; there are Thakurs who once ruled over the village, now working as menials. The perspective of postmodernity looks at caste in an untraditional way. Authoritarianism of social institutions, whether joint family or caste, is outrightly rejected by postmodernity. It is regarded as a rejection of many things. Caste has exercised its traditional power for so many centuries. Its nature has always remained authoritarian. In its present context, postmodernity views caste only as a cultural institution, which prescribes certain norms for caste members. At behavioural level, it has no authority or sanction to oblige the members to follow these norms. Norms are laid down only for creating an image for a particular caste. Violation or deviance does not carry any penalty.

At the village level, the caste exercises some power. Among the lower castes, outcastes are observable in some cases. However, the caste power becomes ineffective in villages where the incidence of migration is greater. Migration is rampant even in the remotest interior villages. Because of the paucity of agricultural land, stagnation and spread of higher and technical education, masses of people are leaving villages for towns and big cities. The restrictions on such caste members are in effect not applicable. The migrant groups are carriers of the values and ethos of modernity.

Sociology has a rich literature on caste and caste ethnicities. This literature was created during the period from fifties to seventies. It is not without its faults. Even Risely who worked extensively on castes admits that the top, rung Brahmin was the only knowledgeable person in the caste-system. He solely depended on Brahminical knowledge: Dirks writes:

> In retrospect, Risely's reliance of Brahminical sociology of knowledge is astounding. He relied almost entirely on Brahmins and other higher castes .... He organized his entire understanding of caste structure and rank according to Brahminical indices ....

The data analyzed by sociologists who worked on caste are not without skepticism. For one thing we are certain that these sociologists were not conversant with the local dialects of the castes they studied. However, there may be some exceptions. The quantum of data given by them can hardly be called authentic. In such a situation, it is dangerous to conclude that castes have not changed but have made some adaptive or assimilative changes.

From the viewpoint of modernity, castes have undergone major changes. Even the traditional hierarchy has experienced and witnessed change. We do not have any empirical data to support the hypothesis since no dependable studies on caste have been added to the repository of sociological research material. In the absence of such data, we cannot make certain statements based on observations and media reports. For the functioning of a caste, in the present context of modernity, order or hierarchy does not come in the way. The statement of a Brahmin who is at the top does not carry any meaning for the castes lower to Brahmins. Perhaps, the statements of the lower caste people, who are at the bottom, are more substantial because they constitute a majority. The perspectives of modernity and postmodernity look at castes as democratic, secular, capitalistic and modern. Description of caste as assimilative and adaptive is only a sociological gimmick. As any other group, each caste has its ethnicity. Hierarchy in this respect is part of ethnicity. Caste is economic, political, secular and ethnicity is its mark of identity.

Who cares for hierarchy? In a modern society, identity of a person is secular. Generally, a man is known by his profession. There was a time in colonial and feudal society when a person's identity was his caste, or sometimes religion. In independent India, feudal identity does not bear any significance. Now, there are no Jagirdars or Zamindars. These have become condemned identities. However, for politicians, caste has some importance for mobilization of masses in election campaigns. The politicians these days woo ethnicities, particularly religious, to gain the support of the followers of certain religions. When in power, they would visit temples, Gurudwaras and mosques. It is an effort to keep the religious groups in good humour. If possible they will dole out some package for the development of a shrine. In all such cases, the sociologists should be told that hierarchy does not come in the way. What matters is not the caste, nor hierarchy but ethnicity. And ethnicity is all restricted to religion and ritual.

The discussion on caste cannot be meaningful if we do not refer to the general social and cultural context of the wider society. It is the method of the application of certain perspectives which turns a caste into an ethnicity or an interest group. There are caste villages in the country, so also there are tribal villages. If, for instance, a village votes by and large for Congress Party, it does not mean that the village has affiliation with that particular party. In fact, a caste is political by its choice. The political role of the caste is that of an interest group, and nothing more. Capitalism, democracy, industrialism and exercise of political power are now not exclusive to higher castes. Like any other group, the castes also aspire to avail of the opportunity. In this respect, when the sociologists say that there is politicization of caste, they should also say that there is criminalization of caste, there is industrialization of caste, there is educational boom in the caste and the like. Such generalization of caste is nothing short of mischievousness. The simple thing is: a caste is a cultural association with its own history, ethnicity, rituals, customs and modes of instruction. Why should it be dragged into politics and other dirty things?

While concluding our discussion on caste, it could be said that by the end of the nineteenth century the colonial society of India experienced several changes. There was rebellion of 1857, followed by general agrarian revolt. The Britishers realized that they must be conversant with the local culture of the Hindus. Caste was considered to be a representative culture of the country as a whole. H.H. Risely came to help the colonial administration and declared India as an ethnographic state. The colonial rule took all the benefits of ethnographic administration.

In independent India, caste also became useful for the parties or people in power. Sociologists made all efforts to study it in all its ramifications and 'avatars'. The studies pertained to the period after 1950. The country during the era took to planned change. There was industrial revolution, community development and above all extension of education, and spread of transport and communication facilities. Caste became an important institution as a beneficiary of development programmes. The sociological data on caste proved very helpful. It became a treasure house of ethnic knowledge. In the census of 1921, there were about three thousand castes in India. The number swelled to more than four thousand as reported by K.S. Singh in his *People of India* project. Data about caste have been analyzed by sociologists – both Indian and foreign. Knowledge about caste is sacred. We do not contest it. But our objection is to the analyses made by sociologists. For Indian sociologists, with the exception of conflict theorists, caste is sacred par excellence. Its sacramental character is maintained by hierarchy which the sociologists call 'order'. The sociologists also admit that modernization has brought about vast structural and cultural changes in the caste. It has been said that modernization has given new strength to caste. There are caste associations, caste constitutions and caste elections.

The position of sociologists in their analyses is that despite massive and forceful changes, caste has not changed. Whatever changes we find in the contemporary caste system itself do not touch its religious core. Religious sanctions are its hierarchy. The caste maintains its order. And order is sacred. The Chamars or the

Bhangis may transform themselves to any extent – become teetotallers, worship the whole range of Gods and deities, observe *vratas* and religious festivals and go to pilgrimage – to four *dhamas*, but they will nevertheless remain Chamars and Bhangis. The diet, dress patterns, living style would not raise their 'position' vis-à-vis caste system. The caste hierarchy, for the sociologists, is like a virgin, which remains untouched. The analysis of caste, as is available to us, is by eminent sociologists including Andre Beteille, Yogendra Singh, Rudolph and Rudolph, A.L. Mayer and on top of the sequence is M.N. Srinivas. They have all interpreted caste from functional perspectives.

How do modernity and postmodernity look at caste? We have analyzed caste in the preceding pages with reference to these perspectives. Indian society is plural and it grants freedom to its several caste-generated ethnicities. What is important for the notion or idea of caste is that its unity and integration are maintained through its various cultural and social institutions. There are linkages which hold the nation together. The ethnicities, though plural, work as linkages. Democracy, progress, secularism, capitalism and technology provide a wide spectrum with which the ethnicities have to identify themselves. In its own field, a particular ethnicity enjoys all freedom. It is like a deity, it may adorn itself with all the gold in the world, the law has no objection. When it comes in the way of the smooth functioning of the state, it becomes objectionable.

Modernity looks at caste as an ethnicity. When the caste groups promote democracy, education and political competitiveness, there is nothing wrong with it. In a democratic society, caste functions as an interest group. It pressurizes political decisions and interprets the issues on the basis of rationality. For instance, Chhatisgarh became an autonomous state after a lot of national argument. What we are pleading is that caste is not a sacrament. It is like any democratic association which struggles to obtain its objectives. Let sociologists not make caste a whipping boy. Its divisive functions have been tabooed. The state does not discriminate anybody on this basis.

## Village Community and Postmodernity

The third important institution of Indian society is the village community. We have in India a sort of romantic euphoria for villages. Rabindra Nath Tagore moved from Calcutta to Shantiniketan, Gandhi shifted from Ahmedabad to Sabarmati and many of our writers in regional languages have written extensively on villages and village life. Villagers are a simple lot of people; they are hard working, all the day toiling in the field. What do we want to make out of these villagers? Do we want to lead them to the road of modernity or keep them isolated in their pristine glory?

Sociologists have studied villages in an exhaustive way. Long back during the colonial period, the British officers-turned anthropologists have described India's villages as 'little republics'. Baden Powell, Karl Marx, Altekar, Radha Kamal Mukerjee all have described villages as autonomous entities. C.T. Metcalfe's observation that village communities are little republics, having nearly everything that they want within themselves, and almost independent of any foreign relations, has become a classic formulation.

Lloyd Rudolph and Susanne Hoeber Rudolph, in their recent work *Postmodern Gandhi* (2006), have discussed Gandhi's postmodernism at length. They particularly refer to the *Hind Swaraj* written by Gandhi when he was on shipboard after three intense and challenging months in London, at the Centre of the British Empire. In *Hind Swaraj*, Gandhi used the concept of *swaraj* or self-rule in a variety of postmodern ways. Rudolph and Rudolph write:

> One way was the critique of modern formal organization such as corporate and state bureaucracies, entities that Max Weber said reduced humans to cogs in the bureaucratic machinery. Gandhi was anti-'Fordist' well before the academy invented its negative analysis of mass production and mass consumption. As we put it, he was for production by the masses and against mass production, that is, production on assembly lines. Gandhi saw early on that assembly line production made workers slaves rather than masters of the machine and that the endless multiplication of wants made consumers slaves rather than masters of their desires.

There was serious thinking about the social form of village in India. Nehru planned to develop India on industrial plane. Gandhi did not agree to it. He was very clear that villages should be made self-reliant. The differences between Gandhi and Nehru came to the surface in October and November, 1947. Gandhi wrote to Nehru that the essence of what he said in *Hind Swaraj* is "that the things required for human life must be individually controlled by every person .... 'You will not understand me,' he continued, 'if you think that I am talking about the villages of today.' 'My villages ... exist in my imagination.' As if to warn Nehru against privileging or naturalizing his vision of a modern industrial India, he continued with the remark that 'After all, every person lives in the world of his imagination'."

"The villager in this imagined village," Gandhi continued, "will not be apathetic .... He will lead his life like an animal in a squalid dark scrum. Men and women will live freely and be prepared to face the whole world .... No one will live indolently or luxuriously.' The village of his imagination would be self-reliant, not self-sufficient.' I can think of many things which will have to be produced on a large scale. May be there will be railways, so also post and telegraph. What it will have and what it will not, I do not know, nor do I care. If I can maintain its essence, the rest will mean free facility to come and settle". Gandhi's imagined village was to be voluntary, another of his experiments with truth. He ended his letter to Nehru by suggesting that they find time to sort out the issues between them.

The structure of Indian village was discussed by our national leaders all through the long period of freedom struggle. When the draft of Constitution was framed, it was referred to Gandhi for his comments. It is said that Gandhi tore off the draft and said that it was meaningless for it did not mention anything about Village Panchayats. The Constituent Assembly took Gandhi's suggestions seriously and made an effective space for Village Panchayats.

The basic questions which agitates India today are: Should our villages be made modern? Should we have industrialization and urbanization in villages? The questions are relevant. The social form of village – traditional or modern – is the basic issue which our sociologists should address. It should also be mentioned that the government policies swing between industrialization and self-reliance in the race of modernization. When the Community Development Programme (CDP) was introduced in 1950, it was declared that India's villages would be made self-reliant. They should be guided to stand on their own legs. They should be developed in a way that they are able to meet their own needs. But self-reliance does not mean self-sufficiency. There are many things which should be brought from outside the village. The development programmes ended with the hope that a nexus should be established between villages and towns.

The national context which surrounds our villages is that the villages have some structural linkages which should be identified and encouraged. This is precisely the message of village-centred development activities. For one thing we are certain: we cannot leave our villages isolated. There cannot be two cultures for one country. The villagers need to be given all facilities so that they can come up at par with other sectors of the society.

## Village Studies

Sociologists have made elaborate studies of villages. One very specific aspect of village is its unity. It is the caste and kinship which keep village unity at territorial level. The territory consists of kinship relations. Normally, marriages are arranged within the specified territory. The territory has co-territories with its own dialect and customs and rituals. Henry Orenstein (*Gaon: Conflict and Cohesion in an Indian Village*, 1965) observed that as territories are cohesive units, the village community still continues to exist. The sense of village identity on many occasions cuts across caste loyalties which usually divide a village. In Gaon, there are important village level rituals in which people as a whole cooperate and participate; for example, when the Gaon wrestlers compete with wrestlers from other villages (in Gaon these wrestlers are untouchables), Rajputs of the village cheer the wrestlers of their own village, even when opponents were Rajputs. Orenstein also mentions that a number of factors, such as neighbourhood, friendship and contiguity of land, brought members of different castes together and united them into a cohesive group.

This is not to say that divisive factors connected with caste do not operate. Orenstein concludes the village unity as under:

> Cohesion is an inclusive phenomenon, but some evidence can be given for its existence. Village identification was not entirely unconscious, at times, concern for the village and for harmonious relations within it was verbalized. One instance of this was given in connection with the Maratha-Rajput conflict on *Hanuman Jayanti*, when a Maratha maligned his own caste in order to prevent an open fight, and Rajputs spoke of the need not to 'hurt the village'. People who professed 'radical' sentiments sometimes said that they could not all of their beliefs, because, they explained, they must live with and get along with their neighbours as smoothly as possible. This kind of statement was not frequent, but it was heard more often in connection with caste. This does not mean that village had more solidarity than it could have through caste. On the contrary, the fact that the need for cooperation was verbalized, might indicate a different kind of solidarity. It is 'organic' rather than mechanical, to use Durkheim's term.

One very important specialty of our villages is the 'Jajmani' system. It is known by different names – *Jajmani* in north India; *Baluta* in Orenstein's Gaon village; *Aya* in K. Ishwaran's study of Mysore. They are all regional variations. It is the system by which economic and ritual mutuality and interdependence of castes bind the villagers together. This binding indicates the solidarity of the villages. Sometimes jajmani relations cover more than one village. For instance, there are villages which do not have a Chamar, a potter or a barber. In this case, a barber may extend his services to the neighbourhood villages.

Yogendra Singh argues that *jajmani* system is not always reciprocal:

> Dominant castes swing the balance of power in their favour in which relationships exist in many villages in India. The institutional changes introduced through land reforms, community development programmes, panchayat elections and national elections have considerably changed the structure of community cohesion and its pattern of inter-group relationship and power structure. But none of these factors have completely eroded the sense of village identity nor do they portend to do so in future.

Yet another factor which has disturbed the jajmani systems all over India's villages is the introduction of cash economy. Now, exchange transactions are carried out on the basis of cash. And, when there is imbalance in the prices of material and services, the jajmani system falls into crisis. The practice of jajmani in advanced villages has almost gone.

Villages are passing through the sieve of large and vital forces of transformation. Development has been one such force. Administration has made many inroads in the structure of villages. School teacher, Gram Sevak, Patwari and development officers have all begun to enter the web of village relationships. Perhaps, one of the major changes has been experienced in the realm of land relations. The intermediaries between the owner of the land and the cultivators have been legally removed. There are now no Zamindars. Land reform in villages has been introduced through (i) abolition of intermediaries; (ii) tenancy reforms; (iii) ceiling on land holdings and redistribution of land; (iv) consolidation of holdings and prevention of holdings from deteriorating to uneconomic size; (v) emphasis on development of cooperative farming; and (vi) religio-economic movement for gift of surplus land by the rich to the poor as *bhoodan*. These measures have been implemented differently in different stages and both have created some uniform sociological consequences.

Reform movements have also brought about changes in the village power structure. There are a large number of village studies which show that the development programmes have brought about tremendous changes in the pattern of relationship. For instance, as Orestein reports, in his village of study, informal leaders are more effective than formal leaders. In the study of Morsali village, in Bangalore district, development programmes have created factionalism. In this village, growth of factions is related with introduction of government sponsored reforms and with interference of government, new factional leaders have gained additional economic autonomy by moving away from subsistence farming to cash crop farming which releases them from dependence upon traditional free cooperative labour as the new farming is done through hired labourers and with the help of outside employees. These processes have given the factional leaders an edge over the traditional leaders, where the only sanction was to manipulate the free, cooperative supply of labour in the case of refusal to comply with their decisions.

Yogendra Singh has critically examined the village studies conducted by sociologists in terms of power and leadership. He has his own perspective which we shall have opportunity to comment upon later. He sums up the village studies as below:

> Now, we have a fairly wider perspective on leadership and power structure of villages in India. Its structure seems still to be dominated by rich and upper caste groups but there is a tendency towards recruitment of younger members to the leadership role in villages and a majority of leaders are literate. An important source to gain leadership in the village and have dominance over its affairs is the landed property; the landed rich are also better educated and have better contacts with the outside world.

Yogendra Singh argues that modernization and sanskritization have brought changes in the village structure. Sanskritization has helped the lower castes to improve their cultural and social status. They are now looked upon as people free from non-vegetarianism and liquor drinking. Their polluted occupations and habits are no more in vogue. The opportunities of development and economic growth, as in the case of Boad and Ganjam distillers of Bailey's Bisipare, have made lower castes improve economically. Though the village studies bring out varying findings, they have similar generalizations. For instance, most of the benefits of development and progress have generally gone to the upper castes and classes in the village. However, the critics of changes in a functional fashion conclude that "changes in rural structure are more adjustive than substantive in significance". Traditionally, influential groups still continue to wield influence and power. Caste privileges still continue to coincide with privileged class status.

## Class in Villages

One very important dimension of Indian society is its class structure. Caste and class comprise to make social stratification. In village social stratification much space has been devoted to the caste. As a matter of fact, class has a recent emergence in villages. Indian village has been described as a habitation of poor and indebted people. The status of an individual in this community is determined by caste. With the permanent land settlements during the British period, land became a decisive factor in the determination of a villager's status. More land means higher status. A queer situation has emerged in villages where caste and class have combined together. For instance, there may be high-castes in a village having larger portions of land. These castes also constitute higher class; and there may be castes that occupy lower status in the caste hierarchy but have larger land holdings. The Patidars of Gujarat are not recognized as higher caste but they have bigger land holdings. In such situations, it is difficult to determine the class or group.

It is certain that class has its origin in property, health, power and prestige. It is precisely Max Weber's mode of stratification. India's social stratification has been overworked. Yogendra Singh, Andre Beteille, Louis Dumont, A.R. Desai, K.L. Sharma and Dipankar Gupta have contributed immensely to the literature pertaining to stratification. But, in the realm of stratification, most of the space used by the sociologists, is occupied by caste. Stratification for these sociologists generally means caste stratification in villages. A strange combination has emerged in Indian sociology. Caste, class, and village are the favourite trinity of studying Indian society. Study of industrial sociology is exceptional. Similar exception is that of class in tribal society. Anthropologists report that with the coming of village development programmes, reservation in services and public institutions, entrepreneurship, education have created classes among the tribals. Five decades have passed and the tribal class system still remains unstudied. The tribal stratification was rudimentary. They had no property, scarce land resources, and what is worse, their forest resource was robbed away by government, its contractors and Hindu caste peasants. But this rudimentary situation is now over. There are rich and middle class tribals and in scheduled areas they are celebrities. Despite the non-availability of research material, we restrict our analysis to whatever little we have in our possession.

Andre Beteille (*Caste, Class and Power*, 1919) has tried to identify classes in his village study of Shivpuram. For Andre, a peasant is one who ploughs his land and where his family members work. Peasantry depends on ecological factors. Technology plays an important part in agriculture. Land distribution, its management and land control are determining factors of village land. In his later work (*Studies in Agrarian Social Structure*, 1974), Andre has analyzed agrarian society from the perspective of status, wealth and power. After considering all the studies on the status of class in villages of India, it could be said that there are five classes of peasants: (1) cash-tenants; (2) share-cash tenant; (3) crop-share tenant; (4) croppers, and (5) other tenants.

The above classification of peasants is based on the mode of agriculture. The Marxist sociologist, A.R. Desai (*Social Background of Indian Nationalism*) categorizes peasants on the basis of land owning: (1) upper class land owners; (2) middle class land owners; and (3) lower class small farmers. Jan Breman, who has worked in Bardoli, Palsana and Valod of Surat district (Gujarat), puts the peasants in three categories: (1) marginal small farmers; (2) middle farmers; and (3) large farmers.

Actually, these studies relate to agrarian classes based on land ownership. No concern is shown for the classes in the villages. Nor these studies refer to class (land owning) with reference to caste. In a broader way, it could be said that land reforms have improved the class status of villagers. In the village, the persons who do not have any land, that is, those who are landless, work as daily wage earners in the fields of big farmers. The class of landless peasants is at the bottom of social stratification. And, those who own larger patches of land belong to higher class.

While discussing the village class structure, it could be said that the village development programmes have largely gone in favour of higher classes. The marginal classes of weaker sections have all been left high and dry. The studies indicate that the village inequality has increased with the introduction of development programmes. Besides development programmes – both community and individual beneficiary programmes – green revolution has also proved to be another source of heightening inequality.

Green revolution came to India in 1966-67. It means introduction of high yielding varieties (HYVs) in agriculture. Improved breed of seeds, improved chemical manure and improved animal husbandry increased the farm production. This movement was largely accepted by progressive and big land owning class of peasants. The infrastructure in the village improved considerably, electric power came to the village, market got enlarged. Frankel Francine, who has analyzed the impact of green revolution on the peasantry, says that it has created new classes. The agriculture became capitalistic and the economic distance between the big farmer and small farmer increased substantively. However, it has changed the economic face of the states, notably Punjab, Haryana, Gujarat, Maharashtra and Andhra Pradesh.

Yogendra Singh has made a penetrating study of the status of class in villages. His finding is that political power is not closely tied to ownership of land as it was in the past. New bases of power have emerged which are to some extent independent of both caste and class. Perhaps, the most important among these is the strength of numerical support.

One very important finding of Yogendra Singh, which has far-reaching consequences, is that

> ....despite the fact that major changes in the system of social stratification have not been widespread, marginal changes in this system have been frequent. This specially refers to the occupational diversification, migration to urban areas and towns and rationalization of agriculture.

Agricultural output has increased, village infrastructure has improved and the lifestyle of people has gone up. Modernity has created for itself space successfully in India's villages. But it is not without its tensions. There is a deep contest to corner as such benefits of development as possible among the higher castes and classes. The inter-village rivalry has also increased. It has disturbed the regional cohesion. But such tensions are normal in any social system. In course of time these are resolved.

## Modern and Postmodern Perspectives on Caste and Village Community

In the present study, we have analyzed Indian society from the perspectives of modernity and postmodernity. The functional ideology of caste and village, which is available to us, presents these institutions as conservative and sterile. Time and again, we are told that caste has not changed. Whatever changes we get in caste system are false. The order of the caste, i.e., the hierarchy, remains unchanged. The villages have become modern; they are secular and democratic. But, despite change, they sentimentally and traditionally remain conservative. Modernization has failed to replace new traditions in place of the old value system. For functionalists, the basic change rests on culture change. And, culture for this purpose consists of values. Beliefs in the transmigration of soul, moral duties and attitudes towards marginal people remain the same. An untouchable may become a minister in the government, he may occupy the chair of professor in a University, but he is traditionally considered as an untouchable. Values determine the status of a person. The impact of achievement is temporal, a short-lived phenomenon. Concluding his analysis of Indian society with inference to the impact of modernization, Yogendra Singh observes:

> Theoretically, if tradition in Indian context consists of the values of hierarchy, holism, continuity and transience, modernity also has certain values. Max Weber argues that individualism, rationality and bureaucracy are the prime contents of modernity. For him, the modern society is rational, democratic, legal and bureaucratic. Constitutionally speaking, the Indian society is democratic and secular. In this context, let us apply the perspective of modernity in the analysis of caste and village community.

Sociology, as any social science, studies the problems of society. If it does not address the societal problems, it is not worth its salt. A country of the kind that India is which has limited resources, cannot afford its social scientists to take up armchair researches which are not concerned with the national needs. If our sociologists define their problems with reference to foreign sociologists, say Robert Radfield or Louis Dumont, they are not rational in their choice of research.

To begin with, let us take caste for our perspectives on modernity and postmodernity. Right from the middle of 19th century, Max Muller and H.H. Risely remarked that caste was a divisive institution and in no case it works for the cohesion of the society. By studying caste along with other ethnic institutions we succeeded to divide the country creating thereby Pakistan. It was a great historical lesson which promoted our constitutional makers to keep caste away from any political-legal consideration. State is constitutionally and legally immune from caste.

The sociologists took to the study of caste at village level. They came out with the finding that caste system is very much in vogue, it still has stronghold on the conservative society, and of course, caste considerations fetch votes handsomely. It also works as a political force. Modern perspective would look at this data in a different way.

Caste is a social group organized on the principle of rationality and bureaucracy. It has its own constitution, sanctions and norms. The caste members are expected to observe its norms and values. Customs of castes are for achieving solidarity and cohesion. The caste members share a common pattern of life, dietary habits and festivals. There are elections to caste associations. In all respects the caste is modern and it maintains its social order.

There is democracy in the caste. Each member is free to exercise his power to vote. If a caste member contests elections, another member is free to enter into the fray against him. Political affiliation is free for all members. There are no restriction. Sociological data are interpreted in term of the politicization of caste. It is not like that. Caste, at its best, is a political interest group. One very important perspective of caste is that it is a political competitor in the race for capital gain. There are lower castes who have amassed enough wealth. Education is no more restricted for them. No social disabilities are attached to caste?

Hierarchy is no problem. A caste has its own merit. Those who volunteer to violate the caste rules, go without punishment. Jan Breman argues that the tribals of Bardoli do not claim a position in the territorial caste hierarchy. They are interested in maintaining their tribal identity. They could be at least, called as constituting tribal castes. When the lower castes imitate the values and beliefs of higher castes, it is not sanskritization; it is the effort of a particular caste, that is, a group, to adapt to modern ways of life. Sanskritization is a misnomer. In the regional society, if education, technology, vegetarianism and teetotalism are considered to be status giving, the lower castes tend to adopt these. It is not imitation of higher castes, it is imitation of the values of castes which are considered to be progressive. It is a mistaken assumption that whatever change comes in society, comes only through caste system.

The sociologists must not forget that in the present social context of the country, it is not holism or collectivity that works. It is the individual who is considered important. Identity of individual is considered by the state, the institutions and the democratic associations. At best, a caste is identified at the local level or in some cases at territorial level. Beyond that caste system is dead.

In a democratic and modern society, the changing structure of caste is irrelevant. Most of the caste studies talk about the changing structure of caste. This has never been the problem of the Indian society nor of the caste itself. It is not the dominant caste which runs the village. Village is run by the groups who wield power. If we look at the caste system from the perspective of modernity, it will immediately bring out the secular nature of our society. Indian sociologists have an obsession with caste and tradition. Thus, the whole society is misunderstood by one and all.

We have argued elsewhere that sometimes modernity and postmodernity are used interchangeably. They are almost synonymous. In the case of caste studies, modernity and postmodernity go together. Postmodernity is against any kind of authoritarianism. Caste, as we find today, does not wield any authority. Its members openly violate the caste norms. Caste commensality, endogamy, traditional occupations and rules of food choices are never taken seriously. For all purposes, the caste today exists only as an ethnic group. Its identity is through ethnicity. However, the caste ethnicity too exists only in its formal form.

When we define caste as any other modern group, we are dragged into a difficulty. And that relates to birth. Membership of caste is by birth. It is not voluntary. Race, likewise, is determined by birth. Long back, Risely defined caste as a racial group. But race is a valid biological concept. So is the caste. But quite like race, caste also has its structural, cultural and value implications. When we discuss caste in terms of the perspectives of modernity, we would refrain from using its biological connotation. A birth is only biological, but ethnicity is the characteristic of caste. Caste politics, caste identity, caste behaviour are all structural and cultural dimensions of the caste system. Biology has nothing to do with the caste behaviour. And, modernity, in this way, underlines birth as the membership criterion of caste. In the new perspectives of modernity and postmodernity, caste in contemporary India is not a biological concept, nor is it hierarchical and religious. It is secular, democratic, capitalistic, working excellently as a pressure group.

This brings us to evaluate the studies of village communities on the perspectives of modernity and postmodernity. The national problem, as indicated by Gandhi and Nehru, with the village community, was to provide self-reliance to these people. The idea was to make the villagers independent for meeting their basic needs. Nehru, however, was of the opinion that villagers need to be modernized. This crucial issue was never raised in the village studies. They raised the problem of village unity and solidarity and in support of their findings they referred to sociological thinkers, particularly Emile Durkheim, who talked of organic solidarity and mechanical solidarity, though it would give academic legitimacy to this interpretation. Secondly, these studies took up the issue of 'jajmani' to stress the point that there has been inter-caste unity in the village. The question of dominant caste has also been taken up. On the whole, the village studies are irrelevant so far as our genuine problems are concerned. The studies make it their central point to move round caste. For them caste and village are synonymous. Who will tell that when the problem of the struggle for independence became immense in the country, it was not caste but the village which participated in the struggle. In all village studies, caste, therefore, was at the centre of analysis.

We do not have book-length studies to inform us about the status of villages when modernity was the idiom of the people. The social or political movements, which emerged in the 30s and the 80s against the high-caste Hindus, were in fact agrarian movements. These movements were against the large land holding higher castes. These castes in the wake of modernization deprived the lower castes of their small patches of lands. Admittedly, the higher castes along with affluent classes enriched themselves through benefits of modernity.

Postmodernity, that is, difference or differentiation, has been the ideological choice of the lower caste tribals belonging to the BPL (below poverty line) categories. They are landless people. Postmodernity is pragmatic, it is down-to-the-earth, that is, realistic. Derrida has used the term 'deconstruction' to clarify the meaning of difference. The village studies do not take into consideration the status of disadvantaged people. Modernity has left these people in a 'capsule society' where there is nobody to take care of them. Postmodernity, in the realm of village studies, considers modernity to be its first-rate enemy. Modernity, it may be reiterated, has made a composite group of higher castes, higher class and creamy layer of lower castes. All the sociologists claim that they study land problems of the agrarian society. P.C. Joshi talks about land reforms in India. But land reforms for whom? Obviously, the reforms are for the composite group.

But, the postmodernity has a tougher time. The lower castes are marching towards composite modern group in a big way. And, there seems no possibility to meet the challenges of modernity in near future. We referred to social movements, which were fragments in the past, have now become fewer and fewer, almost negligible. The trade unions, agrarian revolts, student unrest and movements of any genre are an exception. There are signs of modernity getting increasingly stronger. And, the intensification of modernity means wider gap between the higher and the lower groups. It appears that the future of higher-ups in Indian society is brighter and the lower-ups will have to wait for a brighter future. Their conditions will be bleak for sometime to come.

# IX

## India's Culture: Modernity and Postmodernity

India as a nation or a society has its own culture. It has evolved through centuries. It has passed through a chequered history. It is the composite form of all the variations of culture that we have in the country. Indian society is plural; it has several ethnicities, thousands of castes; languages and dialects. It is multi-ethnic; multi-regional. K.S. Singh has identified 91 culture areas in the country. How shall we define the national culture of India? One very essential characteristic of culture is that it is shared by all the citizens. And, above all, it is learned.

Social anthropologists all over the world have been credited to study simple societies, micro-structures and tribal habitations. Sociologists, on the other hand, have a tradition to study macro-communities, urban and industrial centres. They show their concern for complex organization. Culture in India has been studied at micro level. We do not have any book-length study on national culture carried out by an anthropologist or sociologist. It is on the strength of micro-studies that we can construct some notion or idea about India's culture.

It must be admitted that sociologists are extravagantly fond of the use of culture. For them social and cultural are synonymous terms. These are used interchangeably. Anthropologists have defined culture in a very vague term. For instance, E.B. Tylor's definition of culture is broad than others put forth by both anthropologists and sociologists. For Tylor, anything which is learned as a member of a group is culture. And, there is no limit to learning. Anything or everything from society – a robbery or a sacrifice – can be a subject of learning. The definition is highly vague. It includes all the things which are found between the open sky and the wide earth. There are also some sociologists who have tried to identify the essential characteristics of culture.

Haralambos and Holborn (*Sociology: Themes and Perspectives*, 2000) have given a comprehensive interpretation of culture, referring to Ralph Linton and Clyde Kluckhon:

> Ralph Linton states that "the culture of a society is the way of life of its members, the collection of ideas and habits which they learn, share and transmit from generation to generation". In Clyde Kluckhon's elegant phrase, culture is a 'design for living' held by members of a particular society. Since humans have no instincts to direct their actions, their behaviour must be based on guidelines that are learned effectively; these guidelines must be shared by its members. Without a shared culture, members of society would be unable to communicate and cooperate, and confusion and disorder would result. Culture therefore has two essential qualities: first, it is learned; second, it is shared. Without it there would be no human society.

The definition is precise. When we talk about India's culture, we are certain about two things: it must have sharing of the plural masses of people. The multi-ethnicities, despite having their own culture identity, should have a sense of sharing with the national culture. Thus, two varieties of culture would go simultaneously: ethnicity's own culture and the national culture. For instance, the members of a Brahmin caste would follow the cultural norms of their own caste – they would observe vegetarianism, take daily bath, observe *vratas* and indulge in scriptures. This is all for their caste ethnicity. But, at the same time, they have to share with the national culture which consists of democracy, secularism and scientific ethics. Sharing by the people therefore is essential.

The culture does not develop overnight. It is evolutionary. It has a history. It goes with the process of learning and de-learning.

## Culture and Tradition

Culture and tradition are used interchangably in Indian sociology. Culture is learned, it is shared, whereas tradition is the handing over of beliefs and values from one generation to another. Indian sociologists have worked much on tradition. For instance, Milton Singer refers to India as a traditional society. By tradition, he means Hindu traditions. Yogendra Singh analyzes the impact of modernity on India's traditions. Tradition, according to him, is organized on the themes of hierarchy, holism, continuity and transcendence. What Yogendra Singh calls traditions are actually Hindu traditions? Thus, in the analysis of culture or tradition, the reference invariably is made to Hindu culture and tradition. Does it mean that India's culture is essentially Hindu culture? It would be our mistaken belief if we look at India's culture in the postmodern perspective.

Postmodernity has much to do with what is called popular culture. The Gujarat society has the popular culture of *Dandiya* dance. It is observed during the *Navaratras.* The dance, also called *Garba*, is participated by the mass of people without any caste or class barrier. It is postmodernity. Postmodernity is very closer to aligned with popular culture. John Storey ('Postmodernism and Popular Culture', in *Postmodernism*, ed. by Stuart Sim, 2005) writes:

> Most contributors to the debate on postmodernism agree that whatever else it is or might be, postmodernism has something to do with the development of popular culture in the late twentieth century in the advanced capitalist democracies of the west. That is, whether postmodernism is seen as a new historical moment, a new sensibility or a new cultural style, popular culture is cited as a terrain on which these changes can be most readily found.

The relationship between popular culture and postmodernity would be taken up after we have sorted out the meaning of culture in the context of Indian society. Tylor's definition would not work here. For us, the culture which we have inherited has passed through a long history. We have been arguing that Indian culture is essentially evolutionary.

**History of India's Culture**

To begin with, it must be said that the cultural style of India or its sensibility was that of elites. The higher castes, elites, the Rajas and Maharajas were the torch bearers of culture. The subalterns were condemned of having no culture. But, before we comment on the culture of the higher groups, let us look at its evolution and meaning.

People define culture in a rudimentary way. The sense, in which the term is most frequently used, is good taste and refined manners. But it is also used for material embodiments of good taste and refinement. So, we often refer to the buildings, gardens and paintings of the Mughal period as relics of the Mughal culture. Sometimes, collective institutions, codes and systems are also known as cultural objects. So, the political and educational systems of the Greeks and the legal code of the Romans are often regarded among the most important aspects of their respective culture. And lastly, the term culture has sometimes a still more general and abstract connotation – a system of ultimate ends or norms of life. When people make the disputable assertion that the eastern culture is more spiritual than the western, they use the term in its most general and abstract sense. Without entering into any social science technicalities, the simplest definition of culture is what people call culture. But, for higher-level interpretation, such a simplistic definition of culture would not work.

Culture is a mode of living. And, our living is physical and mental or spiritual. All of us have a physical life – bone and flesh. But we have also external senses. Thoughts and feelings constitute our mental existence. "Those ideas and beliefs, principles which are not confined to a single individual but are shared by others, those collective institutions which are handed down from generation to generation as religion, mortality, law, art, state cannot be said to have a subjective or transitory existence but should be credited with a more permanent objective entity which could be called objective mental existence. A fourth mode of ideal existence could be ascribed to those norms or standards of perfection, those ultimate moral values, by which we judge every object, action, every principle of life – even life itself. The fifth and the highest mode is that of absolute existence which religion knows as God.

Of these the one which interests us here as bearing upon the definition of culture, is ideal existence which we will examine a little more closely."

We have had a preliminary discussion on the definition of culture. S. Abid Hussain (*The National Culture of India*, 1956) has made an attempt to define culture in India's context of philosophy and history. He writes:

> Culture is a sense of ultimate values possessed by a particular society as expressed in its collective institutions, by its individual members in their dispositions, feelings attitudes and manners as well as in significant forms which they give to material objects.

Religion in its wider (Indian) context coincides with, and goes beyond, culture, and in its narrower sense, forms an important part of it. Civilization is sometimes used as just another word for culture but generally in the sense of a higher order of culture. As a matter of fact, civilization is that stage in the cultural development of a people when they begin to live in large habitations called cities, which represent a higher level of material life or a higher standards of living. But, a higher standard of material life has cultural content only when it is imbued with, or serves as a means of attaining some ultimate moral values, or even when it is devoid of any such values, it will prove to be an obstacle to cultural progress. So, civilization is not always an ally but sometimes an enemy too of culture.

It is the culture which keeps a nation united. Geographical units and economic viability hold a society together. Language is also a powerful force to keep the people united. The national culture that maintains us, keeps us moving, is a product of traditions. The evolution of Indian culture goes through different stages of history. It is a composite structure which starts from Indus Valley Civilization to the period after the promulgation of Indian Constitution. The year 1950, when the Constitution came into being, forms the watershed for the final form of India's national culture. We would now look at the formative periods of India's culture.

## Vedic Hindu Culture

What we call as Indian culture today was in fact Vedic Hindu culture, which came into being as a result of the interplay of the Vedic Aryan and pre-Aryan cultures. Indus Valley Civilization was our first cradle of culture. It was Aryan culture which had its sway in north-west of India. Simultaneously, there was development of Dravidian in South India. Actually, there were two streams of culture – Aryan and Dravidian. At a later stage of history, both these streams had interactions resulting in the birth of first national culture of India.

Aryan culture was not accepted fully as it reached the people. The Brahmins exercised their dominance and Buddhism emerged as a new force to combat. It was a new kind of national culture. Although Buddhism had a deep influence over Indian mind, the culture based on it did not last as the national culture for any length of time. Its decay was followed by the rise of a new Hindu culture which again was the result of harmonizing many conflicting tendencies in the cultural life of the country. To distinguish it from the earlier Vedic Hindu culture, it may be called the Puranic culture. At the end of the ancient period, long before the advent of the Muslims, the cultural life in India had again become disorganized. But, after the establishment of the Delhi Sultanate, the process of assimilation and fusion started afresh and by the time the Mughal period commenced the great edifice of a Hindu-Muslim culture – the Hindustani culture – had been erected.

## Hindustani Culture

Akbar was the first Mughal emperor who sought to develop a culture in India which could be called Hindustani. Abul Fazal, who was Akbar's friend, philosopher and guide, wrote in his *Ain-e-Akbari:*

> The king should be above all religious differences and should see that religious considerations should not come in the way of the duty which he owes to every class and every community. Under his all-embracing care everyone should find peace and happiness so that the benefits conferred by the shadow of God are universal.

Akbar adopted a policy which did not discriminate among individuals on the basis of caste and creed. He abolished the pilgrim tax and the 'jizya' in 1563. He thus put an end to distinction between the Hindu and Muslim subjects. But even more significant was the edict issued in 1564 that no resident of India, whatever his caste or creed, should be made a slave. Describing Akbar's secular practices as emperor of India, S. Abid Hussain (*The National Culture of India*, 1956) observes:

> Other important traditions of the old Indian state were revived by the Mughal state under Akbar. Public charity and moral reform, which the Delhi Sultanate had handled only perfunctorily in the limited field of Muslim society, were now carried on systematically and their scope extended to cover all citizens without distinctions. Hindu Pundits and Sadhus were supported by the state more or less like Muslim Ulemas and Figaras (learned men and ascetics) and in many cases mandirs were given grants like masjids by Mughal emperors. Akbar imposed restriction on drinking, gambling and prostitution equally on all sections of the people. At the risk of being accused of interference with religion he even put down some specifically Hindu customs like *sati* (the burning alive of widows).

A national culture is held together by a common language. It was during the Mughal period that Persian mixed with Hindi spoken in and around Delhi had produced a lingua franca known as Hindavi, Hindi or Hindustani, which later on came to be called Urdu. This was now the general medium of interaction between Hindus and Muslims but had yet not acquired the status of a literary language except in the Deccan. In northern India Persian had been the court language of literary expression and conversation among the Muslims. Hindus in government service had started learning Persian during the reign of Sikandar Lodi but, as state accounts were still kept in Hindi, it was not possible for Hindu employees to learn Persian.

Akbar tried to bring Hindus and Muslims together through language. Though Persian was the state language, the general interaction was through Persian as local dialect. He opened schools in which Hindu and Muslim children were taught together through the medium of Persian. These schools imparted education in a variety of subjects such as Persian literature, arithmetic, book-keeping, office work, agriculture, geometry, astrology and history. The educational policy of Akbar was such that it promoted higher cultural understanding between the two communities. Hindu and Muslim scholars were encouraged to translate standard works from Sanskrit to Persian and also to write books on the past and contemporary history.

It must be mentioned that the culture which developed during the Mughal period was very rich in literature, architecture and music. The regional dialects also became rich during the period. Avadhi had produced Malik Mohammad Jayasi, Tulsidas and other such projects. A *sufi* school of poets made valuable contributions to integrate Hindus and Muslims. Abdul Rahim Khan Khanan, Birbal, Ras Khan, Bihari, Keshav Das and a few other poets of Hindi contributed substantially to the fund of knowledge.

Some of the Mughal emperors such as Babur and Humayun had brought with them a purely Persian taste in architecture as well as Persian architects. A few buildings of their times are extant, e.g., the mosques at Panipat and Sambhal built by Babur and that of Fatehabad of Isfahan in Persia. So are the best architectural achievements of Akbar's early reign such as Humayun's tomb in Delhi, designed by the Persian architect Mirza Inayatulla. But, later on, Akbar attempted in this field, as in the political and intellectual fields, a synthesis of the Turko-Persian Muslim conceptions with the Hindu Indian and thus created the graceful Mughal style, pleasing to the eye and restful to the mind. The general design of the Jama Masjid in Fatehpur Sikri is taken from that in Isfahan, etc., imposing lofty gate is characteristic of the classical simplicity of medieval Persia. But its domes reveal the influence of the Jain style and so do the domes of the mosques in Mount Abu.

Mughal architecture was carried to its height during the reign of Shahjahan. He brought architects from Persia and built Taj Mahal. The construction of Taj Mahal exhibits a massive use of marble. The handling of marble requires a delicate expertise. Marble is a soft and fine stone which requires great care, skill and delicacy. Taj Mahal, in fact, weakened the indigenous Hindu style.

During the Mughal period painting and art reached to their zenith. There were some strides also in the field of music. A perfect harmony of taste and sentiment between Hindus and Muslims had already developed during the period of the Delhi Sultanate at the courts of the smaller independent states and the monasteries of the Sufis. The Mughal period influenced the Hindu way of life and culture so intimately that there emerged a culture which combined both Hindu and Muslim ethos of life. Vedic culture had to give away many of its characteristics, and the Muslims its Persian and Arabian cultures. Surely, a new Indian culture, which is called Hindustani, was emerging. It is in this period that Urdu and Hindi developed as link languages and created an edifice for Hindustani culture.

## English or Western Culture in India

Though the British had established their political supremacy in India in the first half of the nineteenth century, the western culture began to influence Indian people with the coming of technology represented by railways, printing machine, telegraph, etc. But, intellectually, the British culture was not immediately acceptable to Indians. Lord MaCaulay introduced English as the medium of instruction but the Indian higher classes did not take it as a matter of status. Indian society, on the other hand, influenced the British. They developed respect for the refinement, culture and scholarship of Indian gentlemen, especially the Brahmins and the Muslims. The reality is that the Englishmen in those days did not try to impose their culture on Indians but were to some extent themselves influenced by Indian culture.

The year 1857 when the sepoy mutiny witnessed a watershed, the Britishers came to realize that the Indian ethnography had its own strength and it should be thoroughly probed. The English missionaries, who worked among the tribals, felt that there was illiteracy and general backwardness all through the country. When the new generation of English civil servants came to India, they were imbibed with the notion of their cultural superiority. They perceived that they were dealing with a depressed lot whom it was their sacred duty to uplift them through western education and culture. They realized that none but the British could grapple with the political chaos in India and establish peace and order; that the medieval Indian culture was out of date and could not meet the economic, political and intellectual demands of the modern age; and that India had to assimilate something of the modern western culture which had helped its rulers to reach their present prosperity and power.

The colonial English culture was built round the state, but it was a peculiar kind of state which India had never known in its history. India had seen the Hindu religious state, the Buddhist moral state and Mughal cultural state which had more or less the same constitutional nature – sovereignty vested in a single individual, the Raja or king, and all people without distinction having the same political status as his subjects. The pivot of social and cultural life used to be royal court. In addition to executive, judicial and legislative functions, the king also had manifold cultural functions like social reform, moral censorship, dispension of charities, patronage of learning arts and crafts, and even the laying down of fashions in dress and manners. The central gravity of the state, even during the reign of the Muslim kings, was inside the country. But, the state which the British set up was in every way different from the traditional Indian state. As a matter of fact, it was not a state at all but a subordinate administration without sovereign power. Sovereignty was vested in the king. Emperor, which had delegated most its authority to the Viceroy, discharged the functions of government with the help of the civil service. This service was for a long time exclusively composed of foreigners who considered themselves socially and culturally superior to the natives and expressed this superiority in every possible way so that the very word 'native' came to be used as a term of contempt.

Looking to the nature of state in colonial rule, it was not possible for the British power to contribute anything to Indian culture. But it gave India peace and order and, what was still more valuable and significant for our future political and cultural development, a new concept of individual and national freedom and a preliminary training in the democratic technique of public life.

English education promoted some Indians to get their education abroad. They read English works and developed a sense for western culture. English works carried much of the first-hand knowledge generated in the west. This has encouraged Indians to fight for their freedom. Our struggle for freedom owes much to the western impact of culture. The impact of western culture on Indian society can be summed up as under:

(1) English language was accepted by higher classes, elites, leaders, Jagirdars and Zamindars. Their children went outside India for higher learning. And, even inside the country, they took admission to English public schools.
(2) Foreign education gave wider exposure to Indians.
(3) Democracy, industrialism, urbanization and technology entered India as a new way of life.
(4) A secular culture developed among the masses. There was also an idea of de-linking religion from the state.
(5) Freedom struggle gave a new national consciousness to the ordinary people. India before independence was not a nation. All India Congress Committee, in its various annual conferences, passed the resolution that when India will get freedom it will build it into a nation. Before the emergence of independent India, the country had a colonial society dominated by British power. The region outside the British territory was dominated by native rulers. We had thus, two Indias – British India and princely states.
    The Indian culture, which developed during the British rule, had also experience of living in a colonial-feudal rule. If this kind of feudal rule gave technology, English education, access to foreign countries and liberalism, it also aroused the feeling of patriotism. For a nation, it is essential to have an alignment to a territory to which people can show their belongingness. The struggle for independence created a strong feeling to mobilize the masses for the attainment of country's freedom. The slogans raised during the struggle brought plurality of people together.
(6) One very unintended consequence of colonial-feudal rule was the mindset of subordination that the people developed in their way of life. Jagirdar, Zamindar and the heads of caste

associations developed authoritarianism as their design of life. The ordinary people were made to respect and obey the commands of superordinate groups. The subordinate groups were oppressed to such an extent that even today they tend to suffer from sycophancy. It is very common to find such groups of flatterers in bureaucracy and other walks of life.

(7) Muslim leaders were against the new type of English education and put a ban on it. Nor they adopted Hindustani culture (a mix of Hindu and Muslim cultures), evolved during Akbar's time, as it was not based on religion.

(8) One very important impact of western culture is the status elevation of English as a medium of communication. Hindi as a national language was not acceptable to Muslims. Nor did the southern states of Kerala, Tamil Nadu, Karnataka and Andhra Pradesh accepted Hindi as a national language. However, Hindi got approval by the parliament in the Devnagari script. In such a situation, English in the long run is used as a common language of interaction.

(9) The impact of west is observable in a variety of ways, such as economic life, recreation, manners, dietary and food ways.

(10) West has also influenced our social sciences. Several of our sociologists and anthropologists were trained in Britain. Functionalism in India has come through England. And, above all, most of our official anthropologists such as Risley, O' Malley and Blunt were from the British civil services.

### National Culture of India: The Constitutional Watershed

Like any other nation, India, too, has its own culture. Culture is manifest in our national society. We very often refer to Indian culture. We talk about our national mainstream. Nowhere, however, we have defined our culture. Nor have we provided any explanation of our national mainstream. Anthropologists and sociologists are considered to be specialists in the field of culture. At best, the anthropologists could talk about culture of simple societies or micro-structures. M.N. Srinivas discussed at length sanskritization or culturalization of the castes. For him, the customs, beliefs and ideology of the high-caste constitute culture.

Caste in itself is culture for him. It is purity of the high-castes, and pollution of the lower castes.

A stock-taking of the literature on sociology would immediately show that ethnography is the lone achievement of sociology and anthropology in India. Micro-descriptions of culture at the level of caste, kin and village do not help us to make long-term generalizations about culture. It is strange that a discipline like sociology, with all its development, hovers around culture. First, we do not have any full-length analysis of our culture. Second, whatever we have is religion-centred culture which considers Hindu culture as the representative culture of the country. Third, in the name of culture, we have restricted ourselves to the description and analysis of tradition. For instance, Milton Singer describes India as traditional India in which Brahmanic ways of living are considered as India's tradition. M.N. Srinivas, as mentioned earlier, looks at Indian society as caste society. Yogendra Singh analyzes modernity with reference to its traditions, namely, hierarchy, holism, continuity and transcendence. All these approaches are oriented to Hinduism and Hindu traditions. Indian culture as is found today is not Vedic culture. In its phases of evolution, it has adopted cultural elements from Mughals and developed an edifice of a Hindu-Muslim culture known as Hindustani culture. The western culture, that is, the culture of the English, also modified Hindu-Muslim culture.

India is inhabited by a large number of communities. K.S. Singh has enumerated more than four thousand communities. Each community has its culture, ethnicity, history and territory. In such a situation, how do we identify the elements of culture which could be called national culture. It creates chaos. The Hindus have their own culture which is drawn from the Vedas, Puranas and epics. The Muslims draw their cultural heritage from Persia and Arabia and similar are the culture patterns of Sikhs, Buddhists, Jains, Parsis and thousands of other communities. What has happened in India is that the anthropologists argue that the analysis of national culture is beyond the scope of anthropology. They are micro-level people. The sociologists have analyzed culture with particular reference to Hindu traditions.

Our objective in the present study is to analyze social institutions of Indian society from the perspective of modernity and postmodernity. Indian culture constitutes the central theme of our society that we have taken up for elaboration.

The best way to identify India's national culture is to look to its Constitution. The Constitution was promulgated in 1950. It is the cutting point. Earlier culture patterns which have developed from Indus Valley Civilization or Vedic period have become irrelevant in the present context. At best, the earlier patterns of culture have made synthesis with the culture elements given by the Constitution. The promulgation of the Constitution is the watershed in the evolutionary history of culture in India.

**Culture Elements in Indian Constitution**

Indian Constitution is a valid document of the elements of national culture. It was framed by Constituent Assembly, which comprised of several of our freedom fighters, legal experts and specialists belonging to various walks of life. *The Constitution declared India a sovereign, socialist, secular, democratic republic*. It aims to secure to all its citizens justice, liberty, equality and fraternity. Justice refers to social, economic and political areas of life. Liberty included freedom of thought, expression, belief, faith and worship. Fraternity assures the dignity of the individual and the unity and integrity of the nation.

The Constitution represents the will of large masses of citizens. There are various ethnicities in the country. People have all the liberty to participate in and celebrate their respective ethnicities. The government does not intervene in the functioning of these ethnicities. However, the people are obliged to integrate and identify themselves with the national culture of the country. If the ethnicities come in the way of national culture, they need to be withdrawn. People's identification with the cultural mainstream of the nation is obligatory.

Our culture is based on democracy. And, the smallest unit of democracy is the individual. The word 'democratic' used in the preamble of the Constitution does not denote merely political democracy but also economic and social democracy. Jawaharlal Nehru once observed:

> Political democracy, as represented by every person having a vote by itself was not enough, except that it may be used to obtain a gradually increasing measure of economic equality.

In fact, social democracy is the basis of political and economic democracy. B.R. Ambedkar, the main architect of Indian Constitution, observes:

> Social democracy is a way of life which recognizes liberty and fraternity as the principles of life.

India's national culture also includes socialism. The word 'socialism' was added to the preamble later on to lay stress on the resolve of the nation to strive for socialism and economic justice that envisages equitable distribution of national income to all sections of the society. The 42nd amendment lays down that the term 'socialism' means that there is freedom from all forms of exploitation – social, political and economic. The state shall endeavour to bring about social and economic equality and keeping this in view it shall try to prevent concentration of wealth in a few hands. The gap between the rich and the poor will have to be narrowed down so that the benefits of independence are brought to every home and hearth. Likewise, the social disparities will have to be done away with so that all have equal opportunities to shape their future.

Yet another element of national culture is secularism. In the 19th century, the British society separated church from state. The state became secular. Secularism in Indian Constitution was put through 42nd amendment simply to reaffirm the faith of the nation in making the Indian politics stay above petty religious considerations while showing the respect to all religions. The 45th amendment lays down that the term 'secular' means that all religions command equal respect and recognition from the state.

In India, no discrimination is ever made against any individual because of his religion. All the people in India, forming different groups, sects, communities, etc., are free to practice, preach and profess any religion. Everybody is equal before law, and enjoys equal rights, no matter to which faith, caste, colour or creed he or she belongs.

The Constitution of India assures to give justice to all. Justice is the quality of treating everybody at par without any privilege or prejudice. It ensures equal opportunities for everyone and gives what is his due. Indians had already suffered much because of the injustice done to them by the imperialist rulers, so the Constitution places great emphasis on justice. Justice should not be limited but should be all-pervading, touching the social, economic and political fields. Social justice occupies an important place in our treatment of disadvantaged groups.

Liberty perhaps is the greatest aspect of our culture. Every citizen of India has liberty of thought, expression, belief, faith and worship. A citizen can choose any religion and can worship in any way he likes. We have suffered a lot because of the 'divide and rule' policy of the colonial power, so the Constitution puts emphasis on the freedom of belief, faith and worship in order to ensure the unity of the nation.

Indian society is characterized by the culture of equality. Our Constitution has done away with all inequalities based on sex, race, religion, caste, creed or colour. Now, all are equal before law and enjoy equal opportunities for their advancement.

The culture of fraternity or brotherhood is yet another dimension of national ethos. It must be mentioned that the slogan of liberty, equality and fraternity was first given by the French revolutionaries. The makers of our Constitution were so much influenced by this slogan that they adopted it for our own Constitution. We all citizens of this country are one. A Bengali, Rajasthani or Punjabi, notwithstanding any residence in any part of country, is an Indian citizen. There is no distinction among them.

## National Culture, Laws and Government Policy

What we call as mainstream of national culture therefore consists of democracy, socialism, secularism, plurality and justice. Added to it are scientific ethics and rationality. Whatever may be the religious culture of people – Hindu, Buddhist, Jain, Muslim or Sikh – it is obligatory on the part of all the citizens of India to follow the culture which is embedded in our Constitution. Scientific ethics do not permit superstitions to have their hold on the individuals. Nor is there any scope for fundamentalism. Rationality, therefore, is an essential part of scientific ethics. The constitutional culture carries with it all the sub-cultures of the country.

India has a body of laws known as Indian penal system. These laws emerge from our constitutional culture. Besides laws, there are government policies, which are implemented to maintain order in the society. No law or government can contradict the national culture. Viewed from wider perspective of national culture, we would define Indian society as democratic, secular, socialistic, rational and sovereign.

The perspective of modernity, when applied to Indian culture, brings out that India would attain progress through economic growth, industrialization, capitalism and urbanism. There would be a modern India, which would cast off conservatism and superstition.

Modern culture has not been accepted by the people in its pure or authentic form. Democracy has been misused and all sorts of benefits are taken by the leaders, high-castes and elites for their own consumption. Fundamentalism flourishes in the name of secularism and religious traditions. Political leaders misuse the public funds on temples and mosques; and encourage religious sentiments of the people for contesting elections. The ideology of socialism has been put to the rear seat. The government at the federal level also takes to disinvestments in the public sectors which were created to promote socialism. There are in India virtually two streams of culture: the national-constitutional-official culture and the varieties of culture manifest in ethnicities spread over to different culture zones. The ethnicities interact with the national culture. These are the little narratives. The sociologists who have studied ethnicities argue on the strength of their empirical findings that these ethnicities are increasingly getting weaker as a result of their interaction with the modern culture accepted by the higher groups of the country. There is a lurking fear among the sociologists that the local cultures or ethnicities would get oblivious and they would hardly retain any of their traces. Modern culture would call the shots.

Modernity created favourable opportunities for the rise of middle class in India. It has been a consumer class which enjoyed much of the benefits of modernity. Yogendra Singh (*Culture Change in India*, 2000) argues that the western culture did not change the core of India's culture. The changes were only adaptive. The Indian society provided enough ground for the identity and continuity of indigenous culture. Yogendra Singh writes:

> A significant quality of social change which relates to structures and processes in societies is that of continuity and existence of the traditional institutions and values. The processes of westernization and modernization have both encountered this phenomenon in all societies. Why is it that despite the overwhelming changes in structures and institutions societies do preserve many elements of their cultural styles, modes of living and the normative and cognitive measures to bring about change, the norms of social hierarchy, degree of empowerment of women and the extent of religious and cultural tolerance remain confounded? Culture changes only slowly and adaptively.

Sociologists and other social scientists have established that the impact of western culture has been so powerful that it has created a crisis in the local culture. Some of the cultural traditions are at the verge of extinction. But, such an interpretation of the impact of western culture seems to be erroneous. The empirical data which are obvious to any observer show that there has been enormous improvement in the lifestyle of the people. Globalization, liberalization and the development of federal markets have given so much money to the people. Modernity's rationality and progress have been misused to create disequalibrium in the society.

During the last fifty years, tourism to religious places has increased manifold. Trains and other means of transport go overcrowded. At the pilgrim centres, there is no space to stand. New gods are created every day; new temples are erected and the old ones are renovated more than often with great fanfare. One fails to understand as to why people have got a new faith in gods and deities. The life of the ordinary man is many times better today than it was during colonial-feudal times. Nor the people have any crisis in their life. What makes them so much inclined to move to gods and celebrate religious functions with all of their enthusiasm, one fails to understand.

It is all a creation of modernity. Modernity has proved to be an enemy of subaltern people. What we have been arguing is that the western contact has not disturbed our age-old traditions. It has rather given new teeth to the upper and middle sections of the society to bite the low segments. Theoretically, it is interesting to note here that culture cannot be compared. It is specific to social structure. In this respect, higher or lower is not the culture; it is the groups practising a particular culture which is higher or lower.

In the present circumstances, there is no danger of the erosion of local cultures. They have rather been strengthened. And, this new strength is largely due to modernity and its various elements. The census of 1931 shows that there were about three thousand castes in the country. Today, the number has risen to more than four thousand. Traditionally, there were four *dhamas* – pilgrim centres – for the Hindus. For a Hindu visiting these pilgrim centres assumed salvation. Today, these pilgrim centres have increased to an astonishing size. The argument is that the material things have changed in the realm of tradition and culture, the values being sidelined. Though sometimes it is argued that Hindu tradition is holistic – oriented to the collectivity. But, there are scholars who argue that Hinduism is invariably oriented to individualism. Jainism and Buddhism stand for the salvation of the individual, and not the collectivity. Transmigration of soul is the sole concern of the individual. It is here that the constitutional value of individualism coincides with the Hindu view of individual salvation.

Summing up the preceding discussion on the national culture of India, we would say that there is a plurality of people belonging to various ethnicities. Taking into consideration the plural culture, we have referred to a composite culture consisting of democracy, secularism, socialism and industrial capitation. Modernity also introduced a new set of values. Studies on India's culture are very scarce. We are familiar with the micro-culture which our anthropologists have strived to bring forth. This micro-culture is limited to a specific group of castes, religious groups and localities. We have not been successful to develop an Indian structure of culture. The constitutional structure, i.e., national culture that we have requires empirical legitimacy.

**High Culture, Popular Culture and Postmodernity**

Popular culture is the central theme of postmodernity. The high culture is the contribution of modernity and feudalism and colonialism. Those who cornered a larger part of modernity developed a high culture. They were English educated gentlemen, Jagirdars, Zamindars and Kulaks, that is, big farmers. High culture includes things like classical music, dance, high art, serious novels, poetry and other cultural products, which are usually appreciated by only a relatively small number of educated people. In the countryside of our society, the higher castes possess this culture. They are educated and observe a sacred life. Vegetarianism, daily bath, wearing of *janeu* (sacred thread) and worship put them to higher class.

Postmodernity encourages popular culture. It is a prime concept of anthropology and denotes all the knowledge, technologies, values, beliefs, customs and behaviour common to people. While simple societies may have only a single integrated culture that is shared by everyone, complex societies can accommodate many layers and levels of cultures and sub-cultures.

Traditionalists have lamented the poor quality of popular culture. Our folk dances and folk songs fall in the category of popular culture. Liberal and radical critics have been more inclined to support the popular culture as an authentic expression of public taste, and to dismiss the remote products of high culture as elitist. Sociologists have become involved in the analysis of popular culture because it provides a window into public consciousness, and is an important element of solidarity within social classes and castes.

One very important dimension of popular culture is the folk literature and folk artists. The folk artists include a large number of specialists. The specialists belong to both the sexes. Dancers, puppeteers, *Bahurupia* and acrobats (*Nat*) are some of the performers of folk culture. The government gives all preference to folk artists on national days. The tribals have folk culture which is unique to the general masses. They have lived in isolation within the cover of forests and hills and this has enabled them to develop their own culture, which is unadulterated from the mainstream culture of the plains. Tribal folk artists are invited on Republic Day at New Delhi. At the state level also, the folk artists are given opportunity to present their culture. On days of sowing and harvesting and other village ceremonies, the popular culture is performed which has mass participation. In the state of Rajasthan, the tribals display *Gavari*, a folk dance, which attracts a huge audience of hundreds of villagers – both tribals and non-tribals – even in the interior villages. In Madhya Pradesh, the folk demonstration of *Pandvani* is a mammoth display of local artists. The artists narrate folk version of epic stories and myths. In Maharashtra, there is *Tamasha* – a folk dance performed by girl artists. Folk art is the expression of popular culture.

Beating of drum in the villages is also an expression of popular culture. It is not merely a source of recreation. Among the tribals the drum beating is used for conveying certain messages which are meant for the common people. For instance, the drum beating of a particular variety conveys that some death has occurred in the village; if there is some raid engineered by the police, there is another variety of drum beating. It is how popular culture works in India's villages.

India's culture is very comprehensive. It has several sub-cultures, for instance, youth culture, village culture, and Brahmin culture. These cultures constitute the general comprehensive culture. As K.S. Singh reports, there are 91 culture zones in India. Rajasthan has, for instance, nine culture zones – Mewar, Marwar, Vagad, Brij, etc. In Gujarat, there are culture zones of Choro Har, Kathiawad, South Gujarat, etc., whereas in Madhya Pradesh, there are Nimach, Malwa and several other zones. Each culture has its specificity which gives identity to it.

## Culture Studies

We do not have in India any authentic culture studies in sociology and social anthropology. Culture studies are "concerned with practices, institutions and modes of classification through which cultural values and norms are instilled in a population. These analyse the forms and representational strategies of social and cultural power through which certain groups dominate other sections of population and control the dissemination of meanings and values. This cultural and interpretative domination is often coterminous with maintaining political and economic power over the dispossessed and the disempowered. Cultural studies offer their methodologies and resources to agents of social change – such as women's movements – and establishes relations with specific cultural institutions and fields of cultural management."

Public culture has not been studied by sociologists in India. There is enough scope of study in public culture. It is a space where meanings are contested, distorted and revived in a continuous process. Public culture, as mentioned above, includes folk culture, folk artists and folk literature. Folk songs are also rich in their content. Iravati Karve refers to folk songs which are sung on the occasion of birth, marriage and death. She finds much similarity in the songs relating to different occasions. Folk culture, in its new form, has taken new dimensions. In an industrial-urban society, folk culture includes cinema, advertisements, television, celebrity gossip in magazines, newspapers, autobiographies of public figures, websites and web-pages of institutions, tourist guides and leaflets, museums, comic strips consumed – sometimes literally – by children, state conography (remember the 'India Shining' ads which provide a textual preface to the 2004 elections), city maps and guides, etc. In public culture, private and state interests, low and high cultural media, and different classes and groups represent and debate what culture is, or should be.

## Public Culture and the Problem of Power

Elitism of modernism always neglected the popular culture. It is because of this that in Europe postmodernity threw a challenge to modernity. Culture has power and the ruling classes did not consider the lower classes or castes. There is a Marxian idiom that says that the culture of the ruling class is the culture of the masses. In India, the culture of higher castes and classes, in natural course, became the culture of lower castes. These neglected sections of society had their own culture, but it is subordinated by the superordinate groups. It is postmodernity, which has come closer to popular culture. The historians, sociologists and anthropologists have never taken into account the culture of lower castes. Their culture is culture of silence. Thus, the culture of ruling classes and dominant castes gets embedded in power. Pramod K. Nayar (*Reading Culture*, 2006) raises some questions about culture, which were initially addressed by Glenn Jordan and Chris Weedon:

> Whose culture would be official one and whose shall be subordinate? What culture shall be regarded as worthy of display and which shall be hidden? Whose history shall be remembered and whose marginalized? What images of social life shall be projected and which shall be marginalized. What voices shall be heard and on what basis? This is the realm of cultural politics.

Nayar describes culture in terms of power relations. Culture is not only art, painting, music and dance. Those who own culture also exercise power. There is much material on the culture of the higher castes. History talks about political elites and celebrities. It turns a blind eye towards the dispossessed, oppressed and marginalized people. Explaining the culture of the downtrodden people , Nayar observes:

> Culture studies are chiefly concerned with the question of the other. It argues that the dominant class has maintained its power through processes of othering, classifying social groups as philistines, savage, and 'uncultured' treating them as object of knowledge and, therefore, subject to power and control. Thus cultural studies are interested in the socio-cultural process through which women, the differently abled, the working classes, the non-white races and queers became 'othered' or marginalized. For an example of the process of power-negotiations within a society, let us look at the marginalization of the *Dalit* culture in India.

Kancha Ilaiah ('Productive Labour' in *Subaltern Studies*, IX, 1996) establishes that Hindu Brahmanism deliberately kept Dalit culture separate from Hinduism itself. It is the culture of the 'Other'. Ilaiah writes:

> They (Hindu Brahamins) decisively thrust us aside ... treated us as the vulgar working mass having no dignity, no self-respect. Our history, our language, our philosophy, our skills, our knowledge of science and technology were all rendered invisible ... the very idea of our caste neglected the idea of history. Our history, therefore, became non-history.

Ilaiah further observes that no Dalit gods figured in stories are studied at school. For the Brahmin or the Bania, the 'prescribed' stories were familiar because Rama and Krishna were the gods they worshipped, while the Dalit knew only Pochamma, Potaraju and Beerappa. Ilaiah writes:

> What difference did it make to us whether we had an English text book that talked about Milton's *Paradise Lost* or *Paradise Regained* ... or Woodsworth's poetry about nature, or a Telgue text book that talks about *Maghasandesham* .... We do not share the contents of either; we do not find our lives reflected in their narratives.

What is said by Ilaiah and other writers belonging to the lower segments of society is that sociologists have always focused on the culture of the higher groups. And, the higher groups for them are invariably Brahmins, Rajputs and Baniyas. The concepts of dominant caste, sanskritization, westernization and hierarchy have all emerged from sociologists who also happen to belong to higher castes. Perhaps, they think that culture is only of higher castes and the lower castes do not have any culture. Such a kind of assumption is unsociological.

We have argued that the values which are contained in our constitution, law, and government policies constitute the cultural mainstream of the country. But, in empirical terms, these elements of culture have not been brought to ground by the people at the grassroots level.

The political parties and the people believing in Hindutva ideology talk about cultural nationalism. By cultural nationalism, they mean the culture of the Hindus or Hindu castes who constitute an overwhelming majority in the country's population. Hindu theory of transmigration of soul characterizes the cultural nationalism. According to it, the Hindu scriptures – Vedas,

Puranas, epics, Brahmans and a large number of sacred texts and rituals constitute the national culture. Sociologists, as is obvious from their discourses, have extended their support to this ideology of Hinduism. Modernity as it belongs to caste elites also follows cultural nationalism.

## Postmodernity is Popular Culture

Postmodernity has created a new sensibility for popular culture. Sensibility means new cultural style as can be seen in religion, tourism and rationality. Writing about the relationship between postmodernity and popular culture, John Storey ('Postmodernism and Popular Culture' in *Postmodernism*, ed. by Stuart Sim (ed.), 2005) writes:

> The postmodernism rejected the cultural elitism of modernism .... The response of the postmodern new sensibility to modernism's canonization was a re-evaluation of popular culture. The postmodernism of the late 1950s and early 1960s was therefore in part a populist attack on the elitism of modernism.

Postmodern technology, rationality and education have promoted the national popular culture in India to new heights and it is expected that no sooner than later, the popular culture would have the form of national culture. The role of film, television, and cell phone, would broaden the scope of popular culture.

# X

## Scheduled Tribes: On the Road to Modernity and Postmodernity

The present chapter is untraditional. The Scheduled Tribes are included in the Eleventh Schedule of Constitution of India. The groups of people which are included in this schedule are described as Scheduled Tribes (STs). They are given certain privileges of protection and development. The total ST population in India, as per 2001 census, is about 8.43 crores which constitutes about 8.20 per cent of the total population of 102.86 crores in the country. The constitutional privileges of reservation are given for a specific period of time by the government.

To argue that STs have attained modernity and postmodernity is to enter into a national debate. If the tribals have become modern, why there is no descheduling? Second, can an ST not attain modernity? Third, can scheduled status and modernity not go together? It is in this respect that our present chapter is controversial. Our position is that the STs are modern and in some respects postmodern also.

Anthropologists have described the present status of tribals in the country. They are not scattered to the whole of country. There are states which do not have any tribal population. And, there are also states which have higher concentration of these people. About 87 percent of them are found in central belt covering eight states of Madhya Pradesh, Orissa, Bihar, Maharashtra, Gujarat, Rajasthan,

Andhra Pradesh and West Bengal. Besides, about 10 per cent are found in the north-eastern region and about 3 per cent in other states. Madhya Pradesh has the highest concentration of 1.22 crores ST population, which is about 20.27 per cent of the total ST population in the country. There are about 360 ST groups speaking more than 100 languages. There are five major tribes, namely, the Bhils, the Gonds, the Santhals, the Oraons and the Minas.

The tribals have their own pockets. They are isolated and generally reside in hills, forest, and undulating terrain. If the SCs have their problem of untouchability, the tribals have the problem of isolation. They live away from the mainstream of castes and other non-tribal groups.

The accounts of tribals which we get from anthropologists present them as savage, backward, illiterate and uncivilized. But, the north-east tribals do not weigh to this portrait. They are more than modern. They utilize most of the benefits of technology and are exposed to English culture. Christian missionaries have been working in the region since the advent of British rule. They have brought them closer to modern culture. Despite modernism, the tribals show all fascination for their indigenous culture. Most of the villages of Naga and Bodo have their own dialect. It would not be wrong to say that each tribal village has its own tribal dialect. A village among these tribals is a sort of 'capsule society'. Despite their differentiated and diverse character, tribal in the north-east are a postmodern society.

Indian society has witnessed colossal change. In this context, it would be wrong to say that the caste Hindus, Sikhs, Jains, Muslims and other non-tribals have demonstrated enough structural and cultural changes, and the tribals have remained unchanged. On any plane of rationality such a proportion cannot be accepted. They too have changed substantially. And, therefore, to describe them as primitive, native and uncivilized, is basically wrong. In some situations, in the heart of tribal mainland, the tribals have moved much ahead of castes. To call tribals as modern communities, might appear to be unanthropological, but empirically, about 71 percent of tribals which inhabit six states of India, namely, Madhya Pradesh, Maharashtra, Rajasthan, Gujarat, Bihar and Orissa, show all characteristics of modern and postmodern life.

We started this chapter with the observation that the government continues to call the tribals as scheduled. STs mean socially, culturally and economically backward. They are not modern. When the government is convinced of the progress made by the tribals on par with the average citizens of the country, the former would be descheduled. And, inspite of their scheduled status, when we call the tribals modern, there is always a fear of being ridiculed by the government and the official sociologists and anthropologists. Despite the fear, we have mustered enough courage to establish that our Indian tribals are modern and in some situations, postmodern. Hence, this part of our present chapter is untraditional.

Among thousands of Indian communities, tribals are the only group which do not have any hierarchy. Bhils, Gonds, Minas are all equals. There is no hierarchy for them. They are an example of an egalitarian society. It is enough to label them as modern. Conventional sociology includes both classical functionalism of Durkheim, Weber and Parsons and dialectical Marxism of Marx and Marxism. The functionalist anthropologist looks at tribals as sterile and practitioners of animism. This view has now changed considerably. It is under political pressure and election strategy that the government also accepts tribals as living a traditional life of primitive world. It is interesting to apply perspectives of modernity and postmodernity to interpret the contemporary tribal life in India.

## Modernity, Postmodernity and Tribals

The definition of tribals has become an ideological issue. The architects of Indian Constitution had witnessed the injustices done to the tribals. They were exploited by the colonial rule and the feudal regime. The British Raj adopted a policy of reconciliation rather than confrontation with tribals. Whenever there were tribal revolts in West Bengal, Orissa and Madhya Pradesh, the British rulers found that the armed forces failed to control the tribals. They, therefore, applied the policy of compromise. In the feudal states of Mewar, Dungarpur and Banswara, whenever there were tribal upheavals, the states always came forward to woo the tribals. Administrative reforms were made to influence the tribals. Recognizing the chivalry of the Bhils, the British government established Mewar Bhil Corps in 1824.

The makers of Constitution were quite aware of the oppression of Bhils. This made them to give special privileges to the tribals. Mentioning about the ill-treatment given to Bhils, R.C. Verma (*Indian Tribes Through the Ages*, 2002) observes:

> The Bhils were ill treated by the Rajputs, the Marathas, and Mohammedans. There were large scale conversions to Islam among the Bhils in western India, particularly in the Khandesh region. The Tadwi Muslims are believed to be the Bhils who were oppressed and exploited and treated like beasts. Consequently, some of them retreated into deep forests and hills and some took to dacoity and highway robbery during the 18th and 19th centuries against the tyranny of the invaders and the exploitation by the local people. In 1818, when Khandesh came under British rule, the Bhils rebelled against the government. But they were suppressed by the use of brutal force.

The Constitution made certain privileges to protect the tribal land and provide safeguards for their development. Reservation for tribals was considered to be a source of assured means of livelihood. More than half a century has gone, and the government still reports that there is no improvement in the tribal people. Our view is that the government is making all efforts to modernize the tribal people. And, it has succeeded to a great extent in this endeavour. There has been a wider process of modernization among the tribals. And, therefore, we take a stand that officially the tribals are scheduled tribes and sociologically they are modern tribals. But, before we establish their modernity and postmodernity, let us hurriedly define modernity. Even, how tribals are defined in ideological terms?

Social anthropologists were not actively involved in the identification of the groups to be included in the scheduled list of tribals. The work was done by social workers, political leaders and state governments. In this connection, it is said that the preparation of scheduled list of tribals is a state subject. And, therefore, each state has its own list of STs. It is possible that a tribe which is included in Gujarat list is not necessarily included in the list of other states. Inclusion is thus state-specific.

What does modernity mean in the case of STs? As discussed elsewhere, modernity is a much disputed concept. Normally, it includes democracy, capitalism, industrialism and secularism. Three different, though interrelated, ideal-type concepts, which characterize the idea of modernity, are given by Rajendra Singh (*Social Movements: Old and New*, 2001):

> First, modernity refers to a passage (i.e., historicity) involving the transformation of the quality and forms of social life. It introduces a notion of movement and change from community to society, from a simple to a complex structure, from fused to differentiated roles, from a closed and relatively immobile social system to an open and mobile system, from particularism to universalism, and from faith and sentiment to science, reason and rationality. From the modernist point of view, capitalism, industrialism and technology heighten the rate of exchange of commodities. Fast communication and the dominance of market relations over all relations of everyday life reveal some of the economic expansions of this modernity.

Rajendra Singh has brought out four interrelated axioms of the evolution of modernity. He draws the axioms from Mats Friberg and Bgorn Hettne. The axioms are given below:

1. *Direction*: The general change of history is directed and cumulative, and it be described as a process of growth and expansion with respect to some particular linear dimensions of society.
2. *Determinism*: The evolutionary process is determined and is irreversible. It is not possible for mankind to influence the course of history except for minor peripheral details. Consequently, the ability of human beings to alter their path in history stands negated.
3. *Progress*: Modernity as an evolutionary concept implies the notion of progress in the normative sense of the word. It gives a message that societies are moving towards a better world.

4. *Immanence*: The evolutionary process is imminent reality in every society. It does not require external intervention. The notion of immanence implies the idea of self-evolution.

The ideal type of modernity very clearly brings out the fact that it is for the progress of the mankind. In our contemporary society, modernity is a state-sponsored programme given by the Constitution to the STs. The safeguards given by the state are meant to improve the status of the tribals. "The lore of the welfare state and policy and planning; development, reform and social intervention have generally emerged as state-produced and state-owned ideological apparatuses .... The lore development involves a linkage between power and knowledge." Zymunt Bauman, in his *Legislators and Interpreters: On Modernity and Postmodernity and Intellectual* (1989), identifies the power-knowledge syndrome of modernity which began with the emergence of a new type of state with resources and will, necessary to shake and administer the social system according to a preconceived model of or, and the establishment of a relatively autonomous, self-managing discourse able to generate such a model complete with the practices its implementation required.

The definition of tribe, so far as Constitution and government policies are concerned, is clear. The groups which are included in the scheduled list are STs. Their development is to lead them to modernity. And, modernity means progress for the tribals. But, there are a few other definitions which are full of ideologies.

G.S. Ghurye *(Scheduled Tribes)* has defined tribals as 'backward caste Hindus'. He argues on the strength of mythological and historical data that there is no specificity of racial strains among tribals. There have been so many admixtures of racial traits that no 'pure' type of race is found among these people. References to tribals are found in our scriptures and history that they came closer to backward caste Hindus. The tribals are not untouchables. Nor are they twice-born. Considering all such things, it can be said that the tribal groups are backward Hindus. Ghurye has been ideologically aligned to Hinduism and therefore he has advocated two propositions: the tribes are Hindus and they would, therefore, be assimilated with the lower Hindu castes.

N.K. Bose, the anthropologist and Gandhian thinker, follows Ghurye's proposition of tribal assimilation among Hindus. Bose analyzes that there is a 'Hindu method' of absorbing tribals in the caste system. Several of the customs and rituals of tribals are such that they would integrate themselves into wider Hinduism. Yet another ethnologist, Hutton also believes that caste system and many cultural traditions of Hindus have organic links with the tribal cultures. However, Risley, O'Malley and Verrier Elwin hold that tribal and Hindu traditions are separate.

The supporters of cultural nationalism, that is, those who propagate the Hindu ideology, argue that tribals are Hindus. Once upon a time, when they lived in hills and forests, they had animism as their religion. But, when they took to settled agriculture, migrated to plains, adopted Hindu gods and goddesses as their cult, they became Hindus. On the other hand, there are also people who do not accept tribals as Hindus. According to them, the crux of Hinduism is caste system and caste system is based on hierarchy. The tribals do not have interdependence among their various tribal groups. Each tribal group is autonomous. And, this differentiates them from caste system of Hindus.

## Verrier Elwin and G.S. Ghurye: The Debate on Isolation and Assimilation

There was a debate in the country over the issue of isolation and assimilation. Assimilation meant to bring the tribals in the colonial mainstream. If the tribals took to their assimilation, they would be closer to caste Hindus and modernization. The caste Hindus, during colonial and feudal period, were becoming modern. They got English education, took to cash economy and benefited from modern technology. The colonial administration wanted to maintain law and order. All these aspects of modernity went a long way in pursuing the high-castes and other non-tribal groups of the country to come closer to one another. The tribals in this process were no exception.

The forests, during the colonial rule, began to decay. The government appointed contractors to cut the forest wood, as it was required in the construction work of railways, factories and several other industrial outfits. It was a major event for the tribals for whom forest was their ancentral home. Their source of livelihood was forest and the colonial rule denied it. The tribals migrated to plains and took to agriculture as their source of living. It was also a schism in their stratification. Those who opted to live a forest life came to be named as authentic original tribes, and those who shifted to plains came to be known tribal\peasants. We would also mention here that the tribal migration to plains marks the beginning of modernity as a way of life and agriculture as the mode of occupation for the tribes.

Shifting of occupation raised the problem of assimilation of tribals in the country's mainstream. The movement of tribals addressed the question: will they remain isolated from the mainstream or will they be assimilated into the caste system? Precisely, it was a problem both for the colonial regime and the body of intellectuals. Verrier Elwin, who was a social worker living in Mandca (Madhya Pradesh), put forward the theory of 'public park'. He argued that the tribal culture which was quite genuine and authentic, when interacted and assimilated with the caste culture, becomes 'polluted'. The urban people, Elwin argued, were full of vices and evils. The tribals should not be allowed to mix with the former. Isolation of the tribals from the caste Hindus, therefore, was injurious. If tribals were allowed to integrate with the caste Hindus, in course of time, they would lose their identity and quality of life. He put his theory in a small book entitled *Loss of Nerve*. He argued that if general people wanted to meet and interact with tribals, the latter should be permitted to reside in a restricted place. They should be used like a 'public park'. His theory is: let us keep the tribals isolated.

G.S. Ghurye contrasted Elwin's theory. Ghurye's book *The Aboriginals: So-called and Their Future* (New Edition: *The Scheduled Tribes*) has a strong response to isolation theory. He said, the future of tribals lies in their assimilation with the caste Hindus. At a later stage, Elwin was convinced of the assimilation theory and he along with Jawaharlal Nehru came out with a solution of the integration of tribals into the national mainstream. It is called 'Panchsheel' – five fundamental principles. These principles contain the document of modernity for the tribals.

Nehru was opposed to imposition of anything on the tribals. He said: "Tribal people should develop along the lines of their genius and we should avoid imposing anything on them. We should try to encourage in every way their own traditional arts and culture." Constitution and government policies laid down the future of tribal people in India. Now, it is stated that the future of tribals is tied down with the future general masses. In the name of protective and development safeguards, the tribals are given a modernization package which will lead to their development.

One very important observation has to be made at this stage of our discussion. To talk about the assimilation of tribals into the country's mainstream, is much far away from reality. Conceptually, integration and assimilation bear different meanings. Integration is the process where there develops cohesiveness among the units for the system. Units do not change their identity but so far they agree with the system, there is identification. The process of assimilation does not allow them to retain their identity. Assimilation is an ideal situation which cannot be attained in any society.

When the tribals integrate themselves with the mainstream, they tend to keep their tribal identity alive. So do the Brahmins and the Baniyas. We have empirical evidence to show that the tribals maintain their identity in the meetings of Panchayat Samiti when the non-tribals are also present Jan Breman (*Of Peasants, Migrants and Paupers,* 1985), who has studied the tribals of Surat district, writes:

> In retrospect, I.P. Desai reaches a somewhat different conclusion in which the element of contest is still further emphasized and counted into resentments arising from economic exploitation and social subservience. He described how the tribals held their own meetings, trying by means of their isolation to make themselves immune to outside influences in order to win self-esteem and to fight for equality.

I.P. Desai ('The Vedchhi Movement' in *History of Rural Development in Modern India,* II), who has been an excellent field worker, much affiliated to grassroots reality, refers to the integration of tribals into the mainstream. It shows that in situations where there is disbelief with the non-tribals, the tribals would maintain and stick to their authentic identity. Desai writes:

> The Adivasis knew the non-Adivasis through the exploiters only, viz., the money lenders, the police, and other government officers, and the liquor shop owners. They, therefore, distrusted all non-Adivasis. They did not want any 'outsider' to be present at their meetings and made a rule that if any 'outsider' come to the meeting the proceedings should stop. The 'outsider' was actually the exploiter primarily. The ugaliak (Baniya) was disliked because he was an exploiter first, non-Adivasi next.

The future of tribals lies, therefore, in their integration into the mainstream of society. The question of their assimilation into the caste society is irrelevant at any stage. There are enough evidences to state that the tribals are increasingly becoming modern. They very much like to practice their cultural and ethnic norms but are simultaneously ready to adapt to the universal practices of modernism. The tribals of Jhabua (Madhya Pradesh), who used to move half naked in the local market armed with bow and arrows, are now a perfect specimen of a modern man. It is difficult to differentiate a Bhil male from a Rajput or a Baniya. He wears trousers and shirts of the same brand. He is conversant with Hindustani language and the younger generation goes to college. The old days of primitive culture have now become obsolete. The description of tribals given by the doctrinaire anthropologists and sociologists does not tally with reality observed by any stranger. A period of more than fifty years is enough to make a group of people progressive and radical. This has happened not with the tribals of India but also elsewhere in South Africa and Australia.

### From Primitiveness to Modernity

The main objective of the present chapter is to identify the watershed that marks the beginning of modernization processes among the tribals of India. We have contested the policy of government which continues to keep the tribals in the scheduled category. It might be due to political constraints or the paternal benefits which the tribals enjoy. It is very interesting to learn that the government even now considers tribals as backward and traditional and sponsors a development programme, which in the real sense is modern and postmodern.

The tribals did not have any property except for a dilapidated *kachha* house, a cow; in rare cases a pair of bullocks, goats and hens. Their stratification was based on the size of the land which in rare cases exceeded five *bighas.* Powerlessness has been the prime characteristic of Indian tribes. There was no power, no prestige, no wealth. It was only a rudimentary form of stratification. And, in some cases, the male population remained unmarried because of its inability to pay the brideprice. Such a situation remained unchanged during the colonial and feudal times.

The watershed came when the tribals came to plains. They were latecomers in the field of agriculture. They learnt ploughing cultivation from caste Hindus. The Constitution, at a later state, provided them opportunities of job, education, entry into government services, employment in industrial sector and a vision for future progressive life. Admittedly, a large number of tribals today are categorized as below poverty line (BPL) people but they have acquired a consciousness, which enables them to agitate against the government and the high-caste Hindus. Now, they do not suffer from the culture of silence. They are vocal. They have scarce money but they know that they are armed with certain privileges. And, this makes them courageous.

The tribals have come in contact with the forces of modernization after the promulgation of Constitution of India. Modernization initiated a process of economic change. The study by B.H. Mehta ('A Summary of the Economic Life of an Aboriginal Tribe of Gujarat', *Journal of University of Bombay*, 1934) indicates that modernization eroded the communal character of the Adivasis. There appeared a differentiation within the tribal groups. Mehta argued that the idea of tribals as an undifferentiated society was misleading. Mehta had studied the house area of the Chaudhris of Surat in 1930. His conclusion of the impact of modernization in creating stratification among the tribals runs as under:

> The enrichment of some meant the impoverishment of the less fortunate, and the latter supplied the growing demand for labour.

Mehta refers to the empirical data generated by him in the field and says that the Chaudhris who could not benefit from modernization had to live a deplorable life. He analyzes that nearly one-third occupied a middle position; one-third formed an upper stratum. He mentions that tribals with substantial holdings even employed bonded labour (*Halis*), usually orphans or unmarried youths from poor households, who were taken on as farm servants on a yearly basis.

Thesis of modernization creating differentiation in the tribal community is further supported by P.K. Bose ('Stratification among Tribals in Gujarat', *EPW*, 1981). He argues that differentiation in the tribal society led to the emergence of class. Ghanshyam Shah ('Traditional Society and Political Mobilization: The Experience of Bardoli Satyagraha,' *Contributions to Indian Sociology*, 1974) reports that only a small minority of large cultivators, the stratum of middle cultivators are becoming constant in size, while the landless and small cultivators are becoming the vast majority. This accumulation at the base of the agrarian hierarchy is confirmed by a survey carried out at the same time among Chaudhris in twenty-one other villages in the tribal areas as reported in Shah's study:

| | |
|---|---|
| Little or no land (< 1 acre) | 24% |
| Small cultivators (1 – 5 acre) | 37% |
| Middle cultivators (5 – 15 acre) | 33% |
| Large cultivators (> 15 acre) | 5% |

### Government Policy Enhances Progressive Inequality

The government adopted policy to help the tribals to increase their farm output. There was green revolution. It increased the production of the big land owners. As a result of modernization and the capitalistic mode of farm product, the process of stratification already existing among the tribals further crystallized. But it did not become rigid class formation. Jan Breman observes on his experiences of South Gujarat cultivators:

> As we have already stated, this process of cumulative inequality has not yet crystallized into rigid class stratification. This does

> not alter the fact that to an increasing degree the separate strata are beginning to distinguish themselves from each other by their lifestyles and living conditions.... Differences in material position create sharply diverging patterns of consumption in food, dress, housing, etc. and also parallel differences in, for instance, the level of education, religious orientation and preferences in politics while the lower strata are condemned by their poverty to follow traditional behaviour patterns, the upper strata model their lifestyles on those of the dominant non-tribal farmers of the plains. Everything of this divergence in lifestyles within the tribal castes.
>
> The upper strata of the tribals attain the position of a higher or middle class. The landless farmers, on the other hand, who do not get any labour in the village, migrate to cities for employment. They do not settle outside as they are not assured to long term work at their place of labour.
>
> A new middle class has also emerged among the tribals. Reservation has opened up new gates of employment. A substantial size of tribals have made their entry into government jobs. They are founding various categories of services. These government jobs are unequally distributed among the tribals. As a result of the unequal spread of jobs in different states or even in a single state there has emerged a new stratum of officers, elites, leaders and technicians who enjoy high status in the tribal society. This new group is called creamy layer of the tribals. As a matter of fact, the creamy layer has taken much of the benefits of development programmes.

### Towards Diversification

Shifts in the livelihood sources of the tribals have taken a long time. When they lived an isolated life in the hills and forests, they depended on stone and wood cutting. Forest was also a source of their livelihood. When they migrated to plains, agriculture became their major occupation. Later on, they took to cash crops. With the facilities of irrigation, some skilled tribal peasants succeeded in growing three crops a year.

With the onset of modernity, there appeared a historical shift in their occupational pattern. There was diversification. And diversification introduced them to a large number of livelihood sources which were untraditional to them. As the occupational situation tells us, the tribals have taken to a large number occupations. They are high-level administrators, technocrats, decision-makers and professionals. It is striking to know that the Minas of Sawai Madhopur district of Rajasthan have the largest number of administrative officers of the cadre of All India Services and state services.

At the lower level, the tribals are found as petty traders, wage earners, drivers, mechanics and truck drivers. Their occupational diversification is so varied that they are found in all walks of national life. They have a well-specified identity in occupational world. The community has a resident character which enables them to adopt any occupation. They exhibit all skills to learn new trades. There are studies which show that tribals have proved to be successful entrepreneurs.

Occupational diversification also shows a change in their lifestyle. Modernity encourages consumption. Before the coming up of modernity in India, that is, promulgation of Constitution and introduction of development programmes, the tribals had a very poor diet. Even, today, a section of them suffers from malnutrition. But there is a clear rise in their consumption level. A section of them do not sell their milk and milk products to market. These are reserved for their own consumption. Earlier, they used to consume inferior cereals. But, now, they grow the cereals which are staple food of the region. Vegetables, eggs, and fruits have entered into their diet. It is a common observation to find a tribal entering into a tea shop for taking snacks. Home distillation of liquor is a rare occurrence. Now, they have become fond of drinking India made foreign liquor.

The dress patterns of both males and females have also undergone change. Now, they prefer synthetic cloth. Women's garments have also witnessed qualitative change. A tribal village today presents a new outlook. The local deity is installed in a temple and some space is created to hold community meetings. Handpumps – two or three – according to the size of the village, are stationed for public water drinking.

Some of the modern facilities are also available in the tribal village. If the size of the village is large, some grocery shops can also be found. One peculiar aspect of such a village is the availability of a beauty parlour and a shop for hair cutting.

Considering all the wider aspects of tribal life in India, it could be safely said that the tribals are fast becoming modern. During the colonial-feudal regime, the tribals were notorious for engineering revolts. Anthropologists have prepared a detailed chronological record of tribal revolts. The first revolt, which took place in 1778, was of the Pahariya Sirdaw of Chhota Nagpur against the British government. There were other movements of Chauri in Bihar (1794-5), Chhota Nagpur tribal revolt (1807-1808), Bhil revolt in Gujarat (1809-1828), Munda revolts in Bihar (1820, 1932 and 1867), Tana Bhagat rebellions in Bihar (1913, 1914 and 1920), Naga revolt (1963-71) and scores of other revolts.

The tribals are not a peace-loving people. Our north-eastern part is known for tribal insurgency. Bonds, Nagas and several other tribal groups continuously threaten one kind of insurgency or the other. Their problem is not economic. They lead a life, which is in all respects modern. Christianity is followed by an overwhelming majority of tribals. Racially also, they are different. They exhibit in many ways that they are not Indians. Their problem is political and territorial. They are modern. Modernity is not a problem for them.

The tribals in the central region of the country have now lost the spirit of rebellion or any movement. The development programmes have given them some relief. If there are some movements, these are only for the sharing of development benefits. The regions, which fall within the dam site area, often create agitation for the release of water for irrigation. Or, there are agitations for increase of seats in professional institutes. Generally, the previously rebellious tribals do not engineer any big or small revolts. They live a peaceful life.

Tribal ethnicity goes with modernity. The Constitution of India does not prevent ethnic processes. Local deities are worshipped with all traditional celebrations. Marriages are celebrated as usual. Even, the Bhopa (magic charmer) performs all his duties. He predicts the oncoming of monsoon, prescribes treatment and works as an arbitrator of village disputes. Normally, his is the first approach of people. Dissatisfied with the performance of Bhopa or village traditional leader, the second choice naturally is secular. Allopathic treatment is preferred by all. For settlement of disputes, courts are open for all. The tribals have acquired skills to handle bureaucracy, political leaders and technocrats.

## Modernity and Reforms

All over the country, there are some proverbs which characterize the social status of the tribes. These proverbs are floated by the high-caste Hindus. For instance, it is said that a Bhil or a Gond would never fail to take revenge for the wrong done to him. He is always drunken; if he has something to eat today, he would never think of tomorrow. He indulges profusely in sex. They are also accused of eating the flesh of dead animals and if there is famine, they would not mind killing a cow and eat its flesh. There are, however, some good things also said for the tribals. It is believed that a tribal would not deceive anybody. If he is given protection, he would sacrifice his life to honour his word.

Modernization has made the tribals conscious about their weaknesses, evils and bad habits. They look at the wider society for their imitation. In Bihar, Madhya Pradesh, Gujarat and Rajasthan, the Bhils, Gonds, and Santhals have started a reform movement. It is known by different names such as Bhagat movement, Tanna Bhagat, etc. These movements are started by tribals themselves. The idea behind them is to reform the tribals. The broader objective is to make them modern. Different caste groups are identified as models for imitation. Mostly high-caste Hindus serve as ideals for imitation.

The Bhagats have a puritanistic way of life. They daily take bath, put on a *janau* (sacred thread), observe *vratas* on sacred days of Hindu calendar, do not eat meat and live a simple life. Liquor is in all cases strictly prohibited. The tribal identity immediately puts them to a higher status in the surrounding region. The Baniya would not hesitate to advance loan to a Bhagat. For a tribal, his best identity in his region is that he is Bhagat.

Functionalists analyze the cult of Bhagatism as a process of Hinduization. They argue that the tribals have become Hindus.

They worship Hindu gods and goddesses. They celebrate Hindu festivals. But, there is yet another perspective to analyze Bhagatism. According to modernity, it shows that the tribals are increasingly becoming modern. They are getting education and adopting ways of life, which are rational, technological and professional. The new reform movement is a craze for the tribals of Central India. One who is not identified as a Bhagat is condemned.

The tribals of north-eastern states – Assam, Arunachal Pradesh, Mizoram, Meghalaya, Nagaland and Tripura – constitute 12.5 per cent to the total tribal population in the country. These tribals follow Christianity as their religion. They do not have any trace of Bhagatism. Their orientation is towards modernization. For their imitation, they refer to the western society. Besides their local dialect, their mode of communication is English language.

Modernity is not equally accepted by all the tribals of the country. So far modernity was released through the Indian Constitution in terms of freedom, equality, fraternity and secularism is acceptable to all. However, the ethnographic practices create diversity among tribals. Despite diversity and occupational fragmentation, there are a few social institutions which are found common to all the tribals. First, the tribals do not have any hierarchy, all are equal among them. Second, though they have embraced alien religions, for instance, Hinduism, Islam and Christianity, they simultaneously also worship their local gods and goddesses. Local deities occupy higher place, followed by alien religions. Third, all the tribals have accepted technology, and the prevailing democratic and capitalistic ethos of life. Fourth, though they have in varying degrees adopted modernity, they continue to celebrate their traditional life, food habits and festivals.

### Extent of Modernity: Some Major Tribal Groups of India

The social status of tribals in India is controversial. The government argues that despite the implementation of development programmes, the tribals have not attained an expected level of progress. The social scientists contest official position and say that the tribals have left behind their primitiveness and backwardness and have adopted fully the modern way of life. Despite the denial of the acceptance of modernity by the tribals, the government itself gives a heavy package of modernity to tribals. In the preceding pages, we have endeavoured to establish that, by and large, the tribals of India are a modern people today.

It is difficult to make broad generalizations on more than seven crores of tribals in India. To overcome this problem we take up some major tribal groups of the country and analyze as to what extent they have come closer to modernity. We hope that such a method would give us a fairly good representation of the modernity status of tribals.

Madhya Pradesh has the largest concentration (22.73%) of tribal population, followed by Maharashtra (10.80%) and Orissa (10.38%). Thus, roughly 44 per cent of the ST population of India lives in these three states only. Then, there are six states which inhabit 71 per cent of the ST population in India. These states include Madhya Pradesh, Maharashtra, Rajasthan, Gujarat, Bihar and Orissa.

There are seven tribes which account for a population of 10 lakhs or more each. These are: the Bhils, the Gonds, the Santhals, the Minas, the Oraons, the Mundas and the Khands. As per 1991 census, the Bhils have the largest population of 97.30 lakhs, followed by the Gonds 93.19 lakhs, the Santhals 49.79 lakhs, the Minas 28.01 lakhs, the Oraons 26.50 lakhs, the Mundas 76.48 lakhs and the Khands about 11.46 lakhs. A brief description of the major tribes is given below to understand the level of modernity attained by them.

### *The Bhils*

Bhils are also known as Bhilala and the Bhil Garasia. According to 1991 census, their population is 97.30 lakhs. Their concentration is found in the states of Madhya Pradesh, Andhra Pradesh, Gujarat, Karnataka, Rajasthan and Tripura. Their main habitation area is comprised of western Madhya Pradesh districts of Jhabua, Dhar, Khargoan, Khandva and Ratlam, east Gujarat districts of Panchmahals, Dong, Bharuch, Sabarkantha, and Banskantha and south Rajasthan districts of Dungarpur, Banswara and Udaipur. Thus, there is a contiguous belt of Bhil population running across the areas of three states of Gujarat, Madhya Pradesh and Rajasthan.

These areas have also been specified as scheduled areas under the Fifth Schedule of the Constitution.

The Bhils trace their origin from the ancient period. Their references are found in Vedic and epic literature. During the medieval period they fought with the Rajputs, especially Maharana Pratap, against the Mughals. History describes them as a martial race. The association of Bhils with the Rajputs became so close that there were inter-marriages between them, particularly with the families of the Bhil chiefs. As a result, a new tribe of the Bhilala came into being.

The medieval period also witnessed Bhils establishing their own kingdoms. They had their kingdoms of Dungarpur, Banswara and Pratapgarh in Rajasthan. The state of Kota was also established by a Bhil chief. It was a custom in the old states of Dungarpur, Banswara, Deolia (Pratapgarh) and also Kota on the part of the Bhil chiefs to put thumb marks in blood on the foreheads on the Rajput kings on the occasion of their coronation. The custom symbolized forceful seizure of power by the Bhils. In Gujarat and Madhya Pradesh also Bhil chiefs were rulers at several places.

The habitation area of the Bhils is scattered. They do not have compact villages. In scattered villages, each house has its own field surrounded from all sides. Thus, the area of single village covers several kilometres. In such villages, some of the development activities are run with difficulty. For instance, it becomes difficult for children to attend a school. And, in between the houses, there are streams, hills and forests.

The Bhils have their deities though they have accepted Hindu gods and goddesses. In Madhya Pradesh, South Rajasthan and Gujarat, some sections of Bhils have even accepted Christianity. The Christian missionaries have erected churches in a cluster of villages. The churches also work as local deities. If the monsoon is late, the Bhil go to church; for minor ailments also they visit church. However, the Christian Bhils show mannerism of a modern city dweller. They speak the local dialect. Their Bhili dialect is at the verge of extinction.

### The Gonds

Gonds are the second largest tribe in the country. They belong to the Dravidian stock of people. They are found in the states of Madhya Pradesh, Andhra Pradesh, Maharashtra, Bihar, Gujarat, Karnataka, Orissa and West Bengal. According to 1991 census, they account for 93.19 lakh people. Their highest concentration is in the central region, popularly known as Gondwana, which includes the Satpura plateau, the portion of the Nagpur plain area and the Narmada valley. The main districts in Madhya Pradesh having significant Gond population are Bastar, Bilaspur, Sarguja, Chhindwara and Mandla.

Verrier Elwin, the British anthropologist, worked among Gonds in the Mandla district. He also married a Gond girl.

The Gonds speak their dialect known as *Gondi.* They also speak *Chattisgarhi* which is the regional dialect. However, Gondi, their own dialect, belongs to Dravidian family of language which is closer to Tamil.

Agriculture is the main occupation of Gonds. However, there is an insignificant portion of Gonds who continue to practise shifting cultivation. Along with agriculture, their secondary occupations include collection of wild fruits, fishing and hunting.

Individual right of ownership over land is recognized among almost all the Gonds who have taken to settled agriculture. There has come a strong consciousness among these people to agitate over their constitutional rights. There is a powerful presence of Christian missionaries among them. This has brought them closer to modernity.

### The Santhals

Santhals are said to be pre-Aryan people. They rank third in the population strength of tribals. According to 1991 census, they constitute 49.79 lakh people. They have been specified as the STs in the states of Bihar, West Bengal, Orissa and Tripura. Their concentration in these three states is contiguous. They speak Santhali language, which has its own script known as *Olchiki.* They are a bi-lingual people. Besides their own language they also speak the regional languages, such as Oriya, Bengali and Hindi.

Santhals are concentrated in Santhal Pargana. Their primary occupation is agriculture though part of their earnings is also derived from minor forest produce, hunting, fishing and shifting cultivation. The dead body among the Santhals is cremated. They mostly follow the rites of caste Hindus.

### The Minas

Minas are found inhabited in the states of Rajasthan and Madhya Pradesh. They are one of the five major tribes of India. Rajasthan has the largest number of Minas, followed by the Bhils. According to 1991 census, their population is 18 lakhs. Quite like the Bhils, the Minas were the ruling tribe. They had several large and small kingdoms. But they could not retain their chieftainship any longer and were defeated several times by the rulers of Amer (Jaipur). Constant warfare shattered their economy. They took to dacoity and criminal activities. They were declared a criminal tribe. The Government of India, in consideration of their educational, economic and political backwardness, provided them constitutional protection by declaring them as the scheduled tribe.

The Minas speak the local dialect though they are also conversant with Hindi. Education is popular with the tribe. They are an intelligent group of people. They have excelled in competitive examination and have also entered into professional careers. In the state of Rajasthan, the Minas occupy the highest place among the tribals. The Bhils lag behind them. The excellence of Minas is also due to the agricultural land they plough. They take cash crops.

Marriage among the Mina as is endogamous. They invite the Brahmin to officiate at the marriage. Ritually, the Minas are included in the category of clean or high-caste Hindus, which include Mahajans, Thakurs and Rajputs. They worship Lord Shiva and also Rama, Krishna and Hanuman. They cremate dead body according to Hindu customs.

### The Oraons

The Oraons belong to Dravidian stock of people. Their language is *Kurukh*. They are declared as an ST in the states of Bihar, Madhya Pradesh, Maharashtra, Orissa and West Bengal. They accounted for 26.50 lakhs in 1991 census. Agriculture is their main occupation. The tragedy of the Oraons is that there has been land alienation among them. This has obliged them to diversify their occupation.

The Bhagats among the Oraons are called Tanabhagats who observe a puritanistic life. Non-vegetarian food and drinks are a taboo for the Oraon people.

### The Mundas

This tribe belongs to Kolarian stock. They are declared as an ST in the states of Bihar, Madhya Pradesh, Orissa, Tripura and West Bengal. As per 1991 census, their population comes to 16.18 lakhs.

The Mundas are an agriculture people. Land is increasingly becoming scarce for them. But, there are other avenues of employment for them. They work as mining labour in industrial and power projects. As a matter of fact, the Mundas have now become industrial people.

### The Khands

The Khands lived a nomadic life. They practised human sacrifices. At present, they have a scheduled status in the states of Orissa, Bihar, Andhra Pradesh, Maharashtra, Madhya Pradesh and West Bengal. According to 1991 census, their population comes to 9.91 lakhs. They are a simple folk of people who speak *Kandhi* as their dialect. They earn their livelihood through cultivation of land. Their agriculture is very crude. They normally do not grow cash crops.

The broad description of some of the major tribes of India brings out clearly that they are agriculturists by occupation. But with the scarcity of land, they have gone in a larger way for diversified occupations, government jobs and jobs in various sectors of industrial life. They are now no more a people living a queer life. Their isolation has been broken. They are in the plains. Government has sponsored many modernity-based development programmes for them. The old resources of livelihood have gone and they are increasingly becoming modern- postmodern.

Theoretically speaking, the tribals of India have already become modern and are also moving towards postmodernity. Postmodernity is diversity and the Panchayat Raj Institutions

(PRIs) have been decentralized. The tribals look after the development of their own village. This differentiates them from tribals of other regions. Basically, the tribal villages all over the country are scattered. The Verrier Elwin Committee has reported that 95 per cent of the tribals in India reside in scattered villages. Living in scattered villages, isolates the tribals from other tribals in the same village. Thus, diversity or isolation is the basic postmodern feature of India's tribals.

The history of the major tribal groups shows that once they were rulers of their land, and never accepted any authoritarianism. There was always antagonism between the Rajputs and the tribals. The tribals constantly rejected the hegemony of the Rajputs. Political authoritarian has never been acceptable to the tribals. The Santhals, Gonds and Bhils have never missed any opportunity to express their rebellion. Denial of institutional authority and rejection of the existing power group appear to be the postmodern tendencies of the tribals.

The tribes of Bihar, Madhya Pradesh, Gujarat and Rajasthan have all through their history opposed high-caste Hindus. But their postmodernism of pragmatism permits them to make compromises of all types in politics, especially at the Panchayat Raj level. Pragmatism is so much embedded in the tribal society that they would not hesitate to have modernity and postmodernity at the same time. We have cited innumerable evidences to show that the former savage tribal has today become modern and postmodern. It is because of his pragmatic attitude towards life.

# XI

# Globalization, Liberalization and Market

We are now on the road to the formation of a global society. The legacy of this society goes back to the enlightenment era. It was during this era that we developed a modern social thought which believed that the universal community of human kind is in all respects the end of object of the highest moral endeavour. Underlying this vision is an assumption that basically the needs and interests of all human beings are universally similar. Such a vision has shaped the emancipatory aspirations of both liberalism and Marxism, which have been committed to the eradication of those structures – the state and capitalism respectively – deemed to suppress the realization of a cosmopolitan world order based upon liberty, justice and equality for all of humanity.

Society is now changing so fast that globalization seems to be the only alternative for the world. Revolution in information technology and the ever-increasing role of mass media have strengthened the ideology put forward by enlightenment and modernity. Moreover, 'surface' events, such as the end of cold war, the collapse of communism and the Soviet Union, the transition from industrialism to post-industrialism, the global diffusion of democratic institutions and practices, together with the intensification of patterns of worldwide economic, financial, technological, ecological interdependence, have all signalled to many observers the final clearing away of the old world order, with all its menacing features, and the inauguration of a new world order which contains the promise of an evolving world, a society, a single global community of fate. Certainly, there can be little doubt that the world is being re-made around us, that radical changes are under way which may be transforming the fundamental parameters of modern human, social and political existence.

There is no single globalization. There are several globalizations. Its avatar is plural, its processes are historical and its outcomes are varying. And, therefore, instead of calling it globalization, we should call it globalizations. Globalization, the world over, is not a cakewalk. Challenges given to it are by no means ordinary. There is always a fear that the nation-state would lose its identity and importance. And, who knows, the state itself might die. There is yet another fear that the gap between the rich and the poor would increase. It is also argued that globalization is nothing short of a cultural bombardment on the developing countries by the western modernity – capitalism, industrialism and the nation-state system. And, the supporters of globalization – its intellectual lobby, keep on threatening, as Fukuyama would say – there is end of history; there is no alternative to capitalism, since socialism has collapsed. And again, to quote a line of Bob Dylan: "You'd better start swimming, or you'll sink like a stone." Where is the alternative? Let us explore globalization from the perspective of sociology.

## Globalization: Meaning and Definitions

Any discussion on globalization – its meaning and content – should necessarily begin with Roland Robertson, who could be said to be father of globalization. It was in the year 1990 that Mike Featherstone edited a book *Global Culture* (Sage Publications, London) which appeared in the market. In this book, Robertson had contributed an article, 'Mapping the Global Condition: Globalization as the Central Concept'. It is here that Robertson for the first time explained the concept of globalization. He says in his introduction: "My primary aim in this discussion is with the analytical and empirical aspects of globalization." Surely, global culture is not the culture of a particular nation-state, say, US or Europe, the culture of a nation-state cannot be global culture because it is homogenous and integrated. Global culture is, therefore, necessarily trans-societal culture, which takes a variety of forms which have preceded the inter-state relations into which nation-states can be regarded as being embedded, and processes which sustain the exchange and flow of goods, people, information, knowledge and images which give rise to communication processes which gain sane autonomy on a global level.

Robertson refers to political upheavals, which took place at the world level in the beginning of 1990. The shaking events which took place in China, the USSR and Europe, disturbed the traditional world order. Robertson writes:

> We have entered a phase of what appears to us in 1990s as great global uncertainty – so much so that the very idea of uncertainty promises to become globally institutionalized. Or to put it in a very different way, there is an eerie relationship between the ideas of postmodernism and postmodernity and the day-by-day geopolitical earthquakes which we (the virtually global we) have recently experienced.

For Robertson, the beginning of the idea of globalization goes back to the global uncertainty of the relations between world nation-states. In his effort to define globalization, Robertson links it with modernity and postmodernity. He also mentions about the politics of the global human conditions. Robertson writes:

> I deal with globalization as a relatively recent phenomenon. In fact, I argue that it is intimately related to modernity and modernization, as well as to postmodernity and postmodernization ... All that I am maintaining is that the concept of globalization per se should be applied to a particular series of developments concerning the concrete structuration of the world as a whole.

In other words, globalization is a comprehensive process, which includes both modernization and postmodernization. It would be wrong to say that the origin of globalization is from intra-societal relations. Nor is it from inter-state relations. Its making, according to Robertson, has been much more complex and culturally richer than that. It is inclusive of both modernity and postmodernity. Robertson (1992) defines it as under:

> I maintain that what has come to be called globalization is, in spite of differing conceptions of that theme, best understood as indicating the problem of the form in terms of which the world becomes united, but by no means integrated in native functionalist mode. Globalization as a topic is, in other words, a conceptual entry to the problem of world order in the most general sense – but, nevertheless, an entry which has no cognitive purchase without considerable discussion of historical and comparative matters.

It is exciting to know that the *International Sociology* decided in the year 200 to bring out a special issue of the journal on 'globalization' for the practice of social science and also for the understanding of world issues. The issue grew out of a multidisciplinary committee on global processes that was set up by the Swedish Council for the Planning and Coordination of Research. Consequently, a thematic research programme on globalization had also been made. The *International Sociology* has shown its concern for the world society as late as 2000. Its guest editor for the June 2000 issue, Goran Therborn has defined globalization as under:

> In comparison with the preoccupations of the social sciences 100 years earlier, the current overriding interest in globalization means two things. First of all, a substitution of the global for the universal, a substitution of space for time ... In a sense, globalization may be interpreted as modernity's flight into space. This issue of *International Sociology* is concerned with the implications of globalizations as plural, historical, social processes both for the practice of social science and for the understanding of world issues.

What Therborn means by globalization is:

1. It is global; it replaces universal.
2. It is space, and replaces time.
3. It is modernity plus a flight into space.
4. It is plural, that is, globalizations.
5. It consists of several social processes.

Therborn has further elaborated the subject matter of globalization and includes in it five major topical discourses, namely, (1) competition economy, (2) socio-critical, (3) state impotence in the face of world economy, (4) cultural, and (5) globe as a whole, i.e., a planetary eco-system. We shall discuss all these discourses on globalization at a later stage.

Anthony Giddens has written extensively on modernization. He assumes importance in the discussion of globalization for the simple reason that for him globalization is the direct consequence of modernization. Robertson did not think this way. He did not link modernization with globalization. Giddens argues that each of the three main dynamics of modernization implies universalizing tendencies which render social relations even more inclusive. They make possible global network of relationships (e.g., the system of international relations or the modern social system of capitalism), but they are also, for Giddens, more fundamental in extending the temporal and spatial distance of social relationships. Time-space distanciation, disembodying and reflexivity mean that complex relationships develop between local activities and interaction across distance. Giddens defines globalization in his book, *The Consequences of Modernity* (1990) as under:

> Globalization can thus be defined as the intensification of worldwide social relations, which links distant localities in such a way that local happenings are shared by events occurring many miles away and vice-versa. This is a dialectical process because such local happenings may move in an obverse direction from the very distanciated relations that shape them. Local transformation is as much a part of globalization as the lateral extension of social connections across time and space.

What is particular about Giddens' definition of globalization is that he links it with modernization. For him, modernization means a capitalist system, which is concerned with the commodity production, where there are social relations between the owners of private capital and non-owners who sell their labour for wages. The second feature of modernity is industrialism, third is the nation-state, and finally, nation-state's power to keep surveillance. All these features of modernity are involved in the process of globalization. He adds to these features the process of time-space distanciation as a prime ingredient of globalization.

Malcolm Waters has done quite a useful work on globalization in his book, *Globalization* (1995). The book has come out after a serious 'grinding' by the author. In this work, Waters has defined globalization as under:

> We can therefore define globalization as a social process in which the constraints of geography on social and cultural arrangements recede and in which people become increasingly aware that they are receding.

Actually, Waters, quite like Giddens, associates globalization with the wider social processes such as post-industrialization, postmodernization and the disorganization of capitalism.

We have argued earlier that globalization has several aspects. Waters has dealt with three major theoretical assumptions or arenas of globalization. These arenas give meaning and content to globalization:

1. *The economy arena*: It includes social arrangements for the production, exchange, distribution and consumption of goods and tangible services.
2. *The polity arena*: It includes social arrangements for the concentration and application of power, especially in so far as it involves the organized exchange of coercion and surveillance (military, police, etc.) as well as such institutionalized transformations of these practices as authority and diplomacy that can establish control over populations and territories.
3. *The cultural arena*: It includes social arrangements for the production, exchange and expression of symbols that represent facts, meanings, beliefs, preferences, tastes and values.

Waters has tried to develop a theory of globalization. The main thrust of his theory is that globalization has relationship between social organization and territoriality. The theorem of globalization in terms of theoretical paradigm as developed by Waters (1995) is as under:

> In summary, the theorem that guides the argument of this book is that: material exchanges localize; political exchanges internationalize; symbolic exchanges globalize. It follows that the globalization of human society is contingent on the extent to

> which cultural arrangements are effective to economic and political arrangements. We can expect the economy and the polity to be globalized to the extent that they are culturalized.

Thus, a broad survey of the definitions of globalization brings forth two major aspects. One is the economic context and the other is non-economic context. The non-economic context broadly includes socio-cultural, historical and political dimensions of globalization. Economic context of globalization seems to be stronger and louder. The European Commission defined globalization as below:

> Globalization is the process by which markets and productions in different countries are becoming increasingly interdependent due to dynamics of trade in goods and services and flows of capital and technology.

However, the economic interpretation of the European Commission is contested by several authors, important among them is Thompson (1999). He argues that the nature of the internationalized world economy would be a non-timed nationally embedded capital. Here, the principal private actors are the multinational corporations having a clear national base and working under the control of the home country. In contrast, the globalized world economy represents a new structure of disembodied economic relationships independent of national economics.

The definition of globalization, which is contested by Thompson, makes five important improvements: (1) private sectors in globalization are international and are independent of national economy; (2) new markets and productions are independent; (3) global economy is controlled by neo-liberal regulations; (4) under globalization, a new world economic system has emerged; and (5) the world economic system is transformed into capitalist system. Actually, the world capitalist system has undergone several changes. The Marxist theory of capitalism, as an explanatory tool to analyze capitalism, has become irrelevant after the disintegration of Soviet Russia. In this context, the economic explanation of globalization has provided a new dynamic capitalism known as 'flexible accumulation'. This capitalism has considerably altered the structure of global financial system, and with the computerization and communication, the significance of instantaneous international coordination of financial flows increased and intensified the reduction of spatial barriers (Harvey, 1989).

I. Wallerstein is a Marxist economist. He has applied Marxian theory to the understanding of globalization. According to him, the existing integrated world capitalist economy dates back to the sixteenth century. Wallerstein (1983) observed:

> The transition from feudalism to capitalism involves first of all (first logically and first temporary) the creation of a world economy. This is to say, social division of labour was brought into being through the transformation of long-distance trade from a trade in 'luxuries' to a trade in 'essentials' or 'bulk goods' which tied together processes that were widely dispersed into long commodity chains .... Such commodity chains were already there in the 16th century, and pre-dated anything that could meaningfully be called 'national economies'.

Wallerstein says that the national economies got a shift during twentieth century. It has ultimately resulted in the shift of capitalist world economy from its primary location in Europe to the entire globe. Wallerstein's main argument in defining globalization revolves round capitalist system. What he argues is that the capitalism, which was restricted to Europe, went beyond it and covered the whole world. Malcolm Waters questions Wallerstein's economic model of globalization and argues that globalization does not end up in the proliferation of capitalism only. It also integrates political and cultural variables.

There is yet another perspective of globalization which does not put emphasis mainly on economic system of capitalism. This approach is best represented by Leslie Sklair in his book, *Sociology of the Global System* (1991). According to him, environmental processes can be analyzed not by inter-state relations but by transnational practices. Sklair has defined transnational practices as those "that cross state boundaries but do not necessarily originate at the level of the state. The transnational corporations, the transnational capitalist class and the culture ideology of consumerism that together constitute transnational practices, are the dominant institutions found in the economic, political and cultural domains respectively as the driving forces of globalization".

What Sklair means by transnational practices is the amalgam of (1) transnational corporations, (2) transnational capitalist class, and (3) consumerism? In globalization, the global capitalist class is likely to operate from a nation-state, which has hegemony over other states. The US seems to be such a hegemonic state which would guide and dominate the transnational practices in all the spheres of economic, political and cultural globalization.

Wallerstein talked about world economy, which has constituted global capitalism. Manual Castells' global economy is different from world economy. Castells is the writer of the multi-volume book, *The Information Age: Economy, Society and Culture: The Rise of the Network Society* (1996). The book discusses elaborately the dynamics of information age. At its core, the information age is the age of new technologies of information, processing and communication. "Information technology is to this revolution what new sources of energy were to the successive industrial revolution .... The technological innovations have been essentially market-driven. The economic process that accompanied the information technology revolution is both informational and global because, under new historical conditions, productivity is generated through and competition is played out in a global network of interaction."

Castells has developed the theory of globalization around his concept of global economy. His definition of global economy runs as under:

> It is an economy with the capacity to work as a unit in real time on a plenary scale.

Castells further explains global economy by saying that "it is capitalist in nature short of, however, a capitalist class structure". Castells and other postmodernists who discuss globalization argue that in postmodern society classes have ceased to exist. According to them, postmodern capitalism is without class structure. Castells writes:

> There is not, sociologically and economically, such a thing as a global capitalist class. But there is an integrated global capital

network whose movements and variable logic ultimately determine economics and influence societies.

Castells further argues that the present capitalist societies are inherently based on information technology, which provides material basis for this society.

The United Nations Development Programme (UNDP) normally publishes Human Development Reports on annual basis. It argues that globalization is not new. There was some kind of globalization in early 16th and the late 19th century. But, the present structure of globalization is totally different from its earlier versions. The present globalization era consists of the following variables:

(1) *New markets*: Foreign exchange and capital markets linked globally, operating 24 hours a day, with dealings at a distance in real time.
(2) *New tools*: Internet links, cellular phone and media networks.
(3) *New actors*: The World Trade Organization (WTO) with authority over national governments, the multinational corporations with more economic power than many states, the global networks of non-governmental organizations (NGOs) and other groups that transcend nation boundaries.
(4) *New rules*: Multilateral agreements on trade, services and intellectual property, backed by strong enforcement mechanism and more binding for national governments, reducing the scope for national policy.

There is also a brighter side to globalization. The Human Development Report says: "Global markets, global technology, global ideas and global solidarity can enrich the lives of people everywhere, greatly expanding their choices. The growing interdependence of people's lives calls for shared values and a shared commitment to the human development of all people." But, the brighter side of globalization is not without its gloom. The same Human Development Report says: "Globalization expands the opportunities for unprecedented human advance for some but shrinks those opportunities for others and erodes human security. It is integrating economy, culture and governance but fragmenting societies. Driven by commercial market forces, globalization in this era seeks to promote economic efficiency, generate growth and yields profits. But it misses out on the goals of equity, poverty eradication and enhanced human security."

The list of negative impacts of globalization is large indeed: "Gaps in income between poorest and richest people; and countries have continued to widen ..... Furthermore, the new rules of globalization – privatization, liberalization and intellectual property rights – are shaping the path of technology, creating new risks of marginalization and vulnerability." Some of the other negative impacts of globalization include global crime in terms of illegal trafficking in weapons, cross-border terrorism, spread of HIV/AIDS, environmental degradation and fundamentalist movements as a part of assertion of local culture. Body-Gendrot (2000) supports Human Development Report's observations by empirical data and says that in Europe and America inequalities and associated problems of violence in cities have worsened under economic globalization.

A.K. Bagchi (1999) reports from India on the basis of field data that "globalization as a policy expression of neo-liberal regime has failed to improve macro-economic management and capacity in the region". It has also been observed that globalization, driven by liberal economic policy in India, has actually increased rural indebtedness, landlessness, food insecurity, child labour, casualization of work, wage gaps between skilled and unskilled labour, and the incidence of social pathologies such as violence and intimidation even as global culture has brought in its wake some changes in the lifestyles of the non-poor.

Yet another economist, Michael Chossudovsky (1991) also reports about the negative impacts of globalization:

> The overall impact of globalization has been a global crisis of which India and many other Asian and Eastern European countries have been made victims.

The British authors Stuart Hall, David Held and Gregor McLennan consider globalization as a complex process which extends the scope of modernization. According to them:

> Modernization is a process which reaches back to the earliest stages of modernity and continues to shape and reshape politics, economics and culture at an accelerated pace and scale. The

> extension of globalizing processes operating through a variety of institutional dimensions (technological, organizational, administrative, cultural and legal), and their increased intensifications, within these spheres, creates new forms and limits within modernity as a distinctive form of life.

Anthony McGrew (1992) views globalization as a process, which operates at a global scale. He writes:

> Globalization refers to those processes, operating at a global scale, which cut across national boundaries, integrating on connecting communities and organizations in space-time combinations, making the world in reality and in experience more interconnected. Globalization implies a movement away from the classifiable sociological idea of a 'society' as a well-bounded system, and its replacement by a perspective which concentrates on "how social life is ordered across time and space".

Thus, what McGrew means by globalization is:

(1) National identities are being eroded as a result of the growth of cultural homogenization and the global postmodernism.
(2) National and other 'local' or particularistic identities are being strengthened by the resistance to globalization.
(3) National identities are declining but new identities of hybridity are taking their place.

We have thus tried to define globalization at length in the above pages and in doing that, we have, as far as possible, included all those scholars who have provided specific perspectives on globalization. Globalization is a vast process taking place at a global scale. But, recently, there are scholars who have developed some theories on globalization. The definitions of globalization also raise certain issues. Some of the major themes, which emerge from the definitions and meaning of globalization, are put below:

(1) Building of a universal community of human kind. The objective goes with the assumption that the needs and interests of mankind all over the world are similar. The vision of globalization as a world community would give liberty, justice and equality for all humanity.
(2) Globalization establishes linkages and interconnections that cut across the nation-states.

(3) Globalization involves a profound reordering of time and space in social life. Giddens refers to it as time-space distanciation or compression. Today, we have to learn how to cope with an overwhelming sense of compression of our spatial and temporal worlds. Harvey argues that there is need to speed up or intensify time-space compression. It is in this context that David Harvey talks about 'global village'.
(4) Capitalism occupies a central place in globalization.
(5) Globalization is associated with technological progress.
(6) Globalization is a product of political factors, in particular, the existence of a permissive global order.
(7) The theory of globalization involves the analytical separation of the factors which have facilitated the shift towards a single world, e.g., the spread of capitalism, western imperialism and the development of a global media system.
(8) Globalization is interrelationship between the political, economic and cultural dimensions of social life.
(9) Globalization is dialectical having both positive and negative consequences. It contains certain dualities or binary oppositions: (i) universalization versus particularization; (ii) homogenization versus differentiation; (iii) integration versus fragmentation; (iv) centralization versus decentralization; and (v) juxtaposition versus syncretization.
(10) It is the expansion of the world system.
(11) It is a necessary accompaniment of modernity.
(12) It is the creation of a single world market.
(13) It is the consequence of modernity.
(14) It is a modern myth.
(15) It is a second modernity

For some sociologists, globalization gives a danger signal. For instance, Ian Roxborough (2002) traces the appropriation of globalization concept by American military strategists. He argues that the end of cold war has raised the question of world hegemony. And, in this race for power, the US has occupied a dominant position in the post-cold war world. After the disintegration of communism in Europe, globalization has come as a ready alternative. It has become a tool in the hands of US. Roxborough writes:

> Of all possible answers, globalization as a diagnosis of the new world order rapidly emerged as the winner, certainly in the rhetoric of the Washington Beltway. It seemed to explain the triumph of free market capitalism over state regulation, it offered a technological underpinning (the internet) for the changes, and most notoriously articulated as the end of history (Fukuyama, 1992), it celebrated the victory of the USA in the cold war. The concept of globalization provided a bridge between past (the cold war) and future by arguing that victory in the cold war had gone to the forces of free market democracies.

And if the US tames globalization, what would be the fate of developing countries?

## History of Globalization

The history of globalization is not very old. It is quite recent. If postmodernism was the concept of the 1980s, globalization is the concept of the 1990s. And, interestingly, postmodernism, despite its longer history, is even today controversial, whereas globalization is not that much debatable. Countries like US and France have accepted globalization as their state policy. The globalization issue of *International Sociology* (June 2000) traces the origin of the concept of globalization. It says that basically globalization is a concern of the second half of the 1990s, although, there were significant sociological contributions in the first half too, such as by Ianni (1992) and Robertson (1992). In the major dictionaries of English, French, Spanish and German of the 1980s or the first half of the 1990s, the word 'globalization' is not listed. In Arabic, at least four different words render the notion. Whereas in Japanese business, the word goes back to the 1980s, it entered Chinese academia only in the mid-1990s. The Social Citation Index records only a few occurrences of globalization in the 1980s but shows its soaring popularity from 1992 onwards, which accelerated in the last years of the past century.

While tracing the history of globalization, we must refer to the work of Anthony Giddens, namely, *The Consequences of Modernity* (1990). In this book, Giddens argues that postmodernity is not actually a break with modernity. The 'radicalized' or 'high' version of modernity is postmodernity. And, globalization, therefore, carries all the elements of modernity and, postmodernity. In fact, when we discuss globalization, we discuss both modernity and postmodernity. However, Giddens makes a difference in modernity and globalization. Modernity and postmodernity are often considered to be culturalistic while globalization is taken as an economic phenomenon. The difference between the three concepts, viz., modernity, postmodernity and globalization is, therefore, only of emphasis. Basically, all the three deal with institutional forms of modern society.

Malcolm Waters has traced the history of globalization in his book, *Globalization* (1995). He says that the word 'global' has been in usage for about 400 years from now. But, it was not used in its technical connotation. The words 'globalization, 'globalize' and 'globalizing' did not exist until about 1960. *The Economist* (4/4/59) reported, "Italy's quota for imports of cars has been increased", and in 1961. Webster became the first major dictionary to offer definitions of globalism and globalization. *The Spectator* (5/10/62) recognized that "globalization is, indeed, a staggering concept". It also mentioned about globalism, globalization, globalize and globalized.

Robertson (2000) reports that the word 'globalization' was not recognized as academically significant until the early or possibly the mid-1980s, but thereafter its use has become well-established. Although he says that its pattern of diffusion is virtually impossible to trace, it is beyond reasonable doubt that he is himself centrally responsible for its currency in sociology. The many items that he himself has published on the topic include what is possibly the first sociological article (1985) to include the word in its title although he had used the concept of 'globality' somewhat earlier. Waters (1995) says that after Robertson, the word 'global' has reached five figures in its use. Waters further informs: "As at February 1994 the catalogue of the Library of Congress contains only 34 items with the term or one of its derivatives in the title." None of these was published before 1987.

### Robertson's Mapping of Globalization History

Robertson argues that the history of globalization is not new. In fact, globalization emerged before the coming of modernity. It came even before capitalism. He has made a mapping of globalization in five major phases. They are discussed below:

### Phase 1: The Germinal Phase (Europe, 1400-1750)

It was the beginning of international trade relations in Europe, churches were considered to be global, i.e., universal, with the coming of enlightenment, the ideas about progress, humanism and individualism were becoming general and Gregorian Calendar had become common for all the western countries. In short, globalization had begun in Europe during the period 1400-1750. The areas, which received the beginning of globalization, include Catholic Church, notions of justice and humanity, universal calendar, and global exploration and colonialism.

### Phase 2: The Incipient Phase (Europe,1750-1825)

There was a sharp shift towards the idea of the homogeneous, unitary state. Formal international relations began to take shape. The areas of life which received some kind of globalization include emergence of nation-states, diplomatic relations between nation-states, international agreements, first non-European nations, and first ideas about internationalism and universalism.

### Phase 3: The Take-off Phase (1975-1925)

It was the period when the idea of acceptable national society came up. There appeared very sharp increase in the number and speed of global forms of communications. Development of global competitions, e.g., Olympics, Nobel Prizes, Implementation of World Time, First World War, League of Nations, etc. also took place. During the take-off time, globalization took the form of conceptualization of the world in terms of the four globalizing reference points: the nation-state, the individual, a single international society, and a single (masculine) humanity.

### Phase 4: The Struggle for Hegemony (1925-1969)

Disputes and wars about the fragile terms of the globalization process were established by the end of the take-off period. Globe-wise international conflicts increased concerning forms of life. Nature of and prospects for humanity were sharply focused by holocaust, atomic bomb and United Nations. Each nation-state in its own way struggled to establish its hegemony. The areas of hegemony include League of Nations and United Nations, Second World War, cold war, conceptions of war crimes and crimes against humanity, and universal nuclear threat of the atomic bomb.

***Phase 5: The Uncertainty Phase (1969-1992)***

There is heightening of global consciousness in the world community. Also, there is an accentuation of post-materialist values and increase in global institutions and movements. Conceptions of individual are rendered more complex by gender, ethnic and racial considerations. The uncertainty phase includes exploration of space, post-materialist values, world communities, international relations, global environmental problems, and global mass media via space technology(satellite television, etc.).

Robertson is a serious analyst of globalization. Earlier, we have called him as the father of globalization. He is credited to have employed the term 'globalization' in its technical sense for the first time. In his book, *Globalization* (1992), he makes certain careful reservations about his argument. The uncertainty phase is one in which the world community itself is not certain about its future direction. Robertson claims that globalization is neither necessarily good nor a bad thing – its moral character will be accomplished by the inhabitants of the planet. He also does not say that the world is, as a consequence of globalization, a more integrated or harmonious place but merely that it is a more unified or systematic place. He means by this, that events in any part of the world will increasingly have consequences for, or will be referenced against events in other distant parts. This relativization may not always be positive. Indeed, the world as a system may well be driven by conflicts that are far more intractable than the previous disputes between nations.

***Some Controversial Issues Regarding Consequences of Globalization***

With the concept of globalization becoming stronger and mature, we are today at the doorsteps of what Mcluhan calls a 'global village'. Our daily life is governed by products originating from all the corners of the world. More and more people are falling within the global mainstream. But, there is yet another scene. On the one hand, globalization is promoting 'uniformization' or 'homogenization', and on the other, there is increasing demand for autonomy and identity. This has resulted in diversity. We all live in diversity and this can hardly be denied. The complexity connected to the diversity is inevitable. Perhaps, this will increase. The two-fold action between the processes which constitute and feed each other, i.e., globalization and localization, is responsible for this. In fact, globalization has given certain challenges to the modern and postmodern societies. These challenges have become controversial for sociologists who have analyzed globalization. We shall mention some of these debatable issues here.

### Globalization and Localization

Wallerstein argues that globalization is the transformation of world system with its own laws and rules. In this process, there is emergence of multinationals and global exchange of people, goods, services and mutual dependencies. Thus, the transcommunication creates a worldwide web of interdependence.

But, globalization also creates favourable conditions for all forms of particularization, localization, and even fragmentation. The challenge given by localization is elaborately discussed by Featherstone, Friedman, Giddens, Hannerz, Latour and Robertson. Arie de Ruizter comments on this problematic issue:

> Apparently, the emergence of a transnational system implies the rebirth of nationalism, regionalism, and ethnicity. Here, we touch the other extreme – the localization. It appears that globalization cannot exist without its corollary, i.e., the processes of localization. Apparently, they constitute and feed each other. In this era of time-space compression distant localities are linked in such a way that local happenings are shaped by events occurring many miles away and vice versa.

The interaction between global and local is also termed as hybridization of institutions or fragmentation of society. Robertson says that the impact of globalization has a great bearing on the local formulations. He refers to the situation of Japan. In this connection, the term 'globalize' is used for indicating global localization. Robertson defines globalization as a term which was developed in particular reference to marketing issues, as Japan became more concerned with, and successful in the global economy against the background of much experience with the general problems of the relationship between the universal and the particular.

The developing countries in Asia and Africa are much scared about the expansion of globalization. They consider it to be a new kind of imperialism, which exercises its hegemony in the field of economy and culture. The US is the leading champion, which subordinates the nation-state cultures. The nation-state and grassroots culture are always in fear of its extinction. The other side of such a notion is that the proliferation of globalization would in the long run establish a uniform social order. The end of this process is homogenization.

### *Globalization Develops Anti-Modernist Ideology*

The issue of nation-state development has gained a fresh dimension in the wake of globalization. Modernization advocated the ideology of progress and development. It became the responsibility of nation-states to lead the people to the goal of development. But, with the coming of postmodernity, the power of nation-state has become quite limited. Postmodernity has now displaced modernity. There is a general understanding among the people that globalization discourses announce the end of the nation-state. In fact, it is this decline of the nation-state, which is responsible for the marginalization of development programmes.

Frans J. Schuurman (2000) is disappointed with the process of globalization. He is among those who argue that globalization has put an end to development. Privatization, which is an ingredient of globalization, does not bother for the marginalized sections of society. His comments run as under:

> When modernity moved into crisis and postmodernity threatened to replace it, development studies also moved into

> what was called 'the impasse' and the notion of development received some serious attacks, various kinds of alternative 'development' notions were presented .... The specific reason why development studies feel challenged by the concept of globalization, is not only because globalization (even more than postmodernity) is heralding the end of the modern age, it is also because there is a changing view on the role of the nation-state.

Schuurman provides a large number of arguments in favour of development programmes. He says that every individual has a right to claim for development. And, this right of development resides in the state. In other words, right to development stems from the people and the people in turn are sovereign and are therefore equated with states. It is, therefore, the view of those who consider development as a part of the state/government. But, there is another side of this argument. The postmodernists claim that the society is run by the market. And, therefore, the market would look into the problem of development. Arguments cannot be alternatives to any programmes of development and, therefore, in the years to come, development would cease to be an active part of state agenda.

### *Crisis for Sociological Theories*

Malcolm Waters argues that globalization is basically a theory of social change. Sociologists have been studying social change through a variety of theories. But, in the context of globalization, is it possible for us to employ Marxian theory of conflict and functionalism to analyze the consequences of globalization? What is worse is that the postmodern social theory is very much critical of mega-narratives and in such a situation will these great theories be able to comprehend globalization? Waters (1995) writes:

> Such controversies as these are appearing to surround the issue of whether old Marxist or functionalist theories can be adapted to explain globalization or whether we need to construct novel arguments. This may be because sociological theories of change have almost always implied the universalization of the processes that they explain. Although, it did not arise without sociology, the concept has therefore found instant appeal across a range of

intellectual interests. It remains for sociology to connect the concept with its own vital theoretical traditions.

Waters has not touched the emergence of social theory but the reality is that globalization along with postmodernity has made conflict and functional theory irrelevant.

### *Risk of Ecological Degradation*

Ulrich Beck has talked about the risks, which is a characteristic of modern and postmodern societies. People in these societies are obliged to experience much of ecological degradation. Capitalism has remained as the only alternative, after the collapse of Soviet Russia. Earlier, technology was predominantly oriented to maximize the production and whatever was gained by massive production was fairly distributed among the masses by the nation-state. But, the process of globalization has made the nation-state quite impotent. As a consequence of it, the weaker sections of the society feel highly victimized. The German sociologist Beck's argument is simple: Earlier, the nation-state was a guardian who could appropriate the benefits of modernization in a justifiable way. But, now, globalization has made the state fragile and replaced it by multinational corporations. Beck (1992) draws our attention to capitalism's global infiltration:

> In the welfare states of the West a double process is taking place now. On the one hand, the struggle for one's 'daily bread' has lost urgency as a cardinal problem overshadowing everything else, compared to material subsistence in the first half of this century, to a third world menaced by hunger. For many people problems of 'overweight' take the place of hunger .... Parallel to that, the knowledge is spreading that the sources of wealth are 'polluted' by growing 'hazardous' side effects.

Globalization has also done the worse in degrading the environment. Capitalism thinks only for its expansion. For Beck, modernization is the primary globalization force. Global risks are the product of global industrialization. But, because risk is itself inherent in globalization, the advent of risk society accelerates the globalization process. It is in terms of this effect that Beck makes his contribution to the conceptualization of globalization. Risk globalizes because it universalizes and equalizes. It affects every member of the society regardless of location and class position. Moreover, it respects no border. Beck (1992) makes his observation as under:

> Food chains connect practically everyone on earth to everyone else. They dip under borders. The acid content of the air is not only nibbling at sculptures and artistic treasures, it also long ago brought about the disintegration of modern customs, barriers. Even in Canada the lakes have become acidified and forests are dying even in the northern reaches of Scandinavia.

What Beck argues is that globalization has cut across the international boundaries, and therefore the risks of modernity travel without any barrier. There is actually a process of risk distribution through the expansion of globalization. This process is called *boomerang curve* by Beck. Here, the effect of risk is of boomerang kind. What actually happens is that the hazardous consequences of risks return to their sources and adversely affect those who produce them. The risks are not only in the field of environment; they also influence other sectors of society such as money, property and legitimation.

### Controversy over Time-Space Compression

Globalization is in no sense an ordinary process of social change. It involves a large number of themes such as modernity, postmodernity, development, risk and time-space compression. There is no general agreement over all these issues and themes covered by globalization. The position taken by Giddens (1990) is that the transformation of society through globalization is a continuation of modernity. There has never been a break in the modernity. Lyotard (1984), on the other hand, disagrees with Giddens. Lyotard's argument is that when modernity failed or, in other words, meta-narratives became irrelevant, the postmodernity or globalization emerged. For Giddens, there is nothing new in globalization. It has only radicalized modernity.

The issue of a connection between postmodernism and globalization is the source of much theoretical speculation. The problem is to link postmodernization with globalization. Perhaps, David

Harvey (1989), a geographer, is the first to link globalization with postmodernity. And, the linkage is through time-space compression. Like Giddens, Harvey begins with an analysis of premodern conceptions of space and time, although the issue of space is here held to be primary. In the feudal context, space was conceived within the terms of relatively autonomous community that involved a fused pattern of economic, political and religious rights and obligations. Space outside the community was only dimly perceived, time even more so. These localized conceptions of time and space were reconstructed during the renaissance.

Harvey argues that the time-space compression bursts out occasionally. Giddens does not agree with Harvey's time-space compression. Rather, he talks about time-space distanciation. Thus, according to Giddens, time and space have become stretched. This is not, of course, the meaning that he intends. What he wants to convey is that social relationships are becoming stretched across great distances. In other words, new communication technologies are ensuring that social relationships between kin or colleagues are becoming more intense and robust. Viewed from such an analysis of time-space compression and time-space distanciation, Harvey and Giddens come closer.

### *Globalization: The Issue of Logics*

A review of the literature on globalization highlights one fundamental disagreement at the level of theory. One group of authors argues that globalization can be explained by the primacy of one causal logic. Among these authors are included Wallerstein, Rosenau and Gilpin. Another group of authors is headed by Giddens. This group argues that theoretically globalization can be explained by four discrete logics instead of single causal logic.

Wallerstein explains globalization by a single logic. He has introduced the concept of the world system and has stressed the centrality of capitalism to the process of globalization. Gilpin and Rosenau consider international relations as the key idiom of globalization. Thus, Rosenau associates globalization with technological progress, whilst Gilpin considers it to be an expression of politico-military factors (power politics). Accordingly, each of these three authors locates the causal logic of globalization in a specific institutional domain, viz., the economic, the technological, and the political respectively.

Instead of a single causal logic, Giddens points to four discrete logics. He says that there are four institutions, which are linked together and which make globalization a possibility. These institutions include capitalism, industrialism, nation-state system and military power. But, the theoretical disagreements should not disturb anybody because globalization is by nature dialectical. The disagreements in fact, constitute the basic pillars of globalization.

### *Controversy over a Global Society*

What should be the shape of a global society? There is controversy over this question. Will globalization develop a society, which would be emancipatory for the mankind as a whole? What we call today liberalism and Marxism have their roots in an enlightened universalism. This universalism is supposed to be charged by a cosmopolitan world society, a global society in which transnational social bonds and universally held notions of peace, justice, equality and freedom would define the conditions of human existence. It is said by some of the propagators of globalization that in its present form it carries most of these objectives. Fukuyama, whom we have referred earlier, said in 1989 that globalization and postmodernity announce the 'triumph' of liberalism across the world as the beginning of a new area of 'perpetual peace'. Fukuyama further says that there is end of history after the cold war, that is, disintegration of Soviet Russia. And, now, the only alternative left with the world is that of capitalism. Capitalism is our future; it is our destiny.

Wallerstein (1983) contested the views of Fukuyama. He argues that the contemporary era is not the triumph of capitalism, nor is it the victory of liberalism. It is an era of crisis, which will bring in its wake emancipation on a global scale. Wallerstein further argues that capitalism is so strong and powerful that it is difficult for nation-states and people to get out of it. He says:

> Despite the appearance of fragmentation (in postmodernity), nature of global markets and the global mobility of capital ensure that few states or people can opt out of the logic of this capitalist world political economy.

Harvey and Jameson support Fukuyama with a tongue in their cheek. They argue that in the last thirty years capitalism has extended its reach and, because of new technologies of communication and control, it has become even more mobile. Furthermore, they argue that this increasingly global form of capitalism is associated with a profound transformation in the nature of the existing world capitalist order. A new form of global capitalism (late capitalism) has extended and deepened its reach across the globe. With this has come an increasing penetration and consolidation of capitalist social relations on a global scale.

### *A Bifurcated World: Rosenau's Views on Globalization*

Globalization is said to bring uniformity. It encourages homogenization. It is centrally capitalistic. All such definitions and meanings of globalization are controversial. For instance, the worldview of Rosenau is different. He argues that the logic of globalization is located in technology. By technology he means specifically the shift to a post-industrial order. Taking technology as his basic thrust of argument, Rosenau draws his conclusions and develops the form of the contemporary global system. He draws heavily from August Comte and says that the world society arises from the global diffusion of techno-industrial civilization. Rosenau has produced a highly original account of the contemporary global condition in his book, *Interdependence and Conflict in World Politics* (1989). He rejects not only the notion of a 'global civilization' but also that of a 'capitalist world society'. Instead, he identifies a complete fracturing of the global system, a structural bifurcation, as the full force of post-industrialism is experienced across the globe. His argument indicates that there is no longer a single global society but rather two: (1) a society of states, in which diplomacy and national power remain the critical variables; and (2) a world in which multifarious organizations, groups and individuals, each pursuing its own interests, create an ever more intricate web of transnational relations which are outside the control of any single nation-state.

Thus, the worldview of Rosenau is bifurcated. He labels this world as multi-centric world. It is a hyper-pluralist transnational society. Its characteristics are:

(1) *Transnational organizations*, such as transnational banks, International Sociological Association, Red Cross, Oxfam, social movements, etc.
(2) *Transnational problems*, such as pollution, drugs, ethnicity, AIDS and environmental degradation.
(3) *Transnational events or happenings*, such as live TV broadcasts during war, attack on Iraq, etc.
(4) *Transnational communities*, based on religion, e.g., Islam, Hinduism, knowledge-based academic networks, culture-art world.
(5) *Transnational structure*, such as those of production, finance and knowledge.

The thrust of Rosenau's theoretical argument is that globalization has bifurcated the contemporary world instead of making it homogenous and single. His bifurcated world thus consists of (1) nation-state-centric world, and (2) multi-centric world having international linkages. This bifurcated world is the world of international politics.

Thus, in this section, we have discussed some of the issues of globalization, which have become controversial. Each scholar has his own logic about the consequences of globalization. What would be the form or shape of global society? The question has been addressed by several sociologists, economists and geographers. The positions taken by these social scientists are varying. There is little common ground for their meeting. It is because each of them delivers his own distinctive response to the consequences and challenges of globalization. None of these positions can be judged to be either fully right or wrong, true or false, since each is essentially attempting little more than claiming to represent the most judicious assessment of where contemporary trends are leading.

Despite disagreements among themselves the authors writing on globalization share some common ground. In particular, while each one of them gives his own model of global society, they all share a belief in the following broad observations:

(1) Modern or postmodern societies can only be understood within a global setting; now, no society is a capsule society.

(2) Whether the nation-state is any longer the most appropriate political unit for organizing human affairs in a more interconnected world system? Nation-state, according to all the authors, is under a serious clout.
(3) With the increase in economic interdependence, the nation-state economy has got a serious setback. Even Gilpin, a staunch champion of realism, acknowledges that the intensification of economic dependence has decreased national economic autonomy. And, what will happen to nation-states when contemporary military power has internationally increased?

It is difficult indeed to make any considered statement about the theme of globalization and its consequences. We can do no better than to close our concluding observations by the quotation of Anthony McGrew ('A Global Society', in *Modernity and Its Futures*, by Stuart Hall et al., 1993):

> As the end of the century draws near, globalization is forcing us to rethink the nature of the 'political community', the basic unit of human affairs. Indeed, globalization appears to be challenging the modern orthodoxy that the nation-state defines the 'good community'.

## Globalization and a Universal Sociology

Globalization has reduced the status of nation-state. The idea of nation-state has today become redundant. Besides globalization, the postmodernism also rejects the notion of 'society' as a totalizing concept. If globalization succeeds in its objective of establishing a world society, what would happen to the concept of Indian society or the Japanese society? The kind of culture, music, architecture, lifestyle and language that we find in India is not genuinely Indian. It is borrowed from different corners of world in the wake of increasing speed of globalization. In such a situation, how does Indian society fulfil the criteria of a society? It appears that the world sociology has to rethink about its definition of society. In this connection, let us refer to Bauman (1992), who defines this problem as:

> It seems that most sociologists of the era of modern orthodoxy believed that all being said – the nation-state is close enough to its own postulate of sovereignty to validate the use of its theoretical expression – the 'society' concept – as an adequate framework for sociological analysis ... In the postmodern world, this belief carries less conviction than ever before.

If we look into the recent writings of Mann (1986), Robertson (2000), Giddens (1990) and Bauman (1992), we would immediately find that they all talk about the redundance of the concept of society in the context of contemporary globalization. Mann, for instance, states: "I would abolish the concept of 'society' altogether." Instead, he conceives of "societies not as unitary social systems or bounded totalities but as constituted by multiple overlapping and intersecting socio-spatial networks of power". Giddens criticizes sociologists for putting undue reliance upon the idea of 'society'. According to him, the concept of society is a bounded system, it should be replaced by a starting point that concentrates upon analyzing how social life is ordered across time and space – the problem of time-space distanciation. McGrew concludes that globalization dislodges society from its focal position in the discourse of modern sociology. But what is there to replace it?

At this stage of our discussion, we must mention that as the concept of society has become irrelevant for the growing strength of globalization, it has become so also for postmodernity. Postmodernism is attached to diversity, difference and the plurality of communities and identities. For it, the notion of 'society' is only totalizing. Bauman's argument runs like this: "Postmodernism is associated with a view of the human world as irreducibly and irrevocably pluralistic, split into a multitude of sovereign units and sites of authority, with no horizontal or vertical order, either in actuality or potency. In such a situation, the sociological concept of society loses its existence."

M.S. Archer gives a serious thinking to the relevance of the concept of society in this era of globalization. He provides a convincing solution for looking at some of the concepts of sociology. These concepts need to be re-examined in the context of globalization. As for society, Archer writes:

> The globalization of society means that societies are no longer the prime units of sociology. What is to replace this focus on societies is a 'sociology of one world' which recognizes that "global processes are now partly constitutive of social reality everywhere".

It is not only about the redundance of the concept of society; in fact, globalization has rendered many of our sociological concepts irrelevant. Archer delivers a radical challenge to both orthodox and postmodernist sociological thinking. She argues that globalization demands a critical rethinking of the sociological enterprise to reflect the arrival of one world. Such rethinking, she proposes, "has to be fired by a commitment to both reason and humanity, and so requires a re-centering of reasoning and the human being within the sociological enterprise". For Archer, reasoning and humanity constitute a bridge to international sociology and so to delivering "sociology for one world".

In the preceding pages, we have discussed the definitions, causal explanations and meaning of globalization. Malcolm Waters and a few other sociologists have argued that globalization has three major perspectives or aspects, namely, economic, political and cultural. In the following pages we will discuss these three perspectives.

### Economic Globalization

Historically speaking, the European dominance had failed to exercise its hegemony over the world by the middle of 20th century. This dominance was, in reality, not in the realm of politics or even culture. It was an economic dominance. It was during this period that European Economic Community (now European Union) was organized. At the level of Asia, Japan had appeared as a powerful economic tiger to combat the European economic market. Europe, in its economic struggle, gave rise to the beginning of globalization. It developed communication networks and physical linkages to different parts of the world. This gave rise to rapid growth of trade. It was during this period that Marx developed the theory of capitalist globalization. Linking economic development with globalization Water (1995) says:

> Capitalism is clearly the vehicle of globalization because its particular institutions – financial markets, commodities, contractualized labour, alienable property – facilitate economic exchanges over great distances. For this reason, we have seen many theories of globalization that take their lead from Marx in stressing its economic foundations. For these authors, as capitalism expands across the globe, it internationalizes the associated pattern of social relations known as class.

We now discuss below the various means by which global economic relationships are accomplished:

### *World Trade*

One of the important factors of economic globalization is the world trade. Trade can link together geographically distant producers and consumers, often establishing a relationship of identification as well as interdependence between them. Overall, in the period since industrialization, world trade between nation-states has expanded very rapidly.

### *International Division of Labour*

World trade means international division of labour. Each country specializes in the production of particular parts of industry. For instance, in international trade of car parts, division of labour has expanded three-fold in twenty years indicating componentization of the car industry. The key feature is Japanese expansion and its investment in the American industry. Quite like the field of automobile, division of labour is also found in the fields of chemicals, construction and memory chips and micro-processors.

### *Multinational Enterprises*

The main focus of many hopes and fears about economic globalization is the multinational corporations (MNCs) and transnational corporations (TNCs). These have become so large and powerful that they undermine the legitimate and often democratically established sovereign authority of the nation-state. In fact, MNCs and TNCs are criticized for their good works as well as for their intolerable and inhuman practices. The multinational enterprises have given a new shift to postmodern capitalism. Now, capitalism has become globalizing capitalism. It has received a shift from resource-based and market-seeking investment to spatial optimization of production and profit opportunities. In fact, the development in multinational enterprises shows that there is end of the old multinationalism.

### Organizational Aspect

Yet another economic adventure, which is observed through globalization, is the organizational aspect of business. Now, business at international plane is run by organizational skills. Earlier, there was Fordism, which meant mass production of standardized items for mass markets. Now, there is the age of post-Fordism. The production at this post-industrial stage is flexible, which requires organizational skills. Thus, flexibility-oriented postmodern production is linked to globalization. As an example of the organizational skills, the case of Japan may be given. The Japanese organizational paradigm argues that the firm must become organization-oriented rather than accountancy-oriented. It should focus on asset building and market share rather than on immediately calculated issues of cost and revenue.

### Floating Finance

One of the major features of globalization is the availability of market for raising loans and capital. Harvey (1989) has specified the role of financing agencies as under:

> Banking is rapidly becoming indifferent to the constrains of time, place and currency ... an English buyer can get a Japanese mortgage, an American can tap his New York bank account through a cash machine in Hong Kong and a Japanese investor can buy shares in a London-based Scandinavian bank whose stock is denominated in Sterling, Dollars, Deutsche Marks and Swiss Francs.

Their effect in globalizing culture and consciousness must, therefore, be equally profound.

Before the onset of globalization in a systematic way during 1990, there was not much of labour migration in the world market. The nation-states kept a vigil on such movements. But, recently, there has been much leniency in allowing labour migration. Presenting the contemporary situation of migration, Waters (1995) observes:

> In a genuinely globalized market, movements of labour and patterns of settlement would be entirely unrestricted by states. However, there are some inklings of evidence that even here the powers of nation-states may be waning. If the restrictions are numerous enough, individual decisions can overwhelm the regulative practices of even the most draconian preventive measure. Several events bear witness to this: The mass illegal migration of Mexicans into the U.S.A., successful migrations by Indo-Chinese 'boat-people', and the collapse of the barbed wire frontier between eastern and western Europe.

### *Transnationalization of Classes*

Classes are traditionally analyzed at the level of nation-state society. Weber argued that the class struggles take place for the distribution of rewards at the level of nation-state. However, Marx had a larger vision of class struggle. He very bravely said: "The working men have no country".

In the context of globalization, there are two situations for class struggle. The first situation is one in which the state society has declined. And, therefore, there is no struggle for the distribution of rewards at the nation-state level. At this level, the classes cease to exist. In the second situation, we have marketization and globalization of the international economy that may be depriving classes of an arena in which to struggle. It is a global economic market that has no centre, there might be no place in which classes can confront one another.

However, Van der Pijl developed an idea about international classes. He argues that as globalization proceeds, the capitalist class pushes itself in an international direction. And, therefore, they assume international status. However, there are few takers of the proposition given by Van der Pijl. On the one hand, it is argued by Malcolm Waters and a few others that though classes in globalization have lost their strength, it should not mean that there is no stratification in the postmodern society. Instead of class, there has emerged a stratification pattern, which is charged by consumption.

### Political Globalization

Daniel Bell, the author of *The Coming of Post-industrial Society* (1976), has made a succinct observation on political globalization:

> The nation-state is becoming too small for the big problems of life, and too big for the small problems of life.

All in all, the status and role of nation-state is being increasingly irrelevant in the era of globalization. Besides Daniel Bell, D. Held (1991) discusses at length the reducing status of nation-state:

(1) The increasing economic and cultural connections reduce the power and effectiveness of governments at the nation-state level. They can no longer control the flow of ideas and economic items at their borders and their internal policy instruments become ineffective.
(2) State power is further reduced because transnational processes grow in scale as well in number.
(3) Many traditional areas of state, for instance, defence, communications and economic management must, therefore, be coordinated on an international or inter-governmental basis.
(4) States are now obliged to surrender their sovereignty within larger political units such as European Union (EU), Association of South-East Asian National (ASEAN), North Atlantic Treaty Organization (NATO), Organization of Petroleum Exporting Countries (OPEC), and international organizations such as United Nations (UN), World Trade Organization (WTO) and International Monetary Fund (IMF).
(5) This provides the basis for the emergence of a supranational state with dominant coercive and legislative power.

#### *Some Planetary Problems and Their Nationalization*

Political globalization has taken up some of the problems which nation-states are required to handle at their level. These problems are so crisis-prone that the problem of one country might affect another country and in the long run engulf the whole globe. Thus, the problems of nation-states are encountered globally. AIDS and environmental degradation are among these crises. We discuss below some of the planetary problems, which have become part of the political globalization:

### Human Rights

One of the most important aspects of political globalization is the consensus on the acceptance of human rights. Earlier to the declaration of human rights, rights were considered only to be political ones in terms of voting rights. Later on, these rights were institutionalized as citizenship rights. It is due to political globalization that the human rights are given priority over other rights. Writing about the importance of human rights, Waters (1995) observes:

> There have been frequent declarations of universal human rights, normally involving freedom of speech and action, freedom of political association and participation, due process under law, minimum access to health, education and material welfare, and control of one's own body, especially its reproductive capacities.

It must be mentioned that the human rights declared globally are taken care of by the nation-states. Normally, the nation-states violate these principles because the conventions offer no means of collective enforcement. Despite the weakness of nation-state in not implementing human rights, at least, it should be appreciated that there has been internationalization of human rights.

### Global Environment

Political globalization has one particularity. It establishes linkages between the globe, the nation-state, the state and the grassroots. Waters (1995) has brought some of the aspects of political globalization, which are related to environment and pollution:

> Global warming is a catcall phrase in contemporary time. The ozone layer is a high level stratum of the atmosphere, which screens the surface of the planet from intense ultra-violet

radiation. Scientists have also found out the effects of both hydrocarbon and emission from cars and industrial sulphur dioxide pollution, which returns as acid rain to destroy forests. O'neill has very successfully drawn out attention to some of our global environmental panics. He calls them globalizing panic.

> By globalizing panic, I understand any practice that traverses the world to reduce its cultural diversity to the generics of coca-cola, tourism and foreign and medical aid, military defence posts, fashion and the international money markets. Since these practices are never quite stabilized, their dynamics include de-globalizing tendencies, which will be reinscribed by the global system as threats to the world order.

### *Development and Inequality*

Inequality has been world's age-old problem. It is the basic aspect of stratification. All through the history of social sciences, inequality has remained a running theme of discussion. But, the emergence of globalization has hastened up the process of insecurity and inequality. It is found that the benefits of globalization have largely been cornered by the countries which have potentiality to invest money. The developing countries have only to satisfy themselves as the consumer society of the rich countries. The poor countries have further experienced a sharp divide between the rich and the poor.

The Human Development Report mentions a large number of insecurities in the developing world resulting from political globalization. These include job and income insecurity, health insecurity, cultural insecurity, personal insecurity and environmental insecurity. The Human Development Report describes the consequences of globalization in the following words:

> Globalization has given new characteristics to conflicts. Feeding these conflicts is the global traffic in weapons, involving new actors and blurring political and business interests. In the power vacuum of the post-cold war era, military companies and mercenary armies began offering training to governments and corporations. Accountable only to those who pay, these hired military services pose a severe threat to human security.

The political consequences of globalization very clearly show that the process of development followed all over the world has created global disparities. There is much political divide in the world today.

### *Peace and Order*

By 1945, the international system had suffered the depredation of two world wars and of consequent revolutions and economic upheavals. When in 1990, there was end of cold war between two big world powers, the political globalization gave some degree of peace and order to the world community. Besides the economic and political globalizations, the United Nations Charter of 1945, consisting of fifty-one nations – mainly the victors in the Second World War – agreed as follows:

(1) War and use of force between states were prohibited.

(2) A monopoly on the use of force was vested in the Security Council of the United Nations Organization, which was expected to use military means to maintain collective security and to constrain aggression.

(3) States could only use force to defend themselves against aggression by another state.

There are several instances, which show that the UN has usually failed to enforce collective security to the world community. The recent example of the violation of security is the US attack on Iraq. Even the Security Council could not exercise its power over US. And, Iraq had to face the attack. Despite its failure, the existence of the UN has established a communicative and normative framework for clearly positive developments in the control of the most destructive means of violence. These include the nuclear test ban treaty of 1961, nuclear non-proliferation treaty of 1968, the various strategic arms reduction agreements of the 1970s and 1980s and the Helsinki Accord that set up the European Council for Security and Cooperation (ECSE).

In the wake of the emergence of international mechanisms to redefine and find solutions for world problems, the nation-state has been assigned a lower status in three ways:

(1) it redirects individual political preferences;

(2) it delegitimates the nation-state as a problem-solver; and

(3) it sets up new international organizations to which some elements of state sovereignty are progressively surrendered.

The era of globalization has resulted in the creation of a borderless world. This has also created a common political culture across societies. The single political culture has been advocated by Fukuyama (1992) and Huntington (1991). These scholars have argued that socialism as a form of government and society has failed totally with the disintegration of Soviet Russia. Huntington says that the national societies are moving towards a political culture of liberal democracy. He gives certain features of such a society: "First that individuals should have rights to autonomy in the spheres of thought and action, for example, the process under law, speech and publication that expresses, political and religious ideas, control of the body, and ownership and disposal of property; and second that the members of any polity should have the right to choose and to participate in their own government by means which roughly give them an equal influence in that choice and an equal chance to participate."

Thus, it is certain that political globalization has created a favourable ground for liberalism, democracy and capitalism. It is argued that at this point of political development in the world, the history has ended. There is nothing beyond democracy, liberalism and capitalism in the world. There are no alternatives to socialism and communism. Concluding the situation of political globalism in contemporary postmodern society, Waters (1995) observes:

> A critical and striking feature of political globalization is that it does not in any area exhibit the extreme level of globalization, for example, in financial markets. Political globalization is most advanced in the areas of international relations and political culture. However, the states remain highly resistant, largely sovereign and critical arena for problem solving.

In the process of political globalization, the nation-state has always remained a debatable issue. Admittedly, state is becoming weak as its sovereignty is continuously encroached upon by international constraints. Despite this, even today, it must be said that the state is the only territorial organization which can solve several problems. And, here, its survival value lies. But, if the state survives globalization, then, it cannot be counted as the force that it currently appears to be. Weakness has definitely crept into it.

### Cultural Globalization

In the earlier sections of this chapter, we have drawn two important conclusions: One is that wherever there are symbols of mediation, the relations at the global level are strong and frequent. In the case of economic globalization, financial markets are mediated by monetary tokens. And, therefore, economic globalization has assumed an important place in globalization. Second, in the situation of material and power exchanges, the economic and political arenas are progressively displaced by symbolic values. In both these situations – economic and political arenas – where there is mediation through symbols or tokens, globalization has become stronger and influential. On this argument, globalization may be considered as a powerful vehicle of culturalization. The cultural globalization, therefore, assumes an important place in our discussion of social change.

Surely, globalization has affected and influenced the world culture. But, in its present form, the globalized culture is chaotic rather than orderly. The absolute globalization of culture would involve the creation of a common hyper differentiated field of value, taste and style opportunities, accessible to each individual without constraint for purposes either of self-expression or consumption. This is simple very difficult. Under a globalized cultural regime, it is not possible to link Islam or Hinduism to the global territories. If we are really keen to develop a global culture, it is essential to have a continuous flow of ideas, information, values and tastes mediated through mobile individuals, symbolic tokens and electronic simulations. The prerequisites for the development of a global culture are difficult indeed to attain. Despite some structural difficulties, globalization has a strong impact on the culture of different world territories. We now discuss some of the arenas of culture which have received influence of globalization.

#### *Development of Fundamentalism and Globalization*

Fundamentalism has developed all over the world along with the extension of globalization. There are reasons for the fresh rise of this religious ideology. Globalization is, in fact, an extension of modernization and postmodernization. Both these movements oppose religious conservatism. The antagonism to modernity finds expression in fundamentalism. This is perhaps the indirect contribution of globalization to religion and religious ideology. Lechner (1992), however, finds direct effects of globalization on religion and fundamentalism. She argues that the fear of modernity motivates the religious leaders to revitalize their religion, so that it can combat effectively, modernity and postmodernity. According to Lechner, the religious revitalization includes the following four points:

(1) The universalization of western culture preferences puts the local religions in identity crisis. For instance, the high-caste hegemony over lower castes and adivasis becomes weak in the wake of the dominance of western secular values. This very conveniently gives rise to Hindu fundamentalism. In the same way, the Islamic ullema must be defended through fundamentalism against the secular ideology.
(2) Nation-state is also responsible for creating a favourable ground for the rise of fundamentalism. The nation-state has become weak owing to globalization and it, therefore, encourages fundamentalism to raise its ugly head.
(3) Fundamentalism also gets currency, as there is predominance of secularism and law.
(4) Fundamentalism, which believes in the superiority of a particular religion, gets defeated by the establishment of the fact that the world is pluralistic and choice-driven and that there is not a single and superior culture.

Thus, fundamentalism is one of the strongest responses to globalization. In the developing countries, where modernity is a latecomer, fundamentalism is a frequent occurrence.

#### *Cosmopolitanism*

As secularism fights against the irrational influence of religion appearing in the form of fundamentalism, modernity also wages war against ethnicity, race and caste. In the premodern world, ethnicity was taken for granted component of identity. The Nazis did all sort of injustices to the Jews in the name of racial ethnicity. In India, the scheduled castes and tribes have been victims of exploitation on the assumption that they were born 'low'.

Ethnicity has been associated with the notion of nation. In the western countries, nation is considered to be ethnic in character. National ethnicity is played upon to convey the superiority of a particular nation. For instance, the British nation is known for its fair play; the Japanese are known for their honourability, the Chinese for industry, the Canadian for decency and the Indians for caste. Wherever we see, we will find the idea of a nation is charged with some kind of ethnicity. Stuart Hall et al. (1992) argue that the political and intellectual elites construct ideological practices to develop national ethnicity. They tell stories or histories of their nation which is full of triumphs and victories. They invent new patterns of rituals, which give collective expression to the nation. They create and construct a large number of myths and legends about the greatness of their nation.

What globalization has done to the culture of ethnicity and nation? Has it developed cosmopolitanism? Hall et al. have summarized the impact of globalization on ethnicity and nationhood on the following counts:

(1) Globalization is full of dialectics: it is a process, which creates differentiation and also homogenization. It has pluralized the world by recognizing the cultural variability.
(2) It weakens the prejudices against the minorities, which have been absorbed in the national mainstream.
(3) The globalization process brings the marginalized groups to the centre. In the case of India, the weaker sections have developed their own elites and groups of middle class people who leave their periphery to move towards the centre of the national mainstream.

Hall et al. have suggested some ways for the weakening of ethnicity and nationhood. One such way for the ethnic groups is to find out their new identity in the process of globalization. The best solution in the global society is to assume a cosmopolitan character where each group should practice its own culture and ethnicity.

### *Emerging Consumer Culture*

A new consumer culture is emerging due to the process of globalization. It must be stressed here that consumer culture means more than simple consumption. In a consumer culture, the items consumed take on a symbolic and not merely a material value. Taking meals in a posh hotel on the weekend by an Indian family gives it symbolic satisfaction which Pierre Bourdieu calls the 'expression of symbolic capital'. Such a kind consumer sovereignty arises in societies where powerful groups encourage consumers to 'want' more than they need. Because consumerism is symbolically mediated, consumer culture liberates values and preferences from particular social and geographical locations and indeed invalidates the social and political structure of modernity. In cosmopolitan cities, consumer culture depends on mass mediated advertising and simulation which exercise sovereignty on the consumer.

### *Global-Local Nexus*

The globalization of economic activity is now associated with a further wave of cultural transformation. Surely, global culture affects and transforms the local culture but the later also makes a place in the global culture. Theodore Levitt explains this as the global standardization of local culture.

Everywhere, there is Chinese food, burger, western music, pizza and jazz. The global pervasiveness of ethnic or local forms represents the cosmopolitanization of speciality. Again, globalization does not mean the end of localism. It means, instead, their expansion to worldwide proportions.

Now, it is the turn of African music, Thai cuisine, aboriginal painting and so on, to be absorbed into the world market and to become cosmopolitan specialities. But, there is also a dark side of globalization of localism. It also happens that in the enthusiasm of borrowing so much from global culture, there is always fear of the extinction of local culture. The local culture faces an identity crisis. At India's level, if western music or remix of cinema music becomes pervasive and popular through the mediation of cinema and TV, there are ample chances of the disappearance of Punjabi *bhangara*, Rajasthan's puppetry, Maharashtra's *tamasha* and

Madhya Pradesh's *pandvani*. Definitely, the interaction between the global culture and local culture is so powerful that there is always a fear of the oblivion of local culture. The fear of the loss of local culture is the consequence of cultural globalization.

And, now, classes are based on consumption pattern.

Thus, it appears that out of the three perspectives of globalization, the economic seems to be strongest. The European Union and the Human Development Report have both stressed on the economic perspective of globalization. Those who highlight the economic perspective, focus mainly on capitalism and its various strands. The fact of the matter is that capitalism has always experienced several shifts. The national economy has now become international economy. The production system has undergone change. It has now become flexible and suits the various taste groups of consumers. Wallerstein very rightly says that the present shift to capitalism has ultimately resulted in the shift of capitalist world economy from its primary location in Europe to the entire world.

Sklair, following Wallerstein, refers to several of the transnational practices. These practices cut across the boundaries of the state and extend to the whole world. Castells, on the other hand, discusses the role of technology in economic globalization. In the realm of technology, information technology occupies the higher place. Castells is credited to have coined the concept of 'global economy' which is basically an economy of capitalism. Recently, Waters has analyzed the economic perspective of globalization. He argues that a larger number of international economic organizations have emerged in the wake of globalization. What Human Development Report calls as new actors are termed as international enterprises by Waters. These include world trade, international division of labour, multinational corporations, management skills, migrant labour and transnational classes.

Some of the major observations of Waters are as below:

(1) Globalization is most advanced in the areas of financial markets and organizational ideologies.
(2) Globalization is least advanced in the labour market.
(3) In globalization, material relationships are localized.

(4) On the other hand, in globalization, power relationships are internationalized. Likewise, symbolic relationships are also globalized.

(5) Economic globalization has entered into a phase, which could be called 'cultural economy'. In this phase, economy has become subordinate to culture, i.e., the choices of the individuals and ethnic groups prevail. This is reflected in the flexible production. In this case, economic commodities have been reduced to signs and media representations.

(6) In a culturalized global economy, world class is displaced by a world status system based on consumption, lifestyle and value commitment.

**India's Perspective on Globalization**

Much has been written on the theme of globalization. Its life has not been very long. At the European level it came in 1990. Its initial objective has been to fulfil the universal needs of the people. The process of globalization supports and extends modernization and recently postmodernization. Liberal democracy, nation-state and capitalism are the major idioms of globalization. In the western world, it is clear from all discussions and debates that the power of nation-state is fast decreasing. It is the private sector, which has taken up most of the functions of the nation-state. It is largely the military power and the maintenance of domestic law and order which remain in the hands of nation-states. The military also has limited functions because of the international constraints on the nation-states.

Arjun Appadurai is an internationally known authority on globalization. Being an Indian, he is much familiar with the form and direction of globalization in India. He says that everywhere in the world globalization is the subject of debate. It is the name of a new industrial revolution (driven by powerful new information and communication technologies), which has barely begun. Because of its newness, it taxes our linguistic and political resources for understanding and managing it. In the United States and other most wealthy countries of the world, globalization is certainly a positive buzzword for corporate elites and their political allies. In the remaining countries of the world – the underdeveloped and the truly destitute ones – there is a double anxiety: fear of inclusion on draconian terms, and fear of exclusion, for that seems like exclusion from history itself.

Research material on India's globalization is very scarce. What is worse, sociologists have paid no attention to the consequences of globalization on Indian culture and society. We have some exceptional studies by sociologists on social consequences of globalization. Out of the exceptions, the studies of Arjun Appadurai (1996) and Yogendra Singh (2000) are in book-length form. Besides these two notable publications, there are a few important articles also which have appeared in the *Economic and Political Weekly* and the *Seminar*. In the field of economic globalization, some noteworthy book-length publications have also appeared. Amit Bhaduri and Deepak Nayar (1996), G.S. Bhalla (1994) and Deepak Nayyar (1995) are some of the economists who have taken long exercises to establish the hegemony of international economic funding agencies over the nation-states. It has been their thrust to conclude that the policy of liberalization adopted by the Indian government in 1990 has seriously fractured and damaged the power of nation-state. Their central theme of discussion is not globalization. They have chosen liberalization as their prime concern of analysis.

Economic globalization is not Yogendra Singh's cup of tea. He restricts himself to the analysis of cultural consequences of globalization. Global versus local is his favourite theme. There is yet another important article by Lloyd Rudolph and Susanne Hoeber Rudolph, the American husband-wife sociologists. This article appeared in the *Economic and Political Weekly* (May 5-11, 2001). Their thrust of enquiry is to discuss the Indian economy's shift from the status of command economy to the federal market economy. According to them, the power of nation-state has shifted to the federal state.

### India's Economic Globalization

International trade has always been a part of India's history. Right from ancient time to medieval and modern, there has been international trade. In a limited sense, we always had some kind of globalization. This globalization was never without its social and cultural consequences. Buddhism spread to most of the Asian countries. South-East Asia was a fertile land for the spread of Hinduism. The globalization that we find in the world today emerged in India during the year 1990s.

The scope of trade and market, which has been accelerated by the process of globalization, poses formidable cultural problems in both the developed and the developing societies. Yogendra Singh (2000) identifies the development of globalization in India as under:

> In India, which traditionally had quite a developed pre-industrial base of trade and market, the impact of the changing role of these institutions has been gradual. The market and trade relations continue to be located in local cultures even today. Also, the economic policy of India upto the 1980s has been that of import substitution and protectionism in trade and market. The full momentum of the globalization of economy started from 1990s onwards, but many checks and balances continue to persist.

The history of globalization in India has gained specificity. Here, it is linked with liberalization and privatization. Both the sociologists and economists talk about liberalization though inevitably their reference is to economic liberalization. They hardly discuss modernization and its extension. However, they focus heavily on the status of nation-state in the new situation of liberalization. Normally, it is asked in India: What is the role of the nation-state in globalization? Do we say the state is dead and publish an obituary to that effect?

Thus, the political globalization in India ends up with the discussion on the survival and weakening of nation-state. Besides the nation-state, another issue relating to globalization is that of political ethnocentrism. We are scared in India that the US would exercise its power over our political decisions. The fear is perpetual about the Americanization of India in most of its political decisions.

Amit Bhaduri and Deepak Nayyar have also characterized economic globalization in Indian perspective. According to them, there are three important dimensions of globalization:

(a) openness to international trade,

(b) openness to international investment, and
(c) international finance.

Commenting on trade, investment and finance, which are at the cutting edge of globalization, Bhaduri and Nayyar (1996) write:

> All these (trade, investment and finance) three aspects of openness have increased with equal or even similar speed.

In such a pattern of economic globalization, which is basically European, the multinational corporations (MNCs) organize the production operations on a global scale. With their branches spread out across different countries of the world, these MNCs can also choose relatively freely, their global investment and employment pattern. The globalization, as it has developed all over the world, gave dominant status to multinationals over the nation-state and national economy. In fact, there has emerged a new ideology of economic liberalization in the west and other parts of the world. Let us see how globalization came to India in the form of liberalization and privatization.

### *Crisis in Indian Economy: Liberalization and Structural Adjustment*

Liberalization in India is a crisis-driven response. There was fiscal crisis with the government. The fiscal gap between growth in output and the rate of interest widened. Explaining the Indian fiscal crisis, Bhaduri and Nayyar (1996) observe:

> The external debt crisis, which surfaced in early 1991, brought India close to default in meeting its international payment obligations. The balance of payments situation was almost unmanageable. The fear of acceleration in the rate of inflation loomed large. The underlying fiscal crisis (an imbalance between income and expenditure of the central government) was acute.

The crisis which the central government had to face in 1991 was not a bolt from the blue. It accumulated over several years through negligent policies driven by a shortsighted politics of convenience. A short span of four months, from November 1990 to March 1991, witnessed the fall of two governments. During the period when Narsimha Rao was Prime Minister and Manmohan

Singh was Finance Minister, the central government had accepted liberalization as its economic policy. All this happened in 1991.

### *Economic Globalization and Structural Reforms in Indian Economy*

In conformity with the orthodox wisdom of the IMF and the World Bank, the government set in motion a process of macro-economic stabilization combined with fiscal adjustment and structural reform.

The meaning of stabilization in economics is much the same as in medicine; just as medical treatment seeks to stabilize the health of a patient in a critical condition, economic management attempts to stabilize an economy in deep crisis. Explaining the method of economic stabilization adopted by the Government of India, Bhaduri and Nayyar (1996) write:

> Any programme of economic stabilization has two fundamental objectives: its first aim is to pre-empt a collapse of the balance of payments situation in the short term by reducing the deficit on current account as much as possible. Its other objective is to curb inflation. While the balance of payments and inflation are deemed as problems, unemployment, poverty or economic deprivation – India's million mutinies – receive no more than passing mention in stabilization.

### *Structural Adjustment of Economic Globalization*

Economic globalization has two basic components: liberalization and privatization. In order to win over the problems of cultural crisis, the government made two structural adjustments:

(1) Structural adjustment and reform seeks to shift resources from the non-traded goods sector to the traded goods sector and within the latter from import competing activities to export activities, and from the government sector to the private sector. Apart from such allocation of resources, structural reform seeks to improve resource utilization.

(2) It changes the structure of incentives and institutions in favour of private initiative and against state intervention. The general economic philosophy is to rely more on market

forces, and wind down the public sector in the hope that the vacuum will be filled by the private sector.

### *Liberalization and Market Forces Occupy the Front Seat*

With the adoption of liberalization as a part of economic globalization, the licence and permit system which rested with the government has been liberalized in favour of private sector. In simple words, liberalization means lesser control of government in matter of trade and investment. It is the beginning of the death of state.

Second, market has been given prior position in the economic globalization. Trade, investment and exchange are determined by the market. All in all, in the context of liberalization, the state has been given the rear seat. The policy does not take into consideration the priorities of the ordinary people, nor does it have a long-term view of development objectives. The public sector, which was considered to be a vehicle to bring socialism by Nehruji, has been given a death blow. It is now closing its shutters.

### ***Privatization: A Part of Liberalization***

The experience of government working in the public sphere has proved that it is inefficient in the management of things. A notion goes around that anything which is running smoothly, if given to the state, it will surely worsen. It would be shattered; doomed. Despite giving enormous subsidies, the public gets degenerated. Indeed, the subsidy is often so large that it provides a basis for some to argue that the state-run system should be abandoned altogether. In fact, the general public is wary of government intervention in the market and see virtue in privatization. Those who are champions of economic liberalization and privatization believe that most economic problems should be left to the market. These ideologies favour the minimalist state and wish to roll back the government whenever possible. Liberalization, privatization and market constitute the central part of India's perspective on economic globalization.

Arundhati Roy (2001), a top-most fiction writer and the one who is associated with a large number of non-government organizations, defines privatization in the context of contemporary economic globalization:

> Privatization is the transfer of public productive assets from the state to private companies. Productive assets include natural resources, earth, forest, water, and air. These are assets that the state holds in trust for the people it represents.

Arundhati narrates the story of Enron of the US, the private power project in India. The Maharashtra government entered into contract with this company. The power that the Enron plant produced was twice as expensive as the cheapest electricity available in Maharashtra. At last, long being caught in several technicalities, the contract with the Enron was cancelled. She makes severe charges on such a kind of privatization adopted by the government. It is looting through liberalization, she says. Privatization is presented as being the only alternative to an inefficient, corrupt state. She gives her assessment of privatization as below:

> India's politicians have virtually mortgaged their country to the World Bank. Today, India pays back more money in interest then repayment installments it receives. It is forced to incur new debts in order to repay old ones. In other words, it is exporting capital.

*Emergence of Federal Market Economy*

When Jawaharlal Nehru was the Prime Minister of the country in 1950s, the nation had a centrally planned economy. It was called command economy. The construction of big dams, public sector factories and development programmes of industrial development were planned and implemented by this command economy. The planned economy received a shift in 1991 when the government accepted liberalization and privatization. This shift is towards federal market economy. Lloyd Rudolph and Susanne Rudolph (2001) define federal market economy as under:

> Our use of the term 'federal market economy' is meant to draw attention to the fact that the new imagined economy evokes not only the decentralization of the market but also new patterns of

> shared sovereignty between the states and the centre for economic and financial decision-making. This increasing sharing shifts India's federal system well beyond the economic provisions of its formal constitution.

The federal market economy has some crucial consequences. It strikes at the centrally planned command economy. In the last decade, it has become clear that if economic liberalization is to prevail, it is the state governments and their chief ministers that can and must break the bottlenecks holding back economic growth. If state chief ministers have become marquee players in the drama of the federal market economy, business leaders, economic regulators and a new breed of policy intellectuals can be found in conspicuous supportive roles.

Federal market economy has also dismantled the permit-licence raj and has put an increasing reliance on markets. All these developments – liberalization, privatization and decentralization of command economy – have given a serious blow to the sovereignty of India's nation-state.

### *India's Cultural Globalization*

Globalization has created the need to reformulate the categories and methods to study culture. There has come a technological revolution in the system of communication. It has compressed both time and space. The increasing use of computers, telephones and Internet has influenced India's social institutions and patterns of relationship. There has come substantial change in our trade, banking and investment. Yogendra Singh, Arjun Appadurai and J.N. Pieterse argue that changes in technology, liberalization and privatization have created social, cultural and institutional forces which surpass the boundaries of the nation-state. Yogendra Singh (2000) elaborates the changes, which have been observed at the level of local culture:

> Paradoxically, however, these changes impact upon the institutions of local culture and social forms such as the family, neighbourhood and the community in a destabilizing manner and generate many forms of social anomie. At the same time, the universal reach of the communication media, such as the

> Internet, telephony, etc., have made it possible to produce and augment 'virtual localities' and 'virtual neighbourhoods'. Thus, the production of locality .... goes hand in hand with the erosion of real-time and real-space bonds of communitarianism and local culture.

What Indian sociologists argue is that technology, communication and market have disintegrated our folk culture and folk societies. The marketization of economy and commodification of production processes through entrenchment of the capitalist mode of production in agriculture converts 'peasants' into 'farmers', eroding the traditional cultural patterns. It is evident, therefore, that in conceptual and theoretical terms, the relationship between the local culture and the processes of globalization should take into account both the analytical and substantive perspectives of the changing cultural realities.

The impact of globalization on local culture and the changing role of the nation-state can be seen in the following areas of cultural life:

### *Plurality of Social Institutions*

India has a plural character in terms of language, geography, ethnicity, religion and culture. The caste system and its related kinship structures have shaped the profile of the culture, economy and power structures within the local communities. The People of India (PoI) project has established the existence of such a kind of cultural plurality. It identifies 91 culture areas in the whole country.

### *Our Diversity is a Sociological Category*

Notwithstanding the plurality of social institutions and culture, there are strong linkages, which keep the India's comprehensive culture intact. The PoI survey affirms that the diversity of communities does not reduce the nature of sociological reality of states/union territories. More than 71 per cent of the communities are localized within the boundaries of states/union territories. It shows that our states/union territories are not only linguistic and cultural but also sociological categories. The survey of PoI also reveals that the diverse local cultures are characterized by linkages and shared commonalities of culture traits, rituals, beliefs and customs. Studies of folk culture across regions have shown remarkable similarity in the ritual styles, songs, and their central themes and symbols.

*Reassertion of Cultural Identity*

The nation-state in India does not seem to have received any substantial change. Nor have the cultural aspects lost their linkages to the total national culture. On the other hand, a new search for cultural identity has started at the regional and linguistic levels. Globalization has made the local culture more assertive in demanding their identity. They have, in fact, consolidated their strength. Yogendra Singh (2000) observes:

> Apart from such empowering impact, the local communities and cultures are also inspired by the new telecommunication media to re-assert their cultural identity and reinforce their residence. It helps them maintain their identity by accessing themselves to cultural meanings and values rather selectively through an adaptive mechanism.

Globalization has thrown challenges in the direction of economy, politics and culture. These are responded by the people with an enhanced sense of self-consciousness and awareness of identity. Yogendra Singh (2000) makes his assessment of the people to cultural globalization:

> Cultural modernization sponsored upon or does not promote the core cultural values of society, its language, social practices and styles of life. The vigour of the renewed sense of self-awareness generated among numbers of the local cultures and communities such as to succeed in making adaptive reconciliation with the forces of globalization.

The study of the impact of cultural globalization on the Indian people is the favourite field of sociologists. But, the sociologists in India are obsessed with the methodology and ideology of functionalism. Most of the so-called 'great' sociologists are functionalists to their every inch. There are some exceptions – Marxists sociologists and a few others. Sociologists have been surpassed by the non-sociologists in the analysis of the challenges of cultural globalization. PoI informs us in categorical terms that regional autonomy has increased to such an extent that people celebrate it. Linguistic rivalries have assumed challenging dimensions. In small villages of no consequence, every year, English medium schools are fantastically increasing in number. Functional vocabulary is very strange and our sociologists have very successfully 'learnt' to use it. Whenever changes have to be analyzed, functionalists talk about 'adaptive' change. 'Core values' of culture are intact, though there is bombardment of values released from globalization. Our folk culture, folk songs, folk literatures have lost their identity.

When we discuss the impact of cultural globalization, we should not forget that modernity and postmodernity came prior to globalization. Postmodernity is given wings and speed by globalization. And, postmodernity is fragmentation, deconstruction, diverse and plural. What globalization has done in India is to play upon our diversity and plurality. These have been enhanced by globalization. We have now become a vulnerable country where everything has taken a hybrid dimension. Perhaps, we are not much aware about the risks involved in globalization. Will our sociologists shed off their adherence to meta-narratives of functionalism?

# Bibliography

Adams, Bert N. and R.A. Sydie, *Sociological Theory*, New Delhi: Vistaar Publications, 2001.

Appadurai, Arjun, *Modernity at Large: Cultural Dimensions of Globalization*, Minneapolis: University of Minnesota Press, 1996.

Baudrillard, Jean, *Simulacres et Simulation*, Paris: Galilee, 1981.

Bauman, Zygmunt, "Sociological Response to Postmodernity", *Thesis Eleven*, 1989.

—, *Intimations of Postmodernity*, London: Routledge, 1992.

Bell, D., *The Coming of Post Industrial Society*, London: Heinneman Educational Books Ltd., 1974.

Beteille, Andre, "Ideas and Interests: Some Conceptual Problems in the Study of Social Stratification in Rural India", *International Social Science Journal*, Vol. 21, No. 2. 1969.

—, *Ideology and Social Change*, New Delhi, 2006.

—, (ed.), *Social Inequality*, Harmondsworth: Penguin Books Ltd., 1969.

—, *Caste, Class and Power*, Berkeley: University of California Press, 1965.

—, *Castes: Old and New: Essays in Social Stratification*, Delhi: Asia Publishing House, 1969.

—, *Inequality and Social Change*, Delhi: Oxford University Press, 1975.

—, and Madan, T. N., (eds.), Encounter and Experience: The Personal Dimension of Social Anthropological Field Work, Delhi.

Bettelheim, C., *India Independent*, London: MacGibbon and Kee, 1968.

Bhaduri, A. and Deepak Nayyar, *An Intelligent Person's Guide to Liberalization*, New Delhi: Penguin, 1996.

Bhatt, Anil, *Caste, Class and Politics: An Empirical Profile of Social Stratification in Modern India*, New Delhi: Manohar Books Service, 1975.

Bourdieu, Pierre and L.J.D. Wacquant, *An Invitation to Reflexive Sociology*, Chicago: University of Chicago Press, 1992.

Breman, Jan, *Of Peasants, Migrants and Paupers*, Delhi: Oxford University, 1985.

Castells, Manuel, *The Information Age: Economy, Sociology and Culture*, 3 Vols., Oxford: Blackwell, 1996.

Chauhan, B.R., "Rural Studies" in *A Survey of Research in Sociology and Social Anthropology*, ICSSR, Vol. I, Bombay: Popular Prakashan, 1974.

Clark, S., *The Fundamentals of Structuralism*, Sussex: Harvester, 1981.

Cohn, Bernard S., "The Changing Status of Depressed Caste" in McKin Marriott (ed.), *Village India*, Chicago: University of Chicago Press, 1955.

—, *India,: The Social Anthropology of a Civilization*, New Jersey: Prentice Hall, 1971.

Collins, Jim, *Uncommon Cultures: Popular Culture and Postmodernism*, 1991.

Connor, S., *Postmodernist Culture*, Oxford: Blackwell, 1989.

Craib. I., *Modern Social Theory: From Parsons to Habermas* (2nd ed.), New York: Harvester Wheatsheaf, 1992.

Das, Verna (ed.), *Oxford Handbook of Indian Sociology*, New Delhi: Oxford University Press, 2004.

Derrida, Jacques, *Of Grammatology*, trans. Gayatri Chakravorty Spivak, Baltimore: Johns Hopkins University Press, 1967, 6th printing, 1984.

—, *Writing and Difference*, London: Routledge, 1981.

—, *The Margins of Philosophy*, Sussex: Harvester Press, 1982.

Desai, A.R. (ed.), *Rural Sociology in India*, Bombay: Popular Prakashan, 1959.

—, *Social Background of Indian Nationalism*, Bombay: Popular Prakashan, 1966.

—, *State and Society in India*, Bombay: Popular Prakashan, 1975.

Desai, I.P., *Some Aspects of Family in Mahuva*, Bombay: Asia Publishing House, 1964.

Doshi, S.L., *Modernity, Postmodernity and Neo-Sociological Theories*, Jaipur: Rawat Publications, 2003.

D'Souza, Alfred, "Dialogue between Religions in India", *Social Action*, XXII, 2, 1972.

D'Souza, Alfred (ed.), *Women in Contemporary India*, New Delhi: Manohar Books Service, 1975.

Dube, Leela, *Sociology of Kinship: An Analytical Survey of Literature*, New Delhi: ICSSR, 1974.

Dube, Saurabh (ed.), *Postcolonial Passages*, New Delhi: Oxford University Press, 2004.

Dube, S.C. (ed.), *Social Sciences and Social Realities: Role of the Social Sciences in Contemporary India*, Simla: Indian Institute of Advanced Study, 1976.

Dumont, Youis, *Homo Hierarchicus*, Delhi: Vikas Publishing House, 1970.

—, *The Elementary Forms of Religious Life*, New York: Macmillan Company, 1915.

Fernandes, Edna, *Holy Warriors*, New Delhi: Penguin Viking, 2006.

Fromm, E., *Escape From Freedom*, London, 1942.

Fukuyama, Francis, *The End of History and the Last Man*. New York: Free Press, 1992.

Giddens, Anthony, *Beyond Left and Right: The Future of Radial Politics*, Stanford, CA: Stanford University Press, 1994.

—, *Modernity and Self-identity: Self and Society in the Late Modern Age*, Cambridge: Polity Press, 1991.

—, *The Consequences of Modernity*, Cambridge: Polity Press, 1990.

—, *The Constitution of Society*, Cambridge: Polity, 1984.

Gorz, A., *Farewell to the Working Class: An Essay on Post-industrial Socialism*, London: Pluto Press, 1982.

Gough, Kathleen, *Class Developments in South India*, Montreal: McGill University Press, 1975.

Gouldner, A., *Coming Crisis in Western Sociology*, New York: The Free Press, 1970.

Gupta, Dipankar, "Can Postmodernism be Universalized? Derrida and Baudrillard in Tropics", *Contributions to Indian Sociology* (n.s) 29, 1 & 2, 1995.

Gupta, Dipankar, *Mistaken Modernity: India between Worlds*, New Delhi: Harper Collins Publishers, India, 2000.

Gutting, Gary (ed.), *The Cambridge Companion to Foucault*, Cambridge: Cambridge University Press, 1994.

Habermas, Jurgen, *The Theory of Communicative Action* (2 Vols.), Cambridge: Polity Press, 1987-88.

Hall, Stuart et al., *Modernity and its Futures*, Oxford: Polity Press, 1993.

Harvey, D., *The Condition of Postmodernity*, Oxford: Basil Blackwell, 1989.

Horkheimer, Max and Adorno, T.W., *Aspects of Sociology*, London: Heinemann Educational Books Ltd., 1973.

Indian Council of Social Science Research, *Third Survey of Research in Sociology and Social Anthropology*, Vols. I & II, New Delhi: Manak Publications, 2000.

Jameson, F., *Postmodernism or the Cultural Logic of Late Capitalism*, London: Verso, 1991.

—, "Postmodernism and Consumer Society", in (ed.), *Posmodernism and its Discontents: Theories and Practices*, by E.A. Kaplan, New York: Verso, 1988.

Jencks, C. (ed.), *The Postmodern Reader*, London: Academy Editions, 1992.

Joshi, P.C. and Damodaran, K., *Marx Comes to India*, New Delhi: Manohar Books Service, 1975.

—, *Land Reform and Agrarian Change in India and Pakistan* (Report), 1971.

—, *Land Reforms in India*, ICSSR Trend Report, 1974.

Kothari, Rajni (ed.), *Caste in Indian Politics*, Delhi: Orient Longman, 1970.

Luhmann, Nklas, *The Differentiation of Society*, New York: Columbia University Press, 1982.

—, *Risk: A Sociological Theory*, New York: Walter de Gruyter, 1993.

—, *Trust and Power*, New York: John Wiley and Sons, 1979.

Lynch, Owen M., *The Politics of Untouchability* (Ph.D. Dissertation), Department of Anthropology, New York: Columbia University Press, 1966.

Lyotard, Jean-Francois, The *Postmodern Condition: A Report on Knowledge*, Minneapolis: University of Minnesota Press, 1984.

Macey, David, *The Lives of Michel Foucault: A Biography*, New York: Pantheon, 1993.

Madan, T.N., *Pathways*, New Delhi: Oxford, 1994.

Majumdar, D.N., *Caste and Communication in an Indian Village*, Bombay: Asia Publishing House, 1958.

Marcuse, H., *Eros and Civilization*, London: The Beacon Press, 1955.

Marcuse, Herbert, *One Dimensional Man*, London: Routledge, 1964.

Merton, R.K., *Social Theory and Social Structure*, The Free Press of Glencoe, 1968.

Mills, C. Wright, *Images of Man*, New York: George Braziller Inc., 1960.

Mukerji, D.P., *Diversities*, New Delhi: People's Publishing House, 1958.

Nicholas, R., "Structure of Politics in Village of Southern Asia", in Milton Singer and B.S. Cohn (eds), *Structure and Change in Indian Society*, Chicago: Aldine Publishing Co., 1968.

Oommen, T.K., "Sociological Issues in the Analysis of Social Movements in Independent India", *Sociological Bulletin*, 1977.

—, "The Concept of Dominant Caste: Some Queries", *Contribution to Indian Sociology*, New Series, No. IV, 1970.

Panini, M.N., "Trends in Cultural Globalization: From Agriculture to Agribusiness in Karnataka", *Economic and Political Weekly*, July 31, 1999.

Poulantzas, N., *Classes in Contemporary Capitalism*, London: New Left Books, 1975.

Ritzer, George, *Postmodern Social Theory*, New York: McGraw-Hill, 1997.

—, *Sociological Theory*, New York: McGraw-Hill, 1996.

—, *The McDonaldization of Society: An Investigation into the Changing Character of Contemporary Serial Life*, Thousand Oaks: Pine Forge Press, 1993.

Robertson, R., *Globalization*, London: Sage, 1992.

—, "Globalization or Globalization", *Journal of International Communication*, Vol. I, No. 1, 1994.

Rosenau, J., *The Study of Global Interdependence*, London, 1980.

Rosenau, P.M., *Postmodernism and the Social Science*, Princeton: Princeton University Press, 1992.

Roy, Arundhati, *Power Politics*, Calcutta: D.C. Books, 2001.

Rudolph, Lloyd and Susanne H. Rudolph, "Iconisation of Chandra Babu", *Economic Political Weekly*, May 5-11, 2001.

—, *Postmodern Gandhi*, New Delhi: Oxford Press, 2006.

—, "Surveys in India: Field Experience in Madras State", *Public Opinion Quarterly*, 22(3), 1958.

Sau, Ranjit, "On the Essence and Manifestation of Capitalism in Indian Agriculture", *Economy and Political Weekly*, Vol. VIII, No. 13, March 31, 1973.

Samuel, P. Huntington, *The Class of Civilization and the Remaking of the World Order*, New York, 1996.

Schuurman, Frans J. (ed.), *Globalization and Development Studies*, New Delhi: Vistaar Publications, 2001.

Sen, Amartya, *Industry and Violence*, Allen Lane (On Imprint of Penguin Books), New Delhi, 2006.

Shah, A.M., "Basic Terms and Concepts in the Study of Family in India", *Economic and Social History Review*, Vol. I, 1964.

—, *The Household Dimension of the Family in India*, New Delhi: Orient Longman, 1973.

Shah, Ghanshyam, "Traditional Society and Political Mobilization: The Experience of Bardoli Satyagraha (1920-28)", *Contributions of Indian Sociology* (NS) 8, 1974.

Shah, Ghanshyam et al., *Untouchability in Rural India*, New Delhi: Sage Publications, 2006.

Sheridan, Alan, *Michel Foucault: The Will to Truth*, London, 1980.

Shumway, David, *Michel Foucault*, Boston, 1989.

Sim, Stuart, *Fundamentalist World, the New Dark Age of Dogma*, Cambridge, 2004.

Singer, Milton (ed.), *Traditional India: Structure and Change*, Chicago: Aldine Publishing Company, 1968.

—, *When a Great Tradition Modernizes*, New York: Praeger Publishers, 1972.

Singh, K.S., *People of India: An Introduction*, Calcutta: Anthropological Survey of India, 1992.

Singh, Rajendra, *Social Movements: Old and New*, New Delhi: Sage, 2001.

Singh, Yogendra, *Culture Change in India*, Jaipur: Rawat Publications, 2000.

—, *Indian Sociology*, New Delhi: Vistaar Publications, 1986.

—, *Modernization of Indian Tradition*, Jaipur: Rawat Publications, Reprint, 1994.

Singh, Yogendra and Oommen, T.K., The *Craft of the Social Sciences in India, Centre for the Study of Social Systems*, Jawaharlal Nehru University, New Delhi.

—, *Image of Man: Ideology and Theory in Indian Sociology*, Delhi: Chanakya Publications, 1983.

—, "Ideology, Theory and Method in Indian Sociology" in *A Quarter Century of International Social Science*, by Rokkan Stein (ed.), New Delhi: Concept Publishing Company, 1979.

—, "Role of Social Sciences in India: Sociology of Knowledge in S.C. Dube (ed.), *Social Sciences and Social Realities: Role of the Social Science in Contemporary India*, Simla: Indian Institute of Advanced Study, 1976.

—, "The Dominant Caste in Rampura", *American Anthropologist* (February).

—, *Religion and Society among the Coorgs of South India*, Bombay: Oxford University Press, 1952.

—, *Social Change in Modern India*, Berkeley: California University Press, 1966.

—, *Social Stratification and Change in India*, New Delhi: Manohar Books Service, 1978.

Sklair, L., *Sociology of the Global System*, Brighton, 1991.

Srinivas, M.N., "Mobility in the Caste System", in Milton Singer and B.S. Cohn (ed.), *Structure and Change in Indian Society*, Chicago: Aldine Publishing Company, 1968.

—, "Village Studies, Participant Observation and Social Science Research in India", *Economic and Political Weekly*, Special Number, 1975.

Thapar, Romesh, *Tribe, Caste and Religion in India*, New Delhi: The Macmillan Company of India Ltd., 1977.

Thorner, D., "The Peasantry Confronted with Industrial Capitalism", 1777-1970,1973.

Touraine, A., *The Post-industrial Sociology*, New York: Random House, 1971.

Touraine, Alain, *Critique of Modernity*, Oxford: Blackwell, 1995.

Vidyarthi, L.P., *Conflict, Tension and Cultural Trends in India*, Calcutta: Punthi Pustak, 1969.

Wallerstein, I., *The End of the World As We Know It*, Minneapolis: University of Minnesota Press, 1999.

Ward, Gleen, *Postmodernism*, London: Teach Yourself Books, 1997.

Waters, Malcolm, *Globalization*, London: Routledge, 1995.

Weber, Max, *Essays in Sociology*, London: Routledge and Kegan Paul Ltd., 1952.

Weiner, M., "Social Science Research and Public Policy in India", *Economic and Political Weekly*, Vol. XIV, No. 38, 1979.

# Index

# Research Methodology in Education and Application of Statistics

# Research Methodology in Education and Application of Statistics

C. Naseema
V. K. Jibin

(2018, First Published 2011)

**Rs. 1400; US$ 56**

ISBN: 978-81-7541-891-2

2023 Impression

*Research Methodology in Education and Application of Statistics*



Published by:
**SHIPRA PUBLICATIONS**
LG 18-19, Pankaj Central Market,
I.P. Ext., Patparganj, Delhi 110092, India
Ph.: +91 11 22235152/6152; 96500 28065
Email: info@shiprapublication.com
www.shiprapublication.com

# Preface

The book is a direct reflection of the exposure to theoretical – academic and practical sides of research, for authors have attempted to provide an overview of the conceptual aspects of research and statistics applied to educational research.

It is directed to students taking a first course in educational research, typically given at the Masters' level as well as doctoral level. It will also help students faced with the necessity to complete a research project or paper without adequate training in research. Educators facing the responsibility to evaluate programmes and study problems through research approach will get benefited by the book. We hope that the topics dealt in different chapters will help to eliminate the current gap between the researcher and practitioners in education. And it may enable us to realize the potential contribution of the research approach to current efforts to evaluate and improve the quality of educational programmes.

Research in Education, as in other fields, is a research for knowledge. Knowledge of research methodology is essential for all those who either take an active role in conducting research or desire to keep themselves abreast of the new developments in education.

Chapter I outlines the nature of research, knowledge and enquiry. It explains the classification of educational research, paradigms in research with reference to positivism, constructivism and phenomenology. Chapter II presents a discussion of problems and its sources, criteria for selecting a problem and survey of related literature.

The sequence of the chapters III to VI follows the steps that a researcher must follow in conducting a research. These include the hypothesis as a starting point, characteristics and different ways of stating a hypothesis. Sampling, tools and techniques of research and methods of research are following it.

Chapter VII deals with qualitative and quantitative techniques of research, internet as an object of research. Chapter VIII discusses the research reporting and Ethics of research.

Section B presents the statistics applied to educational research. It covers fundamental aspects of statistics in Chapter I and inferential statistics in Chapter II.

**Dr. C. Naseema**
**V. K. Jibin**

# Contents

## SECTION B

# SECTION A

# I
# Nature of Research, Knowledge and Enquiry

## 1.1 THE RISE OF RESEARCH IN EDUCATION

Educational research as we now observe it did not evolve independently from other cultural, political and economic developments. As pointed out by Freebody (2003) The interests and procedures of educational researchers have a history. In the twentieth century, across many domains of public life, a particular idea about knowledge was brought to its most forceful expression: that a category of activities termed 'research' is an especially privileged form of public discourse. The claims of research became firmly set against those of folk wisdom, custom, insight, intuition and dogma. Two converging developments attended and accelerated this elevation of research as a special way of knowing: the first is to do with developments in the philosophy of knowledge, particularly debates relating to the kinds of activities that may lay claim to the status of research; the second concerns the victory, however temporary, of interventionist over *laissez-faire* governmental administration. These developments taken together provide us with an account of why and how the special status of research has been put to such extensive public use in the conduct of education.

Research has come to serve several purposes in education. At the most general level, a major purpose is to provide principled bases for 'knowing' to guide practice and policy. Educational research is used to assess the efficacy of targeted initiatives in publicly defensible ways, in terms of both their intended and unintended consequences. Because of pervasive change, and because of education's prominent place in a society and progressive forces, these changes are always at least potentially contentious.

Educational researchers employ empirical inquiry to test out theoretical ideas that inform practice. For example, over the course of the twentieth century, much inquiry was devoted to how children learn, grow and develop in ways that curriculums have been taken to, and are 'supposed to', reflect, and how these changes can be assessed and compared from site to site. In that respect, the curriculum provided a yardstick against which children's 'growth' and 'development' could be assessed. The curriculum, whatever it looks like, moves at a certain pace and has a certain scope of knowledge. In that respect, quantitative techniques can be used to 'measure' the relative position of an individual child or of a collection of children against the curriculum's expectations: 'this much by this time'.

Educational research has been used to inform, advance, or obstruct policy and practice in education. It is difficult to overstate the degree of direct and indirect support given to educational research by educational administrations of various kinds. In education, research conducted in or by educational institutions is most common. The sponsorship of educational researchers by policy-making bodies is one of the crucial ecological factors in the evolution of different theoretical positions and research approaches. Some theories, analytic strategies and reporting formats thrive partly because they provide rationales and 'findings' in forms that they reflect or supplement the preferred ways of the funding and policy making bodies. Other theoretical, analytic and reporting approaches may, by comparison, languish in conditions where funding bodies are either the same as or closely aligned to policy-making bodies in education. Which is to say that, unsurprisingly, educational research is no less political a pursuit than any other form of social inquiry.

## 1.2 WHAT CONSTITUTES RESEARCH?

Research is a systematic activity that is directed towards a discovery and the development of an organized body of knowledge. The chief purposes for conducting research are:

1. To determine the status (both past and present) of a phenomena.
2. To ascertain the nature, comparison and processes that characterize selected phenomena.
3. To trace growth, developmental history, change and status of certain phenomena and
4. To study the cause-and-effect relationships among and between certain phenomena.

The research is a formal, systematic, intensive process used in the investigation of a problem. It may be carried out by an individual, team or an organizer. Research is not limited to laboratory settings. Some of the characteristics of research are:

1. Research is directed towards the solution of a problem.
2. Research emphasizes the development of generations, principles, or theories that will be helpful in predicting future occurrences.
3. Research is based on observable experience or empirical evidence.
4. Research demands accurate observation and description.
5. Research involves gathering new data from primary sources or using existing data for new purpose.
6. It is often characterized by carefully designed procedures that apply rigorous analysis.
7. Research requires expertise.
8. Research attempts to eliminate personal bias in testing rather than proving the hypothesis.
9. It involves the quest for answers to unsolved problems.
10. Research is characterized by patient activity.
11. Research is carefully recorded and reported.
12. Research sometimes require courage.

### 1.3 CLASSIFICATION OF EDUCATIONAL RESEARCH

Actually all research involves the elements of observation, description, and the analysis of what happens under certain circumstances. We can classify educational research into three. Practically all studies fall under one or a combination of these types.

1. *Historical Research*: It describes what was the process involved investigating, recording, analyzing and interpreting the events of the past for the purpose of discovering generalizations that are helpful in understanding the past and the present, and to a limited extent in anticipating the future.
2. *Descriptive Research*: It describes what is describing, recording, analysing and interpreting conditions that exist. It involves some type of comparison or contrast and attempts

to discovery relationships between existing non manipulated variables.

3. *Experimental Research*: It describes what will be, when certain variables are controlled or manipulated. The focus is on variable relationships. As defined here, deliberate manipulation is always a part of the experimental method.

## Types of Research

1. *Fundamental or Basic Research*: Basic research is aimed at the formulation of a theory or a contribution to the existing body of knowledge. Fundamental research is usually carried out in a laboratory situation, often with animals as subjects. For example, if a researcher want to conduct a study using white rats determine the effect of positive versus negative reinforcement on learning to run through a maze successfully, he would be conducting basic research. If he rewarded one group of rats with food pellets for current turns in the maze, but gave an electrical shock to the group of rats making incurrent turns, he could then determine which group mastered the maze in a shorter period of time. Even though this information has no immediate application to motion, it might be useful in the building of a theory concerning motivation and learning.
2. *Applied Research*: Applied research is directed towards the solution of an immediate, specific, practical problem. It has most of the characteristics of fundamental research, including the use of sampling techniques and the subsequent inferences about the target population. However, its purpose is improving a product or a process. For example, a researcher conduct an experiment using praise and criticism as motivational factors in human learning. This would be directed towards solution of a practical problem and classified as applied research.
3. *Action Research*: Action research is focussed on immediate application, not on the development of theory or on general application. It has placed its emphasis on a problem here and now on a local setting. Its findings are to be evaluated in terms of local applicability, not universal validity. Its purpose is to improve school practices.

If most classroom teachers are to be involved in research activity, it will probably be in the area of action research. Fundamental research must continue to make its essential contribution to behavioural theory, and applied research to the improvement of education practices.

Many observers have deprecated action research as nothing more than the application of common sense or good management. But whether or not it is worthy of the term 'research', it does apply scientific thinking and methods to real life problems and represents a great improvement over teachers subjective judgements and divisions based on folklore and limited personal experiences.

## 1.4 PARADIGMS IN RESEARCH

### 1.4.1 Positivism

Positivism is a philosophy which holds that the only authentic knowledge is based on actual sense experience. Metaphysical speculation is avoided. Though the positivist approach has been a recurrent theme in the history of western thought from the Ancient Greeks to the present day and appears in Ibn al-Haytham's 11th Century text *Book of Optics*, the concept was first coined by Auguste Comte, widely considered the first modern sociologist, in the middle of the 19th century.

In the early 20th century, logical positivism—a stricter and more formal version of Comte's basic thesis—sprang up in Vienna and grew to become one of the dominant movements in American and British philosophy. The positivist view is sometimes referred to as a scientific ideology, and is often shared by technocrats who believe in the necessity of progress through scientific progress, and by naturalists, who argue that any method for gaining knowledge should be limited to natural, physical, and material approaches.

Positivism is the most evolved stage of society in anthropological evolutionism, the point where science and rational explanation for scientific phenomena develop.

#### *Logical Positivism*

Logical positivism (later and more accurately called logical empiricism) is a school of philosophy that combines empiricism, the idea that observational evidence is indispensable for knowledge of the world, with a version of rationalism, the idea that our knowledge includes a component that is not derived from observation.

Stephen Hawking has been regarded by some as an advocate of modern positivism, at least in the physical sciences. In *The Universe in a Nutshell* (p. 31) he writes:

Any sound scientific theory, whether of time or of any other concept, should in my opinion be based on the most workable philosophy of science: the positivist approach put forward by Karl Popper and others. According to this way of thinking, a scientific theory is a mathematical model that describes and codifies the observations we make. A good theory will describe a large range of phenomena on the basis of a few simple postulates and will make definite predictions that can be tested.If one takes the positivist position, as I do, one cannot say what time actually is. All one can do is describe what has been found to be a very good mathematical model for time and say what predictions it makes.

### 1.4.2 Characteristics of Positivism

#### *Order and Control*

The scientific method is a systematic approach to problem solving and to the expansion of knowledge. In systematic research, a problem is identified and defined and predictions concerning anticipated outcomes are advanced; information bearing on the solution of the problem is collected according to a pre-designated scheme; the information is subjected to analysis; and finally conclusions are drawn.

The Control is a key element of the scientific approach. The researcher must attempt to control factors that are not under direct investigation.

#### *Empiricism*

The term empiricism refers to the process whereby evidence is rooted in *objective reality* and gathered directly or indirectly through the human senses and is used as the basis for generating knowledge. It involves observations made using our sensory organs and or extensions of our senses e.g. stethoscopes.

#### *Generalisation*

An important goal of science is to understand phenomena. This pursuit of knowledge, however is focussed not on isolated events or situations but rather on more generalised understanding of relationships. Generalisation of research findings is an important criterion for assessing the quality of an investigation.

### *Theory*

Scientific generalisations are facilitated by the development of theories. Theories represent a method of organising, integrating and deriving abstract *conceptualisations* about the manner in which *phenomena* are interrelated.

### Purposes of Research

#### *Description of Phenomena*

Many research studies have, as their main objective, the description of phenomena. The researcher that conducts a descriptive investigation observes, describes, and perhaps classifies.

Exploratory research is an extension of descriptive research. These two types of research share in common the absence of a theory, but exploratory research is more directly orientated toward the discovery of relationships.

### Limitations of Research

#### *Moral or Ethical problems*

Issues that relate to values or ethics are not amenable to the scientific approach because the problems they raise cannot be empirically tested.

#### *Human Complexity*

One of the major obstacles to the conduct of scientific nursing studies is the complexity of the central topic of investigation—human beings. This problem is much less significant in clinical research dealing with bodily processes but very significant in studies dealing with human behaviour or attitudes.

### 1.4.3 Positivism and Construction

This distinction underlies the epistemological discussion of qualitative research quite widely. Positivism as an epistemological programme originally comes from natural sciences, and therefore, is used more as a negative foil to distinguish one's own research from that spelt out in social science discussions.

What is common to all constructionist approaches is that they examine the relationship to reality by dealing with constructive processes in approaching it. Examples of constructions can be found on different levels:

1. In the tradition of Piaget, cognition, perception of the world and knowledge about it are seen as constructs. Radical constructivism (Glasersfeld, 1995) takes this thought to the point where every form of cognition—because of the neurobiological processes involved—has direct access only to images of the world and of reality, but not of both.
2. Social constructivism in the tradition of Schutz (1962), Berger and Luckmann (1966), and Gergen (1985, 1999) inquires after the social conventionalizations, perception, and knowledge in everyday life.

Constructionism is not a unified programme, but is developing in parallel fashion in a number of disciplines: psychology, sociology, philosophy, neurobiology, psychiatry, and information science. It informs a lot of qualitative research programmes with the approach that the realities we study are social products of the actors, of interactions, and institutions.

### *Construction of Knowledge*

Schutz (1962) starts from the following premise: "All our knowledge of the world, in commonsense as well as in scientific thinking, involves constructs, i.e., a set of abstractions, generalizations, formalizations and idealizations, specific to the relevant level of thought organization". Schutz sees every form of knowledge as constructed by selection and structuring. The individual forms differ according to the degree of structuring and idealization, and this depends on their functions. The constructions will be more concrete as the basis of everyday action or more abstract as a model in the construction of scientific theories.

For social constructionism, the processes of social interchange in the genesis of knowledge take on a special significance, and in particular, the concepts that are used.

Knowledge is constructed in processes of social interchange, it is based on the role of language in such relationships, and above all it has social functions. The eventualities of the social processes involved have an influence on what will survive as a valid or useful explanation. Research acts are also part of the social construction of what we can address and find in social research and the acts of writing contribute to this social construction of worlds under study.

***Criticism***

Positivism has also come under fire on religious and philosophical grounds, whose proponents assert that truth begins in sense of experience, but does not end there. Positivism fails to prove that there are no abstract ideas, laws, and principles, beyond particular observable facts and relationships and necessary principles, or that we cannot know them. Nor does it prove that material and corporeal things constitute the whole order of existing beings, and that our knowledge is limited to them. According to positivism, our abstract concepts or general ideas are mere collective representations of the experimental order—for example, the idea of "man" is a kind of blended image of all the men observed in our experience. This runs contrary to a Platonic or Christian ideal, where an idea can be abstracted from any concrete determination, and may be applied identically to an indefinite number of objects of the same class. From the idea's perspective, the latter is more precise as collective images are more or less confused, become more so as the collection represented increases; an idea by definition remains always clear.

***Non Positivism***

Antipositivism evolved in the 19th century, when sociological positivism and sociological naturalism began to be questioned by scientists like Wilhelm Dilthey and Heinrich Rickert, who argued that the world of nature is not the same as the world of society, as human societies have unique aspects like meanings, symbols, rules, norms, and values—all that can be described as the culture.

According to Max Weber view, closely related to antinaturalism, sociological research must use specific tools and methods and concentrate on humans and their cultural values. This has led to some controversy on how one can draw the line between subjective and objective research, much less draw an artificial line between environment and human organization and influenced the study of hermeneutics.

The base concepts of antipositivism have expanded beyond the scope of social science, in fact, phenomenology has the same basic principles at its core.

### 1.4.4 Phenomenology

In a phenomenological study, the researcher attempts to describe the subjective experiences of the participants. Drawing on both theory and methods from early 20th century philosophy and psychology, phenomenological studies are based on extensive interviews in which both the researcher and participant attempt to give up habitual ways of interpreting experience and focus instead on how the participant directly experiences particular situations.

Phenomenology is a branch of philosophy, owing its origin to the work of Husserl and later writers. The aim of phenomenology, as propounded by Husserl, is to study human phenomena without considering questions of their causes, their objective reality, or even their appearances. The aim is to study how human phenomena are experienced in consciousness, in cognitive and perceptual acts, as well as how they may be valued or appreciated aesthetically. Phenomenology seeks to understand how persons construct meaning and a key concept is intersubjectivity. Our experience of the world, upon which our thoughts about the world are based, is intersubjective because we experience the world with and through others. Whatever meaning we create has its roots in human actions, and the totality of social artefacts and cultural objects is grounded in human activity.

Not surprisingly, phenomenology was attractive to psychological investigators in the early part of the 20th century and phenomenological psychology exists as a thriving sub-discipline of psychology where the emphasis is on understanding a person's experience of a problematic situation.

To state one's methodological position is to describe one's view of the nature of reality: for the positivist, the methodological position is that the facts of the world represent real objects, while for the phenomenologist, the world (or at least the world s/he chooses to explore) is one of intersubjectively constructed meanings. Within phenomenology, with its emphasis on understanding the person's experience of the world and his/her situation, the research methods are the methods of philosophy.

Those methods include, for example, conceptual analysis; linguistic analysis; hermeneutical method and praxis; historical-critical method; literary philosophy; and formal logic. These methods also underlie some aspects of qualitative approaches in information science—conceptual analysis is at the base of all 'coding' activities in all methods for analysing qualitative data.

In phenomenological psychology we find the same kinds of research methods as in phenomenology as a philosophical discipline. The emphasis is on understanding the person's experience of the world and their situation and, therefore, narrative accounts, and qualitative interviews are regularly employed research methods. The mode of analysis will vary, of course, according to the theoretical perspective of the researcher, or, perhaps more appropriate to the phenomenological framework, according to the theoretical perspective that arises out of the data.

In psychological research, for example, one may find, through extensive interviews with people suffering from the same diagnosed problem, that some experience the problem as something with which they have to deal in order to cope with the rest of their experience, whereas others find that the structure of their lives is determined by the problem—life is experienced through the problem. In other words, the concepts of structure, coping, 'problem life', and 'normal life', may emerge out of the analysis.

This suggests that methods are capable of being used under different methodological presuppositions, and this would be true. A questionnaire can be used to elicit different things and we can use the data obtained to satisfy our research objectives whether we adopt a positivist or a phenomenological stance.

Having suggested that research methods may be classified in this way, there remains the question, "What methods are appropriate to phenomenological research.", and here we must return to the fundamental methodological issues. Phenomenology demands that we seek to discover the world as it is experienced by those involved in it. It is about the nature of human experience and the meaning that people attach to their experiences. In trying to arrive at this kind of understanding, the researcher is asked to 'bracket', or suspend belief in the phenomena of the external world, to put them aside and focus on the consciousness of that world.

Consequently, phenomenology is not a hypothesis testing mode of research (although it may result in hypotheses that we may wish to test by other means), nor is it one that must be guided by theoretical models. Rather, one is urged to get as close as possible to what the participants in the behaviour of interest are experiencing.

In particular, observation and qualitative interviewing are widely used, as is documentary analysis, although this latter often goes under the heading of hermeneutics, which is closely related to phenomenology.

## 1.5 SCIENTIFIC METHOD

The scientific method involves a double movement of thought. The investigator directs his attention from the partly known toward a meaningful generalization. Secondly, he moves further from suggested whole to the particular parts. The first is induction and the second is deduction.

### Application of the Scientific Method

In employing the use of the scientific method, the investigator starts with a hypothesis as a guide for determining what type of data to gather. On the basis of an analysis of the collected data, the hypothesis is accepted, modified, or rejected. There is a logical sequence to the elements that comprise the scientific method in education.

1. Identification of the problem
2. Definition of the problem
3. Formulation of hypotheses—an assumption or an intelligent guess.
4. Collection of data
5. Organization of data
6. Analysis of data
7. Verification of hypotheses
8. Arriving at conclusion

Research is an endeavour to discover answers to problems (intellectual and practical) through the application of scientific methods to the knowable universe. George Lundberg defines scientific method as one consisting of systematic observation, classification, and interpretation of data. The method of enquiry is the most important factor which distinguishes scientific method from other methods of enquiry.

This method aims only at discovering facts as they actually are and not as they are described to be. It deals with "felt problems" or specific issues. Universality (i.e., not concerned with individual objects but with types, kinds and classes of objects) and predictability are another features of scientific method.

# II
# Problem and its Sources

## 2.1 SELECTION OF PROBLEM

Choice of a problem will depend upon the level at which the research is done. A problem appropriate for a beginner in a first course in research is different from that selected for the more rigorous requirements of the master's dissertation or for doctoral thesis.

Many beginners in research and graduate students are prone to conclude that most of our educational problems have been solved. They may be overawed by the large number of research studies in print.

### 2.1.1 Sources for Identification of Problems

*Advanced Study and Critical Reading*

The background of scholarship resulting from thorough training in a particular field of specialization and research should identify both the available evidence and the unsolved problems. Helpful related activities may include instruction, administration, reading, writing, and investigation.It has been typical for the graduate student to select a thesis problem in his major field of concentration and quite common for the more mature research workers to follow up the area of interest represented in his doctoral dissertation.

Stimulating contacts between professor and student inside and outside the classroom or seminar, or between the senior scholar and younger worker, frequently have been profitable in selection and development of problems for investigation and in encouragement of creativity. Well-known examples are the influence of William James on Dewey, Thorndike, and Woodworth; Wundt on Cattell, Thorndike, and Judd on many educational and psychological investigators active in the mid-twentieth century and later.

In tracing the influence of the senior scholar or teacher on his students, we find Dewey's case especially far-reaching. Some persons have thought that Dewey derived his educational ideas from Rousseau and Froebel, although Dewey told Kilpatrick explicitly that he had not read the works of either man until after he had formed his educational outlook.

Dewey is an example of a scholar whose great influence on his students far exceeded his skill as a teacher and lecturer. Many dozens of his students became pivotal figures in the intellectual life of our country, yet by all the usual criteria of effective instruction Dewey was a poor teacher. Many of these students tell tales of Dewey's dullness as a lecturer and in the next breath say that Dewey's teaching fundamentally changed their thinking.

*Personal Experience*: One of the source of problems for research in the daily experience of the professional educator. The interaction that occurs between teacher and pupil, between pupil and pupil and between pupils and materials, furnishes a rich source of questions to be answered through educational research. The classroom is not the only source of problems for the teacher. The administrator finds himself daily making decisions with little or no objective evidence to guide him in the decision-making process.

Counsellors, consultants, and other professional personnel view the educational scene from different vantage points and are likely to develop research projects that are directed toward the solution of their immediate problems. The daily experience of working in a school setting provides a rich source of possible research problems.

*Professional Literature*: Another means of identifying educational problems is professional journals. It serves as a rich source of ideas in several ways. Many research monographs, dissertations, reports and summaries suggest topics for further research. Opinion articles, theoretical discussions, and reviews of research frequently contain provocative questions that could be developed into significant problems. The 'Encyclopaedia of educational research' gives a review of the research in nearly every area of education.

Technological changes and curricula developments are constantly bringing forth new problems and new opportunities for research Educational innovations as computer assisted instruction, teaching by Television, programmed instruction, modified alphabets, new subject matter concepts and approaches, and team teaching need to be carefully evaluated through the research process.

The graduate academic experience should stimulate the questioning attitude toward prevailing practices and effectively promote problem awareness. Classroom lectures, class discussions, seminar reports and out-of-class exchanges of ideas with fellow students and professors will suggest many problems to be solved.

Some scientists and scholars have considered it undesirable or even unwise to study closely the related literature, fearing that the research worker's mind might be conditioned to see the problem in the same way or in a traditional manner and thus overlook a new or more fruitful approach. It has been said that every laboratory needs one "crackpot" who doesn't know yet what one cant do.

Reading assignments in textbooks special assignments, research reports and term papers will suggest additional areas of need research consultation of with the cause instructor advisor, or major professor is helpful.

Finally, as to the related literature, the poet, Byron, has aptly expressed the dilemma to creative workers: "To be perfectly original one should think much and read little, and this is impossible, for one must have read before one has learnt to think". It would seem that for most graduate students and research workers the solution of this dilemma does depend on critical reading as a stimulus to thinking (see 7.2 of the book).

## 2.2 CRITERIA FOR SELECTING PROBLEM

Following are the criteria for selecting problem of research:

1. It should be really felt.
2. It should have relevance.
3. It should have newness or originality in the context in which the researcher is working.
4. It should have practicability—the problem should yield itself to a study within the scope of the research.
5. The availability of tools, samples, procedure, time factor, less effort and economical.

For selecting a problem,

1. Determine the major area from which the problem arises e g: curriculum.

2. Select a limited area from the major area where you intend to concentrate e.g.: Science curriculum.
3. Determine what aspect of this limited area is going to be studied e.g.: suitability of the curriculum.
4. State the problem in a pinpointed manner, making it unambiguous and meaningful.
   eg: A critical examination of the new secondary school curriculum for Physical science of Kerala State.
5. Operationally define the terms involved i.e., definition in terms of the operation employed.
6. The researcher should possess the necessary financial resources to carry out the study.
7. The researcher should have enough courage and determination to pursue the study in spite of some difficulties and social hazards that may be involved in it.

***Statement of the Problem***

There are different ways for stating problems. They are:

1. Posing a question or
2. Making a declarative statement.

One may choose any of these ways remembering that the question form has an advantage in sharpening and focusing the issue but the declarative statement is perhaps more common and both the ways may be compared easily in an initial statement of the problem.

## 2.3 SURVEY OF RELATED LITERATURE

In the initial stages of research, it is essential that the researcher survey the literature from other research studies and authoritative writings related to the problem under investigation. Identification of a problem, development of research design, and determination of the size and scope of a problem all depend on the care and intensity with which a researcher has examined the literature related to the intended research.

### Selection of Studies to be Reported

The researcher who selects a topic in an area in which much has been written, has the problem of selecting only those studies that are most relevant to his research report. But for the researcher who's topic is in area in which little has been written has the problem of locating material.

A researcher has the responsibility of 'surveying' all writing related to his research, i.e., he must learn to glean from the reference information available (card catalogue, education index, etc) the learner that will help to reveal studies that are most valid and most pertinent to his research. Criteria for selecting references are the following:

1. The data should be recent enough to make the study relevant.
2. The title or subtitle—seem to indicate that report should provide relevant data.
3. The source should have a bibliography that could be helpful in locating further material.

After a substantial list of references has been compiled, a further reduction in the list can be made through a brief scanning of the reports. Scanning means—*reading the headings reading the first sentences in paragraphs, and the abstract or summary, and looking at tables and illustrations*—the researcher can determine whether a reference is relevant enough to conduct a more detailed study. If the reference is not relevant, it can be eliminated from the list. Then the researcher has to select studies relating to areas of limited research.

**Procedure for Reviewing Literature**

The first step in reviewing the literature is the identification of the material that is to be read and evaluated. For this, card catalogue, education index, sociological and psychological abstracts, dissertation abstracts, review of educational research, encyclopaedia of educational research, etc can be used.

The nature of the research project determines the decision concerning where to being the research. If it is a study in an area in which much research has been reported, then a check of primary sources would be a logical first step. A primary source is one in which the writer participated in the experiment. If the study is in an area in which little research has been completed, a check of the secondary sources may be a more logical step. A secondary source is one in which one has compiled the findings of several studies and has given his interpretation of these findings.

## Preparation of the Related Literature Report

The major purpose for reviewing the literature is to demonstrate the relationship between completed research and the topic under investigation. The major value of any research is its contribution to the understanding of a field of study. *Thus the writing of the related literature report should emphasize the relationship that exists between other studies and the research project.*

## Organization of the Report

The beginning researcher often views the writing of a related literature report as simply a compilation of as many research studies as possible that have any remote relationship to the investigation begins with statements. No attempt is made to develop common relationships between the studies or to establish any sort of continuity on the report. This is not the way in which a related literature report should be written.

The body of research can be organized into a logical grouping and sequence. It is the exception rather the rule to find related literature reports divided into major and minor headings (e g: write own topic and the headings).

## Writing the Review

The review of related literature should begin with an introductory paragraph describing the organization of the report. After the introduction, the next step in writing the review is to present studies most relevant to each aspect of the problem outline. All studies cannot and should not be reported in detail. The recentness and quality of the study should be the major criteria on which to base the decision concerning the amount of space to be devoted to the study. Studies with similar or contradictory findings can be reported without using excessive space.

In the final analysis the main purpose of the written report is to convey information to the readers of the report.

# III
# Hypotheses

The explanatory and predictive power of science is enhanced through useful theories and hypotheses, which represent a form of simplification in dealing with detailed items of information. Hypotheses are formulated and tentatively adopted to explain observed facts or conditions and to guide in further investigation in other words, to serve as the investigator's "eyes" in seeking answers to questions. The scientist's hypothesis parallels the common man's personal opinion or hunch.

A hypothesis is an *intelligent or shrewd guess about a relation between variables or a solution to a problem etc. to be subjected to verification before accepting or rejecting it.* An intelligent guess is based on familiarity or knowledge of that field. These statements may or may not be accurate. Therefore each hypothesis is individually tested to determine whether it is tenable.

For the hypothesis to be testable, the variables must be operationally defined i.e., the researcher specifies what operations were conducted, or tests used, to measure each variable. Thus the hypothesis focuses the investigation on a definite target and determines what observations, or measures are to be used.

Hypotheses may serve the following functions: They may contribute as explanations, stimuli to research, sources of methodology, criteria for evaluating experimental and other techniques, and as organizing principles. In thus limiting the area of investigation, sensitizing the worker to pertinent data and relationships, and providing a unifying concept, the single hypothesis should not blind the research worker's observation of all pertinent data, even though some facts may not contribute to validation of the chosen hypothesis. As emphasized later in this chapter, it is common for a particular study to involve formulation and testing of more than one hypothesis.

Factors that contribute to the emergence of hypotheses include generalizing beyond the results of previous investigations, analyzing factual conditions requiring explanation, intellectual equipment and resources of the scientist, and inspiration. Expressed otherwise, hypotheses originate from substantially the same background that serves to identify problems; the insight and imagination that should result from a sound instructional programme, extensive and critical reading, knowledge of existing practices and needs, and meaningful contact with pertinent data.

### 3.1 HYPOTHESIS: A STARTING POINT

Hypothesis enables us to relate theory to observation and observation to theory. The use of hypotheses enables modern man to employ both the ideas of the inductive thinking with their emphasis on observation, and the logic of deductive thinking with their emphasis on reason. The use of hypothesis has united experience and reason to produce a powerful tool for seeking truth.

A hypothesis may be precisely defined as a tentative proposition suggested as a solution to a problem or as an explanation of some phenomenon.

The hypothesis must be structured before the data-gathering phase of the study. This is necessary for two reasons:

1. A well-grounded hypothesis is an indication that the researcher has sufficient knowledge in the area to undertake the investigation.
2. The hypothesis gives direction to the collection and interpretation of the data. It tells us what procedure to follow and the type of data to gather and thus may prevent a great deal of wasted time and effort on the part of the researcher.

Although the necessity of a hypothesis in experimental studies is generally recognized, much descriptive research has been conducted without an explicit hypothesis. In experimental research one makes a prediction about the outcome of the experiment or what the results are expected to show. In descriptive research, however, a hypothesis is recommended to sense as a guide to the aspect of the situation in need of exploration and to the type of data to be gathered.

## 3.2 PURPOSES SERVED BY HYPOTHESIS

1. *Hypothesis Provide Tentative Explanations of Phenomena and Facilitate the Extension of Our Knowledge in an Area*: Well planned hypothesis provide direction and propose explanations. Because they can be tested and validated through scientific enquiry, they permit or to extend knowledge.
2. Hypothesis provide the investigator with a relational statement that is directly testable in a research study.
3. *Hypothesis Provide Direction to the Research*: The hypothesis tells the researcher what to do. It provide a basis for selecting the sample and the research procedures to be used. It indicates the research method required and the sample to use, and even to the statistical test that would be necessary for analysing the data.
4. *Hypothesis Provide a Framework for Reporting the Conclusions of the Study*: The researcher will find it very convenient to take each hypothesis separately and state the conclusions that are relevant to each. This makes a more meaningful and readable presentation.

### Derivation of Hypothesis

The hypothesis are derived—(1) inductively from observations of behaviour or (2) deductively from a theory or other hypotheses.

#### *Inductive Hypothesis*

It involves the researchers formulating a hypothesis as a generation from observed relationships. This reasoning process should be accompanied by an examination of previous research to determine what other investigators have reported on the question. In this process, researcher makes observation, thinks about the problem, turns to the literature for clues, makes additional observation and formulates a hypothesis.

However, these hypotheses may be limited in scope and the results of testing them can lead to a series of worthwhile but unconnected findings, which are limited in the scope of their explanatory power.

#### *Deductive Hypothesis*

A hypothesis derived from a theory is known as a deductive

hypothesis. This can lead to a more useful system of knowledge, as the framework for incorporating them wearing fully into the body of knowledge already exists in the theory itself.

## 3.3 CHARACTERISTICS OF GOOD HYPOTHESIS

### 1. A Hypothesis must have Explanatory Power

A hypothesis must be a possible explanation of what it is attempting to explain. e.g.: Suppose you attempt to start your car and nothing happens. A hypothesis that the car not start because you left the water running in the bathroom sink is not a possible explanation. A hypothesis stating that the battery is dead is a possible explanation.

### 2. A Hypothesis must State the Expected Relationship between Variables

*e.g.*: In the above example, to state "The car will not start and it has a wiring system" would not profitable. A fruitful hypothesis would be "The car will not start because of a fault in the wiring system"

### 3. A Hypothesis must be Testable

The most important characteristic of a "good" hypothesis is testability. This means that the hypothesis is verifiable. i.e., it permits the drawing of deductions, conclusions or implications in such a way that empirical observations will either support or refute the hypothesis. In our example, the hypothesis, 'the car's failure to start is a punishment for my sins" is apparently untestable in this world.

To be testable, a hypothesis must relate variables that are capable of being measured. The indicators of the variables are referred to as operational definitions. The data should be available or there should be suitable techniques for testing.

### 4. A Hypothesis should be Consistent with the Existing Body of Knowledge

Hypothesis should not contradict previously well-established hypothesis, theories and laws. The hypothesis, "my car will not start because the fluid in the battery has changed to gold" satisfies the first three criteria but contrary to the existing knowledge. But the hypothesis, "The car will not start because the fluid in the battery has evaporated to a low level" is consistent with previous knowledge and worthy.

**5. Hypothesis should be stated in clear, simple, precise and in understandable language**

Stating the hypothesis in a single manner not only makes testing of the hypothesis much easier, but also provide a basis for a clear and easily comprehend report at the conclusion of the study. Several hypotheses may needed in a single study. For example "the following hypothesis, "students taught mathematics by means of a programmed text book will show greater learning and retention of mathematical concepts than those using traditional textbooks". These hypothesis would read. (1) Students taught mathematics by means of a programmed text book will show greater learning of mathematical concepts than those using traditional text books and (2) students taught mathematics by means of a programmed textbook will show greater retention of mathematical concepts than those using traditional concepts".

**6. Hypothesis should Involve a Specific Relation or Solution**

**7. Hypothesis should Show a State Relationship Among Variables of the Study**

**Need for Hypothesizing**

1. Hypothesis makes the problem more meaningful and precise
2. Hypothesis provides a researcher with a direction to proceed.
3. Hypothesis helps the researcher with the strength of experience and theory.

Main sources of a hypothesis are:

1. Experience of the researcher,
2. Theory concerning the topic of the researcher i.e., an accepted general truth, and
3. Findings from related studies.

## 3.4 DIFFERENT WAYS OF STATING A HYPOTHESIS

**1. Experimental Hypothesis (Directional Hypothesis)**

It is a hypothesis which states the existence of some phenomena say, group difference, correlation etc or when it favours certain directions regarding selected phenomena.

e.g.:
1. Boys and girls differ in the rate of language acquisition
2. Examination achievement is correlated to anxiety.
3. Giving immediate knowledge of result will enhance achievement motivation.

But in certain cases, we have to negate certain assumptions because it is (1) easy for statistical manipulation and (2) avoid subjectivity.

**2. Null Hypothesis**

A null hypothesis is a non-directional hypothesis that states that no difference or no relationship exists.

e.g.:
1. Boys and girls do not differ in the rate of language acquisition, or Boys and girls almost equal in the rate of language acquisition.
2. There exists no correlation between achievement in examination and examination anxiety.
3. Giving immediate knowledge of result will have no effect on achievement motion.

So a null hypothesis negates the affirmation regarding the existence of a difference, correlation, specific direction of change etc. to indicate that the researcher does not approve any difficulty to a preconception. If the researcher rejects the null hypothesis, it means that he accepts the experimental hypothesis.

The proponents who urge the use of null form in writing hypotheses emphasize the fact that researcher must remain unbiased throughout his research work.

There is some disagreement that some say that it is "too timid". They argue that researcher should indicate the direction of the outcomes of his study whenever possible.

**3. Statistical Hypothesis**

It is different from null and experimental hypothesis. Statistical hypothesis is stated using technical statistical language.

For example, the following statements:

1. The mean speed of language acquisition of boys and girls differ significantly (experimental) or
   There is no significant difference of the mean speed of language acquisition of boys and girls (null).
2. There is significant correlation between examination achievement and examination anxiety or
   There is no significant correlation between examination achievement and examination anxiety.
3. There is significant increase in mean achievement motivation scores when there is immediate knowledge of results or
   There is no significant increase in mean achievement motivation scores when there is immediate knowledge of results.

# IV
# Sampling

In most research instances in the social sciences, it is not possible to collect data from every respondent relevant to our study but only from some fractional part of all the respondents. The process of selecting the fractional part is called 'sampling'.

## 4.1 REASONS FOR SAMPLING

The following are most common reasons for sampling:

- In many cases a complete coverage of the population is not possible.
- It is argued that sampling provides a better option since it addresses the population in a short period of time and produces comparable and equally valid results.
- Studies based on samples require less time and produce quick answers.
- Sampling is less demanding in terms of labour requirements, since it requires a small portion of the target population.
- It is also thought to be more economical, since it contains fewer people and it requires less printed material, fewer general costs (travelling, accommodation, etc.) and of course fewer experts.
- Samples are thought to offer more detailed information and a high degree of accuracy because they deal with relatively small numbers of units.

### Problems of Sampling

Despite these positive qualities, sampling is associated with problems. Two of the most common objections to sampling are that:

1. Sampling procedures require more administration, planning and programming than saturation surveys;
2. Sample studies may not be as valid as saturation surveys.

Despite these problems, sampling offers many advantages, which make it a standard procedure of social research.

## 4.2 PRINCIPLES OF SAMPLING

Samples are expected to be representative. For that reason, samples are expected to be chosen by means of sound methodological principles. With regard to quantitative research, the following are the most important:

- Sample units must be chosen in a systematic and objective manner.
- Sample units must be easily identifiable and clearly defined.
- Sample units must be independent of each other, uniform and of the same size, and should appear only once in the population.
- Sample units are not interchangeable; the same units should be used throughout the study.
- Once selected, units cannot be discarded.
- The selection process should be based on sound criteria and should avoid errors, bias and distortions.
- Researchers should adhere to the principles of research.

## 4.3 STAGES OF SAMPLING

There are free stages or elements in the sampling process. (1) the universe (2) the population (3) the invited sample (4) the accepting sample and (5) the data producing sample.

By universe, it means all possible respondents or measure of a certain kind. eg: 'Study of mentality of Keralites towards strike'. As in usual research we didn't have access to that universe, but has access only to a portion of this because Keralites are everywhere.

The portion of the universe to which a researcher has access is called population. In most research it is the population which is the focus of interest. But we actually collect data only from the sample.

We can divide the general concept of sample into three parts; the invited sample, the accepting sample and the data-producing sample. The invited sample is defined as all elements of the population to which an invitation to participate in the research is extended. The accepting sample is that portion of the invited sample that accepts the uncertain and agrees to participate. The data-producing sample is that portion of the accepting sample that actually produces data.

**The Sample Cycle**

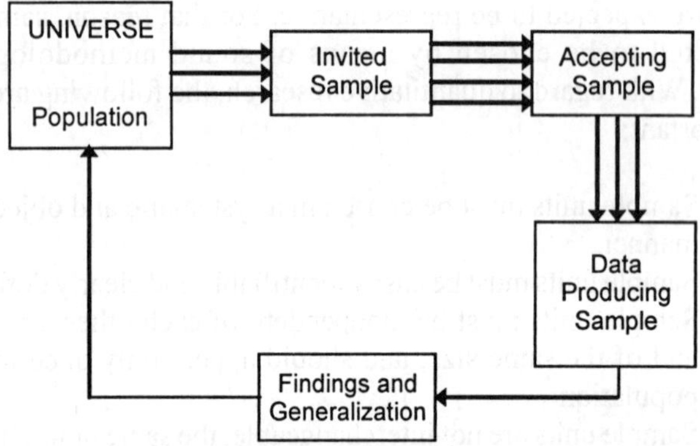


The sampling cycle is completed as the research seeks to use the findings to make estimates of population characteristics and to make generalizations from the sample data which will apply to the populations [Fox, D.J (1969)].

## 4.4 METHODS OF SAMPLING

One of the first steps in designing quantitative research is to choose the subjects – i.e., the individuals who participate in the study. As a group, the subjects are usually referred to as the sample. The sample consists of individuals selected from a larger group of persons called the population. In some studies the sample and population are the same.

Various techniques have been devised for obtaining a sample which will be representative of its population. The adequacy of a sample depends upon our knowledge of the population and the method of sampling.

*Probability Sampling*: In certain studies it is unnecessary to use all individuals in the population as subjects. Then subjects are drawn from a larger population in such a way that the probability of selecting each member of the population is known.

*Availability Sampling*: It involves using whatever subjects are available to the research. These may be two limitations:- sample is not representative of a larger population, so generalizing is more restricted, biased nature.

*Selecting Probability Samples*: The best way to choose a sample that is unbiased is to use random sampling. Sample selection is considered random if every member of the population has an equal chance of being chosen to be in sample. A table of random numbers, computer program for sampling etc. can be used.

### 4.4.1 Random Sampling

It means that we rely upon certain methods of selection to provide an unbiased cross section of the larger group or population. The criterion for randomness is met when (1) every individual in the population has the same chance of being chosen for the sample and (2) when the selection of one individual or thing in no way influences the choice of another.

#### *Mode of Selection*

1. *Use a Table of Random Numbers*: The numbers in such tables have been placed in sequence by a kind of lottery procedure. If individuals in a population have been numbered in sequence and are identified by numbers, selection can be made for a sample by following the random numbers in any systematic way.
2. *Lottery Method*: when the numbers of population are listed, all the names of the numbers are entered on slips of paper. Place them in a container, mix well and then draw sufficient number of slips. The names of the lips identify the sample.
3. If a list is arranged alphabetically or in some other systematic fashion, every $n^{th}$ name may be chosen in the construction of the sample – also known as systematic sampling.

### 4.4.2 Stratified Sampling

One common procedure that is introduced in sampling to prevent biases and to ensure a more representative sample is known as stratification. Having decided which variables are important in sampling, the entire population is studied to see what proportions fall into each category. This requires prior knowledge about the strata of the population. In constructing the sampling the members are drawn at random from the various strata. Stratified sample is likely to be more representative of a population than purely random sample.

### 4.4.3 Proportionate Stratified Random Sampling

If the numbers of the sample are drawn such that the proportions in the various strata in the sample are the same as the proportions in those strata in the population, the sample is proportionate stratified sample.

The population is divided into subgroups, such as gender, age, level of education etc. After dividing the population, samples are drawn randomly from each subgroup. The number of subjects drawn in either proportional/non-proportional.

### 4.4.4 Cluster Sampling

When it is impractical to obtain a list of all members in the population, cluster sampling can be used. The researcher identifies convenient, naturally occurring groups such as neighbourhood, schools, district or regions, not individual subjects and then randomly select some of these units for the study. A researcher can randomly select 12 schools from the 46 schools in a city and then consider the faculty of each of the 12 cluster for a study of teacher altitude.

### 4.4.5 Incidental Sampling

The term incidental sample is applied to those samples which are taken because they are the most available. e.g.: many psychological studies have been made with utilization of students of beginning psychology as sample laboratory animals, etc.

### 4.4.6 Purposive Sampling

Purposive sampling is one arbitrarily selected because there is good evidence that it is very representative of the total population. eg: a sample of house wives as buyers of grocery.

### 4.4.7 Systematic Sampling

Systematic Sampling is similar to random sampling, but the researcher randomly picks a number and then systematically selects subjects from a list of names beginning with the subject arranged the chosen number. eg: every 5th number.

*Proportionate Sampling*: is based on the percentage of subjects in the population that is present in each stratum. For example, 40 per cent of subjects in the population are represented in the first stratum, and then 40 per cent of the final sample should be from that stratum.

### 4.4.8 Multi-Stage Sampling

In this method, a sequence of samples is drawn from samples already selected but only the last sample of subjects is studied. In all other aspects the multi-stage sampling is similar to the simple or systematic sampling.

The main advantage of this sampling procedure is that it allows the establishment of a sample that is directly related to the research object. With every additional drawing, the sample becomes more specific and more relevant to the research question, and the results are expected to become equally relevant and more representative.

The process of choosing a sample through the multi-stage sampling method proceeds as follows:

Step 1: A sampling frame for the target population is identified.

Step 2: A large probability sample is chosen; the units of this sample are usually referred to as *primary selection units*. A sample from the primary selection units is then chosen.

Step 3: After the criteria of the respondents have been identified, another sample is drawn from within the previous sample. The procedure is repeated until the targeted sample size is reached.

Step 4: The last drawing constitutes the sample of the study..

### 4.4.9 Quota Sampling

Quota sampling is a version of stratified sampling with the difference being that instead of dividing the population into strata and randomly choosing a number of respondents, it works on 'quotas' set by the research. It is a non-random stratified sampling procedure.

In simple terms, the researcher sets a 'quota' of respondents to be chosen from specific population groups, by defining the basis of choices (gender, marital status, ethnicity, education, etc.) and by determining its size (e.g., 60 parents of toddlers; 35 policewomen; 66 teachers and so on). The choice of the actual respondents is usually left up to the interviewer.

The way quotas are determined varies, depending on a number of factors related to the nature and type of research. For instance, the researcher might advise the interviewer to survey 50 female students who will attend the next Monday methodology class and 50 male students who walked out of the student union immediately after 5 pm on the last Friday of June; or 100 fathers who attend the local Baby Health Clinic immediately after 9.00 am on the next Monday. The choice is left to the interviewer or left up to chance (as in the last sample).

Another way of determining the quotas based on more strict procedures. One such method is by choosing respondents according to their proportion in the entire population. For instance, if the study is about attitudes of ethnic and non-ethnic Australians to youth homelessness, and the respondents are to be chosen by means of quota sampling, the investigator, after considering the composition of the population, may decide that of the 400 respondents requires for the study 104 should be ethnic and 296 non-ethnic Australians.

In another form, quota sampling considers all significant dimensions of the population and ensures that each dimension will be represented in the sample. This is usually referred to as *dimensional sampling* and is used particularly when the sample is small. In such cases, this procedure guarantees that at least one case from each dimension of the population will be included in the sample.

Quota sampling is quite common in the social sciences because it is less costly than other techniques, does not require sampling frames, is relatively effective, and can be completed in a very short period of time. It is, however, limited, especially with respect to representativeness, control of sampling and fieldwork requirements. Problems of abuse and bias caused by the interviewer, who may turn to the first available, convenient and lest resistant person, are hard to avoid. However, quota sampling is normally not meant to be a random procedure, and should not be expected to provide random data.

### 4.4.10 Snowball Sampling

In this type of sampling researchers begin the research with the few respondents who are available to them. They subsequently ask these respondents to recommend any other persons who meet the criteria of the research and who might be willing to participate in the project. If and when such respondents are recommended, the investigator approaches them, collects the information required and asks them to recommend other persons who might fit the research design and be willing to be studied. This process is continued until the topic is *saturated*, that is, until no more substantial information is achieved through additional respondents, or until no more respondents are discovered.

## 4.5 SAMPLE SIZE

Number of subjects in the study is called sample size. It depends upon:

1. *Type of Research*: eg: correlation research should have a minimum of 30 subjects
2. *Research Hypotheses*: It means that for small relationships large sample is preferred.
3. *Financial Constraints* – Estimate the cost before study.
4. The importance of the results
5. The number of variables studied
6. The methods of data collection and
7. The degree of accuracy needed.

The researcher must determine the size of the sample that will provide sufficient data to answer the research question. The general rule in determining sample size is to use the largest sample possible, since the larger the sample the more representative it will be, of the population.

# V
# Tools and Techniques of Research

Each of the tools of research has its unique characteristics and each should be considered appropriate for collecting certain kinds of data for certain types of problems. The knowledge of instruments is useful not only in choosing the best data collecting methods but also in gaining a better understanding of how the selected tools should be utilized in the study.

The major tools and techniques of research in education are described in this section.

## A. INQUIRY FORMS—METHODS OF QUESTIONING

### 5.1 QUESTIONNAIRE

The questionnaire consists of a series of questions or statements to which individuals are asked to respond. The questions frequently ask for facts, or the opinions, attitudes, or preference of the respondents. It can be used conveniently when large numbers of respondents must be reached; it requires a little time to administer when compared with the interview and it permits the respondents to remain anonymous when they answer the questions.

The common errors observed in questionnaires are:

1. They are often too lengthy;
2. The subject is of trivial importance.
3. The items are vaguely worded and improperly arranged.
4. The form is poorly organized.

#### Characteristics of a Good Questionnaire

1. A good questionnaire will be based on a significant topic and it is so considered by the respondent.

2. It seeks information which is not obtainable from other sources (like school reports or census data etc.)
3. It is as short as possible, though comprehensive and clear enough for securing all the essential information.
4. It is attractive in appearance, neatly arranged and clearly duplicated or printed.
5. It contain directions which are clear and complete.
6. Items are arranged in categories to ensure easy and accurate responses.
7. It avoid annoying or embarrassing questions.
8. It is easy to tabulate and interpret.

## Types of Questionnaire Items

The two commonly used types of questionnaire items are the unrestricted, or open-form item and the restricted or closed-form item.

### *Open-form*

It is also referred to as 'open-end', 'short answer' or free response items. It calls for a free response in the respondent's own words. After the question, there is a space provided in which the respondent is asked to write his answer. This type of item permits explanation, but responses can be difficult to summarize and tabulate. The responses also may be too brief, too ambiguous, or the respondent omitted important information. This type of item is of most value when unrestricted in-depth responses are needed.

e.g.: why did you choose to do your graduate work at this university?

### *Closed Form*

It is also referred to as the "restricted" or "structured" type. It consists of a question or a statement to which a person respond by selecting one or more choices, such as "yes" or "no", write a short response, or check an item from a list of suggested responses. This form facilitate the tabulation and analysis of data. It also improves the reliability and consistency of the data.

One limitation of this kind of item is that the respondent does not have the opportunity to explain whey he has given certain responses and this may be important in some kinds of research studies. This form also limits the scope and depth of responses. So its use in measuring attitudes, feelings and certain aspects of behaviour may be limited.

e.g.: Which of the following is more important as far as a student in a university is considered?

(i) Administrator
(ii) Counsellors
(iii) Teachers

Before the questionnaire is duplicated, it should be examined very carefully by a colleague to eliminate errors and to make necessary modifications. Unless it is absolutely necessary to know the identities of the respondents, the investigator should not ask for their names on the questionnaire because some respondents will provide more accurate data if they believe that others will not know how they answered the questions.

**Limitations**

1. Respondent may not answer all the questions,
2. Carelessness, faulty memory, faulty perception and lack of interest of the respondents.

## 5.2 SCHEDULE

Schedule is usually applied to a set of questions which are asked and filled in by an interviewer in a face to face situation with another person.

A schedule is different from a questionnaire. A questionnaire is usually administered personally to a respondent or a group of respondents. A schedule is administered to a respondent at a time. The advantages this tool has over the questionnaire are that it provide opportunity to establish rapport, to explain the purpose and to make the meaning of items clear. It also economizes time and expense and provides complete and usable returns.

But it may not possible to contact personally all the respondents required, either individually or in a group. Sometimes although personal contact may be possible, it may prove to be too expensive or time consuming.

The characteristics, ways of construction, analysis and interpretation of a schedule is similar to that of a questionnaire.

Its administration in a face to face situation, to an individual or a group is different from the administration of a questionnaire. It is like the administration of an interview.

## 5.3 CHECKLIST

The checklist is a series of phrases or sentences that are to be checked in order to indicate the presence, amount, frequency or order of occurrence of certain kinds of behaviour, characteristics or conditions. Check lists are relatively simple data-collecting devices that are easy to construct and administer. Provided the researcher wishes to limit responses in order to facilitate the analysis and table of data, and to provide that items can be constructed to cover all the areas of inquiry, the check list can be very useful tool of research.

**Example of the Checklist**

Place a check mark besides each of the following facilities that are available in your institution.

| | |
|---|---|
| Drinking water — | Reading room — |
| Seminar hall — | Separate classrooms for all subjects — |
| Library — | Toilet facilities — |

The advantages and disadvantages of the check list are similar to those of the structured questionnaire. They present a good method of obtaining relevant data, which easily can be recorded, analyzed and tabulated. But as in the case of other tools, the researcher cannot be sure that the responses are accurate and truthful.

## 5.4 RATING SCALE

Rating is a term applied to expression of opinion or judgement regarding some situation, object or character. Opinions are usually expressed on a scale of values. Rating techniques are devices by which judgement may be quantified. Rating scale helps to rate something i.e., to find the extent of certain phenomena present in an individual.

Rating scales record judgements or opinions and indicate the degree or amount. Descriptions of different degrees of quality are arranged along a line from high to low or otherwise and this line is the scale.

e.g.: How good was the performance?

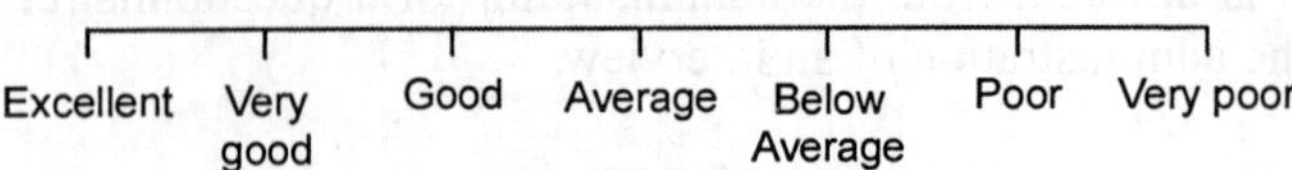


Rating scales have been successfully utilized for the purpose of

1. *Teacher rating*—for selection, evaluation and prediction
2. *Personality rating*—for various purposes
3. Testing the validity of many objective instruments like paper-pencil inventories of personality.
4. *School appraisal*—including appraisal of courses, practices and programmes.

**Limitations of Rating Scale**

***Rating Errors***

Rating scales are subject not only to errors inherent in their design but also to errors that are related to the way in which raters have marked the scale.

1. The hallo effect is an error that occurs. e.g.: If a teacher values highly such traits as neatness and politeness, he may rate a student who displays these traits high on many other traits as well.
2. Personal bias is another error.
3. Logical error results when the rater does not fully understand the terms used in rating scale.
4. Errors of central tendency—occurs when a rater does not have enough information about the individuals to be rated and tends to rate the person as average on all of the characteristics included in the scale.
5. Generosity error occurs because sometimes raters are very reluctant to give any ratings at the low end of the scale. They tend to rate everyone as average or above average.

## 5.5 SCORE CARD

It is an elaborate form of rating scale in which items are always evaluated, usually in numerical terms. The score card provides for the appraisal of a relatively large number of aspects.

It is frequently used in evaluating communities, building-sites, schools, text-books, socio economic status of a family and the worth of any literary or educational work or institution. The rater is provided with a general standard of criteria in detail and has to react and to rate only a single unit of the total situation. At a time a number of raters are employed and their scores build and averaged.

Score cards suffer from limitations and difficulties as in the rating scale. More important one is the suspicion that the whole of a thing may be greater than the sum of its parts.

## 5.6 OPINIONNAIRE OR ATTITUDE SCALE

A research instrument that is similar in some respects to both a questionnaire and a rating scale is the opinionnaire. This is frequently used to measure the attitudes of people towards other people, policies, or situations.

Before constructing an opionnaire, one should study the issue thoroughly. For analysis, divide it into meaningful parts. Then think about the major dimensions of the issue.

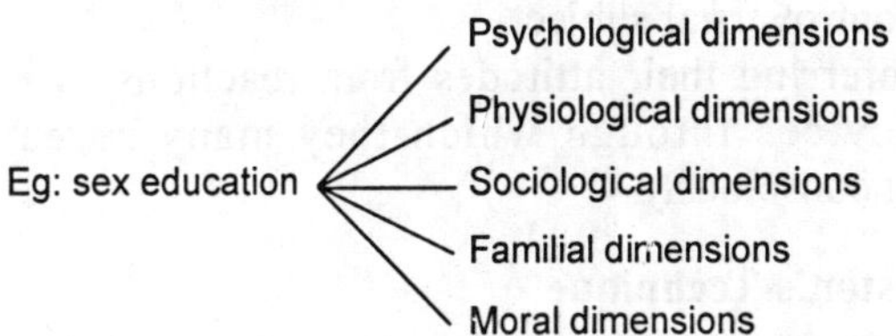


All dimensions should be analyzed ie. thorough and comprehensive analysis on the basis of thorough reading. Analyze each major dimension into specific minor issues. Write down statements on the basis of each specific issue.

### Attitude Scale

Attitude denotes the inner feeling or belief of a person towards a particular phenomenon or it is that particular phenomenon which determines how emotionally one reacts towards an issue. Opinion is what a person say about his attitude towards some phenomena.

Inferring attitude from expressed opinion has many limitations (1) People may conceal their attitudes and express social acceptable opinions. (2) They way not really know how they feel about a social issue, never having given the idea serious consideration. (3) People may be unaware of their attitude about a situation in the abstract; until confronted with a real situation, they may be unable to predict their reaction or behaviour.

Attitudes are revealed in the overt behaviour of an individual. Behaviour also does not always indicate attitude truthfully. Social customs and values make many kinds of behaviour mere formalities quite unrelated or even opposite to the inward feelings of the individual. With these limitations in mind, psychologists and sociologists have explored an interesting area of research, basing their data upon people's expressed opinions. The methods employed are:

1. Asking people directly how they feel about a subject. This technique may employ a schedule or questionnaire of the open or closed form. It may also employ interview process in which the respondent express their opinions orally.
2. Asking people to check in a list the statements with which they agree.
3. Asking people to indicate their degree of agreement or disagreement with a series of statements about a controversial subject.
4. Inferring their attitudes from reactions to a projective devices through which they many reveal attitudes unconsciously.

### 5.6.1 Thurston's Technique

A number of statements, usually 20 or more, are gathered that expresses various points of view toward a group, institution, idea or practice. They are then submitted to a panel of judges each of who arranges them in eleven groups ranging from one extreme to another in position. This sorting by each judge yields a composite position for each of the items. When there has been marked disagreement between the judges in assigning a position to an item, that item is discarded.

**Steps Involved:**

1. Study about the issue.
2. Thorough analysis into minute issues of the issue.
3. Write out statements in unambiguous, precise, simple

language reflecting attitude towards statement. In Thurston's scale only positive attitude statements are there.

4. Find out appropriate judges to evaluate the item i.e., about 30 judges.
5. Rate your items on a 11-point rating scale.
6. Quantify or find out the median of the ratings (responses)
7. Select those items having the median more than 5.

Normally there are 30-40 items

**Defects**

1. We cannot assure that the judges have done their work sincerely.
2. It is difficult to find out a panel of judges i.e., about 30 judges.

### 5.6.2 Likert Attitude Scale

Since the Likert-type scale take much less time to construct, it offers an interesting possibility for the student of opinion research. The subjects are asked to respond to each statement in terms of agreement or disagreement.

First, analyse the major dimensions and then collect a number of statements about a subject. The correctness of the statements is not important as long as they express opinions held by a substantial number of people. It is important that they express favourableness and unfavourableness to a particular point of view and that the number of favourable and unfavourable statements is approximately equal. A trial test should be administered to a number of subjects. Only those items that correlate with the total test should be retained. This testing for internal consistency will help to eliminate statements that are ambiguous or that are not of the same type as the rest of the scale.

#### *Constructing a Likert Attitude Scale*

Before starting construction of scale, the teacher or the test designer must decide what the purpose or objective of the attitude scale is. i.e., the area toward which attitudes are to be measured. Begin with a content outline that identifies the areas in which the attitude will be measured. It is a delineation of the attitude area into topical or subareas that constitutes various aspects of the attitude area to be measured.

When the topical outline is complete, begin writing attitude statements. Write about half of the attitude statements in positive direction with respect to the topic and half in a negative direction.

e.g.: To measure "attitudes towards the emerging and changing role of women"

The sub areas are:

1. relative superiority
2. division of labour
3. claim of education
4. social roles
5. career
6. school
7. Clothes and styles

Start with the subtopical area, in the illustration, "relative superiority". Think of a good positive and negative statement and write one of each, acknowledge to the 12 rules presented in the section 5.6.3.

e.g.: (+) Girls can be leaders just as well as boys can
(–) Girls are the weaker sex.

In constructing the test, do not put all the positive item together. Randomly locate positive and negative items with respect to another to produce a good mix.

***Steps Involved in Lickert's Scale***

1. Analyze the issue into the major dimensions on the basis of theories and previous empirical studies.
2. Write down statements indicating positive and negative attitudes in such a way that their numbers are equal. Fix up the number of items required in the final tool and write statements about double the number.
3. Give five points (or some other convenient number) to each statement. e.g.: Strongly agree, Agree, Undecided, Disagree, Strongly disagree.
4. Arrange these to get a preliminary scale and administer it to a selected sample for preliminary testing (pilot study).
5. This technique allot a scale value to each of the five responses. Say,

| | | SA | A | U | D | SD |
|---|---|---|---|---|---|---|
| Favourable | → | 5 | 4 | 3 | 2 | 1 |
| Unfavourable | → | 1 | 2 | 3 | 4 | 5 |

6. Find the scores of each item for the purpose of item analysis.
7. Correlate the total score with the item score, using any accepted procedure.
   e.g.: In an opinionnaire of 30 items the score values may be $30 \times 5 = 150 \rightarrow$ most favourable and $30 \times 1 = 30 \rightarrow$ Most unfavourable.
8. Select the best items (having maximum correlation) according to the requirement of the final scale.
9. Arrange the items and make the scale complete with suitable instructions.

### *Limitations*

1. It is somewhat inexact and fails to measure opinion with the precision one would desire.
2. We cannot assume that the five positions indicated on the scale are equally spaced. The interval between 'Strongly Agree' and 'Agree' may not be equal to that between 'Disagree' and 'Strongly Disagree'
3. The statements are not of equal value in "for-ness" or "against-ness".
4. With the scale we can determine that there has been a change in attitude, but not the extent of the change.
5. There is the possibility that two individuals who are given the scale may get the same score for an attitude through different combinations of item scores and that this would confound the results.

### *Advantages*

1. It is easier to construct
2. It is more reliable than Thurston's.
3. It permits the use of items that are not manifestly related to the attitude being studied, and
4. It provides more precise information about the subject's opinion on an issue.

### *Writing Attitude Statements*

An attitude scale contains a series of statements or stimuli each of which is responded to by using a scale. Attitude statements are statements about an object, person, issue or experience to which the test taker responds.

### 5.6.3 Guidelines for Writing Attitude Statement (Ebel. 1989)

*1. Avoid Factual Statements*

An attitude statement should require a student to speculate or project, rather than to report on the truth or falsity of facts. Factual statement fit into cognitive measurement and should be excluded from affective measurement.

e.g.: Poor : My teacher punishes children when they misbehave
Better : I am frightened of being punished by my teacher.

*2. Avoid Reference to the Past*

Attitude statements should be written in the present or future tense rather than the past tense since attitude measurement relates to the current state of attitudes that are held and their anticipated effects.

e.g.: Poor : Last year when I got a poor report card, my mother got mad.
Better : If I get a poor report card, my mother will get mad.

Attitude measurement requires that the student project himself into a situation rather than reporting on what was happened in that situation.

*3. Avoid Multiple Interpretations*

An attitude statement must be interpretable in only a single way. If it provokes more than one interpretation, students will not know how to respond to it:

e.g.: Poor : My teacher demands high level of performance
Better : My teacher assists and encourages students to perform well.

In the second example, the first statement could be interpreted as a positive expression of motivation and support or a negative one of excessiveness and overbearing and leads the student into confusion.

### *4. Avoid Irrelevancies*

Attitude scales are written to measure attitude towards a specific object, be that object a person (like "oneself"), a thing (like "a book"), an idea (like "freedom") or an experience (like "school"). All of the statements in that scale must refer to that object and to no other. Statements that refer to any object other than the one under consideration are irrelevant.

e.g.: Poor : The principal in this well-designed building is very supportive of teacher

Better : The principal of this school is very supportive of teachers.

### *5. Avoid Non-distinguishers*

The purpose of an attitude scale is to distinguish between people holding favourable attitude and those holding unfavourable ones.

e.g.: Poor : The United Nations has an important responsibility in the world.

Better : The existence of United Nations makes me confident about the future of the world.

### *6. Cover the Full Range*

The set of attitude statements should reflect the full range in which an object, person or experience can be conceived rather than just one or two facets. To ensure full coverage, it is best to begin with a content outline that identifies the areas in which the attitude will be measured.

### *7. Write Simply, Clearly, Directly*

Do not use big, confusing words when they can be avoided. Attitudes statements must be clear and easy to understand.

e.g.: Poor : As a subject, chemistry provokes my strong involvement

Better : I like to study chemistry

### *8. Write Short Statements*

Attitude statement should rarely exceed twenty words.

e.g.: Poor : When a person find himself in a situation in which he or she can take advantage of another person, he or she can usually be expected to do so.
Better : Basically, people cant be trusted.

***9. One Thought Per Statement***

The statements should restrict to a single thought.

e.g.: Poor : A good teacher knows his or her subject matter and treats all students fairly
Better : A good teacher treats all students fairly

***10. Avoid, "All", "Always", "None" and "Never"***

These words introduce ambiguity into a statement, these words add either confusion or certainty.

e.g.: Poor : I never met a person I didn't like
Better : I find that I like most people I meet

***11. Use "Only", "Just", "Merely" Sparingly***

These words also introduce ambiguity and can often be eliminated.

e.g. Poor : Organized religion is the only way that people can express their faith
Better : Organized religion in the best way that people can express their faith

***12. Avoid Double Negatives***

The use of two negative words (no, not, none) in one sentence scores only to make the sentence more difficult to understand.

e.g.: Poor : No teacher in this school does not respect student rights
Better : Teachers in this school respect students rights

## 5.7 SOCIOMETRY

Sociometric devices are ideally equipped to function in a field where there is much interest in cross-disciplinary integration. A sociometric measure is a measure of assessing the attractions and repulsions within a given group. It usually involves each member of a group privately specifying a number of other persons in the group. With whom he would like to engage in some particular activity and a number of persons with who he would not like to participate in the activity.

Sociometry is a technique for describing the social relationships among individuals is a group. In an indirect way it attempts to describe attractions or repulsions between individuals by asking them to indicate whom they would choose or reject in various situations. Children in a classroom may be asked to name in order to preference (usually 2 or 3) the child or children that they would invite to a party, eat lunch with, sit next to, or home as a close friend. Sociogram is a pictorial representation of the sociometric results.

## 5.8 CRITERIA FOR A GOOD MEASURING TOOL

1. Items should be based upon pre-determined objectives, i.e., objective based tool.
2. *Comprehensiveness*—The test should contain items intended to test all the aspects to be tested.
3. *Objectivity*—Answer should be definite and there should not be the possibility of more than one answer. The answer should not depend upon the likes and dislikes of the examiner or the examinee.
4. *Power of Discrimination*—Test should be efficient enough to discriminate examinees with respect to the degree of the phenomenon being tested.
5. *Validity*—The test should have an established validity.
6. Reliability—Reliability of the test should be ensured.

## 5.9 OBSERVATION

Observation is one of the oldest methods of data collection. (Sarantakos,1998). Until it was introduced to sociology it was largely employed by social anthropologists and ethnologists, with sociologists and other social scientists opting in larger numbers for survey and other techniques. Nevertheless, with time observation gradually became popular outside anthropology and ethnology and particularly in the social sciences. Today, observation is proclaimed to be one of the fundamental techniques of social research.

Literally, observation means a method of data collection that employs vision as its main means of data collection. It is used as the only technique of data collection, or jointly with other techniques, for instance in intensive interviewing, documentary study or case studies. Observation is an indirect method of data collection since in most cases it collects information without the full knowledge of the respondents. Often, even if the respondent knows that he or she is being observed, the actual nature and purpose of observation are not known.

In this chapter we shall explore the nature, types and process of observation and examine its significance for social research.

## Types of Observation

Observation is open to all observable social phenomena. However, there are some limitations. In the first place there are issues that do not lead themselves to an observational analysis, for example personal, sensitive issues or causes and consequences of social phenomena. Also, past or future events cannot be observed. Further, observation is limited by the fact that it can only study observable phenomena.

There are several types of observation, some more popular than others. Although basically similar, they do differ from each other in the degree of the observer's participation in the environment, in the setting in which it occurs, and in the manner in which it is organized. Some examples of observation are given below:

### *Naive and Scientific Observation*

Naive observation refers to everyday, unstructured observation which people use when they interact with others in social situations. Observation becomes scientific when it is systematically planned and executed, when it is related to a certain goal and when it is subjected to tests and controls.

### *Participant and Non-participant Observation*

In general, the degree of the observer's involvement in observation varies from no participation at all to full participation. In the first case, observers study heir subjects from outside the group without becoming a part of the environment of the observed; in the second case, they actually become members of the group they are supposed to study. The first type of observation is known as *non-participant* observation; the other is *participant* observation.

In participant observation, the observers observe from inside the group, and ideally their identity as a researcher is not known. For instance, researchers who want to observe criminals in action manage to become members of criminal gangs; those who wish to study homosexual behaviour pretend to be homosexuals, and are accepted by the members of the group they intend to study; and investigators who want to study the work conditions of labourers in a factory are employed in a plant for a certain time, working along side the workers. As members of these groups, they can study among other things their structure, process, problems and attitudes from the inside, and as experienced by the members of the groups.

In the case of non-participant observation, the observers are not a part of the environment they study. Their position is clearly defined and different from that of the subjects. In ideal terms the observers are invisible, unnoticed and outside the group they observe. The best example of non-participant observation is laboratory observation, where the subjects interact in a laboratory and the researcher observes them from the outside, for example through a one-way vision glass. Observing children playing in the school playground through a window is another example of non-participant observation. In both cases the observer does not actively participate in the group understudy.

Many cases of observation lie somewhat between these two extremes of participant and the non-participant observation. In certain cases investigators are more observers than participants; in others they are more participants than observers – the difference between the various forms of observation is a matter of degree rather than a matter of substance.

### *Structured and Unstructured Observation*

These two types of observation differ in terms of the degree to which they are structured. *Structured observation* employs a formal and strictly organized procedure, with a set of well-defined observation categories, and is subjected to high levels of control and differentiation. It is organized and planned before the study begins. Unstructured observation is loosely organized and the process of observation is largely left up to the observer to define.

*Semi-structured observations* lie somewhere between these two techniques, and may be structured, for instance, in their approach but unstructured in their setting. They are relatively common in social research and combine advantages (and limitations) of both the structured and unstructured techniques of observation.

### *Natural Observations and Laboratory Observations*

The main difference between these two techniques lies in the types of setting in which they unfold. In the former, observations take place in natural settings; in the latter they are performed in a laboratory.

### *Open and Hidden Observation*

The distinction refers to the degree to which the identity of the researcher as an observer as well as the purpose of the study is known to the participants. While in the case of open observation the participants are well informed of the nature of the study and the identity of the researcher, in hidden observation they are not.

### *Active and Passive Observation*

This type of observation refers to the degree to which the observer is involved in the process and purpose of observation. Active observation presupposes full engagement of the observer in the cause of the study, while passive observation sees the role of the observer as being just a strict recording of data. In this case observation is a job to be done in an objective and neutral fashion.

### *Direct and Indirect Observation*

Direct observation studies the subject it intends to explain; for example, if the study intends to explain the patterns of conflict in marital dyads, and observation involves married couples, this is a direct observation. Indirect observation does not involve the object of study, either because the subject refuses to take part in the study or a direct observation is not possible (the subject is deceased). Instead, researchers observe the physical traces the phenomena under study have left behind and make conclusions about the subject. The discussion of physical traces in this volume also applies here.

## Advantages and Limitations of Observation

### *Advantages*

Observation as a method of data collection is generally considered to have the following advantages over other methods:

- It provides information when other methods are not effective.
- It employs a relatively less complicated and less time-consuming procedure of subject selection.
- It can offer data when respondents are unable and/or unwilling to cooperate or to offer information.
- It approaches reality in its natural structure, and studies events as they evolve.
- It offers first-hand information without relying on the reports of others.
- It allows the collection of a wide range of information, even when this information is thought to be, at the time of study, irrelevant. This is particularly true of participant observation.
- It is relatively inexpensive.

***Limitations***

Observation also has some limitations, of which the ones listed below are the most significant. It must be noted that while some limitations occur in qualitative observation and others in quantitative observation, they are often addressed indiscriminately by many writers as they relate to observation as a method.

- It cannot be employed when large groups or extensive events are studied.
- It cannot provide information about past, future or unpredictable events.
- It cannot offer data related to frequency of behaviour.
- It cannot study opinions or attitudes directly.
- It is inadequate when studying certain phenomena, such as sexual behaviour, family violence, etc.
- It is a relatively laborious and time-consuming method.
- It is exposed to the observer's bias, selective perception and selective memory.
- In participant observation the observer is a part of the situation that is being observed.
- It offers no control measures regarding bias, attitudes and opinions of the observer.
- It cannot offer quantitative generalizations on the results.

## 5.10 INTERVIEW

Interviewing is a form of questioning characterized by the fact that it employs verbal questioning as its principal technique of data collection. Together with questionnaires, interviews make up the survey method, which is one of the most popular techniques of social research *(Sarantakos,1998)*.

Interviews are a common occurrence in everyday life, but as a tool of social research, or better as a method of data collection, interviewing is different. This is so with regard to its preparation, construction and execution, first because it is prepared and executed in a *systematic* way, second because it is *controlled* by the researcher to avoid bias and distortion, and third due to the fact that it is related to a specific research question and a specific purpose.

Interviews are employed as methods of data collection in most research designs, regardless of the underlying methodology. Qualitative studies employ unstandardised forms of interviewing, such as intensive interviewing and focused interviewing, while quantitative studies employ predominantly structured interviews. Feminists, finally, consider (especially semi-structured) interviewing a very useful method, value it for its openness, qualitative nature and interviewee-guided mode, employ it often for social reform purposes, and think it is very useful for feminist research. Reinharz (1992), for instance, argues that interviewing is 'particularly suited to female researchers' and feels that it 'draws on skill in the traditional female role'. She goes on to say that this method is very useful when conducted by a woman; for a woman to be understood it may be necessary for her to be interviewed by a woman.

In the discussion that follows we shall examine the most central issues of interviewing, starting with the types of interviews.

### Types of Interviews

There are many types of interviews, each of which differs from the others in structure, purposes, role of the interviewer, number of respondents involved in each interview, and form and frequency of administration. In the international literature, these interview types appear under many and different names. Some types of interviews are employed in both quantitative and qualitative methods; others are used in one research type only. Semi-structured interviews, for instance, are employed in qualitative and quantitative research, but structured interviewing is mostly used in quantitative research.

### *Structured Versus Unstructured Interviews*

*Structured interviews* are based on a strict procedure and a highly structured interview guide, which is not different from a questionnaire. A structured interview is in reality a questionnaire read by the interviewer as prescribed by the researcher. This rigid structure determines the operation of this research instrument and allows no freedom to make adjustments to any of its elements, such as content, wording or order of the questions.

The interview is based on a schedule, and strict adherence to the questions and the instructions is paramount. In this type of interviewing (at least in its extreme form) the interviewer is expected to perform like a 'robot', acting in a neutral manner, keeping the same tone of voice, offering the same impression to the respondents, using the same style, appearance, prompts, probes, etc., and showing no initiative, spontaneity or personal interest in the research topic. The purpose of this is to reduce interviewer bias to a minimum and achieve the highest degree of uniformity in procedure. This form of interview is employed in quantitative research.

*Unstructured interviews* have no strict procedure to follow of the kind described above. In their extreme form they are theoretically inconceivable, for every interview has a structure of some kind, and is structured in some way and to some degree. Nevertheless, the strict control reported above is lacking here. There are no restrictions in the wording of the questions, the order of questions or the interview schedule. The interviewer acts freely in this context, on the basis of certain research points, formulating questions as and when required and employing neutral probing. The structure of these interviews is flexible and the restrictions minimal, being presented in most cases in the form of guides rather than rules. This type of interview is mostly used in qualitative research.

*Semi-structured interviews* lie somewhere between structured and unstructured interviews. They contain elements of both, and while some are closer to structured interviews, others are closer to unstructured interviews. The degree to which interviews are structured depends on the research topic and purpose, resources, methodological standards and preferences, and the type of information sought which of course is determined by the research objective. They can be both qualitative and quantitative techniques.

### *Individual Versus Group Interviews*

When individual interviews are employed the researcher interviews one respondent at a time. This is the most common form of interviewing. The interviewer asks direct or indirect questions to one respondent, who in turn answers these questions. In group interviews more than one respondent is involved in the interview situation. They are also addressed by the interviewer simultaneously. In a small-scale group two people (e.g. husband and wife, or mother and daughter) are interviewed concurrently.

On a larger scale, a group of, say, 20 persons might be interviewed. For example, a class of students might be interviewed together. In such cases, the interviewer hands the students response sheets (e.g. with or without the questions, or computer cards), reads the questions one by one and asks the respondents to enter their answers on their sheet or card. In some cases, the interviewing becomes a dialogue between the interviewer(s) and the respondents. For example, the interviewer ask questions, suggests possible answers (yes, no, I don't know, no answer) and asks respondents to indicate their preferences by raising their hands. The number of positive, negative or neutral answers is counted and recorded in a grouped form. (Adequate measures are taken to ensure that external factors will not affect the answers of the respondents).

Individual and group techniques are employed by both types of methodology, although qualitative studies favour individual interviews.

### Advantages and Limitations of Interview (Sarantakos,1998)

Interviewing is so commonly used in the social sciences that it is quite often considered to be the method of social research. Its popularity is often justified in terms of several of its qualities, which give it an advantage over other methods of data collection. Feminists, for instance, stress among other things the fact that interviewing allows women to speak in their own words and not in the words of the researcher; it allows the study of non-verbal communication which is used by subordinate people to express themselves, is particularly suited to female researchers, avoids alienation between researcher and respondent and encourages the development of a sense of connectedness (Reinharz, 1990).

### *Advantages*

The advantages of interviewing have been stressed by most writers (see Berger *et al.*, 1989; Mahr, 1995; Roth, 1987). Although they refer primarily to standardized forms of interviewing, they also apply in the area of qualitative interviewing. The advantages are:

- *Flexibility*: Interviews can adjusted to meet many diverse situations.
- *High Response Rate*: Interviewing attracts a relatively high response rate.
- *Easy Administration*: Interviews do not require respondents to have the ability to read, handle complex documents or long questionnaires.
- *Opportunity to Observe Non-verbal Behaviour*: Such opportunities are obviously not available when questionnaires or indirect methods are used.
- *Less Patience and Motivation* to complete are needed than are required by questionnaires. Interviews need 'participation', not just 'response'. Participation involves another person with whom the respondent completes the task, so intervening is often perceived as a cooperative venture rather than a one-sided exercise.
- *Control Over the Environment*: Here the interviewer has an opportunity to control the conditions under which the questions are answered.
- *Capacity for Correcting Misunderstandings by respondents*: Such an option is very valuable and not available in other forms of data collection, such as questionnaires.
- *Control Over the Order of the Questions*: Respondents have no opportunity to know what question comes next, or to alter the order of the questions they answer. When the order of the questions is significant, an interview is much more useful than a questionnaire.
- *Opportunity to Record Spontaneous Answers*: The respondent does not have as much time available to answer questions as when questionnaires are employed. When spontaneity is important, interviews offer a real advantage over other methods.
- *Control over the Identity of the Respondent:* When interviews are employed, the identity of the respondent is known; this is not so when other methods (e.g. questionnaires) are used.

- *Completeness of the interview guaranteed* The fact that the interviewer presents the questions guarantees that all questions will be attempted.
- *Control over the time, date and place of the interview* The fact that interviewer presents the questions guarantees that all questions will be attempted.
- *Control over the time, date and place of the interview* If the information must be collected at a certain time (e.g. after the evening news or on Friday evening, etc.), date or place, interviews offer a guarantee that it will be collected according to the specified conditions. Such a guarantee cannot be given when questionnaires are used.
- *More complex questions* can be used because the presence of the interviewer can assist in answering the questions.
- *Greater permissible length* is more possible in interviewing than when other methods (e.g. questionnaires) are used.

***Limitations***

Despite its advantages, interviewing is limited by a number of factors; the following are the most important:

- Interviews are more *costly* and *time consuming* than other methods, such as questionnaires.
- Interviews are affected by the factor 'interviewer' and the possible bias associated with it.
- Interviewing is more *inconvenient* than other methods, such as using questionnaires.
- It offers *less anonymity* than other methods since the interviewer knows the identity, residence, type of housing, family conditions and other personal details of the respondent.
- It is less *effective* than other methods when sensitive issues are discussed. For example, many people prefer to write about sensitive issues than to talk about them.

Apart from these limitations, interviewing is affected by factors common to other techniques of data collection, for example deliberate misrepresentation of facts, genuine mistakes, unwillingness or inability to offer information and similar problems. In such cases, however, it is easier to detect problems when interviewing than when using other methods.

# VI
# Methods of Research

Research can be classified on many bases. It can classify

1. On the basis of ultimate goal, expressed in the nature of results. This is mainly aimed at findings a new theory that could explain a puzzling phenomenon. So it results in a new theory. e.g.: theory of reinforcement. This is the theory oriented research or fundamental research.
2. How to apply a new theory to solve a given practical situation in the result of this type. When we found out a solution, it can be called as Applied Research.

## 6.1 VARIABLES

Variables are the conditions or characteristics that the experimenter manipulates, controls or observes.

The independent variables are the conditions or characteristics that the experimenter manipulates or controls in his or her attempt to ascertain their relationship to observed phenomena. The dependent variables are the conditions or characteristics that appear, disappear, or change as the experimenter introduces, removes or change independent variables.

In educational research usually the dependent variable may be a test score, number of errors, or measured speed in performing a task and independent variables may a particular teaching method, a type of teaching material, a reward, etc.

Then the dependent variables are the measured changes in pupil performance attributable to the influence of the independent variable.

Depending on the way the variables are treated in a study another classification is also possible.

### (1) Causative Study

In this case variables are treated as having cause—effect relation. Here effect is the dependent variable and cause is the independent variable.

e.g.:
1. Intelligence (independent) and mathematics achievement (dependent)
2. Achievement (dependent) depends on intelligence (independent)
3. Effect of achievement motivation on performance in examination

### (2) Correlational Studies

In this case variables are treated as having correlation i.e., the variables have a tendency to co-exist and move together.

e.g.: Effect of education of parents on their views regarding introduction of sex education.

### (3) Analytical Studies

In this case variables are subjected to analysis.

On the basis of research design i.e., the plan/technique of conducting the project.

## 6.2 EXPERIMENTAL RESEARCH

Many problems in education are best investigated by means of experimental research. In experimental research, one or more factors are systematically varied in order to determine what effects this variation produces during the course of the experiment. On the experiment, the condition being evaluated is known as an independent variable and the criterion used to evaluate this condition is referred to as a dependent variable.

In an ideal experiment, there is a direct relationship between the independent and dependent variables. This is impossible to achieve in educational research because there are so many factors or extraneous variables that may operate during an experiment.

## Characteristics of Experimental Research

1. Achieving statistical equivalence of subjects in different groups e.g.: random assignment.
2. At least two groups that can be compared are needed.
3. Manipulation of independent variable.
4. Measurement of dependent variable (Fig. 16.1) and use of inferential statistics.

The only way to hold all variables constant, except the dependent variable is to use two identical groups in the experiment. If the members of the first group (experimental group) are identical to the members of the second group (control group) and if the experimental group receives treatment and the control group does not, any difference in the dependent variable can be attributed only to the manipulation of the independent variable.

## Post-test-Only Design

The experimental and control groups are equated by random assignment. At the end of the experimental period the difference between the mean test scores of the experimental and control groups are subjected to a test of statistical significance, a 't' test or an analysis of variance.

Using a table of random numbers the researcher selects say, 80 students from a school population of 450. These students are randomly assigned to experimental and control treatments using 40 as the experimental group and 40 as the control group.

For the selected two groups, consider that our problem is, "the effect of immediate feedback on scholastic attainment in mathematics". Two groups selected are identical in age, class, sex, intelligence, interest, previous knowledge, socio economic status, achievement, motivation, etc.

Control the variables other than the independent variable that are likely to affect the dependent variable. Now we have the control group (C-group) and the Experimental group (E-group). Select each pair in the two groups matched by controlling the variables. Teach mathematics, same portion taking same time, by the same teacher, same learning experience, etc.—except the nature of feedback. At the end, administer the same test. See Fig. 6.1.

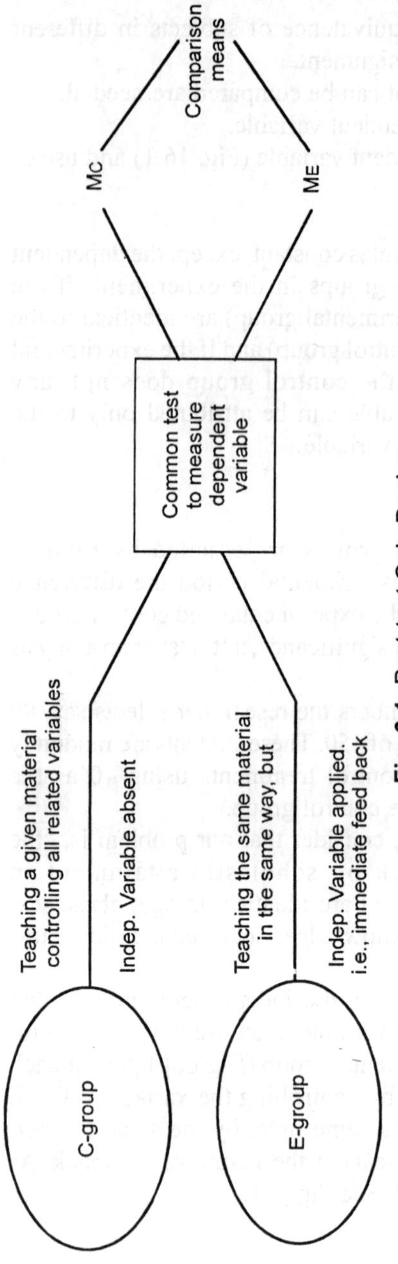


**Fig. 6.1: Post-test Only Design**

After conducting the test find mean value of Dependant variable for the control and experimental groups. Then compare the mean values of the Dependent variable between the groups.

The same procedure can also be symbolized as follows:

| | | |
|---|---|---|
| R X $O_1$ | where, | R – Random sample |
| R C $O_2$ | | X – test for experiment group |
| | | C – test for control group |
| | | O – Observation or test administered |

**Pre Test-Post Test Design**

In this case, the difference is that a pre test is administered to both Control and Experimental group before the treatment starts. The figure 6.2 follows illustrate the procedure.

First, administer a pre-test to find the level of attainment before the experiment for the two groups. Then give training to the two groups adding the independent variable to the experimental group. Then conduct a post test, to find whether there is any difference in the improvement of the level of attainment. After the experiment, the two groups are compared for the 'gain' scores.

**Validity of Experiments**

It is helpful to identify and classify variables that, when not adequately controlled would make it impossible to reach valid conclusion about the outcome of an experiment. Cambell and Stanley organized the variables into two categories: those that pose threats of internal validity and those that pose threats to external validity.

***Factors Affecting Internal Validity***

1. *History*: refers to events occurring in the environment at the same time that experimental variable is being tested. e.g.: a group of students under and they experience simultaneously a high stress by an external event.
2. *Selection*: People factors can introduce a bias—the use of random argument reduces the problems of selection.
3. *Maturation*: Process of change that take place within those persons who are participating in the experimental. For example: age and time.

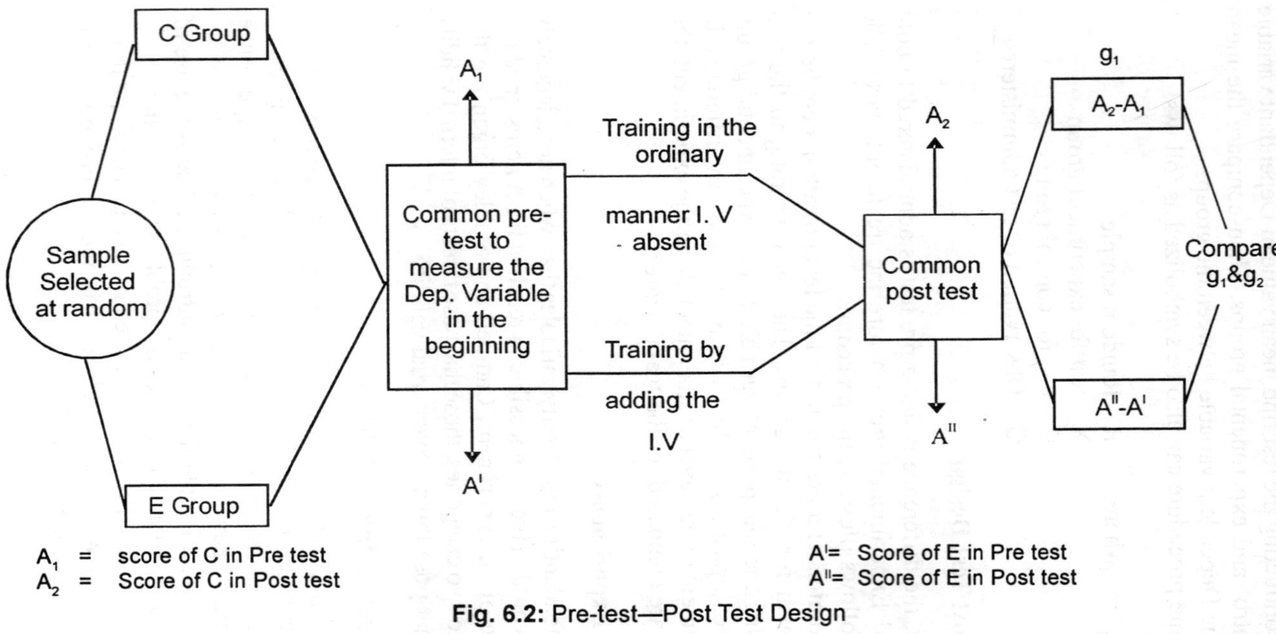


**Fig. 6.2: Pre-test—Post Test Design**

4. *Testing*: refers to the effect of taking a pre test on the subsequent post-test performance of individuals. The effect of taking the pretest may increase the likelihood that the individual will do better on the subsequent pretest.
5. *Instrumentation*: refers to change that occur in the instrument or observation procedures during an experiment. It includes tests, mechanical measuring instruments, and observers, or sensors.
6. *Statistical Regression*: there would be a finding on any possessive measurement for the scores of the higher scorers to decrease toward the mean while the scores of the lower scorers would increase towards the mean. The reason is that chance factors are most likely to contribute to extreme scores than to average scores.
7. *Experimental Mortality*: It is related to the post test date from all of the subjects who were originally included in the study became subjects. Who withdraw from an experimental study may be different from those who remain.

***Factors Affecting External Validity***

Refer to the generalizability or representativeness of the findings of the study. A researcher hopes that the results can be applied during later time periods to groups of people in other geographical area. Factors affecting, external validity are:

*Relative Effects of Testing*: If pretesting that sensitizes the experimental subject to the particular treatment has been used then the effect of treatment may be partially result of the sensitization of the present. Also, subjects often try to help the experimenter by providing the result they think he or she is anticipating. One reason they may react differently to the treatment after a pretest is that they think they then know from the pretest what the experimenter's aim is.

*Interaction Effect of Selection Bias*: If the samples drawn for a study are not representative of the larger population, then it will be difficult to generalize findings from the samples to the population.

*Reactive Effects of Experimental Arrangements*: The arrangements of the experiment or the experience of participating in it may create sufficient artificiality to limit the possibility that the results will be generalizable to a non-experimental test of the treatment.

## 6.3 HISTORICAL RESEARCH

History is the system of organizing and classifying the recorded evidence of past events. Historical research is usually accompanied by an interpretation of these events and of their relevance to present circumstances/provided the factual data of history can be documented in order to insure their validity, historical data once they have been collected.

On the positive side, it may be said that certain historical facts, once they are clearly determined, can be stated quantitatively and, therefore, treated statistically. e.g.. Data obtained from original school records. This historical information may then be used to interpret current events, to identify causes of events, to illustrate developmental trends and to make comparisons.

So, the historical research is, studying the selected phenomena that existed in the past regarding some institution/historical manuscript/monument/organization etc.

### Selection of a Problem

The researcher should exercise due care in selecting a historical problem for investigation. The scope of the problem must be kept within reasonable limits and specific limitations must be set.

*Formulation of Hypothesis*: The hypothesis that the researcher instructs for historical research are useful in explaining and interpreting the events of the historical period in question (The hypothesis are written as statements that tentatively explain given events, situations or phenomena). However, it is likely that a person conducting historical research may not state formal hypotheses to be tested. Rather he may wish to formulate questions and direct his research towards seeking answers to these questions.

e.g.:
1. The monitorial system had no significant effect upon American education?
2. What was the nature of teacher-pupil relationship in Nalanda University?

### Difficulties in Historical Research

A major difficulty is delimiting the problem so that a satisfactory analysis is possible. The historical research must involve a penetrating analysis of a limited problem rather than a superficial examination of a broad area. Since historians may not have lived during the time they are studying and may be removed from the events they investigate. They must often depend upon inference and logical analysis, using the recorded experience of others rather than direct observation.

Finding appropriate primary sources of data requires imagination, hard work and resourcefulness.

**Sources of Data**

A historical research will seek "primary" source materials when they exist. A primary source is an original document or the testimony of an eyewitness. The further back in history the research takes the investigator, the greater becomes his reliance on "secondary" sources.

Secondary source is a reproduction of an original document or of the report of an interviewer other than the original witness. Because of the distortion in passing on information the historians use them only when primary data are not available.

Examples of data:

***(a) Primary Sources:***

1. *Documents*—constitutions, charters, laws, court decisions, official minutes or records.
2. *Remains or relics*—i.e., objects associated with a person, group or period—fossils, skeletons, weapons etc.
3. *Oral Testimony*: oral testimony is the spoken account of a witness or participant in an event.

But in the case of educational data, the main sources are, official records and other documentary materials, oral testimony and relics (building, murals, textbooks, learning materials, etc.)

***(b) Secondary Sources***

Most of history textbooks and encyclopaedia are examples of secondary sources.

**External and Internal Criticism**

External criticism concerns the authenticity and integrity of the document. Examples of unauthentic materials can be found in the many cases of fraud in connection with art anthropological, and historical documents. If a document is fraudulent, biased or in error, it cannot be used as a basis for drawing valid conclusions. The researcher is responsible for checking the origin, objectivity and legality of all sources used in the collection of his data.

If the document is proven to be genuine, the next analysis involves internal criticism. Internal criticism concerned with the authenticity, integrity, and credibility of a content of the document. The researcher must try to determine whether the author know those facts and reported them accurately. e.g., Does the language of the document felt the period in which it was supposedly written? Does the geography/ chronology or other content agree with the evidence from other historical documents?

As in usual cases, after collecting data, the data can be verified with respect to the research questions and arrive in conclusion.

## 6.4 SURVEY

Normally done to gather opinion/existing status or condition of a phenomenon, attitude etc. at present i.e., the time when the study is made.

The survey method gathers data from a relatively large number of case at a particular time. It is concerned with the generalized statistics that result when data are abstracted from a number of individual cases. It is essentially cross-sectional.

School surveys are probably the most widely used form of descriptive research in the field of education.

e.g.: (1) A survey of the opinion of the teachers regarding the suitability of the newly introduced syllabus.

(2) A survey of the opinion of the parents regarding the introduction of a programme for example, compulsory military training to college students.

The surveys can be classified as,

1. *Social Surveys*: e.g.: television viewing habits of school children.
2. *Follow Up Study*: If a school administration is concerned with the drop-out rate from its second school, it may wish to conduct a follow-up study of the recent dropouts in order

to gain a better perspective of the failure of the school system to meet the needs of students.

3. *Public-opinion Surveys*, e.g.: Introduction of Sex education in schools. The public opinion surveys serve a useful purpose in guiding policy in public/school districts. In this case great care should be exercised in selection of sample. It should be a good representative of the population. But there may be sometimes more variation with serious opinions that are expressed as actual decisions.

Steps followed in sample survey:

1. Determine the phenomenon to be studied by the survey. e.g.: opinion of the new syllabus of mathematics
2. Determine the population for the study e.g.: secondary school teachers (mathematics)
3. Decide upon the sample and select it e.g.: number in the sample, subgroups, technique of selection etc.
4. Prepare tool for making survey e.g.: 1000 teachers—male and female, rural and urban, with different categories of experience and qualification etc.
5. Decide upon the strategy for gathering data e.g.: How to collect data—directly or by mail.
6. Gather the data from the sample
7. Analyse the data and draw conclusions
8. Make prediction for the population

## 6.5 CASE STUDY

Case study is a way of organizing social data for the purpose of viewing social reality. It examines a social unit as a whole. The unit may be a person, a family, a social group, a social institution or a community.

It is a study in depth with a vision to diagnose and suggest steps for solving the problem with respect to that case only—the solution has no universal application.

Case studies have been made up of all types of communities. For example, a community study is a thorough observation and analysis of a group of people living together in a particular geographic location in a corporate way. Case study method provide information about specific persons, existing institutions, or concrete entities. This information must include biological, physiological, emotional, psychological and any other kind of data that might help to explain the object of the study.

Steps involved in case study are:

1. Locating the case
2. Analyse the problem associated with the case.
3. Locate most salient aspects of the problem that deserve indepth study. This can be done on the basis of analysis of the case.
4. Determine the sources of data and the tools and techniques by which the data could be collected for the indepth study. For this, a multiple approach is required.
5. Gather enough data required for the indepth study.
6. Analyze the data. Thorough analysis leading to diagnosis and remedial measures is required
7. Make suggestions by way of remedial solution for solving the problem of the case.

Certain precautions have to be taken while conducting case studies.

1. The researcher must be thoroughly familiar with existing theoretical knowledge of the field of inquiry and skillful in isolating the significant variables from many that are irrelevant.
2. Subjective bias is a constant threat to objective data gathering and analysis.
3. Effects may be wrongly attributed to factors that are merely associated rather than causes and-effect related.

### How Does Case Study Methodology Proceed?

#### *Define-Clarifying the Research Question*

As with any research project, it is important to develop some understanding of the focal domain of the research inquiry as a way of entering in the field, and beginning with a set of initial procedures to which the researchers can refer as the project proceeds (Stake, 1995). This preparatory and definitional stage may also entail some initial examinations of the political, historical, cultural and personal factors that have given shape to the setting and to the case in question.

***Design-planning data gathering***

Case study researchers determine in advance whether to study cases that are distinctive or those that are considered somehow 'typical'. That is, those thought to be representative on a set dimension, such as geographic region, cultural composition, socio-economic level and so on. A central design feature concerns the level of analysis attempted. For instance, a Case Study can include more than one unit of embedded analysis, involving study of a single school district and a school in that district, a particular teacher within a faculty, or a parent with in a community. Such studies involve multiple levels of analysis, with each level constituting a case, one nested within the other.

***Analysing data***

Case study methodology uses multiple data collection and analytic procedures. These are aimed at providing researchers with opportunities to:

1. compare and contrast interpretations;
2. expand on the relevance of the project by developing unforeseen findings and interpretations; and
3. explore findings that are anomalous to or disconfirming of original hypotheses and impressions.

Some specific techniques commonly used include information arrays, matrices of categories, tabulating the frequency of events, flow charts and the use of quantitative data that has been collected to corroborate or challenge interpretations from the qualitative data. As well, some case studies have used multiple investigators to provide a variety of perspectives from which to explore patterns in the findings.

***Reporting***

Reports of case studies aim to explore a complex, embedded phenomenon in a way that conveys a coherent experience to the reader reviewed by the participants in the study.

## 6.6 THE NORMATIVE SURVEY METHOD

The historical studies discover, describe and interpret what existed in the past. There are other kinds of investigations which study, interpret and describe what exists at present. The term survey suggest the gathering of evidence relating to current conditions. The term 'normative' implies the determination of normal or typical conditions or practice. The term normative survey is used for the type of research which proposes to ascertain what is the normal or typical condition or practice at the present time.

**Characteristics**

1. It gathers data from a relatively large number of cases
2. It is essentially cross-sectional, mostly of what exists type.
3. It is concerned with the generalized statistics of the whole population or a sample thereof.
4. It is an important type of research involving clearly defined problems and definite objectives. It requires an imaginative planning, a careful analysis and interpretation of the data and a logical and skillful reporting of the findings.
5. It does not aspire to develop an organized body of scientific laws but provides information useful to the solution of local problems.

**Significance**

Scientists do not generally regard the normative survey investigations as research of high order. But

1. It determines the present trends and solves current practical problems.
2. It seems historical perspective through a series of cross-sectional pictures of similar conditions at different times.
3. It suggests the course of future developments.
4. It helps to fashion many of the tools with which we do research.
5. It contributes to advancement of knowledge because it affords penetrating into the nature of what is dealing with.

## 6.7 CONTENT ANALYSIS OR DOCUMENTATION ANALYSIS

Documents are an important source of data in many areas of investigation and the methods of analysis are similar to those used by historians. A document is any valid, written record on an issue or an agreement or procedure. e.g.: thesis, curriculum, text book etc.

Documentation analysis is analysing the content of a document to draw conclusions regarding a public issue or to pass judgements on the acceptability of a document or to gather information regarding past happenings etc. More clearly, it is concerned with the explanation of the status of some phenomenon of a particular time or its development over a period of time.

The following may be used as sources of data: records, reports, printed forms, letters, autobiographies, diaries, compositions, books, periodicals, bulletins, syllabi, court decisions, pictures, films, cartoons etc.

When using documentary sources, one must bear in mind that data appearing in print are not necessarily trust worthy.

e.g.: (i) Analysing the curriculum or text book.
(ii) Gathering details regarding the contribution of an agency to the development of education.

## Main Steps in Content Analysis

### *1. Defining the Unit of Analysis*

The unit (material) may be confined to single word, to phrases to complex sentences. Only those facts should be mentioned which are useful in solving the problem. The units can be considered as the entity whose specified characteristics can be determined and analyzed.

### *2. Specifying Variables and Categories*

Once the unit is defined, the researcher conducts its analysis so as to create reproducible or objective data for scientific treatment and generalization beyond the specific set of symbolic material analyzed. For converting symbolic material into objective data it is necessary to specify the variables explicitly.

There is a need for framing explicit rules specifying what features of the content are to be taken as indication that it fall in one category rather than the other.

### *3. Frequency, Direction and Intensity*

Once the unit is defined and the variables along with their categories to be employed are specified, the analysis will classify units in the material to be analyzed according to frequency, direction and intensity.

For frequency analysis merely counts the number of units which fall into each categories e.g. In the analysis of a public speech by an economist, the number of times 'privatization of higher education' may be employed as an argument for a certain policy of government. In this case 'argument' is taken as recording unit or enumeration unit. Direction refers to whether the reference was favourable, unfavourable, or neutral. It might be pleasant, unpleasant, interesting or uninteresting.

**Purpose of Documentation Analysis**

1. To describe prevailing practices or conditions.
2. To discover the relative importance of, or interest in, certain topics or problems.
3. To discover the level of difficulty of presentation in text books or in other publications.
4. To evaluate bias, prejudice, or propaganda in textbook presentation.
5. To analyze types of errors in student's work.
6. To identify the literary style, concepts or beliefs of a writer.
7. To explain the possible causal factors related to some outcome, action or event.

**Advantages and Disadvantages of Content Analysis**

Content analysis has its own strengths and weaknesses. So, we should be careful in using research technique.

***Advantages***

- Looks directly at communication via texts or transcripts and hence gets at the centre aspect of social interaction.
- Can allow for both quantitative and qualitative operations.
- Can provide valuable historical/cultural insight over time through analysis of text.
- Can be used to interpret texts for purpose such as the development of expert systems.
- Provides insight into complex models of human thought and language use.
- When done well it is considered as a really 'exact' research method.

***Disadvantages***

- Can be extremely time consuming.

- Is subjected to increase error, particularly when relational analysis is used to attain a higher level of interpretation.
- Tends too often to simply consist of word counts.
- Can be difficult to automate or computerized.

## 6.8 CORRELATION METHOD

It is a research approach which analyses the relationship between data, between variables and some results in such a way that the underlying pattern of relationship become clear.

The correlation method is of modern origin, ranked high among research methods in education. This method is a definite improvement on the causal-comparative and the experimental methods. It approaches the problem of cause and effect in terms of degrees and deals with the problems in terms of many variables and reflects the variation of many factors at once.

The chief uses of correlation method are:

1. To measure the strength of association, or the degree to which variation in one factor, is associated with variation in others. Variation between one factor and another may be positively or negatively correlated from +1 through 0 to –1.
2. To predict scholastic success by utilizing available data or special data from the use of aptitude or prognostic tests.
3. To predict teaching success and select teachers according to a composite criterion of teaching success secured through the technique of multiple correlation which takes account of many variables at once.
4. To predict school population which is a necessary aspect of educational planning.
5. To help in fundamental research through (a) the construction of data gathering tools and determination of their validity and reliability. (b) factorial analysis i.e., an analysis of the composition of some psychological phenomenon like intelligence.

The correlation method involves all steps that are involved in other kinds of research. The scores obtained for different variables are analyzed through various statistical techniques. Some factors to keep in mind while calculating correlation coefficient are:

(i) Coefficient of correlation do not represent percentage of anything. They are pure mathematical symbols and not to be mistaken for anything else.
(ii) They are not to be interpreted in a linear sense, i.e., 0.80 should never to be taken to be twice as big as 0.40.
(iii) Errors of measurement are important and should always be taken account of.
(iv) Size of 'r' depends mainly on the range of measurements used in the calculations.

## 6.9 ETHNOGRAPHY AND EDUCATION

The origins of ethnographic research can be traced back to the fifteenth and sixteenth centuries, arising from the interests of Westerners in the new cultures they came across as the European empires expanded (Vidich and Lyman. 1994). Ethnography thus initially expressed, pre-anthropology, a motivation for exploring other, different cultures. Most contemporary definitions of Ethnography are compatible with Denzin's notion that Ethnography is 'that form of inquiry and writing that produces descriptions and accounts about the ways of life of the writer and those written about' (1997). Thus, Ethnography is, by definition, a hybrid approach, characterized by two demands on researchers: one as observing a setting and gathering data, and the other as directly involved in the setting under study, including the researchers, as themselves objects of inquiry (Silverman, 1997: 10).

Ethnography is traditionally associated with the fields of sociology and anthropology. But these fields, it has been taken up by educational researchers to explore ways of describing and interpreting what is happening in formal and informal educational settings. Ethnographic research, with its emphasis on context and 'thick descriptions', has been seen as offering a range of procedures that give it applicability and flexibility in educational settings.

### Steps

As with all research, there are critical decisions to be made concerning the selection of participants whose educational practices or accounts are to be studied. There are a number of approaches to the selection of participants. Each of these approaches follows a particular rationale:

- *Expedient Selection*: These people are available and appropriate to the inquiry, perhaps because they are interested, are engaged in relevant activities, show characteristics of interest to the study, or perceive problems relevant to the terms of the study.

- *Purposeful Selection*: These people are selected because they are taken to represent instances of best cases or worst cases (e.g., according to some external instances of best cases or worst cases (e.g., according to some external criterion such as test scores), clusters of cases (e.g., teachers in small, remote communities), variations commonly encountered (e.g., beginning teachers with 'average' university grades) or special interest (e.g., experienced teachers of severely intellectually impaired students).
- *Probability Selection*: People selected on the basis of knowledge of the larger population to which the researchers wish to generalize the findings. This may involve random selection, or stratified-random selection in which random choice occurs through a proportional selection from within predetermined groupings, in proportions that directly reflect the prevalence of those groupings within the larger population relevant to the study.

Ethnographers put effort into 'breaking' their own cultural knowledge and values, focusing on how the members under observation show their knowledge in the patterns of their practice. They seek to write a 'cultural grammar' that makes visible the logic that connects members' actions with their knowledge and values.

**Characteristics of Ethnographic Research**

1. *Purpose*: The study is concerned with understanding the social phenomena through participation in a research role.
2. *Research Process and Method are Flexible*: It involves various combination of participant observation, in-depth interview and artifact collection. Most of the studies employ emergent design and make decisions about data collection strategies during the study.
3. *Research Role*: Ethnographers become immersed in the situation and the phenomenon. They have interactive social roles and they are involved in interaction with participants.
4. *Context Sensitivity*: Human actions are strongly influenced by settings in which they occur. So generalizations are

context bound. Since it is a field research ethnographers collect data in the setting for a prolonged time.

5. *Concept Analysis*: Ethnographic studies provide an inductive analysis of a single concept.

Educational ethnography is a process, a way of studying human life as it relates to education. It employs qualitative approach and a few quantitative data analysis techniques.

**Steps Involved**

(a) State the purpose and questions to be investigated.

(b) *Select a Site and Research Design*: Site can be selected which is feasible for time, skills and mobility of the ethnographer. After seeking permission, establish a research role, map the field and conduct purposeful sampling.

(c) *Mapping the Field*: Researcher gains a sense of totality and is in a better position to do purposeful sampling of information rich cases.

To get an idea of total context, social, spatial and temporal data should collected from the field.

(d) *Purposeful Sampling*: Choose small groups or individuals required for the information about the problem of interest.

(e) *Data Collection*: Data collection involves observation, interview and artifact collection (which includes beliefs, behaviour the people, values, feelings and perceptions).

(f) Data analysis and Interpretation.

## 6.10 ACTION RESEARCH

The term is used for a family of related techniques that share certain important common ideas, while differing in details of their approach to the research. The differences have led to a variety of names by which such researchers describe their approach—technical action research, practical action research, emanicipatory action research, participatory action research and collaborative action research are examples, along with feminist action research but the generic term action research probably encompasses most of the approaches (Kemmis and Mc Taggart, 2000). This section concentrates on the main common ideas behind the different stands of action research.

The central idea is conveyed by them term 'action research' itself.

Action and research are brought together: action researchers 'engage in careful, diligent inquiry, not for purposes of discovering new facts or revising accepted laws or theories, but to acquire information having practical application to the solution of specific problems related to their work' (Stringer, 2004). Action research brings together the acting (or the doing) and the researching (or the inquiring). In contrast to the ideas of inquiry for its own sake and building knowledge for its own sake, action research aims to design inquiry and build knowledge for use in the service of action to solve practical problems. Therefore, in action research, the inquiry deliberately starts from a specific practical or applied problem or question. Its whole purpose is to lead to action to solve that practical problem or answer that practical question. As Reason and Bradbury (2007) say, action research 'seeks to bring together action and reflection, theory and practice, in participation with others, in the pursuit of practical solutions to issues of pressing concern to people'.

This systematic, disciplined inquiry—this research—is, of course, empirical. Thus action research may involve quantitative data methods and designs. While action research is usually thought of as qualitative approach, and is included here under qualitative research designs, it does not rely only on qualitative data. On the contrary, it uses quantitative data whenever they are appropriate and available. It is like case study research in this respect.

Action Research usually incorporates selected ethnographic and Case Study techniques to document and explore purposeful changes in educational practice. It has been defined Johnson as deliberate, solution-oriented investigation that is group or personally owned and conducted. It is characterized by spiraling cycles of problem identification, systematic data collection, reflection, analysis, data-driven action taken, finally, problem redefinition. The linking of the terms 'action' and 'research' highlights the essential features of this method: trying out ideas in practice as a means of increasing knowledge about and/or improving curriculum, teaching and learning. (1993)

A number of features of this definition show that Action Research aims to advance on Ethnographic and Case Study methodologies:

1. It is a 'deliberate' rather than a purely exploratory entry into a naturally-occurring educational setting. That is, it is planned and self-consciously focused examination of changing practice.

2. It is 'solution-oriented investigation', aimed explicitly at solving particular problems rather than simply documenting their instances, character of consequences.
3. It is 'group or personally owned and conducted'. This is a reference to the politics of knowledge ownership, which is discussed further below, and which emphasizes the importance of the educational practitioners' role as determinants of the description of the problem, what counts as solutions, and what forms the reporting of the project will take.
4. It takes the form of a series of iterations on and around the problem, its documentation and theorization, and the analyses that are used to display how it has been redefined and solved. These iterations are referred to here as 'spirals' but are more commonly known as the Action Research is taken to be central to its core emphasis on the documented improvement of practice.
5. The 'trying out of ideas' is not undertaken solely for the purposes of re-theorizing educational practice or adding to knowledge, but is also aimed at improving educational practice, then and there. In that respect, Action Research is concerned as much with outcomes on the original research site as it is with generalization to other sites or leading to theoretical refinement.

An important characteristic of action research, which sets it apart from other designs, is that it is usually *cyclical* in nature, reflecting the fact that people usually work towards solutions to their problems in cyclical, reflecting the fact that people usually work towards solutions to their problems in cyclical, iterative ways. The words cycle, spiral and (less often) helix are used by writers on action research to describe this. They convey the idea that the one piece of research leading to the one set of actions is not the end of the process, but rather the start of cycle or spiral. The research produces outcomes that lead to the taking of action, but that in turn generates further questions for research, which in turn generates further action, and so on.

**Steps of Action Research**

- Planning a change,
- Acting and observing the consequences of the change,

- Reflecting on these processes and consequences, and then
- Replanning,
- Acting and observing
- Reflecting, and so on.

Stringer begins with the action research cycle, then broadens that to the action research helix and then spiral. Whichever version we consider, the main idea here is that action research is repetitive, continuing and cyclical.

For many people, the spiral of cycles of self-reflection, involving planning, acting and observing, reflecting, replanning and so on, has become the dominant feature of action research as an approach. However, there are seven additional important features of participatory action research. It is a social process, participatory, practical and collaborative, emanicipatory, critical, recursive, and it aims to transform both theory and practice.

Just as action research does not separate inquiring from doing, nor does it separate the researcher from the research.

**Examples of Action Research in Education**

- Hyland and Noffke (2005) report on an action research project investigating the teaching of an elementary social studies methods course for pre-service teachers from a social justice framework.
- Burgess (2006) examines the tensions and challenges of a graduate student dealing with institutional hierarchies in her journey of participatory action research.
- In the article by Kitchen and Stevens (2008), two teacher educators, an instructor and a teaching assistant designed an action research project focused on enhancing their professional practice and the practice of their students by introducing the pre-service teachers to action research.

## 6.11 EX POST FACTO RESEARCH

In cases where manipulation of conditions and random selection are not possible Ex Post Facto or causal comparative study can be conducted. Meaning of the term Ex Post Facto is, 'after the fact' (Latin).

For example, let an accident occur in the road. Then, the reason for occurrence of the accident can be analyzed by Ex Post Facto Method.

Researcher looks for conditions that have already occurred. Here, there is No manipulation of conditions as in experimental study. Because the causes has already occurred.

**Steps to be Followed in the Study**

1. Formulate the problem
   e.g.: Effect of class size on achievement of pupils
2. Identify plausible rival hypotheses.
   The plausible rival hypotheses includes,
   e.g.—better teachers in smaller classes, high ability students, better instructional methods, etc.
   In case of bus accidents, over speed, mechanical failures, break system, driver drunkard, etc. may be the cause and hence plausible hypotheses can be found accordingly.
3. Find and select groups that can be compared
   e.g.: define options, the small and large sample size. Let small sample is about 25 students. Select one group with more than this number. Then compare socio economic status, ability of students, teaching method etc.
4. Collect and analyse data, including data on rival hypotheses
   e.g.: Achievement in small class should be compared with achievement in large class

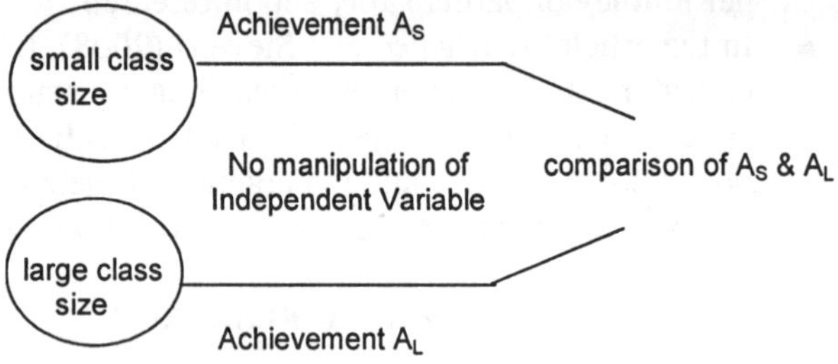


5. Compare the causes obtained and arrive at conclusion.

**Post hoc Fallacy**

This is one of the most serious dangers of ex post facto research. It refers to the conclusion that because factors go together one must be the cause and the other the effect.

e.g.: number of years of education completed and earned income are related—is an assumption for which one may not be the cause for the effect.

## 6.12 PHENOMENOLOGY

In a phenomenological study, the researcher attempts to describe the subjective experience of participants. Drawing on both theory and methods from early 20th century philosophy and psychology, phenomenological studies are based on extensive interviews in which both researcher and participant attempt to give up habitual ways of interpreting experience and focus instead on how the participant directly experiences particular situations. Although ethnographic studies tend to have a phenomenological aspect, what distinguishes the phenomenological approach is more exclusive focus on the subjective experiences of participants and less attention to cultural themes.

For those not familiar with the phenomenological approach, the term refers to a particular group of perspectives and methodologies for carrying out qualitative investigation. These perspectives existed for some time in philosophy before psychological investigators developed a set of methods to go with them. Amodeo Giorgi has termed these methods a "human science" approach, in contrast with the dominantly behavioural and analytically cognitive "natural science" approaches favored by academic psychology. These two sets of attitudes and methods in regard to psychological investigation, one oriented toward "predicting and controlling behaviour," in John B. Watson's words, and the other toward studying consciousness as it is experienced, in oneself or in someone else, are quite different epistemologies.

### Definitions of Phenomenology

A method of learning about another person by listening to their descriptions of what their subjective world is like for them, together with an attempt to understand this in their own terms as fully as possible, free of our preconceptions and interferences.

A method of knowing that "begins with the things themselves, that tries to find a 'first opening' on the world free of our perceptions and interpretations, together with a methodology for reducing the interference of our preconceptions.

Experiences are the basic data with which the phenomenologist works. The experiences of another can be known. Our job is to make them "visible" and true to the subject's own ways of living them.

### Phenomenological Approach

It says that we need to continually examine and reexamine our biases and presuppositions. The attitude is, "I want to understand your world through your eyes and your experiences so far as possible, and together we can probe your experiences fully and understand them.

In this sharing of experiences, in this dialogue, is the "betweenness" we're looking at in phenomenology. It is based on the fact that the experience of others is somehow accessible to us. We can enter into it, into an intimate dialogue. A theme that runs through it is that of interconnectedness.

### Four Approaches to Phenomenology

*Individual Phenomenology*: Researchers use their own actual and imaginary experiences and others' factual and fictional written accounts and theories to develop a thematic description of a phenomenon. This involves INTROSPECTION: a method of inner observation which involves assuming an external viewpoint toward oneself, stating the facts about oneself as others might if they could observe what the introspector observes.

*Empirical Phenomenology*: the researcher examines descriptions written by the co-researcher, and thematizes after collecting the descriptions. In "Empirical and hermeneutic approaches to phenomenological research in psychology," (2001), Serge Hein and Wendy Austin write about the use of bracketing in empirical phenomenology:

The steps of analysis involve in this approaches are:

1. Immersion in the data which requires reading the transcript several times.
2. The statements that are relevant to the phenomenon are identified and thematized.
3. These excerpts and themes are used to develop an exhaustive description of the participant experience of the phenomenon. This description is often referred to as

"situated structural description" (SSD). If there are more than one participant, then additional SSDs are made for each participant, and they are compared in order to identify shared themes and a synthetic general structural description.

**Characteristics of Empirical Phenomenology**

1. Emphasis on commonality that is present in the many diverse appearances of the phenomenon.
2. Reliance on the actual words of the participants
3. Explicitness about the design and the steps taken to obtain the findings.
4. These characteristics leads to verifiability and ability to be replicable.
5. Stressing more on rigor of the approach than on its creative aspects.
6. Acceptance that hermeneutic activity (interpretation) is intrinsic process of research.

**Dialogical Phenomenology**

lt involves interview of the co-researcher, and involving the co-researcher in thematizing during the interview. The researcher may explicitly pay attention to and refer to observations of the co-researcher's behaviour as well as to the co-researcher's descriptions of experience.

A major phenomenological method which their article leaves out, dialogical phenomenology, is of particular interest here for two reasons. One is that it is the easiest to incorporate into a class or training programme, and the other is that it is closer to clinical or counseling intervention than either empirical or hermaneutical phenomenology. One person interviews the other while bracketing his or her own personal reactions as fully as possible, and then after the interview, goes back over the interview notes and involves the co-researcher in the thematizing process.

**Hermaneutic Phenomenology**

Cohen states, "Hermeneutic phenomenology is concerned with understanding texts. In this approach the researcher aims to create rich and deep account of a phenomenon through intuition, while focusing on uncovering rather than accuracy, and amplification with avoidance of prior knowledge. In using this approach we accept the difficulty of bracketing. To overcome this difficulty we acknowledge our implicit assumptions and attempt to make them explicit.

## 6.13 GROUNDED THEORY

As a research strategy, grounded theory is specific and different. At the same time it cuts across the other designs discussed in this chapter, and is 'currently the most widely used and popular qualitative research method across a wide range of disciplines and subject areas' (Brynat and Charmaz, 2007). Grounded theory is both a strategy for research and a way of analyzing data. Grounded theory as a strategy under six headings:

### Grounded Theory Approaches

Traditionally, researchers assumed that one of the main purposes for conducting research is to test a theory. According to this view, the researcher states the theory, collects data, and then decides whether the data support the theory or not. Critics of this view have argued that data collection and data interpretation cannot be so clearly distinguished from each other or from the researcher's theoretical assumptions. Theoretical assumptions influence the formulation of research questions and the selection of methods, which in turn influence the type of data that will be collected and the particular interpretations that are made.

One way that qualitative researchers have responded to these concerns is by means of the grounded theory approach, in which data collection is intended to engender rather than test a theory (Glaser & Strauss, 1967). The grounded theory researcher proceeds as inductively as possible, with no preconceived ideas at the outset of the study. As data are collected, the results guide the development of tentative explanations that are explored through further data collection. This is a cyclical process in which data are collected in order to evaluate and refine the emerging theory. Data collection needs when no new insight emerge, and the constant comparative method is used for data analysis.

### Meaning

The first point to make is that grounded theory is not a theory at all. It is a method, an approach, a strategy. Grounded theory is a research strategy whose purpose is to generate theory from data. 'Grounded' means that the theory will be generated on the basis of data; the theory will therefore be grounded in data (Punch, K.F., 2009). 'Theory' means that the objective of collecting and analyzing the research data is to generate theory to explain the data. The essential idea in grounded theory is that theory will be developed inductively from data. Grounded theory, then, is an overall strategy for doing research. To implement that strategy, grounded theory has a particular set of techniques and procedures. As well as the grounded theory strategy, we can therefore talk also about grounded theory analysis—that style of analysis which uses procedures to develop a theory grounded in the data.

Grounded theory has its explicit purpose the generation of theory from data. This raises the contrast between research that aims to generate theory and research that aims to verify theory. Many research methods texts insisted that hypotheses were central to research and that, since the hypothesis was deduced from some more general theory, the point of the research was the testing of theory.

In the grounded theory approach, which aims to generate theory, no 'up-front' theory is proposed, and no hypotheses are formulated for testing ahead of the research. The research does not start with a theory from which it deduces hypotheses for testing. It starts with some research questions and an open mind, aiming to end up with a theory.

Another way of saying this is that grounded theory is essentially an inductive technique, but is uses deduction as well. Its tresses induction as the main tool for theory development, but, in developing the theory, deduction will also often be necessary.

In the traditional view of research, data collection is a discrete stage in the research, usually to be completed before data analysis beings. In grounded theory, the patterns is different. Guided by some initial research questions, the researcher will collect a first set of data, preferably quite small. The second set of data will be collected after the first analysis of data, guided by emerging directions in that analysis. This is the principle of theoretical sampling—the idea that subsequent data collection should be guided by theoretical developments that emerge in the analysis. This cycle alternation between data collection and analysis will not step a two repetitions. It continues until theoretical saturation is achieved—that is, until new data are not showing new theoretical elements, but are rather confirming what has already been found.

This pattern is shown in the following figure:

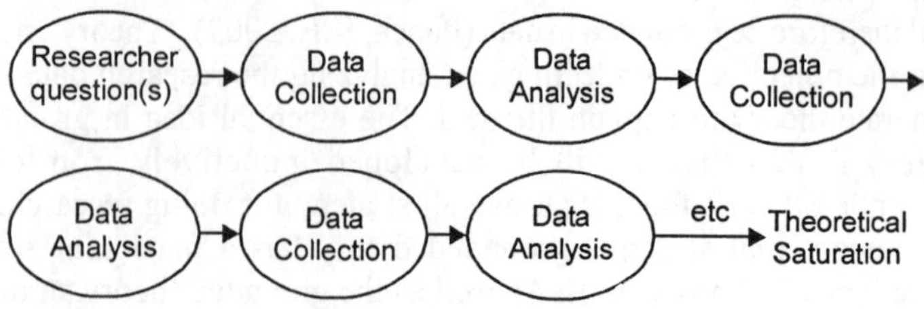


It is becoming more common to find this sort of data-collection/ data-analysis relationship in qualitative research today. It is different from traditional research, but it resembles what we normally do in everyday life, when we encounter a puzzling situation. Like much else in grounded theory, it models the way humans have always learned. In this respect, grounded theory is faithful to its philosophical roots in pragmatism (Glaser and Strauss, 1967).

## Importance of Grounded Theory Research

It is not surprising that grounded theory has become a widely used approach in qualitative research. According to Punch there are the following main reasons for this.

1. While much is said in the research methodology literature about the need to generate theory in research, very little is said about *how* to do that. Grounded theory explicitly addresses that question.
2. It represents a coordinated, systematic but flexible overall research strategy, in contrast to the ad hoc and uncoordinated approaches that have sometimes characterized qualitative research.
3. It brings a disciplined and organized approach to the analysis of qualitative data. In the qualitative research context, with its history of a lack of well-formulated methods for the analysis of data, this point has great appeal.
4. A fourth reason—very relevant to education—has to do with the identification of research problems from professional practice, and form organizational and institutional contexts. Grounded theory appeals because it concentrates on discovering concepts, hypotheses and theories.

**Example of Grounded Theory Studies**

1. Blasé and Blasé (2002) used grounded theory methods to study 50 US teachers who believed they were subjected to long-term mistreatment by school principals.
2. Fleishmann (2005) reports a grounded theory study of 33 websites self-published on the Internet by parents of children with autism.

## 6.14 EVALUATION RESEARCH

Evaluation research is a type of research which is usually conducted by practitioners, social workers, psychologists and economists. It is a form of applied research, which by nature aims to search for solutions to problem, assess the significance of existing policies and practices, and evaluate the need for new approaches, plans and programs. In this sense, evaluation research is expected to be systematic and precise in its operations, and this requires a clear plan, program or design.

In the area of psychology, psychotherapy and social work, evaluation research can look at clinical programs and interventions concerning individuals with mental illness or interpersonal difficulties (family conflicts and violence) (Ellis, 1994).

The purpose of evaluation research varies with many factors. The goals of evaluation research are (Ellis, 1994; Bauer; Bauer, 1994):

1. To discover gaps in services and to investigate the alternatives employed to meet the unmet needs.
2. To predict whether a planned programme will be successful.
3. To assess the quality and effectiveness of a programme, and the impact it has on the community.
4. To establish whether the programme is cost effective, and whether benefits outweigh the costs.
5. To identify the need for and ways of improving the effectiveness of an existing programme.

This list of goals indicates that there are many types of evaluation research. The most common are *feasibility studies or needs analysis, process analysis and impact analysis.*

## The Steps of Evaluation Research

As stated above, in evaluation research the steps of the research process are the same as those described above for any research project. Details regarding the content of the various steps of the model may vary; however, the basic structure of the model remains the same.

### Preparation

The first task to be accomplished is to define the research topic. There are two major topics investigated in this type of research. These are program and/or community. For instance, program evaluation research studies programs; feasibility studies or needs analysis studies investigate communities with a view to identifying gaps in services, evaluating their offerings and looking for ways of improving them, including need identification and need assessment.

The next items in the list of tasks of the preparation step of the research model are *definition* and *operationslisation*, which are part and parcel of evaluation research. The extent to which definition and operationalisation will go depends among other things on the type of evaluation. Programs are often conceived as formally defined by the government, and operationalisation will be geared towards the aspect of the program to be evaluated. Some might study the *process* and others the *outcomes* of the program.

Finally, hypotheses can be formulated as much in evaluation research as in any other type of research.

### Design

As in other research types, during this step evaluation research will consider two major questions, namely those regarding sampling procedures and methods of data collection and analysis.

1. *Sampling*: The study will address respondents who will be in a position to provide useful information about the program or needs in question. These will be: (a) persons who have knowledge of the program and its effects on the community, (b) the persons responsible for its development and/or introduction, (c) those working with the program or who are responsible for the services it provides, (d) stakeholders, (e) experts, (f) government authorities, and (g) community groups. The *methods of sampling* which will

be employed in evaluation research to identify the respondents will be taken from those available to other researchers.

2. *Methods*: The methods of data collection vary significantly from one type of research to another. Overall, the main methods used in evaluation research are those employed by other researchers and in most cases are observation (observing clients, agency employees, practices and intervention strategies), case studies, documentary analysis (service records, files, agency records, log books, statistics, etc.), community surveys, interviews with employees and clients, social indicators and experimental research (Ellis, 1994). Service evaluation techniques and cost-benefit analysis are also used.

**Data Collection**

The actual collection of data varies slightly from the way it is conducted by other researchers in that it uses additional practices and procedures and relies more on respondent participation than other studies. Such practices are the use of:

1. *Steering committees* consisting of members from sponsors, management of agency, staff and clientele which are established for the duration of the study and offer advice on many important issues;
2. *focus groups* which are small groups called for a one-off meeting and consultation/discussion of problems; and
3. *Delphi groups*, which act in a similar manner to steering committees.

It must be noted that the difference here is not that evaluation research employs methods which other studies do not use, but rather it uses these methods to a greater extent and it gives them more weight than other types of research.

**Data Processing**

This step depends entirely on the type of methodology, methods and techniques chosen by the researcher. In most cases, analysis is qualitative but community surveys, surveys of clients, etc. often are analysed by means of quantitative methods or a combination of both.

This is common when attitude surveys or experimental designs are used, which lend themselves to advanced statistical analysis. Following this, the findings will be interpreted to show whether the evaluation is positive or negative, that is, whether the program succeeded in achieving the intended outcomes or not.

**Reporting**

As in any other research type, the findings of the study will be communicated through all possible channels. The final report will clearly show the trends identified in the research, the conclusions and eventual recommendations, for example whether the program should be continued in its present form, continued in a modified form, or be discontinued. In many cases, evaluation research takes place in the context of *action research*, which by nature not only involves the participants but also takes steps towards changing conditions, influencing government and the community in their decision regarding the issue in question, and working towards implementing the recommendations contained in the report. Policy recommendations, advocacy and action often are corollaries of the research outcomes of evaluation research.

# VII
# Qualitative and Quantitative Techniques

## 7.1 QUALITATIVE AND QUANTITATIVE TECHNIQUES

It is important to note at this point that every piece of educational research is predicated upon a set of propositions concerning what can properly count as 'an educated person'—for that study, and in a particular society at a particular moment in its history. The attributes comprising such a characterization are *qualities*. These qualities may end up being talked about as scales or continuums, and they may be tested, scored and measured; they may be correlated among themselves or with other qualities. But regardless of all that, these quantitative manoeuvres do not circumvent the qualitative work that needed to have been undertaken in order to identify, demarcate and name those attributes in the first place, that is, in advance of any counting. So all educational research is necessarily founded on qualitative analysis, a set of decisions, theorized and explicit or otherwise, about the basic moving parts that the project will take to be the objects of its study.

As indicated by Freebody (2003), like 'education', 'qualitative' is a slippery term, put to a variety of uses, and carrying a variety of conceptual associations. Qualitative research methods grew in popularity, into what Gitlin (1994) termed 'a tremendous flood', out of a particular concern with the ways in which quantitative research methods, and their attendant techniques evident in experimental and survey research in the Social Sciences, were being applied to the study of education. To put it bluntly, many educational researchers came to feel that research activities structured through the logics of quantification leave out lots of interesting and potentially consequential things about the phenomenon—interesting and consequential not just in terms of the concerns and understandings of educators, but also in terms of the richness of the accounts of educators' experiences. By comparison, many have felt the quantitative research projects made available relatively stripped-down portrayals that seriously limit the potential for application to professional practice.

To explore the nature of educational research that is 'qualitative', therefore, we need to consider the ways it has been used to distinguish one set of research practices from other sets—the contrastive games in which it has played. If we scan the field of educational research, we find a number of polarities relating to the quantitative-qualitative distinction. A variety of aims, procedures and outcomes of research methods and dispositions have become attached to the term 'qualitative', as have, often indirectly, a variety of theories and ideologies about the individual, society and education.

Sometimes, as in Taylor and Bogdan's (1984) influential account, we find that, 'qualitative methodology' is taken to refer most generally to research that produces descriptive data bout people's words and their observable behaviour. In this sense, these authors aligned the descriptor 'qualitative' with a domain of data, a set of interests, rather than, primarily, with a philosophy of knowledge or theories of the individual, society or ideology, or even set of analytic procedures or techniques. Taylor and Bogdan listed the following central characteristics. Qualitative research, they claimed:

1. is inductive and holistic (e.g., develops from such positions as 'grounded theory' as opposed to operating by deduction from set premises, and by attention to the atomistic components of cultural practice):
2. is sensitive to researcher effects (as opposed to insensitive);
3. draws on 'natural settings' as the source of data (as opposed to, say, laboratories) and the researcher is the key instrument of data collection (as opposed to assessment 'instruments' such surveys);
4. is interested in the subject's point of view (as opposed to uninterested or disinterested);
5. is descriptive (rather than neglectful) of the taken-for-granted experience of members;
6. reports all valuable perspective available (as opposed to omitting some 'valuable' perspectives, or deciding in advance that some are insufficiently 'valuable' to warrant inclusion);

7. is humanistic (as opposed to depersonalized, one-dimensional or anti-subjective; see Atkinson, 1990: 8, 21);
8. is interested in 'the inner life of the person' (as opposed to the observable 'outer life' of the person or the group's 'averaged' life); and
9. has an emphasis on validity, regards all settings and people as worthy of study, and regards research as a craft (as opposed to emphasizing reliability, selective sampling of settings and people, and a regard for itself as a science, an art, a trade or perhaps a business).

A number of characteristics that come along the qualitative study, according to Freebody are: First, qualitative research approaches are interested in *unintended as well as intended consequences*. This does not amount to a neglect or a dismissal of cause-and-effect based research in education, but rather to an insistence on the inevitability of the unintended consequences of interventions into a shifting environment, and moreover, of the unforeseeable nature of some of those consequences.

Second, qualitative research approaches have a particular attitude to the issue of statistical '*normality*'. This is a professional and cultural attitude, but it is also an important theoretical issue. It has two aspects: first, it is in examining anomalous or borderline cases that we can see how theories need to be refined and how certain assumptions about contextual factors may beholding the original theoretical idea in place.

Third, there is an axiomatic understanding that *the phenomenon of interest can escape* when it decontextualized or when it is mistaken for a pre-theorized variable. This escape has typically been discussed in two senses. The first sense is derived from social science's perennial concern with the ethnographic history of a practice, and the relevance of this history to what the practice is and how it is recognizable. In this sense, we can consider educational practices as having material, interactional, institutional and ideological histories—histories of things (the materials and props of educational activities, such as books, blackboards, websites); histories of ways of talking, reading and writing (e.g., between teachers and students); histories of institutional practices (the ways of organizing the learning experiences of students of different kinds in different settings); and histories of assumptions that may serve the interests of some cultural groups more fully that others. One commitment within a qualitative approach is to ensure that the phenomenon as it is observed is not artificially disentangled from these life-giving histories.

Fourthly, qualitative researchers show determination to *identify the phenomenon in situ* and to understand that its location is separated from it only at the peril of rendering conclusion thoroughly invalid. That is, the qualitative researchers understands that research can be immobilized by a lack of interest in the very issues that render an event a valid instance of a particular educational practice—its sense in the precise location in which it occurred.

Finally, qualitative research is characterized by an understanding that *contextual considerations should not be assumed to operate as distinctive 'variables' consistently or independently* across a range of sites, somehow in isolation from one another. Resorting to the use of sociological variables such as ethnicity, social economic status or gender, does not solve explanatory problems for the qualitative researcher.

So when quantitative and qualitative research approaches are enacted in educational research, they are taken to signify more than simply a focus on the countable features of an event versus the distinctive qualities of the event. For some, the relationship of quantitative and qualitative traditions in education is a contrast between approaches of competing philosophical approaches to cultural experience. Depending on how profoundly the contrast is taken to be between qualitative research approaches and their neighbours, researchers will or will not admit to the possibility (or, again, for some, the necessary) of projects and programmes that attempt to combine them.

## Qualitative and Quantitative Research Comparison

One major difference is that the quantitative scientist's philosophical point of view is neutral. Data are gathered objectively from the perspective of a hypothesis or question that is deductively derived from theory or other observation. The view point of the persons observed or whose behaviour is measured is not considered. The standpoint of the qualitative researcher is more typically humanistic, as reflected in the importance given to the observed persons' own perspective as it exists in their circumstances and environment. It is a holistic approach that is usually inductive and designed to answer general questions. In a sense, the human experience or point of view is seen as more important than the scientific point of view. Further, quantitative research hypotheses are often deduced from theory, and the research designed to lead to knowledge of facts and causes. On the other hand, qualitative descriptions may lead to general statements or theories designed to understand phenomena. The difference between the quantitative focus on facts and causes and the qualitative stress on understanding is also based on the neutral-versus-humanistic underpinnings of the two approaches. The following table represents an attempt to summarize briefly the differences between the qualitative and quantitative approaches.

| | *Quantitative Research* | *Qualitative Research* |
|---|---|---|
| Basic approach | Deductive theory leads to hypothesis reduced to measured variables (occasionnally inductive) | Inductive: descriptions are holistic, yet detailed, and may lead to generalization or theory |
| Philosophical approach | Neutral | Humanistic |
| Starting point | Hypothesis or specific question: "If A then B", or "If A, what does B do?" | Non-specific research question: "What is the nature of A?" |
| Purpose | To discover facts and causes objectively derived from data gathered; based on the scientist's perspective | To subjectively derive understanding from the perspective of observed persons in their own milieu |
| Data | Numerical, derived from surveys, questionnaires, and other objective measures | Descriptive; derived from observation, interviews, and a person's written or spoken words |
| Analysis | Statistical | Descriptive |
| Outcome | Decision with respect to hypothesis; may relate to practice or theory | Description, but may involve analysis or theory development |

Whenever possible, the qualitative research tries to gather data unobtrusively, or in ways that keep the observed people from knowing that they are being observed. As was mentioned earlier this is designed to reduce the potential bias that could be introduced by the observation process itself. Of course, that isn't always possible, and the qualitative researcher may, as indicated previously, do interviews or gather data obtrusively, or in ways that may be known to the subjects in the research.

Sometimes the researcher may act as participant observer, actually participating and socially interacting with research subjects in the setting normally occupied by the subjects. During these interactions, the participant observer tries to gather data in a systematic and unobtrusive way. The researcher keeps notes in as detailed a fashion as possible, frequently writing observations from memory between observation periods to keep the observation unobtrusive yet accurate.

## 7.2 OBJECTIVITY IN QUALITATIVE RESEARCH

Qualitative researches reject fundamentally the notion of objectivity. (Sarantakos,1998). As we shall see later, the notion of establishing inter subjective reliability (so that if a research study is carried out by two or more researchers the same results are achieved) is neither desirable nor possible. This attitude is based on methodological and theoretical grounds.

In the first place, objectivity is associated with and results from standardization- a methodological tool that is incompatible with the main principles of qualitative research

In addition, objectivity requires that the researcher remains distant from and neutral to the research object, the respondents, the methods and techniques of data collection and analysis, and to the findings – requirements that are against the fundamental principle of qualitative research, which encourages inter subjectivity, closeness between the elements of the research and involvement of the researcher in the whole research process.

For the qualitative researcher, social reality does not exist objectively but is created in interaction and through interpretation, of which the researcher is an integral part. The researcher experiences reality through interaction and interpretation. Our world is something we make, not something we discover (Rorty, 1989). In this sense, objectivity is impossible in qualitative research.

For some qualitative researchers, objectivity seems to take on a different meaning in qualitative research. Here, objectivity is 'emergent', that is, it evolves out of the subjectivity of the parties of interaction. Qualitative research uses an inter subjective concept of objectivity in as far as one wants to break away from the subjectivity through generalization.

For other qualitative researchers, what is important is validity, and if validity is assured – as it is believed to be – research should be reliable as well as objective. Finally, it is argued that instead of attempting to neutralize the relationship between researcher and researched by means of artificial techniques, which is unachievable anyway, one should look for 'transparency', that is, stating openly the course and elements of the research process, and let others judge its quality.

## 7.3 THE INTERNET AS AN OBJECT OF RESEARCH

As the rather vague formulations in the previous paragraph may have shown already, there is still a need to study who is really using the Internet and who is not. Also, there is still a need to develop knowledge about how different people use the Internet and how this varies across social groups (e.g., across age, social class, education, or gender). For such research, you can carry out traditional projects of media use and audience research. For example, you may interview potential or real users of the Internet about their experiences and practices with it. Methods can be standardized or open-ended interviews or focus groups. You can also do (participant) observations in Internet cafes to analyze how people use the computers and the Internet, or you can do conversation analyses of how people use the net collaboratively (e.g., analyzing children's talk in front of the screen in a computer class at school). Mitra and Cohen (1999) see the analysis of the numbers and experiences of users as the first approach to studying the Internet and the analysis of the text exchanged by users as the second. Common to such projects is that they use qualitative methods in a traditional way. Here, the Internet is only an object that people talk about or use in your study, but it is not in itself part of your study (as a methodological tool).

### 7.3.1 Preconditions of Qualitative Online Research

If you want to do your research online, some conditions should be given. First, you should be able to use a computer not only as a luxurious typewriter, but in a more comprehensive way. You should also have some experience using computers and software. Also you should have access to the internet and you should enjoy being and working online and you should be (or become) familiar with the different forms of online communication like e-mail, chat rooms, mailing lists, and blogs. If these conditions are met on your side, you should consider whether your research is an issue that you can only study by using qualitative online research. For example, if you are interested in the social construction of an illness in online discussion groups, you should analyze their communication or interview the members of such groups and this can be done most easily if you address them online. Following from these two preconditions, a third becomes evident. The prospective participants of your study should have access to the Internet and they should be accessible via the Internet. If you want to study why people decide to stop using the Internet, you will have to find other ways of accessing you prospective participants and you should not plan your study as an online study. Another precondition is that you know about the methods of qualitative research independent from their online use before you transfer them to internet research.

### 7.3.2 Transferring Qualitative Research and Methods to the Internet

Most research using the Internet is still quantitative-online surveys, Web-based questionnaires, or Internet experiments (see Hewson, *et al.*, 2003). But the use of qualitative research on the Web is expanding, too (see Mann and Stewart, 2000). We can observe that researchers have transferred many qualitative methods to Internet research. We find forms of online interviewing, the use of online focus groups, participant observation, virtual ethnography (Hine 2000), and studies of interaction and traces of interaction (Bergmann and Meier, 2004; Denzin, 1999). Some of these methods can be transferred and applied in Internet research more easily; some of them and some of the principles of qualitative research can be transferred to the Web only with modification.

### 7.3.3 Ways of Using Computers in Qualitative Research

Although most of the software and computers in qualitative research are used for analyzing data, there are also other steps in the qualitative research process for which computers can be employed. In general, the following ways of using computers and software in the context of qualitative research are mentioned:

1. Making notes in the field;
2. Writing or transcribing field notes;

3. Editing—correcting, extending, or revising field notes;
4. Coding—attaching keywords or tags to segments of text to permit later retrieval;
5. Storage–keeping text in an organized database;
6. Search and retrieval—locating relevant segments of text and making them available for inspection;
7. Data "linking"—connecting relevant data segments to each other, forming categories, clusters, or networks of information;
8. Memo writing—writing reflective commentaries on some aspect of the data, as a basis for deeper analysis;
9. Content analysis—counting frequencies, sequence, or locations of words and phrases;
10. Data display—placing selected or reduced data in a condensed, organized format, such as matrix or network, for inspection;
11. Conclusion drawing and verification-aiding the analyst to interpret displayed data and to test or confirm findings;
12. Theory building—developing systematic, conceptually coherent explanations of findings; testing hypotheses;
13. Graphic mapping—creating diagrams that depict findings or theories;
14. Report writing—interim and final reports.

Some other aspects could be added to this list; most notably, the transcription of interviews, the writing of a research diary, the communication with other researchers through computer networks, e-mail, using the internet, and writing articles about one's own research or its methods and so on.

### 7.3.4 Types of Software for Analyzing Qualitative Data

The programmes available at the moment can be summarized in various types:

- Word processors, which allow one not only to write but also to edit texts, to search for words, or word sequences at least in a limited way.
- Text retrieval programmes, which specifically allow one to search, summarize, list, and so on certain word sequences.
- Text-base managers for administering, searching, sorting and ordering text passages.

- Code-and-retrieve-programmes for splitting the text into segments, to which codes are assigned and for retrieving or listing all segments of the text, which were marked with each code; marking, ordering, sorting and linking texts and codes are supported and both (text and code) are presented and administered together.
- Code-based theory building. Additionally, these programmes support theory building by supporting steps and operations at the level of the text (attachment of one or more passages to a code) but also at the conceptual level (relations between codes, superior and subcategories, networks of categories), always going back to the attached text passages. In some programmes, more ore less luxurious graphic editors are included and it is possible to integrate video data.
- Conceptual networking is possible in the last group, which offer extensive options for developing and presenting conceptual networks, network of categories, and various ways to visualize relations among the various parts of the network.

# VIII
# Research Reporting

The major purpose of documentation is, to give proper credit to the researchers and theories who have preceded. As a bonus, it is also very helpful to the reader who is interested in a more detailed discussion of the topic. Proper referencing directs the reader to the appropriate journal or book where he or she can learn more about the specifics of the work being cited.

Now let's look at the specifics of standardized documentation. The standard documentation procedure established by the APA is used throughout the field of education and, not coincidentally, throughout, this text. This style requires that the last name of the author(s) and the year of publication be inserted in the text at an appropriate point. For example, consider the following:

Erikson (1959) felt that adolescence was a time of ...........

Or

In a discussion of adolescence (Erikson, 1959), it was suggested that....,

If, however, there happens to be more than one author for a single work, separate the second or last author from the other(s) by and if the author's names are not enclosed by parentheses, and by the ampersand (&) if they are so enclosed. Here are a couple of examples:

Sternberg and Nigro (1980) found.........

In a developmental study (Sternberg & Nigro, 1980) it was found that ......

If a work has more than two authors, the names of all the authors only have to be listed the first time that reference is made to them. For example:

Everston, Emmer, Clements, Sanford, and Worsham (1984) stated that...

Subsequent references to the same study should only list the name of the first author, followed by *et al.* and the year of publication. For the previous example, the next time these authors are mentioned you'd only have to write.

Everston *et al.* (1984) suggested that...............

When more than one study is involved, the citations are listed in alphabetical order on the basis of the first author's last name, and then the studies themselves are separated by semicolons:

Recent studies (Anderson, Klossen, and Johnson, 1982; Bowman, 1982; Senter, 1981) have stated that...

## 8.1 FORMAT OF THE RESEARCH REPORT

The key features of the research report are outlined in the *Publication Manual of American Psychological Association* (American Psychological Association, 1983), and the organization of the features are as follows:

1. Title
2. Name and affiliation of author(s)
3. Abstract
4. Introduction
5. Method
6. Results
7. Discussion
8. References
9. Appendix

To aid you in identifying the major sections of a report, we have reprinted an actual journal article and pointed out the key points as they appear (see the section Reading Reports Firsthand, in this chapter). Please do yourself a favour and refer to this as you read through the rest of this chapter.

### The Title (What is it?)

Do not overlook the importance of the title of your research report. Overly creative or "cutesy" titles should be avoided in favour of more descriptive ones that will provide the reader with a at least some idea of what you're doing. Usually the title conveys to the reader the major independent variable(s) as well as the major dependent variable(s). For instance, in the study by Harrison, Strauss, and Glabman (1981) entitled, "The Impact of Open and Traditional Classrooms on

Achievement and Creativity: The Israeli Case", the independent and dependent variables are readily identified. In this case the type of classroom is the independent variable, and we can easily gather from the title that the researchers attempted to discover whether it might influence the dependent variables, which were measures of achievement and creativity.

The title is also important in that the key words can be used for cataloguing your report in the event that it is someday published. (Listed, you never know). If it is published it will usually find its way into such summary publications as Educational Resources Information Center (ERIC), Psychological Abstracts, and Sociological Abstracts.

Also in this, the age of the computer, automated literature searches can now be done by accessing the key words in the title of a journal article or book. As you can well imagine, computerized literature searches can save us a lot of time, which we can use for doing other things—such as more research!

### The Author(s) (Who Did it?)

By far, the easiest section of your report to write is the listing of the *Author(s) and their affiliations*. Typically, the author who has made the most significant contribution is listed first, along with his or her personal affiliation (i.e., college, university, school, or other educational institution). In deciding how you would like to have your name appear in print, keep in mind that you should stick to your decision. Using alternate forms of your name such as Ingrid M. Smart, I.M. Smart, or I. Melissa Smart on subsequent publications may add to confusion on the part of the reader. Titles, such as Dr. or Ms., and degrees, such as B.S. or Ed.D., should be omitted.

### The Introduction (What's It All About?)

If you have managed to whet the intellectual curiosity of your reader with your abstract, a difficult task at best, you want to maintain your hold by presenting a clear, cogent *introduction* to your research. This section should first and foremost inform the reader of the problem under study. By citing previous research or theories pertinent to your problem, you are able to set the stage for showing where your particular study fits into the overall scheme of things.

To accomplish this, you will need to spend some time in the library. Familiarize yourself with those reference books that list the abstracts of studies done in the field of education, for example, *ERIC*, *Psychological Abstracts*, and *Sociological Abstracts*.

*ERIC* is a national information system that serves as a major source of documents on education. Most libraries have access to the entire *ERIC* file every month as new documents become available. This publication includes a document section, which is divided according to sixteen major content areas in education. The area covered are career education; counseling and personnel services; early childhood education; educational management; handicapped and gifted children; higher education; information resources; junior colleges; languages and linguistics; reading and communication skills; rural education and small schools; science, mathematics, and environmental education; social studies and social-science education; teacher education; tests, measurement and evaluation; and urban. The content areas in this document section are then broken down into (1) the abstracts of all the *ERIC* documents; (2) "descriptors", which identify the documents' essential subject matter; and (3) the corresponding ED number, which is used to identify each *ERIC* document.

In addition to the document section, *RIE* also has an index section, which catalogues each entry alphabetically into a subject index by major descriptor. The index section also includes an author index, which is arranged alphabetically by the authors' last name, and even an institution index, which is arranged alphabetically by the institution responsible for the document. Each of these three indexes includes the documents' ED number, but not the abstracts themselves (since they have already appeared in the document section).

## The Method (What Was Done?)

In the method section you get the opportunity to tell the education community exactly how you conducted your study. Here you can showcase your creativity and all that you have learned about experimental design, confounding variables, and overall precision. The method section should include the operational definitions of your variables, and these should be written in sufficient detail to allow another researcher to replicate your study in all its essential details. In a study designed to measure the effect of computer-assisted instruction on the acquisition of math skills, for example, the colour of the walls in the classroom is probably not an essential detail to be included. However, such variable as the sex, grade level, and aptitudes of the students are like to be important and should be included in your write-up.

When reading an article that does contain flaws or confounding variables, it is usually in this method section that they become most clearly visible. Did the researcher use an appropriate control group to warrant his or her conclusions? Were the influential extraneous variables appropriately kept from clouding the results? Since the information necessary to answer these types of questions must be included in the method section, you should read this section with special care to properly evaluate the study.

The method section is usually divided into labelled subsections for the sake of organization and enhanced readability. The most commonly used subsections are (1) subjects, (2) apparatus or materials, and (3) procedure.

### The Subjects (Sample)

Obviously, in this section we describe the characteristics of the subjects under study, including relevant demographic information. In almost all studies, it is important to note the age and sex of the subjects. Depending on the particular study, characteristics such as race, aptitudes, and socio-economic status may also be vital.

In any case, you must always indicate how may subjects were used and how they were selected: were they randomly chosen from the population of, or were they selected purposefully, etc.

How were the subjects assigned to the research conditions? How many subjects failed to complete the entire experiment, and why did this attrition occur? What was the final number of subjects that participated in each research condition? All these questions should be answered in the subjects section.

### The Tools or Materials

In this section you must describe the equipment and materials used in your study. Obvious materials such as furniture, tape recorders, and projection screens need only be mentioned and do not have to be described in minute detail. Keep in mind that in conducting educational research your materials may consist simply of a specially designed questionnaire, but even this needs some measure of description. When conducting research for a class assignment, you should include a copy of the actual questionnaire in the Appendix. For a published study, the journal editor will usually decide whether it is appropriate for the appendix.

**The Procedure**

The procedure subsection should provide a step-by-step account of the happenings in your study. You should account for the subjects' time from the moment they show up for the study until they are dismissed. This will include the instructions the subjects received. These may be summarized or paraphrased, but if in any way important to the understanding of the study, they should be presented verbatim.

Various design specifications such as randomization and counterbalancing should be described here, and in experimental studies the manipulation of the independent variable should be detailed. For instance, how was test anxiety induced in some students and not in others?

**The Results (What Was Found?)**

This is what the reader has been waiting for. What did you find? In the *results section* you summarize your data and describe the statistical tests you have conducted to determined the possible significance of your findings. All the pertinent results should be presented here, regardless of whether or not they support your hypotheses. Even though the results may be contrary to your expectations, they may be important in and of themselves or as groundwork for future research.

Your goal in presenting your results is to do so in a clear and objective manner, without attempting to interpret or evaluate them. The general format is to begin by describing your dependent variable, how it was scored, and what unit of measurement was used in your analyses. Example of opening phrase is,

Educational aspirations were measured by responses to three questions on the College Student Questionnaire…

**The Discussion (What Does It Mean?)**

Now it's time to pupil it all together. You have stated your problem, explained what you did to address it, presented what you have found, and now you must put it into perspective and explain what it all means. The *discussion section* contains your interpretation of your findings. Your results are discussed in the light of any recent literature that can be shown to be specifically related to the problem presented in your introduction. Any theoretical consequences of your results should be presented here as well.

In the discussion section you will have the opportunity to discuss any important flaws or weaknesses that may have existed in your study. Try to identify the limitations that most likely affected your study.

Another mistake is to provide elegant reasons for why your results did not occur as expected and then go on to draw the same conclusions that you had hoped to draw in the first place (Warm, 1973). Explaining, or over explaining, your flaws does not, alas, make them disappear. It is quite possible that your data reflect the true state of the world, and that your original expecations were wrong.

You may find it helpful to keep the following major pints in mind when organizng your discussion section. All these points may not apply for every study that you conduct, but they should serve you well as a general framework.

1. Restate your research question so that the reader is reminded of your major purpose.
2. Briefly review your major findings in a sentence or two without refernce to statistics.
3. Indicate specifically whether your findings confirmed or disconfirmed your hypotheses.
4. Indicate whether your study is in agreement or disagreement with previous related research.
5. If there is disagreement with previous work, try to account for this discrepancy.
6. Explain your results. Tie them in with any existing theories that may apply to your study.
7. Briefly summarize your study and suggest, in a few sentences, some possibilities for further research.

Your discussion should leave the reader with a clear indication of what your study has contributed and what conclusions and theoretical implications you have drawn.

## The References (Who Did Something Like It?)

The most difficult and also most interesting part of the report is now behind you, but an important section still remains. The references section is a listing of every study that was cited in your report. However, don't overdo it by confusing the references section with a general bibliography. Whereas a bibliography contains a reference to all background material read, the references section lists only those works that have been directly referred to elsewhere in the paper. The purpose is to enable the reader to find any study or book you have referred to and then, if needed, read it firsthand.

Although this section is quite mundane, it is nonetheless important. Here is where you will feel that the specific format guidelines set forth by the American Psychological Association were purposely designed to ruin your day. The details are necessary, however to ensure that all the important information is included and presented in a consistently uniform way. References are listed alphabetically by the last name of the first author of each study. For a journal article, the general format is as follows:

Author's (s') Last Name(s), Initials (Year). Title of article. *Name of Journal, Volume, Number, pages.*

Perfetti, C.A., and Hogaboam, T. (1975). The relationship between single word decoding and reading comprehension skill. *Journal of Educational Psychology, 67,* 461-469.

For a book, it looks like this:

Author's(s') Last Name(s), Initials. (Year). *Title of book.* City where published: Publisher.

Dewey, J. (1956). *The child and the curriculum: The school and society.* Chicago: University of Chicago Press.

### The Appendix (What Else Do You Want to Know?)

An appendix is an optional supplement to your report. In most instances it is omitted altogether. If there are lengthy details of your study that you feel are essential for understanding, evaluation, or replication, they probably should be included in an appendix—for example, complicated mathematical proofs, customized questionnaires, and innovative computer programmes. When writing research reports for class assignments, theses, or dissertations, you should probably include summary tables of statistical tests, copies of printed materials given to the subjects, instructions, debriefings, and so on.

### References

1. Best, J.W. and Kahn, J.V. (1995). *Research in Education (7th ed)*. New Delhi: Prentice Hall.

2. Koul, L. (2005). *Methods of Educational Research.* New Delhi: Vikas Publishing House.
3. Fox, D.J. (1969). *The Research process in Education.* USA: Holt, Rinehart and Winston.
4. Garrett, H.E. and Woodworth, R.S. (1961). *Statistics in Psychology and Education.* New York: Vakils, Feffer and Simons Ltd.
5. Chandra, S. and Sharma, R.K. (2002). *Research in Education.* New Delhi: Atlantic Publishers and Distributors.
6. Springer, K. (2010). *Educational Research—Acontextual approach.* Chennai: John Wiley and sons, inc.
7. Fielding, N., Lee, R.M. and Blank, G. (2008). The sage handbook of Online Research Methods.Singapore:SAGE.
8. Stemler, S. (2001). *An Overview of Content Analysis. Practical Assessment Research and Evaluation*, 7 (17). Retrieved July 25, 2006 from http://PAREonline.net.
9. Encyclopaedia of Wikipedia.
10. "Writing Guides—Conducting Content Analysis" Colorado State University, writing @CSV home page.
11. http://writing.colostate.edu/idex.cfm.
12. www.gsu.edu/www.com/content.htm.
13. www.comp.lanes.ac.uk/computing/research.txt.
14. www.library.miami.edu/staff/imc/psymeth.html.

# IX
# Ethics in Social Research

Social research is a dynamic process, which involves researchers and respondents, and which is based on mutual trust and cooperation, as well as on promises and well-accepted conventions and expectations (Sarantakos,1998). On the basis of this, researchers enter the research field with relatively few limits and many options for action. This freedom of action has always been thought to offer the best opportunities for answering the research question or solving the problem under investigation.

Nevertheless, research practice has shown that this freedom can have adverse effects on the participants, causing serious problems to the subjects and the community in general. Often uncontrolled freedom violates directly and/or indirectly the rights of those involved in the research process- a violation that is often benefits to the public that greatly outweigh the problems and hardship suffered by a relatively small number of respondents. For example, forwarding confidential information to the police, thereby violating promises and hurting the respondents concerned, may be justified by the fact that such information helps authorities to prevent crime or to restore justice; or resting certain drugs on people without their knowledge, although this may affect their health adversely, may be justified by the fact that promises and hurting the respondents concerned, may be justified by the fact that such information helps authorities to prevent crime or to restore justice; or testing certain drugs on people without their knowledge, although this may affect their health adversely, may be justified by the fact that it may help to produce medicine that could improve public health and save lives.

But is such action permissible? The answer to this question is by no means uniform; while the majority of social researchers are in favour of upholding promises and avoiding at all costs violation of the rights of the respondents and the community in any way, others still believe that 'after all the end justifies the means'. Consequently, there may be researchers who still misuse the power and privileges of their position, and carry out research that hurts respondents and the community in many ways.

As stated earlier, research bodies as well as contractors and consumers of research are aware of the possibility that such malpractices can happen and have raised their objections and made concrete suggestions about how malpractices can be avoided or prevented. Nevertheless, such suggestions were answered by the claim that 'ethics' should be the controlling factors, with research being guided by unwritten standards and principles, which were left to the researcher to accept or reject.

With the passing of time, and with research becoming not only more frequent but also more intrusive, pluralistic (i.e., including several researchers in the same project) and highly computerized, and with the findings becoming increasingly more open to abuse than before, the need for some regulation of the research process beyond self-regulatory mechanisms of the researcher became a necessity.

## 9.1 PROFESSIONAL PRACTICE AND ETHICAL STANDARDS

The following issues relate to ethical standards in professional practice:

- *Accuracy in Data Gathering and Data Processing*: With regard to collection and processing of data, ethical codes contain a clause suggesting that researchers are expected to plan, collect and process data by employing high professional standards, a systematic and objective procedure and well accepted ethical standards.
- *Relevant Research*: Further, methods and techniques should be chosen as required by the research objective and not for other reasons.
- *Appropriate Interpretation of the Data*: The researcher is expected to interpret the data in full according to general methodological standards.
- *Accurate Reporting*: Researchers are expected to include in a report the research findings accurately expressed and in an unbiased manner and also to explain the methods employed in the collection and analysis of the data.

Research problems, errors or distortions known to the researcher should be stated in the report.

- *Fabrication of Data is Misconduct*: Researchers should not publish findings on data they did not collect.
- *Falsification of Data is Misconduct*: Researchers should abstain from falsifying data, or even changing words.

***The Researcher-Respondent Relationship***

- *Proper Identification*: Codes of ethics suggest that the researcher should identify herself or himself to the respondent and avoid giving false impressions of the researcher or the project sponsor.
- *Clear Outset*: Researchers should inform the respondent of the type of questions, the degree of question sensitivity or stress and the possible (true) consequences that the questioning and the research in general might have on the respondent.
- *Welfare of the Respondent:* The researcher should always be concerned with the welfare of the respondent, including mental and physical health and safety, and take all possible precautions to avoid incidental injury. The researcher should also avoid questions or issues that may cause embarrassment, guilt, discomfort, hazards or risks to the respondent.Where such conditions might occur, the researcher should inform the respondent accordingly at the outset of the study.
- *Free and Informed Consent*: Respondents should participate in the research freely and not be pressured to do so or deceived in any way. They should also be fully informed about the nature and goals of the study before they are asked to take part in the project
- '*Right to Privacy*: Researchers should respect respondents' privacy when entering their private sphere and when asking questions, and should allow respondents to leave unanswered questions for which they do not wish to provide the information required.
- *The Right to Anonymity*: Data collected by researcher should be anonymous, that is, not related to names or other forms of identification.
- *The Right to Confidentiality*: Information offered by the

respondent should be used by the researcher only, and only for the purpose of the study; it should not be made available to other people for any reason or purpose.

***The Researcher-Researcher Relationship***

- *Misleading Ascription of Authorship*: Researchers should not list authors in their report without their permission, should not attribute work to persons who have not contributed and should attribute adequately work completed by students, trainees or associates.
- *Misuse of Authority or Role*: Authority given by a researcher to a colleague should not be misused, and when criticizing works or research studies of others this should be guided by 'honesty, sincerity, justice, and responsibility rather than by polemic, personal bias or collective interests'.
- *Plagiarism*: Researchers should abstain from using other people's work without appropriate acknowledgement.

# SECTION B

# X
# Statistics

## 10.1 WHAT IS STATISTICS?

Think for a moment of the thousands of complex tasks you perform each and every day and stand in awe at the marvel you represent. You are absolutely unique. No one else possesses your physical features, your intelligence, your personality, or your values. What is perhaps even more impressive is that your ensuing actions reveal a wisdom that is statistically correct on most occasions. In short, you are a finely tuned and enormously sophisticated decision making statistical instrument.

In daily living, our statistical functioning is usually informal and loosely structured. We behave statistically, even though we may be only vaguely aware of the formal laws of probability. This section will help you learn about collecting and analyzing data. As you will see, the data for behavioural scientists are the numbers and measurements collected as a result of making careful and systematic observations. In addition, it help you learn how to make decisions or inferences based on careful analysis of the data.

You have been calculating arithmetic means almost all of your life—whenever you find the average of your test scores in a course or calculate the batting average of your favourite player on the women's or men's ball team. There is no reason to fear statistics. Much of what you will be learning to do you are already doing in an informal manner.

**Definition:** *Statistics is a branch of scientific methodology which deals with the collection, classification, description and interpretation of data by the conduct of surveys and experiments.* Its purpose is to describe and draw inferences about the numerical properties of population. Population means a group or aggregate of any kind.

### Why You Should Study Statistics

Perhaps the reason that many students dread taking statistics is that they do not understand why they have to take the course.

All psychologists use the scientific method to understand behaviour and mental processes. An essential aspect of any scientific work is collecting data and making decisions based on these data. As we noted previously, statistics is the process of collecting data and making decisions based on the analysis of these data. Therefore, statistics is a tool that helps you to solve complex problems and think rationally about various problems addressed in psychology.

You may object and say that your personal experiences have allowed you to learn a lot about human behaviour. If personal experiences are so valued, why should they be replaced with empirical methods and statistics? The truth is the personal experience has its limitations for learning more about the world around us. Although personal experience may be beneficial to us in our daily lives, the procedure is haphazard at best. Personal experience is useful, but as we shall see, the empirical method is far more satisfactory in addressing specific questions.

Psychologists base their knowledge of human behaviour on empirical evidence. Any student who wishes to become a professional psychologist must be familiar with statistical procedures and research techniques in order to perform their job effectively. Even if you do not pursue a professional career as a psychologist, you will constantly be confronted with opportunities to make decisions based on empirical evidence. Your knowledge of statistical reasoning will help you to make good decisions.

If statistics is approached with positive expectations and attitudes, it can be one of the most exciting fields of study.

## 10.2 SCALES OF MEASUREMENT

### What is a Number?

Symbols denoting amounts, things that can be added, subtracted, multiplied and divided.

Numbers are used in a variety of ways to achieve different goals

1. To name or identify—Nominal
2. To represent position or order in a series—Ordinal

3. To represent quantities such as how many or how much—Interval or Ratio

*Variables*: Observation and measurement are very essential in physical and social sciences.

The things we observe are referred as variables and any particular observation as value of the variable.

Independent ↓      Dependent ↓

e.g.: Effect of Sex difference on the amount of time spent on studying

↓ Nominal      ↓ ratio scale

**Measurement**

It is an act of assigning numbers to the qualitative or quantitative aspects of objects, events or constructs in a systematic, reliable and valid manner.

Scales of measurement falls under four broad categories namely, 1) Ratio or Absolute scale 2) Interval scale 3) Ordinal scale and 4) Nominal scale depending upon the attributes possessed by the set up measures like, **magnitude, equal intervals** and **absolute zero point.**

When a scale has magnitude, one instant of the attribute (variate) can be judged as greater than (>), Less than (<) or equal to ( = ) another instance of the attribute.

e.g.: measurements of height, weight, family size etc.

Equal intervals denote that the magnitude of the attribute represented by a unit of measurement on the scale is equal regardless of these on the scale that the unit falls. e.g.: height

An absolute zero point is a value that indicates, nothing at all of the attribute being measured exists. e.g.: intelligence

A scale of measurement which possesses attributes like magnitude, equal intervals and absolute zero point is called a *ratio scale or an absolute scale*. This scale is termed 'ratio" because the collection of properties that it possesses allow ratio statements to be made about the attribute being measured.

An *interval scale* possesses the attribute of magnitude and equal intervals but not an absolute zero point e.g.: temperature.

An *ordinal scale* reflects only magnitude. A nominal scale refers to be classified of items into discrete groups which do not bear any magnitude relationships to one another.

1. Nominal scale: e.g.: classification of data into groups say, group 1, 2, 3, etc.
2. Ordinal scale: e.g.:Physical measurements ranked in order of marks (ranks) 1, 2, 3, etc.
3. Interval scale: e.g.: Psychological measurement, like Intelligence, aggressiveness etc.
4. Ratio scale: e.g.: CGS and MKS scales of measurement.

## 10.3 FREQUENCY DISTRIBUTION

The following are the scores obtained on an English test. Convert this into frequency distribution.

52, 28, 42, 56, 47, 78, 82, 55, 56, 41, 62, 38, 57, 55, 50, 37, 72, 65, 66, 52, 54, 62, 68, 42, 47, 39, 44, 47, 52, 48, 62, 54, 42, 48, 53, 60, 42, 56, 48, 68.

Range = (82 – 28) + 1 = 55

The procedure or steps in organizing a frequency distribution are the following:

1. Determine the range. (range = highest score – lowest score + 1)
2. Divide this by a number between 10 and 20 (the convention is that the number of class interval between 10 and 20) to estimate the appropriate size of the interval.
3. List the intervals beginning at the bottom left. The lowest interval begin with a number which is a multiple of the interval size.
4. Tally the frequency.
5. Summarize these under column labelled ‘f’.
6. Total this column and record the number of cases at the bottom as N.

| *Class* | *Tally* | *f* |
|---|---|---|
| 80-84 | I | 1 |
| 75-79 | I | 1 |
| 70-74 | I | 1 |
| 65-69 | IIII | 4 |
| 60-64 | IIII | 4 |
| 55-59 | ~~IIII~~ II | 7 |
| 50-54 | ~~IIII~~ I | 6 |
| 45-49 | ~~IIII~~ I | 6 |
| 40-44 | ~~IIII~~ I | 6 |
| 35-39 | III | 3 |
| 30-34 | – | 0 |
| 25-29 | I | 1 |
| | | N = 40 |

## Graphical Representation of Frequency Distribution

Graphical representation is used for the comparison of two or more data. Measurement of the variable is represented along the horizontal axis and the respective frequencies along the vertical line. Height of a graph should be less than the length or in the ratio 3:5.

### *Some Conventions for the Construction of Graphs*

1. It is customary to let the horizontal axis (abscissa) represent measures of the variable under construction and the vertical axis represent the frequency.
2. The arrangement of the graph should proceed from left to right i.e., the low numbers on the horizontal axis should be on the left. Similarly the low numbers at the ordinate should start from the bottom.
3. Select the units of representation along the axes in such a way that the ratio of height to length is roughly 3:5.
4. Whenever possible the vertical scale should be so selected that a zero point falls at the intersection of the axes. When this is not possible designate the point of intersection as zero and make a small break in the vertical axis to represent the units of frequencies.
5. Both the horizontal and vertical axes should be appropriately labelled.
6. Assign a descriptive title which states previously what it is meant.

7. The break "∫∫" on x axis indicates that the vertical axis has been moved for convenience.

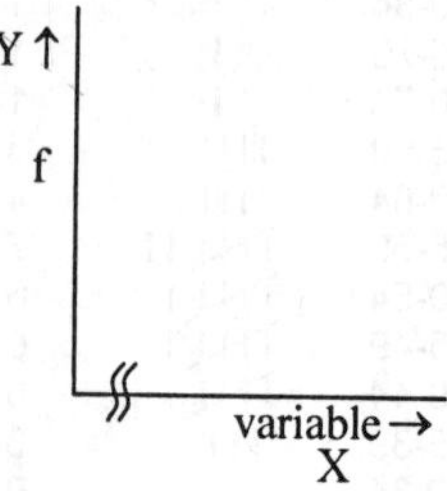


### *Histogram*

For a histogram the exact class limits are marked along the horizontal axis and the frequencies along the vertical axis. Draw bars on these exact limits with area being equal to that of the respective frequencies.

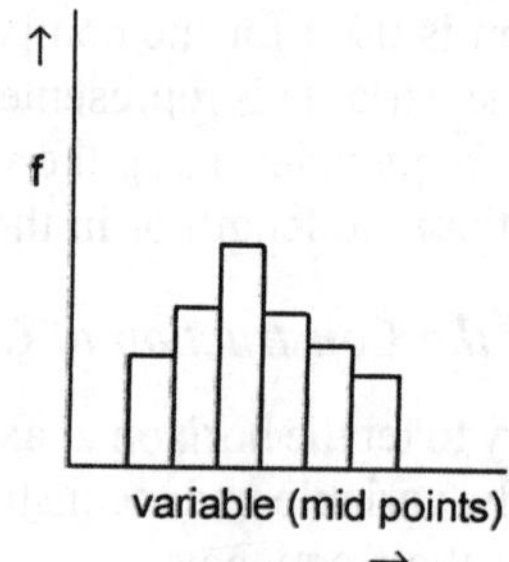


### *Frequency Polygon*

To draw a frequency polygon, the midpoints of class intervals are marked along the horizontal axis (instead of the exact limit in the histogram). The respective frequencies are plotted above the midpoint. Join these points by broken lines. The figure thus obtained is the frequency polygon.

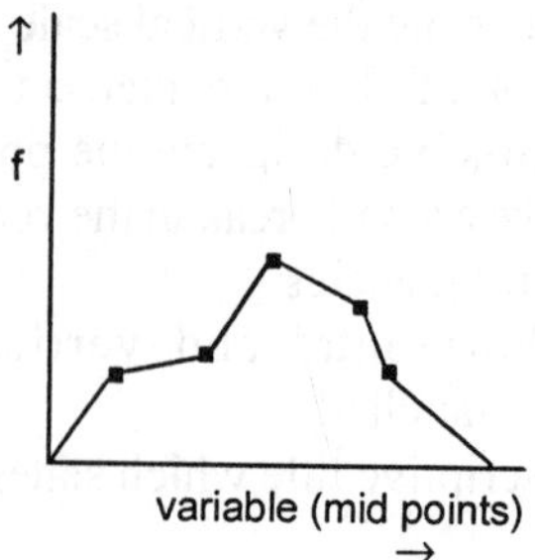

***Cumulative Frequency Polygon***

In a cumulative frequency distribution, the frequency are successively added. Along the abscissa, exact upper limits are marked.

*Smoothing*

To get an idea how the figure might look if the data were more numerous, the frequency polygon may be smoothed. For this adjusted frequencies are determined. To find adjusted or smoothed f, add frequency 'f' on the given interval and 'f' s on the two adjacent intervals.

## 10.4 MEASURES OF CENTRAL TENDENCY

**Mean**

***(1) Ungrouped data: Mean*** $= \dfrac{\sum X}{N}$

In an ungrouped data, arithmetic mean equals ΣX where $\dfrac{\sum X}{N}$ denotes the sum of all the observations and N, the number of observations.

Find the mean of the measures 10,12,15,18,20

Mean = $^{75}/_{5}$ = 15

***(2) Grouped data***

Consider the following frequency distribution

***Assumed Mean Method***

In this method, we are assuming a mean and calculate the mean according to the following formula.

Let the assumed mean be A = 62,

Then, $\overline{X} = A + i\dfrac{\sum fx'}{N}$

Where $x' = \dfrac{X - A}{i}$

| x′ | Fx′ |
|---|---|
| 4 | 4 |
| 3 | 3 |
| 2 | 2 |
| 1 | 4 |
| 0 | 0 |
| –1 | –7 |
| –2 | –12 |
| –3 | –18 |
| –4 | –24 |
| –5 | –15 |
| –6 | –0 |
| –7 | –7 |
| | $\Sigma fx' = -70$ |

$$\text{Mean} = A + i\frac{\sum fx'}{N}$$

$$= 62 + 5 \times -70/40$$

$$= 62 - 35/4 = 62 - 8.7 = 53.3$$

***Combined Mean of Two Groups***

Consider a set of $N_1$ measurements with mean $\overline{X}_1$, and another set of $N_2$ measurement with arithmetic mean $\overline{X}_2$, then the arithmetic mean of the N combined group can be computed by the formula

$$\overline{X}_{comb} = \frac{N_1\overline{X}_1 + N_2\overline{X}_2}{N_1 + N_2}$$

This formula can be extended to any number of groups. Thus when there are three groups, the formula becomes $\overline{X}_{comb} = \frac{N_1\overline{X}_1 + N_2\overline{X}_2 + N_3\overline{X}_3}{N_1 + N_2 + N_3}$ for a group of N = 50, mean is 25 and for another group with N = 40, Mean is 40

$$\text{Then, Comb. Mean} = \frac{50\times25+40\times40}{25+40} = \frac{2850}{65} = 43.85$$

***Major Properties of Arithmetic Mean***

1. Sum of deviation of measures taken from the mean = 0
2. Sum of squares of deviations of the measures taken from the mean is minimum i.e. it is less than the sum of squares of the deviations taken from any measurement from the data.

In the above problem, sum of squares of deviations of mean = 16+, 4+, 0+, 4+, 16 = 40

If we take deviations from 20 or 12, and square is 0,4,16,36,64 sum = 120

So it is always greater than that the mean.

**Median**

It is the middle most value of a set of observations when arranged in the order of magnitude.

When n is odd, median is the middle most value. It is the $\frac{n+1}{2}$ th value, when 'n' is even, median is the arithmetic mean of the two middle values.

***Calculating Median from a Frequency Distribution***

| *Class* | *f* | *Cum. Frequency* |
|---|---|---|
| 45-49 | 1 | 76 |
| 40-44 | 2 | 75 |
| 35-39 | 3 | 73 |
| 30-34 | 6 | 70 |
| 25-29 | 8 | 64 |
| 20-24 | 17 | 56 |
| 15-19 | 26 | 39 |
| 10-14 | 11 | 13 |
| 05-09 | 2 | 2 |
| 0-04 | 0 | 0 |

Median $= l + i \dfrac{\left(N/2 - F\right)}{f}$ in a frequency distribution where

l = Lower limit of the median class
i = Size of the class interval
N = Size of the sample
F = Cumulative frequency corresponding to l
f = Actual frequency of the median class

l = 14.5; F = 13; i = 5; f = 26; N/2 = 76/2 = 38

$$\text{Median} = 14.5 + \frac{(38-13)\times 5}{26}$$
$$= 14.5 + 25 \times 5/26 = 14.5 + 4.8$$
$$= 19.3$$

Median $= l + i \dfrac{\left(N/2 - F\right)}{f}$

Median is in the class, $\left(N/2\right)$ = 20. Cumulative frequency of 20 is coming in the class 70-74

| *Class* | *f* | *Cum f* |
|---|---|---|
| 95-99 | 2 | 40 |
| 90-94 | 2 | 38 |
| 85-89 | 4 | 36 |
| 80-84 | 6 | 32 |
| 75-79 | 3 | 26 |
| 70-74 | 4 | 21 |
| 65-69 | 5 | 17 |
| 60-64 | 2 | 12 |
| 55-59 | 2 | 10 |
| 50-54 | 4 | 8 |
| 45-49 | 1 | 4 |
| 40-44 | 2 | 3 |
| 35-39 | 1 | 1 |
| | N = 40 | |

$$\text{Median} = 69.5 + 5 \times \frac{(20-17)}{4}$$

$$= 69.5 + 5 \times 3/4 = 69.5 + 3.75$$

$$= 73.25$$

**Mode**

**Mode is that measure which occurs most frequently. In the ungrouped data, 2, 6, 7, 8, 10, 11, 8, 8**

**Mode = 8**

**In a frequency distribution mode is the midpoint of the class having the highest frequency.**

**A frequency distribution, having two equal high frequencies not in the adjacent classes is called bimodal frequency distribution. Mode of a frequency distribution can be calculated by the formula.**

$$\text{Mode} = l + \frac{c.f_2}{f_1 + f_2}$$

**Where**

**l = is the lower limit of the modal class**
**C = is the size of the class interval**
**$f_1$ = is the frequency of the class preceding to the model class**
**$f_2$ = is the frequency of the class succeeding to the model class**

**Mode can be calculated using another formula**

**Mode = 3 Median – 2 Mean**

## 10.5 MEASURES OF DISPERSION

**All researchers encounter and are interested in the variability of the data they collect. Consider some simple examples. When an instructor gives an exam, there is variance among the grades: Some students do better than others. The instructor may be interested in why some students receive good grades whereas others struggle to pass. A**

researcher may want to show that a new drug is effective for the treatment of depression. She want to find out whether people treated with the drug differ from people given a placebo. The differences between the people in the two treatment groups is another form of variability. Therefore, measure of dispersion, like measures of central tendency, are descriptive statistics that all researchers use to understand their data.

Studying the variability of data is essential to the use and interpretation of many statistics. We can see that a score by itself is meaningless and takes on meaning only when it is compared with other scores or other statistics. Consequently, if we know the mean of the distribution of a variable, we can determine whether a particular score is higher or lower than the mean. Now comes the next important question, How much higher or lower? What if the mean of the distribution is 100 and an individual's score is 105? Obviously, there is a 5-point difference and the individual's score is above the mean. Does this 5-point difference represent an exceptional difference or a trivial difference? We can answer these questions directly by examining the relative dispersion of the data.

Consider the following Figure, which shows two distributions of data. In both cases the mean of the distribution is 100 and the number of observations is the same. How should we interpret a score of 105 in the two distributions? In distribution A, the data are more broadly dispersed than the data in distribution B. In other words the data in distribution A is more variable than the data in distribution B. what is the relative position of 105 in each of the distributions? In distribution A, the score is relatively close to the mean. That is, the percentile ranking of the score is only slightly above the mean. In distribution B, however, the same score of 105 appears to be exceptionally far from the mean and close to the most extreme score. We would expect the percentile ranking to be high in this case. Therefore, a score of 105 can be considered to be only slightly greater than the mean or much greater than the mean depending upon the overall dispersion of the data.

This example illustrates our need to calculate a measure of dispersion. Knowing the measure of central tendency and the measure of dispersion of the data, we can better interpret the meaning of individual scores in a set of data. In this chapter we will discuss four measures of dispersion or variability: the range, the semi-interquartile range, the variance, and the standard deviation.

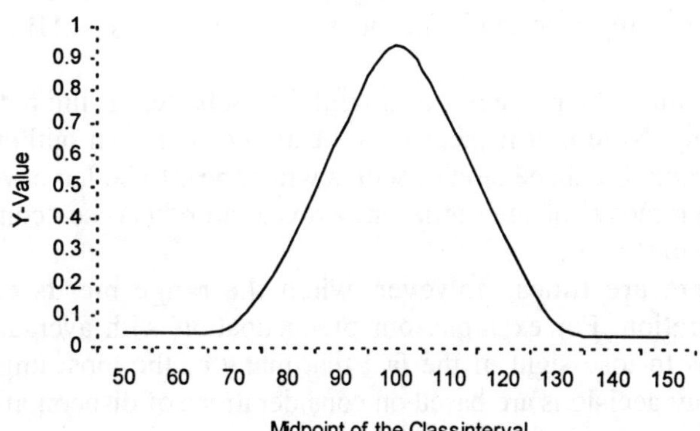


Distribution B

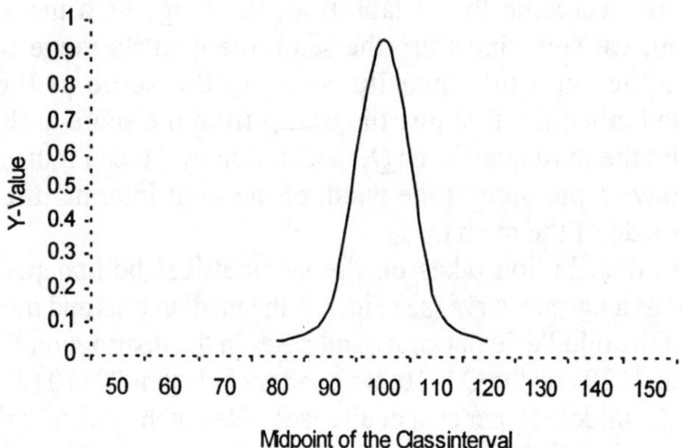


## The Range

When you calculate the various measures of central tendency, you locate a single point along the scale of scores and identify it as the mean, the median, or the mode. When your interest shifts to measures of dispersion, however, you must look for an index of variability that indicates the spread of scores around that central location.

One of the first measure of dispersion—the range. It consists simply of the scale distance between the largest and smallest scores; that is, the range is equal to the highest score minus the lowest score.

Thus, if the highest score is 140 and the lowest is 30, the range is 140 – 30 = 110. Note that the range is a single value, not two values as is commonly reported in the media. Thus, the range is 110, not 30 to 140.

Although the range is meaningful, its usefulness is limited by its instability. Note that if there is one extreme score (an outlier) in a distribution, the dispersion of scores will appear to be large when in fact the removal of the outlier may reveal an otherwise "compact" distribution.

There are times, however, when the range merits careful consideration. For example, our preoccupation with averages can cause us to lose sight of the fact that many of the most important workaday decisions are based on considerations of dispersion rather than on measures of central tendency.

## Quartile Deviation (The Semi-interquartile Range)

In order to overcome the instability of the range as a measure of dispersion, we sometimes use the semi-interquartile range (Q). To calculate the semi-interquartile, subtract the score at the 25th percentile (called the first quartile or $Q_1$) from the score at the 75th percentile (the third quartile or $Q_3$) and divide by 2 (see Figure). Then we will have a measure of the width of the semi-interquartile range on either side of the median.

If the distribution takes on the symmetrical bell-shaped form identified as a normal curve (see Figure), the median plus and minus the Q cuts off the middle 50 per cent of all cases in the distribution. Thus, if the median is 70 and the Q is 10, we can conclude that $70 \pm 10$ (60 to 80) includes the middle 50 per cent of all cases. Even with markedly skewed distributions (see figure), the median plus and minus the Q accounts for the middle 50 per cent of cases. Thus, $65 \pm 6.5$ yields 58.5 and 71.5 as the values that bracket the middle 50 per cent of cases. For this reason, the Q is most frequently used in conjunction with the median when extreme skew rules out the use of mean and the standard deviation as measures of central tendency and variability, respectively.

In the behavioural sciences, we find that some interval-and ratio-scaled data such as reaction time scores, heart rate measures, and income figures are usually sufficiently skewed to justify the use of the median as the measure of central tendency, and the semi-interquartile range as the index of dispersion. These measure are often used to describe ordinally scaled data as well.

$$\text{Semi-interquartile Range} = \frac{73-60}{2} = 6.5$$

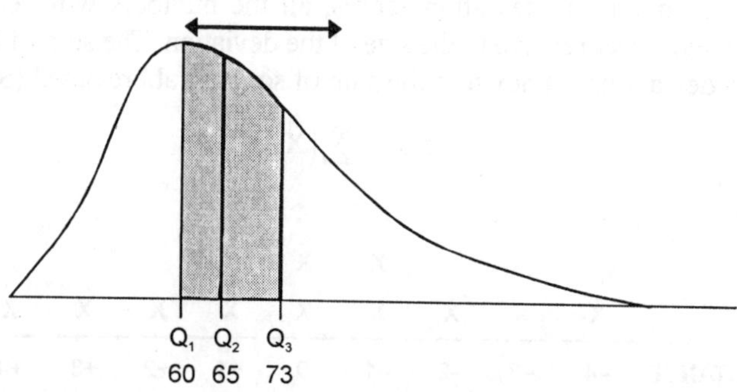


Although the Q is far more meaningful than the crude range, it has two significant shortcomings: (1) Like the crude range, it does not by itself permit the precise interpretation of a score within a distribution, and (2) like the median, it does not enter into any of the higher mathematical relationships that are basic to inferential statistics. As a consequences, we need to turn our attention to the most frequently used measures of dispersion, variance and the standard deviation.

**Variance ($s^2$) and the Standard Deviation(s)**

Before we begin to discuss these topics, we need to review some material covered in previous sections. The sum of the mean subtracted from all values of a variable is equal to zero (i.e., $\Sigma(X - \overline{X}) = 0$). When divided by N, this sum is said to be the first moment about the mean. The word "moment" is a technical term that represents the point where there is equilibrium between opposite forces. We said that the mean represents the balance point in the distribution. That is why the sum of the deviation scores is always 0; the mean is the point of equilibrium between high and low scores. The first moment about the mean describes the mean along the measurement scale. Specifically, the first moment about the mean is calculated as

$$0 = \frac{\sum(X-\overline{X})}{N}$$

Note that the first moment about the mean always equals 0 because the mean is the point in the distribution that balances the opposing forces of large and small numbers.

If we square the deviation scores, all the numbers will become positive and larger relative to the size of the deviation. The sum of these squared deviations is known as the sum of squares, abbreviated (SS).

$$SS = \sum(X - \overline{X})^2$$

| | X | X | X | X | X | X | X | X | X |
|---|---|---|---|---|---|---|---|---|---|
| | | | | X | X | X | | | |
| | | | | | X | | | | |
| DISTANCE | –4 | –3 | –2 | –1 | 0 | +1 | +2 | +3 | +4 |
| (DISTANCE)$^2$ | 16 | 9 | 4 | 1 | 0 | 1 | 4 | 9 | 16 |

$\Sigma$ (DISTANCE)$^2$ = 60

Before proceeding with the procedures for calculating measures of dispersion, it will be advantageous to think more about the notion of distance from a mean and the impact of squaring each deviation. The above figure illustrates a distribution of scores. It is clear that the scores farther from the mean will contribute more to the overall total when these squared deviations or distances are summed. Small deviations, when squared, increase by relatively small amounts ($2^2 = 4$, $3^2 = 9$). Numbers that are a greater distance from the mean, when squared, become much larger ($9^2 = 81$, $11^2 = 121$). This fact suggests that scores further from the mean have a greater effect on the sum of squares than scores closer to the mean.

As should be obvious, as we add more scores to the set, the sum of squares becomes larger, especially if these scores deviate from the mean. As a consequence, we cannot use the sum of squares as a direct measure of dispersion. To make a more useful measure of dispersion, we divide the sum by the total number of scores (N). In effect, we are calculating the average squared deviations. Consequently, we have a statistic that represents the average squared deviation for a set of data. This average is called the variance of a sample and is represented by $s^2$.

Specifically, the variance of a set of data is calculated by

$$s^2 = \frac{\sum(X - \overline{X})^2}{N}$$

and may also be represented as the sum of squares (SS) divided by N. i.e., $\frac{SS}{N}$

Statisticians also call this equation the second moment about the mean. Again it is critical to recognize the concept of equilibrium between opposing forces. The variance averages the effects of large and small deviations from the mean. We can use this fact to our advantage because we can use the variance to help us characterize how much the typical score deviates from the mean.

Because we squared all the deviation scores before dividing by N, the variance represents the average of the sum of *squared* difference between each score and the mean. If we take the square root of the variance, we will convert the variance to a score that represents our measurement scale. The result of this transformation is called the standard deviations and is represented by s.

$$s = \sqrt{\frac{\sum(X-\overline{X})^2}{N}}$$

Therefore, most researchers report the standard deviation because it represents the average deviation between the mean and the observed score.

**Calculation of the Variance and Standard Deviation from an Array of Scores**

You are now ready to apply these formulas to some examples. It encourage you to use a calculator or a computer to help you with the calculations. Our experience has been that many people are prone to make mistakes when trying to do these calculations by hand. You should also get into the habit of preparing a neat, step-by-step account of your work. As you will find, the calculations for most statistics are easy and do not require complicated mathematical procedures.

The computational equation produces the same result as the definitional equation. The only real difference is that the computational equation takes less time to perform.

***Definitional Equation for Variance:***

$$s^2 = \frac{\sum(X-\overline{X})^2}{N} \text{ and standard deviation, } s = \sqrt{\frac{\sum(X-\overline{X})^2}{N}}$$

computational equation for standard deviation is,

$$\Sigma = \frac{1}{N}\sqrt{N\sum X^2 - (\sum X)^2}$$

It is the measure of the scatter or spread of the separate observations around the central tendency, especially the mean.

***Homogeneous Groups:***

Two groups are said to be homogenous if the variability of the two groups are equal.

**Standard deviation—Definition**

The standard deviation of a group of measurements is defined as the square root of the sum of squares of deviations of each observations from the mean divided by the size of the sample

Thus,

$$s \text{ or } \sigma = \sqrt{\frac{\left(\sum X-\overline{X}\right)^2}{N}}$$

$$= \sqrt{\frac{\sum x^2}{N}} \quad \text{Where } x = X - \overline{X}$$

$$= \sqrt{\frac{\sum X^2}{N} - \frac{\left(\sum X\right)^2}{N}}$$

$$= \frac{1}{N}\sqrt{N\sum X^2 - \left(\sum X\right)^2}$$

**Percentile Points**

The method of calculating percentiles is the same as that employed in finding the median. Percentile points are points below which lies a given percentage of cases. In general percentile points are denoted by Pp. This implies that Pp is the Pth percentile which again denotes point below which lie P percentage of cases

Pp is calculated by the formula $Pp = l + i\,\dfrac{\left(P\dfrac{N}{100} - F\right)}{f}$

Where,

l – exact lower limit of the class in which the pth percentile lies

F – the cumulative frequency corresponding to l

f – actual frequency of the class containing the pth percentile point

N – size of the sample.

The percentile points are $p_1$, $p_2$.... Among these the percentile points lie $p_{10}$, $p_{20}$, $p_{30}$.... $p_{90}$ are called deciles.

$P_{25}$, the 25th percentile, the point below which lie 25 per cent of the cases of the distribution is called the first quartile of the distribution denoted by $Q_1$

$P_{50}$, the 50th percentile, the point which lie 50 per cent of the cases of the distribution is called the second quartile and is denoted by $Q_2$.

$P_{75}$, the 75th percentile, the point below which the 75 per cent of the cases of the distribution which is called as the 3rd quartile, $Q_3$.

**Quartile Deviation**

Q, the quartile deviation has been defined as half the range between Q1 and Q3

i.e. $$Q = \frac{Q_3 - Q_1}{2} \text{ or } \frac{P_{75} - P_{25}}{2}$$

Since in the calculation of quartile deviation, we are considering the range between the first and third quartiles only, i.e., (the middle portion of the continuum of measurements), Q is the measure of variability at the middle portion of the distribution.

Calculate Q from the following:

| c | f | cum. f |
|---|---|---|
| 136-139 | 3 | 200 |
| 132-135 | 5 | 197 |
| 128-131 | 16 | 192 |
| 124-127 | 23 | 176 |
| 120-123 | 52 | 153 |
| 116-119 | 49 | 101 |
| 112-115 | 27 | 52 |
| 108-111 | 18 | 25 |
| 104-107 | 7 | 7 |
| | 200 | |

$$Q = Q_3 - \frac{Q_3 - Q_1}{2} \text{ or } \frac{P_{75} - P_{25}}{2}$$

$P_{75}$:

$$P_{75} = l + \frac{i\left(\frac{3N}{4} - F\right)}{f}$$

$\frac{PN}{100} = 75 \times 200/100 = 150, l = 119.5, F = 101, f = 52, i = 4$

$$P_{75} = 119.5 + 4\,\frac{(150 - 101)}{52} = 123.26$$

$$P_{25} = l + \frac{i\left(N/4 - F\right)}{f}$$

$\frac{PN}{100} = 25 \times 200/100 = 50$

$P_{25} = 111.35 + 4\ (50 - 25)/27 = 115.203$

$$Q = \frac{P_{75} - P_{25}}{2} = 123.26 - 115.20/2$$

$$= 4.03$$

## Average or Mean Deviation

It is the arithmetic mean of absolute deviations of all the observations from the mean. (Absolute deviations means deviations disregarding the sign) Mean deviation is calculated by:

1. In an ungrouped data, M.D. = $\frac{\sum|x|}{N}$

   where $x = X - \overline{X}$ 52, 50, 56, 68, 65, 62, 57, 70

2. In a grouped data, frequency distribution MD = $\frac{\sum|fx|}{N}$

   where $x = X - \overline{X}$

Calculate Mean Deviation:

| Class | f | X | $x' = \frac{X - A}{i}$ | fx′ | $X - \overline{X}$ | fx |
|---|---|---|---|---|---|---|
| 195-199 | 1 | 197 | 5 | 5 | 26 | 26 |
| 190-194 | 2 | 192 | 4 | 8 | 27 | 42 |
| 185-189 | 4 | 187 | 3 | 12 | 16 | 64 |
| 180-184 | 5 | 182 | 2 | 10 | 11 | 55 |
| 175-179 | 8 | 177 | 1 | 8 | 6 | 48 |
| 170-174 | 10 | 172 | 0 | 0 | 1 | 10 |
| 165-169 | 6 | 167 | –1 | –6 | –4 | –24 |
| 160-164 | 4 | 162 | –2 | –8 | –9 | –36 |
| 155-159 | 4 | 157 | –3 | –12 | –14 | –56 |
| 150-154 | 2 | 152 | –4 | –8 | –19 | –38 |
| 145-149 | 3 | 147 | –5 | –15 | –24 | –72 |
| 140-144 | 1 | 142 | –6 | –6 | –29 | –29 |
| | N = 50 | | | –12 | | $\Sigma|fx| = 500$ |

$$\text{Mean} = A + \frac{i\sum fx'}{N}$$

$$= 172 + \frac{5 \times -12}{50} = 170.8 = 171$$

$$\text{MD} = \frac{\sum|fx|}{N} = 500/50 = 10$$

**Combined Standard Deviation**

$$\sigma_{Comb} = \frac{\sqrt{N_1(\sigma_1^{\;2}+d_1^{\;2})+N_2(\sigma_2^2+d_2^2)+..........}}{N_1+N_2+............}$$

Where $d_1 = \overline{X}_1 - \overline{X}_{comb}$

$d_2 = \overline{X}_2 - \overline{X}_{comb}$

Mean, standard deviation and size of three groups A, B and C are given below. Compute the mean and standard deviation of the three groups combined, which group is more consistent?

| *Group* | $\overline{X}$ | $\sigma$ | *N* |
|---|---|---|---|
| A | 82 | 10 | 25 |
| B | 86 | 12 | 35 |
| C | 88 | 16 | 20 |

$$\overline{X}_{comb} = \frac{N_1\overline{X}_1 + N_2\overline{X}_2 + N_3\overline{X}_3}{N_1+N_2+N_3}$$

$$= \frac{25\times 82+35\times 86+26\times 88}{25+35+20} = 85.25$$

$d1 = X_1 - \overline{X}_{comb} = 82 - 85.25 = -3.25$

$d2 = X_2 - \overline{X}_{comb} = 86 - 85.25 = 0.75$

$d3 = X_3 - \overline{X}_{comb} = 88 - 85.25 = 2.75$

$$s_{comb} = \frac{\sqrt{N_1(\sigma_1^{\;2}+d_1^{\;2})+N_2(\sigma_2^2+d_2^2)+..........}}{N_1+N_2+............}$$

$$= \frac{\sqrt{25\times(100+3.252)+35(122+0.752+20(162+2.752))}}{80}$$

$= 12.794$

***Effect upon Mean and б when a constant is added***

| X | $X - \overline{X}$ | $(X - \overline{X})^2$ |
|---|---|---|
| 9 | 2 | 4 |
| 8 | 1 | 1 |
| 7 | 0 | 0 |
| 6 | –1 | 1 |
| 5 | –2 | 4 |
| X = 7 | | $\Sigma x^2 = 10$ |

$$\sigma = \sqrt{\frac{10}{5}} = \sqrt{2}$$

***Adding 5 to each value,***

| X | $X - \overline{X}$ | $x^2$ |
|---|---|---|
| 14 | 2 | 4 |
| 13 | 2 | 4 |
| 12 | 1 | 1 |
| 11 | 0 | 0 |
| 10 | -2 | 4 |
| M = 12 | | 10 |

$$\sigma = \sqrt{\frac{10}{5}} = \sqrt{2}$$

***Effect upon $\overline{X}$ and б on multiplication: Multiply each by 10.***

| X | | $X_1$ |
|---|---|---|
| 9 | | 90 |
| 8 | | 80 |
| 7 | $\sigma = \sqrt{2}$ | 70 |
| 6 | | 60 |
| 5 | | 50 |
| $\overline{X} = 7$ | | $\overline{X}_1 = 70$ |

| $X_1$ | $X_2$ |
|---|---|
| 20<br>10<br>0<br>–10<br>–20 | 400<br>100<br>0<br>100<br>400 |
| $\overline{X}1 = 70 = 10 \times \overline{X}$ | $\sigma_1 = \sqrt{2} \times 10$ |

When each measure is added by the same constant $\overline{X}$ becomes $\overline{X}$ + constant and б is changed when each measure is multiplied by a constant. $\overline{X}$ and б are multiplied by the same constant.

**When to Use Various Measures of Central Tendency**

***Mean***

1. when most of the measures are distributed around a central point.
2. when other measures like SD, MD, correlation etc. involving mean are to be computed.
3. when a measure of central tendency of greatest stability is needed.

***Median***

1. when the exact midpoint of distribution is needed.
2. when there are extreme scores which would affect the mean.

***Mode***

1. when a quick and approximate measure of central tendency is needed.
2. when the measure of central tendency should be the most typical value.

**When to Use Measure of Variability**

*Range*: When the data are too scattered, when a type of extreme scores or of a total spread is wanted.

QD: 1. When median is used as the measure of central tendency.
2. When there are extreme scores which would affect the standard deviation disproportionately.

3. When the measure at the middle of the distribution is wanted.

AD: 1. When it is devised to get all the deviations from the mean.
2. When there are extreme scores which may influence SD.

SD: 1. When the statistic having the greatest stability is needed.
2. When extreme deviation should exercise a proportionately greater effect on the variability.
3. When coefficient of correlation and other statistics are subsequently to be computed.

## 10.6 PERCENTILE RANKS (GARRETT, 1961)

| Class | f | F |
|---|---|---|
| 195-199 | 1 | 50 |
| 190-194 | 2 | 49 |
| 185-189 | 4 | 47 |
| 180-184 | 5 | 43 |
| 175-179 | 8 | 38 |
| 170-174 | 10 | 30 |
| 165-169 | 6 | 20 |
| 160-164 | 4 | 14 |
| 155-159 | 4 | 10 |
| 150-154 | 2 | 6 |
| 145-149 | 3 | 4 |
| 140-144 | 1 | 1 |

### Calculation of Percentile Rank of Score – 163

The score 163 lies in the interval 160–164. i.e., 159.5–164.5. From the given data we can see that up to the score 159.5. (the exact lower limit of the interval containing the score 163) the cumulative frequency is 10.

The interval 159.5 – 164.5 has 5 units of interval and 4 scores are distributed in this interval. Then one unit of interval when converted into score gives us.

$4/5$ = 0.8 distance

The score 163 is 3.5 units distance from 159.5. These 3.5 units of interval equals 3.5x0.8 score distance. Thus on the whole the number of scores below 163 is $(10 + 3.5 \times 0.8)$. This figure is for the given sample size of N = 50. When this is converted into a percentage.

The percentile rank of 163 = $\frac{(10+3.5\times0.8)}{50}\times100 = 25.6 = 26$

**Question:** Calculate the percentile rank of 171,188 and 156

*Percentile Rank of 171 (PR)*

It lies in the interval 170–174

$$PR = \frac{(20+2\times1.5)}{50}\times100 = 46$$

*PR of 188*

It is in the interval 185–189

$$PR = \frac{(43+3.5\times0.8)}{50}\times100 = 91.6 = 92$$

*PR of 156*

It is in the interval 155–159

$$\frac{(6+1.5\times0.8)}{50}\times100 = 14.4 = 14$$

$$PR = \frac{F+(\text{given score}-l)}{N}\times100$$

F → Cum. Frequency up to lower limit of the class interval
l → lower limit,
i → class interval,
f → freq. of the interval containing the given score
N → number (size)
PR of upper limit = Cum. freq. F × 100/N

**Calculating PRs from Ordered Data**

Ordinary ranks can be converted into percentile ranks using the formula,

$$PR = 100 - \frac{(100R-50)}{N}$$

Where R → rank position

**20 children are put in order of merits for scores on a LG test. Compute the PR of each child**

For 1: $PR = 100 - \frac{100\times1-50}{20} = 100 - 2.5 = 97.5$

For 2: $PR = 100 - \frac{100\times2-50}{20} = 92.5$

For 3: $PR = 100 - \frac{100\times3-50}{20} = 87.5$

For 4: $PR = 100 - \frac{100\times4-50}{20} = 82.5$

For 5: $PR = 100 - \frac{100\times5-50}{20} = 77.5$

For 6: $PR = 100 - \frac{100\times6-50}{20} = 72.5$

For 7: $PR = 100 - \frac{100\times7-50}{20} = 67.5$

For 8: $PR = 100 - \frac{100\times8-50}{20} = 62.5$

For 9: $PR = 100 - \frac{100\times9-50}{20} = 57.5$

For10: $PR = 100 - \frac{100\times10-50}{20} = 52.5$

For11: $PR = 100 - \frac{100\times11-50}{20} = 47.5$

For12: $PR = 100 - \frac{100\times12-50}{20} = 42.5$

For13: $PR = 100 - \frac{100\times13-50}{20} = 37.5$

For14: $PR = 100 - \frac{100\times14-50}{20} = 32.5$

For15: $PR = 100 - \frac{100 \times 15 - 50}{20} = 27.5$

For16: $PR = 100 - \frac{100 \times 16 - 50}{20} = 22.5$

For17: $PR = 100 - \frac{100 \times 17 - 50}{20} = 17.5$

For18: $PR = 100 - \frac{100 \times 18 - 50}{20} = 12.5$

For19: $PR = 100 - \frac{100 \times 19 - 50}{20} = 7.5$

For20: $PR = 100 - \frac{100 \times 20 - 50}{20} = 2.5$

## 10.7 SKEWNESS

It refers to the symmetry or asymmetry of the frequency distribution. A frequency distribution or curve is said to be symmetrical if at the highest point of a curve, we draw a curve to the x-axis, then this line of separation splits the curve into two equal halves exactly.

If a distribution is asymmetrical and the larger frequencies tend to be concentrated toward the low end of the variable and smaller frequencies toward the high and, it is said to be positively skewed or skewed to the right. If the opposite poles ie. if the larger frequencies being concentrated towards the high end of the variable and the smaller frequencies toward the low end, the distribution is said to be negatively skewed or skewed to the left.

Skewness can be calculated by the formula

$$\text{Skewness} = 3\frac{(\text{Mean} - \text{Median})}{\text{SD}}$$

$$SK = \frac{(P_{90} + p_{10})}{2} - P_{50}$$

In a positively skewed distribution the mean lies to the right of the median and mode represents the point of highest frequency.

Therefore, the points of mean, median and mode in a positively skewed distribution will be as in the figure.

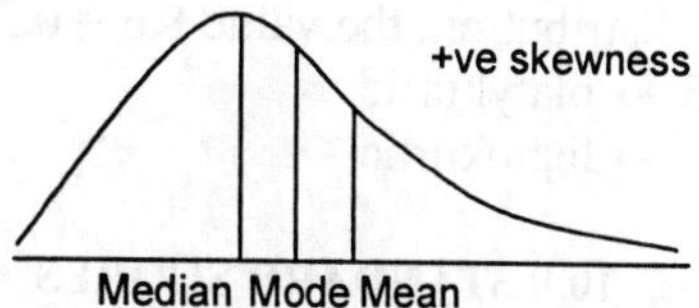


In a negatively skewed distribution, mean lies to the left of the median and since mode represents the highest point of frequency, the position of mean, median and mode will be as in the figure.

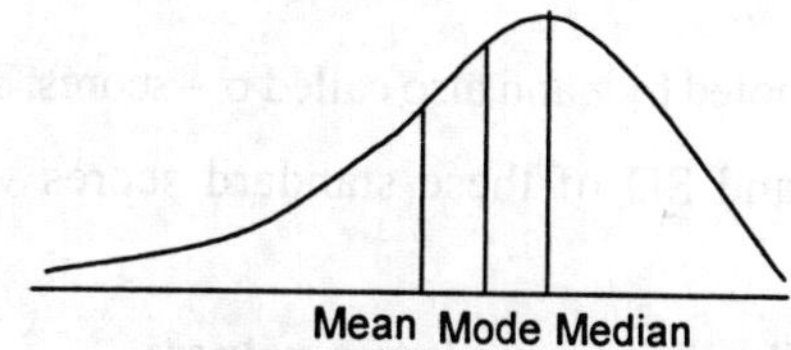


## 10.8 KURTOSIS

It refers to the flatness or peakedness of one distribution in relation to another. It is conventional to speak of a distribution as leptokurtic if it is more peaked than a particular type of distribution known as the normal distribution (mesokurtic) and platy kurtic if it is less peaked. This means that a mesokurtic or normal distribution falls between a leptokurtic and platykurtic distribution.

$$Ku = Q/D = \frac{P_{75} - P_{25}}{2(P_{90} - P_{10})}$$

where Ku is the range between 90th and 10th percentile.

Thus the formula $Ku = \frac{P_{75} - P_{25}}{2(P_{90} - P_{10})}$

For a normal distribution, the value Ku = 0.263
If Ku > 0.263 → platykurtic
If Ku < 0.263 → leptokurtic

## 10.9 STANDARD SCORES

For a variable X if a set of measures are given then their mean will be denoted by $\overline{X}$ and Std deviation by σ or s. Then $X - \overline{X}$ are called deviation scores. When these deviation scores are divided by the std deviation of X we get Std scores.

They are denoted by z and also called σ – scores. Thus $z = \frac{X - \overline{X}}{\sigma}$

The mean and SD of these standard scores will be 0 and 1 respectively.

**Convert the following scores into z values**

| X | $X - \overline{X}$ | $(X - \overline{X}^2)$ | $Z = \frac{X - \overline{X}}{\sigma}$ | $(z - \overline{z}^2)$ |
|---|---|---|---|---|
| 70 | 14 | 196 | 1.668 | 2.782 |
| 60 | 4 | 16 | 0.476 | 0.226 |
| 50 | –6 | 36 | –0.715 | 0.5112 |
| 54 | –2 | 4 | –0.238 | 0.566 |
| 46 | –10 | 100 | –1.192 | 1.420 |
| | | 332 | | 4.9975 |

$\overline{X} = 56 \quad \sigma = \frac{\sqrt{\Sigma(X - \overline{X}^2)}}{N} = \frac{\sqrt{352}}{5} = 8.39$

$\text{Mean of } z = \frac{-0.001}{5} = 0 \text{ and SD, } s = \frac{\sqrt{4.9975}}{5} = \frac{\sqrt{5}}{5} = 1$

**i.e., the mean and SD of standard scores are 0 and 1**

## 10.10 NORMAL DISTRIBUTION

1. The normal probability distribution or simply, normal curve is expressed by the equation.

$$y = \frac{N}{\sigma\sqrt{2\pi}} e^{\frac{-x^2}{2\sigma^2}}$$

This equation when written in standard score form as

$$y = \frac{N}{\sigma\sqrt{2\pi}} e^{\frac{-z^2}{2}}$$

Where X stands for the given variable and Y → respective frequencies

2. The normal distribution is symmetrical about the ordinate at $X = \overline{X}$ and appears on a smooth curve. Since the ordinate at $X = \overline{X}$ divides the curve into two equal parts the mean, median, and mode will coincide at one point.
3. For a normal distribution, Sk = 0 Ku = 0.263
4. The curve is asymptotic i.e. the curve extends to infinity on either side of the mean.
5. The curve will be maximum at the ordinate $X = \overline{X}$ and hence the maximum ordinate is given by $Y = \frac{1}{\sqrt{2\pi}} = 0.3989$
6. The curve has points of inflexion at $X = \overline{X} \pm \sigma$ (turning points)
   Practically X = X+3, X–3
7. The total area under the curve has considered as N. For practical purposes this area is treated as 1.
8. 68.26 per cent of the total area under the normal curve lies between $X - \sigma$ and $X + \sigma$
9. 95.44 per cent i.e. 95 per cent of the total area under the normal curve lies between $X - 2\sigma$ and $X + 2\sigma$
10. Quartile deviation of a normal distribution is $\frac{2}{3}\sigma = 0.6745\sigma$
11. Mean deviation = $4\frac{\sigma}{5}$

**Applications of the Normal Probability Curve**

*I. Find the height of the ordinate of the normal curve at the following z values*

$-2.15, \quad -1.53, \quad +0.07, \quad +0.99, \quad +2.76$

The height of the ordinate from the table of areas and the ordinates of the normal curve.

The height at z = +2.15 = 0.0395. Since the curve is symmetrical,
the height of the ordinate at z = –2.15 = 0.0395
height of the ordinate at –1.53 is 0.1238
height of the ordinate at +0.07 is 0.3980
height of the ordinate at +0.99 is 0.2444
height of the ordinate at +2.76 is 0.0088

*II. Consider a normally distributed variable with* $\overline{X} = 50$, $\sigma = 10$, *For N = 200. Find the height of the ordinate at the following value of X: 25, 87, 49, 57, 63*

1. $z = \dfrac{X - \overline{X}}{\sigma} = \dfrac{25 - 50}{10} = -2.5$

2. $z = \dfrac{35 - 50}{10} = -1.5$

3. $z = \dfrac{49 - 50}{10} = -0.1$

4. $z = \dfrac{57 - 50}{10} = -0.7$

5. $z = \dfrac{63 - 50}{10} = 1.3$

1. At z = 2.15, height of the ordinate = 0.715
   when N = 200, height of the ordinate at z = –2.15 = 0.0175 × 200 = 3.5
2. At z = – 1.5, height of ordinate = 0.1295
   when N = 200, height of the ordinate at z = 0.1295 × 200 = 25.9

3. At X = 49, z = – 0.1, height of the ordinate = 0.2420
   when N = 200, height of ordinate = 200 × 0.2420 = 48.4
4. At X = 57, z = 0.7, height of ordinate = 0.3123
   when N = 200, height of ordinate = 200 × 0.3123 = 62.46
5. At X = 63, z = 1.3 height of ordinate = 0.1714
   when N = 200, height of ordinate = 200 × 0.1714 = 34.28

*III. Find the proportion of the area of the normal curve*

(a) Between mean and z = 1.49

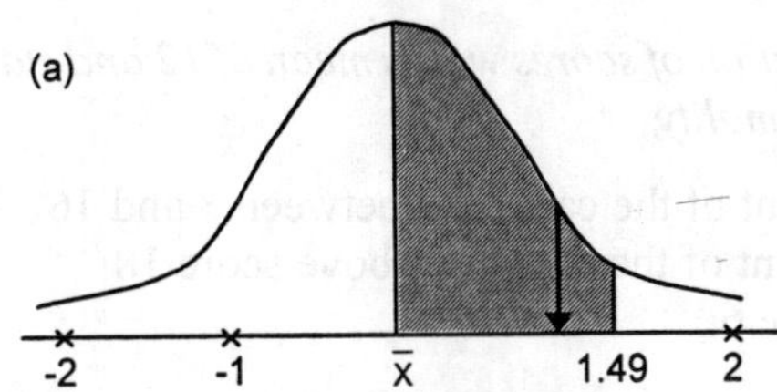


(b) Between mean and z = 1.26

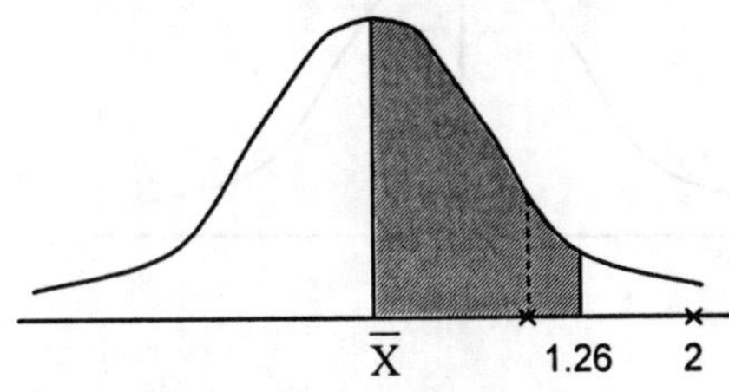


(c) To the right of z = 0.25
(d) To the right of z = 1.50
(e) To the left of z = –1.26
(f) To the left of z = 0.95
(g) Between z = ± 0.50
(h) Between z = –0.75 and z = 1.50
(i) Between z = 1.00 and z = 1.96
(j) Between z = 1.00 and z = 1.01

(a) Up to z = 1.49 (i.e. between z = 0 and z = 1.49) the area = 0.4319
(b) Area between mean and z = 1.26 = 0.3962
(c) To the right of 0.25 means the area between 3 and 0.25 i.e., ½ of total area – area of 0.25 = 0.5 – 0.0987 = 0.4013

(d) To the right of z = 1.50 0.5 – 0.4332 = 0.0668
(e) To the left of z = –1.26 = 0.5–0.3962 = 0.1038
(f) To the left of z = 0.95 0.5+0.3790 = 0.8289
(g) Between z = +0.50 = 2 × 0.1915 = 0.3830
(h) Between z = –0.75 and z = 1.5 = 0.2734 + 0.4332 = 0.7066
(i) Between z = 1.00 and z = 1.96 = area of z = 1.96 – area of 1.00 = 0.4750 – 0.3413 = 0.1337
(j) Between z = 1.00 and z = 1.01 area of z = 1.01 – area of 1.00 = 0.3438 – 0.3413 = 0.0025

*(1) Given a distribution of scores with a mean of 12 and std deviation of 4. Assuming normality,*

(a) What percent of the cases fall between 8 and 16
(b) What percent of the cases lie above score 18
(c) Below score 6.
X = 12 б = 4

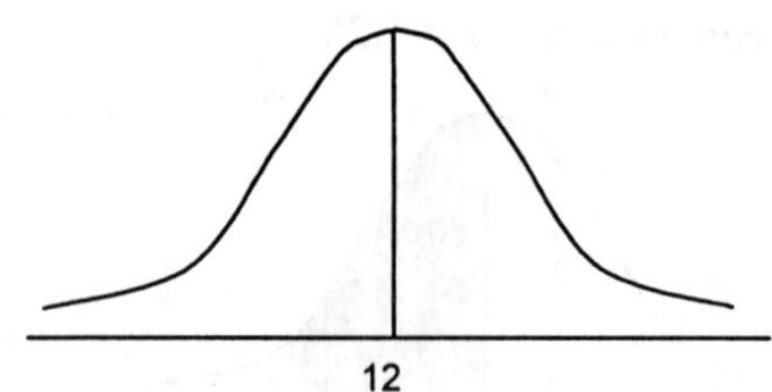


(a) $\dfrac{X - \overline{X}}{\sigma}$

for 8 $\dfrac{8-12}{4} = -1 = z$

for 16, $\dfrac{16-12}{4} = 1 = z$

area between –1 and +1 = 0.3413 × 2 = 0.6826, i.e., 68.26 per cent of the cases falls between 8 and 16

(b) For X = 18 z = $\dfrac{8-12}{4}$ = 1.5. Area above z = 1.5 is 0.5–0.4332 = 0.0668, 0.68 per cent of the cases above 18.

(c) For X = 6, $z = \frac{6-12}{4} = -1.5$. Area below –1.5 is, 0.5 – 0.4332 = 0.0668 i.e., 6.68 per cent of cases are below score 6

*(2) Given $\overline{X}$ = 80 and б = 16, and N = 510, what percent of the scores in this distribution fall above a score of 110 assuming a normal distribution* $z = \frac{110-80}{16} = 1.875$ N = 510

Area above 1.875 = 0.5 – 0.4693 = 0.0307,
When N = 510, Percent of scores fall above the score 110 = 0.0307 × 510 = 15.657 = 1565.7
Area = 0.5 – 0.4696 = 0.0304 For N = 510, area = 15.504

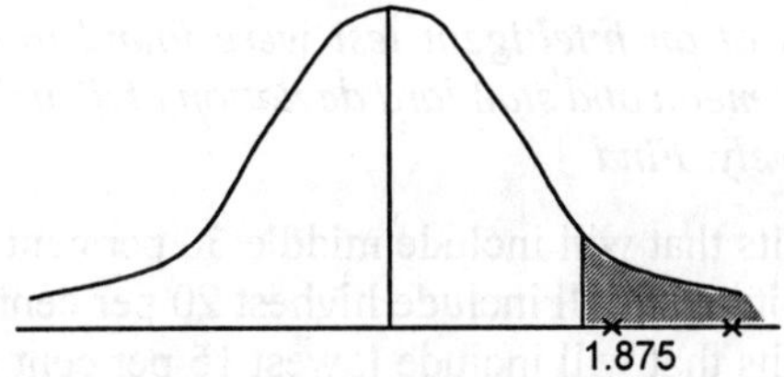


*3) Given a distribution of scores with $\overline{X}$ – 16 and б – 4. If we assume normality, what links will include the middle 75 per cent of the cases.*

From the table area of 37.5 per cent or 0.375 corresponding to z = 1.15 so z = 1.15

$$Z = \frac{X-\overline{X}}{\sigma};\ 1.15 = \frac{X-16}{4} = 20.6$$

The middle 75 per cent of the cases means 37.5 per cent cases on either sides of the curve from the ordinate at z = 0. Therefore limits that will include the middle 75 per cent of the cases means, the limit having the area between z = 0, and covering the area 37.5 per cent. Using the table, we can see the z value corresponding to the area 0.3750 is z = 1.15

Since the curve is symmetrical, the lower limit containing the left 37.5 per cent of the cases is, z = –1.15.

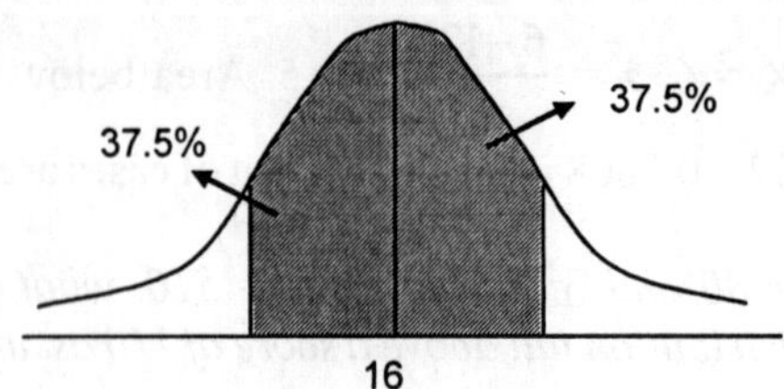


Since $z = \dfrac{X - \overline{X}}{\sigma}$ i.e., $1.15 = \dfrac{X - 16}{4}$ $X = 20.6$

For $z = -1.15$, $-1.15 = \dfrac{X - 16}{4}$ $X = 11.4$

So the area of 75 per cent of cases lies between scores 20.6 and 11.4

*(4) The scores of an intelligent test were found to be distributed normally. If the mean and standard deviation of distribution were 40 and 8 respectively. Find*

(a) the limits that will include middle 50 per cent of the cases
(b) the limits that will include highest 20 per cent of the cases
(c) the limits that will include lowest 15 per cent of cases

(a) z corresponds 25 per cent or 0.25 is $z = 0.675$

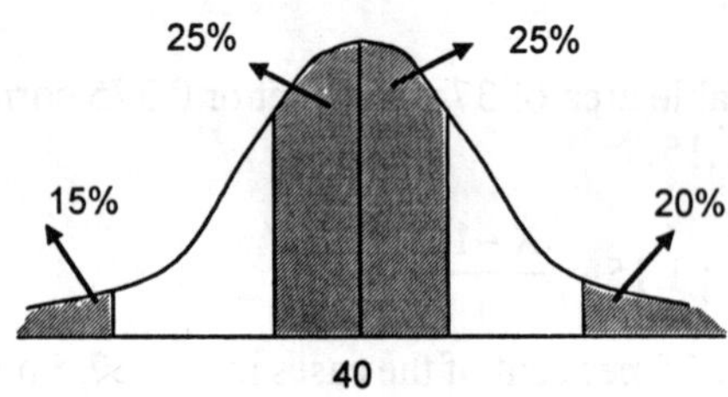


So limits are $z = .0.675$ and $z = -0.675$

The score for $z = 0.675$, $0.075 = \dfrac{X - 40}{8}$, $X = 45.4$

for $z = -0.675$, $X = 34.6$
So the limits are 34.6 and 45.4

(b) Highest 20 per cent means, 0.5 – 0.2 = 0.3 z = 0.845 0.845

$= \frac{X-40}{8}$ i.e., X = 46.76

For z = 0.5, X = (3 × 8) +40 = = 64 i.e., between 46.76 and 64

(c) Lowest 15 per cent means, 0.5 – 0.15 = 0.35

For area 0.35, z = –1.4

$-1.4 = \frac{X-40}{8}$; X = 31.68; for z = –3, X = 16 so the limits are 16 and 31.68

*(5) A teacher decides to fail 25 per cent of the students in a class. Examination marks are roughly normally distributed with a mean of 72 and a SD of 6. What marks should a student get to pass?*

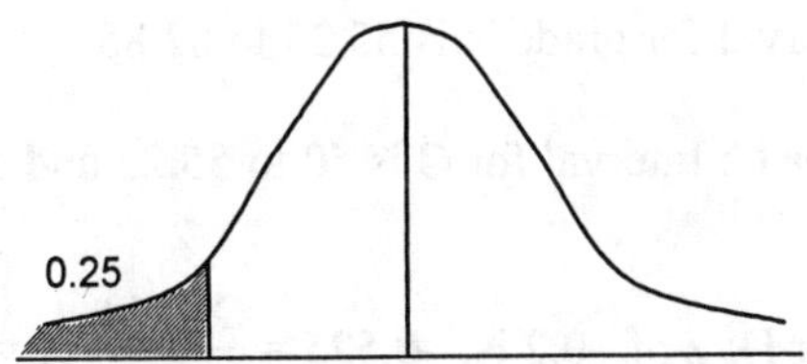


Area = 0.5 – 0.25 = 0.25

z corresponds to 0.25 = 0.675 $\frac{X-\overline{X}}{\sigma} = 0.675 = \frac{X-72}{6}$, X = 67.95 ≈ 68

[The minimum mark required for a pass is the z corresponding to which first 25 per cent denotes for a fail]

So, minimum marks required for a pass is 68

*(6) Scores on a particular physical test are normally distributed with a mean of 50 and a standard deviation of 10. The decision is made to use a letter grade system A, B, C, D, E with the proportion. 0.10, 0.20, 0.40, 0.20 and 0.10 in the five grades respectively. Find the score intervals for the five letter grades.*

*Intervals for A*: 0.5–0.1 = 0.4 z = 1.285 $\frac{X-50}{10} = 1.285$; X = 62.85

$\frac{X-50}{10} = 3 \quad X = 80$

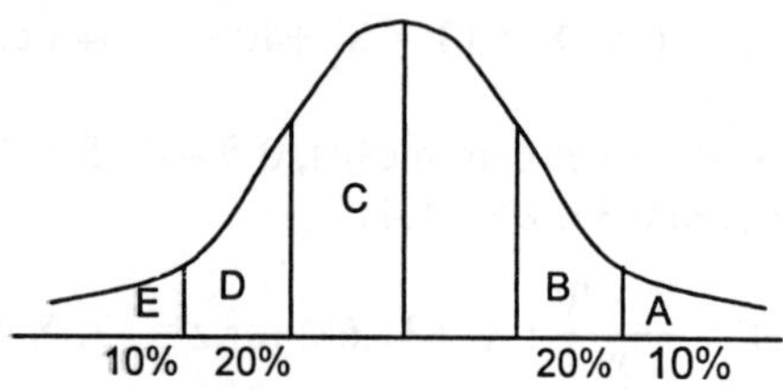


So the interval for grade A is 62.85 to 80

*Interval for B*: area of B = 0.5 – 0.3 = 0.2

$z = 0.525 \quad 0.525 = \frac{X-50}{10} \quad X = 55.25$

So the interval for grade B is 55.25 to 62.85

*Interval for C*: Interval for C is 50 to 55.25 and 50 to 44.75 i.e. 44.75 to 55.25

Interval for D: z of –0.2 is, $-0.525 = \frac{X-50}{10} \quad X = 44.75$

So interval for D grade is from 44.75 to 37.15

*Interval for E*: $z = -1.285 \quad \frac{X-50}{10}$ or $X = 37.15$

$-3 = \frac{X-50}{10}$ or $X = 20$

So interval for E is 20 to 37.15

*(7) The following are data for test scores for two age groups*

| | *11 Year Group* | *14 Year Group* |
|---|---|---|
| $\bar{X}$ | 48 | 56 |
| S | 8 | 12 |
| N | 500 | 800 |

Assuming normality, estimate how many of the 11 year old do better than the average 14 year old and how many of the 14 year old do worse than the average 11 year old.

(a) 11 year olds do better than the average 14 year old means, 11 year olds do better than the score 56

z score equation of 56 is: $z = \frac{X - \overline{X}}{\sigma} = \frac{56 - 48}{8} = 1$

Area corresponding to the z value 1 is 0.3413. So the area above the z value i is 0.5 – 0.3413 = 0.1587

Therefore 15.87 per cent of the cases lies above the score 56. When N = 500, the no. of 11 year group = 500 × 0.1587 = 79.35

(b) 14 year olds do worse than the average 11 year old means, 14 year olds do worse than the score 48.

z score corresponding to 48 is, z = 48 – 56÷12 = –0.666

Area corresponding to z = –0.666 is, 0.2486

Therefore area below the z value 0.666 is, 0.5 – 0.2454 = 0.2514. When N = 800, the no. of 14 year group children below score 48 is, 0.2546 × 800 = 201.12

So 201.12 of the 14 year pupils lie below the score 48.

*(8) A normal distribution has the mean 95 Find its standard deviation if 20 per cent of the area under the curve lies to the right of 103.4.*

X = – 95, z corresponding to 0.3 is z = 0.84

But $z = \frac{X - \overline{X}}{\sigma}$  $0.84 = \frac{103.4 - 95}{\sigma} = \frac{8.4}{\sigma}$

Given the area under the curve to the right of the score 103.4 is 20 per cent. Therefore the area under the curve from the mean (z = 0) to the score 103.4 will be 30 per cent. From the table of areas and ordinates the z – score up to which the area is 30 per cent from the mean is, z = 0.84. Thus z = 0.84 and the score 103.4 are the same.

z = 0.84 means, $\frac{X - \overline{X}}{\sigma} = 0.84$ substituting the values of X and $\overline{X}$, we get

$$\frac{103.4-95}{\sigma} = 0.84 \text{ or } \sigma = 10$$

*(9) Given the distribution of the scores made on a logical memory test by 300 boys and 250 girls. The boys mean score is 21.49 with a σ of 3.63. Girls mean score is 23.68 and s is 5.12. The median of boys is 21.41. Median of girls is 23.66. What percent of the boys exceed the median of the girl's distribution?*

| | *Boys* | *Girls* |
|---|---|---|
| N | 300 | 250 |
| M | 21.49 | 23.68 |
| σ | 3.63 | 5.12 |
| Mdn | 21.41 | 23.66 |

we have to calculate the area of the curve above the raw score X = 23.66 which is the median of the girl's scores. So z value corresponding to X = 23.66 is,

$\overline{X}$ of boys = 21.49

σ of boys = 3.63 $z = \frac{X-\overline{X}}{\sigma} = \frac{23.66-21.49}{3.63} = 0.5978$

Area of the curve up to z = 0.5978 is from the tables, 0.2258. The area above the z score 0.5978 is equal to 0.5 – 0.2258 = 0.2742. But N = 300. Therefore the percentage of the boys exceeding the mean score of girls is, 0.2742 × 300 = 82.26. So 82 boys out of 300 lies above the score 23.66.

*(10) In a normal distribution with mean 45, and б – 10, at what percentile rank does a score of 58 fall? Also find 23rd percentile.*

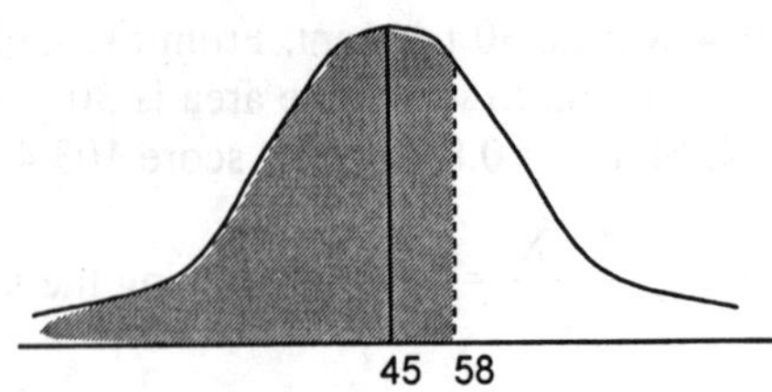

We have to find out the number of cases lies below the score 58. i.e. the area under the curve from mean to score 58 and + 0.5

$$\text{z value corresponding to } 58 = \frac{58-45}{10} = 1.3$$

Area from z = 0 to z = 1.3 = 0.4032. So the total area up to z = 4.3 is, 0.4032 +0.5 = 0.9032

The percentage of cases lies below z = 1.3 is 90.32 = 90 per cent. So the percentile rank is 90.32

**To Find 23rd Percentile:** To find the 23rd percentile, z corresponds to area 0.23 is, the 23rd percentile mean the point below which lie 23 per cent of the cases. The area of the curve up to the 23 per cent is 0.5 – 0.23 = 0.27. z value corresponding to area 0.27 is

$$-0.74 \quad \frac{X-\overline{X}}{\sigma} = \frac{X-45}{10} = -0.74 \text{ or } X = 37.6$$

So the 23rd percentile = 37.6

**To Determine the Relative Difficulty of Test Questions, Problems and Other Test Items:**

**Problem:** (1) Given a test question solved by 10 per cent of a large unselected group. A second problem solved by 20 per cent of the same group and a third problem solved by 30 per cent. If we assume the capacity measured by the test problems to be distributed normally, what is the relative difficulty of questions 1, 2, and 3?

The first item has been solved by 10 per cent of the group. Since the capacity measured by the test problem is assumed to be distributed normally, this 10 per cent is the extreme right 10 per cent under a normal distribution. Therefore, the difficulty value of this item will be the lower limit of this extreme right 10 per cent. From the table, the lower limit we can see that such lower limit is –z = 1.28. i.e. the lower limit is at a distance 1.286 from the mean and hence we can say the difficulty value of the item or 1.28σ.

The second item has been solved by 20 per cent of the same group. Therefore, the difficulty value of this item will be the lower limit of the extreme 20 per cent group. From the table, this lower limit is, z = 0.84. i.e., this point is 0.846 distance from the mean and the difficulty value of the test item is 0.846.

The third item has been solved by 30 per cent of the group. Therefore, the difficulty value of this item will be the lower limit of the extreme 30 per cent group. From the table, this lower limit is z = 0.52 i.e., the point is 0.526 distance from the mean and hence the difficulty value of the item is 0.526.

$$\text{Relative difficulty} \quad \begin{matrix} 1)\ 1.28\sigma \\ 2)\ 0.84\sigma \\ 3)\ 6.52\sigma \end{matrix} \quad \begin{matrix} 0.44 \\ 0.32 \end{matrix}$$

*(2) Given 3 test items 1,2 and 3 panel by 50 per cent, 40 per cent, and 30 per cent respectively of a large group on the assumption of normality of distribution, what percentage of this group must pass test item 4 in order for it to be as much more difficult than 3 or 2 is more difficult than 1.*

For the Ist, 50 per cent of the group has passed. So z = 0

For the 2nd item, 40 per cent z value is, z = 0.255. The difficulty level is 0.2556

$$\begin{matrix} 1 - 0 \\ 2 - 0.255\sigma \\ 3 - 0.525\sigma \end{matrix} \quad \begin{matrix} 0.255\sigma \\ 0.270\sigma \end{matrix}$$

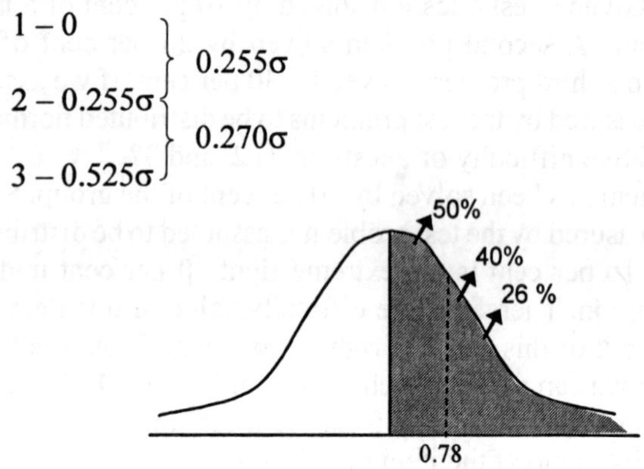


2 is 0.255 σ more difficult than 1, so 4th item is 0.255σ more difficult than 3.

So difficulty value of 4th item is, = 0.525 σ + 0.255 σ = 0.780 σ from the mean

The area corresponding to the z value z = 0.780 is, 0.2823

The area passed by 20 per cent is, 0.5 – 0.2823 = 0.2177

Therefore 21.77 per cent of the students passed the 4th item

Note: 1 50 per cent $z = 0$
2 40 per cent $z = 0.25$
3 30 per cent $z = 0.52$

Looking to the above values, since item 2 is 0.25 б further along the difficulty scale, than item 1, it is clear that item 4 must be 0.25 б above item 3 if it is to be much farther than item z as item 2 is farther than item 2.

Therefore item 4 must have a difficulty value 0.52 б + 0.25 б away from the mean. i.e., 0.77 á distance away from the mean, which is represented by $z = 0.77$.

The pass percentage of item 4 means the no. of cases i.e., the area under the curve from $z = 0.77$ onwards. From the table, this area is 0.5–area from $z = 0$ to $z = 0.77$. i.e. 0.5 – 0.280 = 0.2177. Hence, the required pass percentage of the item 4 is, 21.77 per cent.

**Problems**

1. What proportion of the cases of a normal distribution will fall 1) to the left of $z = 0$, 2) to the right of $z = 0$, 3) to the right of $z = +1.00$, 4) to the left of $z = 1.00$
2. Determine the proportion of cases falling under the normal curve to the left of $z = -1.96$ + to the cases to the right of $z = 1.96$.
3. If the mean of a normal distribution is 43, σ– 2, with how many SDs of the mean would you except almost all of the cases to fall?
   What score values correspond to these points?
4. In a normal distribution with mean – 50 and б – 8, what score is likely to fall at the 95th percentile.
5. (a) In a normal distribution, determine $P_{25}$, $P_{46}$ and P81 is s units.
   (b) What are the percentile ranks of scores at –1.23 б, –0.50 б, 0.84 σ
6. In a certain achievement test, the 7th grade mean is 28.00 and б – 4.80 and 8th grade mean is 31.06 and S.D. is 4.00. What per cent of the 7th grade is above the mean of the 8th grade.

What per cent of the 8th grade is below the mean of the 7th grade.

7. Assume that the distribution of grades in a class of 500 freshmen is normal with M = 72 and б–10. The instructor wants to give letter grades as follows. 10 per cent A's, 30 per cent B's, 40 per cent C's, 15 per cent D's, and 5 per cent E's. Compute to the closest score the divisions between A's and B's, B's and C's; C's and D's; D's and E's.

## 10.11 DEGREES OF FREEDOM

It refers to the number of observations that are free to vary after we have placed certain restrictions on the data. Imagine that we have a sample with four number 18, 23, 27, 32. The sum is 100 and the mean is 25. If we subtract the mean from each score, the sum of the deviation must equal zero $\sum\left(X_i - \overline{X}\right) = 0$.

Let four numbers were drawn at random from a population and are independent of each other because the selection of one number had no influence on the selection of another. i.e., each observation is free to assume any value in the population.

The deviation scores are not independent. Current definition of means requires the sum of the deviation scores to equal 0. therefore the mean restricts the freedom of potential values the deviation scores can take.

In the above example, we must impose the restriction that the deviations are based on the mean, the values of only three deviations are free to vary. As soon as 3 deviations are known, the 4th is determined by the fact that its addition to the other deviation scores must sum to 0. i.e., the fourth score is restricted by the definition of mean.

In general, if we have placed a single restriction, df is N–1. In the example, N–1 = 3.

### Comparison of Normal Distribution and Students' t-distribution

When N is less than 30 's' will under estimate 'σ'. The famous biologist William Gossett resolved the problem of small sample sizes (he published his work under the pseudo name, "student"). In such cases the scores will follow students' t distribution.

**t-distributions**: t-distributions are theoretical symmetrical distributions with a mean of zero and a standard deviation that becomes smaller when degrees of freedom increases.

**Similarities with Normal Distribution**

1. Both are sampling distributions—one for large sample, other for small sample.
2. Both distributions are symmetrical and bell-shaped.
3. Both have a mean of 0

## 10.12 CORRELATION AND REGRESSION

Correlation is an index of the degree of relationship between two variables. By relationship we mean pattern of consistent variation in the two variables. There are two types of variations.

1. When one variable increases, so also the other. This is a linear positive relationship.
2. When one variable increases and the other decreases. This is called a linear negative relationship.

Relationships can be linear or curvilinear. If the pair of measurements when plotted on a graph, seems to cluster around a line the relationship is said to be linear. While one variable increases regularly the other variable increases upto a particular stage and then begin to decrease such a relationship is called currvilinear.

The coefficient of correlation will be between –1 and +1. If a coefficient of correlation is 0, it means that there is no relationship between the variables. If a coefficient of correlation is +1, the relationship is perfect and positive. e.g.: Consider the following set of measurements

| | X | Y |
|---|---|---|
| 1 | 20 | 10 |
| 2 | 18 | 9 |
| 3 | 16 | 8 |
| 4 | 14 | 7 |
| 5 | 12 | 6 |
| 6 | 10 | 5 |

Here pairs of measurements for two variables X and Y are given for six subjects. Each pair of measurement can be plotted as a point when represented graphically. These six pair of measurements when represented graphically will be as in the figure.

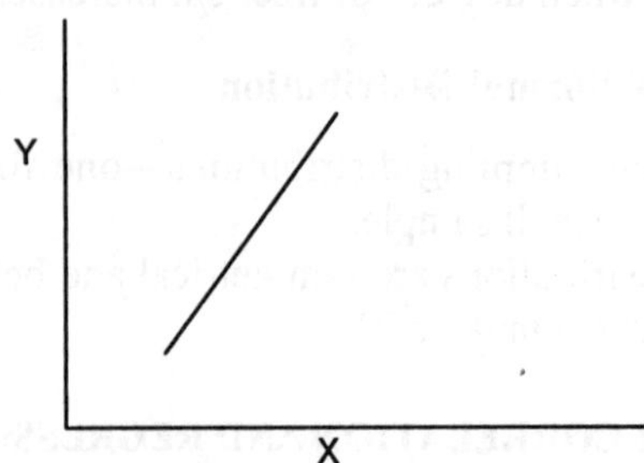


In this example, we can see that for every two units of increase is the X variable there is a corresponding one unit of increases in the Y variable and hence the measurer when plotted extends from lower left of the side to upper right. Such relationship is a good example of perfect +ve relationship represents by r = +1.

| | X | Y |
|---|---|---|
| 1 | 20 | 5 |
| 2 | 18 | 6 |
| 3 | 16 | 7 |
| 4 | 14 | 8 |
| 5 | 12 | 9 |

In this example, for every two units of increase in the X variable there is a corresponding decrease of one unit in the Y variable and hence when these measures plotted graphically, will extend from upper left to lower right as figure. Such relationship is an example of perfect –ve relationship represented by r = –1.

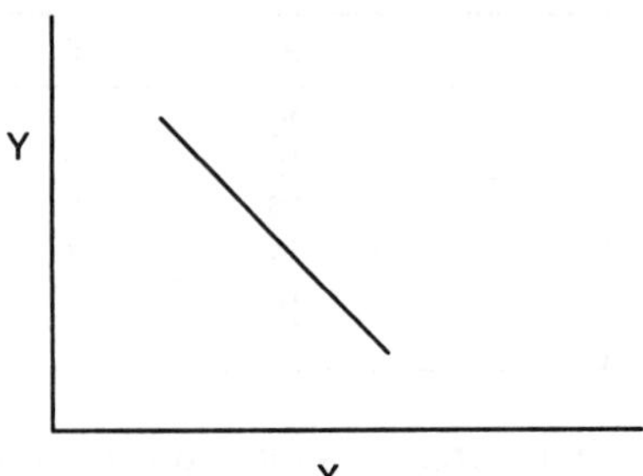

If the pair of measures when plotted graphically seems to scatter all over the region, then we can say there is no relationship between the two variables and in such case the coefficient of correlation = 0 or very near to 0. A standard coefficient of correlation used to calculate linear correlation is the Pearson's Product Moment coefficient of correlation. This correlation when calculated for a population is denoted by 'ρ' and if calculated from a sample is denoted by 'r'. If we have to find the relationship between X and Y for a sample, the symbol will be $r_{xy}$ and the formula is

$$r_{xy} = \frac{1}{N}\frac{\sum xy}{\sigma_x \sigma_y}$$

where $x = X - \overline{X}$; $y = Y - \overline{Y}$

$\sigma_x$ = Standard deviation of X

$\sigma_y$ = Standard deviation of Y

Compute the coefficient of correlation for following data.

| X | Y | $x = X - \overline{X}$ | $y = Y - \overline{Y}$ | xy |
|---|---|---|---|---|
| 12 | 7 | 5 | −1.5 | −7.5 |
| 10 | 3 | 3 | −5.5 | −16.5 |
| 9 | 8 | 2 | −0.5 | −1.0 |
| 8 | 5 | 1 | −3.5 | −3.5 |
| 7 | 7 | 0 | −1.5 | 0 |
| 7 | 12 | 0 | 3.5 | 0 |
| 6 | 10 | −1 | 1.5 | −1.5 |
| 5 | 9 | −2 | 0.5 | −1.0 |
| 4 | 13 | −3 | 4.5 | −13.5 |
| 2 | 11 | −5 | 2.5 | −12.5 |
| | | | | −57.0 |

$\overline{X} = 7 \quad \overline{Y} = 8.5$

$$r_{xy} = \frac{1}{N}\frac{\sum xy}{\sigma_x \sigma_y}$$

$$= \sqrt{78/10} = 2.793$$

$$r_{xy} = \frac{1}{10} \times \frac{-57}{2.793 \times 2.975} = -0.6859$$

**Machine Formula for Calculation of 'r' is,**

$$r_{xy} = \frac{N\sum XY - \sum X \sum Y}{\sqrt{\left[N\sum X^2 - (\sum X)^2\right]\left[N\sum Y^2 - (\sum Y)^2\right]}}$$

**Prediction in Relation to Correlation**

An educational psychologist is interested in predicting his scholatisic performance of a child from a type of intelligent test scores. An employer may be interested in predicting the job performance based on information available to him at the time of selection. A clinical psychologist may be interested in predicting his patients receptivity to treatment from information obtained prior to treatment. To predict all these, there is a statistical technique and that is regression equations based on correlation between the variables.

Any set of paired observations may be plotted on a graph paper each pair of observations being represented by a point. Then we can fix a straight line to this set of points by the method of least squares. (The method of least square states that the sum of squarer of deviations from the points to the line is a minimum).

We may concern with estimating or predicting one variable from knowledge of another. This is the prediction—problems of predicting one variable from a knowledge of another are usually referred to as regression problems. We are dealing with linear regression. It is assumed that a straight line is an appropriate model for describing the relation between two variables.

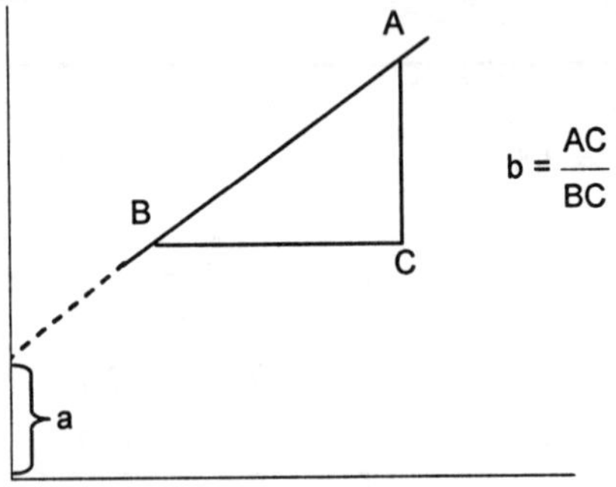

$$b = \frac{AC}{BC}$$

The general equation for any straight line is given by

$$Y = a + bX$$

Where a is a constant. It is the distance on the Y-axis (y-intercept) from the origin to the point where the line meets the Y-axis and b is the slope of the line. The slope describes the rate of increase in Y with increase in X. if a and b are known, the location of the line is uniquely fixed. For any given value of X, we can compute a corresponding value of Y.

**Regression Line of Y on X**

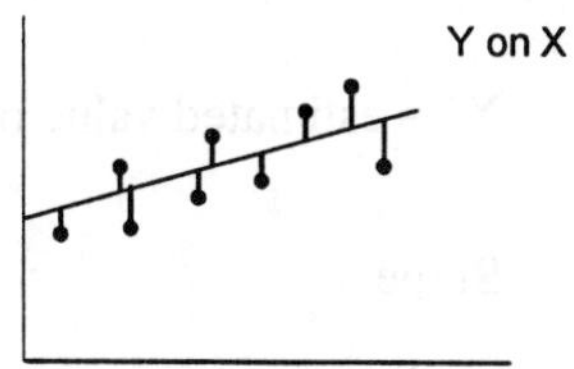


If our interest is in predicting Y from X, the method of least squares locates the line in a position such that the sums of squares of distances from the points to the line taken parallel to the y axis is a minimum. This line is known is the regression line of Y on X.

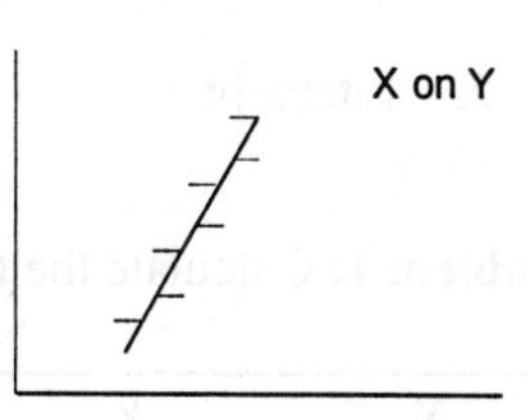


If our interest is in predicting X from Y, the method of least square locates the line in a position such that the sum of squares of distances from the points to the line taken parallel to the X axis is a minimum. This line is known as regression line of X on Y.

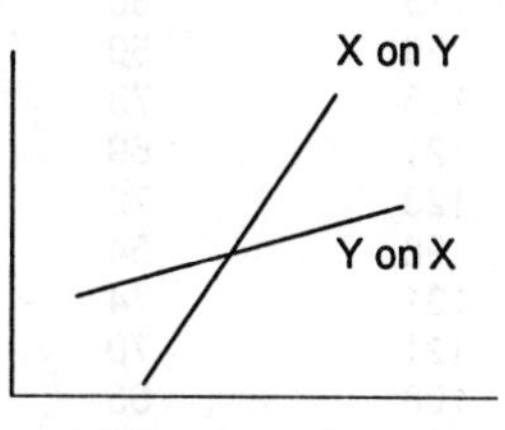


For a bivariate frequency distribution, the two regression lines will be as in figure. When the correlation is perfect, the two regression lines coincides throughout their lengths. The higher the correlation, the closer they be. All regression lines intersect at a point representing the means of X and Y.

**Regression Equations and Regression Coefficients**

Equation for a straight line is,

$$Y = a + bX$$

Equation for the regression line of Y on X is

$$Y' = a_{yx} + b_{yx}X$$

where Y′ = estimated value of Y

Slope, $$b_{yx} = \frac{N\sum XY - \sum X \sum Y}{N\sum X^2 - (\sum X)^2}$$

Y-intercept $$a_{yx} = \frac{\sum Y - b_{yx}\sum X}{N}$$

Equation for the regression line of X on Y is,

$$X' = a_{xy} + b_{xy} Y$$

X′ = estimated value of X.

Slope $$b_{xy} = \frac{N\sum XY - \sum X \sum Y}{N\sum Y^2 - (\sum Y)^2}$$ and

X – intercept $$a_{xy} = \frac{\sum X - b_{xy}\sum Y}{N}$$

**Problem 1:** Calculate the two equations of the regression lines:

| *X* | *Y* | *XY* | *X²* | *Y²* |
|---|---|---|---|---|
| 118 | 66 | 7788 | 13924 | 4356 |
| 99 | 50 | 4950 | 9801 | 2500 |
| 118 | 73 | 8614 | 13924 | 5329 |
| 121 | 69 | 8349 | 14641 | 4761 |
| 123 | 72 | 8856 | 15129 | 5184 |
| 98 | 54 | 5292 | 9604 | 2916 |
| 131 | 74 | 9694 | 17161 | 5476 |
| 121 | 70 | 8470 | 14641 | 4900 |
| 108 | 65 | 7020 | 11664 | 4225 |
| 111 | 62 | 6882 | 12321 | 3844 |
| 1148 | 655 | 75915 | 132810 | 43491 |

$$b_{yx} = \frac{N\sum XY - \sum X \sum Y}{N\sum X^2 - (\sum X)^2}$$

$$= \frac{10 \times 75915 - 1148 \times 655}{10 \times 132810 - (1148)^2}$$

$$= 0.70714$$

$$a_{yx} = \frac{\sum Y - b_{yx}\sum X}{N}$$

$$= \frac{655 - 0.70714 \times 1148}{10} = -15.679$$

Equation to the regression line of Y on X is Y′ = 0.70714X – 15.679

$$b_{xy} = \frac{N\sum XY - \sum X\sum Y}{N\sum Y^2 - (\sum Y)^2}$$

$$= \frac{10 \times 75915 - 1148 \times 655}{10 \times 43791 - (655)^2}$$

$$= 1.22514$$

$$a_{xy} = \frac{\sum X - b_{xy}\sum Y}{N}$$

$$= \frac{1148 - 1.22514 \times 655}{10}$$

$$= 34.552761$$

The equation of regression line of X on Y is, X′ = 1.22514 Y + 34.5528

Calculate the estimated values of Y for the given values of X.

$$Y' = 0.71X - 15.68$$

| X | Estimated Value of Y |
|---|---|
| 118 | Y' = 0.71 × 118 – 15.68 = 68.1 |
| 99 | Y' = 0.71 × 99 – 15.68 = 54.61 |
| 118 | Y' = 0.71 × 118 – 15.68 = 68.1 |
| 121 | Y' = 0.71 × 121 – 15.68 = 70.23 |
| 123 | Y' = 0.71 × 123 – 15.68 = 71.65 |
| 98 | Y' = 0.71 × 98 – 15.68 = 53.9 |
| 131 | Y' = 0.71 × 131 – 15.68 = 77.33 |
| 121 | Y' = 0.71 × 121 – 15.68 = 70.23 |
| 108 | Y' = 0.71 × 108 – 15.68 = 61.00 |
| 111 | Y' = 0.71 × 111 – 15.68 = 63.13 |

In the given problem, X = 118. So substitute in equation, we can calculate the corresponding value of Y estimated value of Y → y1 from the equation by distribution for X. Thus Y = 0.71 × 118 – 15.68

For the above given problem, compute predicted values of X for the given Y values

X' = 1.22 Y + 34.55 is the equation to the regression line of X on Y.

| Y | Predicted value of X |
|---|---|
| 66 | X' = 1.22 × 66 + 34.55 = 115.07 |
| 50 | X' = 1.22 × 50 + 34.55 = 95.55 |
| 73 | X' = 1.22 × 73 + 34.55 = 123.61 |
| 69 | X' = 1.22 × 69 + 34.55 = 118. 73 |
| 72 | X' = 1.22 × 72 + 34.55 = 122.39 |
| 54 | X' = 1.22 × 54 + 34.55 = 100.43 |
| 74 | X' = 1.22 × 74 + 34.55 = 124.83 |
| 70 | X' = 1.22 × 70 + 34.55 = 119.95 |
| 65 | X' = 1.22 × 65 + 34.55 = 113.85 |
| 62 | X' = 1.22 × 62 + 34.55 = 110.19 |

**Problem 2: The following are paired measurements:**

| X | Y |
|---|---|
| 1 | 2 |
| 5 | 4 |
| 6 | 5 |
| 6 | 3 |
| 2 | 1 |

Compute (a) The correlation between X and Y.

(b) The slope of regression line for predicting X from a type of Y.

(c) The slope of regression line for predicting Y from a type of X.

(d) The regression equation for predicting a rare score as X from a row score as Y.

| X | Y | XY | $X^2$ | $Y^2$ |
|---|---|---|---|---|
| 1 | 2 | 2 | 1 | 4 |
| 5 | 4 | 20 | 25 | 16 |
| 6 | 5 | 30 | 36 | 25 |
| 6 | 3 | 18 | 36 | 9 |
| 2 | 1 | 2 | 4 | 1 |
| 20 | 15 | 72 | 102 | 55 |

(1) The correlation between X and Y is

$$r_{xy} = \frac{N\sum XY - \sum X \sum Y}{\sqrt{\left[N\sum X^2 - (\sum X)^2\right]\left[N\sum Y^2 - (\sum Y)^2\right]}}$$

$$= \frac{5\times 72 - 20\times 15}{\sqrt{(5\times 102 - 20^2)(5\times 55 - 15^2)}} = \frac{60}{\sqrt{110\times 50}} = 0.809$$

(2) The regression line for predicting X from a knowledge of Y is the regression line of X on Y i.e.

$$b_{xy} = \frac{N\sum XY - \sum X \sum Y}{N\sum Y^2 - (\sum Y)^2}$$

$$= \frac{5\times 72 - 20\times 15}{5\times 55 - (15)^2} = 1.2$$

(3) The slope of regression line for predicting Y from X is, the slope of Y′

$$= b_{yx} X + a$$

$$b_{yx} = \frac{N\sum XY - \sum X \sum Y}{N\sum X^2 - (\sum X)^2}$$

$$= \frac{5\times 72 - 20\times 15}{5\times 102 - 400} = 0.5455$$

(4) The regression equation for predicting a raw score of X from a raw score of Y is,

$$X' = b_{xy} Y + a_{xy}$$

(5) Here $$a_{xy} = \frac{\sum X - b_{xy}\sum Y}{N}$$

$$= \frac{20 - 1.2 \times 15}{5} = 0.4$$

Therefore, the regression equation for predicting X is X' = 1.2Y + 0.4

**Relation of Regression to Correlation**

If all points in a scatter diagram fall exactly along a straight line the two regression lines coincide. ie. when there is perfect relationships the two lines coincide. When this is not so the two regression lines have an angular separation. When the degree of relationship between the variables decreases, the angular separation between the two lines increases.

Thus we can see that a relationship between r and the slopes of the two regression lines. Hence the following formula

(1) $$b_{yx} = \frac{r\sigma_y}{\sigma_x}$$

(2) $$b_{xy} = \frac{r\sigma_x}{\sigma_y}$$

From these two equations, we can see that $b_{yx} = r^2$ i.e. $r = \sqrt{b_{yx}.b_{xy}}$
Using these formulae, equation to the two regression lines are

(1) The line of Y on X is, $$Y' = \frac{r\sigma_y}{\sigma_x}(X - \bar{X}) + \bar{Y}$$

(2) The line of X on Y is, $$X' = \frac{r\sigma_x}{\sigma_y}(Y - \bar{Y}) + \bar{X}$$

These two equations are known as equations in the deviation score form.

From the data $\overline{X} = 40.3$; $\overline{Y} = 12.5$ $\sigma x = 12.6$ $\sigma y = 3.6$ and $r_{xy} = 0.60$, Find the regression equations for predicting Y from X and X from Y.

The regression equation for predicting Y from X is,

$$Y' = \frac{r\sigma_y}{\sigma_x}(X - \overline{X}) + \overline{Y}$$

$$Y' = 0.60 \times 3.6/12.6\,(X - 40.3) + 12.5$$

$$Y' = 0.17143\,(X - 40.3) + 12.5$$

The regression equation for predicting X from Y is,

$$X' = \frac{r\sigma_x}{\sigma_y}(Y - \overline{Y}) + \overline{X}$$

$$= 0.60 \times 12.6/3.6\,(Y - 12.5) + 40.3$$

$$X' = 2.1\,(Y - 12.5) + 40.3$$

If the measurements are represented in standard score form, the coefficient of correlation can be calculated by, $r = \frac{1}{N}\sum ZxZy$

Regression equation with standard measures are,

$$Zy' = r\,Zx$$

where Z′x, Z′y stands for the Z′x = r Zy i.e.,

predicted or estimated standard scores. Here, both the regression lines have the same slope and is equal to r, coefficient of correlation between the variables.

**Standard Error of Estimate**

The difference between an observed value and a predicted value is an error of estimate from the regression equations, Y–Y′ is an error of estimate of Y and X–X′ that of X. Perfect prediction is possible when error of estimate is zero. Hence variance of error of estimate or standard error of estimate is taken as a measure of the accuracy of estimate.

The variance of errors of estimate (in predicting Y from X) is, (variance means square of standard deviation)

$$Sy.x^2 = \sigma y.x^2 = \sum \frac{(Y-Y')^2}{N-1}$$

∴ Std error of estimate of Y, when X is given is,

$$Sy.x = \sigma y.x = \sqrt{\frac{\sum(X-X')^2}{N-1}}$$

Secondly, std error of estimate of X when given Y is

$$Sx.y = \sigma x.y = \sqrt{\frac{\sum(X-X')^2}{N-1}}$$

Error of estimate in terms of r

$\sigma y.x = \sigma y \sqrt{1-r^2}$ when r = 0, sy.x = sy, no meaning for prediction

$\sigma x.y = 6 \times \sqrt{1-r^2}$ when r = 1, sy.x = sx.y = 0

**e.g.:** (1) Given the following data for two tests:

| History (X) | English (Y) |
|---|---|
| $M_x = 75$ (60) | $M_y = 70$ (75) |
| 6x = 6 | 6y = 8.00 |

$r_{xy} = 0.72$

(a) Work out the regression equations in score form

(b) Predict the probable grade in English of a student whose history mark is 65. Find the standard error of estimate of this prediction (0.92)

(c) If $r_{xy}$ had been 0.84 (σ's and M's are the same) what is the standard error of estimate?

Ans: (a) Y′ = 0.96 X – 2.00; X′ = 0.54 Y + 37.2

(b) Y? = 0.96 X – 2.00 = 60.4 $S_{y.x} = \sigma y \sqrt{1-r^2}$

$= 8\sqrt{1-(0.72)^2} = 5.55$

(c) $S_{y.x} = 8\sqrt{1-(0.84)^2} = 4.34$

(2) Standard scores on variables X for four individuals are –2.0, –1.68, 0.18 and 1.16. $r_{xy} = 0.5$. what are the estimated standard scores on Y?

(3) What is the standard error in estimating standard scores on Y from standard scores on X?

$S_{y.x} = \sigma y\ \sqrt{1-r^2}$ . Here a set of standard scores are given. Their mean = 0, standard deviation = 1 always.

r = 0.5 $\therefore S_{y.x} = 1\sqrt{1-0.5^2} = 0.866$

(4) A variance $Sy^2 = 400$ and $r_{xy} = 0.5$. What is the variance of errors of estimation in predicting Y from X?

Given, $Sy^2 = 400$ $r_{xy} = 0.5$. we have to find $S_{y.x}$.

↓

$Sy = 20$ $S_{y.x.} = 20\ \sqrt{1-(0.72)^2} = 17.32$

$S_{y.x}{}^2 = 17.32^2 \gg 300$

(5) Explain the term correlation and regression. Set up the regression equation

(a) for Y on X and (b) X on Y

| X: | 6 | 9 | 12 | 15 | 18 |
|---|---|---|---|---|---|
| Y: | 18 | 10 | 24 | 20 | 28 |

(b) Given the following data on two tests:

| Maths (x) | Reading (y) |
|---|---|
| Mean = 50 | Mean = 60 |
| SD = 10.00 | S.D. = 8 |
| r = 0.05 | |

Work out regression equations in score form and also predict the probable scores in reading of a boy whose scores in mathematics is 40.

# XI
# Inferential Statistics

## 11.1 SAMPLING

Statistics is the study of population. It deals with the collection, classification, description and interpretation of data obtained by the conduct of surveys and experiments. Its essential purpose is to describe and draw inferences about the numerical properties of population.

In every day language the term 'population' is used to refer to groups or aggregates of people. But to a statistician the term population refers not only to a defined group of people, but also to define groups or aggregates of animals, objects, materials, measurements and happenings of any kind.

The statistician's concern is with properties which are descriptive of the group rather than with properties of particular members.

Population can be finite or infinite. When the number of a population can be counted and a finite number obtained, the population is infinite. When the number of members are not countable, it is an infinite population. In many situations the population the statistician proposes to describe are finite but so large that for all practical purposes they may be regarded as infinite.

Because of the large size of many populations, it may be either impracticable or impossible for the investigator to produce statistics based on all members. So the investigator draws a sample from a population.

A sample is any subgroup or sub aggregates drawn by some appropriate method from a population. The method used is important. Having drawn the sample, the investigator utilizes appropriate statistical methods to describe its property. He then proceeds to make statements about the properties of the population from his knowledge of the properties of the sample i.e., he proceeds to generalize from the sample to the population.

The fact that inferences can be made about the properties of population from a knowledge of properties of samples is basic in research thinking. Such statements are of course subject to error. The magnitude of the error involved in drawing such inferences can in most cases be estimated by appropriate procedures. Where no standard error of any kind can be made, generalization about population form sample data are worthless.

## 11.2 METHOD OF SAMPLING

In drawing inferences about the characteristics of population, from sample statistics, the assumption is frequently made that the sample should be drawn at random from the population. The word random is used in a theoretical sense and in operational sense. In theoretical sense, the word refer to an assumption about the equii-probability of events i.e., a random sample is one such that every member of the population has an equal probability of being included in it.

The word random in operational sense is used to describe certain operation of method (i.e., the drawing of members from a container after they have been thoroughly mixed or drawing of cards from a deck after they have been shuffled).

**Mode of Selection**

1. Use a table of random numbers. This is the more convenient form. Label the members of population at first. Then draw the members directly from a table of random numbers. i.e., to use the table of random numbers in getting a sample of 50 from a line of 3000 students, assign each student a number between 1 and 3000. Then go to the random number table and mentally block the table off to convenient columns. Read down the columns until you obtain 50 number that fall between 1 and 3000. The students assigned corresponding to these 50 members constitute a randomly selected sample.
2. When the members of population are listed, all the names of some odd number be entered on slips of paper. Place these in a container and mix it well. Then draw sufficient number of slips. The names of the slips identify the sample (this method is also known as Lottery method).

3. If a list is arranged alphabetically or in some other systematic fashion every n'th name may be chosen in the construction of the sample.

   This is sometimes known as systematic sampling. Forms of modified random sampling are sometime used.
4. Stratified Sampling: This requires prior knowledge about the strata of the population in constructing the sample and the members are drawn at random from the various strata.

   If the members are drawn such that the proportions in the various strata in the sample are the same as proportion in those strata in the population, the sample is proportionate stratified sample.

## 11.3 SAMPLING DISTRIBUTION

Even when a sample is random, it is likely to be different from the population. Samples of a population may also differ just because they are composed of different individuals.

Suppose we draw several samples from a population and statistics (say, mean, σ, etc.) are computed for each of these samples. Then the distribution of each of these statistics is called a sampling distribution of the statistic computed. Since mean is a statistic the distribution of the means of several samples of a population forms a sampling distribution of the mean.

### Standard Error

Just as a distribution scores has certain characteristics (mean and variance) so too does a sampling distribution. The standard deviation of a sampling distribution of a statistic is called the standard error of that statistic.

Hence the standard deviation of the sampling distribution of mean is known as the standard error of the mean. This is denoted or SE, $\sigma_{\bar{x}}$, SE ($\bar{x}$).

### Sampling Error

The statistics of one sample may not be equal to the statistics of other sample from a population.

**e.g.:** Mean of a sample will not be equal to the mean of other samples taken from the same population even though samples are selected randomly from the population. The fact that means differ in value from one sample to another justify the fact that there is variability in such a distribution of means. Since standard deviation is the most appropriate index of variability, the standard deviation of sampling distribution of means. $\sigma_{\bar{x}}$ is a numerical index of the extent to which means will vary from sample. More generally standard error is an index of the amount of sampling error with reference to a given statistic.

**Standard Error of the Mean**

The standard Error of the mean i.e., $\sigma_{\bar{x}}$ can be calculated by the formula.

$\sigma_{\bar{x}} = \dfrac{\sigma_x}{\sqrt{N}}$ where $\sigma x$ stands for the standard deviation of the population and N – sample size.

In cases when population standard deviation is unknown $\sigma \bar{x}$ is calculated by the formula, $\sigma \bar{x} = \dfrac{s_x}{\sqrt{N}}$

Where $s_x$ stands for standard deviation of the sample and N – sample size.

**Problem:** If the population standard deviation is as given below, what would be the standard error of sampling distribution of the mean for sample of size N?

(a) $\sigma_x = 12$ N = 16
(b) $\sigma_x = 10$ N = 25
(c) $\sigma_x = 8$ N = 36

a) $\sigma_{\bar{x}} = \dfrac{\sigma_x}{\sqrt{N}} = \dfrac{12}{\sqrt{16}} = \dfrac{12}{4} = 3$

(b) $\sigma_{\bar{x}} = \dfrac{\sigma_x}{\sqrt{N}} = \dfrac{10}{5} = 2$

(c) $\sigma_{\bar{x}} = \dfrac{\sigma_x}{\sqrt{N}} = \dfrac{8}{6} = \dfrac{4}{3} = 1.33$

## 11.4 APPLICATION OF THE CONCEPT OF STANDARD ERROR

**Sampling Distribution and Normality:**

Given random sampling, the sampling distribution of the mean (1) is a normal distribution if the population distribution of raw scores is normal (2) approaches a normal distribution if the size of the sample is large.

The degree to which a sample mean represents its parameter is an index of the significant or trustworthiness of the computed sample mean. Therefore, when we have calculated a statistic, we may ask ourselves a question how good an estimate is if the statistic of the parameter is based upon the entire population from which the sample was drawn. The answer to this question depends on the standard error.

Estimation of a parameter by means of a statistic can be done in two ways. (1) point estimation and (2) interval estimation. A point estimate is the value obtained by direct calculation of the sample values. e.g.—If in a particular sample, $\overline{X} = 26.38$. This is a point estimate of the population.

Fixing up an interval with given degree of confidence within which the population mean may lie is the process of interval estimation.

If the sample taken is large, the sampling distribution will follow a normal distribution and hence we can say 68.26 per cent of the statistic will be within $\pm$ 1 SE of the statistic from the parameter 95.44 per cent of the statistic will be within $\pm$ 1.96 SE of the static from the parameter. 99.74 per cent of the statistic will lie within $\pm$ 2.58 SE of the statistic from the parameter.

i.e., If there are 100 sample, and hence 100 sample means, then, (1) 68 per cent sample means will not miss the population mean by $\pm 1\, \sigma_{\bar{x}}$ of mean. (2) 95 of 100 sample means will not miss the population mean by $\pm$ 1.96 × SE of the mean (3) 99 of 100 sample means will not miss the population mean by $\pm$ 2.58 SE of the mean.

Stated in terms of probability, these will become (1) the probability is 0.68 that our sample mean does not miss the population mean by $\pm$ 1 S.E. of the mean (2) the probability is 0.95 that the sample mean does not miss the population mean by $\pm$ 1.96 × SE of the mean. (3) the probability is 0.99 that our sample mean does not miss the population mean by $\pm$ 2.58 × S.E. of the mean or (1) the probability is 0.05 level, that our single mean misses the population mean by $\pm$ 1.96 × S.E. of mean. (2) the probability is 0.01 that our sample mean misses the population mean by $\pm$ 2.58 S.E. of mean.

Two confidence intervals are in general use and are accepted by most statisticians. There are the 0.95 confidence interval and 0.99 confidence interval.

We know that 95 per cent of the cases in a normal distribution form within the limit, $\pm 1.96\,\sigma_{\bar{x}}$ and hence 0.95 confidence interval of the population mean is ($\bar{X} \pm 1.96\,\sigma_{\bar{x}}$) when $\bar{X}$ is the sample mean.

Similarly, since 99 per cent of the cases form within the limit $\pm$ 2.58 $\sigma_{\bar{x}}$ the 0.99 confidence interval of population mean is ($\bar{X} \pm 2.58\,\sigma_{\bar{x}}$).

The limits of the confidence interval of a parameter have been called as fiduciary limits and the confidence placed in the interval defined by the limits, or containing the parameter is called the fiduciary parameter and thus,

1. The probability is 0.95 that the population mean lies within the interval ($\bar{X} \pm 1.96\,\sigma_{\bar{x}}$) or the probability is 0.05 that the population mean falls outside the interval ($\bar{X} \pm 1.96\,\sigma_{\bar{x}}$).
2. The probability is 0.99 that the mean population lies within the interval ($\bar{X} \pm 2.58\,\sigma_{\bar{x}}$) or the probability is 0.01 that the population mean fall outside the interval ($\bar{X} \pm 2.58\,\sigma_{\bar{x}}$).

(1) Given M = 26.40; s = 5.20; N = 100

(a) Compute the 0.95 confidence interval and 0.99 confidence interval of the mean.

$$\sigma_{\bar{x}} = \frac{\sigma}{\sqrt{N}} = \frac{5.2}{\sqrt{100}} = \frac{5.2}{10} = 0.52$$

0.95 confidence interval is, $\bar{X} \pm 1.96\,\sigma_{\bar{x}}$

i.e., (26.4 + 1.96 × 0.52) = 27.4192

(26.4 – 1.96 × 0.52) = 25.3808

Therefore, the 0.95 confidence interval of the mean is, 25.3808 to 27.4192

**0.99 Confidence Interval** $\overline{X} \pm 2.58\,\sigma_{\bar{x}}$

$$26.4 - 2.58 \times 0.52 = 25.0584$$

$$26.4 + 2.56 \times 0.52 = 27.7416$$

Therefore, 0.99 confidence interval is, (25.0584, 27.7416)

For a given group of 500 soldiers, the mean score is 95 and standard deviation is 25. Determine the 0.99 interval for the true mean.

0.99 confidence interval is, $\sigma_{\bar{x}} = \frac{25}{\sqrt{500}} = 1.198$

$(\overline{X} \pm 2.58\,\sigma\overline{x})$ i.e.,

$(95 - 2.58 \times 1.118,\ \ 95 + 2.58 \times 1.118)$

i.e., (92.1156, 97.884)

**Standard Error of the Mean for Small Samples**

When sample is small, the sampling distribution of mean does not follow normal distribution and will follow a student's t-distribution. Standard Error of the mean is given by the formula.

$$\sigma\overline{x} = \frac{s}{\sqrt{N}} \qquad \text{where, } s = \sqrt{\frac{\sum x^2}{N-1}}$$

Here the degrees of freedom is N–1

**Problem:** 10 measures of reaction time to light are taken from a practiced observer. The mean is 175.50 milliseconds and standard deviation is, 5.82 milliseconds. Determine the 0.95 confidence interval and 0.99 confidence interval of the population mean.

$$N = 10,\ s = 5.82,\ \overline{X} = 175.50$$

$$\sigma\overline{x} = \frac{s}{\sqrt{N}} = \frac{5.82}{\sqrt{10}} = 1.84$$

Here degrees of freedom is 10 – 1 = 9

From Table of t-distribution, for 9 degrees of freedom and for the probably level. 0.05, the value is 2.262. for the probability level 0.01, value = 3.250. The 0.95 confidence interval of the population mean is

$(\overline{X} \pm 2.26\ \sigma_{\bar{x}})$
$(175.5 - 2.26 \times 1.84, 175.5 + 2.26 \times 1.84)$
i.e., (171.342, 179.658)
0.99 confidence interval is,

$(\overline{X} \pm 3.25\,\sigma_{\bar{x}})$
i.e., $(1755 - 3.25 \times 1.84, \quad 175.5 + 3.25 \times 1.84)$
i.e., (169. 52, 181.48)

(1) The mean of 16 independent observations of a certain sample is 100 and standard deviation is 24.
   (a) At the 0.05 confidence interval, what are the fiduciary limits of the true mean?
   (b) Taking the 0.99 confidence interval as our standard we may be assumed that the true mean is at least as large as what value?

(a) $N = 16,\ \overline{X} = 100,\ s = 24$

$$\sigma_{\bar{x}} = \frac{s}{\sqrt{N}} = \frac{24}{\sqrt{10}} = 6$$

Degrees of Freedom 16 – 1 = 15

From Table, for 15 degrees of freedom, for the probability 0.05, value is 2.131 and for 0.01 level value is, 2.947.

(a) Fiduciary limits at 0.05 level is

$(\overline{X} \pm 2.131\ \sigma_{\bar{x}})$
i.e., $(100 - 2.131 \times 6, 100 + 2.131 \times 6)$
i.e., (87.214, 112.786)

(b) The confidence interval at 0.01 level

$(\overline{X} \pm 2.947\,\sigma_{\bar{x}})$. Here we have to calculate the large value of the mean.

i.e., $\overline{X} + 2.947 \times 6 = 100 + 2.947 \times 6 = 117.682$
So the true mean can be as large as 117.682.

**Standard Error of Random Sample**

| | *Large sample* | *Small sample* |
|---|---|---|
| (1) $\sigma_{\bar{x}}$ | $\sigma/\sqrt{N}$ | $\frac{S}{\sqrt{N}}$ with N-′1df and $S = \sqrt{\frac{\sum x^2}{N-1}}$ |
| (2) $s_{Mdn}$ | (i) $\frac{1.253\sigma}{\sqrt{N}}$ (ii) $\frac{1.858\ Q}{\sqrt{N}}$ | |
| (3) $s_{\sigma}$ | $\frac{0.71\sigma}{\sqrt{N}}$ | |
| (4) $s_Q$ | (i) $\frac{0.786\sigma}{\sqrt{N}}$, (ii) $\frac{1.17Q}{\sqrt{N}}$ | |
| (5) $\sigma\%$ | $\sqrt{\frac{PQ}{N}}$ where P is the percent of occurrence of the behaviour and Q is 100–P | |
| (6) $s_r$ | (i) $\frac{1-r^2}{\sqrt{N}}$ * where r is the coefficient of correlation in the population (ii) ** test against the null hypotheses (r = 0) compare the sample 'n' with the tabled value of r for N–2 df and for the required level of probability. | |

**Note:**

1. Standard error of median $s_{Mdn} = 1.25\,\sigma_{\bar{x}}$, this shows that mean is more dependable than the median.
2. When N< 25 the sampling distribution of s is skewed. i.e., the distribution is normal only when N>25.
3. $\sigma_{\sigma} = 0.71\,\sigma_{\bar{x}}$

4. Sampling distribution of percent is normal when N>50 and when p lies between 5 percent and 95 percent.
5. There are two serious objection to this formula
   (a) The 'r' in this formula is population. since this r is not known, r in the sample is to be substantiated. Therefore, if our sample is in error, $s_r$ will also be in error.
   (b) The sampling distribution of r is not normal except when r = 0 and N is large. When $r \geq 0.80$, (high correlation) and N is small, the sampling distribution of r is skewed. And the standard error from this formula is quite misleading. This is true also when $r \leq 0.20$.
6. The function of z has two advantages over r
   (i) Its sampling distribution is approximately normal.
   (ii) Its standard error depends upon the size of the sample and is independent of r. This formula is specially useful when r is very high or very low.
7. If the computed r is large enough this procedure is good. This test does not consider the size of r. This test is especially useful when N is small.

**Problem:** In a study of cheating, among elementary school children, 44 or 41.4 per cent of the 348 children from homes of high SES were found to have cheated on various tests. Assuring our sample is to be representation of children from good homes, how much confidence can be placed in this percentage? How well does it represent the population percentage?

$P = 41.4\%$

$Q = 100 - P = 100 - 41.4 = 58.61\%$

$$s\% = \sqrt{PQ/N} = \sqrt{\frac{41.4 \times 58.6}{348}} = 2.6\%$$

Since the sample is large, the 0.99 confidence interval of the population percentage is

Given sample percentage $\pm$ 2.58 σ%

i.e., $(41.4 \pm 2.58 \times 2.6)$

i.e., $(41.4 \pm 6.708)$

i.e., (34.64, 48.20)

Thus the probability is 0.99 that the population percent lies within the limits 34.6 and 48.2 i.e., The population percentage can be at least 34.6 and as large as 48.2.

**Significance of the Coefficient of Correlation**

(1) Given an r of 0.45 based upon 60 cases.

(a) Find the $s_r$, determine the limits of the 0.99 confidence interval for the population r.

*I. Method*

$$\sigma r = \frac{1-r^2}{\sqrt{N}} = \frac{1-0.45^2}{\sqrt{60}} = 0.103$$

the limits of 0.99 confidence interval is $(r \pm 2.58 \times 0.103)$
i.e., $(0.45 \pm 2.58 \times 0.103)$
i.e., (0.185, 0.715)
From the table of Fischer's z the equivalent of r = 0.45 is 0.48

The standard error of z is, $\frac{1}{\sqrt{N-3}}$

$$\sigma_z = \frac{1}{\sqrt{60-3}} = 0.1324$$

The 0.99 confidence interval of r is $(z \pm 2.58 \times 0.132)$
i.e., $(0.48 \pm 2.58 \times 0.132)$
i.e., (0.139, 0.820)
0.99 confidence interval of r is (0.1384, 0.675)

*II. Method*

(58 degrees of freedom corresponding to 0.01 level of probability)

For N – 2 df, i.e., 60 – 2 = 58df, and for 0.01 level of probability. The value of r from the table is 0.325.

(If the given statistic is less than the tabled value, it is not significant).

The given coefficient of correlation is 0.45 > 0.325 which is the tabled value of r.

i.e., ∴ the given r is significant at 0.01 level of significance.

(1) Using a large sample procedure estimate for the following data the 0.95 and 0.99 percent confidence interval for means.

| | $\overline{X}$ | N | $\Sigma(X-\overline{X})^2$ |
|---|---|---|---|
| a | 26.2 | 7 | 77 |
| b | 58.3 | 11 | 249.0 |
| c | 46.3 | 25 | 1.525 |
| d | 8.4 | 16 | 444.7 |

(a) For the first case, $\overline{X} = 26.2$ and $N = 7$, $Sx^2 = 77$

$$\text{for large sample } \sigma = \sqrt{\frac{\sum x^2}{N}} = \sqrt{\frac{77}{7}} = 3.3166$$

$$\sigma x = \frac{\sigma}{\sqrt{N}} = \frac{3.32}{\sqrt{7}} = 1.255$$

0.95 confidence interval is $(\overline{X} \pm 1.96\,\sigma_{\bar{x}})$
i.e., $(26.2 \pm 1.96 \times 1.255)$
i.e., (23.74, 28.6598)

0.99 confidence interval is, $(\overline{X} \pm 2.58\,\sigma_{\bar{x}})$
i.e., $(26.2 \pm 2.58 \times 1.255)$
i.e., (22.962, 29.438)

(b) $\overline{X} = 58.3$ $N = 11$ $\Sigma(X - \overline{X})^2 = 249$

$$\sigma = \sqrt{\frac{\sum x^2}{N}} = \sqrt{\frac{249}{11}} = 4.758$$

$$\sigma_{\bar{x}} = \frac{\sigma}{\sqrt{N}} = \frac{4.758}{\sqrt{11}} = 1.435$$

0.95 confidence interval is, $(\overline{X} \pm 1.96\,\sigma_{\bar{x}})$
i.e., $(58.3 \pm 1.96 \times 1.435)$
i.e., (55.487, 61.113)

0.99 confidence interval is, $(\overline{X} \pm 2.58\,\sigma_{\bar{x}})$

i.e., (58.3 $\pm$ 2.58 × 1.435)
i.e., (54.598, 62.00)

(c) $\overline{X} = 46.3 \quad N = 25 \quad \Sigma(X - \overline{X})^2 = 1.525$

$$\sigma = \sqrt{\frac{\sum x^2}{N}} = \sqrt{\frac{1.525}{25}} = 0.2469$$

$$\sigma_{\bar{x}} = \frac{\sigma}{\sqrt{N}} = \frac{0.2469}{\sqrt{25}} = 0.0494$$

0.95 confidence interval is, ($\overline{X} \pm 1.96\,\sigma_{\bar{x}}$)
i.e., (46.3 $\pm$ 1.96 × 0.0494)
i.e., (46.203, 46.3968)

0.99 confidence interval is, ($\overline{X} \pm 2.58\,\sigma_{\bar{x}}$)
i.e., (46.173, 46.427)

(d) $\overline{X} = 8.4 \qquad N = 16 \quad \Sigma x^2 = 444.7$

$$s = \sqrt{\frac{\sum x^2}{N}} = \sqrt{\frac{444.7}{16}} = 5.272$$

$$\sigma_{\bar{x}} = \frac{\sigma}{\sqrt{N}} = \frac{5.272}{\sqrt{16}} = 1.318$$

0.95 confidence interval is, ($\overline{X} \pm 1.96 \times \sigma_{\bar{x}}$)
i.e., (8.4 $\pm$ 1.96 × 1.318)
i.e., (5.817, 10.983)

0.99 confidence interval is, ($\overline{X} \pm 2.58\,\sigma_{\bar{x}}$)
i.e., (8.4 $\pm$ 2.58 × 1.318)
i.e., (4.999, 11.800)

(2) Using a large sample procedure obtain the 95 and 99 per cent confidence interval for a mean of 105 where N = 100 and S = 10. Obtain also the 75 and 85 per cent confidence intervals.

$$S = 10 \quad N = 100 \quad \therefore \sigma_{\bar{x}} = \frac{S}{\sqrt{N}} = \frac{10}{10} = 1$$

0.95 confidence interval is, $(\overline{X} \pm 1.96\ \sigma_{\bar{x}})$
i.e., $(105 \pm 1.96 \times 1)$
i.e., (103.04, 106.96)

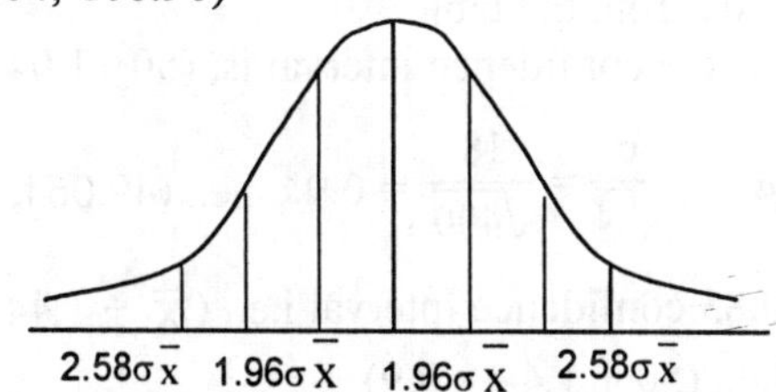


0.99 confidence interval is, $(\overline{X} \pm 2.58\,\sigma_{\bar{x}})$
i.e., $(105 \pm 2.58 \times 1)$
i.e., (102.42, 107.58)

To find 75 per cent of the confidence interval of the mean, by theory, the cut off points of the 75 per cent confidence interval can be found from the table of areas and ordinates under a normal curve in such a way that 37.5 per cent of the area lies on either side of the ordinate at the mean of the sampling distribution of the mean. From the table, we can see that the limit points covering 37.5 per cent of the case on either sides of the mean are $-1.15\,\sigma_{\bar{x}}$ and $+1.15\,\sigma_{\bar{x}}$. Hence the 75 per cent confidence interval of the mean is $(\overline{X} \pm 1.15\,\sigma_{\bar{x}})$.

i.e., $(105 \pm 1.15\,\sigma_{\bar{x}})$ i.e., (103.85, 106.15)

To find 85 per cent confidence interval of the mean from the table of areas and ordinates under a normal curve, the limit points which include 85 per cent of the area are: (i.e., 42.5% of the area on either sides of the mean) are $-1.44\,\sigma_{\bar{x}}$ and $+1.44\,\sigma_{\bar{x}}$. So the 85% confidence interval of the mean is, $(\overline{X} \pm 1.44\,\sigma_{\bar{x}})$ i.e., $(105 \pm 1.44\,\sigma_{\bar{x}})$ i.e., (103.56, 106.44).

(1) A random sample of 400 observations has a mean of 50 and a standard deviation of 18. Estimate the 70 per cent,

85 per cent, 90 per cent, 95 per cent and 99 per cent confidence interval of the mean.

$$\overline{X} = 50 \quad \sigma = 18 \quad N = 400$$

(1) 0.70 confidence interval of the mean is, ($\overline{X} \pm 1.04\ \sigma_{\bar{x}}$) since 35 per cent of area corresponds to the limit 1.04 from the table.

∴, the confidence interval is, ($50 \pm 1.04 \times 0.9$)

$$\sigma_{\bar{x}} = \frac{\sigma}{\sqrt{N}} = \frac{18}{\sqrt{400}} = 0.9 \quad \text{i.e., } (49.064, 50.936)$$

(2) 0.85 confidence interval i.e., ($\overline{X} \pm 1.44\,\sigma_{\bar{x}}$) 0.425
i.e., ($50 \pm 1.44 \times 0.9$)
i.e., (48.704, 51.296)

(3) 0.90 confidence interval is, ($\overline{X} \pm 1.65\,\sigma_{\bar{x}}$)
i.e., ($50 \pm 1.65 \times 0.9$)
i.e., (48.52, 51.485)

(4) 0.95 confidence interval is, ($\overline{X} \pm 1.96\,\sigma_{\bar{x}}$)
i.e., ($50 \pm 1.96 \times 0.9$)
i.e., (48.24, 51.76)

(5) 0.99 confidence interval in ($\overline{X} \pm 2.58\,\sigma_{\bar{x}}$)
i.e., ($50 \pm 2.58 \times 0.9$)
i.e., (47.68, 52.32)

## 11.5 TESTS OF SIGNIFICANCE OF DIFFERENCE BETWEEN STATISTICS

A hypothesis is a tentative assumption put forward by the investigator which is to be tested and verified for its validity. Hypothesis can be stated either in declarative form or in null hypothesis.

**e.g.:** When there are two groups. A and B when we are comparing their achievement levels, if we say the groups A and B differ in their achievement is a hypothesis in the declarative form and when we say there is no difference between A and B with respect to achievement, then it is a hypothesis in the null form.

Sample means vary from sample to sample eventhough they are taken randomly from a population. i.e., there is an observed difference between means. Whether this difference is a real one i.e., a considerable one or due to sampling error only, this can be considered by the test of significance of difference between statistics.

**Levels of Significance**

The purpose of inferential statistics is to assist in making influence and judgments about what exists on the basis of partial evidence. This is accomplished by using probability. The level of significance is the probability value that form the boundary between rejecting or not rejecting the null hypothesis.

We have seen that for large samples the sampling distribution or statistic is normal and hence 95 per cent of the cases lie within $\pm 1.96\,\sigma_{\bar{x}}$ so also 99 per cent of cases. Within $\pm 2.58\,\sigma_{\bar{x}}$; i.e., 5 per cent of the cases lie outside the region of $\pm 1.96\,\sigma_{\bar{x}}$; 1 per cent of cases lie $\pm 2.58\,\sigma_{\bar{x}}$ outside. These two regions are called regions of rejection and they are counted in terms of the probability below 1.96 and 2.58 respectively. Then we may say for the 0.04 level of significance, the boundary between region of acceptance and region of rejection is 1.96 for a large sample. So also for the 0.01 level of significance. The boundary between the region of acceptance and rejection is 2.58 for a large sample.

The null hypothesis ($H_0$) can be stated in three ways

(1) $\mu_1 = \mu_2$, i.e., $\mu_1 - \mu_2 = 0$. In this case the alternative hypothesis ($H_1$) will be $\mu_1 \neq \mu_2$.

(2) $H_0 - \mu_1 \geq \mu_2$ then $H_1$, is $\mu_1 < \mu_2$ i.e., $\mu_1 - \mu_2 < 0$

(3) $H_0 - \mu_1 \leq \mu_2$ i.e., $H_1 \rightarrow \mu_1 > \mu_2$ or $\mu_1 - \mu_2 > 0$ where $\mu_1$ and $\mu_2$ are the parameters of two populations.

When $H_0$ is $\mu_1 = \mu_2$, critical region lies evenly on both sides of the normal distribution and hence test of significance in this case is called a two-tailed or two-sided test.

In the case of stating hypothesis in the form $H_0 - \mu_1 \geq \mu_2$ or $\mu_1 \leq \mu_2$. i.e., when we are indicating the direction of the difference, the critical regions falls only on either the left side or right side of distribution and hence test of significance in this case is called a one-tailed test or one-sided test.

| *One-tailed (Directional)* | *Two-tailed (Non-directional)* |
|---|---|
| (1) used for comparison of two groups<br>(2) when $H_0$ is $\mu_1 \geq \mu_2$ i.e., when $H_1$ is – $\mu_1 < \mu_2$ or $\mu_1 > \mu_2$.<br>(3) For large samples, the critical value for 0.05 level of significance is 1.65 and for 0.01 level of significance it is 2.33<br>(4) For small samples, refer the table of t-distribution with the degrees of freedom available for each case. | (1) used for comparison of two groups<br>(2) when $H_0 \rightarrow \mu_1 = \mu_2$ i.e., when $H_1$ $\mu_1 \neq \mu_2$.<br>(3) For large samples, the critical value for 0.05 level of significance is 1.96 and for 0.01 level of significance is 2.58.<br>(4) For small samples, refer the table of t-distribution for critical values under 0.05 and 0.01 level of significant against the df available in each case. |

## Errors in Hypothesis Testing

Two types of errors are possible. There are: (1) Type I error and (2) Type II error.

Type I error is rejecting $H_o$ when $H_o$ is true.

Type II error is accepting $H_0$ is when $H_0$ is false. The probability of type I error is denoted by '$\alpha$'. The probability of type II error by '$\beta$'.

Type I and Type II error can also be represented as follows.

| | $H_o$ is true | $H_1$ is true |
|---|---|---|
| Accept $H_1$ | $\alpha$ | Correct decision |
| Accept $H_0$ | Correct decision | $\beta$ |

***(A) Test of Significance of Difference between Means for Large Independent Samples:***

In this case, the critical region CR for difference between statistics is found by the formula, $CR = \frac{D}{SE_D}$ where D = difference between statistics. In the case of difference between means, the CR is calculated by the formula,

$$CR = \frac{\overline{X}_1 - \overline{X}_2}{\sqrt{\frac{\sigma_1^2}{N_1} + \frac{\sigma_2^2}{N_2}}}$$

If the CR is greater than or equal to $\pm 1.96$, the difference between means is said to be significant at the 5 per cent level of significance. i.e., at 0.05 level of significance. If C.R. is greater than or equal to 2.58, the difference is said to be significant at 0.01 level. For a one-tailed test, if the CR is $\geq 1.65$, the difference between means is said to be significant at 5 per cent level and if CR $\geq 2.33$ the difference between means is said to be significant at 0.01 level.

**Question:** In a study of abstract reasoning, a sample of 83 twelfth grade boys and a sample of 95, 12th grade girls scored as shown below on a test of abstract reasoning.

| *Sex* | *N* | *Mean* | *S.D* |
|---|---|---|---|
| Girls | 95 | 29.21 | 11.56 |
| Boys | 83 | 30.92 | 7.8 |

Test the significance of difference between means

$$\text{The critical ratio is } CR = \frac{\overline{X}_1 - \overline{X}_2}{\sqrt{\frac{\sigma_1^2}{N_1} + \frac{\sigma_2^2}{N_2}}}$$

$$CR = \frac{30.92 - 29.21}{\sqrt{\frac{(7.8)^2}{83} + \frac{(11.56)^2}{95}}}$$

$$= \frac{1.71}{1.463} = 1.169$$

The CR is not significant at 0.05 level and 0.01 level since the critical ratio is less than 1.96. The difference between means is not significant. Also CR < 1.65, the difference between means is not significant at 5 per cent level if we making use of a one-tailed test. Thus the test is not significant for one-tailed or two-tailed.

**(2)** On an arithmetic reasoning test, thirty one 10 year old boys and forty two 10 year old girls made the following scores. Is the mean difference of 4.58, in favour of the boys significant at the 0.05 level?

| *Sex* | *M* | *σ* | *N* |
|---|---|---|---|
| Boys | 40.39 | 8.69 | 31 |
| Girls | 35.81 | 8.33 | 42 |

$$CR = \frac{\overline{X}_1 - \overline{X}_2}{\sqrt{\frac{\sigma_1^2}{N_1} + \frac{\sigma_2^2}{N_2}}}$$

$$CR = \frac{40.39 - 35.81}{\sqrt{\frac{(8.69)^2}{31} + \frac{(8.33)^2}{42}}}$$

Let the null hypothesis ($H_0$) be, "there is no significant difference between the observed means of the two samples". The CR for large independent samples is

$$CR = \frac{4.58}{2.022} = 2.265$$

Since CR is greater than 1.96, the difference between means is in favour of boys and is significant at 0.05 level.

*One–Tailed Test*: In this case CR is greater than 1.65. So it is also significant at 0.05 level.

***(B) Test of Significance of Difference between Means for Small Independent Samples***

$$CR = \frac{M_1 - M_2}{\sqrt{\frac{\sum\left(X_1 - \overline{X}_1\right)^2 + \sum\left(X_2 - \overline{X}_2\right)^2}{N_1 + N_2 - 2}\left(\frac{N_1 + N_2}{N_1 N_2}\right)}}$$

$$= \frac{M_1 - M_2}{\sqrt{\frac{(N_1 - 1)S_1^2 + (N_2 - 1)S_2^2}{N_1 + N_2 - 2}\left(\frac{N_1 + N_2}{N_1 N_2}\right)}}$$

Here the df is, $N_1 + N_2 - 2$

**(1)** On an arithmetic reasoning test thirty one 10 year old boys and forty two 10 year old girls made the scores below

| *Sex* | *M* | $\sigma$ | *N* |
|---|---|---|---|
| Girls | 40.39 | 8.69 | 31 |
| Boys | 35.81 | 8.33 | 42 |

Using a small sample test, test whether the difference between means is significant or not.

$$CR = \frac{M_1 - M_2}{\sqrt{\frac{(N_1-1)S_1^2+(N_2-1)S_2^2}{N_1+N_2-2}\left(\frac{N_1+N_2}{N_1N_2}\right)}}$$

$$= \frac{4.58}{\frac{\sqrt{5110.43}}{71}\times 0.0561}$$

$$= \frac{4.58}{2.0088} = 2.279$$

The CR is significant at 0.05 level since it is greater than 2.00 (from table of t-distributions) for 71 degree of freedom. It is significant at 0.01 level of significance (2.65). comparing CR, with the tabled value, the difference between means is not significant at 0.01 level of significance.

***(C) Test of Significance of Difference between Means for Large Dependent Samples***

Here $$t = \frac{M_1 - M_2}{\sqrt{\frac{\sigma_1^2}{N_1}+\frac{\sigma_2^2}{N_2}-2r\frac{\sigma_1\sigma_2}{N_1N_2}}}$$

**(1)** Two groups of high school students are matched for M and s upon a group intelligence test. There are 58 subjects in group A and 71 in group B. The records of these two groups upon a battery of learning tests are as follows.

| | Group A | Group B |
|---|---|---|
| M | 48.62 | 53.61 |
| σ | 10.60 | 15.35 |
| N | 58 | 72 |

The correlation of the group intelligence test and the learning battery is the entire group from which A and B were drawn is 0.50. Is the difference between groups A and B significant at 0.05 level? At the 0.01 level? Since matched groups are dependent, the critical ratio is given by,

$$t = \frac{M_1 - M_2}{\sqrt{\frac{\sigma_1^2}{N_1} + \frac{\sigma_2^2}{N_2} - 2r\frac{\sigma_1\sigma_2}{N_1N_2}}}$$

Substituting the values,

$$t = \frac{48.52 - 53.61}{\sqrt{\frac{(10.60)^2}{58} + \frac{(15.35)^2}{72} - \frac{2 \times 0.5 \times 10.6 \times 15.35}{58 \times 72}}}$$

$$= \frac{-5.09}{\sqrt{\frac{(10.60)^2}{58} + \frac{(15.35)^2}{72} - 0.03896}}$$

$$= \frac{-5.09}{\sqrt{5.1708}} = 2.238$$

The t-value is –2.238

Since the CR is greater than 1.96, the difference between means is significant at 0.05 level. But the critical ratio (difference between means) is not significant at 0.01 level of significance since it is less than 2.58.

**(2)** At the beginning of school year the mean score of a group of 64, 6th grade children upon an educational achievement test, in reading was 45 with a s of 6. At the end of the school year the mean score on an equivalent form of the same test was 50 with a s of 5. The correlation between scores made on the initial and final testing was

0.60. Has the class made significant progress in reading during the year?

Given that, $N_1 = N_2 = 64$, $M_1 = 45$, $s_1 = 6$, $r = 0.60$, $M_2 = 50$, $\sigma_2 = 5$

Let the hypothesis be "let the mean scores at the end of the class is significantly higher than the mean scores at the beginning of the class" (Therefore we have to make use of a one-tailed test).

Critical Ratio is given by

$$t = \frac{M_1 - M_2}{\sqrt{\frac{\sigma_1^2}{N_1} + \frac{\sigma_2^2}{N_2} - 2r\frac{\sigma_1\sigma_2}{N_1N_2}}}$$

Substitute the values

$$t = \frac{45-50}{\sqrt{\frac{6^2}{64} + \frac{5^2}{64} - 2\times\frac{0.6\times 6\times 5}{64\times 64}}}$$

$$= \frac{-5}{\sqrt{0.5625 + 0.3906 - 0.008789}}$$

$$= \frac{-5}{\sqrt{0.9443}} = -5.1453$$

The difference between means is significant beyond 0.01 level of significance because the critical ratio is greater than 2.53 or 1.65.

Therefore the progress in means scores is significant at 0.05 level and at 0.01 level.

### *Test of Significance of Difference between Means for Small Dependent Samples*

*Problem:* 12 subjects are given 5 successive trials upon a digit symbol test of which only the scores for trials 1 and 5 are shown. Is the mean gain from initial to final trial significant?

| *Trial 1* | *Trial 5* | *D* |
|---|---|---|
| 50 | 62 | 12 |
| 42 | 40 | –2 |
| 51 | 61 | 10 |
| 26 | 35 | 9 |
| 35 | 30 | –5 |
| 42 | 52 | 10 |
| 60 | 68 | 8 |
| 41 | 51 | 10 |
| 70 | 84 | 14 |
| 55 | 63 | 8 |
| 62 | 72 | 10 |
| 38 | 50 | 12 |

Let the hypothesis be, "there is no difference between the mean scores of trial 1 (initial trial) and trial 5 (final trial)

$$D = \frac{96}{12} = 8$$

$SE_{\overline{D}} = \sqrt{\frac{\sum\left(D-\overline{D}\right)^2}{N\text{-}1}}$ the standard error of a mean = $\frac{\sigma}{\sqrt{N}}$ where

σ stands for the SD of the given set of scores. Therefore $SE_{\overline{D}}$ =

$\frac{\text{S.D. of D's}}{\sqrt{N}}$

When X is the given variable, $\sigma x = \sqrt{\frac{\sum\left(X-\overline{X}\right)}{N\text{-}1}}$

when the sample is small. In this techniques X = D, and $\overline{X} = \overline{D}$

$$\therefore \text{S.D. of D's} = \sqrt{\frac{\sum\left(D-\overline{D}\right)^2}{N-1}}$$

| $D-\bar{D}$ | $(D-\bar{D})^2$ |
|---|---|
| 4 | 16 |
| −10 | 100 |
| 2 | 4 |
| 1 | 1 |
| −13 | 169 |
| 2 | 4 |
| 0 | 0 |
| 2 | 4 |
| 6 | 36 |
| 0 | 0 |
| 2 | 4 |
| 4 | 16 |
| | 354 |

$$\text{S.D. of D's} = \sqrt{\frac{354}{11}} = 5.673$$

$$\text{S.E. of } \bar{D} = \frac{\text{S.D. of D's}}{\sqrt{N}}$$

$$= \frac{5.673}{\sqrt{12}}$$

$$= 1.63$$

The CR, $$t = \frac{\bar{D}}{S.E_{\bar{D}}}$$

$$= \frac{8}{1.63} = 4.90$$

Since the sample is small and N = 12 the CR follows students t-distribution with 11(12–1) degrees of freedom. Therefore to find the t values for 11 df, we have to refer the table of t. From the table of t, for 11 degrees of freedom and for 0.05 level of significance, the value of t is 2.20.

The obtained CR is greater than the tabled value of t at 0.05 level of significance and hence, we may say the difference between means of trial 1 and trial 5 is significant at 0.05 level of significance.

The tabled value of t for 11df and for 0.01 level of significance is, 3.11. Here also the obtained CR is greater than the tabled value of

t. and hence we may say the difference between mean scores of initial trial and final trial is significant at 0.01 level of significance.

**(3)** Two groups X and Y of VIIth grade children comes 72 in each group are paired child for age and score as form A of the Otis group intelligence scale. Three weeks later both groups are given form B of the same test. Before the second test, group X i.e., experimental group is praised for its performance on the first test and urged to try to better its score group Y, the controlled group is given the second test without comment. Will the incentive (praise) cause the final scores of group X and group Y to differ significantly. The relevant data are given below.

| | Group X | Group Y |
|---|---|---|
| (1) Number of students | 72 | 72 |
| (2) Mean scores on form A | 80.42 | 80.51 |
| (3) Standard deviation on form A | 23.61 | 23.46 |
| (4) Mean scores on form B | 88.63 | 83.24 |
| (5) Standard deviation on form B | 24.36 | 21.62 |
| Correlation between final scores | 0.65 | |

Let the hypothesis be, "there is no significant difference in the mean scores on form B of the intelligence test". Since form B of the intelligence test is given, after the incentive between the experimental group (group x) and the control group (Y).

Since the samples are matched pairs,

$$\text{CR} = \frac{M_1 - M_2}{\sqrt{\frac{\sigma_1^2}{N_1} + \frac{\sigma_2^2}{N_2} - 2r\frac{\sigma_1\sigma_2}{N_1N_2}}}$$

Here $M_1 = 88.63, M_2 = 83.24, \sigma_1 = 24.36, \sigma_2 = 21.62, r = 0.65$
Submitting these values, the CR is,

$$t = \frac{88.63 - 83.24}{\sqrt{\frac{(24.36)^2}{72} + \frac{(21.62)^2}{72} - \frac{2 \times 0.65 \times 24.36 \times 21.62}{72 \times 72}}}$$

$$= \frac{5.39}{\sqrt{8.2418 + 6.492 - 0.1321}} = \frac{5.39}{\sqrt{14.734 - 0.1321}}$$

$$= \frac{5.39}{\sqrt{14.602}} = 1.411$$

The CR, 1.411 is less than 1.96 or 2.58. The incentive will not cause any significant change on the final scores. Between group X and group Y, since t value is not significant at 0.05 level. It is not significant at form B of intelligence scores on X and Y at 0.01 level. Thus we can infer that the incentive given to the that experimental group does not cause a significant change in mean scores of group X than of Group Y.

***(D) Test of Significance of Difference between Percentages***

When $P_1$ and $P_2$ are the percentages of occurrence of certain behaviour, than critical ratio for the test of significance of difference between two percentages is calculated by the formula,

$$CR = \frac{P_1 - P_2}{\sqrt{PQ\left(\frac{1}{N_1} + \frac{1}{N_2}\right)}}$$

where P—the combined percentage for the population is calculated as

$$P = \frac{N_1P_1 + N_2P_2}{N_1 + N_2} \text{ and}$$

$$Q = 100 - P \text{ (}Q = 1 - P \text{ — when P is in proportion)}$$

**Problem:** In a study of cheating among elementary school children 144 or 41.4 per cent of 348 children from homes of good S.E.S. were found to have cheated on various tests. In the same study, 133 or 50.2 per cent of 265 children from homes of poor S.E.S. also cheated on the same test. Is there a true difference in the incident of cheating in these two groups?

Here $P_1 = 41.4\%$, $P_2 = 50.2\%$

$$P = \frac{N_1P_1 + N_2P_2}{N_1 + N_2}$$

$$= \frac{348 \times 41.4 + 265 \times 50.2}{348 + 265}$$

$$= \frac{27710.2}{613}$$

$$P = 5.20\%$$

$$\therefore Q = 100 - P = 54.8\%$$

$$\text{Critical ratio} = \frac{P_1 - P_2}{\sqrt{PQ\left(\frac{1}{N_1} + \frac{1}{N_2}\right)}}$$

$$= \frac{41.4 - 50.2}{\sqrt{45.2 \times 54.8\left(\frac{1}{348} + \frac{1}{265}\right)}}$$

$$= \frac{-8.8}{\sqrt{2476.96 \times 6.64714 \times 10^{-3}}}$$

$$= \frac{-8.8}{4.058}$$

$$CR = -2.17$$

Here the critical ratio is –2.17. The value exceeds 1.96. So the difference between percentage is significant at 5 per cent level. Since CR is less than 2.58; it is not significant at 1 per cent level.

*Note*: (This test is for uncorrelated samples)

**(1)** In a school of 500 pupils, 52.3 per cent are girls and in a second school of 300 pupils 47.7 per cent are girls. Is there a significant difference between the percentage of girls enrolled in two schools.

$N_1 = 500, N_2 = 300, P_1 = 52.3\%, P_2 = 47.7\%$

$$P = \frac{P_1N_1 + P_2N_2}{N_1 + N_2}$$

$$= \frac{52.3 \times 500 + 47.7 \times 300}{500 + 300}$$

$$= 50.58$$

$Q = 100–50.58 = 49.42$

$$\text{Critical Ratio} = \frac{P_1 - P_2}{\sqrt{PQ\left(\frac{1}{N_1} + \frac{1}{N_2}\right)}}$$

$$= \frac{52.3 - 47.7}{\sqrt{50.58 \times 49.42\left(\frac{1}{500} + \frac{1}{300}\right)}}$$

$$= \frac{4.6}{3.65}$$

$$CR = 1.26$$

The CR = 1.26. The value is less than both 1.96 and 2.58. So it is not significant at 5 per cent and 1 per cent levels of significance. There is not a significant difference between the percentage of girls enrolled in the two-schools.

The two groups are almost equal.

### *(E) Test of Significance of Difference between Two Correlations*

Let the given correlation coefficients be $r_1$ and $r_2$. To test the significance of the difference between $r_1$ and $r_2$, convert $r_1$ and $r_2$ to Fischer's z-functions. Let them be $z_1$ and $z_2$ respectively. Then the CR is calculated by

$$CR = \frac{z_1 - z_2}{\sqrt{\frac{1}{N_1 - 3} + \frac{1}{N2 - 3}}}$$

**(1)** The r between intelligence and achievement in the freshness class of college A is 0.40. for N = 147 and r between intelligence and achievement in the freshman class of college B is 0.60 for N = 125. Is the relationship between intelligence and achievement higher in college B than in College A?

$r_1 = 0.4$ $\quad N_1 = 147$ $\quad z_1 = 0.42$

$r_2 = 0.6$ $\quad N_2 = 15$ $\quad z_2 = 0.69$

"Let there is no significant difference"

$$CR = \frac{z_1 - z_2}{\sqrt{\frac{1}{N_1 - 3} + \frac{1}{N2 - 3}}}$$

$$= \frac{0.42 - 0.69}{\sqrt{\frac{1}{144} + \frac{1}{122}}} = -2.194$$

Since the value exçeeds 1.96, it is significant at 0.05 level. Thus the correlation differ significantly.

## 11.6 ANALYSIS OF VARIANCE (ANOVA)

This is one of the most powerful and most common tests employed in the social sciences and is suitable for interval/ratio level distributions. It is known either as ANOVA or as F-test. These tests are also known as single or one-way (when one criterion is used), as two-way (when two criteria are used), or as N-way (factorial) analysis when more criteria are used. It is called F-test after its creator, Sir R.D. Fischer.

ANOVA is similar to the t-test. The main characteristics and the advantage of the F-test over other tests is that it is employed when more than two variables are studied. It is a parsimonious test i.e., a single test that produces results which would otherwise have required several tests.

### Conditions/Basic Assumption of ANOVA

ANOVA is employed if certain condition are met. Three such conditions are:

1. *Independence*: that scores are independent from each other.
2. *Normality*: that scores are normally distributed.
3. *Homogeneity*: the variances are equal.

There are several types of ANOVA. The most common are one-way and two-way ANOVA. One way is employed when there is one-independent variable (factor) and one dependent. We are looking at whether the sample groups vary systematically in one way, or with regard to one aspect only.

| | | | Independent | Dependent |
|---|---|---|---|---|
| e.g.: | 1) | Factor | : Marital status — affect— | overall happiness |
| | | Levels | : Single, married, divorced | very happy, happy, unhappy, very unhappy |
| | 2) | Factor | : Gender ——affect—— | Scholastic Achievement |
| | | Male, female | | Very high, High, Moderate, Low, Very Low |
| i.e., | Effect of marital status on overall happiness,<br>Effect of gender on scholastic achievement. | | | |

A two way-ANOVA includes two criteria of classification as well as two independent variables and one dependent variable.

**e.g.:** Effect of Gender and Experience on Teaching Competence.
Effect of Social Class and Marital Status on Overall Happiness.

**Computing ANOVA**

ANOVA works on the following assumptions:

1. The total variation (TV) can split into two components—each of which has a certain source of variation: small components are the within-sample variation (WV) and between sample variation (BV) i.e., TV = WV + BV.
2. The samples are randomly selected.
3. The population is normally distributed.
4. The samples are independent.
5. The samples have a common variance.

F-test is computed by the formula,

$$F = \frac{\frac{BV}{k-1}}{\frac{WV}{N-k}} \qquad \dots (1)$$

(Total sample N – 1 = N – k + k – 1)
where k is the number of categories (groups) and N is the total sample

***Steps in Computation***

1. A table is set up with scores and squared scores for each group.

*Effect of Type of Text Book on Achievement*

| Group A | | Group B | | Group C | | Group D | | Group E | |
|---|---|---|---|---|---|---|---|---|---|
| $X_1$ | $X_1^2$ | $X_2$ | $X_2^2$ | $X_3$ | $X_3^2$ | $X_4$ | $X_4^2$ | $X_5$ | $X_5^2$ |
| 7 | 49 | 4 | 16 | 6 | 36 | 7 | 49 | 8 | 64 |
| 4 | 16 | 9 | 81 | 5 | 25 | 9 | 81 | 6 | 36 |
| 5 | 25 | 3 | 9 | 4 | 16 | 8 | 64 | 7 | 49 |
| 4 | 16 | 5 | 25 | 6 | 36 | 7 | 49 | 9 | 49 |
| 6 | 36 | 5 | 25 | 6 | 36 | 7 | 49 | 9 | 81 |
| $\Sigma X_1$= 26 | $\Sigma X_1^2$= 142 | $\Sigma X_2$= 26 | $\Sigma X_2^2$= 156 | $\Sigma X_3$= 27 | $\Sigma X_3^2$= 149 | $\Sigma X_4$= 38 | $\Sigma X_4^2$= 292 | $\Sigma X_5$= 39 | $\Sigma X_5^2$= 311 |

2. The sums for all columns (for scores and squared scores) are computed.
   i.e., the means of scores and squared scores are computed.
3. The total variation (TV) is computed by the formula

$$TV = \sum x^2 - \frac{\left(\sum x\right)^2}{N}$$

Where, $\sum x^2$ — is obtained by adding the squared scores of each group.

$\left(\sum x\right)^2$ — is obtained by squaring the sum of the scores of each group.

in the example, $TV = 1050 - \frac{24336}{25} = 76.56$

4. The values of WV are computed for the five groups by employing the above formula for each group separately and adding up the scores for each group.

$$WV = \sum x^2 - \frac{\left(\sum x\right)^2}{n}$$

Where n – the number of respondents in the group for which WV is computed.

For A: $WV = 142 - \frac{(26)^2}{5} = 6.8$

B: $WV = 156 - \frac{26^2}{5} = 20.8$

Thus WV = 6.8 + 20.8 + 3.2 + 3.2 + 6.8 = 40.8

5. The between-samples variation (BV) is computed by the formula

$$BV = TV - WV$$

i.e., BV = 76.56 – 40.8 = 35.76

6. k–1 which is the df for BV and N–k; the df for WV, are computed k is the no. of groups, N is the total sample.

i.e., k –1 = 5 –1 = 4

N – k = 25 – 5 = 20

$$\frac{W}{k-1} = \text{mean square for Between groups}$$

$$\frac{BV}{k-1} = \text{mean square for Within groups}$$

7. The values obtained above are substituted in formula (1) to obtain F-score.

$$F = \frac{BV/_{k-1}}{WV/_{N-k}} = \frac{35.76/_{4}}{40.8/_{20}} = 4.3824$$

The values obtained from the above computation are usually represented in a summary table, known as ANOVA summary table

*The ANOVA Summary Table*

| *Source of Variation* | *Sum of Squares* | *df* | *Mean Square* | *F* |
|---|---|---|---|---|
| Between groups (BV) | 35.76 | 4 | 8.94 | 4.3824 |
| Within groups (WV) | 40.80 | 20 | 2.04 | |
| Total | 76.56 | 24 | | |

8. *Interpretation of F:* Critical value of F is located from Table of F. df of BV is across the table and df for WV is down the left-hand column. If the F value is greater than critical value of F, the null hypothesis is rejected.

In our example, df for BV and WV are 4 and 20 respectively CVF at 0.05 level is 2.87. since our F value is > CVF, null hypothesis is rejected.

## Questions

I. An ANOVA summary table is given below: Fill the missing material and continue with the following questions.

| *Source of Variance* | *Sum of Squares* | *df* | *Mean Square* | *F* |
|---|---|---|---|---|
| Between groups (BV) | 39.636 | 3 | 13.212 | 6.25 |
| Within groups (WV) | 33.824 | 16 | 2.114 | |
| Total | 73.460 | 19 | | |

1. How many levels of the independent variable were there?
2. Assuming equal sample sizes, how many subjects were in each treatment condition?
3. What are the degrees of freedom for the F-ratio?
4. Assuming a = 0.05, what is the CVF required to reject the null hypothesis?
5. Can the null hypothesis be rejected in this case? Yes 6.25> 3.63
6. How should the F-ratio be reported according to APA style?

**Ans:** (1) Four levels; (2) 5; (3) 3, 16; (4) 3.63; (5) Yes since 6.25>3.63; 6) Publication manual of American Psychological Association (1994) recommended for reporting the results of an F-test as, F ($df_B$, $df_W$) = F, = 6.25, P < 0.05

II. Fill in the Blanks

| *Source of Variations* | *Sum of Squares* | *df* | *Mean Square* | *F* |
|---|---|---|---|---|
| Between groups (BV) | 12.450 | — | 6225 | |
| Within groups (WV) | — | 27 | — | |
| **Total** | **60.609** | **29** | | |

**One-Way ANOVA**

Consider an experiment involving k experimental treatments. Let the number of members in the k groups be $N_1, N_2, \ldots\ldots N_k$. Total number of members in all groups combined is, $N_1 + N_2 + \ldots N_k = N$.

**Sum of Measurements**

Group I: $X_{11}, X_{21}, X_{31} \ldots\ldots X_{N1}$ i.e., $\sum_{i=1}^{N} X_{i1}$

Group II: $X_{12}, X_{22}, X_{32} \ldots\ldots X_{N2}$ i.e., $\sum_{i=1}^{N} X_{i2}$

i.e., $\sum_{i=1}^{N} X_{ik}$

**Group Means:** $\overline{X}_1, \overline{X}_2, \ldots\ldots\ldots \overline{X}_k$ Grand mean = $\overline{X}$

Total variation in the data is represented by the sum of squares of deviations of all the observations from the grand man.

For the first group observations, sum of squares (SS) is,

$$\sum_{i=1}^{N} \left(X_{i1} - \overline{X}\right)^2$$

Total sum of squares may be divided into two parts:

1. Within groups –
2. Between groups –

**Components of Variance:** The variance of all scores in the data set regardless of experimental group is called the total variance. We can partition the total variance into two smaller components.

1. *Between group variance*: estimate of variance based upon variability between groups (index of the degree to which the independent is associated with differences among the subjects as well as some chance differences between the groups due to sampling error).
2. *Within group variance*: Estimate of variance based upon the variability within groups.

**Mean Squares**

Each sum of squares has an associated number of df.

1. Total sum of squares has N–1 df (one df is lost by taking deviation about the grand mean)
2. df associated with the within-groups, sum of squares is, $(N_1-1)+(N_2-1)+\ldots(N_k-1) = N-k$.
3. df associated with the between groups sum of squares is, k – 1, (we have k means)

$$\underset{\text{Total}}{N-1} = \underset{\text{within}}{(N-k)} + \underset{\text{between}}{(k-1)}$$

Sum of squares within group is, $s_w^2 = \dfrac{\sum_{j=1}^{k}\sum_{i=1}^{Nj}\left(Xij-\overline{X}_j\right)^2}{N-k}$

Sum of squares between group is, $s_b^2 = \sum_{j=1}^{k}\dfrac{N_j\left(\overline{X}_j-\overline{X}\right)^2}{k-1}$

To test the hypothesis, $H_o: \mu_1 = \mu_2$,

Find F – ratio $F = \dfrac{sb^2}{s_w^2}$

Test significance F ratio from the Table,

$$F = \frac{\text{between group variance}}{\text{within group variance}}$$

**Summary of ANOVA**

To test the significant difference between k mean using the analysis of variance, the following steps are involved

1. Partition the total sum of squares into two components—a within groups and a between-groups sum of squares, using the appropriate computation formulae.
2. Divide these sum of squares by the associated number of degrees of freedom to obtain $s_w^2$ and $s_b^2$ the within—and between—group mean squares.
3. Calculate F ratio $s_b^2/s_w^2$ and refer this to the Table of F. Consult the Table F associated with the numerator and with (k–1) df and with the denominator with N – k df.
4. If the probability of obtaining the observed F value is small, say, less than 0.05 or 0.01, under the null hypothesis rejected the hypothesis.

## 11.7 CHI-SQUARE ($\chi^2$) TEST

When a coin is tossed 200 times, the theoretical consideration lead us to expect 100 heads and 100 tails. But in practice, these results are rarely achieved. The quantity $\chi^2$ (a Greek letter, pronounced as chi-square) describes the magnitude of discrepancy between theory and observation. If c = 0, the observed and expected frequencies, the greater is the value of $\chi^2$. Thus $\chi^2$ affords a measure of the correspondence between theory the observation.

If $O_i$ ($I$ = 1, 2, ......, n) is a set of observed (experimental) frequencies and $E_i$ ($I$ = 1, 2, ......., n) is the corresponding set of expected (theoretical or hypothetical) frequencies, then $\chi^2$ is defined as

$$\chi^2 = \sum_{i-1}^{n}\left(\frac{(O_i - E_i)^2}{E_1}\right)$$

Where $\Sigma O_i = \Sigma E_i$ = N (total frequency) and degrees of freedom (*df*) = (n–1).

*Note*: (i) If $\chi^2 = 0$, the observed and theoretical frequencies agree exactly.

(ii) if $\chi^2 > 0$ they do not agree exactly.

**Degree of Freedom**

While comparing the calculated value of $\chi^2$ with the table value, we have to determine the degrees of freedom.

If we have to choose any four numbers whose sum is 50, we can exercise our independent choice for any three numbers only, the fourth being 50 minus the total of the three numbers selected. Thus, though we were to choose any four numbers, our choice was reduced to three because of one condition imposed. There was only one restraint on our freedom and our degrees of freedom where 4–1 = 3. If two restrictions are imposed, our freedom to choose will be further curtailed and degrees of freedom will be 4–2 = 2.

In general, the number of degrees of freedom is the total number of observations less the number of independent constraints imposed on the observations. Degree of freedom (*d.f.*) are usually denoted by $v$ (the letter 'nu' of the Greek alphabet).

Thus, $v = n - k$, where $k$ is the number of independent constraints in a set of data $n$ observations.

*Note*: (*i*) For a p × q contingency table (*p* columns and *q* rows), $v = (p-1)(q-1)$

(ii) In the case of a contingency table, the expected frequency of any class.

$$= \frac{\text{Total of row in which it occurs} \times \text{Total columns in which it occurs}}{\text{Total number of observations}}$$

$\chi^2$ test is one of the simplest and the most general test known. It is applicable to a very large number of problems in practice which can be summed up under the following heads:

(i) as a test of goodness of attributes

(ii) as a test of independence of attributes

(iii) as a test of homogeneity of independent estimates of population variance.

(iv) as a test of hypothetical value of the population variance $\sigma^2$.

(v) as a list to the homogeneity of independent estimates of the population correlation coefficient.

## Conditions for Applying $\chi^2$ Test

Following are the conditions which should be satisfied before $\chi^2$ test can be applied.

(a) N, the total number of frequencies should be large. It is difficult to say what constitutes largeness, but as an arbitrary figure, we may say that N should be at least 50, however, few the cells.

(b) No theoretical cell-frequency should be small. Here again, it is difficult to say what constitutes smallness, but 5 should be regarded as the very minimum and 10 is better. If small theoretical frequencies occur (i.e., $< 10$), the difficulty is overcome by grouping two or more classes together before calculating (O–E). It is important to remember that the number of degrees of freedom is determined with the number of classes after regrouping.

(c) The constraints on the cell frequencies, if any, should be linear.

*Note*: If any one of the theoretical frequency is less than 5, then we apply a correction given by F Yates, which is usually known as 'Yates correction for continuity', we add 0.5 to the cell frequency which is less tan 5 and adjust the remaining cell frequency suitably so that the marginal total is not changed.

## The $\chi^2$ Distribution

For large sample sizes, the sampling distribution of $\chi^2$ can be closely approximated by a continuous curve known as the chi-square distribution. The probability function of $\chi^2$ distribution is given by.

$$f(\chi^2) = c\,(\chi^2)^{(v/2-1)}\,e^{-x^2/2}$$

where $e = 2.71828$, $\nu$ = number of degrees of freedom; c = a constant depending only on $\nu$.

Symbolically, the degree of freedom are denoted by the symbol $v$ or by d.f. and are obtained b the rule $v = n - k$, where k refers to the number of independent constraints.

In general, when we fit a binomial distribution the number of degree of freedom is one less than the number of classes; when we fit a Poisson distribution the degrees of freedom are 2 less than the number of classes, because we use the total frequency and the arithmetic mean to get the parameter of the Poisson distribution. When we fit a normal curve the number of degrees of freedom are 3 less than the number of classes, because in this fitting we use the total frequency, mean and standard deviation.

If the data is given in a series of "n" number then degrees of freedom = n–1

In the case of Binomial distribution d.f. = n – 2

In the case of Poisson distribution d.f. = n – 2

In the case of Normal distribution d.f. = n – 3

## $\chi^2$ Test as a Test of Goodness of Fit

$\chi^2$ test enables us to ascertain how well the theoretical distributions such as Binomial, Poisson or Normal etc. fit empirical distributions, i.e., distributions obtained from sample data. If the calculated value of $c^2$ is less than the table value at a specified level (generally 5%) of significance, the fit is considered to be good i.e., the divergence between actual and expected frequencies is attributed to fluctuations of simple sampling. If the calculated value of $c^2$ is greater than the table value, the fit is considered to be poor.

### EXAMPLES

**Example 1:** The following table gives the number of accidents that took place in an industry during various days of the week. Test if accidents are uniformly distributed over the week.

| *Day* | *Mon* | *Tue* | *Wed* | *Thu* | *Fri* | *Sat* | *Total* |
|---|---|---|---|---|---|---|---|
| No. of Accidents | 14 | 18 | 12 | 11 | 15 | 14 | 84 |

**Let the Null Hypothesis $H_0$.** is, "The accidents are uniformly distributed over the week". Under this $H_0$, the expected frequencies

of the accidents on each of these days $= \frac{84}{6} = 14$.

| *Observed frequency O* | *14* | *18* | *12* | *11* | *15* | *14* |
|---|---|---|---|---|---|---|
| Expected frequency E | 14 | 14 | 14 | 14 | 14 | 14 |
| $(O_1\text{-}E_i)^2$ | 0 | 16 | 4 | 9 | 1 | 0 |

$$\chi^2 = \sum_{i-1}^{n}\left(\frac{(0_i - E_i)^2}{E_1}\right) = \frac{30}{14} = 2.1428$$

*Conclusion.* Table value of $\chi^2$ at 5 per cent level for (6 – 1 = 5d.f.) is 11.09.

Since the calculated value of $\chi^2$ is less than the tabulated value, $H_0$ is accepted i.e., the accidents are uniformly distributed over the week.

**Example 2.** A die is thrown 270 times and the results of these throws are given below:

| No. appeared on the die | 1 | 2 | 3 | 4 | 5 | 6 | Total |
|---|---|---|---|---|---|---|---|
| Frequency | 40 | 32 | 29 | 59 | 57 | 59 | 276 |

Test whether the die is biased or not.The Null hypothesis $H_0$. is "Die is unbiased".

Under this $H_0$, the expected frequencies for each digit is $\frac{276}{6} = 46$

To find the value of $\chi^2$

| O | 40 | 32 | 29 | 59 | 57 | 59 |
|---|---|---|---|---|---|---|
| E | 46 | 46 | 46 | 46 | 46 | 46 |
| $(O-E)^2$ | 36 | 196 | 289 | 169 | 121 | 169 |

$$\chi^2 = \sum_{i-1}^{n}\left(\frac{(0_i - E_i)^2}{E_1}\right) = \frac{980}{46} = 21.30$$

*Conclusion*: Tabulated value of $\chi^2$ at 5 per cent level of significance for (6–1 = 5) d.f. is 11.09. Since the calculated value of $\chi^2$ = 21.30 > 11.07 the tabulated value, $H_0$ is rejected i.e., die is not unbiased or die is biased.

**Example 3.** The following table shows the distribution of digits in numbers chosen at random from a telephone directory:

| Digits | 0 | 1 | 2 | 3 | 4 | 5 | 6 | 7 | 8 | 9 |
|---|---|---|---|---|---|---|---|---|---|---|
| Frequency | 1026 | 1107 | 997 | 966 | 1075 | 933 | 1107 | 972 | 964 | 853 |

Test whether the digits may be taken to occur equally frequently in the directory.

*Null hypothesis $H_0$*: The digits taken in the directory occur equally frequency. i.e., there is no significant difference between the observed and unexpected frequency. i.e., there is no significant difference between the observed and expected frequency. Under $H_0$, the expected frequency is given by $= \frac{10,000}{10} = 1000$ To find the value of $\chi^2$

| O | 1026 | 1107 | 997 | 996 | 1075 | 1107 | 933 | 972 | 964 | 853 |
|---|---|---|---|---|---|---|---|---|---|---|
| E | 1000 | 1000 | 1000 | 1000 | 1000 | 1000 | 1000 | 1000 | 1000 | 1000 |
| $(O-E)^2$ | 676 | 11449 | 9 | 1156 | 5625 | 11449 | 4489 | 784 | 1296 | 21609 |

$$\chi^2 = \sum_{i-1}^{n}\left(\frac{(0_i - E_i)^2}{E_1}\right) = \frac{58542}{1000} = 58.542$$

*Conclusion*: The tabulated value of $\chi^2$ at 5 per cent level of significance for 9 d.f. is 16.919. Since the calculated value of $\chi^2$ is greater than the tabulated value, $H_0$ is rejected.

i.e., there is significant difference between the observed and theoretical frequency.

**Example 4:** Let theory predicts the proportion of students in the four groups as per their achievement is, $G_1$, $G_2$, $G_3$, $G_4$ should be in the ratio 9: 3: 3: 1. In an experiment with 1600 students the numbers in the four groups were 882, 313, 287 and 118. Does the experimental result support the theory.

**Sol.** $H_0$. The experimental result support the theory. i.e., there is no significant difference between the observed and theoretical frequency under $H_0$, the theoretical frequency can be calculated as follows:

$$E(G_1) = \frac{1600 \times 9}{16} = 900; \; E(G_2) = \frac{1600 \times 3}{16} = 300;$$

$$E(G_4) = \frac{1600 \times 3}{16} = 300; \; E(G_4) = \frac{1600 \times 1}{16} = 100$$

To calculate the value of $\chi^2$.

| Observed frequency O | 882 | 313 | 287 | 118 |
|---|---|---|---|---|
| Expected frequency E | 900 | 300 | 300 | 100 |
| $\frac{(O-E)^2}{E}$ | 0.36 | 0.5633 | 0.5633 | 3.24 |

$$\chi^2 = 4.7266$$

*Conclusion*: Table value of $\chi^2$ at 5 per cent level of significance for 3 d.f. is 7.815. Since the calculated value of $\chi^2$ is less than that of the tabulated value. Hence $H_0$ is accepted. i.e., the experimental result support the theory.

## 11.8 SPSS (STATISTICAL PACKAGE FOR THE SOCIAL SCIENCES)

SPSS is a very widely used package, especially in University social science departments and among social scientists in government and in private organisations. It is developed by SPSS Inc. with headquarters in USA but with a world-wide network of supplying organisations and support teams.

Originally, Statistical Package for the Social Sciences (SPSS) was released in its first version in 1968 after being developed by Norman H. Nie and C. Hadlai Hull. Norman Nie was then a Political Science postgraduate at Stanford University, and now Research Professor in the Department of Political Science at Stanford and Professor Emeritus of Political Science at the University of Chicago. SPSS is among the most widely used programs for statistical analysis in social science. It is used by market researchers, health researchers, survey companies, government, education researchers, marketing organizations and others. The original SPSS manual (Nie, Bent & Hull, 1970) has been described as one of "sociology's most influential books". In addition to statistical analysis, data management (case selection, file reshaping, creating derived data) and data documentation (a metadata dictionary is stored in the data file) are features of the base software.

The developers of the Statistical Package for the Social Sciences (SPSS) made every effort to make the software easy to use. This prevents you from making mistakes or even forgetting something.

That's not to say it's impossible to do something wrong, but the SPSS software works hard to keep you from running into the ditch. To foul things up, you almost have to work at figuring out a way of doing something wrong.

You always begin by defining a set of *variables,* and then you enter data for the variables to create a number of *cases*. For example, if you are doing an analysis of automobiles, each car in your study would be a case. The variables that define the cases could be things such as the year of manufacture, horsepower, and cubic inches of displacement. Each car in the study is defined as a single case, and each case is defined as a set of values assigned to the collection of variables. Every case has a value for each variable

Variables have types. That is, each variable is defined as containing a specific kind of number. For example, a *scale* variable is a numeric measurement, such as weight or miles per gallon. A *categorical* variable contains values that define a category; for example, a variable named *gender* could be a categorical variable defined to contain only values 1 for female and 2 for male. Things that make sense for one type of variable don't necessarily make sense for another. For example, it makes sense to calculate the average miles per gallon, but not the average gender.

After your data is entered into SPSS — your cases are all defined by values stored in the variables — you can run an analysis. You have already finished the hard part. Running an analysis on the data is much easier than entering the data. To run an analysis, you select the one you want to run from the menu, select appropriate variables, and click the OK button. SPSS reads through all your cases, performs the analysis, and presents you with the output.

You can instruct SPSS to draw graphs and charts the same way you instruct it to do an analysis. You select the desired graph from the menu, assign variables to it, and click OK.

You have made all the choices necessary to produce output. Not only does SPSS require that you select a sufficient number of variables to produce output, it also requires that you choose the right kinds of variables. If a categorical variable is required for a certain slot, SPSS will not allow you to choose any other kind. Whether the output makes sense is up to you and your data, but SPSS makes certain that the choices you make can be used to produce some kind of result.

Pull-down Menu
Tool Bar
Each Column is a variable
Each Row is a Case
Data Editor has two views
Status Bar

**Fig.:** Entering data in SPSS

All output from SPSS goes to the same place — a dialog box named SPSS Viewer. It opens to display the results of whatever you've done. After you have output, if you perform some action that produces more output, the new output is displayed in the same dialog box and almost anything you do produces output.

## REFERENCES

1. Garrett, H.E. and Woodworth, R.S. (1961). *Statistics in Psychology and Education.* New York: Vakils, Feffer and SimonLtd.
2. Springer, K (2010). *Educational Research-Acontextual approach*. Chennai: John Wiley and Sons, Inc.
3. Ferguson, G.A. (1971) Statistical analysis in Psychology and Education (3rd Edn.) Tokyo: Mc Graw Hill.
4. Sarantakos, S. (2nd Ed.) (1998) Social Research-. Hong Kong :MC Millan.

# Appendix I

## Standard Normal (Z) Table

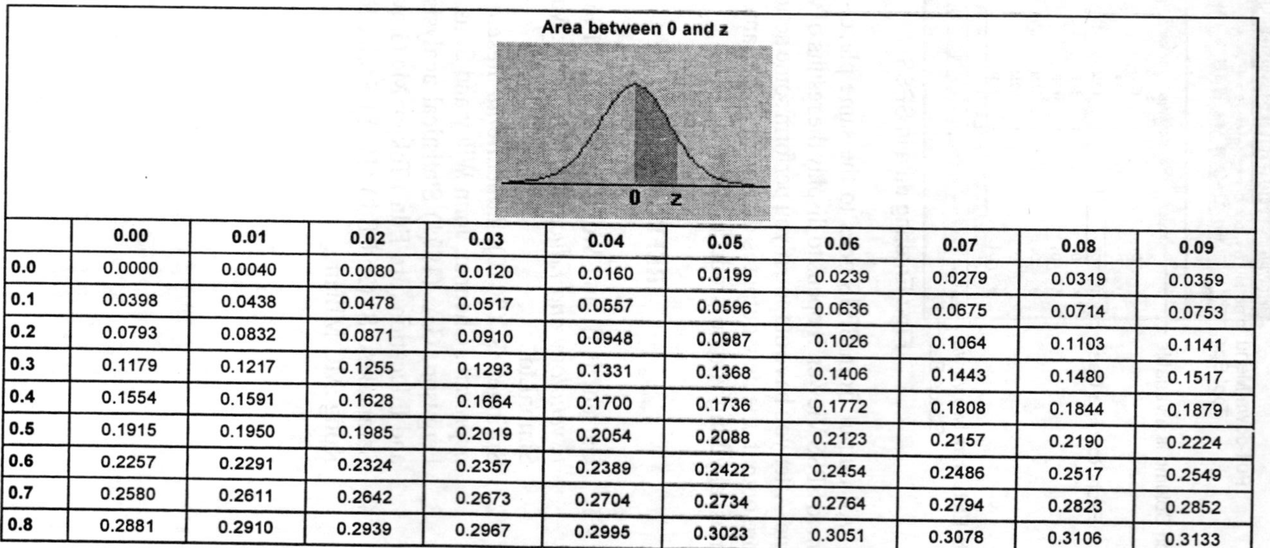


| | 0.00 | 0.01 | 0.02 | 0.03 | 0.04 | 0.05 | 0.06 | 0.07 | 0.08 | 0.09 |
|---|---|---|---|---|---|---|---|---|---|---|
| 0.0 | 0.0000 | 0.0040 | 0.0080 | 0.0120 | 0.0160 | 0.0199 | 0.0239 | 0.0279 | 0.0319 | 0.0359 |
| 0.1 | 0.0398 | 0.0438 | 0.0478 | 0.0517 | 0.0557 | 0.0596 | 0.0636 | 0.0675 | 0.0714 | 0.0753 |
| 0.2 | 0.0793 | 0.0832 | 0.0871 | 0.0910 | 0.0948 | 0.0987 | 0.1026 | 0.1064 | 0.1103 | 0.1141 |
| 0.3 | 0.1179 | 0.1217 | 0.1255 | 0.1293 | 0.1331 | 0.1368 | 0.1406 | 0.1443 | 0.1480 | 0.1517 |
| 0.4 | 0.1554 | 0.1591 | 0.1628 | 0.1664 | 0.1700 | 0.1736 | 0.1772 | 0.1808 | 0.1844 | 0.1879 |
| 0.5 | 0.1915 | 0.1950 | 0.1985 | 0.2019 | 0.2054 | 0.2088 | 0.2123 | 0.2157 | 0.2190 | 0.2224 |
| 0.6 | 0.2257 | 0.2291 | 0.2324 | 0.2357 | 0.2389 | 0.2422 | 0.2454 | 0.2486 | 0.2517 | 0.2549 |
| 0.7 | 0.2580 | 0.2611 | 0.2642 | 0.2673 | 0.2704 | 0.2734 | 0.2764 | 0.2794 | 0.2823 | 0.2852 |
| 0.8 | 0.2881 | 0.2910 | 0.2939 | 0.2967 | 0.2995 | 0.3023 | 0.3051 | 0.3078 | 0.3106 | 0.3133 |

| 0.9 | 0.3159 | 0.3186 | 0.3212 | 0.3238 | 0.3264 | 0.3289 | 0.3315 | 0.3340 | 0.3365 | 0.3389 |
|---|---|---|---|---|---|---|---|---|---|---|
| 1.0 | 0.3413 | 0.3438 | 0.3461 | 0.3485 | 0.3508 | 0.3531 | 0.3554 | 0.3577 | 0.3599 | 0.3621 |
| 1.1 | 0.3643 | 0.3665 | 0.3686 | 0.3708 | 0.3729 | 0.3749 | 0.3770 | 0.3790 | 0.3810 | 0.3830 |
| 1.2 | 0.3849 | 0.3869 | 0.3888 | 0.3907 | 0.3925 | 0.3944 | 0.3962 | 0.3980 | 0.3997 | 0.4015 |
| 1.3 | 0.4032 | 0.4049 | 0.4066 | 0.4082 | 0.4099 | 0.4115 | 0.4131 | 0.4147 | 0.4162 | 0.4177 |
| 1.4 | 0.4192 | 0.4207 | 0.4222 | 0.4236 | 0.4251 | 0.4265 | 0.4279 | 0.4292 | 0.4306 | 0.4319 |
| 1.5 | 0.4332 | 0.4345 | 0.4357 | 0.4370 | 0.4382 | 0.4394 | 0.4406 | 0.4418 | 0.4429 | 0.4441 |
| 1.6 | 0.4452 | 0.4463 | 0.4474 | 0.4484 | 0.4495 | 0.4505 | 0.4515 | 0.4525 | 0.4535 | 0.4545 |
| 1.7 | 0.4554 | 0.4564 | 0.4573 | 0.4582 | 0.4591 | 0.4599 | 0.4608 | 0.4616 | 0.4625 | 0.4633 |
| 1.8 | 0.4641 | 0.4649 | 0.4656 | 0.4664 | 0.4671 | 0.4678 | 0.4686 | 0.4693 | 0.4699 | 0.4706 |
| 1.9 | 0.4713 | 0.4719 | 0.4726 | 0.4732 | 0.4738 | 0.4744 | 0.4750 | 0.4756 | 0.4761 | 0.4767 |
| 2.0 | 0.4772 | 0.4778 | 0.4783 | 0.4788 | 0.4793 | 0.4798 | 0.4803 | 0.4808 | 0.4812 | 0.4817 |
| 2.1 | 0.4821 | 0.4826 | 0.4830 | 0.4834 | 0.4838 | 0.4842 | 0.4846 | 0.4850 | 0.4854 | 0.4857 |
| 2.2 | 0.4861 | 0.4864 | 0.4868 | 0.4871 | 0.4875 | 0.4878 | 0.4881 | 0.4884 | 0.4887 | 0.4890 |
| 2.3 | 0.4893 | 0.4896 | 0.4898 | 0.4901 | 0.4904 | 0.4906 | 0.4909 | 0.4911 | 0.4913 | 0.4916 |
| 2.4 | 0.4918 | 0.4920 | 0.4922 | 0.4925 | 0.4927 | 0.4929 | 0.4931 | 0.4932 | 0.4934 | 0.4936 |
| 2.5 | 0.4938 | 0.4940 | 0.4941 | 0.4943 | 0.4945 | 0.4946 | 0.4948 | 0.4949 | 0.4951 | 0.4952 |
| 2.6 | 0.4953 | 0.4955 | 0.4956 | 0.4957 | 0.4959 | 0.4960 | 0.4961 | 0.4962 | 0.4963 | 0.4964 |
| 2.7 | 0.4965 | 0.4966 | 0.4967 | 0.4968 | 0.4969 | 0.4970 | 0.4971 | 0.4972 | 0.4973 | 0.4974 |
| 2.8 | 0.4974 | 0.4975 | 0.4976 | 0.4977 | 0.4977 | 0.4978 | 0.4979 | 0.4979 | 0.4980 | 0.4981 |
| 2.9 | 0.4981 | 0.4982 | 0.4982 | 0.4983 | 0.4984 | 0.4984 | 0.4985 | 0.4985 | 0.4986 | 0.4986 |
| 3.0 | 0.4987 | 0.4987 | 0.4987 | 0.4988 | 0.4988 | 0.4989 | 0.4989 | 0.4989 | 0.4990 | 0.4990 |

# Appendix II

## Student's t Table

**t table with right tail probabilities**

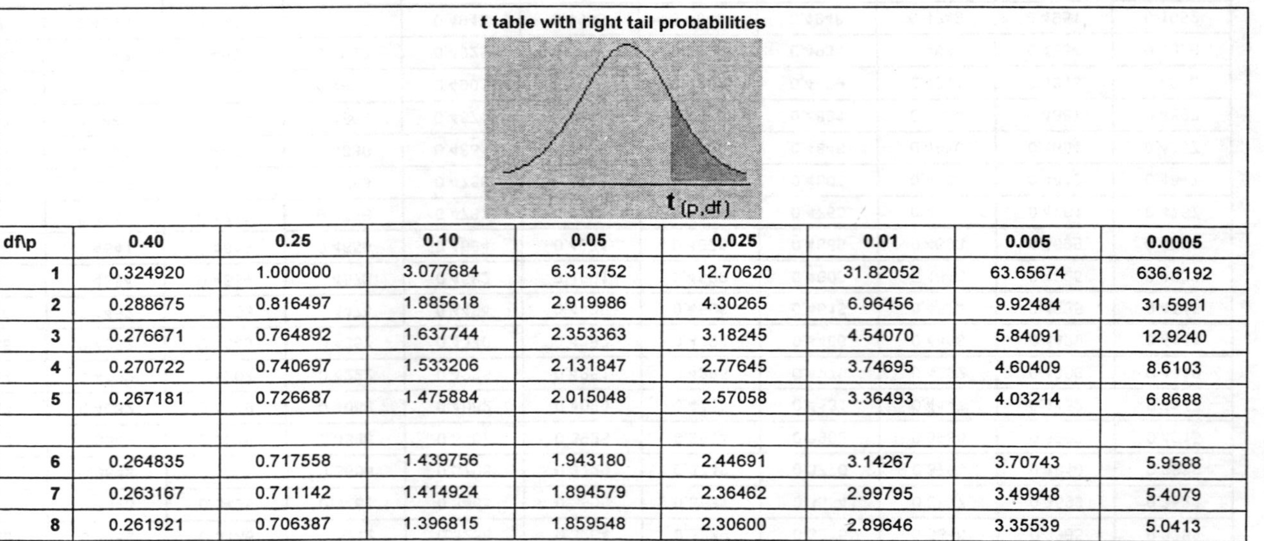


| df\p | 0.40 | 0.25 | 0.10 | 0.05 | 0.025 | 0.01 | 0.005 | 0.0005 |
|---|---|---|---|---|---|---|---|---|
| 1 | 0.324920 | 1.000000 | 3.077684 | 6.313752 | 12.70620 | 31.82052 | 63.65674 | 636.6192 |
| 2 | 0.288675 | 0.816497 | 1.885618 | 2.919986 | 4.30265 | 6.96456 | 9.92484 | 31.5991 |
| 3 | 0.276671 | 0.764892 | 1.637744 | 2.353363 | 3.18245 | 4.54070 | 5.84091 | 12.9240 |
| 4 | 0.270722 | 0.740697 | 1.533206 | 2.131847 | 2.77645 | 3.74695 | 4.60409 | 8.6103 |
| 5 | 0.267181 | 0.726687 | 1.475884 | 2.015048 | 2.57058 | 3.36493 | 4.03214 | 6.8688 |
| | | | | | | | | |
| 6 | 0.264835 | 0.717558 | 1.439756 | 1.943180 | 2.44691 | 3.14267 | 3.70743 | 5.9588 |
| 7 | 0.263167 | 0.711142 | 1.414924 | 1.894579 | 2.36462 | 2.99795 | 3.49948 | 5.4079 |
| 8 | 0.261921 | 0.706387 | 1.396815 | 1.859548 | 2.30600 | 2.89646 | 3.35539 | 5.0413 |

| | | | | | | | | |
|---|---|---|---|---|---|---|---|---|
| **9** | 0.260955 | 0.702722 | 1.383029 | 1.833113 | 2.26216 | 2.82144 | 3.24984 | 4.7809 |
| **10** | 0.260185 | 0.699812 | 1.372184 | 1.812461 | 2.22814 | 2.76377 | 3.16927 | 4.5869 |
| | | | | | | | | |
| **11** | 0.259556 | 0.697445 | 1.363430 | 1.795885 | 2.20099 | 2.71808 | 3.10581 | 4.4370 |
| **12** | 0.259033 | 0.695483 | 1.356217 | 1.782288 | 2.17881 | 2.68100 | 3.05454 | 4.3178 |
| **13** | 0.258591 | 0.693829 | 1.350171 | 1.770933 | 2.16037 | 2.65031 | 3.01228 | 4.2208 |
| **14** | 0.258213 | 0.692417 | 1.345030 | 1.761310 | 2.14479 | 2.62449 | 2.97684 | 4.1405 |
| **15** | 0.257885 | 0.691197 | 1.340606 | 1.753050 | 2.13145 | 2.60248 | 2.94671 | 4.0728 |
| | | | | | | | | |
| **16** | 0.257599 | 0.690132 | 1.336757 | 1.745884 | 2.11991 | 2.58349 | 2.92078 | 4.0150 |
| **17** | 0.257347 | 0.689195 | 1.333379 | 1.739607 | 2.10982 | 2.56693 | 2.89823 | 3.9651 |
| **18** | 0.257123 | 0.688364 | 1.330391 | 1.734064 | 2.10092 | 2.55238 | 2.87844 | 3.9216 |
| **19** | 0.256923 | 0.687621 | 1.327728 | 1.729133 | 2.09302 | 2.53948 | 2.86093 | 3.8834 |
| **20** | 0.256743 | 0.686954 | 1.325341 | 1.724718 | 2.08596 | 2.52798 | 2.84534 | 3.8495 |
| | | | | | | | | |
| **21** | 0.256580 | 0.686352 | 1.323188 | 1.720743 | 2.07961 | 2.51765 | 2.83136 | 3.8193 |
| **22** | 0.256432 | 0.685805 | 1.321237 | 1.717144 | 2.07387 | 2.50832 | 2.81876 | 3.7921 |
| **23** | 0.256297 | 0.685306 | 1.319460 | 1.713872 | 2.06866 | 2.49987 | 2.80734 | 3.7676 |
| **24** | 0.256173 | 0.684850 | 1.317836 | 1.710882 | 2.06390 | 2.49216 | 2.79694 | 3.7454 |
| **25** | 0.256060 | 0.684430 | 1.316345 | 1.708141 | 2.05954 | 2.48511 | 2.78744 | 3.7251 |
| | | | | | | | | |
| **26** | 0.255955 | 0.684043 | 1.314972 | 1.705618 | 2.05553 | 2.47863 | 2.77871 | 3.7066 |

| | | | | | | | | |
|---|---|---|---|---|---|---|---|---|
| **27** | 0.255858 | 0.683685 | 1.313703 | 1.703288 | 2.05183 | 2.47266 | 2.77068 | 3.6896 |
| **28** | 0.255768 | 0.683353 | 1.312527 | 1.701131 | 2.04841 | 2.46714 | 2.76326 | 3.6739 |
| **29** | 0.255684 | 0.683044 | 1.311434 | 1.699127 | 2.04523 | 2.46202 | 2.75639 | 3.6594 |
| **30** | 0.255605 | 0.682756 | 1.310415 | 1.697261 | 2.04227 | 2.45726 | 2.75000 | 3.6460 |
| | | | | | | | | |
| **inf** | 0.253347 | 0.674490 | 1.281552 | 1.644854 | 1.95996 | 2.32635 | 2.57583 | 3.2905 |

# Appendix III
## Right tail areas for the *Chi-square* Distribution

**Right tail areas for the *Chi-square* Distribution**

| df\ area | .995 | .990 | .975 | .950 | .900 | .750 | .500 | .250 | .100 | .050 | .025 | .010 | .005 |
|---|---|---|---|---|---|---|---|---|---|---|---|---|---|
| 1 | 0.00004 | 0.00016 | 0.00098 | 0.00393 | 0.01579 | 0.10153 | 0.45494 | 1.32330 | 2.70554 | 3.84146 | 5.02389 | 6.63490 | 7.87944 |
| 2 | 0.01003 | 0.02010 | 0.05064 | 0.10259 | 0.21072 | 0.57536 | 1.38629 | 2.77259 | 4.60517 | 5.99146 | 7.37776 | 9.21034 | 10.59663 |
| 3 | 0.07172 | 0.11483 | 0.21580 | 0.35185 | 0.58437 | 1.21253 | 2.36597 | 4.10834 | 6.25139 | 7.81473 | 9.34840 | 11.34487 | 12.83816 |
| 4 | 0.20699 | 0.29711 | 0.48442 | 0.71072 | 1.06362 | 1.92256 | 3.35669 | 5.38527 | 7.77944 | 9.48773 | 11.14329 | 13.27670 | 14.86026 |
| 5 | 0.41174 | 0.55430 | 0.83121 | 1.14548 | 1.61031 | 2.67460 | 4.35146 | 6.62568 | 9.23636 | 11.07050 | 12.83250 | 15.08627 | 16.74960 |
| | | | | | | | | | | | | | |
| 6 | 0.67573 | 0.87209 | 1.23734 | 1.63538 | 2.20413 | 3.45460 | 5.34812 | 7.84080 | 10.64464 | 12.59159 | 14.44938 | 16.81189 | 18.54758 |
| 7 | 0.98926 | 1.23904 | 1.68987 | 2.16735 | 2.83311 | 4.25485 | 6.34581 | 9.03715 | 12.01704 | 14.06714 | 16.01276 | 18.47531 | 20.27774 |

| | | | | | | | | | | | | | |
|---|---|---|---|---|---|---|---|---|---|---|---|---|---|
| **8** | 1.34441 | 1.64650 | 2.17973 | 2.73264 | 3.48954 | 5.07064 | 7.34412 | 10.21885 | 13.36157 | 15.50731 | 17.53455 | 20.09024 | 21.95495 |
| **9** | 1.73493 | 2.08790 | 2.70039 | 3.32511 | 4.16816 | 5.89883 | 8.34283 | 11.38875 | 14.68366 | 16.91898 | 19.02277 | 21.66599 | 23.58935 |
| **10** | 2.15586 | 2.55821 | 3.24697 | 3.94030 | 4.86518 | 6.73720 | 9.34182 | 12.54886 | 15.98718 | 18.30704 | 20.48318 | 23.20925 | 25.18818 |
| | | | | | | | | | | | | | |
| **11** | 2.60322 | 3.05348 | 3.81575 | 4.57481 | 5.57778 | 7.58414 | 10.34100 | 13.70069 | 17.27501 | 19.67514 | 21.92005 | 24.72497 | 26.75685 |
| **12** | 3.07382 | 3.57057 | 4.40379 | 5.22603 | 6.30380 | 8.43842 | 11.34032 | 14.84540 | 18.54935 | 21.02607 | 23.33666 | 26.21697 | 28.29952 |
| **13** | 3.56503 | 4.10692 | 5.00875 | 5.89186 | 7.04150 | 9.29907 | 12.33976 | 15.98391 | 19.81193 | 22.36203 | 24.73560 | 27.68825 | 29.81947 |
| **14** | 4.07467 | 4.66043 | 5.62873 | 6.57063 | 7.78953 | 10.16531 | 13.33927 | 17.11693 | 21.06414 | 23.68479 | 26.11895 | 29.14124 | 31.31935 |
| **15** | 4.60092 | 5.22935 | 6.26214 | 7.26094 | 8.54676 | 11.03654 | 14.33886 | 18.24509 | 22.30713 | 24.99579 | 27.48839 | 30.57791 | 32.80132 |
| | | | | | | | | | | | | | |
| **16** | 5.14221 | 5.81221 | 6.90766 | 7.96165 | 9.31224 | 11.91222 | 15.33850 | 19.36886 | 23.54183 | 26.29623 | 28.84535 | 31.99993 | 34.26719 |
| **17** | 5.69722 | 6.40776 | 7.56419 | 8.67176 | 10.08519 | 12.79193 | 16.33818 | 20.48868 | 24.76904 | 27.58711 | 30.19101 | 33.40866 | 35.71847 |
| **18** | 6.26480 | 7.01491 | 8.23075 | 9.39046 | 10.86494 | 13.67529 | 17.33790 | 21.60489 | 25.98942 | 28.86930 | 31.52638 | 34.80531 | 37.15645 |
| **19** | 6.84397 | 7.63273 | 8.90652 | 10.11701 | 11.65091 | 14.56200 | 18.33765 | 22.71781 | 27.20357 | 30.14353 | 32.85233 | 36.19087 | 38.58226 |
| **20** | 7.43384 | 8.26040 | 9.59078 | 10.85081 | 12.44261 | 15.45177 | 19.33743 | 23.82769 | 28.41198 | 31.41043 | 34.16961 | 37.56623 | 39.99685 |
| | | | | | | | | | | | | | |
| **21** | 8.03365 | 8.89720 | 10.28290 | 11.59131 | 13.23960 | 16.34438 | 20.33723 | 24.93478 | 29.61509 | 32.67057 | 35.47888 | 38.93217 | 41.40106 |
| **22** | 8.64272 | 9.54249 | 10.98232 | 12.33801 | 14.04149 | 17.23962 | 21.33704 | 26.03927 | 30.81328 | 33.92444 | 36.78071 | 40.28936 | 42.79565 |
| **23** | 9.26042 | 10.19572 | 11.68855 | 13.09051 | 14.84796 | 18.13730 | 22.33688 | 27.14134 | 32.00690 | 35.17246 | 38.07563 | 41.63840 | 44.18128 |
| **24** | 9.88623 | 10.85636 | 12.40115 | 13.84843 | 15.65868 | 19.03725 | 23.33673 | 28.24115 | 33.19624 | 36.41503 | 39.36408 | 42.97982 | 45.55851 |
| **25** | 10.51965 | 11.52398 | 13.11972 | 14.61141 | 16.47341 | 19.93934 | 24.33659 | 29.33885 | 34.38159 | 37.65248 | 40.64647 | 44.31410 | 46.92789 |
| | | | | | | | | | | | | | |

| | | | | | | | | | | | | | |
|---|---|---|---|---|---|---|---|---|---|---|---|---|---|
| **26** | 11.16024 | 12.19815 | 13.84390 | 15.37916 | 17.29188 | 20.84343 | 25.33646 | 30.43457 | 35.56317 | 38.88514 | 41.92317 | 45.64168 | 48.28988 |
| **27** | 11.80759 | 12.87850 | 14.57338 | 16.15140 | 18.11390 | 21.74940 | 26.33634 | 31.52841 | 36.74122 | 40.11327 | 43.19451 | 46.96294 | 49.64492 |
| **28** | 12.46134 | 13.56471 | 15.30786 | 16.92788 | 18.93924 | 22.65716 | 27.33623 | 32.62049 | 37.91592 | 41.33714 | 44.46079 | 48.27824 | 50.99338 |
| **29** | 13.12115 | 14.25645 | 16.04707 | 17.70837 | 19.76774 | 23.56659 | 28.33613 | 33.71091 | 39.08747 | 42.55697 | 45.72229 | 49.58788 | 52.33562 |
| **30** | 13.78672 | 14.95346 | 16.79077 | 18.49266 | 20.59923 | 24.47761 | 29.33603 | 34.79974 | 40.25602 | 43.77297 | 46.97924 | 50.89218 | |

# Appendix IV

## F Distribution Critical Values

### F Distribution critical values for P=0.01

| Denominator | | | | | | | | | | | | | | |
|---|---|---|---|---|---|---|---|---|---|---|---|---|---|---|
| | Numerator DF | | | | | | | | | | | | | |
| **DF** | **1** | **2** | **3** | **4** | **5** | **7** | **10** | **15** | **20** | **30** | **60** | **120** | **500** | **1000** |
| **1** | 4052.2 | 4999.5 | 5403.4 | 5624.6 | 5763.6 | 5928.4 | 6055.8 | 6157.3 | 6208.7 | 6260.6 | 6313.0 | 6339.4 | 6359.5 | 6362.7 |
| **2** | 98.503 | 99.000 | 99.166 | 99.249 | 99.299 | 99.356 | 99.399 | 99.433 | 99.449 | 99.466 | 99.482 | 99.491 | 99.497 | 99.498 |
| **3** | 34.116 | 30.817 | 29.457 | 28.710 | 28.237 | 27.672 | 27.229 | 26.872 | 26.690 | 26.504 | 26.316 | 26.221 | 26.148 | 26.137 |
| **4** | 21.198 | 18.000 | 16.694 | 15.977 | 15.522 | 14.976 | 14.546 | 14.198 | 14.020 | 13.838 | 13.652 | 13.558 | 13.486 | 13.474 |
| **5** | 16.258 | 13.274 | 12.060 | 11.392 | 10.967 | 10.455 | 10.051 | 9.7222 | 9.5526 | 9.3793 | 9.2020 | 9.1118 | 9.0424 | 9.0314 |
| **7** | 12.246 | 9.5467 | 8.4513 | 7.8466 | 7.4605 | 6.9929 | 6.6201 | 6.3143 | 6.1554 | 5.9920 | 5.8236 | 5.7373 | 5.6707 | 5.6601 |
| **10** | 10.044 | 7.5594 | 6.5523 | 5.9944 | 5.6363 | 5.2001 | 4.8492 | 4.5582 | 4.4055 | 4.2469 | 4.0818 | 3.9964 | 3.9303 | 3.9195 |

| **15** | 8.6831 | 6.3588 | 5.4169 | 4.8932 | 4.5557 | 4.1416 | 3.8049 | 3.5223 | 3.3719 | 3.2141 | 3.0471 | 2.9594 | 2.8906 | 2.8796 |
|---|---|---|---|---|---|---|---|---|---|---|---|---|---|---|
| **20** | 8.0960 | 5.8489 | 4.9382 | 4.4306 | 4.1027 | 3.6987 | 3.3682 | 3.0880 | 2.9377 | 2.7785 | 2.6078 | 2.5167 | 2.4446 | 2.4330 |
| **30** | 7.5624 | 5.3903 | 4.5098 | 4.0179 | 3.6990 | 3.3046 | 2.9791 | 2.7002 | 2.5486 | 2.3859 | 2.2078 | 2.1108 | 2.0321 | 2.0192 |
| **60** | 7.0771 | 4.9774 | 4.1259 | 3.6491 | 3.3388 | 2.9530 | 2.6318 | 2.3522 | 2.1978 | 2.0284 | 1.8362 | 1.7264 | 1.6328 | 1.6169 |
| **120** | 6.8509 | 4.7865 | 3.9490 | 3.4795 | 3.1736 | 2.7918 | 2.4720 | 2.1914 | 2.0345 | 1.8600 | 1.6557 | 1.5330 | 1.4215 | 1.4015 |
| **500** | 6.6858 | 4.6479 | 3.8210 | 3.3569 | 3.0539 | 2.6751 | 2.3564 | 2.0746 | 1.9152 | 1.7353 | 1.5175 | 1.3774 | 1.2317 | 1.2007 |
| **1000** | 6.6603 | 4.6264 | 3.8012 | 3.3379 | 3.0356 | 2.6571 | 2.3387 | 2.0564 | 1.8967 | 1.7158 | 1.4953 | 1.3513 | 1.1947 | 1.1586 |

# Appendix V

## F Distribution critical values for P = 0.05

| Denominator | | | | | | | | | | | | | | |
|---|---|---|---|---|---|---|---|---|---|---|---|---|---|---|
| | Numerator DF | | | | | | | | | | | | | |
| DF | 1 | 2 | 3 | 4 | 5 | 7 | 10 | 15 | 20 | 30 | 60 | 120 | 500 | 1000 |
| 1 | 161.45 | 199.50 | 215.71 | 224.58 | 230.16 | 236.77 | 241.88 | 245.95 | 248.01 | 250.10 | 252.20 | 253.25 | 254.06 | 254.19 |
| 2 | 18.513 | 19.000 | 19.164 | 19.247 | 19.296 | 19.353 | 19.396 | 19.429 | 19.446 | 19.462 | 19.479 | 19.487 | 19.494 | 19.495 |
| 3 | 10.128 | 9.5522 | 9.2766 | 9.1172 | 9.0135 | 8.8867 | 8.7855 | 8.7028 | 8.6602 | 8.6165 | 8.5720 | 8.5493 | 8.5320 | 8.5292 |
| 4 | 7.7086 | 6.9443 | 6.5915 | 6.3882 | 6.2560 | 6.0942 | 5.9644 | 5.8579 | 5.8026 | 5.7458 | 5.6877 | 5.6580 | 5.6352 | 5.6317 |
| 5 | 6.6078 | 5.7862 | 5.4095 | 5.1922 | 5.0504 | 4.8759 | 4.7351 | 4.6187 | 4.5582 | 4.4958 | 4.4314 | 4.3985 | 4.3731 | 4.3691 |
| 7 | 5.5914 | 4.7375 | 4.3469 | 4.1202 | 3.9715 | 3.7871 | 3.6366 | 3.5108 | 3.4445 | 3.3758 | 3.3043 | 3.2675 | 3.2388 | 3.2344 |
| 10 | 4.9645 | 4.1028 | 3.7082 | 3.4780 | 3.3259 | 3.1354 | 2.9782 | 2.8450 | 2.7741 | 2.6996 | 2.6210 | 2.5801 | 2.5482 | 2.5430 |
| 15 | 4.5431 | 3.6823 | 3.2874 | 3.0556 | 2.9013 | 2.7066 | 2.5437 | 2.4035 | 2.3275 | 2.2467 | 2.1601 | 2.1141 | 2.0776 | 2.0718 |

| | | | | | | | | | | | | | | |
|---|---|---|---|---|---|---|---|---|---|---|---|---|---|---|
| **20** | 4.3512 | 3.4928 | 3.0983 | 2.8660 | 2.7109 | 2.5140 | 2.3479 | 2.2032 | 2.1241 | 2.0391 | 1.9463 | 1.8962 | 1.8563 | 1.8498 |
| **30** | 4.1709 | 3.3159 | 2.9223 | 2.6896 | 2.5336 | 2.3343 | 2.1646 | 2.0149 | 1.9317 | 1.8408 | 1.7396 | 1.6835 | 1.6376 | 1.6300 |
| **60** | 4.0012 | 3.1505 | 2.7581 | 2.5252 | 2.3683 | 2.1666 | 1.9927 | 1.8365 | 1.7480 | 1.6492 | 1.5343 | 1.4672 | 1.4093 | 1.3994 |
| **120** | 3.9201 | 3.0718 | 2.6802 | 2.4473 | 2.2898 | 2.0868 | 1.9104 | 1.7505 | 1.6587 | 1.5544 | 1.4289 | 1.3519 | 1.2804 | 1.2674 |
| **500** | 3.8601 | 3.0137 | 2.6227 | 2.3898 | 2.2320 | 2.0278 | 1.8496 | 1.6864 | 1.5917 | 1.4820 | 1.3455 | 1.2552 | 1.1586 | 1.1378 |
| **1000** | 3.8508 | 3.0047 | 2.6137 | 2.3808 | 2.2230 | 2.0187 | 1.8402 | 1.6765 | 1.5811 | 1.4705 | 1.3318 | 1.2385 | 1.1342 | 1.1096 |

# Appendix VI

## Conversion of Pearson's r to Fischer's z

| *r* | *z'* |
|---|---|
| 0.00 | 0.0000 |
| 0.01 | 0.0100 |
| 0.02 | 0.0200 |
| 0.03 | 0.0300 |
| 0.04 | 0.0400 |
| 0.05 | 0.0500 |
| 0.06 | 0.0601 |
| 0.07 | 0.0701 |
| 0.08 | 0.0802 |
| 0.09 | 0.0902 |
| 0.10 | 0.1003 |
| 0.11 | 0.1104 |
| 0.12 | 0.1206 |
| 0.13 | 0.1307 |
| 0.14 | 0.1409 |
| 0.15 | 0.1511 |
| 0.16 | 0.1614 |
| 0.17 | 0.1717 |
| 0.18 | 0.1820 |
| 0.19 | 0.1923 |
| 0.20 | 0.2027 |
| 0.21 | 0.2132 |
| 0.22 | 0.2237 |
| 0.23 | 0.2342 |
| 0.24 | 0.2448 |
| 0.25 | 0.2554 |
| 0.26 | 0.2661 |
| 0.27 | 0.2769 |
| 0.28 | 0.2877 |
| 0.29 | 0.2986 |
| 0.30 | 0.3095 |
| 0.31 | 0.3205 |
| 0.32 | 0.3316 |
| 0.33 | 0.3428 |
| 0.34 | 0.3541 |
| 0.35 | 0.3654 |
| 0.36 | 0.3769 |
| 0.37 | 0.3884 |
| 0.38 | 0.4001 |
| 0.39 | 0.4118 |
| 0.40 | 0.4236 |

| | |
|---|---|
| 0.41 | 0.4356 |
| 0.42 | 0.4477 |
| 0.43 | 0.4599 |
| 0.44 | 0.4722 |
| 0.45 | 0.4847 |
| 0.46 | 0.4973 |
| 0.47 | 0.5101 |
| 0.48 | 0.5230 |
| 0.49 | 0.5361 |
| 0.50 | 0.5493 |
| 0.51 | 0.5627 |
| 0.52 | 0.5763 |
| 0.53 | 0.5901 |
| 0.54 | 0.6042 |
| 0.55 | 0.6184 |
| 0.56 | 0.6328 |
| 0.57 | 0.6475 |
| 0.58 | 0.6625 |
| 0.59 | 0.6777 |
| 0.60 | 0.6931 |
| 0.61 | 0.7089 |
| 0.62 | 0.7250 |
| 0.63 | 0.7414 |
| 0.64 | 0.7582 |
| 0.65 | 0.7753 |
| 0.66 | 0.7928 |
| 0.67 | 0.8107 |
| 0.68 | 0.8291 |
| 0.69 | 0.8480 |
| 0.70 | 0.8673 |
| 0.71 | 0.8872 |
| 0.72 | 0.9076 |
| 0.73 | 0.9287 |
| 0.74 | 0.9505 |
| 0.75 | 0.9730 |
| 0.76 | 0.9962 |
| 0.77 | 1.0203 |
| 0.78 | 1.0454 |
| 0.79 | 1.0714 |
| 0.80 | 1.0986 |
| 0.81 | 1.1270 |
| 0.82 | 1.1568 |
| 0.83 | 1.1881 |
| 0.84 | 1.2212 |
| 0.85 | 1.2562 |
| 0.86 | 1.2933 |
| 0.87 | 1.3331 |
| 0.88 | 1.3758 |
| 0.89 | 1.4219 |
| 0.90 | 1.4722 |
| 0.91 | 1.5275 |
| 0.92 | 1.5890 |

| | |
|---|---|
| 0.93 | 1.6584 |
| 0.94 | 1.7380 |
| 0.95 | 1.8318 |
| 0.96 | 1.9459 |
| 0.97 | 2.0923 |
| 0.98 | 2.2976 |
| 0.99 | 2.6467 |